Building Quality Shaders for Unity®

Using Shader Graphs and HLSL Shaders

Daniel Ilett

Apress®

Building Quality Shaders for Unity®: Using Shader Graphs and HLSL Shaders

Daniel Ilett
Coventry, UK

ISBN-13 (pbk): 978-1-4842-8651-7   ISBN-13 (electronic): 978-1-4842-8652-4
https://doi.org/10.1007/978-1-4842-8652-4

Managing Director, Apress Media LLC: Welmoed Spahr
Acquisitions Editor: Spandana Chatterjee
Development Editor: Spandana Chatterjee
Coordinating Editor: Shrikant Vishwakarma

Cover designed by eStudioCalamar

Cover image designed by Freepik (www.freepik.com)

Distributed to the book trade worldwide by Springer Science+Business Media New York, 1 New York Plaza, Suite 4600, New York, NY 10004-1562, USA. Phone 1-800-SPRINGER, fax (201) 348-4505, e-mail orders-ny@springer-sbm.com, or visit www.springeronline.com. Apress Media, LLC is a California LLC and the sole member (owner) is Springer Science + Business Media Finance Inc (SSBM Finance Inc). SSBM Finance Inc is a **Delaware** corporation.

For information on translations, please e-mail booktranslations@springernature.com; for reprint, paperback, or audio rights, please e-mail bookpermissions@springernature.com.

Apress titles may be purchased in bulk for academic, corporate, or promotional use. eBook versions and licenses are also available for most titles. For more information, reference our Print and eBook Bulk Sales web page at http://www.apress.com/bulk-sales.

Any source code or other supplementary material referenced by the author in this book is available to readers on GitHub via the book's product page, located at www.apress.com/. For more detailed information, please visit http://www.apress.com/source-code.

Printed on acid-free paper

To Lewis.

Table of Contents

About the Author

Daniel Ilett is an ambitious and motivated PhD student at the University of Warwick. He is a passionate game developer, specializing in shaders and technical art. He publishes a range of educational and tutorial content, including videos and written work, aimed at beginners and intermediate developers. He also does freelance work on shaders and visual effects for games.

About the Technical Reviewer

Simon Jackson is a long-time software engineer and architect with many years of Unity game development experience, as well as an author of several Unity game development titles. He loves to both create Unity projects and lend a hand to help educate others, whether it's via a blog, vlog, user group, or major speaking event.

His primary focus at the moment is on the XRTK (Mixed Reality Toolkit) project. This is aimed at building a cross-platform Mixed Reality framework to enable both VR and AR developers to build efficient solutions in Unity and then build/distribute them to as many platforms as possible.

Acknowledgments

With thanks to Lewis, who reads all my tweets out loud back to me seconds after posting. Something tells me he won't be reading this whole book to me. You also had to deal with me in the morning before I'd had a coffee, which couldn't have been easy.

Thank you also to my family, especially my mum, who has apparently been saying "Did you know he's writing a book?" whenever my name comes up in conversation with people.

With thanks to the Warwick Game Design Society and its members, who have given me a space to flourish and work on games while at university. You also showed me how to eat a gigantic slice of chocolate fudge cake in under a minute, which surely got us some strange looks from other pubgoers. There are too many of you to count!

Finally, my thanks to the Apress team and everyone who was involved in writing this book with me. From the first invitation to write the book to every bit of advice and correction, you've all been invaluable partners on this journey.

Introduction

So you've decided to start writing shaders in Unity. That's a good decision if I do say so myself! Before I started writing shaders, I saw many people in the game development space talk about them in hushed tones, as if they were some kind of arcane secret bestowed from the heavens, but it's my belief that anyone can write shaders with a soft introduction. It's like learning any other skill; you don't learn to ride a push-bike by imitating Evel Knievel right off the bat.

This is the kind of book I wish I had when I was learning to write shaders in Unity. The early chapters establish the core concepts and syntax you'll need to know when writing shaders, and throughout the course of the book, I will steadily introduce more complex topics until we have covered some of the lesser-known shader topics in Unity. By that point, you should be able to create complicated, versatile effects by yourself.

Who This Book Is For

This book covers topics ranging from the beginner to the intermediate level. I'll assume you already know your way around the Unity Editor, but I will explain the interface of unfamiliar sections such as the Shader Graph editor. Here are a few hypothetical readers I think will enjoy this book:

- I've never written a shader before.

  If this is you, then I definitely recommend starting with Chapter 1 and working through the book in order, and you should start your project with the Universal Render Pipeline (URP; if you don't know what that means, all is explained in Chapter 1). Chapter 2 is optional – it covers all the math related to shaders, but not everyone learns math easily by reading it all up front, so feel free to skip it to start with and come back whenever later chapters introduce math that you're unfamiliar with.

- I wrote shaders a few years ago for old Unity versions, but I'm unfamiliar with Unity versions past 2018–2019 or so.

The early chapters will serve as a good refresher, but you can probably skim-read Chapter 1 at the very least, perhaps more. Pick out a few of the examples and give them a go just to remind yourself of the syntax and concepts before diving into later chapters head-on!

- I'm experienced with writing shaders in code, but I'd like to transition to using Shader Graph (or vice versa).

    Every example in the book is presented in both shader code and Shader Graph where possible (there are a small number of effects and features that, for various reasons, are only possible in one of those tools). It may be helpful to read through examples you are familiar with and use that as a springboard to learn the tool you're not as experienced with.

- I've grasped the basics, but I want to move on to more difficult topics like compute shaders and tessellation shaders.

    Although the earlier chapters will be useful as a reference should you need it, you will want to skip or skim-read Chapters 1–4, which cover the basics, and then choose to read subsequent chapters on a case-by-case basis. The most advanced topics start from Chapter 10 onward, but I've attempted to sprinkle in intermediate features throughout the book.

Recommended Software

Every example in the book *will* work in **Unity 2021.3**, which is the latest Long-Term Support (LTS) version of the engine at the time of the writing of this book. If you are reading this book in the future and there is a later LTS version, then every example will most likely still work, although you may potentially need to change the names of functions and macros. If you are using an earlier version than 2021.3, most of the effects will work, but there are features that are completely missing in certain versions. The book will still be helpful if you are working on a project started in an earlier Unity version and you are unable to upgrade to a newer version, and I will warn you when I am using a recently added feature.

CHAPTER 1

Introduction to Shaders in Unity

Everybody wants to make gorgeous games, and shaders are one of the most powerful tools in the technical artist's toolkit to achieve just that. In this chapter, we will take a step back and explore, briefly, how rendering in Unity works and where shaders fit into the story. By the end of the chapter, you will understand the basics of the rendering process, what Unity's different render pipelines are, and how we will use programs called shaders to control how our games look.

Rendering

A *game engine* is nothing but a toolbox filled with software geared toward making games, and the bit of software we're most interested in is the *renderer* – the code that takes meshes, sprites, and shaders and turns them all into the images you see on your screen. Unity is no different from other engines in this regard. At a high level, the renderer processes a set of data through a series of distinct steps, as seen in Figure 1-1. Some of the stages are handled automatically by Unity, so we won't need to worry about them, while others are controlled entirely by using shaders that we will write. As we will see, each stage has a specific purpose, and some are even optional. Let's briefly explore the history of the graphics pipeline and see how shaders came about in the first place.

© Daniel Ilett 2022
D. Ilett, *Building Quality Shaders for Unity*®, https://doi.org/10.1007/978-1-4842-8652-4_1

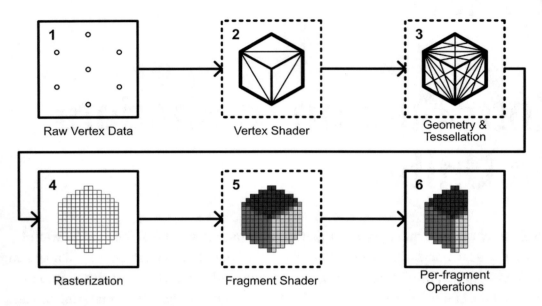

Figure 1-1. *The stages of the graphics pipeline. The stages surrounded by a dotted line indicate parts of the pipeline we can customize using shaders*

In ancient times (the 1990s), with the advent of real-time 3D graphics, the functionality afforded to graphics programmers was limited. We had what's called the *fixed-function pipeline*, where we could configure a relatively small set of specialized functions (such as "do lighting," "add textures," and so on) that ran on the GPUs of the time. This was faster than previous software rendering methods, which ran on the CPU, but came with heavy limitations. The fixed-function pipeline is akin to building a car with five options for the body shape, seven for color, and three for the engine size; it covered a lot of use cases, but we need finer control to build a car with any shape imaginable with all the colors of the rainbow and beyond.

Enter the *programmable pipeline*. In modern computer graphics, we can completely control the behavior of certain parts of the rendering process using small programs called *shaders*. No longer are we constrained to a limited set of functions – now, we can write C-style code to instruct the graphics card to do any combination of effects. The impossible became possible. Whereas the fixed-function pipeline is like flicking a bunch of levers someone else made for us, the programmable pipeline is like building an entire machine from scratch using raw materials to our exact specifications.

As you can see from Figure 1-1, there are several stages, each of which carries out a specific purpose:

- The *vertex shader* lets us control how objects get placed on-screen. This type of shader typically receives vertex data from a mesh and uses mathematical transformations to position them on-screen properly. You can also use this shader stage to animate vertex positions over time.

- The *tessellation shader* can be used to subdivide a mesh into smaller triangles, creating additional vertices. This is useful when combined with vertex shaders that offset the positions of vertices, as you can get more detailed results.

- The *geometry shader* can be used to create whatever new primitive shapes you want, anywhere you want. Although this stage can incur a performance hit, it can do things that are difficult to achieve with the other shader stages.

- The *fragment shader* is used to color each pixel of the object. Here, we can apply color tint, texture, and lighting to each part of the object – for that reason, most of the "interesting" work is often carried out in the fragment shader.

- Compute shaders are another kind of shader that exist outside the pipeline and can be used for arbitrary computation on the GPU. These computations don't necessarily need to involve graphics at all, although compute shaders still have a use in some graphics-only contexts.

The vertex shader and fragment shader stages are the two most important stages that we have control over, so we'll be seeing them in almost every shader we write. The other stages are optional. In Unity, we will primarily be using HLSL (High-Level Shading Language) to write our shader code. There are several kinds of shading language available, and the way we write shaders in Unity has changed over time, so we will explore this in greater detail in Chapter 3 when we write our very first shader file. Now that we know what a shader is, let's look deeper at the flow of data throughout the rendering process.

Game Data

At the very start of the pipeline, we have a bunch of data. When we place objects such as characters or landscapes into a scene in Unity, we are implicitly adding data that needs to be passed to the first stages of the graphics pipeline. Here's a brief list of the kinds of data the graphics pipeline needs:

- The position and orientation of the *camera* defines how every other object will appear on the screen. Some objects will be obscured from view if they are behind the camera, outside of its field of view, or if they are too far from or too close to the camera.

- *Meshes*, or 3D models, can be defined by a set of *vertices* (points), connected by *edges*, three of which make up a *triangle*. These vertices are passed to the vertex shader, alongside data such as vertex colors and *texture coordinates*. In Unity, the *Mesh Renderer* component is responsible for passing this data to the shader.

- *Sprites* in 2D can be considered a square *quad* made up of two triangles. Unity's *Sprite Renderer* component passes the two triangles to the vertex shader.

- Objects on the *UI* (user interface), such as text or images, use specialized components to pass data to the shader in a similar manner.

Objects are processed one at a time through each stage of the graphics pipeline. Before processing, Unity may sort the data in certain ways. For instance, a typical graphics pipeline will render all opaque objects and then will render semitransparent objects over the top, starting from the furthest transparent object from the camera (i.e., back to front). Once the preprocessing stage is completed, the next step is to render each object in turn, starting with the vertex shader.

The Vertex Shader

As I mentioned, Unity's renderer components are responsible for passing data to the vertex shader. Here's where things start to get exciting for technical artists like us! Most vertex shaders will look the same: we take vertex positions, which start relative to the object being rendered, and use a series of matrix transformations to put them in the correct position on-screen. We can also implement some effects at the vertex stage. For example, we can generate waves to animate a water plane or expand the mesh to create an inflation or explosion effect.

Alongside positions, the vertex shader also transforms other vertex data. Meshes can have several pieces of information attached to each vertex, such as vertex colors, texture coordinates, and other arbitrary data we might choose to add. The vertex shader doesn't just perform these transformations; it also passes the data to subsequent shader stages, so we can modify data however we want. For example, in some of the shaders we'll see later, we will pass the world position of vertices so we can use it in the fragment shader.

Between the vertex and fragment shader stages, a process called *rasterization* takes place, in which the triangles that make up a mesh are sliced into a 2D grid of *fragments*. In most cases, a fragment corresponds to one pixel on your screen. Think of the rasterizer as an advanced version of MS Paint, which takes the triangles of the mesh and converts them into an image the size of the game window – that image is called the *frame buffer*. During rasterization, other properties are interpolated between vertices. For example, if we consider an edge where the two vertices have black and white vertex colors, respectively, then the new colors of pixels along that edge will be varying shades of gray. Once rasterization has finished, we move on to the fragment shader.

The Fragment Shader

This is sometimes called the *pixel shader*, and it is perhaps the most powerful and flexible stage of the graphical pipeline. The fragment shader is responsible for coloring each pixel on the screen, so we can implement a wide variety of effects here, from textures to lighting, to transparency, and so on. Special kinds of shaders called post-processing shaders, which can operate on the entire screen, can be used for additional effects, such as simple color mapping, screen animations, depth-based effects, and special types of screen-space shading.

Once the fragment shader has finished, a final round of processing occurs. These processes include depth testing, where opaque fragments may be discarded if they would otherwise be drawn behind another opaque fragment from another object, and blending, where the colors of semitransparent objects are mixed – blended – with colors that have already been drawn to the screen. We may also use a *stencil*, which stops certain pixels from being rendered to the screen, as you can see in stage 6 of Figure 1-1.

Of course, I've simplified many of the stages for this brief primer. Later on in the book, we'll explore the vertex and fragment shaders to the fullest, and we'll see optional types of shader designed for highly specialized tasks. That said, most of the shaders you will write throughout your shader career will involve moving vertices around and coloring fragments. So far, we've seen how the graphics pipeline operates in general, but there are a few other things to be aware of before we dive in.

Unity's Render Pipelines

Now we come to the elephant in the room. Before 2017, Unity had a single rendering pipeline for all use cases: modern high-end PC and console, virtual reality, low-end mobile devices, and everything in between. According to Unity themselves, this involved compromises, which sacrifice performance for flexibility. On top of that, Unity's rendering code was something of a "black box," which was impenetrable without a Unity source code license, even with comprehensive documentation and an active developer community.

Unity chose to overhaul its renderer by introducing *Scriptable Render Pipelines (SRPs)*. To keep things brief, a SRP gives developers control over exactly how Unity renders everything, letting us add or remove stages to or from the rendering loop as required. Realizing that not all developers want to spend the time building a renderer from scratch (indeed, one of the key reasons many people choose a game engine in the first place is that all the work on the rendering code is done for you), Unity provides two template render pipelines: the *High-Definition Render Pipeline (HDRP)*, which targets high-end console and PC gaming, and the *Universal Render Pipeline*, which is designed for lower-end machines and mobiles, although it can also run on more powerful hardware. All SRPs, including custom SRPs you write and the two template render pipelines, bring exclusive support for new systems, which I will mention throughout the book.

The legacy rendering system is also available for those who already started their projects in older Unity versions and is now called the *built-in render pipeline*. For most new projects targeting a broad set of hardware, it is recommended that you start a project with URP – eventually, Unity will make this the default for new projects. Unfortunately for us, shaders sometimes differ slightly between all three pipelines, which is why I feel it's important to make the distinction between them early on. In this book, I will do my best to explain the differences between each and present you with shader examples that work in all three where possible.

Note   Although it is possible to swap pipelines partway through development, it can be painful to do so, especially with larger projects. If you have already started a project, I recommend sticking with the render pipeline you chose unless there is a feature only supported by a different pipeline that you absolutely require.

Shader Graph

With the advent of the SRPs came a few exclusive features. For us, none of those features are quite as impactful as Shader Graph, Unity's node-based shader editor. Traditionally, shaders have existed only as code, which puts them firmly on the "programmer" side of the "programmer-to-artist" spectrum. But in the last decade or so, one of the biggest innovations in the field of technical art has been the shift to visual editors for shaders. These editors are somewhat akin to visual coding tools, which replace lines of code with nodes, which are bundles of functionality that can be connected into a graph. For many, visual editors like these are far easier to get to grips with than code, because you can visualize the progression of a shader at each step. Unlike code shaders, a visual editor can preview what your shader looks like at each node so you can debug your game's visuals with ease.

Note   Originally, Shader Graph was exclusive to SRP-based pipelines. In Unity 2021.2, however, support for Shader Graph was ported to the built-in pipeline. Unity seems to be keeping it a bit quiet, as most of the online documentation for Shader Graph seems to avoid saying so!

Throughout this book, I will show you examples in both shader code and Shader Graph, because I believe that both will be important to technical artists going forward. Chapter 3 will focus on shader code, while Chapter 4 will serve as your introduction to Shader Graph.

Summary

We covered a lot in this chapter! You should now be aware of the key terminology that will be used throughout the rest of this book. Here's a rundown of what we learned:

- The rendering/graphics pipeline is a series of stages that operate on data.

- Vertex shaders are used to position objects on-screen.

- Triangle faces are converted to fragments/pixels during rasterization.

- Data is interpolated between vertices during the rasterization stage.

CHAPTER 2

Math for Shader Development

People learn in different ways. While many people reading this book will want to learn every single bit of math related to shader development before jumping into making shaders, others will be happy to skim-read the important bits and pick up the rest as they go along. In this book, I've opted to give you a comprehensive look at shader math early on, with the understanding that you can skip the chapter and flick back here whenever you see fit. Throughout the book, I will provide references back to the appropriate section of this chapter whenever a new concept is introduced for those who want to pick up the important bits as they go.

In this chapter, I will introduce you to the fundamental math that you will encounter when making shaders: from vectors and matrices to trigonometry and coordinate spaces and everything in between.

Vectors

Vectors are a fundamental building block for shaders – almost everything you do inside a shader will involve a vector somewhere. So what are they? Let's imagine we're on a treasure hunt and we're given a map of the local area. We're starting at the base camp in the bottom-left corner, and we'll represent this with the vector $(0, 0)$, since this map has two dimensions. If this map measures distances in miles, let's say there's an extremely large tree two miles east and one mile north, plus a rocky hill one mile east and four miles north and a sandy beach three miles east and five miles to the north. Charting everything on our map, it'll look something like Figure 2-1.

© Daniel Ilett 2022
D. Ilett, *Building Quality Shaders for Unity*®, https://doi.org/10.1007/978-1-4842-8652-4_2

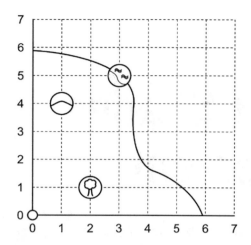

Figure 2-1. *A map containing a few landmarks*

Position and Direction Vectors

We can use vectors to represent the offset between our starting point and each of those three locations – the vector between our starting point and the tree is (2, 1), because it's two miles to the east, or the *x-direction*, and one mile to the north, the *y-direction*. In fact, vectors are great at representing the offset between any two points simply because that's what a vector is: a quantity that has a length and a direction. That's the one-line description almost every textbook gives, at least! In this example, the direction is pointing toward the tree, and the length is about 2.24 miles. You might have noticed that the vector starting at the rocky hill and ending at the sandy beach is also (2, 1).

There are a few things to grasp already. Firstly, we can represent any position using its offset from some origin point, which in 2D is (0, 0) – that's why I conveniently chose that as the starting point on our map. A vector containing only zeroes is always special, as it's the only vector with a length of zero and without a particular direction – both properties will become relevant as we explore operations on vectors. It's got a special name too: the *zero vector*. Secondly, vectors can start at any point on the map. Not only are they useful at telling us where some point is in relation to the origin point but they can tell us about the displacement between two points that are not (0, 0). This is important because saying "the vector (2, 1)" could mean several different things on the same map.

Vector Addition and Subtraction

Now let's go hiking. From our starting point, we'll go and explore the rocky hill first, because we think the treasure might be buried on the top. Luckily, there's a well-trodden dirt path heading directly there. Bad news for us: After an hour of digging, we don't find anything. Darn. Our next best guess is that the sandy beach might have some clues to the treasure's location. So, exhausted, we pack up our shovel and metal detector and trek to the beach; this time, there's a stone path with no bends that leads to the beach. The route we took can be seen in Figure 2-2. Now, how far from the starting point are we?

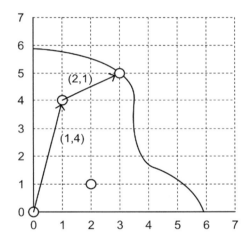

Figure 2-2. *The first leg of the journey*

Vectors can easily be added to one another by taking each of the numbers inside the first vector and adding them to the corresponding numbers from the other vector (although both vectors must have the same dimension). Each of the values inside a vector is called a *component*, and they're named like the axes of a graph: the first is the *x*-component, then *y*, then in higher dimensions *z*, and then *w*. Adding two vectors in 2D, then, is just a case of adding the x-components together and then the y-components. To figure out our position vector on the beach, let's add up the components of the journey we took.

Equation 2-1: Adding two vectors

$$(1,4)+(2,1)=(1+2,4+1)=(3,5)$$

The sandy beach is indeed at $(3,5)$. Subtraction works the same way. We found a clue on the beach that's directing us toward the tallest object in the area, so we'll head over to the tree next – amazingly, there's a perfectly straight concrete path that passes just by the tree. Whoever built these paths sure knows how to set up contrived math questions. Given the beach is at $(3,5)$ and the tree is at $(2,1)$, what's the vector from the beach to the tree?

Remember that vectors have direction. We can get the answer by taking the destination vector and subtracting the starting vector. The same logic applies here: apply the subtractions component-wise.

Equation 2-2: Subtracting two vectors

$$(2,1)-(3,5)=(2-3,1-5)=(-1,-4)$$

In the context of our map, the vector $(-1,-4)$ means "–1 miles east and –4 miles north" or, more simply, "one mile west and four miles south."

Scalar Multiplication

This time, we're pretty sure that we'll strike gold here. The metal detector goes off at the base of the towering tree, so, with great anticipation, we'll dig into the ground with our shovels. And wouldn't you know it? After 5 minutes, we hear a *kathunk*, and we drag out a chest with the treasure inside. Success! With the treasure in our grubby hands, it's time to head back to base camp, where we started. We already know the tree is at $(2,1)$, as seen in Figure 2-3, so what's the easiest way to figure out the vector from the tree to base camp? We can *negate* a vector to flip its direction. All positive components become negative and vice versa. That's exactly what we need to do here – therefore, the vector for the final leg of our journey is $(-2,-1)$.

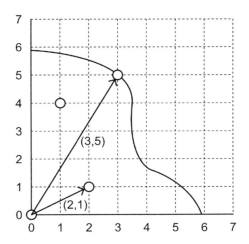

Figure 2-3. *Point vectors for the start and end positions of the next leg of the journey*

Equation 2-3: Reversing a vector's direction

$$-(2,1) = (-2,-1)$$

This is an example of *multiplication by a scalar*. If a vector has several components, then a single number by itself is called a scalar, and they are helpful when it comes to vector math. Multiplication can be used to change the length of a vector – for example, multiplying the vector $(2, 1)$ by 3 results in the vector $(6, 3)$, which is three times longer, and multiplying by 0.5 instead results in $(1, 0.5)$, which is half as long. Multiplying by 1 always results in the same vector; for that reason, 1 is called the *multiplicative identity*, just as the vector $(0, 0)$ is the *additive identity*. Multiplying a vector by –1, like we just did, will always reverse the vector's direction but preserve its length. Multiplying by other negative numbers will reverse the direction, but the length will change. And multiplying by 0 always results in the zero vector, which we discussed before. Dividing is the same thing as multiplication – just multiply by the reciprocal instead.

Equation 2-4: Examples of scalar multiplication

$$3 * (2,1) = (6,3)$$

$$1 * (2,1) = (2,1)$$

$$-1 * (2,1) = (-2,1)$$

$$0 * (2,1) = (0,0)$$

Vector Magnitude

I've mentioned the *length* of a vector a few times, so how do we calculate it? The advantage of tracing out vectors on a graph like this is that it makes it easy to see that a vector is always the hypotenuse (the longest edge) of a right-angled triangle, as shown in Figure 2-4.

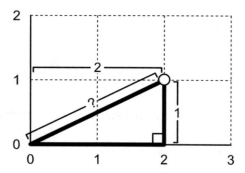

Figure 2-4. *The longest side length of a right-angled triangle can be calculated using the other two side lengths*

You'll likely be familiar with the *Pythagorean Theorem*, which is exactly what we use to calculate vector length (or, as it's often called, *magnitude*). I'll use the terms *length* and *magnitude* interchangeably throughout the book. With vectors, we'll take the square of each component of the vector, add them together, and then take the square root of the result. We represent magnitude of a vector in formulas by putting vertical bars around it. So, for the vector $(-2, -1)$, its length is represented by $|(-2, -1)|$ and calculated like so:

Equation 2-5: Calculating the magnitude of a vector

$$|(-2, -1)| = \sqrt{2^2 + 1^2} = \sqrt{5} \approx 2.24$$

So there you have it: when your teachers said Pythagoras would be useful in later life, this is what they meant. Now we know that the last leg of our treasure hunt was about 2.24 miles long, which is quite the trek. In fact, the total distance we walked throughout the day was 12.72 miles, so I hope we can afford a shower and a long rest using all that treasure.

Vector Normalization

We've seen how the magnitude of a vector might be useful, but what if we are only interested in its direction? For any given vector (except the zero vector), there are infinite other vectors that point in the same direction – we just need to multiply by any positive scalar value to get one of those vectors. As it turns out, many calculations we're going to make throughout this book are going to work a lot better if the vectors have a length of 1. This is called a unit vector, and the process to turn one vector into a unit vector with the same direction is called normalization. You can see a vector and its normalized counterpart in Figure 2-5.

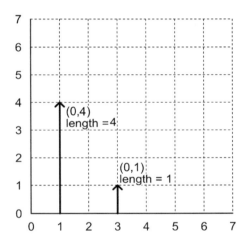

Figure 2-5. *A vector of length 4 and its normalized counterpart, which has length 1*

To normalize a vector, all we need to do is divide by its magnitude; we've seen how to do each bit before, so let's put them together. I'm going to start with the vector $(3, 4)$, which I'm going to call A. The corresponding unit vector is denoted $\hat{A}$.

Equation 2-6: Normalizing a vector

$$\hat{A} = \frac{A}{|A|} = \frac{(3,4)}{\sqrt{3^2 + 4^2}} = \frac{1}{5}(3,4) = \left(\frac{3}{5}, \frac{4}{5}\right)$$

If we were to relate this back to the treasure hunt, then if we had set off from base camp toward the hill at $(1, 4)$, got tired after exactly one mile of walking, and took a rest, then we'd be at $\frac{1}{\sqrt{17}}(1,4) \approx (0.24, 0.97)$.

Basis Vectors and Linear Combinations

So far we've been discussing the properties of the vectors themselves, but now it's time to talk about the map as a whole. Earlier, I mentioned that there are infinite vectors that point in the same direction as a given nonzero vector, but what does that mean? Our map is in 2D, and as a physical object, it will have a certain size. Let's imagine the map extends infinitely in each direction. We can represent any position on this infinite map using a real number in each of the vector's two components. We call the map a *vector space* (in fact, this space in particular is called $\mathbb{R}^2$ because it's two-dimensional and it's made up of real numbers, $\mathbb{R}$).

In many contexts we'll see throughout the book, it will be useful to represent position vectors as a combination of vectors that are perpendicular to each other. For example, the point $(1, 1, 1)$ in 3D (in the space $\mathbb{R}^3$) can be obtained by adding $(1, 0, 0)$, $(0, 1, 0)$, and $(0, 0, 1)$ together. We say that the vectors $(1, 0, 0)$, $(0, 1, 0)$, and $(0, 0, 1)$ form a *basis* for the vector space $\mathbb{R}^3$, because these three vectors have the following properties: they are *linearly independent*, because we can't add multiples of any two of those vectors to form the third one; and they *span* the entire space, because we can form any vector in $\mathbb{R}^3$ by combining multiples of these three vectors. We may not use these terms very often in computer graphics, but we will see how sets of perpendicular vectors become important in later sections.

Dot Product

At this point, you should be comfortable with adding vectors, multiplying by scalars, and normalizing vectors. Each of these operations results in a new vector. What other information can we discern from vectors? Often, we are interested in the angle between two vectors, as seen in Figure 2-6.

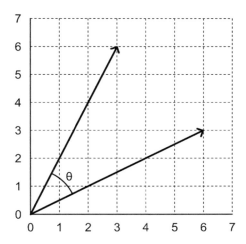

Figure 2-6. *The angle between two vectors*

There are plenty of contexts where the angle between two vectors becomes useful, such as lighting, where the angle between a light ray and a surface normal vector influences the amount of illumination falling on the object. In these contexts, we use an operation called the *dot product*, denoted by **a** · **b** for the vectors *a* and *b*.

Equation 2-7: Dot product of two vectors in 2D

$$\boldsymbol{a} \cdot \boldsymbol{b} = |\boldsymbol{a}||\boldsymbol{b}| \cos \theta$$

$$\boldsymbol{a} \cdot \boldsymbol{b} = \boldsymbol{a}_x \boldsymbol{b}_x + \boldsymbol{a}_y \boldsymbol{b}_y$$

Recall that |*a*| and |*b*| are the magnitudes of *a* and *b*, respectively. *θ* is the angle between the two vectors. There are two ways of calculating the dot product, and both ways result in a scalar value. Neat! For that reason, the dot product is sometimes called the *scalar product*. So what can we do with the dot product? Well, it provides an extremely efficient way of evaluating the angle between two vectors. If we combine the preceding two formulas and rearrange them, then we have a good way of calculating the cosine of the angle between the two vectors.

Equation 2-8: Finding the cosine between two vectors

$$|\boldsymbol{a}||\boldsymbol{b}| \cos \theta = \boldsymbol{a}_x \boldsymbol{b}_x + \boldsymbol{a}_y \boldsymbol{b}_y$$

$$\cos \theta = \left(\frac{\boldsymbol{a}_x \boldsymbol{b}_x + \boldsymbol{a}_y \boldsymbol{b}_y}{|\boldsymbol{a}| \times |\boldsymbol{b}|} \right)$$

We can evaluate the angle between the two vectors using just the cosine of the angle. For instance, if $\cos \theta$ equals zero (and therefore if the dot product equals zero), the two vectors are at right angles to each other – they are *perpendicular*. In the lighting example I mentioned previously, the amount of light would be zero. Else, if $\cos \theta$ equals 1, then the two vectors are parallel – they have the same direction. –1 means they are still parallel but point in opposite directions. We can see this if we calculate the dot product between $(2, 1)$ and $(-2, -1)$:

Equation 2-9: Calculating the cosine of the angle between two vectors

$$\cos \theta = \left(\frac{2 \times -2 + 1 \times -1}{\sqrt{5} \times \sqrt{5}} \right)$$

$$\cos \theta = \left(\frac{-5}{5} \right)$$

$$\cos \theta = -1$$

Any values of $\cos \theta$ between 0 and 1 mean θ is between 0° and 90°, and when $\cos \theta$ is between –1 and 0, θ is between 90° and 180°. However, you will notice we had to do quite a bit of rearranging to get a formula for the cosine. What if we could avoid needing to do that? You'll see that the denominator in Equation 2-8 relates to the length of both vectors – if that equals 1, then the dot product is exactly equal to the cosine. We have already seen a method for making sure the input vectors have a length of 1: normalization! In many of the operations we'll be doing throughout the book, it will be important to make sure all vectors are normalized first so that we don't need to divide after doing the dot product. Since normalization involves dividing by the length anyway, this will only be more efficient if we use the dot product on the vectors more than once, but it's a good habit to get into regardless.

Cross Product

We've seen a type of vector multiplication that results in a scalar value. What if we wanted to get a vector result instead? What would that look like? Enter the *cross product*, also known as the *vector product*. For two vectors in 3D space, the cross product between them will produce a third vector, which is perpendicular to both original vectors. There are a few caveats. Firstly, the cross product of any vector with the zero vector always results in the zero vector – perpendicularity isn't well-defined for the zero vector. Secondly, the cross product of a vector with any vector parallel to it (including itself) also results in the zero vector. In this instance, there isn't a single direction perpendicular to both input vectors – in fact, there are infinite directions such a vector could point in. Also, the cross product isn't defined in 2D because you can never obtain a third vector perpendicular to both input vectors. For two vectors in 3D, the cross product looks like this:

Equation 2-10: Cross product of two vectors in 3D

$$\boldsymbol{a} \times \boldsymbol{b} = |\boldsymbol{a}||\boldsymbol{b}|\sin\theta\ \boldsymbol{n}$$

$$\boldsymbol{a} \times \boldsymbol{b} = \begin{pmatrix} a_y b_z - a_z b_y \\ a_z b_x - a_x b_z \\ a_x b_y - a_y b_x \end{pmatrix}$$

In the first equation, $\boldsymbol{n}$ is the unit vector perpendicular to both $\boldsymbol{a}$ and $\boldsymbol{b}$, and θ is the angle between $\boldsymbol{a}$ and $\boldsymbol{b}$. A useful property of the cross product equation is that if both $\boldsymbol{a}$ and $\boldsymbol{b}$ are unit vectors and are themselves perpendicular to one another, then $|\boldsymbol{a}|$, $|\boldsymbol{b}|$, and $\sin\theta$ all equal zero, and the equation becomes $\boldsymbol{a} \times \boldsymbol{b} = \boldsymbol{n}$. In most cases when calculating the cross product inside shaders, we can just normalize the output if we are certain that the resulting $\boldsymbol{n}$ is not the zero vector.

Matrices

We have seen how vectors work, but they are not expressive enough for us to carry out every operation that computer graphics demands of us. To get the best performance out of our graphics card, we will be using matrices for some of the most expensive calculations in the graphics pipeline. Let's start with the most obvious question: what are matrices?

A *matrix* (the singular form of the word – the plural is *matrices*) is a rectangular array of numbers organized into *rows* and *columns*. They can have any size, and we refer to the matrix size by saying a matrix is *m* by *n*, where *m* is the number of rows and *n* is the number of columns. They're kind of like tiny *Excel* spreadsheets.

Equation 2-11: An example of two 2 × 3 matrices

$$A = \begin{bmatrix} -7 & 4 & 2 \\ 8 & 0 & -1 \end{bmatrix} \qquad B = \begin{bmatrix} 5 & 2 & 3 \\ -8 & 1 & 1 \end{bmatrix}$$

Each number inside the matrix – each *element* of the matrix – is usually a real number in shaders. Matrices are usually denoted by a capital letter (in this example, we have matrices *A* and *B*), whereas individual matrix elements are denoted by a lowercase letter and subscripts to indicate which row and column of the matrix an element is from. For example, $a_{1,2}$ is the element of *A* in the first row and the second column, which is 4. $b_{2,1}$ is in the second row and first column of matrix *B*, which is –8. Unlike many programming languages, matrices are one-indexed – sorry.

As we will see later, matrices are used heavily in computer graphics to represent transformations required for taking data from a mesh and converting it into positions on-screen. If you are writing basic shaders, it is not necessary to know how each and every matrix operation works, because Unity will provide helper functions for us – in which case, you might wish to skip to a later section on space transformations to see how matrices generally help us in the computer graphics pipeline. However, some of the shaders we will see later rely on matrix operations, so I believe it is still useful to understand how to manipulate matrices ourselves.

Note   Sometimes, it takes a while for matrices to stick in your brain if it's your first time using them. If you need extra worked examples or if you'd like to go further with matrices than this chapter does, then cuemath.com/algebra/solve-matrices/ is a great resource.

Matrix Addition and Subtraction

There are many operations we can do with matrices, so let's start with the basics. The size of the matrix is crucial because some operations become incompatible between matrices of certain sizes. Let's take addition as an example. To add two matrices, they must be the same size. Adding is simple – just take each element from the first matrix and add it with the element in the same position from the second matrix.

Equation 2-12: Adding two 2 × 3 matrices

$$A + B = \begin{bmatrix} -7+5 & 4+2 & 2+3 \\ 8+(-8) & 0+1 & -1+1 \end{bmatrix} = \begin{bmatrix} -2 & 6 & 5 \\ 0 & 1 & 0 \end{bmatrix}$$

Subtracting two matrices works in a similar way – both matrices must be the same size. We can think of subtracting a matrix as adding the negative of that matrix; finding the negative of a matrix is as easy as negating each element of the matrix.

Equation 2-13: Subtracting a 2 × 3 matrix from another 2 × 3 matrix

$$A - B = \begin{bmatrix} -7-5 & 4-2 & 2-3 \\ 8-(-8) & 0-1 & -1-1 \end{bmatrix} = \begin{bmatrix} -12 & 2 & -1 \\ 16 & -1 & -2 \end{bmatrix}$$

Scalar Multiplication

Just like we could with vectors, we can multiply a matrix by a scalar value. We take every element of the matrix and multiply each one by the scalar value, resulting in a new matrix the same size as the original one.

Equation 2-14: Multiplying a 2 × 3 matrix by a scalar value

$$2 \times A = 2 \begin{bmatrix} -7 & 4 & 2 \\ 8 & 0 & -1 \end{bmatrix} = \begin{bmatrix} 2\times(-7) & 2\times 4 & 2\times 2 \\ 2\times 8 & 2\times 0 & 2\times(-1) \end{bmatrix} = \begin{bmatrix} -14 & 8 & 4 \\ 16 & 0 & -2 \end{bmatrix}$$

This is called *scalar multiplication*. We will see how *matrix multiplication* works in a bit, but first, let's look at some operations and terminology that are unique to matrices.

Square, Diagonal, and Identity Matrices

We saw how matrices are rectangular, but there is a special type of matrix called a *square matrix*, where there is the same number of rows as columns, such as a 2 × 2, 3 × 3, or 4 × 4 matrix. A *diagonal matrix* is even more special – it is a square matrix where every element must equal zero, except the elements on the diagonal line from the top left to the bottom right (this is called the *leading diagonal*). The elements on the leading diagonal could still equal zero. We'll see later that these kinds of matrix have different behavior under certain operations.

Equation 2-15: A diagonal matrix

$$C = \begin{bmatrix} 7 & 0 & 0 \\ 0 & -2 & 0 \\ 0 & 0 & 6 \end{bmatrix}$$

An extremely important kind of matrix, the *identity matrix*, denoted *I*, is a diagonal matrix where all elements on the leading diagonal equal one. There is only one identity matrix for any given matrix dimension – here are the 2 × 2, 3 × 3, and 4 × 4 identity matrices:

Equation 2-16: Identity matrices in two, three, and four dimensions

$$I_2 = \begin{bmatrix} 1 & 0 \\ 0 & 1 \end{bmatrix} \quad I_3 = \begin{bmatrix} 1 & 0 & 0 \\ 0 & 1 & 0 \\ 0 & 0 & 1 \end{bmatrix} \quad I_4 = \begin{bmatrix} 1 & 0 & 0 & 0 \\ 0 & 1 & 0 & 0 \\ 0 & 0 & 1 & 0 \\ 0 & 0 & 0 & 1 \end{bmatrix}$$

Matrix Transpose

These are all interesting types of matrices, but let's see some other matrix operations. First, there is the *matrix transpose* operation, denoted with a superscript T, such as A^T (sometimes A' is used), which effectively mirrors the matrix in the leading diagonal (remember – this is a diagonal line that starts in the top-left corner). The element $a_{1,2}$ in the new transposed matrix is equal to element $a_{2,1}$ in the original matrix. For the matrix A, which was 2 × 3, the matrix A^T is 3 × 2.

Equation 2-17: Transposing a matrix

$$A = \begin{bmatrix} -7 & 4 & 2 \\ 8 & 0 & -1 \end{bmatrix} \quad A^T = \begin{bmatrix} -7 & 8 \\ 4 & 0 \\ 2 & -1 \end{bmatrix}$$

There are a few properties of the matrix transpose operation to note. The transpose of the transpose of a matrix will return the original matrix. This makes sense – if we mirror a matrix in the leading diagonal and then mirror again, we expect to get back what we had originally.

Equation 2-18: Transposing a transpose matrix

$$\left(A^T\right)^T = \begin{bmatrix} -7 & 8 \\ 4 & 0 \\ 2 & -1 \end{bmatrix}^T = \begin{bmatrix} -7 & 4 & 2 \\ 8 & 0 & -1 \end{bmatrix}$$

We also find that if we add two matrices together and then take the transpose, the result is the same as if we had taken the transpose of the two matrices individually and then added them. Intuitively, this also makes sense if you think of the transpose as just moving the matrix elements to a new position: it doesn't matter if we add elements and then move them or if we move elements and then add them – we are still adding exactly the same elements together.

Equation 2-19: Transposing the addition is the same as adding the transposes

$$A^T + B^T = \left(A+B\right)^T = \begin{bmatrix} -2 & 6 & 5 \\ 0 & 1 & 0 \end{bmatrix}^T = \begin{bmatrix} -2 & 0 \\ 6 & 1 \\ 5 & 0 \end{bmatrix}$$

If we multiply a matrix by a scalar value and then take the transpose, we get the same result as if we had taken the transpose of the matrix and then multiplied by the scalar. If you think about this in the same way as the previous example involving addition, the transpose is just moving elements around, so we are multiplying the elements by the same value in either scenario.

Equation 2-20: Transposing the scalar multiple is the same as scalar multiplying the transpose

$$\left(xA\right)^T = x\left(A^T\right) = \begin{bmatrix} -7x & 8x \\ 4x & 0 \\ 2x & -x \end{bmatrix}$$

Matrix Determinant

Transposing is not the only useful matrix operation of course! We can also calculate the *matrix determinant*, denoted *det*(A) or |A| for the matrix A. The determinant only exists for square matrices – those with the same number of rows as columns. We rarely need to calculate this ourselves, but I will include the process here for completion. Let's start with the determinant of a 2 × 2 matrix:

Equation 2-21: Determinant of a 2 × 2 matrix

$$\det\left(\begin{bmatrix} a & b \\ c & d \end{bmatrix}\right) = ad - bc$$

As you can see, the determinant of a matrix is a scalar value. If the determinant of a matrix equals zero, then the matrix has no inverse (we will learn about invertible matrices later). What about larger matrices, such as a 3 × 3 matrix?

$$\det\left(\begin{bmatrix} a & b & c \\ d & e & f \\ g & h & i \end{bmatrix}\right)$$

There are a few methods for calculating the determinant, but we will use the *Laplace expansion*, which is recursive and uses the 2 × 2 matrix determinant as its base case. The process is like this: We will take any given column or row of the 3 × 3 matrix. Let's choose the top row. For each element of the row, if we "cross out" the row and column containing that element temporarily, we are left with a 2 × 2 submatrix, which we will calculate the determinant of using the preceding equation. Then, multiply by the element you started with.

In our case, we will be left with three values: $a(ei - hf)$; $b(di - gf)$; and $c(dh - ge)$. We will combine these like so: add the value corresponding to the leftmost element, then subtract the next one, and then add the last one. Therefore, the determinant of this 3 × 3 matrix is $a(ei - hf) - b(di - gf) + c(dh - ge)$.

In fact, if we were carrying out this process for a 4 × 4 matrix, the same rules would apply: calculate the determinant of the submatrices you obtain through "crossing out" each element of the row, then add the first, subtract the second, add the third, and subtract the fourth. This $+ - + -$ pattern extends to any size matrix. Don't worry too much about needing to remember all this – it's helpful to know what's happening under the hood, but there are shader functions that do this for you.

So far, we've looked at some great matrix operations, but none are quite as useful as the next one we'll look at. This one is the backbone of the entire graphics pipeline, and without it, we would struggle to build an efficient method of transforming data onto the screen.

Matrix Multiplication

Multiplying a matrix by another matrix can be a little tricky at first, but I'll go through it step by step. Like many other matrix operations, there are restrictions on the sizes of the two matrices: the number of columns of the first matrix must equal the number of rows in the second one due to the way matrix multiplication works. As it turns out, the result will have as many rows as the first matrix and as many columns as the second. Let's take matrices A and B^T as examples:

$$A = \begin{bmatrix} -7 & 4 & 2 \\ 8 & 0 & -1 \end{bmatrix} \qquad B^T = \begin{bmatrix} 5 & -8 \\ 2 & 1 \\ 3 & 1 \end{bmatrix}$$

If we were to calculate $A \times B^T$, then this would work because A has three columns and B^T has three rows. The resulting matrix will be 2×2. On the other hand, $A \times B$ is not a valid operation, because B only has two rows. Before even seeing how matrix multiplication works, we can already make an interesting observation: by the same rules, $B^T \times A$ is also a valid multiplication, but it will result in a 3×3 matrix. Matrix multiplication is said to be *noncommutative* because the order of the inputs matters. This is different from multiplying real numbers, which is *commutative* – for example, $3 \times 9 = 9 \times 3$. On the other hand, matrix multiplication is *associative* like real number multiplication – that is, for three matrices L, M, and N, it doesn't matter which order we resolve the following chain of multiplications: $L \times M \times N = (L \times M) \times N = L \times (M \times N)$.

Equation 2-22: Matrix multiplication sizes

$$A \times B^T = \begin{bmatrix} z_{1,1} & z_{1,2} \\ z_{2,1} & z_{2,2} \end{bmatrix} \qquad B^T \times A = \begin{bmatrix} y_{1,1} & y_{1,2} & y_{1,3} \\ y_{2,1} & y_{2,2} & y_{2,3} \\ y_{3,1} & y_{3,2} & y_{3,3} \end{bmatrix}$$

How do we carry out the multiplication operation? Let's calculate $A \times B^T$. We already know this will be a 2×2 matrix. To calculate the top-left element, $z_{1,1}$, we will perform a product of the first row of the first matrix with the first column of the second matrix. Similarly, the bottom-left element, $z_{2,1}$, is the product of the second row of matrix A and the first column of matrix B^T. The product works by taking the first element of the row and the first element of the column and multiplying them, then moving across the row and down the column and adding their product, and so on until you've reached the end of both the row and the column, resulting in a single scalar value to put in the result matrix. In fact, it works the same way as the dot product for vectors that we saw earlier.

Equation 2-23: Calculating the matrix multiplication

$$A \times B^T = \begin{bmatrix} -7 \times 5 + 4 \times 2 + 2 \times 3 & -7 \times (-8) + 4 \times 1 + 2 \times 1 \\ 8 \times 5 + 0 \times 2 + (-1) \times 3 & 8 \times (-8) + 0 \times 1 + (-1) \times 1 \end{bmatrix} = \begin{bmatrix} -21 & 62 \\ 37 & -65 \end{bmatrix}$$

Earlier, I introduced identity matrices. Recall that an identity matrix is square and has ones down the leading diagonal, with zeroes everywhere else. If we multiply any matrix by an identity matrix, then it is left unchanged by the operation. It doesn't matter if the identity is first or second (as long as the sizes are compatible).

Equation 2-24: Multiplying by the identity matrix

$$A \times I_2 = \begin{bmatrix} -7 \times 1 + 0 + 0 & 0 + 4 \times 1 + 0 & 0 + 0 + 2 \times 1 \\ 8 \times 1 + 0 + 0 & 0 + 0 \times 1 + 0 & 0 + 0 + (-1) \times 1 \end{bmatrix} = \begin{bmatrix} -7 & 4 & 2 \\ 8 & 0 & -1 \end{bmatrix}$$

One last property of matrix multiplication is that taking the transpose after matrix multiplication is the same as taking the transpose of the individual matrices and then multiplying *in the opposite order*.

Equation 2-25: Matrix multiplication and transpose interaction

$$(C \times D)^T = D^T \times C^T$$

Matrix Inverse

The final major matrix operation we will explore is the *inverse* of a matrix. I briefly mentioned that a matrix is *invertible* if its determinant is nonzero. But what is the inverse of a matrix? If we multiply a matrix, *E*, by its inverse, denoted E^{-1}, then the result will be an identity matrix. The order of multiplication does not matter – an identity matrix is always the result, and it will have the same size as E. Let's say that *E* is a 3 × 3 matrix.

Equation 2-26: Multiplying a matrix by its inverse

$$A \times A^{-1} = \begin{bmatrix} 1 & 0 & 0 \\ 0 & 1 & 0 \\ 0 & 0 & 1 \end{bmatrix} \qquad A^{-1} \times A = \begin{bmatrix} 1 & 0 \\ 0 & 1 \end{bmatrix}$$

And how do we calculate the inverse? For a 2×2 matrix, this is not too complicated to do by hand. It requires us to calculate the determinant first. Recall that the determinant of a matrix only exists if the matrix is square; this means that non-square matrices do not have an inverse. Matrices that do not have an inverse are also sometimes called *singular* or *degenerate*.

Equation 2-27: Inverting a 2×2 matrix

$$\begin{bmatrix} a & b \\ c & d \end{bmatrix}^{-1} = \frac{1}{ad - bc} \begin{bmatrix} d & -b \\ -c & a \end{bmatrix}$$

As you can see, we are dividing by the determinant of the matrix to obtain the result. Inside the matrix, we have swapped the positions of *a* and *d* and negated *b* and *c*. Let's try an example.

Equation 2-28: Matrix inverse example

$$\begin{bmatrix} 2 & -1 \\ 4 & -3 \end{bmatrix}^{-1} = \frac{1}{2 \times (-3) - 4 \times (-1)} \begin{bmatrix} -3 & 1 \\ -4 & 2 \end{bmatrix} = \left(-\frac{1}{2}\right) \begin{bmatrix} -3 & 1 \\ -4 & 2 \end{bmatrix} = \begin{bmatrix} 1.5 & -0.5 \\ 2 & -1 \end{bmatrix}$$

And what about inverting a 3×3 or 4×4 matrix? Calculating the inverse gets longer and more complicated the larger the matrix is, and it's not worth learning how to do it, since shaders provide a function to do this for you. I've shown you the example for 2×2 matrices because they are more manageable, but the process for 3×3 matrices and beyond will take a lot of space to explain with little payoff.

We have now seen the basic building blocks of math we will need for the rest of the book. Vector and matrix operations will form the building blocks upon which we will build the next bit of knowledge. So far, we have considered both vectors and matrices in a general sense, but now we are going to see how we can use both for purposes that are directly relevant to computer graphics.

Matrix Transformations

I mentioned previously that matrices are going to be powerful enough for us to use them in the graphics pipeline. Usually, we represent points (or vertices) in space using vectors. As it turns out, and as I have hinted toward slightly, we can consider vectors to be a special case of matrix, which has only one column or one row, depending on which way round it is written. We'll call them *column vectors* and *row vectors*. With that in mind, it becomes possible to manipulate point vectors using matrix multiplications – there are certain operations we can represent easily using matrices, and we're going to see how they all work, starting with scaling.

Note   If you need an extra resource to get to grips with matrix transformations, then I recommend learnopengl.com/Getting-started/Transformations. Although the website is geared toward learning OpenGL, this section is applicable to learning computer graphics in general.

Scaling Matrices

Scaling is the process of making an object larger or smaller. If we have a cube and we scale it by a factor of two, we have made it twice as large in each axis, as seen in Figure 2-7.

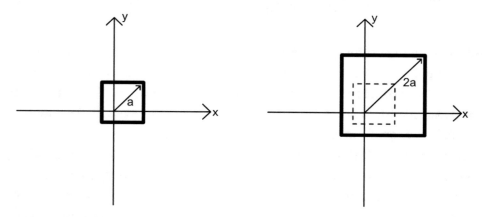

Figure 2-7. *Scaling an object in 2D by a uniform amount in each axis*

Of course, we can choose to scale in any of the x-, y-, or z-axis independently. Let's say we have a vector $v = (v_x, v_y, v_z)$ that we want to scale in each axis. If we wish to represent this using just vectors, we can define another vector $s = (s_x, s_y, s_z)$ to represent the scaling factor in each axis (if we want to uniformly scale in all axes, then $s_x = s_y = s_z$). Then, we can multiply the two together component-wise. This operation is called the *Hadamard product*, which isn't often discussed alongside other vector operations – we'll denote it as $v \circ s$.

Equation 2-29: Scaling a point via component-wise multiplication

$$\boldsymbol{v} \circ \boldsymbol{s} = \left(v_x s_x, v_y s_y, v_z s_z \right)$$

This is an efficient way to perform a scaling operation, but there's a drawback: it's not easy to combine this with other operations. In computer graphics, we often need to apply several transformations to an object at once (e.g., translation, rotation, and scaling). If we have a thousand vertices on our object, then we can do each of those operations one after the other on all vertices, or we can combine the operations into a single matrix via matrix multiplication and perform one pass over the vertices. The latter is far more efficient, and that's why we use matrices. So how do we represent scaling using a matrix? If you recall, the identity matrix has ones down the diagonal. If we multiply a vector by the identity matrix, it is the same as scaling by 1. Hence, if we swap out those ones for other values, we can scale by different amounts.

Equation 2-30: Scaling using a matrix

$$\begin{bmatrix} s_x & 0 & 0 \\ 0 & s_y & 0 \\ 0 & 0 & s_z \end{bmatrix} \begin{pmatrix} v_x \\ v_y \\ v_z \end{pmatrix} = \begin{pmatrix} v_x s_x \\ v_y s_y \\ v_z s_z \end{pmatrix}$$

Remember the rules for matrix multiplication: we have a 3×1 matrix (or column vector), and we wish to get another 3×1 matrix back out, so we need a 3×3 matrix for the scaling operation, and we need it to be on the left of the vector. I'll note here that, for brevity, I've only described how to scale about the origin. You could, theoretically, scale relative to any point in 3D space, but the math gets a lot trickier. One trick we can use in this case is to translate all points in space so that the origin is now at the desired scaling point, perform the scale, and then undo the original translation (we will see how translation works soon). Of course, scaling is not the only transformation we can apply to vertices. Let's also see how rotation works.

Rotation Matrices

Rotation is a bit more complicated than scaling. We can perform rotations around each of the x-, y-, and z-axes, like how we can scale nonuniformly in each of those directions, but now we'll end up with sine and cosine involved – that's a step-up in difficulty from just swapping out a few entries in a matrix. Figure 2-8 shows us what a rotation of angle θ looks like in 2D.

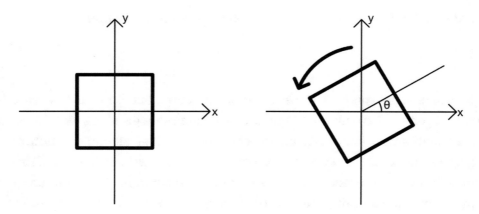

Figure 2-8. *Rotating counterclockwise by θ around the origin*

Let's see how a rotation around the z-axis works in 3D. A rotation around z will preserve the z-component of any point vector while changing the x- and y-components. A nice corollary of that fact is that any rotation in 2D can be thought of as a rotation around z, because you can think of 2D points as 3D points that have forgotten they have a z-axis (i.e., z = 0). If we wanted to carry out a rotation by angle θ around the z-axis, then conventionally the rotation would happen *anticlockwise* (or *counterclockwise* depending on where in the world you're reading this), and it looks like this when working solely with vectors:

Equation 2-31: Rotating by angle θ around the z-axis

$$R_{z,\theta}\left(v_x,v_y,v_z\right)=\left(v_x\cos\theta - v_y\sin\theta, v_x\sin\theta + v_y\cos\theta, v_z\right)$$

And, for completion, here are the similar rotations of angle θ around the y-axis and x-axis:

Equation 2-32: Rotating by angle θ around the y-axis and x-axis

$$R_{y,\theta}\left(v_x,v_y,v_z\right)=\left(v_x\cos\theta + v_z\sin\theta, v_y, -v_x\sin\theta + v_z\cos\theta\right)$$

$$R_{x,\theta}\left(v_x,v_y,v_z\right)=\left(v_x, v_y\cos\theta - v_z\sin\theta, v_y\sin\theta + v_z\cos\theta\right)$$

How would we represent these as matrices? As we can see, it's trickier to work out than the scaling matrix was because each output vector component sometimes depends on multiple input components. For example, when rotating about the z-axis, if the input x-component is v_x, then the output x-component is $v_x \cos \theta - v_y \sin \theta$. The rotation matrices, then, are not diagonal. In order, the rotations around the z-axis, y-axis, and x-axis by angle θ are represented by a matrix as such:

Equation 2-33: Rotating by angle θ around each axis using a matrix

$$R_{z,\theta} = \begin{bmatrix} \cos\theta & -\sin\theta & 0 \\ \sin\theta & \cos\theta & 0 \\ 0 & 0 & 1 \end{bmatrix}$$

$$R_{y,\theta} = \begin{bmatrix} \cos\theta & 0 & \sin\theta \\ 0 & 1 & 0 \\ -\sin\theta & 0 & \cos\theta \end{bmatrix}$$

$$R_{x,\theta} = \begin{bmatrix} 1 & 0 & 0 \\ 0 & \cos\theta & -\sin\theta \\ 0 & \sin\theta & \cos\theta \end{bmatrix}$$

Take a few minutes to try out a few example rotations by yourself by multiplying a vector by any of these matrices. If you follow the matrix multiplication steps, take note of which calculations you're doing – it's the Hadamard product we saw earlier in the scaling step. And what if we wanted to rotate by angle θ about an arbitrary axis other than the x-, y-, or z-axis? Like we saw with scaling, we need to transform the entire world so that the desired rotation axis aligns with one of those three, then perform the rotation around that axis, and then undo the transformations we did in the first place. In this case, we can perform rotations around the x-axis by angle ψ and y-axis by angle φ to do the initial alignment such that the desired rotation axis lies on the z-axis, then rotate around the z-axis by angle θ, and then rotate around the y-axis by angle $(-\varphi)$ and the x-axis by angle $(-\psi)$. Let's call the arbitrary rotation R_{new}.

Equation 2-34: Rotation around an arbitrary axis

$$R_{new} = R_{x,-\psi} \times R_{y,-\varphi} \times R_{z,\theta} \times R_{y,\varphi} \times R_{x,\psi}$$

This is a great example of how matrix multiplication can help us. Instead of needing to perform each of these rotations on each and every vertex one after the other, we can combine all five rotations into a single matrix via multiplication like this so we only need to multiply each vertex by one matrix. Note the order of rotations – since matrix multiplication is commutative, we must put the matrices in this order. That said, matrix multiplication is associative, so it doesn't matter which order we resolve each multiplication operation in once they've been written out like this. If we want to rotate about an arbitrary point other than the origin, then the process is like scaling – you can translate the entire space such that the arbitrary point lies at the origin, perform your desired rotation, and then undo the translation. On that note, it's time to see how translation in 3D space works.

Translation Matrices

Translation is probably the easiest of these three transformations to understand. Translation is the process of moving a point vector to a different position – all we need to do is specify an offset. Figure 2-9 shows us what translation in 2D looks like.

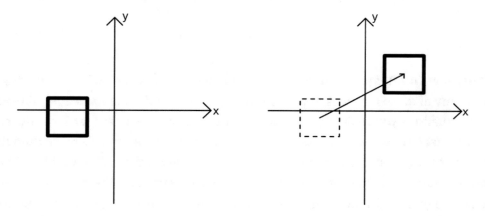

Figure 2-9. *Translation moves all vertices of a shape by the same offset*

With vectors, this is very easy to represent using vector addition; if we wish to move a point vector $v = (v_x, v_y, v_z)$ by an offset $t = (t_x, t_y, t_z)$, then we can represent that like so:

Equation 2-35: Translating a point vector

$$v + t = \left(v_x + t_x, v_y + t_y, v_z + t_z\right)$$

Since it's so easy to represent translation using vector addition, we can now go ahead and do the same thing we did with rotation and scaling and turn this into a matrix. But wait – we run into a problem if we try. With a 3 × 3 matrix, putting any value other than 1 along the leading diagonal will scale the points, which we don't want, and putting any value other than 0 in any of the other positions means that the output value for one of the components will depend in part on the input value of a different component, which we also don't want. That's because the rotation and scaling matrices we wrote assume that we are rotating or scaling around the origin, but translation is *moving the origin*. Unfortunately for us, we really need to represent translation as a matrix operation if we are to harness the full benefit of using matrices, so we are going to need more information.

Homogeneous Coordinates

Let's rethink the way we represent points using vectors. Right now, if we wish to represent a 2D point using a vector, we use a vector with two elements, x and y. For 3D, we add the component z. This is the most intuitive way to represent points (and directions) because we can separate out each component and see exactly where a point is along each axis. But this is not the only way of representing points. Let's say we have the point (x, y, z) in *Cartesian coordinates* (the system we've been implicitly using until now). I could just as easily represent it using the vector $(x, y, z, 1)$, which has four components instead of three. These are called *homogeneous coordinates*, and the fourth component is usually labeled w.

There are some quirks to using the new system over the old one. Firstly, any two vectors that are scalar multiples of one another represent the same point in 3D space. The vectors $(1, 2, 3, 1)$ and $(2, 4, 6, 2)$ represent the same point because each element of the second is twice the corresponding element of the first. This won't be relevant just yet, but we will revisit this fact later. For now, all we will do is set the w component to 1. It's also worth noting that we can get back to Cartesian coordinates by dividing each component by w and then removing the fourth component.

Now, what impact does this have on the hypothetical translation matrix? Since we are now using four-element vectors (which could be considered 4×1 matrices), we will need to use a 4×4 matrix. As we established previously, the translation values can't be inside the upper-left 3×3 part of the matrix, and we have the added constraint that we need the w component to stay as 1 after the transformation. Let's see what such a matrix looks like – I'll include my working out for the intermediate steps.

Equation 2-36: Translating a point in homogeneous coordinates using a matrix

$$\begin{bmatrix} 1 & 0 & 0 & t_x \\ 0 & 1 & 0 & t_y \\ 0 & 0 & 1 & t_z \\ 0 & 0 & 0 & 1 \end{bmatrix}\begin{pmatrix} v_x \\ v_y \\ v_z \\ 1 \end{pmatrix} = \begin{pmatrix} v_x+0+0+t_x \\ 0+v_y+0+t_y \\ 0+0+v_z+t_z \\ 0+0+0+1 \end{pmatrix} = \begin{pmatrix} v_x+t_x \\ v_y+t_y \\ v_z+t_z \\ 1 \end{pmatrix}$$

Fantastic! Now we have a matrix for translation. Take a couple of minutes to step through each bit of the multiplication to understand why this wasn't possible with just a 3 × 3 matrix. On that note, we won't be able to multiply the 3 × 3 transformation matrices for rotation and scaling that we previously worked out by the new 4 × 4 translation matrix, because the sizes are now incompatible. We need to pad out the matrices with something – in each case, we add a fourth column and fourth row containing zeroes, apart from the lower-right element, which is always 1.

Equation 2-37: 4 × 4 rotation and scaling matrices

$$S = \begin{bmatrix} s_x & 0 & 0 & 0 \\ 0 & s_y & 0 & 0 \\ 0 & 0 & s_z & 0 \\ 0 & 0 & 0 & 1 \end{bmatrix}$$

$$R_{z,\theta} = \begin{bmatrix} \cos\theta & -\sin\theta & 0 & 0 \\ \sin\theta & \cos\theta & 0 & 0 \\ 0 & 0 & 1 & 0 \\ 0 & 0 & 0 & 1 \end{bmatrix}$$

$$R_{y,\theta} = \begin{bmatrix} \cos\theta & 0 & \sin\theta & 0 \\ 0 & 1 & 0 & 0 \\ -\sin\theta & 0 & \cos\theta & 0 \\ 0 & 0 & 0 & 1 \end{bmatrix}$$

$$R_{x,\theta} = \begin{bmatrix} 1 & 0 & 0 & 0 \\ 0 & \cos\theta & -\sin\theta & 0 \\ 0 & \sin\theta & \cos\theta & 0 \\ 0 & 0 & 0 & 1 \end{bmatrix}$$

By now, we are armed with the basic knowledge we'll need for tackling the computer graphics pipeline. It's time to see how each piece of the puzzle we've seen so far fits into the pipeline as a whole and understand how the math we've seen helps us move data from one stage of the pipeline to the next.

Space Transformations

The graphics pipeline is all about spaces. Don't worry. This isn't rocket science, and we're not going into actual *outer space*, but we are going to learn about many different types of space that exist throughout the graphics pipeline and how we can use matrices to convert from one space to another. In the graphics pipeline, each vertex on a mesh is initially defined relative to a local origin point. This is called *object space* (or sometimes *model space*). This is how your mesh looks when loaded in an external modeling program such as *Blender* or *Maya*, as seen in Figure 2-10.

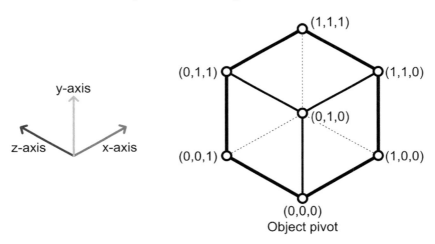

Figure 2-10. *In object space, all vertices of the object are defined relative to the pivot point of the object*

However, in Unity, you will have many objects in the scene, and they will not share a common origin point; when objects are placed at different positions in the world, with individual rotations and scales, this is called *world space*. All vertices are now relative to a common world origin, and each individual object has a pivot point, with each vertex relative to that point, as seen in Figure 2-11. However, this doesn't happen magically – we need to supply a matrix ourselves to do this transformation.

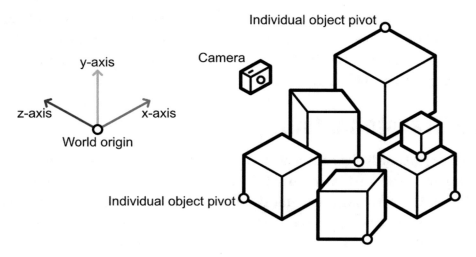

Figure 2-11. *In world space, objects appear relative to a world origin point*

Note   Learn OpenGL has a dedicated section about coordinate transforms at learnopengl.com/Getting-started/Coordinate-Systems.

Object-to-World Space Transformation

Relating this to Unity in particular, each GameObject in your scene has a Transform component, which specifies the position, rotation, and scale of the object. The *model matrix* – the one that transforms from object to world space – contains each of these transformations inside a single matrix. Thankfully, we've covered each of these transformations already, so we will work through an example using what we learned previously.

We are going to transform the point $v = (v_x, v_y, v_z)$ by translating it by $t = (t_x, t_y, t_z)$ and scaling it by a factor of $s = (s_x, s_y, s_z)$, and, for the sake of simplicity, we'll rotate only around the z-axis by an angle of θ (the real graphics pipeline can rotate around an arbitrary axis or perform multiple rotations). Matrix multiplication is noncommutative, so the order of each operation is important – which order should we do them in? In general, it shouldn't matter if we are consistent. However, in this context, we know that the scaling and rotation operations assume that our point is relative to the origin, so it will be best if we leave the translation as the final operation. Let's work through the example. Remember that we're using homogeneous coordinates, so we'll be transforming a slightly modified point $\boldsymbol{v}' = (v_x, v_y, v_z, 1)$.

Equation 2-38: Object-to-world transformation example (model transformation)

$$
\begin{bmatrix} 1 & 0 & 0 & t_x \\ 0 & 1 & 0 & t_y \\ 0 & 0 & 1 & t_z \\ 0 & 0 & 0 & 1 \end{bmatrix}
\begin{bmatrix} s_x & 0 & 0 & 0 \\ 0 & s_y & 0 & 0 \\ 0 & 0 & s_z & 0 \\ 0 & 0 & 0 & 1 \end{bmatrix}
\begin{bmatrix} \cos\theta & -\sin\theta & 0 & 0 \\ \sin\theta & \cos\theta & 0 & 0 \\ 0 & 0 & 1 & 0 \\ 0 & 0 & 0 & 1 \end{bmatrix}
\begin{bmatrix} v_x \\ v_y \\ v_z \\ 1 \end{bmatrix}
$$

$$
= \begin{bmatrix} s_x\cos\theta & -s_x\sin\theta & 0 & t_x \\ s_y\sin\theta & s_y\cos\theta & 0 & t_y \\ 0 & 0 & s_z & t_z \\ 0 & 0 & 0 & 1 \end{bmatrix}
\begin{bmatrix} v_x \\ v_y \\ v_z \\ 1 \end{bmatrix}
$$

$$
= \begin{bmatrix} v_x s_x\cos\theta - v_y s_x\sin\theta + t_x \\ v_x s_y\sin\theta + v_y s_y\cos\theta + t_y \\ v_z s_z + t_z \\ 1 \end{bmatrix}
$$

We won't only be transforming this single point, however. These matrices operate on every point in the mesh, but as I mentioned, we will multiply all the matrices together once and use that on every vertex. There is an extra wrinkle involved – what if the GameObject under consideration is a child object of some other GameObject? In that case, we can just evaluate from the bottom of the hierarchy upward: we apply the model for the object under consideration, then apply the model matrix of its parent, and so on until you reach the topmost object. This process can be optimized by calculating the model matrix for each GameObject only once and keeping it in memory, since the model matrix of any one object might be used several times.

Now that every vertex is in world space, let's think about the next step. When rendering objects to the screen, we need some viewpoint within the world to use as our frame of reference, and we usually call this the *camera*. You can see it in Figure 2-11. Unity provides a Camera component we can attach to a GameObject for this reason; although we can have more than one, for the sake of simplicity, let's assume there is only one and that it will render to the full screen. The next step is to transform everything relative to the camera.

World-to-View Space Transformation

When all objects in the scene are relative to the camera, we call this *view space* (sometimes it's called *camera space* or *eye space*). When converting vertex positions in the scene from world space to view space, we don't really do anything we haven't seen before – we just need to transform the entire scene such that the camera's local right, up, and forward directions align with the world's x-, y-, and z-axes and the camera is positioned at the world origin. Hence, the *view matrix*, which is applied to every object in the scene, ends up being the inverse of the camera's model matrix. Figure 2-12 shows a scene in view space from the camera's perspective. There's not much else to say about this transformation, so let's move on to the next step, where we define which objects will be drawn by the camera and which won't.

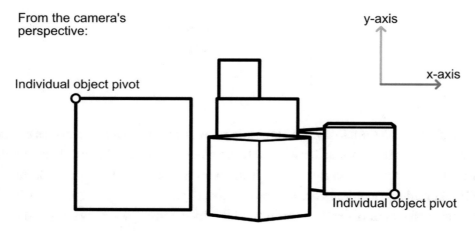

Figure 2-12. *A representation of view space from the camera's point of view. Objects seen in this view have a z-position greater than 0. View space is like world space, but the origin is at the camera's position. Not all objects represented here will necessarily be rendered*

View-to-Clip Space Transformation

Game cameras come in two flavors: *orthographic* and *perspective* (although strawberry and chocolate would be better in my opinion). Each type dictates the shape of the view volume of the camera – in other words, objects outside this volume will not be "seen" by the camera.

An orthographic camera's view volume is a cuboid defined by six planes. The near clip plane and far clip plane, respectively, define a minimum and maximum distance along the camera's forward direction, and objects must lie between those two distances to be drawn. The other four faces, which lie parallel to the camera's forward direction, are defined by the aspect ratio of the screen and the "size" of the camera (which is a setting in Unity). Objects seen by an orthographic camera will have the same size no matter where inside the view volume they appear (see Figure 2-13), which isn't how your own vision works. However, this is usually preferable for 2D games.

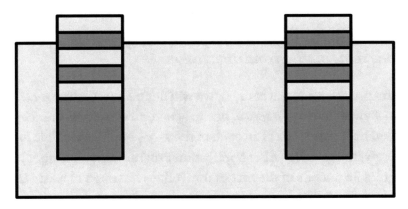

Figure 2-13. *Six lit cubes on top of a plane, as captured by an orthographic camera*

On the other hand, a perspective camera's view volume is a *frustum*, which is like a pyramid shape with the tip sliced off. The near and far clip planes work the same way, but the shape of the other four planes is defined by the aspect ratio and the *field of view (FOV)* of the camera (which is also a setting in Unity). Unlike an orthographic camera, objects seen by a perspective camera look smaller when further away, like in real life. An example of a scene captured by a perspective camera is seen in Figure 2-14.

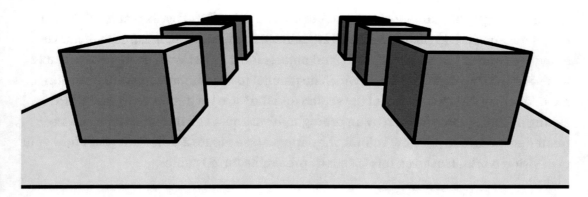

Figure 2-14. *The same six lit cubes on a plane, as captured by a perspective camera with the same position and orientation*

Based on the properties of the camera, we will define a *projection matrix* to transform from view space to *clip space*. In clip space, all objects in the scene will exist in a box bounded between –1 and 1 in each of the x-, y-, and z-axes. This has a few advantages: Firstly, the graphics API (Application Programming Interface) can efficiently clip all objects that lie outside of the box so that it does not need to waste GPU resources on further steps. Secondly, these positions are independent of the screen's or the game window's resolution. Figure 2-15 shows what clip space might look like.

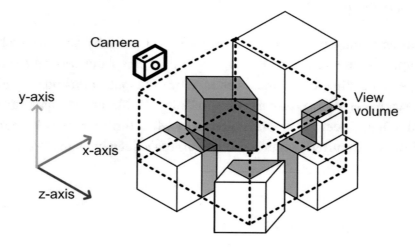

Figure 2-15. *Clip space places all objects inside a virtual box. Gray objects are inside the box; white ones are outside. Although the box dimensions are bounded between –1 and 1 in each direction, the box can still be a cuboid when visualized in world space. Objects are "stretched" to fill the clip volume*

The projection matrix for an orthographic camera is constructed differently from one for a perspective camera. The orthographic variant is easier to create, and it looks like the following:

Equation 2-39: Orthographic projection matrix

$$
P_{ortho} = \begin{bmatrix}
\left(\dfrac{2}{right - left} \right) & 0 & 0 & -\left(\dfrac{right + left}{right - left} \right) \\
0 & \left(\dfrac{2}{top - bottom} \right) & 0 & -\left(\dfrac{top + bottom}{top - bottom} \right) \\
0 & 0 & \left(\dfrac{2}{far - near} \right) & -\left(\dfrac{far + near}{far - near} \right) \\
0 & 0 & 0 & 1
\end{bmatrix}
$$

Here, the *right, left, top,* and *bottom* variables represent the distance in Unity units of each respective side plane from the center of the near plane, and the *near* and *far* variables, unsurprisingly, represent the distances of the near and far clip planes from the camera. Figure 2-16 shows some of these distances in a top-down view.

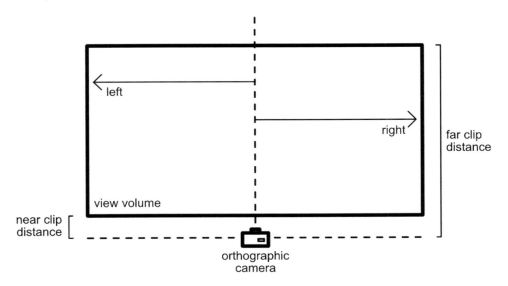

Figure 2-16. *A top-down view of an orthographic camera view volume*

We can discern a lot about what the orthographic projection matrix is doing just by looking at it. On the right-hand side, we can see classic signs of a translation – this is repositioning each vertex such that the center of the view volume becomes (0, 0). The values along the leading diagonal represent a scaling operation such that the edges of the viewing volume are bounded between –1 and 1 in each axis. This matrix will also preserve the value of the w component of the point vector – if it is 1 before the multiplication, it will be 1 afterward.

The equivalent matrix for perspective projection is a little more complicated to understand. An orthographic camera did not need to account for the field of view of the camera, because objects don't appear smaller the further away they are. For a perspective camera, however, objects *do* appear smaller when further away, and the field of view is responsible for how strong the shrinking effect is. Figure 2-17 is a 2D representation of a perspective camera view volume.

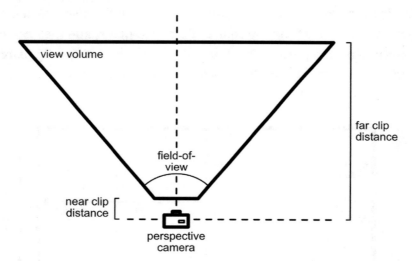

Figure 2-17. *A top-down view of a perspective camera view volume*

The perspective projection matrix is calculated like so:

Equation 2-40: Perspective projection matrix

$$P_{persp} = \begin{bmatrix} \left(\dfrac{2 \cdot near}{right - left}\right) & 0 & \left(\dfrac{right + left}{right - left}\right) & 0 \\ 0 & \left(\dfrac{2 \cdot near}{top - bottom}\right) & \left(\dfrac{top + bottom}{top - bottom}\right) & 0 \\ 0 & 0 & \left(\dfrac{far + near}{far - near}\right) & -\left(\dfrac{2 \cdot far \cdot near}{far - near}\right) \\ 0 & 0 & 1 & 0 \end{bmatrix}$$

Applying the perspective projection matrix also ends up with each vertex position inside a bounded box, but it must account for the field of view of the camera. We define the top, bottom, left, and right values relative to the vertical field of view (or FOV) in radians and aspect ratio using a bit of trigonometry like so:

Equation 2-41: Calculating values for the perspective projection matrix

$$top = near \cdot \tan\left(\frac{FOV}{2}\right)$$

$$bottom = -top$$

$$right = aspect \cdot top$$

$$left = -right$$

The most interesting part of the matrix is that it will set the w component of the output vector to the z component of the input vector, which will be important later. For the first time, we will see values of w other than 1.

These transformations are the backbone of the vertex shader stage, which we will see in the next chapter, and there is another trick we can do to make the pipeline run as efficiently as possible. The view and projection matrices are based on the camera's properties, which usually stay consistent while drawing a frame – that means we can multiply the two together. On top of that, the model matrix stays consistent for every vertex of an object, so we can multiply the model, view, and projection matrices together for drawing each object. The combination *model-view-projection (MVP) matrix*, as it's called, is used in vertex shaders to perform all transformations in one fell swoop. It looks like this:

Equation 2-42: The model-view-projection matrix

$$M_{MVP} = M_{projection} \times M_{view} \times M_{model}$$

There is one last step after each transformation has been performed. We are still in homogeneous coordinates, so we need to transform back into Cartesian coordinates. At the same time, we need to collapse our 3D points onto a 2D screen.

Perspective Divide

Recall that, in homogeneous coordinates, any point that is a scalar multiple of another point represents the same thing. $(1, 2, 3, 1)$ is the same as $(2, 4, 6, 2)$. When using a perspective camera, the MVP transformation ended up setting the position's w component equal to z. What we want to do now is collapse all points in the world onto a plane located at $z = 1$ – this is called the *perspective divide*. The reason for this is that two objects in the scene with the same (x, y) coordinates in the world shouldn't necessarily appear at the same (x, y) point on your screen due to the perspective effect, where objects further back appear smaller. Figure 2-18 shows how two such points will get projected onto a plane differently.

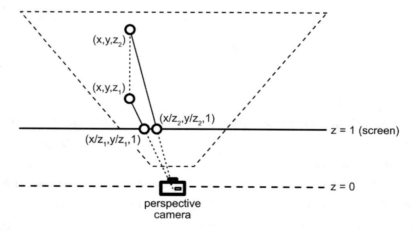

Figure 2-18. *Two points with the same (x, y) coordinates may not be projected onto the same point on the screen if they have a different z coordinate, due to the way perspective projection collapses points onto the screen (i.e., the z = 1 plane)*

By dividing homogeneous coordinates by the w component, we end up with the vector $\left(\frac{x}{w},\frac{y}{w},\frac{z}{w},1\right)$. Since we had previously set $w = z$, this is equivalent to $\left(\frac{x}{z},\frac{y}{z},1,1\right)$, which puts all positions on the plane z=1, like we wanted. Once we have divided by w, we can ignore the last two components of the vector to end up with the final normalized screen position of the point: this is called *normalized device coordinates*, a 2D representation that maps the top edge of your screen to $y = 1$, the lower edge to $y = -1$, the left edge to $x = -1$, and the right edge to $x = 1$. The perspective divide happens automatically between the vertex and fragment shader stages.

Summary

This chapter has served as your introduction to the math involved in computer graphics. I hope you're still intact! The basic building blocks are vectors, and we can manipulate them in many ways, including using matrices to multiply vectors. Matrix multiplication is indispensable in the graphics pipeline because it allows us to combine operations efficiently. Using matrices, we will apply a series of transformations to take vertices of a mesh from object space all the way to device coordinates. Here is a summary of what we learned:

- Vectors can be used to represent points in any dimension.

- There are many operations you can carry out on vectors, such as addition, scalar multiplication, normalization, dot product, and cross product.

- Matrices are 2D arrays of numbers with a number of rows and columns.

- Some matrix operations, such as determinant and inverse, only exist on square matrices. Some matrices do not have an inverse, and they are called singular.

- Homogeneous coordinates add a fourth component to facilitate matrix transformations that would otherwise be impossible, such as translating 3D points.

- A series of matrix transformations operate on vertex data, taking it from object space to world space, to view space, to clip space, and to normalized device coordinates.

CHAPTER 3

Your Very First Shader

It's finally time to make our first shader! If you've ever followed a tutorial to learn a new programming language, then your first program was probably logging "Hello, World!" to the console or the screen. It's a bit harder to do that with shaders, so we'll settle with displaying a mesh and applying a basic color to it. In this chapter, I will show you how to set up your scene and explain which components need to be attached to objects. Then, we will see how shaders in Unity work, and we will write our very first vertex and fragment shader functions. The differences between shaders in each of Unity's render pipelines are explored. Finally, I will cover the basic shader syntax that you will be seeing throughout the book.

Shader code isn't the only way to write shaders in Unity. If you prefer to avoid programming, then the next chapter will introduce Shader Graph, Unity's visual shader editor. However, you will still find the first part of this chapter useful. To prepare for writing our very first shader, let's set up a new Unity project.

Project Setup

Before we can jump into writing our first shader, we have an important decision to make: which render pipeline will we use? I briefly described these in Chapter 1, but to recap, there are three pipelines:

- The built-in render pipeline was Unity's only rendering code up until 2017. Most older learning resources available regarding shaders use the built-in pipeline, although some are very outdated.

- The Universal Render Pipeline, URP, is a more "lightweight" pipeline aimed at lower-end machines and cross-platform development. It used to be named the "Lightweight Render Pipeline," or LWRP.

- The High-Definition Render Pipeline, HDRP, is intended for games that require high-fidelity rendering and lighting quality. A restricted number of platforms support HDRP.

© Daniel Ilett 2022
D. Ilett, *Building Quality Shaders for Unity*®, https://doi.org/10.1007/978-1-4842-8652-4_3

If you don't know much about each render pipeline, then it can be very tricky to make this decision up front. After all, while it is possible to switch from one pipeline to another mid-development, it can be difficult to untangle your work from the original pipeline and rework it into the new one. With that in mind, here are a few use cases that I hope will assist you in making your choice:

- If you're just starting out with Unity and are here to learn shaders without having a specific project in mind, **I recommend starting with URP**. Unity intends to make URP the default pipeline for new projects in the future, so an increasing proportion of learning resources will move away from the built-in pipeline and toward URP.

- If you are working on a multi-platform project targeting high-end consoles (e.g., PS5, PS4, Xbox One, Xbox Series X/S) and PC, then you can choose any pipeline, subject to other requirements. These are the platforms that currently support HDRP, which is the best choice if you want to use cutting-edge graphics.

- If you plan to target mobile, web, or other consoles (e.g., Nintendo Switch), then *do not* use HDRP.

- If you plan only to use shader code and not Shader Graph, then I recommend not using HDRP. Although code-based shaders are possible in HDRP, learning resources are lacking compared with the other two pipelines; Unity themselves recommend using Shader Graph when working in HDRP. That's what I'll be doing throughout the book!

- If you are left with a choice between the built-in pipeline and URP, it can be difficult to fall on either side of the fence. I still recommend URP because it is going to receive the most active development in the future, but if you do pick the built-in pipeline, then rest assured almost all the book's examples will still work!

Once you have picked a pipeline, let's create a new project via the Unity Hub.

Creating a Project

When you open the Unity Hub, you will see the screen like that in Figure 3-1, which lists all your existing Unity projects if you have any. I've blurred out my project names – sorry if you wanted to snoop on what I've been working on!

Figure 3-1. *The Unity Hub, which opens on the Projects tab*

Click the *New project* button in the top-right corner of this window. You'll see another window where we are presented with many templates, as shown in Figure 3-2. I'm going to show you how to build shaders primarily in 3D, so let's pick the respective 3D option for the pipeline you will be using:

- If you're using the built-in pipeline, pick the template simply called "3D."

- In URP, pick the template called "3D Sample Scene (URP)." This template contains an example scene with a few assets already set up for you.

- Similarly, in HDRP, pick "3D Sample Scene (HDRP)."

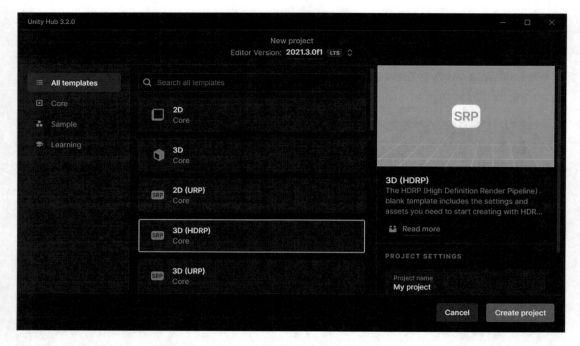

Figure 3-2. *The New project screen of the Unity Hub*

Type a project name and save location into the fields on the right-hand side of the screen and click the *Create project* button. Unity will create a new folder and populate it with the template files. Then the Unity Editor will open. We can now set up a scene ready to create and test our shaders.

Setting Up the Scene

If we are going to start writing shaders, we'll need to attach them to an object in the scene to see what it looks like at runtime. I usually add a humble sphere to test most of my 3D shaders, so let's add one now by following these steps:

- Add the Unity primitive sphere to your scene, which you can do via the toolbar through *GameObject* ➤ *3D Object* ➤ *Sphere*. You may find it useful at times to use other meshes, but a sphere is perfect for quickly testing most effects.

- We use materials in Unity to attach shaders to objects. Materials are contained in the Assets folder alongside other assets like textures, scripts, and meshes. Create one by right-clicking in the Project View and selecting *Create* ➤ *Material*. Name it something like "HelloWorld", since we'll be making our very first shader.

    - Unity automatically uses a default shader: the Standard shader in the built-in pipeline and the Lit shader in URP and HDRP.

- Drag the material onto the sphere mesh you added. The appearance of the sphere may change slightly when you do so.

Note   At this point, if you are using HDRP or want to only use Shader Graph, skip to the next chapter to make your first shader. Writing shaders with code is possible in HDRP, but it is a magnitude more difficult to do due to a lack of learning resources and the increased complexity in using HDRP.

- Create a new shader file by right-clicking in the Project View and choosing *Create* ➤ *Shader* ➤ *Unlit Shader*, which copies a template shader into the new file with a *.shader* file extension. Name it "HelloWorld.shader" since it's our first shader. You don't need to type the extension.

- Select the HelloWorld material we created previously, and in the Shader drop-down at the top of the Inspector window, find "Unlit/HelloWorld". See Figure 3-3 to see an example material in Unity.

Figure 3-3. *A material created in Unity. From top to bottom, this window features a drop-down to pick the shader used by the material, a section for shader properties that we can tweak, and a preview window at the bottom*

Tip   You can change how the preview window on a material behaves using the row of buttons just above the preview. Click the play button to animate the material over time. Use the next button along to change to a different preview mesh. Use the button with yellow dots on it to tweak how many light sources are simulated. Use the drop-down with the half-blue sphere icon to specify a reflection probe for the preview. And use the menu on the right-hand side to dock and undock the preview window.

The template shader is already a completed shader, but it's no use to start off with a completed shader since we're here to learn. Open the shader file by double-clicking it in the Project View and delete the file contents – any material using the shader will turn magenta, which happens whenever the shader fails to compile properly. Now that our scene is set up, we can focus on writing the shader file. We will start by discussing shader syntax.

Note   If you installed Unity with the default settings, you most likely have Visual Studio or Visual Studio Code installed. Therefore, when you double-click a shader file, Unity will open it in one of those. You can customize which editor is used via *Preferences ➤ External Tools.*

Writing a Shader in Unity

There are several popular graphics APIs (*Application Programming Interfaces*) that are used by programs, such as Unity, to handle graphics for us. Each graphics API has a corresponding *shading language*:

- The OpenGL API, a popular cross-platform graphics library, uses a shading language called GLSL (for OpenGL Shading Language).

- DirectX, which is designed for use on Microsoft's platforms, uses HLSL (High-Level Shading Language).

- Cg, a deprecated shading language developed by Nvidia, uses the common feature set of GLSL and HLSL and can cross-compile to each depending on the target hardware.

The shading language is what you write shader code in. A game or game engine will compile shaders written in one of those languages to run on the GPU. Although it is possible to write shaders using any one of GLSL, HLSL, or Cg, modern Unity shaders are written in HLSL.

Note   In the past, Unity shaders used Cg as the primary shading language. Over time, the default has switched to HLSL. Unity will automatically cross-compile your shader code for the target platform.

There is an extra layer to it in Unity. Unity uses a proprietary language called *ShaderLab*, which acts as a wrapper around the shading languages I just mentioned. All code-based shaders in Unity are written in ShaderLab syntax, and it achieves several aims at once:

- ShaderLab provides ways to communicate between the Unity Editor, C# scripts, and the underlying shader language.

- It provides an easy way to override common shader settings. In other game engines, you might need to delve into settings windows or write graphics API code to change blend, clipping, or culling settings, but in Unity, we can write those commands directly in ShaderLab.

- ShaderLab provides a cascading system that allows us to write several shaders in the same file, and Unity will pick the first compatible shader to run. This means we can write shaders for different hardware or render pipelines and the one that matches up with the user's hardware and your project's chosen render pipeline will get picked.

It'll become a lot easier to understand how this all works with a practical example, so let's start writing some ShaderLab.

Writing ShaderLab Code

In this example, we will write a shader to display an object with a single color, and we'll add the option to change that color from within the Unity Editor. Most of the code required for this shader is the same between the built-in and Universal render pipelines, but there are a few differences, which I will explain when we reach them.

Note   When there is a difference between the code required for each pipeline, I will present you with two code blocks labeled with the pipeline they are intended for. Choose only the one for your pipeline.

Open the HelloWorld.shader file. Inside the file, we'll start by naming the shader using the Shader keyword. This name will appear when viewing any material in the Inspector if you use the *Shader* drop-down at the top of the material (see Figure 3-3). After declaring the name, the rest of the shader is enclosed within a pair of curly braces, so we will put any subsequent code inside these braces.

Tip   You can include folders inside the name – for example, naming the shader "Examples/HelloWorld" places the shader under the folder "Example" alongside any other shaders that use that folder in their path.

Listing 3-1. Beginning a shader file

```
Shader "Examples/HelloWorld"
{

}
```

Inside the braces, we will declare a list of *material properties*. These can be thought of as the shader's variables, as this list of properties will appear in the Unity Editor on any selected material that uses this shader. Properties are powerful, because they let us create several materials that use the same shader, but with different variable values. There are several types of property we will see throughout the book, but to start with, we will add a single Color property. The syntax is similar to declaring the Shader – we will write the Properties keyword, followed by a set of curly braces. The syntax for the properties themselves looks a bit strange at first.

Listing 3-2. Declaring properties in ShaderLab

```
Shader "Examples/HelloWorld"
{
    Properties
    {
        _BaseColor("Base Color", Color) = (1,1,1,1)
    }
}
```

The line of code declaring the property has lots of parts to it, so let's break down the weird syntax:

- Conventionally, shader property names start with an underscore, and we capitalize the start of each word. In this case, _BaseColor is the *computer-readable* name of the property, and we will refer to it in shader code later as _BaseColor.

- Inside the parentheses, we first specify a *human-readable* name in double quotes, which Unity uses in the Inspector. In this case, the name we chose is "Base Color", which is like the code-readable name anyway.

- Next comes the type of the variable, which is Color. We could also have types like Texture2D, Cubemap, Float, and so on – these are all types we'll see later.

- Finally, we give the property a default value after the equals sign, which is used when you create a new material with this shader.

Note   It seems strange to have two different names for each property, but it's useful to have both types of names like this because we might want to use certain technical names within the code, but another person working with this shader to create materials in the Inspector might not understand (or need to know) what the code name means. A human-readable name makes it clearer what the property is for.

Colors are made up of four components: red, green, blue, and alpha/transparency. In this example, the color is opaque white by default since all four components have a value of 1. You may have encountered different standards for color values before, so here's how Unity deals with them:

- Colors are often stored as unsigned (positive) integers between 0 and 255. This requires 8 bits of storage space. 0 means no color, and 255 means full color.

- Colors are made up of a mix of red, green, and blue. Plus we have an "alpha" value that represents transparency. Therefore, we use four channels of 8 bits each for colors.

- In Unity, especially in shaders, we instead use floating-point values between 0 and 1 to represent each color channel. A floating-point number has a fractional part. A color value of (1, 1, 1, 1) means all four channels use the maximum value, which appears as fully opaque white.

- We use this representation in shaders for higher precision. All you need to remember is that a regular color value is between 0 and 1.

Now that we've dealt with the Properties block, we will add a SubShader.

Adding a SubShader

With ShaderLab, we can add several SubShader blocks with different features to ensure that this shader will work on different kinds of hardware or different render pipelines, but in this example, we will only add one.

Listing 3-3. Adding a SubShader in ShaderLab

```
Shader "Examples/HelloWorld"
{
      Properties { ... }

      SubShader
      {

      }
}
```

If you define multiple SubShader blocks, Unity picks the first one that works on your combination of hardware and render pipeline. When your hardware is incompatible with every SubShader, the shader will fail to compile, and Unity will display the error material, which is magenta.

Note   Always put the SubShader with the highest requirements first. There doesn't seem to be a hard limit on the number of SubShaders you can include in one file, but you'll find it difficult to maintain the file if you add too many.

There's also the Fallback system, which you can use to specify the name of an alternative shader file to use if every SubShader in this shader file is incompatible – Unity carries out the same process of checking every SubShader in that file (and if they don't work, every Fallback too) and picks the first that works. Fallback shaders should be specified *after the closing brace* of the final SubShader block. If you decide you don't want to use a Fallback, you can choose not to include the keyword or explicitly write Fallback Off.

Listing 3-4. Specifying the Unlit/Color shader as a fallback

```
Shader "Examples/HelloWorld"
{
      Properties { ... }

      SubShader { ... }
      SubShader { ... }

      Fallback "Unlit/Color"
}
```

Inside the SubShader, we will start to add settings that control how the shader will operate – there are a lot of possible options, but we'll add only one for now: Tags.

SubShader Tags

The Tags block lets us specify whether the shader is opaque or transparent, set whether this object is rendered after others, and specify which render pipeline this SubShader works with. Each tag is a key-value pair of two strings, where the first string is the name of the tag and the second string is its value. Let's add a RenderType tag to specify we want to use *opaque rendering* for this object.

Note   We can add code comments in ShaderLab in a similar manner to C-style languages: single-line comments start with a double forward slash //, and multiline comments are enclosed between /* and */.

Listing 3-5. Adding Tags inside a SubShader in ShaderLab

```
SubShader
{
    Tags
    {
        // Render alongside other opaque objects.
        "RenderType" = "Opaque"
    }
}
```

Inside the Tags block, we can also specify the Queue to determine when this object gets drawn. Earlier, I gave a simplified explanation of how Unity draws objects: all opaque objects first and then all transparent objects. It's a bit more in-depth than that. The Queue is an integer value, where lower values get rendered first. There are a few preset values:

- Background = 1000

- Geometry = 2000

- AlphaTest = 2450

- Transparent = 3000

- Overlay = 4000

If you would like to use a value other than these presets, we can add or subtract values. To set a Queue value of 1500, we can say Background+500 or Geometry-500. Using these default values, you can see that any objects in the Background, Geometry, or AlphaTest queue get rendered before anything in the Transparent queue. For opaque objects like this one, we usually stick with Geometry, so we will insert the following line inside the Tags block.

Listing 3-6. Setting the rendering queue in the Tags block

```
Tags
{
    "RenderType" = "Opaque"
    "Queue" = "Geometry"
}
```

The last tag I want to add for now is the `RenderPipeline` tag. This tag can be used to restrict a SubShader to a specific pipeline, which is extremely useful if you're using features or syntax exclusive to one pipeline. You can even include multiple SubShaders in the file, each one supporting a different pipeline. Here are the values you should use:

- For URP, the tag value is "UniversalPipeline".

- In HDRP, the tag value is "HDRenderPipeline".

- In the built-in pipeline, there is no corresponding tag value. Place any SubShader blocks for the built-in pipeline at the bottom of the list.

With that in mind, if you are using URP, we'll add the following tag to our shader. This is the first pipeline-dependent piece of code we're adding. In the built-in pipeline, you shouldn't add this.

Listing 3-7. Adding a RenderPipeline tag in the Tags block in URP

```
Tags
{
        "RenderType" = "Opaque"
        "Queue" = "Geometry"
        "RenderPipeline" = "UniversalPipeline"
}
```

With the Tags block out of the way, the last bit of ShaderLab we need to add is a Pass block.

Adding a Pass

A Pass is where we add the "proper" shader code and start making things appear on-screen. A pass is one complete cycle of rendering an object; a SubShader can contain multiple Pass blocks, and if there is more than one, then Unity will run all of them from top to bottom.

Listing 3-8. Creating a shader pass inside the SubShader

```
SubShader
{
        Tags { ... }
```

```
Pass
{

}
}
```

It's also possible to add a second Tags block inside a Pass block. The most common reason for doing so is to label passes with a `LightMode` tag, which tells Unity what the pass will be used for. We don't always need to add one, although when I'm working in URP, I like to explicitly add one to each pass because URP only allows you to add one pass with each valid `LightMode` tag. We'll explore those tags in later sections. For now, if you are using URP, we will add a `LightMode` tag called `UniversalForward`, which is used for "standard" geometry rendering with the Forward Renderer. In the built-in pipeline, don't worry about adding a `LightMode` tag for now.

Listing 3-9. Using the UniversalForward LightMode tag in URP

```
Pass
{
        Tags
        {
                "LightMode" = "UniversalForward"
        }
}
```

Inside the Pass, we will also specify which shading language we are using. In the past, Unity used the Cg language for its shaders, but the language has since been discontinued, and Unity shaders now use HLSL (although it is also possible to write GLSL shaders too). I'm mentioning this here because we are going to use two enclosing keywords to wrap our shader code – `HLSLPROGRAM` and `ENDHLSL`.

Note   You might find tutorials online that still use the Cg language, which requires code to be enclosed in `CGPROGRAM` and `ENDCG`. Most of the syntax is identical between Cg and HLSL, but we're going to exclusively do things the modern way in HLSL.

Listing 3-10. Specifying the shading language

```
SubShader
{
    Tags { ... }
    Pass
    {
        HLSLPROGRAM
                // HLSL code goes in here.
    ENDHLSL
    }
}
```

We're finally ready to write some HLSL code. How exciting! From this point, all code will be written between the HLSLPROGRAM and ENDHLSL keywords. We'll no longer be writing in Unity's proprietary ShaderLab language and will instead be writing in the HLSL shading language. Next, let's do some setup for our shader.

Pragma Directives and Includes

We're going to write *vertex* and *fragment* functions to determine what the shader does. I usually name them vert and frag, respectively. These are just regular HLSL functions that we can name however we want, so to tell Unity which functions are the vertex and fragment shaders, respectively, we use special preprocessing directives like the following.

Listing 3-11. #pragma statements for declaring vertex and fragment functions

```
HLSLPROGRAM
    #pragma vertex vert
    #pragma fragment frag
ENDHLSL
```

#pragma statements pop up quite often when writing shaders. We use them to define shader functions, like Listing 3-11, as well as to compile shaders for certain platforms or require certain hardware features. We also use a different preprocessor statement, #include, to include other shader files inside this one. It's in the name really! Quite helpfully, Unity provides a large number of shader include files containing useful functions, matrices, and macros that we frequently need. The location of these files differs depending on the pipeline you're using:

- In the built-in pipeline, it's not easy to access these within the engine directly. They can be found at *[Unity root installation folder]/Editor/ Data/CGIncludes*.

  - The most important and frequently used file is *UnityCG.cginc*. Don't let the *cginc* file extension confuse you – it's still compatible with HLSL.

- In URP and HDRP, include files can be accessed in-Editor. In the Project View, scroll down to the Packages section and find the following folders:

  - *Core RP Library/ShaderLibrary* contains core shader files common to both pipelines.

  - *Universal RP/ShaderLibrary* contains URP's shader files.

  - *High Definition RP/Runtime/Material* contains HDRP's shader files in a series of subfolders.

In each shader, we will include a standard library helper file containing the most useful macros and functions that are key to writing shaders. In the built-in pipeline, we must include the *UnityCG.cginc* file I mentioned, and in URP, we'll include the *Core.hlsl* file from the URP shader library. Pick the following code that corresponds to your pipeline.

Listing 3-12. Including Unity's standard shader library in the built-in pipeline

```
#pragma vertex vert
#pragma fragment frag

#include "UnityCG.cginc"
```

Listing 3-13. Including Unity's standard shader library in URP

```
#pragma vertex vert
#pragma fragment frag

#include "Packages/com.unity.render-pipelines.universal/ShaderLibrary/Core.hlsl"
```

The first step of the graphics pipeline involves collecting all the data from the scene to pass to the shader, so we need to devise some way of obtaining the data here on the shader side. We'll do that via *structs*.

Controlling Data Flow with Structs

We pass data between shader stages via containers called structs, which contain a bunch of variables. The first struct contains all the data we want to pull from the mesh and pass to the vertex shader.

The appdata Struct

We usually name this struct `appdata`, `VertexInput`, or `Attributes`; I will stick with the name `appdata` throughout the book because Unity's built-in structs are named similarly, although you can name this whatever you want. Each instance of `appdata` contains data about one vertex of the mesh, and for now, all we need is the *position* of the vertex. Vertex positions are defined in object space, where each position is relative to the origin point of the mesh (for a refresher on object space, see Figure 2-10).

HLSL requires us to add what's called a *semantic* to each variable. It's just a bit of added information that tells Unity what each variable will be used for in the next shader stage – for example, vertex positions need to use the `POSITION` semantic. Semantic names don't need to be capitalized, although most documentation will use capitalized names. We will make it clear that the vertex position is in object space by naming the variable `positionOS`.

Note   A full list of semantics can be found on the Microsoft HLSL website. At the time of writing, it can be found here: `https://docs.microsoft.com/en-us/windows/win32/direct3dhlsl/dx-graphics-hlsl-semantics`.

Listing 3-14. The appdata struct for passing data to the vertex shader

```
#include "include-file-for-your-pipeline"

struct appdata
{
    float4 positionOS : POSITION;
};
```

Take note of the semicolon after the closing brace! The type of the `positionOS` variable is `float4` because we are using floating-point values to represent each component of the position, and there are four components. We will cover the core types in HLSL and how to use them later in the chapter. While we are thinking about structs, we will also write the struct for data being passed between the vertex and fragment shaders.

The v2f Struct

This struct is commonly called `v2f`, `VertexOutput`, or `Varyings`, but I will be sticking with `v2f`, which stands for "vertex-to-fragment." Recall that the rasterization step happens after the vertex shader and before the fragment shader, so we need to know which types of data will be output from the vertex shader. This might not be the same as the data input to the vertex shader – for instance, we may calculate or generate our own types of data from scratch inside the vertex shader. For our first shader, we'll only be outputting the clip-space position of each vertex, so we will name this variable `positionCS` (see Figure 2-15 for a look at clip space).

Listing 3-15. The v2f struct for passing data from the vertex shader to the fragment shader

```
struct appdata { ... };

struct v2f
{
       float4 positionCS : SV_POSITION;
};
```

You'll notice that the semantic is different here. HLSL makes a distinction between a position being input to and output by the vertex shader, so we use the `SV_POSITION` semantic instead. Like all semantics, other learning resources might choose not to capitalize the name. Next, we will deal with variables.

Variables in HLSL

Although we declared the `_BaseColor` property back in the `Properties` block, we need to declare it again inside HLSL. It's also possible to declare variables here that are not specified in the `Properties` block – in that case, we would need to use C# scripting to set the values of those variables rather than modifying values in the material's Inspector. _BaseColor is, obviously, a color, which doesn't have a special type in HLSL. It's just a four-element vector of floating-point numbers, for which we use the float4 type. We declare these variables just below the structs we just wrote.

Note   Unity may also generate certain shader variables for us. We need to declare some of them inside HLSL, but we won't need to include them in Properties or pass the data to the shader ourselves with scripting. An example of this kind of variable is _CameraDepthTexture, which we will see later.

Listing 3-16. Declaring variables in HLSL in the built-in pipeline

```
struct v2f { ... };

float4 _BaseColor;
```

The rules regarding variables are slightly different when using URP. This code will still work, but I'm including a section once we've finished the shader explaining how to tweak the code to make use of features exclusive to URP and HDRP. With that change aside, everything is set up for us to start writing the two shader functions, vert and frag.

The Vertex Shader

The vertex shader function needs to transform the vertex positions from object space to clip space, which would usually involve a series of transformations from object to world space, then from world to view space, and then from view to clip space. A full description of this process is available in Chapter 2. The combined transformation is called the *model-view-projection* transformation, and Unity provides a function to apply the transformation for us.

- In the built-in pipeline, this function is called UnityObjectToClipPos:
  - The name is long, but it intends to clarify what it is doing: it's carrying out the object-to-clip transformation, and it's operating on positions.

- There are similarly named functions in the built-in pipeline, such as UnityObjectToWorldDir, which performs the object-to-world transformation and operates on direction vectors.

  - In URP, this function is called TransformObjectToHClip:

    - Similarly, the name is meant to tell you what the function is doing, and other functions in the core shader library are named using similar conventions.

  - In both pipelines, the respective function takes the object-space position as input and returns the clip-space position as output.

The vert function, which is our vertex shader, is just like any regular function, with a return type (in this case, v2f) and a list of parameters (we accept an appdata instance as input). Pick the correct code for the pipeline you're using.

Listing 3-17. The vertex shader in the built-in pipeline

```
v2f vert (appdata v)
{
    v2f o;
    o.positionCS = UnityObjectToClipPos(v.positionOS);
    return o;
}
```

Listing 3-18. The vertex shader in URP

```
v2f vert (appdata v)
{
    v2f o;
    o.positionCS = TransformObjectToHClip(v.positionOS);
    return o;
}
```

Finally, we will write the fragment shader function, frag.

The Fragment Shader

The only argument to the function is the v2f struct that was output by the vert function, and we have a float4 return type, because the fragment shader will calculate and return the color of each fragment. The key difference between the two functions is that we need to specify a semantic for the fragment output, which is SV_TARGET. Inside the function, the only thing we need to do is return the _BaseColor, which was input to the shader as a property.

Listing 3-19. The fragment shader

```
float4 frag (v2f i) : SV_TARGET
{
    return _BaseColor;
}
```

Although we didn't use any of the data from the v2f input ourselves, Unity automatically uses the variable with the SV_POSITION semantic to rasterize the object into fragments, so we didn't set up the v2f struct for nothing! If you've followed each step correctly, then your shader will compile, and the Inspector should display the correct shader properties when you select the material, as seen in Figure 3-4. Success!

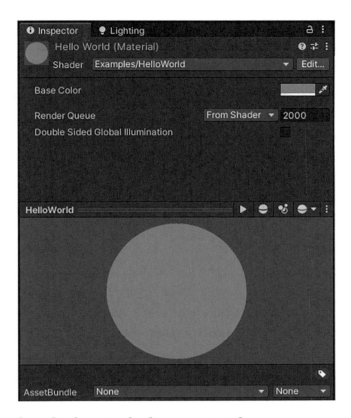

Figure 3-4. *Our first shader attached to a material*

We can change the behavior of the material in a few ways through the Inspector window:

- You can see the Base Color property on the material, which we can tweak to change the color of the preview at the bottom of the window and any object that uses this material.

- It is also possible to override the Queue we defined within the shader – instead of using the Geometry queue, which has a value of 2000, we can set any integer value here to modify how Unity renders the object. There may be edge cases where this is necessary, but I usually leave this field alone and let it inherit the value from the shader.

- If we tick the *Double Sided Global Illumination* option, then Unity will account for both sides of each face of the mesh while lightmapping, even if only one side of each face is rendered normally.

We have successfully written a shader that renders an object in a single color with no lighting, which is about as "Hello World" as you can get. Congratulations for making it to this stage! Now that we've written our first shader, let's revisit one of the key differences between writing shaders for the built-in pipeline and URP.

The SRP Batcher and Constant Buffers

As we have seen, there are sometimes differences between shaders designed for each of Unity's render pipelines. Some of these differences amount to changing a specific function name because the core libraries differ slightly between pipelines, and other differences represent a fundamental change in how the pipelines operate. In this section, I want to provide an overview of one difference in particular: the *SRP Batcher*.

Note   If you are just starting out with Unity, you may find it useful to stick with the built-in pipeline for now and come back to the Universal Render Pipeline later, since a lot of tutorials out there were written for the built-in pipeline. However, if you are planning on using Shader Graph, then you will *require* URP or HDRP. Eventually, URP will become the default for new projects in Unity, and future learning materials will focus on it.

This is a system supported by all Scriptable Render Pipelines (including URP and HDRP) to render objects more efficiently than traditional methods, but our shaders need to conform to a handful of rules to be compatible with the SRP Batcher. Namely, we need to include most of our variable declarations inside a special structure called a *constant buffer*.

This type of buffer lets us specify that the variables within stay constant throughout the shader pass – in other words, the value of the variables won't abruptly change at any point while the shader is running. We use a pair of macros, CBUFFER_START(name) and CBUFFER_END, to enclose our constant buffer, and we provide the special name UnityPerMaterial for the buffer containing all properties that might change between materials. In place of Listing 3-16, we will use the following code instead.

Listing 3-20. The CBUFFER for declaring variables in URP

```
struct v2f { ... };
CBUFFER_START(UnityPerMaterial)
        float4 _BaseColor;
CBUFFER_END
```

We don't need to change the variable names or types in any way – we just need to enclose them in the constant buffer. By making this change, Unity can batch together objects that use the same shader and the same mesh and render them using a single draw call. I'll be going into much more detail about optimizations like this in Chapter 13, but this is one SRP-exclusive feature I want to keep in mind throughout the book! Now that we have written our first shader, let's cover basic shader features that we didn't see in that shader.

Common Shader Syntax

Shaders come with many types, operators, and functions, which we'll be seeing a lot throughout the book, so I will introduce the most important ones here. By the end of this section, you should understand the difference between similar variable types and what they are used for, as well as operators that work on those types.

Scalar Types

There are three main data types that are used for floating-point numbers: float, double, and half. We've seen float before – it uses 32 bits to represent numbers. The half type uses 16 bits, which makes it great for low-precision values with at most three digits after the decimal point, but some platforms map them to float anyway. And the double type uses 64 bits, but you will rarely need that much precision. When writing numbers inside a shader (a raw number written down is called a *literal*), we can add a postfix character to specify the type – f for float, h for half, and d for double.

Listing 3-21. The float, half, and double data types

```
float x = 3.7f;
half y = 9.4h;
double z = 27.047d;
```

You may also see the `fixed` type in some older shaders, which is supported by Cg and uses 11 bits for representing low-precision data like non-HDR colors, but it's not part of HLSL. There are also integer data types – `int` and `uint` represent *signed* and *unsigned* integers, respectively. Both types use 32 bits. A signed integer can represent negative numbers, while unsigned integers cannot; both can represent the same number of numbers, but their range is shifted.

Listing 3-22. The int and uint types

```
int a = -7;
uint b = 9;
```

We can use common math operators with these types. If we mix types, then HLSL will intelligently interpret what type the output should be. We can add using the + operator, subtract using -, multiply with *, and divide using the / operator. The unary – operator is also defined, and we can use it to make a single value negative. These operators follow the same precedence rules as regular math; brackets are evaluated first, then powers, then multiplication and division, and then addition and subtraction. There's also the modulus operator, %, which returns the remainder after division. Unlike many languages, HLSL defines the modulus operation for both integers and floating-point types.

Listing 3-23. Valid math operations in HLSL

```
7 * 4        // = 28
-19          // = -19
6.4f + 9     // = 15.4f
14 / 4       // = 3 (integer types truncate the fractional part)
7 % 3        // = 1
7.4f % 3     // = 1.4f
```

Vector Types

Vector types in HLSL are made by combining the scalar types we just covered. The way we construct these types is simple: take the name of the scalar type we are basing the vector type on and add a number to the end that represents the number of elements. If we need a two-element vector of floating-point numbers, we use the `float2` type. A three-element vector of integers? That's an `int3`.

Note   Personally, I wish conventional programming languages commonly supported these kinds of types out of the box.

To declare any of these types, we can use a constructor like the following.

Listing 3-24. Vector types in HLSL

```
float2 x = float2(5.4f, 9.2f);
int3 y = int3(2, -4);
uint1 = uint1(3);
```

The number of elements must be between 1 and 4 inclusive. As you can see in Listing 3-24, it's possible to use a vector type with one element, like `int1`, which is practically the same as the scalar type it is based on. We already saw `float4` being used to represent positions when we wrote the example shader earlier in this chapter. Vectors are used to represent all manner of things in HLSL such as colors, positions, and directions, so there are operations on vectors that you should be aware of. Like scalars, we can use common math operators with vectors. The +, -, *, /, and % operators work *element-wise*. This means, for example, that the * operator works very differently from the dot product, which is typically thought of as "multiplying" vectors.

Listing 3-25. Vector math operations

```
float2 x = float2(1.2f, 2.4f);
float2 y = float2(-3.1f, 4.6f);

x * y;      // = (-3.72f, 11.04f)
x - y;      // = (4.3f, -2.2f)
y + x;      // = (-1.9f, 7.0f)
y / x;      // = (-2.58333f, 1.91666f)
```

We can access the individual elements of a vector in many ways. Vectors can have a size anywhere between 1 and 4, and we can access those four elements using {VectorName}.x, .y, .z, and .w to get the first, second, third, and fourth component, respectively, as long as the vector contains the element you're trying to access. Vectors can also contain color data, so, helpfully, we can use {VectorName}.r, .g, .b, and .a to get each of the four components – the two naming systems are aliases for one another.

Otherwise, we can use array indexing syntax like a classic programming language to access elements, where the indices start from zero. We can perform operations on those individual components as if they were scalar values or assign values to those components.

Listing 3-26. Accessing vector components

```
float3 example = float3(1.9f, -2.7f, 3.5f);
example.x + example.z;      // = 5.4f
example.y = 2.4f;           // example = (1.9f, 2.4f, 3.5f)
example.b;                  // = 3.5f
example[0] + example[2];    // = 5.4f
```

What if we need to access multiple components of a vector? There are several ways to do that. For instance, if we need to convert the first three parts of a float4 into a new float3, then we can access those components one by one using any of the methods we just covered.

Listing 3-27. Accessing multiple vector components

```
float4 example = float4(1.2f, 2.4f, -5.2f, -0.7f);
float3 other = float3(example.x, example.y, example.z);
```

However, this is cumbersome to type out every time. Thankfully, it is possible to access multiple vector components at once, in any order, with possible repetition – this is called *swizzling*, and frankly, it's one of the best features of shading languages. This allows us to create a new vector of up to four components by mixing and matching the components of an existing vector. The following are all valid statements in HLSL.

Listing 3-28. Using swizzling to access multiple vector components

```
float4 example = float4(1.2f, 2.4f, -5.2f, -0.7f);
float3 ex1 = example.xyz;  // = (1.2f, 2.4f, -5.2f)
float3 ex2 = example.rgb;  // = (1.2f, 2.4f, -5.2f)
float3 ex3 = example.xxx;  // = (1.2f, 1.2f, 1.2f)
float4 ex4 = example.wzyx; // = (-0.7f, -5.2f, 2.4f, 1.2f)
float4 ex5 = example.yyxx; // = (2.4f, 2.4f, 1.2f, 1.2f)
```

Swizzling makes writing shaders far quicker than it otherwise would be, as you will constantly need to access more than one vector component like this. Unfortunately, you can't swizzle using array index syntax, so you don't tend to see that syntax used as often in shaders as the other accessing methods. You may also need to create vectors that are made up of parts of multiple existing vectors, which is also easy to do in HLSL.

Listing 3-29. Combining parts of multiple vectors into new vectors

```
float4 example1 = float4(-7.4f, 2.1f, 3.2f, 3.3f);
float3 example2 = float3(2.2f, 8.9f, 9.0f);

float4 example3 = float4(example1.xy, example2.xy);

// example3 = (-7.4f, 2.1f, 2.2f, 8.9f)
```

Matrix Types

Matrix types are a bit more complicated than vector types. We can define matrices in a similar way to vectors by writing the scalar type that the matrix will contain, followed by the dimension. As you may recall from Chapter 2, matrices are referred to by their size by writing the number of rows by the number of columns, so a 3 × 2 matrix of floating-point numbers has three rows and two columns, and we use the type `float3x2` to represent it. We construct matrices by listing the elements of each row in a list, like the following.

Listing 3-30. Constructing the 3 × 3 identity matrix in HLSL

```
float3x3 example = float3x3
(
    1, 0, 0,        // First row
    0, 1, 0,        // Second row
    0, 0, 1         // Third row
);
```

It's not necessary to space out a matrix like this by stating each row on a separate line. We can just as easily condense Listing 3-30 onto a single line, but you will find it easier to read a matrix that has been written out like so. Now that we have a matrix, how do we access its elements? We can access elements using array indexing syntax like we could with vectors. However, like with vectors, it's not possible to swizzle with that syntax. Since matrices are two-dimensional structures, we need two array indices to access a single element: first for the row and second for the column. Or, if we want to grab an entire row at a time, we can supply just one index for the row.

Listing 3-31. Accessing matrix elements in HLSL

```
float ex1 = example[0][0];                    // = 1
float ex2 = example[0][1] + example[0][2];    // = 0
float ex3 = example[2][2];                    // = 1
float ex4 = example[3][3];                    // invalid syntax
float3 ex5 = example[0];                      // = (1, 0, 0)
```

So what about swizzling? There are two other ways to access matrix elements. First, we can say {MatrixName}._mxy, where xy are the zero-indexed row and column you want to access. For instance, example._m00 gets the top-left element of the example matrix. The syntax is a bit unwieldy, but bear with it! The other way to access elements is to say {MatrixName}._xy, where xy are now the one-indexed row and column you want. Writing example._11 *also* gets the top-left element of the example matrix. If you don't like the discrepancy between both those incredibly similar schemes, I'd say learn one and stick to it – throughout this book, I will use the zero-indexed version that uses m in the name. But be aware that other resources could use either syntax. Using these two methods, we can swizzle to create new vectors or matrices (up to four elements can be pulled from the matrix at a time using swizzling).

Listing 3-32. Swizzling matrix elements in HLSL

```
float2 ex1 = example._m11_m11;             // = (1, 1)
float4 ex2 = example._m00_m01_m10_m11;     // = (1, 0, 0, 1)
float2x2 ex3 = example._m00_m01_m10_m11;   // = 2x2 identity
```

Finally, like vectors, matrices support common math operators, which work per component. This means, among other things, that the * operator is not the same as doing matrix multiplication as I described in Chapter 2. There's a dedicated mul function for matrix multiplication, which we will see later.

Listing 3-33. The * operator on matrices

```
float3x3 a =
(
    1, 0, 1,
    0, 3, 0,
    0, 0, 2
);

float3x3 b =
(
    2, 0, 0,
    0, 2, 0,
    0, 0, 2
);

float3x3 result = a * b;

// result = ( 2, 0, 0,
//            0, 6, 0,
//            0, 0, 4 )
```

Included Variables

Unity includes several variables to aid your shader programing. While it is possible to send arbitrary data to a shader ourselves through C# scripting, Unity sends a lot of data to the shader automatically, such as time-based variables, transformation matrices, and camera properties. Some of these will be explored in detail in their respective chapters, so we will cover only a selection of the variables here.

Transformation Matrices

Transformation matrices are the backbone of the graphics pipeline, so it makes sense for Unity to declare the key matrices for us and make them available inside shaders. The syntax for the name of most of these matrices is UNITY_MATRIX_{NAME}. Table 3-1 is a non-exhaustive list of the most important matrices that are available; each one is of type float4x4.

Table 3-1. *Matrices provided by Unity*

Matrix name	Description
UNITY_MATRIX_M unity_ObjectToWorld	The model matrix that transforms from object space to world space. These two names are aliases for one another.
UNITY_MATRIX_I_M unity_WorldToObject	The inverse model matrix that transforms from world space to object space. These two names are aliases for one another only on URP; for the built-in pipeline, only unity_WorldToObject exists.
UNITY_MATRIX_V	The view matrix that transforms from world space to view/camera space.
UNITY_MATRIX_P	The projection matrix that transforms from view space to clip space.
UNITY_MATRIX_MV	The model-view matrix that transforms from object space directly to view space.
UNITY_MATRIX_VP	The view-projection matrix that transforms from world space to clip space. This can be considered the "camera matrix" since both view and projection are reliant on the camera properties.
UNITY_MATRIX_MVP	The model-view-projection matrix that transforms from object space directly to clip space. This matrix is often used in the vertex shader.

Time-Based Variables

Shaders can be animated over time without requiring us to write external time data to the shader. Unity already provides plenty of time variables for our shaders, covering the time since the level was loaded and the time since the last frame execution. Let's see these variables in action.

The variable _Time is a float4 that contains the time since level load in four commonly used formats. Let's say the time since level load is called *t*. The x-component of _Time stores *t*/20, which is useful if you need a slow timer in your shader. The y-component stores an unedited *t* value, so you'll use _Time.y if you need the exact number of seconds since level load. _Time.z stores 2*t*, and _Time.w stores 3*t*, which are both useful if you need a fast timer in your shader. Of course, not all these variables will work in all cases, so a good solution is to include a property in your shader, perhaps called _Speed, and use _Time * _Speed in your calculations. The advantage of writing your shaders in that way is that you can modify the speed of animations per material.

Listing 3-34. The _Time variable

```
float t = _Time.y;
float fastT = _Time.w;
```

Another useful application of _Time is to create a clock that ticks up to a certain value and loops back round to zero. The following code snippet will count to 1 second and then loop back to zero and start counting to 1 again.

Listing 3-35. Creating a looping timer using _Time

```
float loopedTime = _Time.y % 1.0f;
```

Surprisingly often, you will use sin(_Time.y) or cos(_Time.y) in your shaders. A shorthand for both functions can be found in the additional variables _SinTime and _CosTime, respectively. Both are of type float4, and they respectively contain the sine and cosine of $t/8$, $t/4$, $t/2$, and t, in that order.

Listing 3-36. Using the sine of _Time. The following two statements are equivalent

```
float sineTime1 = sin(_Time);
float sineTime2 = _SinTime.w;
```

Finally, we can access the time since the previous frame was rendered, which is conventionally called *delta time*. This is also a float4, where each value contains the time in seconds since last frame in different formats. Let's call the delta time in seconds *dt*. The variable unity_DeltaTime stores *dt* in the x-component and $1/dt$ in the y-component. We can also access the *smoothed* delta time, which is *dt* averaged out over a handful of frames – this avoids the value of *dt* spiking temporarily when a single frame takes unusually long to process. Let's call the smoothed delta time *sdt*. Unity stores *sdt* in unity_DeltaTime.z and $1/sdt$ in unity_DeltaTime.w. I don't often find myself needing delta time in shaders, but it's useful to know it's there.

Listing 3-37. Using delta time in shaders

```
float deltaTime = unity_DeltaTime.x;
```

Summary

In this chapter, we saw how to create a basic unlit color shader in Unity in the built-in and Universal render pipelines. Shaders must take data about the scene and transform the position of each vertex into a different coordinate space using the functions provided by Unity. Then, we can color each pixel, or fragment. A language called ShaderLab acts as a wrapper around the shader code, and it lets us define the macroscopic features of the shader and provides an interface between the Unity Editor and the shader. In the next chapter, we will see these same concepts in the context of Shader Graph. In this chapter, we learned the following points:

- Shaders must be attached to a material to be applied to a mesh.

- HLSL, GLSL, and Cg are examples of shader languages. The standard shader language in Unity is HLSL, since Cg has been deprecated.

- Unity's proprietary language, ShaderLab, wraps around shader code and provides an interface between the shader and the rest of Unity.

- Properties are shader variables that we can edit on a material.

- A ShaderLab file can contain many SubShaders, and Unity picks the first one that is valid on the hardware.

- Tags can be used to customize the rendering order and render pipeline for a specific SubShader or Pass.

- Unity provides helpful macros and functions that are commonly used in shaders.

- URP shaders must declare most variables inside a constant buffer.

- HDRP uses Shader Graph instead of code for most user-generated shaders.

- There are several core variable types in HLSL that represent scalars, vectors, and matrices of different dimensions.

- Swizzling can be used as a shorthand to access vector components in any order or combination, with possible repetition.

CHAPTER 4

Shader Graph

Shader programming is at a somewhat strange crossing of disciplines. Obviously, since there is code involved, you need some amount of programming ability, but many people who write shaders bring their programming experience from other languages rather than learning shaders from scratch as their first language. If you are only interested in writing shaders, then there are many concepts you may need to learn from scratch, which increase the barrier to entry. If you're an artist wishing to write shaders, but you have no programming experience, then shaders can seem daunting. There's a tool that is perhaps more approachable for artists due to the lack of programming while still being usable by programmers: *Shader Graph*.

With the advent of Scriptable Render Pipelines, Unity also released a new node-based visual shader editor called Shader Graph. Instead of using code, the logic required for shaders is now packed into visual elements called *nodes*, which you can drag around the graph environment and connect to form a chain of behavior that makes up the shader – each node is executed starting from the left-hand side and traveling to the right until you reach the graph outputs. An example of a shader made with Shader Graph can be seen in Figure 4-1. You can think of each node as standing in for a line of code or a function, and connecting them together is like writing those lines of code one after another in a shader code file.

© Daniel Ilett 2022
D. Ilett, *Building Quality Shaders for Unity*®, https://doi.org/10.1007/978-1-4842-8652-4_4

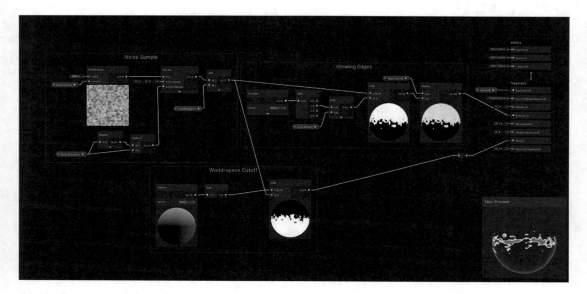

Figure 4-1. *A zoomed-out view of a Shader Graph that dissolves the edge of a mesh*

Shader Graph Overview

Shader Graph has several advantages over traditional code. First, and most obviously, code is no longer required. Artists who wish to avoid coding, or programmers who prefer a change of pace from staring at lines of code, will be able to put together many of the same shaders that shader programmers have had access to for years.

Second, it becomes easier to see at a glance what the shader is doing at each stage. With code shaders, it can be difficult to debug problems or visualize what the result will be until you have finished writing the entire shader (although there are tools that you can use to assist with shader debugging), but Shader Graph displays a preview window on many of its nodes, which gives you immediate feedback without needing additional windows or tabs open in Unity.

And, third, Shader Graph does some of the boilerplate work for you. We saw in the previous chapter that, for example, we need to handle some of the matrix transformations during the vertex stage if we're using code (although we are supplied with macros and functions to make it easier), but with Shader Graph we don't even have to worry about that. Furthermore, some of the nodes included in Shader Graph give us access to some complex behavior that otherwise would take a nontrivial amount of work to implement ourselves in code.

Shader Graph is not without its drawbacks. Shader Graph does not support every kind of shader, such as geometry shaders or compute shaders, although support for these *could* be added in future updates. Also, your graphs are compiled into shader code in the end, but as with many other systems that automatically generate code, you can usually get better performance out of a hand-authored code shader than an equivalent graph.

Note   This book was written for Unity 2021.3 in mind, so versions of Shader Graph before and after this version may look different. If the things I talk about don't quite match up to what you see, then you might need to spend a little time looking up the differences between versions, but the information in this book will almost certainly still be relevant.

Creating a Basic Shader in Shader Graph

In Chapter 3, we learned how to use shader code to build a basic shader, which lets us customize the color of an unlit object. In this section, we will see how to create a similar effect in Shader Graph.

Scene Setup

To set up my scene, I'll follow the same process I outlined near the start of the previous chapter. If you created a project with the URP or HDRP template, the Shader Graph package should already be installed, but in the built-in pipeline it won't be, and there is every chance that something could go wrong with installation, so first let's check that Shader Graph is installed via the Package Manager.

- Go to *Window* ➤ *Package Manager* to open the Package Manager window. This window is shown in Figure 4-2.

Figure 4-2. *The Package Manager window, which we use to install Shader Graph*

- Use the *Packages* drop-down at the top to pick "Unity Registry,"
  which lists all possible packages.

- Scroll down to find the entry for Shader Graph. If it's installed, it
  will have a green tick beside it. If not, click the *Install* button in the
  bottom left of the window.

Once Shader Graph is installed, follow the steps from the start of Chapter 3 to set up the scene. The main difference is that we won't be creating a shader file because we're using Shader Graph instead. If you right-click in the Project View and go to *Create ➤ Shader Graph*, there will be different options to create your graph based on which pipeline you are using:

- In all pipelines, you will see the option to create a Blank Shader Graph
  or a Sub Graph. We'll explore the latter option later in the book.

- In the built-in pipeline, there are also Lit and Unlit options.

- In URP, you have an expanded set of options, including Lit, Unlit,
  Decal, Sprite Lit, and Sprite Unlit. The latter two are intended for use
  with 2D sprites.

- In HDRP, you have the most options: Lit, Unlit, StackLit, Decal, Eye,
  Fabric, and Hair.

No matter which render pipeline you are using, we will pick the *Unlit* option (we will see the other options in later chapters). This creates a new asset with a *.shadergraph* extension, which I'll call "HelloShaderGraph".

Note   The types of preset that are available will change between versions. Notably, if you see an option called PBR Graph, then this was renamed to Lit Graph in Unity 2020.1, but it does broadly the same thing.

Like we did for the shader code examples, we will also add a sphere to the scene and create a new material to use our shader. In the Shader drop-down at the top of the Inspector on the material, all graphs are included in a folder called "Shader Graphs" by default – it'll have the same name here as the one you gave to the file when creating it, which in my case is "HelloShaderGraph".

The Shader Graph Interface

When you double-click a Shader Graph in the Project View, the Shader Graph editor will open in a dockable window, as seen in Figure 4-3. Like other windows in Unity, you can position it wherever you want, tabify it alongside other windows, and resize or maximize the window. Each Shader Graph you are working on will open in a separate tab, so you can even work on multiple graphs at once.

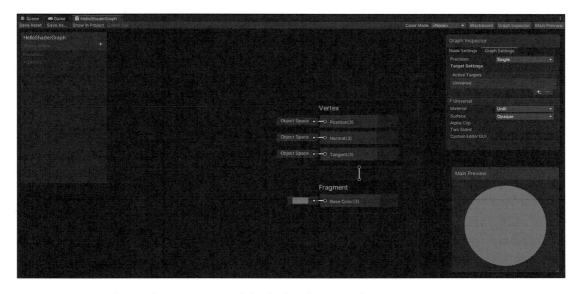

Figure 4-3. *A brand-new, unmodified Shader Graph*

Inside the Shader Graph editor, there are several sub-windows and toolbars, so let's explore each one in turn.

The Toolbar

First, there is the toolbar that runs along the top of the window. Starting with the left, you will find the following operations:

- Click the *Save Asset* button if you want changes to your graph to be visible back in the Scene View.

- *Save As* is similar and lets you save the graph under a new filename.

- *Show in Project* focuses the editor on the file that the current graph is saved in.

- The *Check Out* button checks out the current file with source control (this option is grayed out if source control is not enabled).

There is also a separate section on the right-hand side of the toolbar:

- The *Color Mode* option controls how Shader Graph displays some nodes. By changing this option to something other than *None*, Unity adds a small colored ribbon to the top of each node depending on the option chosen.

- The other three options (*Blackboard*, *Graph Inspector*, and *Main Preview*) are toggles that turn on or off the corresponding window.

Speaking of which, let's explore those windows now.

Togglable Windows

The *Blackboard* is a separate draggable mini window where we can define *properties* and *keywords*, which act as the inputs to the graph, like we saw in shader code. It can be found on the left-hand side of the editor (see Figure 4-3). By default, a property can be overridden on any material that uses this shader, so we can create several materials with this shader with different behavior. We will see how to add properties soon.

The *Graph Inspector*, like the main Inspector window in the Unity Editor, will display information about anything we click within Shader Graph. By default, it is on the right-hand side of the editor, but it can be moved anywhere you want. It contains two tabs:

- *Graph Settings*, which displays graph-wide information and lets us customize the macroscopic behavior of the graph.

- *Node Settings*, which displays options for any node or property we have highlighted.

The Graph Settings tab contains the all-important *Precision* option, which controls the types of variables Unity uses under the hood to process the logic we write in our graph:

- *Single*, contrary to how it sounds, is the higher-precision type.

- *Half* is lower-precision type.

- I usually stick with *Single*, but *Half* may have better performance (while impacting quality), especially on mobile devices.

Finally, there is the *Main Preview* window, which displays what your graph will broadly look like when added to your game. You can right-click this box to change the type of mesh used in the preview, including a custom mesh of your own. There are a few limitations to this, however. This window will simulate only one directional light, so if you expect this material to exist near many light sources, then it may not be an accurate representation of how the object will appear in-game. For most use cases, it's a good approximation. All of this is important of course, but we're most interested in the middle of the window.

The Graph Environment

The graph environment in the center of the Shader Graph editor window is where we will construct the graph, and you should see a small list of rectangles enclosed in two groups already on the graph. This is called the *master stack*, and it is filled with a few *blocks*, which represent the outputs of your graph. The master stack is split into two sections:

- The *vertex stage* is like the graph's vertex shader. Here, we can influence the individual vertices of the mesh.

- The *fragment stage* operates on fragments (or pixels). We can apply color, lighting, and texture to an object here.

- Each section can be moved independently, although there will always be a link between the two. Since each block is an output from the graph, I sometimes refer to the master stack as the "output stack," the "graph outputs," or just the "outputs."

Inside both sections of the master stack, you will see a few graph outputs called *blocks*. The vertex stage section always contains three blocks for the vertex position, normal, and tangent vectors by default. These blocks have default values attached to them, so if we want our effect to use a basic vertex shader that just places vertices into the correct place on-screen, we don't need to add any nodes or make any changes whatsoever to the vertex stage. This is quite different from shader code, where even the simplest vertex shader requires a relatively high amount of boilerplate code. We also don't need to define any of the graph input data such as positions and texture coordinates like we do when writing shader code, so it is often faster to make a basic shader effect using Shader Graph than using shader code.

Since we picked the Unlit preset, the fragment stage only contains the *Base Color* block. It uses a default light-gray color if we don't attach anything to it, but we can click the tiny color block next to it to modify the color. By adding zero nodes or properties, we already have a shader that we can use to output a basic color of our choosing. However, it is preferable to modify settings like this per material, for which we require properties.

Adding Properties

Properties allow us to control the flow of data between the Unity Editor and the graph. There are many types of property that can be added to a graph, which you will see if you click the plus icon on the Blackboard (see Figure 4-4).

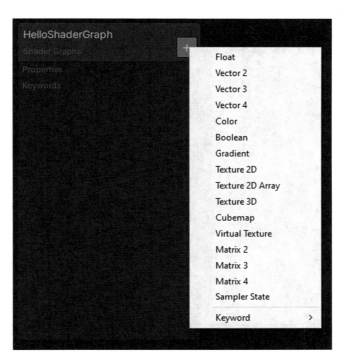

Figure 4-4. *Clicking the "+" button on the Blackboard brings up a list of property types*

These property types match those we saw in Chapter 3 when we wrote a code-based shader. Let's start by adding one of the most common kinds of property: a Color. When you first add a property, Unity will automatically select the name of the new property so that you can edit it – I'm going to call mine "Base Color". This is a human-readable name that will appear in the material Inspector and on the graph. Under the hood, Unity uses an alternative machine-readable reference string to handle properties. We can see the reference, and other settings for the property, if we left click the property name and navigate to the Node Settings tab on the Graph Inspector window (see Figure 4-5).

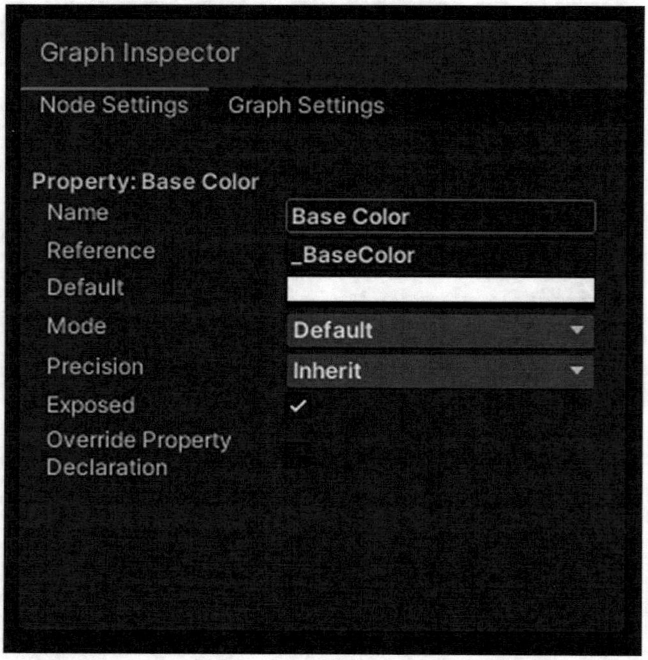

Graph Inspector

Node Settings   Graph Settings

Property: Base Color

Name   Base Color

Reference   _BaseColor

Default

Mode   Default   ▼

Precision   Inherit   ▼

Exposed   ✓

Override Property
Declaration

Figure 4-5. *When a property is selected, the Node Settings window displays options for the property*

Let's go over each setting.

Property Naming

Some of the settings are specific to certain types of property, but you will always see *Name* and *Reference* options. You can set whatever *Name* you want, and it will appear when you drag the property onto the central Shader Graph surface. The *Reference* string is the name Unity gives to the property when it autogenerates code based on our graph. For the *Reference* string, the convention is to start with an underscore – Unity will prepend one to the name invisibly if you miss it out here. I usually name it the same as, or similar to, the *Name*, but without spaces and with an underscore at the start.

To reset a property name if you make changes to it, right-click the property on the Blackboard and select *Reset Reference*. I will change the reference value of my property to _BaseColor. Next, we'll go over other common options seen on most property types.

Common Property Options

We can change the default value of the property with the *Default* option. This setting obviously changes based on the property type! In the case of Color properties, clicking the box will bring up Unity's color picker window and let you choose any RGB color you'd like. I change the default to white in most cases, but this will depend on what you're using the color for.

The *Exposed* checkbox is available on most property types, and it controls whether the property appears in the material Inspector. It might seem strange to have properties that we can't modify outside Shader Graph, but you can think of these as "global" variables, which we can plug into the graph at any stage.

- These properties can still be modified externally at runtime through C# scripting, as we will see later.

- Helpfully, any property that is exposed will have a small green dot next to its name to help you distinguish between exposed and non-exposed properties.

- Some property types, such as Gradient, cannot be exposed; even though the option appears, the checkbox can't be ticked.

The *Override Property Declaration* option, which is at the bottom of the list and is available on all property types, controls how the property is declared in code.

- *Per Material* is the default option, which means that the value of this property can differ between material instances.

- The *Global* option means that the variable is declared globally instead, but this can break compatibility with the SRP Batcher, so only use this option if you know what you're doing.

- The *Hybrid Per Instance* option is related to the *DOTS Hybrid Renderer*, which is outside the scope of this book.

Next, let's see the options that are exclusive to Color properties.

Color Property Options

The next setting for a `Color` is the *Mode*, which has two values: *Default*, which we use for regular colors, and *HDR*, which lets us use values beyond the typical 0–1 range. The HDR setting adds an additional *Intensity* value to the color picker, where intensities above zero may push the RGB values above 1. HDR colors are useful for emissive color, which we will see later. I will leave it as Default for now.

The *Precision* option refers to the underlying type used to represent the property when the graph is converted to code behind the scenes.

- I briefly covered the types used in shader code at the end of Chapter 3. The options in Shader Graph are *Single* and *Half*, which map to the `float` and `half` types, respectively.

- The *Inherit* option uses the graph's global precision setting. Half-precision floats use half the number of bits as single-precision floats, but the optimization impact is small, so don't worry about overzealously managing which setting you use on each node and property.

Other types might have more options, but you should have a good understanding of the kinds of settings available on properties in Shader Graph. Now that we have added a Color property, let's start using it in the graph.

Building the Graph

In the middle of the graph environment, we can chain nodes together to build up the behavior of the shader. Eventually, our chains of nodes need to link up to one of the outputs on the master stack, but first, we need to put some nodes on the graph to link up in the first place.

If you right-click an empty part of the graph, then an option window will appear. The one we're interested in is *Create Node*, which brings up another window with a search box and a list of drop-downs, as shown in Figure 4-6. Every node you can add can be found somewhere within the categories listed, or you can just type the name into the search box, which is what I usually do. Alternatively, the shortcut to skip straight to the Create Node dialog is to press the spacebar while hovering your mouse over empty space on the graph.

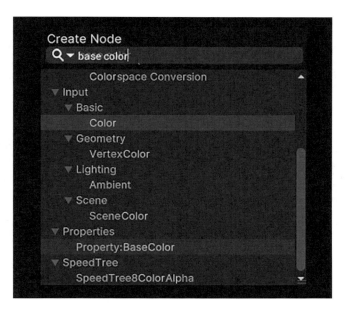

Figure 4-6. *Adding a node to the graph by searching its name*

If we want to add the Base Color property we created to the graph, we can use the Create Node window and type in "Base Color," or we can click the *Properties* drop-down and choose *Property:BaseColor*. You can also left-click and drag the property from the Blackboard onto the graph surface. Once you have added it using one of those methods, you will see it on the graph as a small, rounded box. It won't do much on its own, so we need to connect it with something.

You should see a small pink circle on the right-hand side of the node. This is called a *pin* (although I'll often just refer to it as an output), and if you left-click and drag from it, you will start dragging a wire from it. We can connect this wire to the corresponding pin on the left side of the *Base Color* output on the master stack. If you do that and then click the Save Asset button in the top-left corner of the Shader Graph window, then you will have created your very first shader using Shader Graph! The full graph, complete with the Blackboard and the settings used on the Base Color property, can be seen in Figure 4-7.

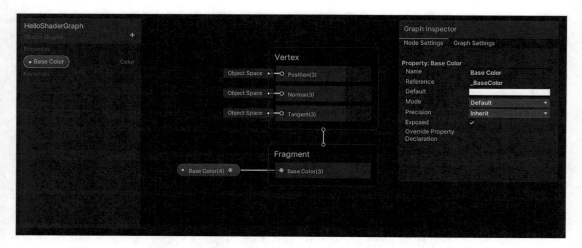

Figure 4-7. *A basic graph that lets us tint an unlit object a specific color*

This shader works like the one we built in Chapter 3, as you can see in Figure 4-8. We can change the properties of the material like before, and you should see the changes reflected on any object that uses that material.

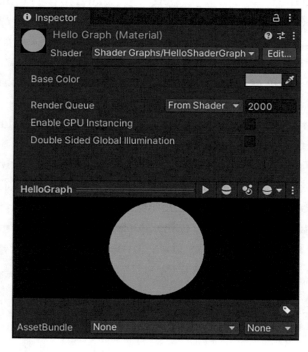

Figure 4-8. *When this shader is attached to a material, we can tint it using the Base Color property*

Congratulations! You just finished creating your first shader with Shader Graph! Now, let's see some of the other unique features of Shader Graph and how to use them.

Shader Graph Features

Shader Graph has several features to help you with making shaders. Some of them are like features you would find in shader code, such as Sub Graphs, which are an abstraction of functions. Others only make sense in a graph environment. Let's see what these features are and understand how we can use them to organize graphs and speed up our shader design workflow.

Adding Blocks to the Master Stack

Blocks on the master stack act as the outputs from your graph. The blocks that are available to you will be different depending on the render pipeline you are using and which of the two shader stages you are adding a block to. There are two ways of changing the blocks available on your master stack. We can add blocks manually by right-clicking the shader stage within the master stack that you want to add the block to and selecting *Create Node* (or using the spacebar shortcut). The list contains all blocks available on your current pipeline.

Alternatively, in *Edit* ➤ *Preferences* ➤ *Shader Graph*, make sure the *Automatically Add and Remove Block Nodes* option is ticked. When you do this, if you modify certain options in the Graph Settings, Unity will automatically add required blocks and remove redundant ones. In Figure 4-9, you can see me change the *Surface* from *Opaque* to *Transparent*, which makes Unity add an *Alpha* block to the fragment stage. The reverse is true; changing from *Transparent* back to *Opaque* will remove the *Alpha* block.

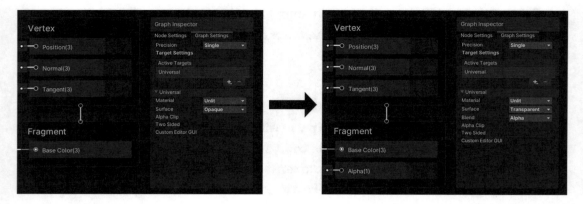

Figure 4-9. *Changing from Opaque to Transparent rendering adds an Alpha block*

Redirect Node

When creating larger graphs, you might end up with a spaghetti mess of wires crossing everywhere, which makes it harder to work out what the graph is doing. In recent versions of Shader Graph, there is an easy way to sort this out. If you double-click any wire, then a `Redirect` node will appear, and we can move this around to organize our graph more effectively. If you no longer need it, just delete it, and the wire will return to its original state. Figure 4-10 shows the redirect node in action.

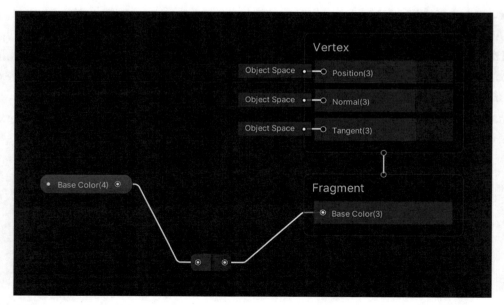

Figure 4-10. *The redirect node can be used to organize graphs such that connections between nodes can be followed more easily on complicated graphs*

Preview Node

One of the major advantages of Shader Graph is the immediate visual feedback you get on many nodes. However, you might prefer to collapse the preview window on nodes using the small up arrow at the top of the preview to prevent graphs from becoming too sprawling (you can reopen the preview using the new down arrow at the bottom of the node). If you have created a graph with many tightly packed nodes, it is time-consuming to move the nodes around just to reopen a preview. Using the Preview node, you can drag a wire off any of those tightly packed nodes to bring up a preview window detached from the other nodes. Preview acts as a passthrough, so any inputs are displayed visually and then output by the node. Figure 4-11 shows an example of where a Preview node is helpful.

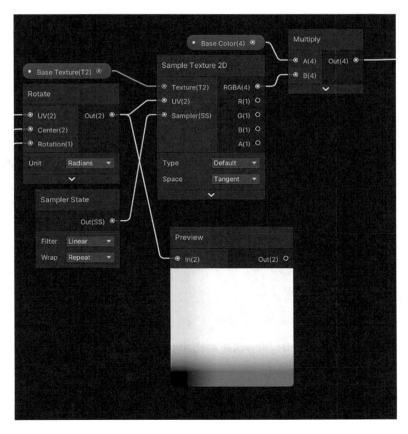

Figure 4-11. *To expand the Rotate node in this graph snippet to see its preview window, you would have to move the Sampler State node out of the way. It is potentially easier to drag out a Preview node instead*

Color Mode

One of the options on the toolbar of the Shader Graph window is the *Color Mode*, which can be used to identify nodes more easily. By switching to an option other than *None*, you will see a small ribbon of color below the name of each node. If you select *User Defined*, then you will need to set the color on each node yourself by right-clicking it and choosing the new *Color* option from the menu and setting whatever color you'd like.

Shader Path

By default, any graph you create will appear in the Shader drop-down on a material under the "Shader Graph" folder. Figure 4-12 shows where our *HelloShaderGraph* graph will appear. This makes it easy to find all your graph-based shaders in one place, but you can change this on the top of the Blackboard on your graph and by double-clicking just below your graph name, where it says "Shader Graphs" by default. It's not clear just by looking at it, but this is an editable string field where you are able to specify a file path for your graph.

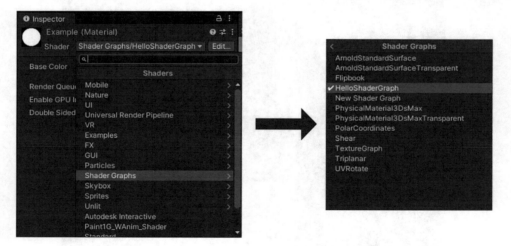

Figure 4-12. *The default path for your graphs is Shader Graphs/{YourGraph}*

Node Groups

Organizing your graphs is important to make sure you can follow what the graph is doing. When you are creating larger graphs, you'll often find that clusters of nodes are being used to carry out larger functions. For example, you might be using a group of around ten nodes that set up options for eventually sampling a texture. In cases like those, you can select all the nodes in the cluster by left-click dragging over them all, then right-click, and select *Group Selection* from the menu to create a *node group*. You can give the group a title by double-clicking at the top of it, which I often use as a short comment to explain what the group is doing. Figure 4-13 shows you an example of a group.

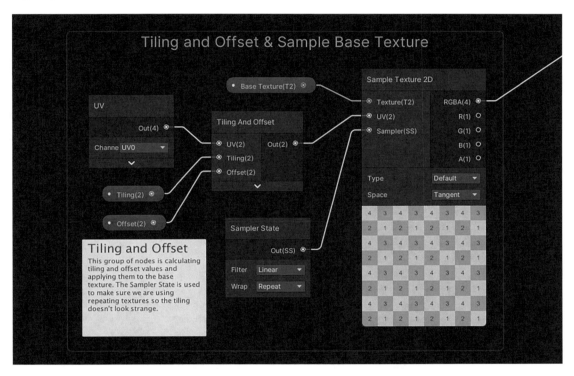

Figure 4-13. *Groups can be used to encapsulate nodes that work together toward a single goal. Sticky notes can be used to add more context to nodes in case it is not immediately obvious why you made your graph in a certain way*

Sticky Notes

In shader code, it is easy to add code comments using // for single-line comments and /* */ pairs for multiline comments. The equivalent mechanism in Shader Graph is *sticky notes*. To add one, right-click an empty section of the graph and select *Create Sticky Note* from the menu. You can edit the title and body of the note separately, resize the note, and move it around anywhere on the graph. This lets you give a little more context to someone looking at your graph if there's a section of nodes that are particularly complicated. I often use them in combination with groups by using the note to describe what the group is doing in more detail than the group title can. Figure 4-13 shows you what a sticky note might look like.

Node Snapping

Node snapping is a relatively recent Shader Graph feature that snaps nodes to line up with nearby nodes while dragging them. To enable this feature, go to *Edit ➤ Preferences* in the Unity Editor and then select the *General* tab and tick the *Graph Snapping* option. Now, when dragging a node around, you will notice blue guidelines appear, and the node will snap to those lines instead of freely moving about. If you see the lines but the nodes don't snap, then go into the Preferences menu and toggle the Graph Snapping option twice, which should fix it. Figure 4-14 shows what node snapping looks like.

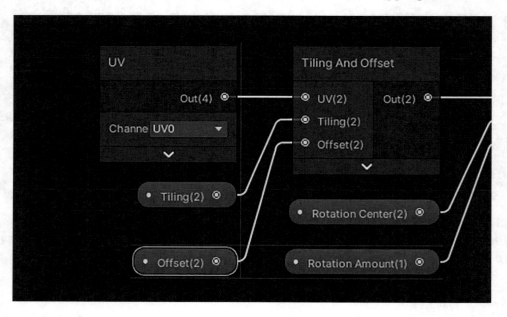

Figure 4-14. *The Offset property node in this example is being actively dragged. The guidelines are snapping its right-hand side to the UV node and its top and bottom edges to the Rotation Amount property node*

Sub Graphs

Sub Graphs are Shader Graph's replacement for functions. While creating a graph, you might find yourself repeating the same group of nodes several times. When this happens, consider bundling that group of nodes into a separate Sub Graph that can be referenced by the main graph. We can use a single Sub Graph in several other graphs or even use Sub Graphs within Sub Graphs. Although they are officially called "Sub Graphs," I often refer to them as subgraphs, without the space.

There are a couple of ways to create a new subgraph:

- The first is to right-click in the Project View and select *Create* ➤ *Shader* ➤ *Sub Graph*, which creates an empty subgraph.

- The other method is to select a group of nodes on any existing graph, then right-click, and select *Convert To* ➤ *Sub Graph*, which automatically creates the subgraph for you, complete with the correct inputs and outputs.

Let's make a subgraph from scratch that takes a color as input and inverts its RGB value.

Color Invert Sub Graph

First, create the subgraph using the first method I just mentioned. I'll call it "InvertColors". The environment looks like a regular graph, except you will see an `Output` node in place of the master stack. If you click it and look at the Node Settings, you'll see a section called *Outputs* – we can add or remove entries and change the name and type of each output. Left-click a name to edit it. For this subgraph, we only need a single output color, so make sure there is a single output, rename it to "Output", and make sure its type is `Vector 4`.

To change the inputs to the graph, we can add properties using the Blackboard – they act the same as on a standard graph. I'll add a `Color` property called "Input Color". The graph surface in the center of the screen acts just like a regular graph, so I will drag the `Input Color` property onto it and drag a pin off the property to add an `Invert Color` node. This node has four tick boxes, one for each color channel, to control which ones become inverted; I'll tick all four. The output of the `Invert Color` node should be linked to the single graph output. Figure 4-15 shows the entire graph.

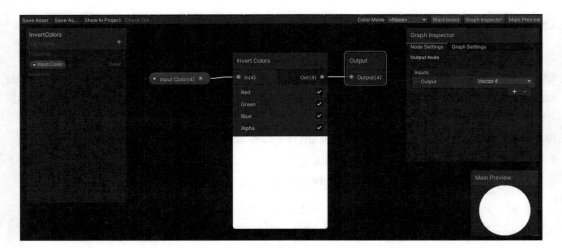

Figure 4-15. *A Sub Graph for inverting any color that is input to the graph*

To use the subgraph within another graph, we can add it using the Create Node menu, under the new Sub Graphs section that has appeared. Or we can drag the Sub Graph asset from the Project View onto the graph. We could modify the HelloShaderGraph shader using the new `InvertColors` subgraph by inserting it between the `Base Color` node and the output – by default, `Base Color` is white, and the preview on the `InvertColors` subgraph correctly appears black. Figure 4-16 shows what this would look like.

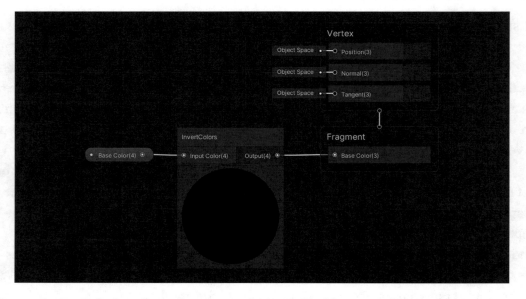

Figure 4-16. *Sub Graph nodes are used in graphs like any other regular type of node*

Custom Function Node

Shader Graph does not ship with a node for every shader function imaginable. Although it comes with over 200 nodes for a multitude of uses, you might sometimes find that a node just doesn't exist for what you want to do. In that case, you have two choices. You can recreate the feature yourself by using the other nodes that exist and packaging them together in a Sub Graph or node group. Or, if you're coming to Shader Graph from a shader code background, you can use the `Custom Function` node. You won't use this node very often unless you need to run some very specialized code that isn't provided by any of Shader Graph's nodes, but I will mention it now because it is a very powerful tool in our arsenal that partially crosses the gap between code and graph. Let's try the invert color example again, but this time we will use a `Custom Function` node.

Color Invert Custom Function

When you add a `Custom Function` node to your graph, the preview will look like a magenta and black checkerboard, and there will be a little red error mark next to it because we haven't specified any custom code yet. When the node is selected, you will see many options appear in the Node Settings (see Figure 4-17). There are sections for *Inputs* and *Outputs* to the node, and when you add or remove entries from either list, you will see those changes reflected on the node itself. There doesn't seem to be a restriction on the number of inputs and outputs you can add. For our custom color inversion node, we will need one input called "Color" and one output called "Out", both of which are of type `Vector 4`.

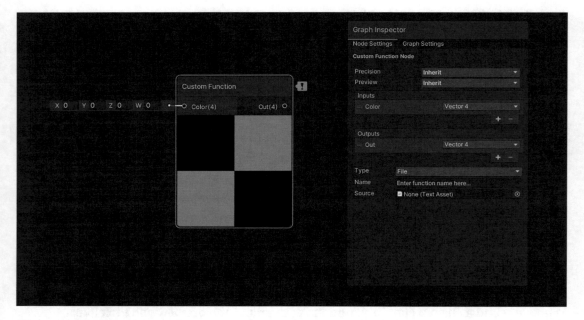

Figure 4-17. *A custom function node with one input and one output defined, but no code body*

The next option is the *Type*. There are two settings – first, we will explore the *String* setting, which lets us write the custom code directly inside the Node Settings window.

Custom Function String Mode

When this mode is selected, Shader Graph will automatically generate a function for us under the hood using the code we write inside the *Body* field and the function name we provide in the *Name* field. I will name my function "invert", and I will use the following code for the body, taking care to ensure that the variables I use match up with the names of my input and output.

Listing 4-1. A snippet of custom code that takes each color channel of the Color input and outputs one minus the channel value, respectively

```
Out = 1.0f - Color;
```

Shader Graph generates a function based on what we just wrote and the *Precision* setting for this `Custom Function` node. Based on the snippet we just wrote, Unity will generate the following code.

Listing 4-2. Two versions of a function that inverts a color using either single or half precision, generated by the Custom Function node

```
void invert_float (float4 Color, out float4 Out)
{
    Out = 1.0f - Color;
}

void invert_half (half4 Color, out half4 Out)
{
    Out = 1.0f - Color;
}
```

This interface is restrictive because you can only type a single function inside the body. There may also be instances where your code needs to differ between precision settings, but it's impossible to do this in *String* mode. Let's see how to remedy this.

Custom Function File Mode

In *File* mode, we solve both these problems: we can define several functions inside a single file and then pick one to use in the Custom Function node. In most cases I would recommend using *File* mode. If we were to copy and paste Listing 4-2 into a separate file named "Invert.hlsl" and save it inside your project's Assets folder, we could drag that file onto the *Source* field, and all errors on the node should disappear.

Note   You'll have to create the Invert.hlsl file in an external program, because Unity doesn't have an option to create HLSL files directly.

For any function you write in the file, it must have either _float or _half at the end of its name (although you don't need to include both versions for every function), but in the Node Settings, write the name without either suffix. Figure 4-18 shows a completed Custom Function node with the color white being used as input.

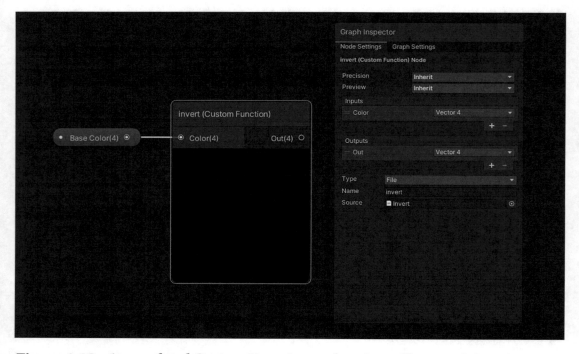

Figure 4-18. *A completed Custom Function node using a file containing custom code*

Here, Unity will pick between the `invert_float` and `invert_half` functions based on the *Precision* of the node, which you can change using the option at the top of the Graph Inspector.

Summary

In this chapter, we saw that Shader Graph is a very powerful and, to many people, a more approachable tool for creating shaders in Unity. It comes bundled with over 200 nodes for most of the operations you will need and provides ways of filling some of the gaps. Even if you prefer shader code, Shader Graph can be an effective tool for rapidly prototyping ideas and getting real-time visual feedback from within the graph environment. Here's a summary of the key points from this chapter:

- In Shader Graph, we connect nodes together to create a shader.

- The master stack is a list of shader outputs that we can modify.

- Graphs are eventually compiled to shader code under the hood, although the generated code is often less optimized than an equivalent hand-authored shader.

- Most nodes provide a real-time preview of the output, which makes it easy to see what each stage of the shader is doing.

- We can define shader properties on the Blackboard and expose most property types to the Inspector.

- The Graph Inspector provides options for the graph as a whole and for individual nodes when they are selected.

- Shader Graph provides multiple features for organizing your graphs such as redirect nodes, node snapping, node groups, and sticky notes.

- Sub Graphs can be used to bundle together commonly used groups of nodes, like functions in shader code.

- The Custom Function node can be used to inject custom shader code into nodes.

CHAPTER 5

Textures and UV Coordinates

Now we have seen how basic shaders are made in Unity using both shader code and Shader Graph. It's possible to add complex color patterns to the surface of an object by generating those patterns within the shader itself, but this is not always possible, so sometimes we will need to create such patterns externally and import them into the shader. We do this using *textures*.

The most common type of texture is a 2D array of color data that a shader can read. You can think of a texture as a regular image – *texture* is the technical term we use in computer graphics to refer to them. We apply textures to objects using a process called *texture mapping*, where we match up each part of the 2D texture to parts of the surface of a 3D object and apply those bits of the texture to those bits of the model. What we do with the values from the texture after mapping them depends on the context. Or we might mess with the way the mapping works inside the shader itself to achieve certain effects.

Note Unity supports many file formats for textures, such as PNG, TIFF, and JPEG. I use PNG for most textures I create.

In this chapter, you will learn everything you need to know about texture mapping. We will tweak the basic shader we wrote earlier to include texture support. Then we will see some techniques to modify the mapping between textures and meshes. Later, we will see different kinds of textures other than regular 2D textures and use them in a slightly different way.

© Daniel Ilett 2022
D. Ilett, *Building Quality Shaders for Unity®*, https://doi.org/10.1007/978-1-4842-8652-4_5

Basic Texturing

A basic type of texture contains data about the color of the surface of an object. If I wanted to create a model of a wooden table and apply a texture to the surface, then the bulk of the texture would probably be some shade of brown and contain a wood grain pattern using different shades of brown. You can create a texture using most image editing programs or download them from the Internet – there are many sources of images in the public domain that may be appropriate for use in shaders, or you can find them on the Unity Asset Store.

Tip   When using images from the Internet, check the license attached to the image to ensure you have the rights to use it in your game. For example, some types of Creative Commons license like CC0 (CC-zero) are extremely permissive and allow redistribution, commercial use, and derivative versions of game assets. Other licenses may restrict some of those rights.

Adding texture support to an existing shader requires modifying many parts of the shader such the properties and the main body – let's see how it works in HLSL first and then create a Shader Graph to do the same.

Texture Support in HLSL

Let's start by creating a shader that is very similar in structure to the HelloWorld shader we wrote in Chapter 3. We'll be aiming to build a shader that uses a single texture to determine the base color of the object, along with a single color that we use to tint the texture color. Since HelloWorld already applies a tint color (without the texture), it's a good place to start. Figure 5-1 shows what we are aiming for.

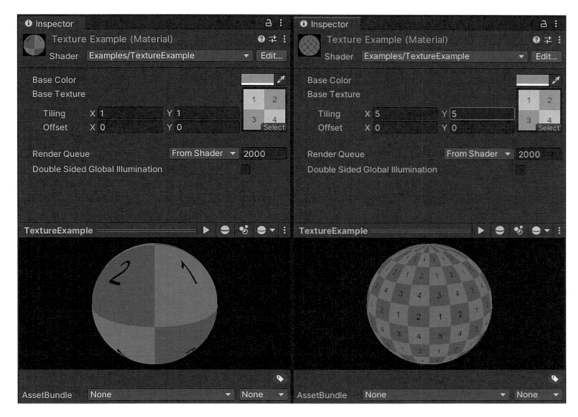

Figure 5-1. *The completed TextureExample shader with a textured preview, using 1× tiling (left) and 5× tiling (right)*

Remember that we should give each shader a unique name at the top of each shader file, so I'll be calling this one "TextureExample". Start by creating a new shader file called "TextureExample.shader", and replace the file contents with the following code.

Listing 5-1. The TextureExample shader code skeleton

```
Shader "Examples/TextureExample"
{
    Properties
    {
        _BaseColor ("Base Color", Color) = (1, 1, 1, 1)
    }
    SubShader
    {
```

111

```
        Tags
        {
                "RenderType" = "Opaque"
                "Queue" = "Geometry"
        }

        Pass
        {
                HLSLPROGRAM
                #pragma vertex vert
                #pragma fragment frag

                struct appdata { ... };
                struct v2f { ... };
                v2f vert (appdata v) { ... }
                float4 frag (v2f i) : SV_Target { ... }

                ENDHLSL
        }
    }
}
```

There are a few gaps in this shader currently, so think of it as a skeleton that we're going to put some meat onto throughout this section. Let's start by adding the tags and include files required by the shader – we'll need to do this in each shader we write.

- In the built-in pipeline, let's just include the UnityCG.cginc file inside HLSLPROGRAM. We don't need to add any tags.

- In URP, we must add some additional tags alongside the include file:

  - Add a RenderPipeline tag to the existing Tags block in the SubShader.

  - Insert an additional Tags block in the Pass to contain a LightMode tag.

  - Include the Core.hlsl file inside HLSLPROGRAM.

Listing 5-2. Adding the UnityCG.cginc include file in the built-in pipeline

```
Pass
{
    HLSLPROGRAM
    #pragma vertex vert
    #pragma fragment frag
    #include "UnityCG.cginc"
```

Listing 5-3. Adding tags and including files in URP

```
Tags
{
    "RenderType" = "Opaque"
    "Queue" = "Geometry"
    "RenderPipeline" = "UniversalPipeline"
}
Pass
{
    Tags
    {
        "LightMode" = "UniversalForward"
    }

    HLSLPROGRAM
    #pragma vertex vert
    #pragma fragment frag

    #include "Packages/com.unity.render-pipelines.universal/
    ShaderLibrary/Core.hlsl"
```

Now we are ready to add a new entry to the Properties list.

Adding Texture Properties

Recall that, in shaders, properties are variables that we use as inputs, and we can assign values to these variables inside the Unity Editor. In ShaderLab, adding a texture property looks the same no matter which render pipeline you are using, but the syntax is a bit strange.

113

Listing 5-4. Adding a texture to the Properties block

```
Properties
{
        _BaseColor("Base Color", 2D) = (1,1,1,1)
        _BaseTex("Base Texture", 2D) = "white" {}
}
```

Back in Chapter 3, we saw how properties work; the process of declaring a Texture2D has many moving parts, so let's go through each in turn:

- The reference value we'll use in the shader code is _BaseTex.

- The human-readable name that will be visible in the Inspector window is "Base Texture".

- The type of this property is 2D, which we use for Texture2D properties.

- After the equals sign, we specify the default value if no texture is assigned:

    - The choices for color textures are "white", "gray", "black", and "red", which generate a texture filled with the corresponding color.

    - For normal maps, we can use "bump", which generates a flat normal map. We will see how normal mapping works in a later chapter.

    - If no color name is specified or an invalid name is supplied, Unity defaults to "gray".

- The curly braces after the default value are required.

Once we have added the texture to Properties, we also need to declare it inside the HLSL code block. Colors use the float4 type because they are simply a four-element vector of values, but textures are a bit more complicated. They are a 2D array of colors, and they could have an arbitrary size; they might not even be square. The type we use is called sampler2D, and we will define _BaseTex alongside the other variable declarations.

In Chapter 3, we saw that in URP, we must put variable declarations inside a constant buffer to ensure our shader is compatible with the SPR Batcher. You might, therefore, be tempted to put this texture declaration inside the buffer too. However, textures are an exception – they can be defined outside the buffer, and your shader will still comply with the restrictions required by the batcher. Your shader won't actually break if you do happen to declare them inside the constant buffer, so don't worry if you do that by mistake. In the built-in pipeline, they can be declared alongside all other variables as normal. I'll be placing all variable declarations underneath the v2f struct definition (although we haven't yet filled in the contents of that struct).

Listing 5-5. Declaring a texture in HLSL in the built-in pipeline

```
struct v2f { ... };

sampler2D _BaseTex;
float4 _BaseColor;
```

Listing 5-6. Declaring a texture in HLSL in URP

```
struct v2f { ... };

sampler2D _BaseTex;

CBUFFER_START(UnityPerMaterial)
        float4 _BaseColor;
CBUFFER_END
```

Currently, your shader will not compile since we've left many blank sections. However, if you were to use the same structs and vert and frag function code as the HelloWorld shader, your material would look like Figure 5-2 in the Inspector.

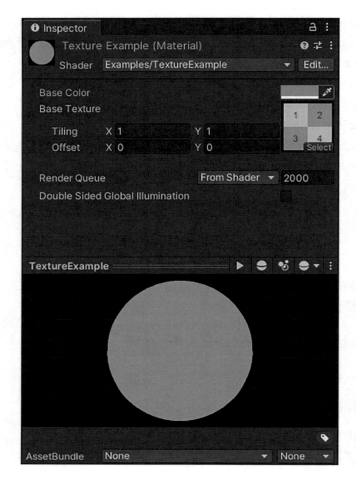

Figure 5-2. *A theoretical version of the TextureExample shader attached to a material*

In this screenshot, you can see the Base Texture property is now visible. I have attached a checkerboard texture to the property – you can use the small "Select" button on the texture preview to open a window containing all textures in your project. We haven't modified the fragment shader to make use of the texture yet, so the preview at the bottom is still a solid color.

When you add a Texture2D property to an HLSL shader, you will also see *Tiling* and *Offset* settings attached to that texture. Both options modify how Unity maps the textures to objects. If we change the tiling setting, then the texture will get stretched or repeated across the surface of your mesh, and if you change the offset setting, the texture will be scrolled across the object's surface. To use these inside the shader, Unity generates a set of optional variables for every texture as follows:

116

- For any texture named {TextureName}, Unity creates a variable called {TextureName}_ST.

  - This variable contains the tiling and offset values inside a four-dimensional vector.

  - The (x,y) components store the tiling vector, and the (z,w) components store the offset vector.

  - "S" stands for "scale," while "T" stands for "translation."

- Unity also generates the variable {TextureName}_TexelSize.

  - *Texel* is a term that stands for "texture element," the same way *pixel* stands for "picture element."

  - The (x,y) components store 1.0/width and 1.0/height, respectively. That may seem strange, but these values are used often in calculations.

  - The (z,w) components store the unmodified width and height, respectively.

- Lastly, the variable {TextureName}_HDR is generated, but it is only helpful on High Dynamic Range–encoded textures.

  - An HDR texture (and HDR technology in general) represents each color channel of each texel with more than the standard 8 bits of data.

  - This lets us encode a greater range of values, and we can reproduce images with more accurate color and lighting details.

  - This variable can be used with the DecodeHDR function to properly extract HDR data from such a texture.

To use these variables in the shader, we must declare them the same way we would declare any other variable. Since they are each float4 variables, we must follow the SRP Batcher rules in URP to ensure the shader stays batcher-compatible. In the following code snippet, we will declare the tiling and offset variable for our shader.

Listing 5-7. Declaring optional texture variables

```
float4 _BaseColor;
float4 _BaseTex_ST;
```

Now that we can send textures to the shader via properties, it's time to talk about how exactly we will map those textures onto the surface of the object.

Texture Coordinates

To sample a texture at a specific position, we use *texture coordinates* (also commonly called *UV coordinates*, or colloquially just "UVs"), which are a mapping between a 3D model and 2D textures – each vertex of the mesh is assigned a UV coordinate, which defines where on the texture we should read data from. For any other point on the mesh surface that isn't a vertex, we *interpolate* the UVs between the nearest vertices. A demonstration of how UV mapping might work is seen in Figure 5-3.

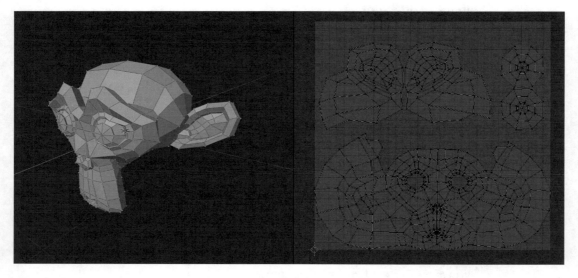

Figure 5-3. *On the left, a 3D model in Blender, a 3D modeling software package. On the right, its associated UV mapping*

The mapping doesn't need to be contiguous – two adjacent faces on the mesh could map to opposite parts of the texture. As you can imagine, UV coordinates are a bit like trying to wrap a square sheet of wrapping paper around any weirdly shaped 3D object imaginable, but we're allowed to cheat and cut the paper into tiny bits and stick them around the object however we want. 3D artists wrap people's birthday presents creatively!

To use these UVs, we need to input them to the shader. In Chapter 3, we saw how to pass vertex positions to the vertex shader as part of the appdata struct – we use the same struct to pass UV data by adding an extra variable.

- For UV coordinates, the type is float2, and the shader semantic is TEXCOORD0 (which stands for "texture coordinate 0").

- Unity supports more than one set of UVs, so if you wanted to use different UV channels for different textures, then you could specify multiple additional channels using the semantics TEXCOORD1, TEXCOORD2, and so on up to TEXCOORD7.

- Some platforms may support more UV channels, but you will always have these eight available. Each of these texture coordinate slots is called an *interpolator*.

Listing 5-8. Passing texture coordinates to the vertex shader

```
struct appdata
{
    float4 positionOS : Position;
    float2 uv : TEXCOORD0;
};
```

Note   The "standard" set of UVs, which is most commonly used for texture mapping, is TEXCOORD0. You can author UV channels on a mesh however you want, but almost every shader will assume you are using TEXCOORD0 for mapping regular textures to your mesh, so we will stick with that for our shaders.

The fragment shader requires these UVs, so we will also need to modify the v2f struct to include them. Unlike vertex positions, we don't need to change the semantic we use for UVs – we can use TEXCOORD0 again. These edits to the appdata and v2f structs are the same whether you are using the built-in pipeline or URP.

Listing 5-9. Passing texture coordinates from the vertex shader to the fragment shader

```
struct v2f
{
    float4 positionCS : SV_Position;
    float2 uv : TEXCOORD0;
};
```

We process these UVs in the vertex shader between the two structs, which means we can modify them before sending them to the fragment shader. This is where we usually apply tiling and offset to the UVs depending on the tiling and offset settings of the textures we're using, although you don't have to. The easiest way to pass UVs from vertex to fragment is to just send them through unchanged, as this line of code would do.

Listing 5-10. Passing UV data to the fragment shader without modification

```
o.uv = v.uv;
```

No matter how you change the tiling and offset values in the Inspector, your texture won't look any different if you use this shader. Thankfully, one of the macros included in Unity's shader include files will apply the transformations for us. The macro is called TRANSFORM_TEX, and it automatically uses the {TextureName}_ST variable to apply the mapping. TRANSFORM_TEX takes the input UVs and the texture name as inputs. Thankfully, this macro uses the same name in the built-in and Universal pipelines.

Caution   If you don't define {TextureName}_ST anywhere and try to use the TRANSFORM_TEX macro with the corresponding texture {TextureName}, then you will get an "undeclared identifier" compile error. Unity will helpfully let you know which variable is undeclared.

Listing 5-11. Passing UV data to the fragment shader using TRANSFORM_TEX in the built-in pipeline

```
v2f vert (appdata v)
{
    v2f o;
    o.positionCS = UnityObjectToClipPos(v.positionOS);
    o.uv = TRANSFORM_TEX(v.uv, _BaseTex);
    return o;
}
```

Listing 5-12. Passing UV data to the fragment shader using TRANSFORM_TEX in URP

```
v2f vert (appdata v)
{
    v2f o;
    o.positionCS = TransformObjectToHClip(v.positionOS);
    o.uv = TRANSFORM_TEX(v.uv, _BaseTex);
    return o;
}
```

We will be able to access these UV coordinates in the fragment shader. During the rasterization process, which happens between the vertex and fragment stages, Unity will interpolate the per-vertex UVs we just calculated to give us per-fragment UVs, which we can use to apply the right bits of the texture to the mesh. The process by which we grab values from the texture is called *texture sampling*.

Texture Sampling

We use UVs to sample textures. The basic function for sampling 2D textures is tex2D, which takes the name of the texture and the UVs as parameters. Unity takes those UVs, finds the position on the texture corresponding to the UVs, and returns the color at that location. The color is a float4. We're going to modify the fragment shader to sample _BaseTex in the first line.

Listing 5-13. Sampling a texture using tex2D

```
float4 frag (v2f i) : SV_Target
{
        float4 textureSample = tex2D(_BaseTex, i.uv);
        ...
}
```

Recall that vectors in shaders, like the `float4` vector here, are just a collection of numbers – we can add or multiply them together. We had previously used the `_BaseColor` property to output only a solid color, so we can multiply that by the texture sample we just did to output a texture with a tint. It's common in shaders to supply both a base texture and a base color because you may want to create a handful of materials with the same basic pattern (such as a checkerboard like I used in Figure 5-1), but with different coloration.

The alternative is to supply multiple different textures that were tinted differently when they were created and sample them without tinting, but this wastes texture memory on the GPU and increases the build size of your game, because you need to include all those textures. To multiply colors together, we use the asterisk (*) operator.

Listing 5-14. A fragment shader that outputs a tinted texture

```
float4 frag (v2f i) : SV_Target
{
        float4 textureSample = tex2D(_BaseTex, i.uv);
        return textureSample * _BaseColor;
}
```

This code is identical between the built-in pipeline and URP. If you look at the material's Inspector window now (see Figure 5-1), then the preview will display the texture tinted with the base color you chose. If you tweak the tiling and offset settings, then the preview window will update to reflect your changes.

Texture Support in Shader Graph

We will follow roughly the same steps to create this shader in Shader Graph. To start off with, create a new Unlit graph and name it "TextureGraph". We'll start by adding the same Base Color property we used in HelloShaderGraph. Then we'll need to add a new texture property.

Creating a texture property is as easy as selecting the plus arrow on the Blackboard and selecting `Texture2D` as the variable type. The name of the variable should be "Base Texture", and the reference value is `_BaseTex`, complete with underscore. Figure 5-4 shows what the property should look like. Unity compiles each Shader Graph into ShaderLab behind the scenes, so the properties in the generated file will be set up the same way we wrote our code, with a declaration in the `Properties` block and another one in HLSL.

Figure 5-4. *The Base Color and Base Texture properties for TextureGraph*

In Unity versions from 2021.2 and up, you will see a *Use Tiling and Offset* option on all texture properties, which adds the *Tiling* and *Offset* vectors to the Inspector window. However, in versions below 2021.2, Unity won't display the tiling and offset vectors for a texture on the material Inspector window, so you must create those properties yourself.

Applying Tiling and Offset Vectors

When working in versions prior to 2021.2, I usually add two separate `Vector2` properties called `Tiling` and `Offset` and set the default values to $(1, 1)$ and $(0, 0)$, respectively. Unity will display both your `Vector2` properties in the Inspector with four components, as if they were `Vector4` properties (see Figure 5-5), so we must ignore the third and fourth components of each property.

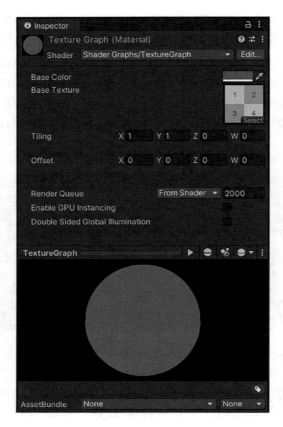

Figure 5-5. *A material that uses the TextureGraph shader. So far, we have not sampled the texture inside the shader, so it only uses a block color for its output*

Let's see how to apply these values in Shader Graph. We don't need to do these steps if you're in Unity 2021.2 and above, but it will still be useful to read this section anyway. Unlike with shader code, we don't need to deal with passing the UV data between shader stages. Unity does all of that behind the scenes and provides a UV node to obtain texture coordinate data about the mesh. To make use of the `Tiling` and `Offset` properties, we can add a node called `Tiling And Offset`, which acts somewhat like the `TRANSFORM_TEX` macro we used in code; it takes a base set of UV coordinates and scales it by the *Tiling* input and then translates by the *Offset* input.

By default, the *UV* input of the node uses the first set of texture coordinates attached to the mesh. Shader Graph calls these UVs `UV0`, which corresponds to `TEXCOORD0` in shader code. The drop-down lets you pick which set of UVs to use, but Shader Graph only supports UV0–UV3, whereas we can access at least eight sets of UVs with code. For now, we will use the default value. You could also explicitly add a UV node and connect that to the *UV* input. Figure 5-6 shows how these nodes and properties fit together.

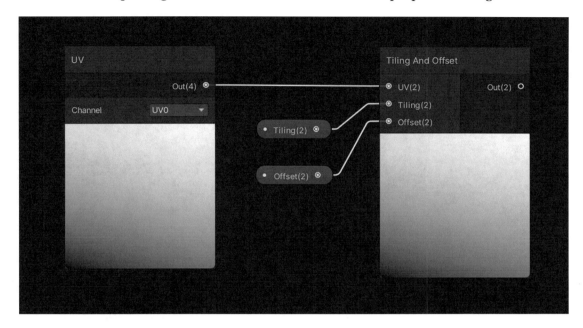

Figure 5-6. *Using tiling and offset values to modify UVs in Shader Graph*

The output of the Tiling And Offset node is a new set of UV coordinates with those transformations applied to the original UVs. If we wanted to, we could pass *any* Vector2 into the Tiling And Offset node and treat those as UVs, even if they didn't originate from a UV node – in fact, that's how many custom effects are made. We'll see how to do that later.

If you dislike using two separate properties for Tiling and Offset, you could instead create a single Vector4 property called TilingAndOffset with a default value of $(1, 1, 0, 0)$, but this entails more work on the graph to separate the two Vector2 parts. In such a scenario, you would use the first two components for the tiling and the other two for the offset. Figure 5-7 shows how you might achieve that using the Swizzle node:

- We output the TilingAndOffset property directly to the *Tiling* slot.

- Since the *Tiling* slot expects a Vector2, it will truncate the property to its first two components (x, y).

- We output `TilingAndOffset` into a `Swizzle` node. The *Red Out* is set to *Blue*, and the *Green Out* is set to *Alpha*. Then we connect the `Swizzle` output to the *Offset* slot.

- In all, the `Swizzle` node will output (z, w, x, x), but it is truncated to just (z, w).

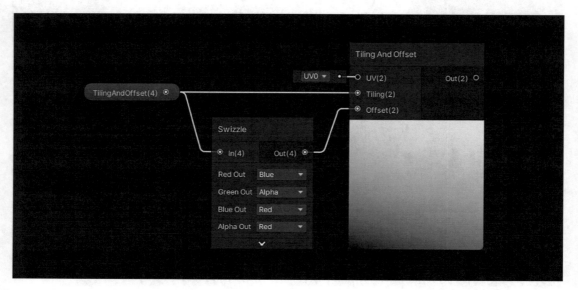

Figure 5-7. *The Swizzle node lets you rearrange the components of a vector*

Now that we have our UVs, we will use them to sample the texture.

Sampling Textures

Like the `tex2D` function in shader code, Shader Graph has the `Sample Texture 2D` node for sampling textures. It takes a texture, a set of UVs, and a sampler as inputs and outputs a color, as seen in Figure 5-8. The color is available as a full vector, with the *RGBA* output, as well as the four individual components as floats. We will use the `Base Texture` property and the output from `Tiling And Offset` as the inputs and skip over the sampler for now.

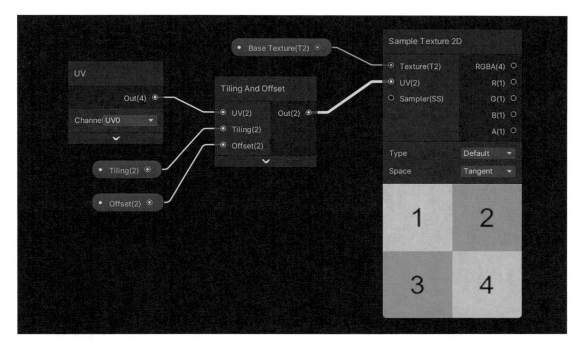

Figure 5-8. *Sampling a texture using tiling and offset in Shader Graph*

If you're using Unity 2021.2 or above and you ticked the *Use Tiling and Offset* option in the settings for Base Texture, then the Sample Texture 2D node automatically applies those tiling and offset options. That's a lot more convenient as we avoid needing to add so many nodes to the graph! Although it's not much of a problem because this graph is small, when we start making larger graphs, space-saving features like this are going to become invaluable.

In this example, I have attached a similar checkerboard texture to the default value for Base Texture. Sample Texture 2D displays a preview of what the texture looks like if it were sampled using the currently attached inputs with their default values. This node is more complicated than those we have seen so far, due to the options at the bottom of the node:

- The *Type* dropdown is used to determine whether the node will output colors (in *Default* mode) or normal vectors (in *Normal* mode).

- The *Space* dropdown determines which sampling space is used. This option is only relevant for normal mapping, which we will revisit in a later chapter.

I will leave both options alone for now. After sampling the texture, we can multiply it with the `Base Color` property, which already existed on the graph. This works the same way as shader code: colors are just four-element vectors, and when we multiply two of them together, each element is multiplied by the corresponding element of the other vector. We will output the result to the *Base Color* option on the graph's master stack, as shown in Figure 5-9.

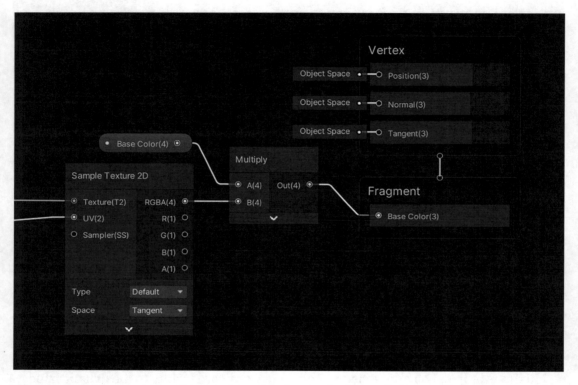

Figure 5-9. *Outputting the combined color to the Base Color on the master stack*

If you select the material and look at its Inspector window, then it will be slightly different from the code equivalent if you added the `Tiling` and `Offset` properties manually. Unfortunately, Unity will display these as four-element vectors even though we specified that they are of type `Vector2`, so the z and w components will be ignored (see Figure 5-10).

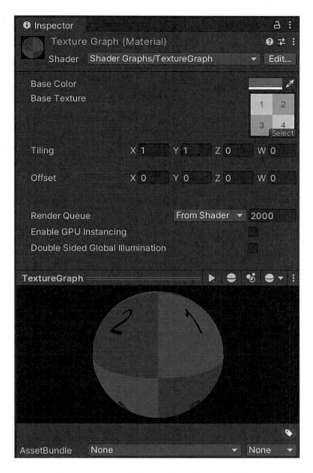

Figure 5-10. *The material Inspector for a shader made with Shader Graph*

At this point, the graph we just made should have parity with the shader code we wrote. However, there's a lot more to textures in Unity than just simple sampling like this. Let's look at some of the technical details of texturing and then customize how each texture is read while sampling.

Mipmaps and Level of Detail

By default, Unity uses a technique called *mipmapping*, whereby higher-resolution versions of a texture are used for close objects and lower-resolution versions of the same texture are used for faraway objects. Typically, Unity precalculates each of the *mipmap levels* ahead of time: the 0th mipmap level leaves the texture unchanged, the 1st level is half the size in each axis, the 2nd level is a quarter the size of the original in each axis, and so on, as in Figure 5-11. This increases the amount of texture memory required by a third, but it is faster to sample the lower-resolution mipmap levels when an object is far away, where there wouldn't be a perceptible difference if you chose to sample a high-resolution mipmap level instead.

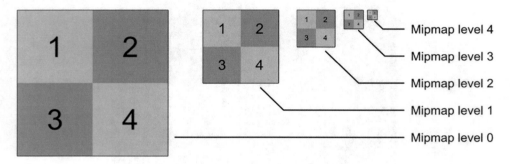

Figure 5-11. *A texture with different mipmap levels. Each time the mipmap level increases by one, the texture is scaled by a factor of half along both axes, resulting in a texture that is one quarter the size*

A single large object with parts that are both close to and far away from the camera could be textured using more than one mipmap level. It is also possible to manually control which mipmap level is sampled inside a shader using alternative versions of the tex2D function and the `Sample Texture 2D` node in HLSL and Shader Graph, respectively.

Level of Detail

The term *Level of Detail (LOD)* usually applies to 3D meshes. In this context, when a mesh is far away from the camera, we can swap it for a version with fewer triangles, so we save precious rendering resources for close-up details we can actually perceive. It is also applicable to texturing. You can think of mipmaps as the 2D analogue of a 3D mesh LOD system because we use mipmaps to sample faraway objects with lower-resolution textures.

Texture LOD in HLSL

In code shaders, we can force Unity to use a specific mipmap level by using the `tex2Dlod` function in place of `tex2D`. Rather than supplying UV coordinates using a `float2`, we use a `float4` – the UVs you know and love go in the (x, y) components, and then we stick an extra value representing the numbered mipmap level we want to sample (0 for the original texture, 1 for the 1st mipmap level, and so on) into the fourth (`w`) component.

Listing 5-15. Using tex2Dlod to sample a specific mipmap level (in this case, the 3rd level)

```
float4 sampleUVs = float4(i.uv, 0.0f, 3.0f);
float4 textureSample = tex2Dlod(_BaseTex, sampleUVs);
```

The `tex2Dlod` function, unlike `tex2D`, can be used within the vertex shader. It might seem strange, given what we've learned so far, to be using textures within the vertex shader, but it can certainly be helpful. There are many effects with work on object geometry that can benefit from reading precalculated values from a texture and applying those values to each object, such as a vertex shader that simulates rolling waves on the surface of the sea by reading wave data from a texture – we will see effects like that later.

Texture LOD in Shader Graph

Let's see how this works in Shader Graph too. Instead of using a `Sample Texture 2D` node, we can use the alternative `Sample Texture 2D LOD` node. Both nodes have the same inputs, except the `LOD` variant has an extra *LOD* option, which works the same as in shader code. We can replace the set of nodes in Figure 5-8 with the nodes in Figure 5-12. Using higher *LOD* values will decrease the quality of the image, and a value of 0 would sample the highest-quality mipmap level.

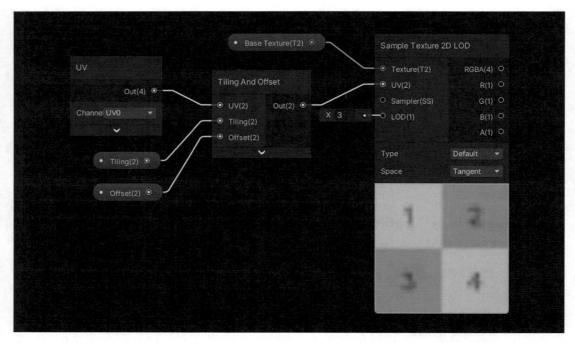

Figure 5-12. *Using Sample Texture 2D LOD in place of Sample Texture 2D. The 3rd mipmap level has been specified in the LOD input, so the preview's resolution is noticeably lower than the original texture*

Note   While using Shader Graph, you will find that some nodes will refuse to connect their outputs to either the vertex stage or fragment stage outputs on the master stack. This means that those nodes are incompatible with that stage. For example, `Sample Texture 2D` will not connect to any nodes in the vertex stage, but `Sample Texture 2D LOD` will connect to nodes in either stage.

Sampling Options

Before we even create the shader, we can influence how textures will get sampled. If you've used Unity for a while, you will probably be familiar with the texture import window; if you click a texture in the Project View, then the Inspector will list many options related to how the texture gets used during rendering (see Figure 5-13). The ones we are most interested in right now are *Wrap Mode* and *Filter Mode*.

Figure 5-13. *The texture import window of an example texture. The Wrap Mode and Filter Mode settings are seen roughly in the middle of the list of settings*

Wrap Mode

The Wrap Mode of a texture defines what happens when you attempt to sample the texture using UVs outside the 0–1 range in either axis. There are five sampling modes:

- The default behavior is to *Repeat*, which acts like the texture gets repeated infinitely, so sampling at $(1.5, 3.5)$ is the same as sampling at $(0.5, 0.5)$. Otherwise, we can pick the following modes.

- The *Clamp* option locks your UVs to the 0–1 range. Sampling at
  $(1.5, 3.5)$ is the same as sampling at $(1.0, 1.0)$, and sampling at
  $(−7.0, 0.3)$ is the same as sampling at $(0.0, 0.3)$.

- *Mirror* will sample normally between the 0 and 1 range, then mirror
  the UVs between 1 and 2, then sample normally again between 2 and
  3, and so on. Sampling at $(1.2, 1.3)$ is like sampling at $(0.8, 0.7)$.

- *Mirror Once* is like Mirror, but it will only mirror one time and then
  clamp. Sampling at $(−0.1, 0.2)$ is like sampling at $(0.1, 0.2)$, but
  sampling at $(−2.3, −1.0)$ is like sampling at $(−1.0, −1.0)$.

- Finally, the *Per Axis* sampling mode lets you define one of the
  preceding four options for each of the two axes independently. You
  could Repeat along the u-axis and Clamp on the v-axis, for instance.

Figure 5-14 illustrates what each sampling mode might look like when applied to an
example checkerboard texture with a number in each quadrant.

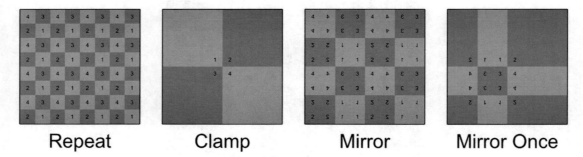

Figure 5-14. *Wrap modes applied to an example texture. The material used to
render these textures uses the TextureExample shader with 4× tiling and an offset
of –1.5 in both axes*

Filter Mode

The Filter Mode, on the other hand, defines what type of blurring is used on the texture.
One of the problems with texture mapping is that the pixel density of your screen (or, at
least, the pixel density of the portion of your screen taken up by an object) doesn't always
line up with the texel density of the texture on that object. In a perfect world, pixels and
texels would always line up 1:1 so that we can sample the texture, apply that color to the
screen pixel, and sleep easy knowing that the mapping was absolutely perfect.

The real world, sadly, is messy. Sometimes, we will find ourselves with an object that takes up a large portion of the screen that uses a low-resolution texture or vice versa – in those cases, we must decide how sampling will operate. We use filtering to do that. Let's look at the three settings available for Filter Mode:

- *Point filtering* is perhaps the easiest to understand. If a UV coordinate does not line up exactly with the center point of a texel on the texture, then the UV gets rounded to the nearest one, and the color of that texel is sampled. For that reason, point filtering is sometimes called *nearest-neighbor filtering*.

- *Bilinear filtering*, which is the default option, will interpolate between the (up to) four closest texels to the specified UV coordinate. If the UVs match up to the center of a texel exactly, that texel's color is sampled. Otherwise, this filter works by taking a weighted average of the color of the four closest texels to the UV coordinate.

- *Trilinear filtering* works like bilinear filtering with an added step. If the UV coordinate is being used to sample on the overlap between two mipmap levels on an object, then the resulting color is interpolated between those mipmaps. In effect, this is the result of using bilinear filtering on both mipmap levels and then interpolating between both those values.

Each combination of Wrap Mode and Filter Mode looks different. By default, when sampling a texture inside a shader, the behavior specified in the texture import settings will be used, but it's possible to override those settings using sampler states.

Sampler States

Sometimes it will be necessary to override a texture's default filter and wrap settings for a specific shader effect. Both HLSL and Shader Graph have mechanisms for doing so.

Sampler States in HLSL

So far, we have seen the `sampler2D` type, which bundles together the texture data (the texels that make up the texture) and the sampler data (the combination of wrap and filter settings) into one object, and the `tex2D` function that reads from a `sampler2D`. However, sometimes we want to separate the texture data from the sampling settings. For instance, we might find that we're using many textures on an object, but we only want to use one set of wrap and filter settings for all of them.

We can use the `Texture2D` type in HLSL to declare the texture data by itself using the same naming conventions we previously used for `sampler2D` (such as naming a texture _BaseTex). Then, to define a sampler that uses the wrap and filter settings from a specific texture, we use the SamplerState type. The workflow looks like this:

- Add a texture to your Assets folder and tweak the Wrap and Filter modes as you like.

- Include the texture inside Properties in ShaderLab using the syntax we have seen before.

- In HLSL, define the texture in your Properties list using the `Texture2D` keyword instead of `sampler2D`. `Texture2D` can be placed outside the `UnityPerMaterial` buffer in URP, like `sampler2D`.

- Add an extra variable of type `SamplerState`. The name of this variable is `sampler_BaseTex`; in general, the variable `sampler_{TextureName}` accesses the wrap and filter modes associated with the `{TextureName}` texture.

- Instead of using tex2D, use the Sample function. This function is defined on the Texture2D object directly, so to sample _BaseTex, we now say `_BaseTex.Sample(sampler_BaseTex, i.uv)`.

Although this approach requires more typing, the advantage is that we can go on to define several textures and sample them all using a single `SamplerState`, as in the following code listing.

Listing 5-16. Sampling multiple textures using only one SamplerState object

```
// Defining multiple textures and one sampler.
Texture2D _BaseTex;
```

```
Texture2D _AnotherTex;
Texture2D _ThirdTex;
SamplerState sampler_BaseTex; //_BaseTex's sampler.

// Sampling textures within the fragment shader.
float4 baseCol = _BaseTex.Sample(sampler_BaseTex, i.uv);
float4 anotherCol = _AnotherTex.Sample(sampler_BaseTex, i.uv);
float4 thirdCol = _ThirdTex.Sample(sampler_BaseTex, i.uv);
```

Note   Some older graphics APIs (such as OpenGL ES) only support the use of `sampler2D`. You cannot separate textures and samplers using those APIs.

It is also possible to create custom `SamplerState` objects that are not tied to any texture's import settings. First, declare the `SamplerState` type. Then, we must name the sampler carefully. We build the name using the settings we want to use: if we want to use point filtering, the name will contain the word *Point*, and if we want to use repeat wrapping, it will contain the word *Repeat*. These names are case-insensitive and can be specified in any order, and we don't need to include spacing characters between the words, so the following variables do the same thing:

- `SamplerState pointrepeat;`

- `SamplerState Point_Repeat;`

- `SamplerState sampler_RepeatPoint;`

You can specify wrap modes per axis by naming the sampler "RepeatUClampV", for example, which would repeat along the u-axis and clamp along the v-axis. The available names are the same as the filter and wrap options on the texture import window.

Sampler States in Shader Graph

`SamplerState` objects are also supported by Shader Graph. We can create a `Sampler State` node, which has drop-down options for *Wrap* and *Filter*. They are the same as before, except "Bilinear" is renamed "Linear" in the filter settings. We can link the output to the `Sample Texture 2D` node, which accepts a *Sampler* input.

Alternatively, we can create a property of type `Sampler State` and drag that onto the graph and then connect it to the `Sample Texture 2D` node. The only difference is that we define the sampler options in the Node Settings window when using properties. Despite it being a property, it is impossible to expose it to the material Inspector, so it acts more like a private variable than a public property. Figure 5-15 shows how you might connect a `Sampler State` node to the existing TextureGraph shader.

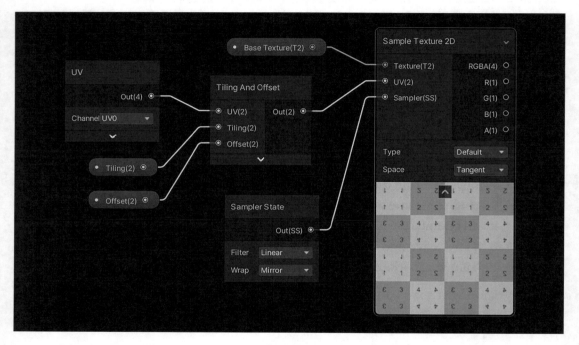

Figure 5-15. *Using a sampler state to override texture settings in Shader Graph*

Try out different combinations of Filter and Wrap settings to see what effects you can create. For example, point filtering works great for pixel art, but bilinear filtering may work better for high-resolution organic textures.

Summary

Textures form the backbone of many shader effects. We have now seen several ways of manipulating the way textures are read in Unity shaders. In the next chapter, we will introduce some common ways of modifying the UVs used for sampling, such as rotating, scaling, shearing, and offsetting the UVs. We will then see a whole host of special shader effects and then look at `Texture3D` and `Cubemap` textures. Here's what we learned in this chapter:

- Basic textures contain color data about the surface of an object. We can sample them using `tex2D` or a `Sample Texture 2D` node.

- Textures are mapped onto objects according to a set of coordinates called UVs.

- Unity provides the `TRANSFORM_TEX` macro to assist with scaling and offsetting textures.

- The `Tiling And Offset` node does the same thing in Shader Graph as `TRANSFORM_TEX` does in shader code.

- Mipmaps are smaller versions of a texture that are automatically generated by Unity. We can access them using `tex2Dlod` or a `Sample Texture 2D LOD` node.

- We can modify the Wrap Mode of the texture to influence what happens when we sample the texture outside of the typical 0–1 UV boundaries. We could clamp to a boundary texel, repeat the texture, or mirror across the texture boundary.

- The Filter Mode controls what happens when we use UV coordinates that don't quite match up exactly to the centroid of a particular texel. We can snap to the nearest neighbor with point sampling or blend between adjacent texels with bilinear or trilinear filtering.

- Sampler states can be used to modify the wrap and filter settings of a texture within an individual shader.

CHAPTER 6

Advanced Texturing

Textures are extremely versatile. We can encode practically any color data we want inside
a texture and use it in any number of ways, and in this chapter, we will learn about some
methods of using textures for interesting and varied effects. These methods include
modifying the UVs to map textures in different ways and sampling a texture multiple
times with different sets of UVs and then compositing the results. Later, we will see
different kinds of texture than the standard `Texture2D`, such as `Texture3D` and `Cubemap`.
Before we dive into new methods of texturing, I'm going to set up a base shader in
ShaderLab and HLSL. If you're going to be using Shader Graph, you can skip this section.

Base Shader in HLSL

This chapter is slightly different from most of the others in the book because each of
the HLSL shaders starts with the same base code, so I will start each shader with the
following code. This code is very similar to the TextureExample shader from the previous
chapter, so all the content should be familiar to you. Each new shader will require a
different name, so I'll leave it empty in this example.

Listing 6-1. The skeleton code for HLSL examples in Chapter 6

```
Shader ""
{
    Properties
    {
        _BaseColor ("Base Color", Color) = (1, 1, 1, 1)
        _BaseTex("Base Texture", 2D) = "white" {}
    }
    SubShader
    {
```

© Daniel Ilett 2022
D. Ilett, *Building Quality Shaders for Unity*®, https://doi.org/10.1007/978-1-4842-8652-4_6

```
        Tags
        {
                "RenderType" = "Opaque"
                "Queue" = "Geometry"
        }
        Pass
        {
                HLSLPROGRAM
                #pragma vertex vert
                #pragma fragment frag

                struct appdata
                {
                        float4 positionOS : Position;
                        float2 uv : TEXCOORD0;
                };

                struct v2f
                {
                        float4 positionCS : SV_Position;
                        float2 uv : TEXCOORD0;
                };

                v2f vert (appdata v) { ... }

                float4 frag (v2f i) : SV_Target
                {
                        float4 textureSample = tex2D(_BaseTex, i.uv);
                        return textureSample * _BaseColor;
                }
                ENDHLSL
        }
    }
}
```

There are differences between the built-in pipeline and URP. Each one uses a different include file, and in URP, we must include an extra RenderPipeline tag inside the Tags block.

Listing 6-2. Adding tags and include files in the built-in pipeline

```
Pass
{
      HLSLPROGRAM
      #pragma vertex vert
      #pragma fragment frag

      #include "UnityCG.cginc"
```

Listing 6-3. Adding tags and include files in URP

```
Tags
{
      "RenderType" = "Opaque"
      "Queue" = "Geometry"
      "RenderPipeline" = "UniversalPipeline"
}
Pass
{
      Tags
      {
            "LightMode" = "UniversalForward"
      }
      HLSLPROGRAM
      #pragma vertex vert
      #pragma fragment frag

      #include "Packages/com.unity.render-pipelines.universal/
      ShaderLibrary/Core.hlsl"
```

We must declare the variables from the Properties block again in the HLSLPROGRAM block. In URP, all non-texture variables should be defined inside a constant buffer. We'll add the properties right below the v2f struct definition.

Listing 6-4. Declaring variables in the built-in pipeline

```
struct v2f { ... };
```

sampler2D _BaseTex;
float4 _BaseColor;
float4 _BaseTex_ST;

Listing 6-5. Declaring properties in URP

```
struct v2f { ... };
```

sampler2D _BaseTex;

CBUFFER_START(UnityPerMaterial)
      float4 _BaseColor;
      float4 _BaseTex_ST;
CBUFFER_END

We will also fill the `vert` function with different code for each pipeline. For transforming vertex positions from object space to clip space, the built-in pipeline uses the `UnityObjectToClipPos` function, whereas URP uses `TransformObjectToHClip`.

Listing 6-6. The vert function in the built-in pipeline

```
v2f vert (appdata v)
{
    v2f o;
    o.positionCS = UnityObjectToClipPos(v.positionOS.xyz);
    o.uv = TRANSFORM_TEX(v.uv, _BaseTex);
    return o;
}
```

Listing 6-7. The vert function in URP

```
v2f vert (appdata v)
{
    v2f o;
    o.positionCS = TransformObjectToHClip(v.positionOS.xyz);
```

```
    o.uv = TRANSFORM_TEX(v.uv, _BaseTex);
    return o;
}
```

Note   Interestingly, if you don't specify a name for the shader, it will still work. In the Shader drop-down, Unity will display the name of the shader file. However, you should name every shader properly.

Although this is a fully functional shader, we're more interested in seeing what happens when we make changes to the code. With that in mind, let's play around with the texture coordinates in different ways.

Modifying Texture Coordinates

A mesh usually comes with at least one set of UVs attached to the vertex data. As we have established, each UV coordinate is just a two-dimensional vector specifying a point in UV space, and like all vectors, we can manipulate it. A common transformation for UVs that we have not yet covered is rotation.

UV Rotation

The most efficient way to perform rotations in shaders is to create a rotation matrix – recall that a rotation matrix for 2D data looks like this, where θ is the angle of rotation:

$$\begin{bmatrix} \cos\theta & -\sin\theta \\ \sin\theta & \cos\theta \end{bmatrix}$$

Figure 6-1 shows you how different angles of rotation impact the appearance of a checkerboard texture. We'll be applying a rotation matrix like this one to the UVs before sampling the main texture. Let's see how this works in shader code first and then move on to Shader Graph.

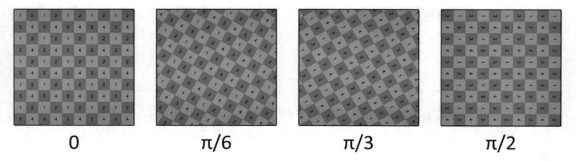

$$0 \qquad \pi/6 \qquad \pi/3 \qquad \pi/2$$

Figure 6-1. *Rotations applied to a texture. The numbers below each texture represent the rotation in radians being applied to the UVs. Note that the rotations in this example are applied around the origin, which is in the bottom-left corner*

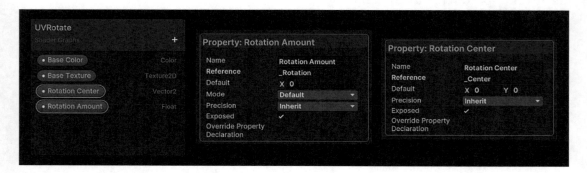

Figure 6-2. *Adding UV rotation properties in Shader Graph*

UV Rotation in HLSL

Start with the base shader from the start of this chapter and name the file "UVRotation. shader". We can rename the shader on the first line of the file accordingly.

Listing 6-8. Renaming the UV rotation shader at the start of the file

```
Shader "Examples/UVRotation"
```

First, we will need to add two new shader properties to control the amount of rotation and the center of rotation. The _Rotation property represents the rotation in radians, and the _Center vector property controls the center of rotation in UV space. We can declare both properties inside the Properties block.

Listing 6-9. Declaring UV rotation properties in the Properties block

```
Properties
{
    _BaseColor ("Base Color", Color) = (1, 1, 1, 1)
    _BaseTex("Base Texture", 2D) = "white" {}
    _Rotation("Rotation Amount", Float) = 0.0
    _Center("Rotation Center", Vector) = (0,0,0,0)
}
```

We must then declare both variables again inside the HLSLPROGRAM block. These declarations should be placed alongside the existing variable declarations (in URP, they go inside the constant buffer).

Listing 6-10. Declaring UV rotation properties in the HLSLPROGRAM block

```
float4 _BaseColor;
float4 _BaseTex_ST;
float _Rotation;
float2 _Center;
```

In HLSL, there exist special types for creating matrices. The type's name is made up of the data type that will be contained in the matrix and the dimensions of the matrix. We will be using floating-point numbers inside a 2×2 matrix, so the type we are using is float2x2. Its constructor takes four elements; the first two are the first row, and the last two are the second row. Since a basic rotation like this preserves parallel lines, it doesn't matter whether we do the following calculations in the vertex or fragment shader, so I will do them at the start of the vertex shader for efficiency's sake.

Listing 6-11. Creating a rotation matrix in HLSL

```
v2f vert (appdata v)
{
    float c = cos(_Rotation);
    float s = sin(_Rotation);
    float2x2 rotMatrix = float2x2(c, -s, s, c);
```

147

With the rotation matrix ready, we just need to multiply it with the UV coordinates. In HLSL, we use a function called `mul` to perform matrix multiplication. Order matters – we need to make sure that the rotation matrix is the leftmost function parameter and the UVs are the rightmost parameter. Assuming you are also writing this code in the vertex shader, we will apply the rotation to the UVs after the `TRANSFORM_TEX` macro has been applied. To rotate around an arbitrary center point, we subtract the `_Center` vector prior to the matrix multiplication step and add it back afterward.

Listing 6-12. Using the mul function to multiply matrices in HLSL

```
    o.uv = TRANSFORM_TEX(v.uv, _BaseTex);
    o.uv -= _Center;
    o.uv = mul(rotMatrix, o.uv);
    o.uv += _Center;

    return o;
}
```

Caution   A silly mistake I make quite often is using the * operator to try and multiply matrices instead of using `mul`. If you get compiler errors when using matrices, it's likely you could be making the same error.

If this shader were applied to a quad and the rotation setting were changed on the material Inspector, you would see the texture mapping change according to Figure 6-1. Next, let's see how this works in Shader Graph.

UV Rotation in Shader Graph

Start by creating a new Unlit graph and naming it "UVRotation.shadergraph". I'll add `Rotation Amount` and `Rotation Center` properties based on the `_Rotation` and `_Center` properties that we saw in the shader code version of this effect. Figure 6-2 shows the settings required for these properties.

As is often the case in Shader Graph, there's a node that does exactly what we want. In fact, the `Rotate` node can be found under *Create Node* ➤ *UV* ➤ *Rotate* so we can be certain this is the correct one! Make sure you don't confuse it with `Rotate Around Axis`, which is intended for 3D vectors. A node tree containing this node can be seen in Figure 6-3, where I have inserted it just before a `Sample Texture 2D` node.

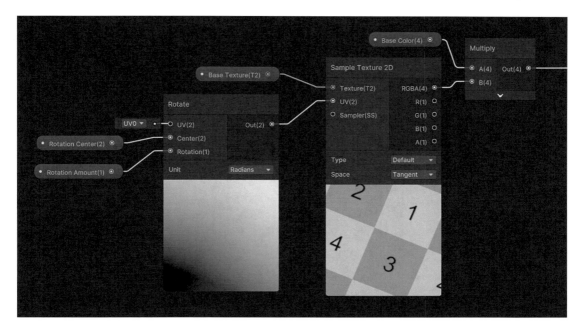

Figure 6-3. *The Rotate node rotates UVs around a specified center point*

Shader Graph does a lot of the heavy lifting for us. We can specify *Center* and *Rotation* inputs that work the same way as our shader code, and we can switch the type of units we're using between radians and degrees using the *Unit* drop-down just above the node's preview window. The preview window itself displays what the rotated UVs look like by representing the u-axis with red and the v-axis with green.

`Rotate` is not the only node available under *Create Node ➤ UV*. Shader Graph provides an arsenal of methods for playing around with UVs and texture mapping, which can be helpful in all manner of scenarios, so we're going to dig in and look at some of the most useful ones. Plus, we'll recreate them in HLSL shader code.

Flipbook Mapping

It's common to use *flipbook animations* in games. Although it's seen more often in 2D games, we can still use animated textures in 3D games if we wish. So what is a flipbook? Outside of computer graphics, you may have seen people draw slightly different pictures on each page of a booklet and then flip between the pages quickly from the front of the booklet to the back to create the illusion of animation. We can translate the same concept to textures by including all the different animation frames in a big texture, sampling a tiny part of the full texture corresponding to a single frame, and then jumping to the next frame by shifting the UVs at a regular timestep. Figure 6-4 shows an example flipbook texture sheet.

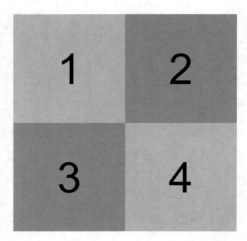

Figure 6-4. *An example flipbook texture. We have been using this texture throughout the chapter, but now we will consider each quadrant of the image to be a flipbook animation frame*

Figure 6-5. *Properties for the Flipbook graph*

Let's see how flipbooks work in HLSL and then see how much easier it is in Shader Graph.

Flipbooks in HLSL

I'll start by creating a new shader file called "Flipbook.shader" containing the base shader from the start of this chapter. The first thing we'll do is change the name at the top of the file to "Examples/Flipbook".

Listing 6-13. Changing the name of the shader at the top of the file

```
Shader "Examples/Flipbook"
```

We'll need extra shader properties to tell the shader how large the texture sheet is and to control the speed of the flipbook animation. The _FlipbookSize property is a float2, and _Speed is a float. We must first declare these properties in the Properties block using ShaderLab syntax.

Listing 6-14. Adding size and speed properties in the Properties block

```
Properties
{
    _BaseColor ("Base Color", Color) = (1, 1, 1, 1)
    _BaseTex("Base Texture", 2D) = "white" {}
    _FlipbookSize("Flipbook Size", Vector) = (1,1,0,0)
    _Speed("Animation Speed", Float) = 1
}
```

We then redeclare each variable alongside the existing variable declarations in the HLSLPROGRAM block. Remember that we need to put variables inside a constant buffer in URP.

Listing 6-15. Adding size and speed properties in the HLSLPROGRAM block

```
float4 _BaseColor;
float4 _BaseTex_ST;
float2 _FlipbookSize;
float _Speed;
```

The remaining calculations belong in the vertex shader, and thankfully, the code is the same for both the built-in and Universal pipelines. Instead of using TRANSFORM_TEX to deal with the UVs, we will be calculating UVs on the texture sheet manually. First, we'll set up a few variables to help us and then carry out the rest of the calculations like so:

- The `tileSize` variable will store the size in UV space that each flipbook frame takes up, so if we had 4 × 2 frames, `tileSize` would be $(0.25, 0.5)$.

- The `tileCount` variable will store the total number of tiles.

- To determine which `tileID` to sample from at the current time, we can multiply `_Time.y` by `_Speed` to get a clock that ticks upward, modulo by `tileCount` to make it loop, and then take the `floor` to lock the values to integers.

- Using `tileID`, we can calculate which tile to sample in the x- and y-axes. We'll store this inside two UV offset variables, `tileX` and `tileY`.

- Finally, we take the original UVs, scale them to the size of one tile, and add the `tileX` and `tileY` offsets to each axis.

Putting all these steps together, the code for the vertex shader looks like the following.

Listing 6-16. The flipbook vertex shader

```
v2f vert (appdata v)
{
    v2f o;
    o.positionCS = // existing code for your pipeline;

    float2 tileSize = float2(1.0f, 1.0f) / _FlipbookSize;
    float width = _FlipbookSize.x;
    float height = _FlipbookSize.y;
    float tileCount = width * height;

    float tileID = floor((_Time.y * _Speed) % tileCount);
```

```
float tileX = (tileID % width) * tileSize.x;
float tileY = (floor(tileID / width)) * tileSize.y;

o.uv = float2(v.uv.x / width + tileX,
        v.uv.y / height + tileY);

return o;
}
```

Once you've written this shader up and attached it to an object in the scene, you should see the texture animate over time as long as the Speed property is above zero.

Flipbooks in Shader Graph

Shader Graph provides a node for texture sheet animations called Flipbook, which handles the fiddly UV calculations for us. Here's how it works:

- The *Width* and *Height* inputs represent the number of tiles in the x- and y-axes, respectively.

- The *Tile* input is used to control which tile should be output. This value is zero-indexed.

  - The node uses modulo arithmetic to automatically loop back to zero if you specify a tile ID that exceeds the width and height values.

- The Flipbook node includes options to invert the x- or y-direction when looping over tiles.

  - By default, *Invert Y* is ticked because UVs start at (0, 0) in the bottom left, whereas it's most common to draw animation frames starting on the top row and ending at the bottom.

  - Likewise, if your animation frames are drawn left to right, leave *Invert X* unticked.

- It's important to remember that the Flipbook node takes UVs as input and outputs a fresh set of UVs, so we still need to use a Sample Texture 2D node to sample the texture.

Let's start making the graph. I'm going to create a new Unlit graph and name it "Flipbook.shadergraph". We will include four properties on this graph:

- The Base Color and Base Texture properties that we are familiar with

- A Flipbook Size property of type Vector2 to control width and height, in number of tiles, of the flipbook texture

- A Speed property of type Float that we use alongside a Time node to scroll through the flipbook automatically over time

These properties can be seen in Figure 6-5. I'll avoid using tiling and offset settings with this graph since they won't play nicely with the Flipbook node. Speaking of which, here's how we'll use the Flipbook node:

- Add a Flipbook node, which can be found under Create Node ➤ UV ➤ Flipbook.

- Use a Split node to separate the components of the Flipbook Size property and use the first outputs as the *Width* and *Height* parameters of the Flipbook node.

- For the *Tile* input, which we want to change over time, we can make use of the Time node, which outputs various time formats. Just use the regular *Time* output and multiply it by the Speed property.

Figure 6-6 shows what the node tree for this section of the graph would look like. In this example, I'm using a checkerboard texture with numbers on each tile – there are 2 × 2 tiles, and I took the snapshot when the third tile was active, hence the number 3 on the Sample Texture 2D preview.

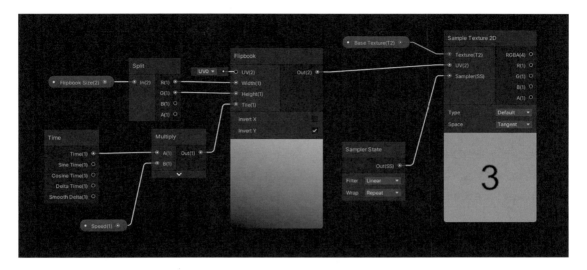

Figure 6-6. *Creating flipbook animations in Shader Graph*

If you were to set up these nodes and supply your own texture sheet, then you would see the preview windows animate on your screen. HLSL doesn't include its own functions for flipbook textures, so we'll build our own.

Polar Coordinate Mapping

So far, we have used Cartesian coordinates for most of our applications. In a Cartesian coordinate system, every point in space can be represented by exactly one set of coordinates, and we represent the point using a distance along each cardinal axis. This isn't the only possible coordinate system, although at a glance it's the one that seems to make sense for UV mapping. Let's look at another system and see what we can do with it.

Polar coordinates represent points in 2D space using an angle of rotation around the origin and a radius, such as $(\pi, 3)$. Now, each point in space can be represented using an infinite number of coordinates – for example, the point $(5, 0)$ in Cartesian space can be represented using the polar coordinate $(0, 5)$ or $(2\pi, 5)$ or $(4\pi, 5)$ and so on. It's an interesting system, but what does this mean for UV mapping?

We can convert from Cartesian to polar coordinates inside shaders and use them as UVs directly. When we do so, our mappings will work quite differently – what used to be straight lines will now appear circular, which makes for some interesting visual effects. Polar coordinates are particularly effective at representing *radial* patterns compared with Cartesian coordinates, as you tend to introduce *aliasing* in textures containing

155

circles when using Cartesian coordinates, which forces you to increase the resolution to avoid aliasing artifacts. I'll show you an example, but I'd encourage you to play around with different textures yourself to see what polar coordinates can do. Let's explore polar coordinates with HLSL and then in Shader Graph.

Polar Coordinates in HLSL

I'm going to create a new shader file using the template from the start of this chapter and name it "PolarCoordinates.shader". Inside the new shader, the first change we must make is to rename it at the top of the file.

Listing 6-17. Renaming the polar coordinate mapping shader

```
Shader "Examples/PolarCoordinates"
```

Once that's done, we'll need to add a few properties:

- The _Center property is a float2 and is used to change the origin point where we calculate polar distances and angles from. Make this (0.5, 0.5) by default, which is in the center of the usual [0,1] range for UVs.

- The _RadialScale property, which is a float, is used to scale the polar radius.

- The _LengthScale is a float that is used to scale the polar angle.

First, we will add these properties to the Properties block.

Listing 6-18. Adding properties for polar mapping to the Properties block

```
Properties
{
    _BaseColor ("Base Color", Color) = (1, 1, 1, 1)
    _BaseTex("Base Texture", 2D) = "white" {}
    _Center("Center", Vector) = (0.5,0.5,0,0)
    _RadialScale("Radial Scale", Float) = 1
    _LengthScale("Length Scale", Float) = 1
}
```

Then, we will add them to the HLSLPROGRAM code block alongside the existing variables. Thankfully, we don't need to do any edits to the vertex shader this time, nor do we need to mess with the contents of either of the structs.

Listing 6-19. Adding properties in the HLSLPROGRAM block

```
float4 _BaseColor;
float4 _BaseTex_ST;
float2 _Center;
float _RadialScale;
float _LengthScale;
```

Let's now write a function called cartesianToPolar, which will deal with the mapping between the two coordinate systems for us. It'll need to take a set of UVs as both input and output, but it won't need to take any other inputs. Then, we can use the function inside the fragment shader to perform the mapping. It won't be enough to calculate these UVs in the vertex shader like we could for the flipbook shader, because HLSL simply couldn't interpolate the UVs properly if we calculated them per vertex. We also need to declare the cartesianToPolar function before we write the frag function, because functions can only see and utilize other functions declared before themselves.

Listing 6-20. The cartesianToPolar mapping function and the fragment shader

```
float2 cartesianToPolar(float2 cartUV)
{
     float2 offset = cartUV - _Center;
     float radius = length(offset) * 2;
     float angle = atan2(offset.x, offset.y) / (2.0f * PI);

     return float2(radius, angle);
}

float4 frag (v2f i) : SV_Target
{
     float2 radialUV = cartesianToPolar(i.uv);
     radialUV.x *= _RadialScale;
     radialUV.y *= _LengthScale;
```

```
        float4 textureSample = tex2D(_BaseTex, radialUV);
        return textureSample * _BaseColor;
}
```

There's one small note about this code – in URP, we have access to a constant named PI, which is declared in a file called *Macros.hlsl* (which is included in *Common.hlsl*, which is itself included in the *Core.hlsl* file we imported). If you use this exact code in the built-in render pipeline, you will get a compile error because PI will be undeclared – it's not included in *UnityCG.cginc*. The easiest way to solve this is to add a line at the start of cartesianToPolar to declare PI if you are using the built-in render pipeline.

Listing 6-21. Adding a PI declaration in the built-in render pipeline

```
float2 cartesianToPolar(float2 cartUV)
{
        const float PI = 3.14159235f;
        float2 offset = cartUV - _Center;
```

Once you've added this line, the shader is complete and will look like the example in Figure 6-7. Play around with different textures and change the scale properties to get a feel for how polar coordinates work. Next, let's see how to use polar coordinates in Shader Graph.

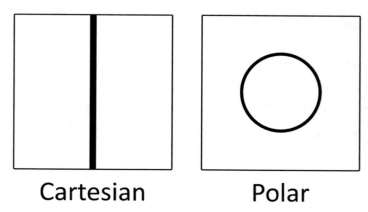

Figure 6-7. *Comparison of a texture seen in Cartesian space (left) and the same texture using the Polar Coordinate shader (right)*

Figure 6-8. *Properties for the Polar Coordinates graph*

Polar Coordinates in Shader Graph

Shader Graph comes with a node called `Polar Coordinates`, found under *Create Node* ➤ *UV* ➤ *Polar Coordinates*, for converting between Cartesian and polar coordinate systems. Here's how it works:

- The main input and output of the node is a set of UVs, but there are extra inputs to change how the mapping works.

- The *Center* input can be used to change what point the polar distances and angles are calculated from – by default, this is (0.5,0.5), in the middle of the usual 0–1 range for UVs.

- The *Radial Scale* option scales the polar radius.

- The *Length Scale* option scales the polar angle.

I'll create another new Unlit graph and name it "PolarCoordinates.shadergraph". Alongside the `Base Color` and `Base Texture` properties we have used on most of our graphs so far, I'll also include three extra properties:

- The `Center` property is a `Vector2` and is used to control the polar center.

- The `Radial Scale` property, which is a `float`, will be used for the *Radial Scale* parameter on the `Polar Coordinates` node.

- Likewise, the `Length Scale` property, which is also a `float`, will be used for the *Length Scale* parameter of the `Polar Coordinates` node.

These properties can be seen in Figure 6-8. Once we've added each of the properties to the Blackboard, we'll use them to control a `Polar Coordinates` node as seen in Figure 6-9.

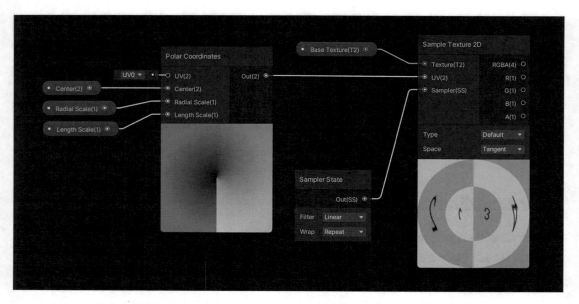

Figure 6-9. *Using the Polar Coordinates node to change UVs*

In the preview window on `Sample Texture 2D`, you can see how different the sampling is for my example texture compared with Cartesian coordinate UVs – everything now looks very circular. In fact, any straight line that runs from the top to the bottom of the texture becomes a perfect circle with this shader – Figure 6-7 shows another example texture with a single black line down the center in Cartesian coordinates and the output of the shader using that texture on a quad mesh.

Note   If you see slight gaps in the texture sampling with polar coordinates, especially along the cardinal axes, then it may help if you disable mipmaps on the texture.

Let's see another example of a special kind of mapping that we can use in some scenarios to improve the appearance of our objects.

Triplanar Mapping

So far, we have sampled a texture once to apply it to a mesh. This has involved using the object's baked-in UV coordinates (with a little bit of modification). However, this isn't the only way to map textures to objects. Sometimes, your mesh won't have UVs, especially if you've generated the mesh procedurally in Unity. In those cases, it's possible to generate UVs inside either the vertex shader or fragment shader, which gives us free reign to define whatever mapping we want, or we can use other forms of data for mapping other than UVs. *Triplanar mapping* does just that – mapping without using UVs. So what's triplanar mapping?

The "planar" bit of the name refers to mapping a texture across a plane. Imagine taking a texture and panning it across space along its "z-axis." When it encounters an object, the surface of that object gets painted with whichever bit of the texture it intersects – that's how a planar map works. The texture applied to a surface isn't dependent on UVs, but instead uses the world-space position of the object's surface points for mapping.

The "tri" bit means that we use three such maps, locked to the three cardinal axes: x, y, and z. Based on the orientation of the surface at any point, we will apply the planar map that most closely aligns with the surface normal direction, with a degree of blending between maps when the surface normal is at the midpoint between two cardinal directions. This process is illustrated in Figure 6-10.

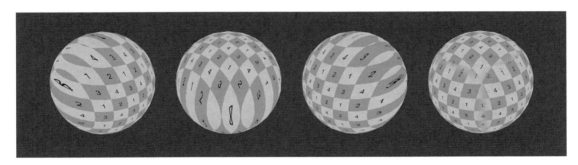

Figure 6-10. *From left to right: planar mapping along the x-, y-, and z-axes, respectively, and a mapping that blends together the first three, known as triplanar mapping*

The advantage of triplanar mapping is that we, ideally, get a mapping across an object that isn't significantly stretched on any part of the object's surface since the planar map that aligns best with the surface at any point gets picked. However, the technique requires sampling the same texture three times, so it comes with a performance impact compared with regular UV mapping. This becomes more apparent the more textures you are sampling, so if we wanted to use normal mapping and specular mapping, for instance, you'd need three samples of each of those maps too, and your shader may become significantly slower.

Triplanar Mapping in HLSL

Let's recap what we will need for triplanar mapping. Unlike traditional UV texture mapping, triplanar mapping relies on the world-space position and normal vector of each fragment of the mesh. None of the shaders we have written so far have required vertex normal data, so we will see how to pass that to the shader program. Usually, the vertex shader will transform directly from object space to clip space using the `UnityObjectToClipPos` or `TransformObjectToHClip` function, depending on your chosen pipeline, but we require *world-space* positions and normals specifically. We will see how to transform position and direction vectors from object to world space.

I will create a new shader file called "Triplanar.shader" and replace its contents with the template at the start of this chapter. I will also change the name at the top of the file to "Examples/Triplanar" – from there, let's go through the changes and additions we'll need to make across both built-in and URP.

Listing 6-22. Renaming the triplanar mapping shader file

```
Shader "Examples/Triplanar"
```

We're going to need new properties. Alongside the `_BaseColor` and `_BaseTex` properties, we will need two more, both of which are of type `Float`:

- The `_Tile` property is used to control the tiling of the three texture samples.

- The `_BlendPower` property is used to control how strongly each of the texture samples gets blended together at the boundary between them.

These properties should first be added to the Properties block near the top of the file.

Listing 6-23. Adding tiling and blending properties to the Properties block

```
Properties
{
    _BaseColor ("Base Color", Color) = (1, 1, 1, 1)
    _BaseTex("Base Texture", 2D) = "white" {}
    _Tile ("Texture Tiling", Float) = 1
    _BlendPower ("Triplanar Blending", Float) = 10
}
```

Afterward, add both these properties to the HLSLPROGRAM block alongside other variable declarations. Remember to put them both inside the constant buffer if you're using URP.

Listing 6-24. Adding tiling and blending properties to the HLSLPROGRAM block

```
float4 _BaseColor;
float4 _BaseTex_ST;
float _Tile;
float _BlendPower;
```

We'll be creating our own mapping, so we no longer need to read UVs into the shader. In the appdata struct, remove the UVs. We also need to include the vertex normals as an input variable, which requires us to use the NORMAL semantic. I'll call this variable normalOS for these object-space normals (to follow the naming convention we've been using for positions), and its type is float3. These normals are attached to each vertex, so we can change them by editing the mesh in an external modeling program, through scripting, or in the import settings of the mesh.

Listing 6-25. The triplanar shader needs vertex positions and normals as inputs in appdata

```
struct appdata
{
      float4 positionOS : POSITION;
      float3 normalOS : NORMAL;
};
```

In the v2f struct, it's a similar story – we no longer need to pass UV coordinates between the vertex shader and fragment shader. But we do need to pass *something* over. We're going to calculate the world-space position of each vertex and pass that to the fragment shader, so we'll include that in place of the UVs, but what semantic do we use? We're already using SV_POSITION for the clip-space position, which we still need to include in v2f, so we can't use that (or POSITION).

It's common in shaders to use the TEXCOORD channels for arbitrary data, not just UVs, so we'll define a float3 variable called positionWS (WS means world space) and use TEXCOORD0. In a roundabout way, we're transmitting data in place of UVs, using the semantic normally used for UVs, for mapping textures without UVs. How about that!

On top of that, we also need to send over normals. Our fragment shader also requires the normals in world space, but we can't use the NORMAL semantic again in v2f, so we will stuff this data into another TEXCOORD interpolator. Let's choose TEXCOORD1 since it's the next one and name the variable normalWS, following our naming conventions.

Listing 6-26. Using the TEXCOORD semantic for non-UV data in the v2f struct

```
struct v2f
{
    float4 positionCS : SV_POSITION;
    float3 positionWS : TEXCOORD0;
    float3 normalWS : TEXCOORD1;
};
```

In the vertex shader, we need to calculate positionWS. We are given the object position, positionOS, in appdata, so we just need to transform from object to world space. Strangely, Unity doesn't provide a UnityObjectToWorldPos function in the built-in include files, so we'll need to perform the matrix multiplication ourselves. Unity defines many transformation matrices for us, including unity_ObjectToWorld, so we can use that. In the Universal Render Pipeline, there is a helper function defined for us called TransformObjectToWorld.

Similarly, we must calculate normalWS. We have access to normalOS, so we can pass this into the UnityObjectToWorldDir function, which *does* exist in the built-in pipeline, or the TransformObjectToWorldNormal function in URP.

Listing 6-27. Transforming from object- to world-space positions and normals in the built-in pipeline

```
v2f vert (appdata v)
{
    v2f o;
    o.positionCS = UnityObjectToClipPos(v.positionOS.xyz);
    o.positionWS = mul(unity_ObjectToWorld, v.positionOS);
    o.normalWS = UnityObjectToWorldDir(v.normalOS);
    return o;
}
```

Listing 6-28. Transforming from object- to world-space positions and normals in URP

```
v2f vert (appdata v)
{
    v2f o;
    o.positionCS = TransformObjectToHClip(v.positionOS.xyz);
    o.positionWS = TransformObjectToWorld(v.positionOS.xyz);
    o.normalWS = TransformObjectToWorldNormal(v.normalOS);
    return o;
}
```

Everything is now set up for us to start sampling the triplanar maps in the fragment shader. We need to sample across the three cardinal axes – in effect, we need to construct three sets of UVs from the world position. Since UVs are two-dimensional, we will define three 2D planes, and the easiest way to do that is use the YZ plane for the x-axis, the XZ plane for the y-axis, and the XY plane for the z-axis, respectively. The only special case is the x-axis. If we were to sample across the YZ plane, then the resulting texture would be rotated 90°, so we use ZY instead. The fragment's position on any of these three planes will define the UVs used for sampling. We'll multiply all three sets of UVs by _Tile.

Listing 6-29. Creating three sets of UVs from the world position

```
float4 frag (v2f i) : SV_TARGET
{
    float2 xAxisUV = i.positionWS.zy * _Tile;
    float2 yAxisUV = i.positionWS.xz * _Tile;
    float2 zAxisUV = i.positionWS.xy * _Tile;
```

With these UVs, we can sample the texture three times. Since we're adapting this shader from TextureExample.shader, we should have _BaseTex already defined in the properties. These three samples represent the three planar maps that we've been talking about.

165

Listing 6-30. Sampling the texture three times

```
float2 zAxisUV = i.positionWS.xy * _Tile;

float4 xSample = tex2D(_BaseTex, xAxisUV);
float4 ySample = tex2D(_BaseTex, yAxisUV);
float4 zSample = tex2D(_BaseTex, zAxisUV);
```

To pick between the three samples, we will use the world normals. Using a few mathematical tricks, we can calculate a set of weights based on the normals, which represent how strongly the shader should blend each sample. Firstly, we will use the abs (absolute value) function on the normals to ensure that our calculations always end up with positive weights for each of the three samples (without it, normals pointing in the negative direction will result in a negative weight). Then, we will raise the normals to the power of _BlendPower in each axis – the higher the value, the smaller the blending region between maps. Finally, we will divide everything so far by the sum of the components.

Listing 6-31. Calculating the blend weights

```
float4 zSample = tex2D(_BaseTex, zAxisUV);

float3 weights = pow(abs(i.normalWS), _BlendPower);
weights /= (weights.x + weights.y + weights.z);
```

Finally, we can multiply each weight by the corresponding texture sample to obtain the final color.

Listing 6-32. Blending the three texture samples together

```
        float4 outColor = xSample * weights.x + ySample * weights.y + zSample
        * weights.z;
        return outColor;
}
```

Once you have done this step and applied the shader to an object in the Scene View, you should see something like Figure 6-10 if you use the correct settings. Next, let's see how to do triplanar mapping in Shader Graph.

Triplanar Node in Shader Graph

In Shader Graph, the `Triplanar` node carries out triplanar mapping using the world-space position and normal vector of each fragment, as seen in Figure 6-11. Additionally, you can scale the mapping using the *Tile* input and control the amount of blending at the border between the planar maps using the *Blend* option – the higher this value is, the sharper the seams become. Like many other texture sampling nodes, this one can accept a *Sampler State* input too.

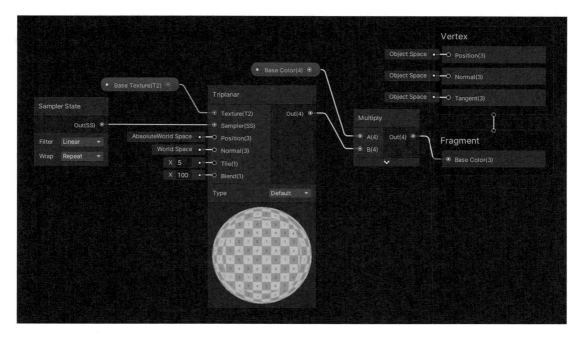

Figure 6-11.   *Triplanar mapping using the Triplanar node in Shader Graph*

I'll create a new Unlit graph and name it "Triplanar.shadergraph". This will be a relatively simple graph, so I'll just add Base Color and Base Texture properties and then add a Triplanar node to the surface, as shown in Figure 6-11.

The preview window on the `Triplanar` node does not give you a very good idea of what the node looks like in-game because the camera view is in a fixed location. Triplanar mapping uses world-space positions so we should look at an object in the Scene View, as in Figure 6-12.

Figure 6-12. *Triplanar mapping as seen on a sphere in the Scene View*

In this example, I used a very high value for the *Blend* input, so the seams between each planar map are rather visible. However, there is minimal warping of the texture across the object's surface; any warping that does exist is most apparent near the seams. There are many nodes included in Shader Graph that are nontrivial to reproduce in shader code, as we're about to find out by porting the triplanar mapping effect to HLSL.

There are several effects that we might want to implement that don't come with a prepackaged node in Shader Graph or a helpful function made for us in HLSL. For these effects, we'll need to think carefully about what we need to make the effect – what properties will be important, and what calculations will we need for the effect? Let's look at an example – the *shear* transformation.

UV Shear

The shear transformation is one that we didn't cover in Chapter 2. You see this often in math textbooks as a basic transformation, but in computer graphics it's not nearly as important as the translation, scaling, and rotation transformations. Shearing matrices are used to shift positions by some distance – the further away a position is from the shear axis, the further along the axis it becomes shifted. A shear matrix that would work on 2D UV coordinates looks like this:

$$\begin{bmatrix} 1 & sh_u \\ sh_v & 1 \end{bmatrix}$$

Figure 6-13 demonstrates how shearing works along the x- and y-axes.

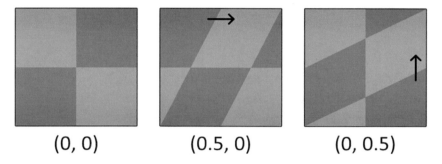

(0, 0)   (0.5, 0)   (0, 0.5)

Figure 6-13. *Shearing works by moving positions along an axis more the further from the axis they originally were*

Figure 6-14. *The Shear graph properties*

Shear in HLSL

This looks like it ought to be simple to implement in HLSL – after all, we just implemented rotation using a matrix like this. It's a similar process for shear. I'll start by using the template code from the start of this chapter in a new file called "Shear.shader". Inside this file, change the shader's name to `Examples/Shear`.

Listing 6-33. Changing the name of the shear shader

```
Shader "Examples/Shear"
```

Next, we will use a property to control the amount of shearing along the u- and v-axes of the UVs. We only need to add one, and I'll call it _Shear – the x-component will store the u-shear amount, and the y-component stores the v-shear amount. By default, the vector should be zeroed out, representing no shear.

Listing 6-34. Shearing properties

```
Properties
{
    _BaseColor ("Base Color", Color) = (1, 1, 1, 1)
    _BaseTex("Base Texture", 2D) = "white" {}
    _Shear("Shear Amount", Vector) = (0, 0, 0, 0)
}
```

Then, we will define this property again in the HLSLPROGRAM block, using the float2 type. Place it alongside other variable declarations.

Listing 6-35. Declaring shear properties in the HLSLPROGRAM block

```
float2 _Shear;
```

Now we can implement the shear itself in the vertex shader. Like rotations, shearing will preserve parallel lines on any texture we use, so we can perform the operation in the vertex shader rather than the fragment shader for efficiency's sake. We will construct a new float2x2 matrix for the shear and then use the mul function to multiply our UV coordinates (after we have used TRANSFORM_TEX on them). The other thing to note is that we need to invert the values used in the shear matrix to ensure the shear operates in the correct direction.

Listing 6-36. Shearing in the vertex shader

```
v2f vert (appdata v)
{
    float2x2 shearMatrix = float2x2
      (
          1, -_Shear.x,
```

```
        -_Shear.y, 1
    );

    v2f o;
    o.positionCS = // Existing code for your platform;
    o.uv = TRANSFORM_TEX(v.uv, _BaseTex);
    o.uv = mul(shearMatrix, o.uv);
    return o;
}
```

That's all we need to do for this shader. It's like using a rotation matrix, isn't it? In the Scene View, you will now be able to play around with the material and see how different shear values impact the appearance of the object. By changing the x- and y-components independently, you will see a shear like one of those in Figure 6-13. If you shear along both axes at once, you'll be able to create more interesting effects.

Shear in Shader Graph

This is one instance where Shader Graph is arguably more complicated to use than the HLSL equivalent because of how the nodes work. We will still need to construct a matrix since there is no Shear node (there is a Radial Shear node, but that works very differently), and the way we create matrices in Shader Graph can sometimes be a bit finicky.

I'll start with a new Unlit graph, which I'll name "Shear.shadergraph". To start, we will add a Vector2 property called Shear Amount, which controls the shear distance along the two axes. Alongside this, also add Base Color and Base Texture properties, which you should be familiar with by now. These properties are shown in Figure 6-14.

Next, let's start adding nodes to the graph surface. We need to use a Matrix Construction node to build the matrix – at first glance, it may look a bit complicated, as shown in Figure 6-15. Here's how it works:

- There is an option at the bottom of the node to control whether this matrix is row-major or column-major – whichever one you pick will change whether the four inputs are for rows or columns. I'll keep it as *Row*.

- Each input represents a row of the output matrix. However, there are not separate construction nodes for 2 × 2, 3 × 3, or 4 × 4 matrices – all sizes are constructed with this one type of node.

- We want to output a 2 × 2 matrix, so I'll be inputting a Vector2 to each of the first two inputs. We can ignore the third and fourth inputs.

- There are different outputs for different matrix sizes, so we will use the bottommost 2 × 2 output.

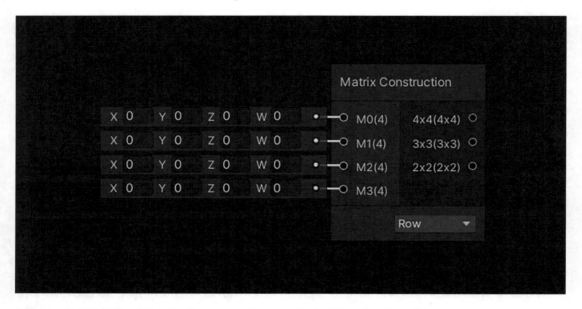

Figure 6-15. *The Matrix Construction node in Shader Graph*

I will take the Shear Amount property and use a Negate node to reverse its direction. The Negate node reverses the direction for the shear, but using it is a matter of personal choice depending on which direction you think positive values of Shear Amount should shear in. We can then split the two components of the vector to use them for the upper-right and lower-left elements of the matrix, with ones in the remaining positions. Figure 6-16 shows how these nodes should be connected.

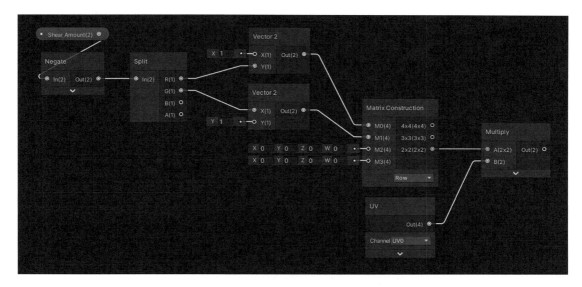

Figure 6-16. *Creating a shear matrix and applying it to UVs to obtain sheared UVs*

Once we have created the matrix, we can multiply it by the UVs using a UV node and use the output in the `Sample Texture 2D` node's *UV* input. You should now see a result in the Scene View like that in Figure 6-13 if you modify the `Shear Amount` of the material.

So far, we have covered textures in 2D. These are easily the most common type of texture, but it is not the only one. We can also use 3D texture data and cubemap data.

Texture3D

A 3D texture is conceptually like a 2D texture, except now we have an additional dimension of data. We don't see them all that often in shaders due to the vastly increased texture memory requirements over a standard 2D texture, but they are useful for applications such as volumetric effects and animated 2D textures where each frame of the animation is stored in the 3D texture like a stack. Before we can use a `Texture3D` inside a shader, we must first create one. It's possible to save a 2D texture in your Assets folder and then convert it to a `Texture3D`.

Importing 3D Textures from 2D Textures

Earlier in this chapter, we saw how flipbook animations can be made using shaders by importing a 2D texture that contains each frame of the animation in a grid. Similarly, we can create a Texture3D asset by importing such a 2D texture and changing some of the import settings on that texture. Figure 6-17 shows you an example of such a texture, where each sub-texture in the grid corresponds to a frame of a smoke particle effect. The frames start from the top left and advance along the x-direction and then the y-direction.

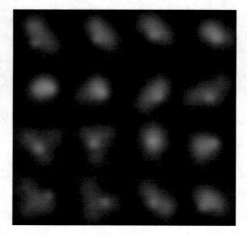

Figure 6-17. *An example 2D texture sheet that can be converted to Texture3D. This sheet has a resolution of 512 × 512 and contains 16 frames, so the resulting Texture3D will have a resolution of 128 × 128 × 16*

In Figure 6-18, you can see the import settings required to convert a Texture2D into a Texture3D. Here is the list of steps you'll need to follow to create your own Texture3D:

- Create a 2D texture sheet of your own, where each "frame" is aligned along a grid, in an external tool such as Photoshop.

- Change the *Texture Shape* setting from 2D to 3D.

- Set the *Columns* and *Rows* settings, which should have now appeared, to the size of your frame grid.

- Tweak the other options however you see fit.

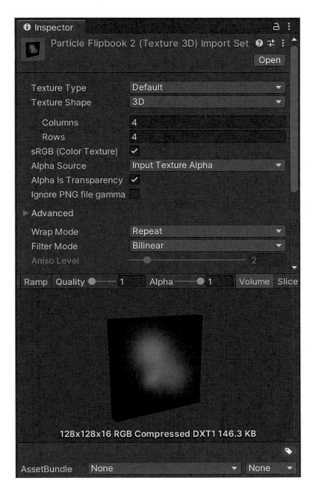

Figure 6-18. *An example Inspector window for a Texture3D asset*

Note   Each "frame" of the `Texture2D` you create must have the same dimensions as each other. However, they do not need to be square (e.g., each frame can be 128 × 256).

We now have a `Texture3D` asset, which contains texture data in three dimensions rather than two. Let's use it inside a shader that can blend between each frame of the texture to achieve a smoothed particle animation.

Blended Particles Using Texture3D

A key benefit of using Texture3D is that they support many of the features of Texture2D, with an added dimension. If we think of each 2D "slice" of a Texture3D as an animation frame, then we can use bilinear filtering to not only blend the texels of the 2D frames themselves but also blend *between* those frames, with minimal additional overhead. We can get a color between two frames using only a single texture sample. This is different from the flipbook approach we saw earlier in this chapter, which would not be able to blend between frames without using two texture samples and blending between them manually. To use bilinear filtering, change the *Filter Mode* of the texture to *Bilinear*.

Both HLSL and Shader Graph support ways of sampling a Texture3D that work like sampling a Texture2D, but now we need to specify a three-dimensional UV coordinate due to the added dimension. Let's see how it works in HLSL and then in Shader Graph. Note that usually this kind of shader would support transparency, but we will be covering that topic in the next chapter.

Blended Particles in HLSL

I will create a new shader file named "ParticleFlipbook.shader" and then copy the template from the start of this chapter. Inside this file, change the shader's name to "Examples/ParticleFlipbook".

Listing 6-37. Changing the name of the ParticleFlipbook shader

```
Shader "Examples/ParticleFlipbook"
```

Next, we will deal with the properties. As you may have guessed, there are special types associated with Texture3D – in the Properties block, we will change the definition of the _BaseTex property so that the type is 3D instead of 2D.

Listing 6-38. Changing the _BaseTex property type from 2D to 3D

```
_BaseTex ("Base Texture", 3D) = "white" {}
```

In the shader code, we also swap out the sampler2D type for sampler3D instead. In URP, we can leave all sampler3D objects outside the constant buffer, like we did with sampler2D.

Listing 6-39. Changing the type of the _BaseTex sampler

```
sampler3D _BaseTex;
```

Despite using `Texture3D` now, we still pass two-dimensional UV coordinates through the `appdata` and `v2f` structs because our 3D models still only have 2D UV data attached to them. To obtain the third UV component, which is required for sampling, we will generate it in the fragment shader.

In this example, we will be using `_Time.y` for the third UV component, which has the effect of animating through each frame over time. If you recall from Chapter 3, `_Time.y` gives us the time in seconds since the game started. After calculating the new UVs, we can sample _BaseTex using the `tex3D` function. `tex3D` takes a sampler and a set of UVs as input, like `tex2D`, but the UVs must now have three components instead of two.

Listing 6-40. A fragment shader that samples a 3D texture using tex3D and time-based UVs

```
float4 frag (v2f i) : SV_Target
{
    float3 animUV = float3(i.uv, _Time.y);
    float4 textureSample = tex3D(_BaseTex, animUV);
    return textureSample * _BaseColor;
}
```

We can create a material with this shader and attach the particle `Texture3D` we imported into Unity. Then any object that uses the material will start to animate through each animation frame over time. The shader blends between each frame due to the bilinear texture filtering we are using on the `Texture3D`. As it turns out, setting the *Filter Mode* to *Point* instead will cause this shader to act just like the flipbook shader we wrote earlier in the chapter. The same is true of the Shader Graph version of the shader.

Blended Particles in Shader Graph

To create this effect in Shader Graph, we will start with a fresh graph. Create a new Unlit graph and name it "ParticleFlipbook.shadergraph".

This graph requires only one property of type Texture3D, which I will name Particle Flipbook. We can drag it onto the graph surface and output it to a Sample Texture 3D node, which is analogous to the tex3D function in HLSL. Connect the Particle Flipbook property to the *Texture* pin. The output of the sampling node can be connected directly to the Base Color output on the master stack – see Figure 6-19.

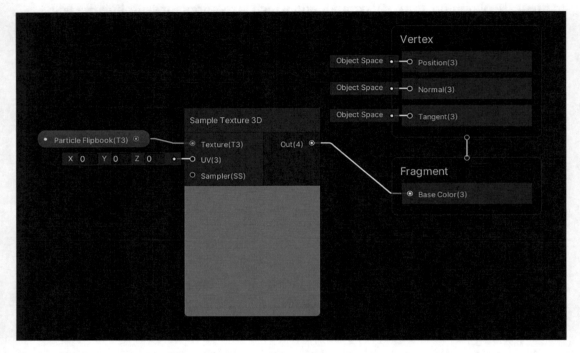

Figure 6-19. *Using a Sample Texture 3D node to sample a Texture3D*

Now let's deal with the three-dimensional UVs required by Sample Texture 3D. For the first two components, we can add a UV node to the graph and use a Split node to feed the first two components to a Vector 3 node. Then, in the third component of the Vector 3 node, we can use a Time node's regular Time output. This completes the UVs we need, and we can connect the output of the Vector 3 node to the *UV* slot on Sample Texture 3D. Figure 6-20 shows the entire graph.

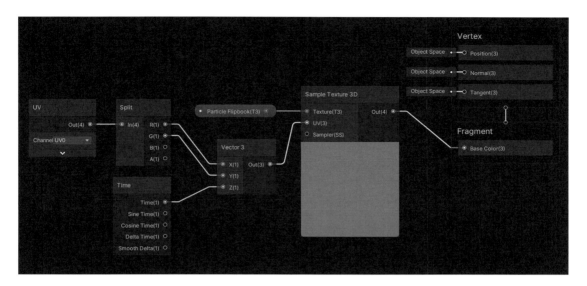

Figure 6-20. *The complete ParticleFlipbook graph, which reads slices of a Texture3D over time*

Like with the HLSL version of this shader, we can create a material that uses it, and you should see it animate over time. Now that we have seen how `Texture3D` can be used, let's talk about another special type of texturing that we can apply to objects: cubemaps.

Cubemaps

A *cubemap*, conceptually, is a textured box that we use to approximate the reflections on an object from the environment around it. We commonly use cubemaps for the *skybox* for this reason; the sky is usually the most prominent source of light in an outdoor scene. Rendering the sky pixels directly using a cubemap and rendering reflections onto the surface of an object involve slightly different calculations, so let's explore both. First, we need a way to create a cubemap object in the first place.

Importing Cubemaps from 2D Textures

When you were much younger, you probably saw how it's possible to cut out the net of a cube on a 2D piece of paper and then fold it together to make a 3D cube. By a similar process, we can convert a 2D texture containing six square textures into a cubemap. There are many formats that we can use for our 2D textures to import them as cubemaps, but for simplicity's sake, I'll focus on one here. Figure 6-21 lists some of the texture orientations we can use for cubemaps.

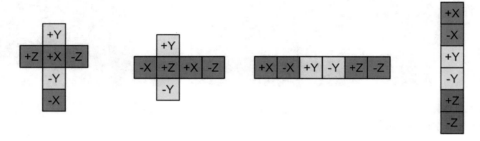

Figure 6-21. *Four texture orientations that Unity can automatically convert to a cubemap. Each one contains six square texture sections, covering the positive and negative directions on the three cardinal axes, as indicated on the diagram*

Unity chooses the correct unpacking method based on the aspect ratio of the image. We will use the third orientation, which features the cubemap faces laid out in a horizontal line. Figure 6-22 shows the example cubemap we will use.

Figure 6-22. *A cubemap texture we can import into Unity and automatically convert to a cubemap. This cubemap data was originally captured inside a Unity scene*

To import the texture as a cubemap, drag it into your Assets folder like any other texture. Then in the import settings window, choose *Texture Shape* ➤ *Cube*. The preview window will update to show a visualization of the cubemap that you can pan around, as seen in Figure 6-23.

Figure 6-23. *The import settings required for a cubemap. Not all texture settings are shown in this screenshot. You can pan the preview around using the left mouse button*

Figure 6-24. *A cubemap that has been sampled directly and mapped to a sphere*

Now that we have a cubemap texture, let's use it inside a couple of shaders. We can sample cubemaps in both Shader Graph and HLSL, so let's start with some examples in HLSL.

Using Cubemaps in HLSL

This task is a bit harder in HLSL because there is a lot more boilerplate code we need to set up. Let's take it step by step and see how to sample cubemaps directly first and then deal with reflections. Figure 6-24 shows what happens when a cubemap is sampled directly and displayed on a sphere.

Sampling a Cubemap in HLSL

I'll start by creating a new shader file, naming it "CubemapExample.shader", and copying the template code from the start of this chapter to overwrite the file's contents. As always, start by renaming the shader at the top of the file.

Listing 6-41. Renaming the shader

```
Shader "Examples/CubemapExample"
```

Let's remove the existing _BaseTex property and add a cubemap property, which I will name _Cubemap for simplicity. This looks a lot like adding other types of textures, except the type is now CUBE. I'll do this in the Properties block first.

Listing 6-42. Adding a cubemap property in Properties

```
Properties
{
    _BaseColor ("Base Color", Color) = (1, 1, 1, 1)
    _Cubemap("Cubemap", CUBE) = "white" {}
}
```

We also need to add the _Cubemap property inside the HLSLPROGRAM code block. Cubemaps use the samplerCUBE type in HLSL. Like other textures, we don't need to define this inside the CBUFFER if we are using URP. I'll declare it underneath the v2f struct definition.

Listing 6-43. Adding a cubemap property in HLSL

```
struct v2f { ... };

samplerCUBE _Cubemap;
```

Now let's deal with the appdata and v2f structs. In both structs, we no longer require UV information since we are not using texture coordinates for sampling the cubemap. We do, however, need to include the surface normal vector as an input to the vertex shader in object space and as an input to the fragment shader in world space. We will add entries to both structs accordingly. Note that in the appdata struct, we can use the Normal semantic for the normalOS variable, but in v2f we will need to use the TEXCOORD0 semantic, even though it is not a texture coordinate.

Listing 6-44. Modifying the appdata and v2f structs to include normal data

```
struct appdata
{
      float4 positionOS : Position;
      float3 normalOS : Normal;
};

struct v2f
{
      float4 positionCS : SV_Position;
      float3 normalWS : TEXCOORD0;
};
```

To pass the normals between the vertex and fragment shaders, we must convert them from object to world space inside the vertex shader. As we saw previously with position data, the functions we use to transform normal data are slightly different in the built-in pipeline and URP; in built-in, we use UnityObjectToWorldNormal, whereas in URP we use TransformObjectToWorldNormal. We need to remove all code relating to UVs from the vertex shader and then add a single line depending on your render pipeline.

Listing 6-45. Transforming the normals from object to world space in the vertex shader in the built-in pipeline

```
v2f vert (appdata v)
{
     v2f o;
     o.positionCS = TransformObjectToHClip(v.positionOS.xyz);
     o.normalWS = UnityObjectToWorldNormal(v.normalOS);
     return o;
}
```

Listing 6-46. Transforming the normals from object to world space in the vertex shader in URP

```
v2f vert (appdata v)
{
    v2f o;
    o.positionCS = TransformObjectToHClip(v.positionOS.xyz);
    o.normalWS = TransformObjectToWorldNormal(v.normalOS);
    return o;
}
```

Now we can modify the fragment shader. Let's remove all code inside it and rewrite it from scratch. We want to sample the cubemap at the correct position and then output the color that we sampled; Unity supplies the texCUBE function for this, which takes a samplerCUBE and a normal vector as input. Here is the entire fragment shader.

Listing 6-47. Sampling a cubemap

```
float4 frag (v2f i) : SV_Target
{
    float4 cubemapSample = texCUBE(_Cubemap, i.normalWS);
    return cubemapSample;
}
```

With this shader, we can sample the cubemap and apply it to a mesh. We could conceivably use this shader for a skybox mesh, where we add a giant sphere around the camera and use a cubemap to represent the sky.

If we want to use the cubemap for reflections, there is a little more work to be done. Whereas in Shader Graph we would just need to swap out one node for a different one, in HLSL there is a bit more work to be done.

Sampling a Reflected Cubemap in HLSL

A reflected cubemap treats the surface of an object as if it was extremely shiny and uses the cubemap to determine what light gets reflected off its surface. If you think of the cubemap itself as a kind of skybox, then a "reflected cubemap" is just the result when that skybox reflects off a sphere. Figure 6-25 shows what a reflected cubemap looks like.

Figure 6-25. *A cubemap that has been mapped onto a sphere using the reflection technique. The cubemap was originally captured inside this scene, so the sphere appears as if it was extremely shiny*

For this example, I will start by creating a new shader named "CubemapReflections. shader" and replace the file contents with the template code at the start of the chapter. Rename the shader at the top of the file too.

Listing 6-48. Renaming the shader

```
Shader "Examples/CubemapReflections"
```

We'll be using the same cubemap property as the previous example, so follow Listings 6-42 and 6-43 to add it to our shader. Now let's think about the data we will need to pass between the vertex and fragment shaders.

- The vertex shader still requires the normal vector, so follow Listing 6-44 to set up the appdata struct correctly.

- The fragment shader will no longer be using the world normal vector to sample the cubemap; instead, it will use a reflected vector, which we calculate in the vertex shader.

- The v2f struct, therefore, uses a variable named reflectWS in place of normalWS in the TEXCOORD0 semantic.

Listing 6-49. Replacing world normals with a world-space reflection vector in v2f

```
struct v2f
{
    float4 positionCS : SV_Position;
    float3 reflectWS : TEXCOORD0;
};
```

In the fragment shader, we can quickly swap out the variable we use for sampling the cubemap from i.normalWS to i.reflectWS too. Compared to the previous cubemap example, there are no other differences in the fragment shader, as most of the difference is in the vertex shader.

Listing 6-50. Tweaking the variable we use for sampling the cubemap

```
float4 frag (v2f i) : SV_Target
{
    float4 cubemapSample = texCUBE(_Cubemap, i.reflectWS);
    return cubemapSample;
}

float4 cubemapSample = texCUBE(_Cubemap, i.reflectWS);
```

Let's turn our attention to the vertex shader. There's a bit more work to be done here than in the other cubemap example:

- To calculate the reflection vector, we take the view vector (which is the vector between the camera and the surface of the object) and reflect it in the surface normal vector.

- Therefore, we need access to the world-space normal vector for this calculation. The code is almost the same as the previous cubemap example, except now it's a local variable instead of a member of v2f.

    - In the built-in pipeline, we use the UnityObjectToWorldNormal function. In URP, we instead use TransformObjectToWorldNormal.

187

- Next, we need to get the view vector.

  - We can derive it from the world-space position. To get this, we multiply the object-space position by the `unity_ObjectToWorld` built-in matrix.

  - We pass this into a method that returns the view vector. In the built-in pipeline, the method is called `UnityWorldSpaceViewDir`, and we must manually normalize the result. In URP, it's called `GetWorldSpaceNormalizeViewDir`.

  - This vector points in the opposite direction from what we need, so negate it with the "`-`" operator.

- To obtain the final reflected vector, we use the `reflect` function using the view vector and the normal vector.

Listing 6-51. The reflected cubemap vertex shader in the built-in pipeline

```
v2f vert (appdata v)
{
    v2f o;
    o.positionCS = UnityObjectToClipPos(v.positionOS.xyz);
    float3 normalWS = UnityObjectToWorldNormal(v.normalOS);

    float3 positionWS = mul(unity_ObjectToWorld, v.positionOS).xyz;
    float3 viewDirWS = UnityWorldSpaceViewDir(positionWS);
    viewDirWS = normalize(viewDirWS);

    o.reflectWS = reflect(-viewDirWS, normalWS);
    return o;
}
```

Listing 6-52. The reflected cubemap vertex shader in URP

```
v2f vert (appdata v)
{
    v2f o;
    o.positionCS = TransformObjectToHClip(v.positionOS.xyz);
    float3 normalWS = TransformObjectToWorldNormal(v.normalOS);
```

```
    float3 positionWS = mul(unity_ObjectToWorld, v.positionOS).xyz;
    float3 viewDirWS = GetWorldSpaceNormalizeViewDir(positionWS);

    o.reflectWS = reflect(-viewDirWS, normalWS);
    return o;
}
```

Now we have completed the shader. If we attach a material with this shader to, say, a sphere, we can see how the reflections work by panning the camera around it. Obviously, it's hard to pan the camera in a book, but I hope Figure 6-25 gets the point across!

Using Cubemaps in Shader Graph

I'm going to use a new unlit Shader Graph to create this shader, so create one and name it "CubemapExample.shadergraph". Let's talk about directly sampling the cubemap first.

Sampling a Cubemap in Shader Graph

We need to expose a property for the cubemap, so add a new Cubemap property and name it Scene Cubemap. Drag this onto the graph, and then drag out a new Sample Cubemap node from it. To sample a cubemap directly, we require the world-space normal vector on the surface of the object, which Unity handily supplies for us by default. If we output this to the Base Color output on the master stack, as seen in Figure 6-26, then the Main Preview will update to show you what the shader looks like.

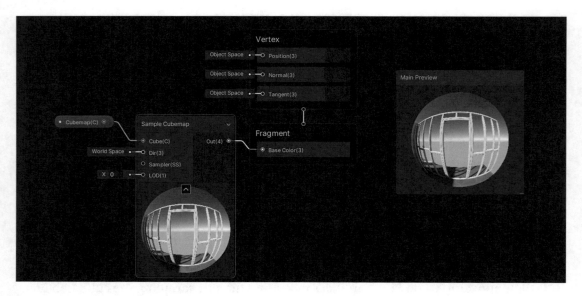

Figure 6-26. *A graph that can be used to sample the cubemap*

This is not the only way to sample a cubemap. This method of sampling is great for use on a skybox, as we are directly polling the values inside the cubemap. Often, however, we wish to use cubemaps for reflections, which is a bit more complex. Let's see how that works now.

Sampling a Reflected Cubemap in Shader Graph

Conceptually, sampling a reflected cubemap is like taking your object and imagining that the skybox – the cubemap – is surrounding it on all sides. The color on the surface of your object is equal to the light reflecting from the skybox/cubemap. To sample the cubemap in this manner, we now require the normal vector, this time in object space, and the *view vector* from the camera to the surface of the object. Shader Graph once again supplies a node for this called Sample Reflected Cubemap and has the correct inputs on the graph by default. In fact, we just need to swap out the Sample Cubemap node on our graph with a Sample Reflected Cubemap node, as in Figure 6-27.

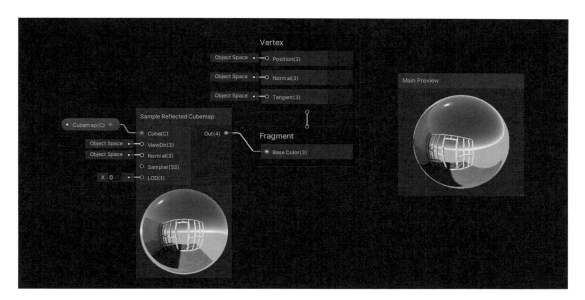

Figure 6-27. *Sampling the cubemap to apply reflections to an object*

When we sample like this, the preview looks like a perfectly reflective sphere, and when attached to an object in the scene, it will look like the sphere in Figure 6-25.

Summary

Texturing is one of the core features of shaders. This chapter has not covered every use case and every technique related to textures by any stretch of the imagination, but we have seen how basic texturing works, how UV mapping is performed, and how we can modify UVs to create a range of graphical effects. Here's what we learned in this chapter:

- We can modify UV coordinates in the vertex or fragment shader to change how sampling works. Rotation and shearing of UVs are possible using transformation matrices.

- Polar coordinates are used to define points using an angle and a distance. Using polar coordinates in place of UVs when sampling can lead to interesting texture patterns.

- Flipbooks can be used to animate a texture over time.

- Triplanar mapping uses three texture samples in different world-space planes to ensure minimal distortion of a texture on the surface of an object.

- We can create 3D textures from 2D textures and sample them using tex3D or Sample Texture 3D.

- Similarly, we can create cubemaps from 2D textures comprised of six square sub-textures and sample them inside a shader using texCUBE or Sample Cubemap.

- We can reflect cubemap data onto the surface of an object by reflecting the view vector in the surface normal of an object and then using that as the sampling vector in texCUBE. In Shader Graph, we can use Sample Reflected Cubemap.

CHAPTER 7

The Depth Buffer

How do you make sure objects get rendered in the correct order if they overlap in the viewport? What if an object is only partially obscured by another one? When attempting to render a given pixel, we need a system in place that allows us to check whether a pixel has already been drawn at the same position and determine whether it is in front of or behind the one we are currently drawing. This requires us to store additional data every time we draw a pixel. We can't just store the color of the pixel; we also need to store the *depth* of the last pixel drawn to that position. Unity stores the color data inside a 2D array the size of the screen called the *color buffer*, and similarly, the depth information is stored in the *depth buffer*, which has the same dimensions as the color buffer. In this chapter, we will learn how the depth buffer works and create some shader effects that interact with it in different ways.

How Rendering Opaque Objects Works

In practically every game you work on, there will be several objects each scene, some of which will overlap the same screen position. Which one will be rendered on top? Setting aside transparent objects for now, as we will explore those in the next chapter, Unity needs to choose one of the objects to render at each pixel position on-screen. We can't just draw the objects in an arbitrary order, as you will inevitably end up with objects incorrectly drawn over other objects that are in front of them.

Unity requires extra information to render the objects. The typical solution is to store depth information about each pixel in an extra data structure called the depth buffer. It's also called the *z-buffer* because it stores the distance along the z-axis relative to the camera. The idea here is that whenever we want to render an object, we compute its z-distance from the camera and compare it with the value in the depth buffer. If the

© Daniel Ilett 2022
D. Ilett, *Building Quality Shaders for Unity*®, https://doi.org/10.1007/978-1-4842-8652-4_7

z-distance is less than the value in the depth buffer, the object gets rendered (i.e., its colors get written to the color buffer), and we store the z-distance in the depth buffer. The rendering loop looks like this:

- Initialize all values in the depth buffer to a maximum value, 1.0. This is called *clearing* the depth buffer.

- Pick the next opaque object in the scene that hasn't been rendered yet.

- Apply the vertex and fragment shaders to the object to figure out which colors *might* be rendered to the screen and at what screen position.

- Calculate the distance of each pixel of the object from the camera along the camera's z-axis.

- Compare that distance with the value in the z-buffer at this location. This is called the *depth test*:

  - If the new depth is less than or equal to the old depth, write the new color and depth to the color buffer and depth buffer, respectively.

  - Else, if the new depth is greater than the old depth, discard the pixel we are trying to render and do not modify either of the buffers.

- Pick the next opaque object that has not been rendered and repeat the rest of the steps until all objects have been rendered.

This relatively simple loop ensures that only the object closest to the camera gets rendered at every pixel position. There is an additional memory requirement related to the depth buffer since we need to store an entire second texture the size of the game window in memory, but the trade-off is that depth testing is a relatively time-efficient method for correctly rendering opaque objects in the correct order.

Now that we know at a high level how a depth buffer can be used to solve some of the problems associated with rendering objects correctly, how exactly is it implemented in Unity?

How the Depth Buffer Works

As I mentioned, the depth buffer stores a depth value per pixel. However, it's not quite as simple as storing the distance of each pixel in Unity units (if you recall, one Unity unit is commonly understood to represent one meter of real-world space). Unity takes the distance of a pixel from the camera, which we can call the *z-value*, where the minimum distance is the near clip distance of the camera and the maximum is the far clip distance. All pixels outside that range are culled. The z-value is then transformed into a depth value to be stored in the depth buffer by transforming the range from [*near, far*] to [0, 1]. This means each value inside the depth buffer is a floating-point number between 0 and 1, inclusive.

There are various ways we could achieve a mapping between z-values measured in Unity units and depth values between 0 and 1. For example, if this mapping were linear, then it would be easy to compute, but we run into issues with precision. Essentially, we want to use as much precision as possible to represent objects closer to the screen, because the distances between these objects are a lot more noticeable than the distances of objects far from the screen. Any loss of precision when depth testing close objects may lead to incorrect ordering of objects and result in the same graphical issues we were trying to avoid.

Consequently, we use a nonlinear depth buffer where depth values are calculated using the following equation:

Equation 7-1: Calculating depth values from z-values

$$depth = \left(\frac{1/z - 1/near}{1/far - 1/near} \right)$$

The distribution of z-values to depth values is illustrated in Figure 7-1. This means that objects close to the camera use a far higher proportion of the range of possible values, so we can make depth comparisons on those objects with higher precision than we would with a linear depth buffer. In fact, with Unity's default values of 0.3 and 1000 for the near and far clip distances, respectively, around 70% of the precision is taken up by objects that are up to one Unity unit away from the camera.

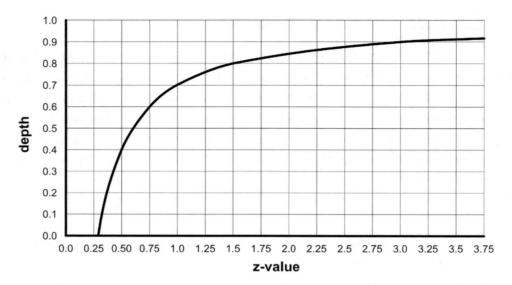

Figure 7-1. *Converting camera distances (z-values) to depth values to store in the depth buffer. In this example, the near clip distance is 0.3, and the far clip distance is 1000*

All of this is to say we must be careful when reading values from the depth buffer within our shaders and be mindful of what those values represent. As we will see later, there are ways to easily convert the values from the depth buffer into formats that will be more helpful to us. Next, we will look at render queues and see how Unity uses them to enforce an ordering on objects being rendered.

Render Queues

Unity uses a queue system when rendering objects. When you create a shader, you must specify a queue tag, which tells Unity at which stage during the rendering loop to render objects that use that shader. The queue is rendered in order, so if you create two shaders with different queue values, all objects with the lower queue value are rendered before anything that uses the higher queue value. In Chapter 3, I briefly listed the named queues available in Unity and their respective queue values:

- Background = 1000

- Geometry = 2000

- AlphaTest = 2450

- Transparent = 3000

- Overlay = 4000

To specify a queue in HLSL, we use one of these preceding values. We can add or subtract values to or from them, so if we wanted to make a shader that runs just before the Geometry queue, we could give it a Queue value of Geometry-1.

Listing 7-1. Specifying queue values inside a Tags block in HLSL

```
Tags
{
    // Other tags go here.
    ...
    "Queue" = "Geometry-1"
}
```

In Shader Graph, we are only able to specify whether an object uses the Geometry queue or the Transparent queue by changing the Surface option in the Graph Settings. In the following example in Figure 7-2, the shader is using the *Opaque* Surface option, which corresponds to the Geometry queue.

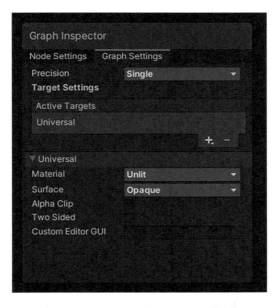

Figure 7-2. *Setting the Surface option to Opaque, which corresponds to the Geometry queue. The other option is Transparent*

Any object with a queue value of 2500 or below is considered to be opaque, and anything above that is considered to be transparent (we will be talking about transparent rendering in a future chapter). Now that we know how objects are rendered in queue order, let's talk about how depth testing is performed.

Depth Testing and Writing

To determine which pixels should get drawn, we carry out *depth testing* to compare the depth of a pixel we wish to draw to the screen with the depth of the pixel that has already been rendered at that position. We can customize how the depth test works using ShaderLab syntax, but first, let's see how the standard "less-equal" depth test operates.

The ZTest Keyword

I will be using the TextureExample shader from Chapter 5 as a basis for this shader. Inside the Pass, we can specify the type of depth test we would like to use with the ZTest keyword. The default value is ZTest LEqual, which means that the depth test passes if the tested pixel's depth is less than or equal to the value in the depth buffer (i.e., the object is closer than or at the same distance as the previously drawn object). We can specify this in ShaderLab syntax like the following.

Listing 7-2. Specifying a ZTest inside a Pass

```
Pass
{
    ZTest LEqual

    // All other Pass code here.
    ...
}
```

If we don't specify a ZTest at all, then LEqual is the default behavior. Figure 7-3 gives an example of two objects drawn using this type of depth testing. Thankfully, this syntax is the same in HLSL no matter which render pipeline we are using.

Figure 7-3. *In the left image, we see that one of the cubes is rendered over the other. The front cube is closer to the camera than the back cube, so it is rendered in front. Panning the camera to the side, as in the right image, confirms the relative positioning of the two cubes*

LEqual is not the only type of depth test. The other possible values are as follows:

- Less – The depth test passes if the tested depth is strictly less than, and not equal to, the depth buffer value.

- GEqual – The depth test passes if the tested depth is greater than or equal to the depth buffer value.

- Greater – The depth test passes if the tested depth is strictly greater than, and not equal to, the depth buffer value.

- Equal – The depth test passes if the tested depth is exactly equal to the depth buffer value.

- NotEqual – The depth test passes if the tested depth value is not equal to the depth buffer value.

- Always – The depth test always passes, and the object is always rendered.

- Never – The depth test always fails, and the object is never rendered.

You can use these values to render geometry in interesting ways, although almost every shader you write will use ZTest LEqual – your game would look bizarre if you routinely used the others! I would suggest using the other modes sparingly and for specific purposes. As an example, if we use ZTest Always, this is a great way to ensure objects are always visible, so you could use it for quest markers or x-ray vision, as seen in Figure 7-4.

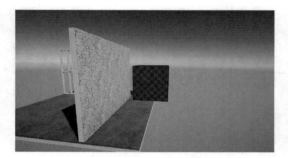

Figure 7-4. *Using ZTest Always on a cube. In the left image, the cube is drawn on top of the wall. However, panning the camera to the side (as in the right image), we see that the cube is behind that wall in 3D space*

Tip   The ZTest Equal depth test can be useful when you are using a multipass shader or you are using multiple materials on one object – if each pass uses a similar vertex shader, your geometry will line up perfectly, and ZTest Equal will trigger on any subsequent passes, provided the first pass writes to the depth buffer successfully.

Try out different values to see what kind of visual effects you can come up with. Now that we have explored the ZTest keyword, let's look at ZWrite.

The ZWrite Keyword

When the depth test passes, the object geometry will be drawn to the screen. For opaque objects, we usually want to also write the depth of the object to the depth buffer so that subsequent objects can check their own depth values against it. However, there are circumstances where we don't want to perform the write. In ShaderLab, we have access to the handy ZWrite keyword, which controls whether we write to the depth buffer: ZWrite On will write depth when the depth test passes, and ZWrite Off will not. We usually specify this keyword just below the ZTest keyword.

Listing 7-3. Specifying a ZWrite inside a Pass, just below a ZTest

```
Pass
{
    ZTest LEqual
    ZWrite On

    // All other Pass code here.
    ...
}
```

ZWrite On is the default behavior for opaque objects if we don't specify the keyword at all. The result is that the rendering order of opaque objects in the scene does not matter, because each object writes its own depth; and therefore, when combined with an appropriate ZTest, all objects are rendered in the correct order. However, when rendering transparent objects, which we will be covering in the next chapter, we almost always use ZWrite Off because of the way transparent objects work.

Now that we have seen how configuring depth testing works in ShaderLab, let's see how it works in Shader Graph.

Depth Settings with Shader Graph

Support for custom depth testing in Shader Graph isn't quite as straightforward. By default, opaque graphs will use ZWrite On and ZTest LEqual, and transparent graphs will use ZWrite Off and ZTest LEqual. This is the same default behavior as shader code, but in many versions of Shader Graph, this can't be customized at all.

However, versions of HDRP from 7.1 onward (for Unity 2019.3) support *Depth Test* and *Depth Write* options if you are using a transparent graph, as seen in Figure 7-5.

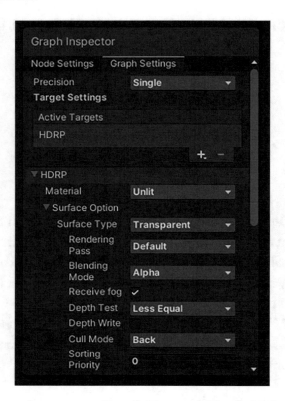

Figure 7-5. *HDRP graphs support Depth Test and Depth Write, but only on transparent objects*

Prior to Unity 2021.2, URP Shader Graph did not support these options. However, in versions of URP for 2021.2 and above, you will have access to the Depth Test and Depth Write options, even on opaque objects, as seen in Figure 7-6.

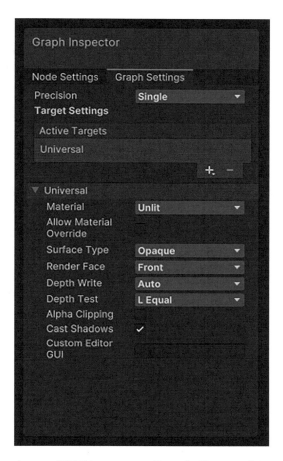

Figure 7-6. *Later versions of URP support Depth Test and Depth Write on both opaque and transparent graphs*

Although custom depth testing support in Shader Graph is a little shaky as of the writing of this book, there is every chance that the full suite of options will become available on both URP and HDRP in the future, regardless of the surface type of the shader you are creating. Now that we have established what options are available for depth testing in our shaders, let's talk about early depth testing.

Early Depth Testing

With conventional depth testing, which follows the algorithm that I described at the start of this chapter, Unity needs to run the entire shader – both the vertex and fragment stages – on the object before running the depth test and determining whether the object should be drawn. This ensures that Unity can be absolutely certain that the depth test executes correctly, since the fragment shader is capable of writing to the depth buffer directly or discarding pixels, thereby influencing the results of the depth test.

However, you've probably realized that most shaders don't do either of those things. In cases like those, it does not make much sense to evaluate the (expensive) fragment shader at all! As a result, many GPUs support *early depth testing*, where Unity carries out the vertex shader to establish the position of an object, then performs a special depth-only rendering pass, and culls objects based on that. For the objects that pass this stripped-down depth test, the fragment shader is evaluated. This optimization is especially useful if you have a complicated fragment shader or you are performing several shader passes on each object. The best part is that you don't need to turn this feature on, as it will happen automatically.

We have now covered how Unity performs depth testing in detail. Before we move on to creating shader effects that utilize depth, let's talk about a graphical artifact that appears commonly in games and discuss techniques for avoiding and mitigating it.

Z-Fighting

Z-Fighting is a phenomenon caused by uncertainty during depth testing. When two surfaces overlap or are very (extremely!) close to each other, Unity won't be able to definitively pick which of the two should be rendered over the other, so parts of both may be rendered, usually in a "stripy" pattern. These artifacts usually look unstable, and moving the camera will drastically change the fighting "pattern" of the two objects, so the effect is described as the two objects "fighting" for dominance over the other, hence the name. Figure 7-7 is an example of two objects z-fighting.

Figure 7-7. *Z-Fighting on two cubes. In the central section, the surfaces of the cubes intersect, so Unity cannot be sure which one is closer to the camera. In motion, the z-fighting effect is usually erratic, and the fighting pattern changes constantly*

So how can we avoid z-fighting in our games? Of course, we can make sure we never place two objects in a scene such that they are overlapping, and in cases where it is unavoidable, we could add a small offset to the position of one of the objects to make sure it is always rendered first. However, it's not always easy to check every object to verify that z-fighting will not occur, especially if your scene contains many objects. We can exploit the behavior of the depth buffer to at least reduce the likelihood of z-fighting occurring.

One of the key features of the depth buffer is that its bounds are described by the camera's near and far clip planes. As a result, if we would like to increase the precision of depth comparisons between objects (and therefore reduce the likelihood of z-fighting on close objects), we can make the camera's near clip distance as high as possible and the far clip distance as low as possible. By default, a Unity camera has a near distance of 0.3 and a far distance of 1000 (see Figure 7-8), but you may be able to tweak these values for your game. If you are experiencing z-fighting issues, changing these values is one of the easiest changes you can make in your game, although this is not a definitive solution to the problem.

Figure 7-8. *The default clipping planes for a camera in Unity are 0.3 and 1000 for the near and far clip planes, respectively*

We have now covered the depth buffer in detail. From this point onward, we will explore shader effects that use depth.

Shader Effects Using Depth

Now that we have seen plenty of ways of interacting with the depth buffer, let's try our hand at writing shader effects that interact with it. The first effect we will write is a silhouette effect, during which we will learn exactly how to access depth values for use within a shader. After that, we will cover other effects that utilize depth.

Silhouette

A silhouette effect is one where foreground objects are colored in a dark color – usually pitch black – and the background elements use a lighter color like white. The result is that we lose all detailed information about the scene except the edges of the foreground elements, which we can exploit if we want to stylistically render certain parts of a scene. In this example, we are going to create a silhouette shader, which will access the depth of each object behind the mesh being rendered and output those depth values as the base color of the mesh (with the option to remap the colors). Let's see how we can create this effect in HLSL first and then Shader Graph.

Silhouette Effect in HLSL

To create a silhouette effect using HLSL, we will be using a few new concepts that we have not yet seen. As the first step, we need to know how to access depth values that we can use within our shaders, and for that, we introduce the *depth texture.*

Figure 7-9. *A sample scene with the Silhouette shader attached to a cube. The shapes of the wooden construction frame and the floor can clearly be seen on the cube*

Preparing the Depth Texture

If you are working in the built-in pipeline, then you're good to go – you can move on to the next subsection and start writing the shader.

However, if you are working in URP, we must enable the depth texture before we can use it in shaders. Here are the steps required to enable it:

- In the Unity Editor's Project window, find your URP Asset – this is usually under *Assets* ➤ *Settings* (there will be multiple URP Assets, so perform the following changes on all of them).

- If you installed URP manually through the Package Manager, your URP Assets might be elsewhere within the Assets folder.

- At the top of each asset, ensure the *Depth Texture* option is ticked. Figure 7-10 shows you what the asset looks like when selected.

Caution   If you do not enable the depth texture in URP, then the Silhouette effect will not work properly, as the camera depth texture will be unfilled.

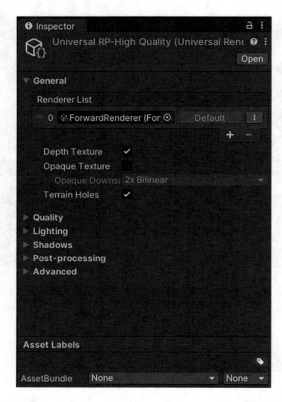

Figure 7-10. *Enabling the depth texture in the Universal Render Pipeline*

Once you have enabled the depth texture, we can start thinking about how to use it to write the Silhouette shader.

Camera Depth Texture

When we render opaque objects, we typically write the depth value of each pixel to the depth buffer. On the other hand, transparent objects, which are drawn after all opaques have been rendered, usually do not have their depth information written to the depth buffer. Therefore, if we want access to complete depth information for the current frame, we need to do it after all opaque objects have been rendered.

Note   We will be covering transparent rendering in much more detail in Chapter 8.

However, we can't directly access those depth buffer values from within the fragment shader. Instead, Unity will carry out an extra depth-only pass on all the opaque objects and render those depth values into a special texture called `_CameraDepthTexture`, which we can access within our shaders.

There is a subtle distinction here: the depth buffer and the camera depth texture are *not* the same thing, but they do contain similar information. The depth buffer is used internally by the graphics pipeline to perform depth testing and culling, while the depth texture is used by us inside shaders for depth-based effects. With that out of the way, let's see how we can access and sample the depth texture inside a shader.

Note   After completing the Silhouette effect in both HLSL and Shader Graph, we'll see how to write this depth-only pass to make sure our custom opaque shaders write their depth information into the camera depth texture.

Reading Depth Values

The `_CameraDepthTexture` is a `Texture2D` like any other. We use UVs to sample it at a specific position – the only difference now is that those UVs are in screen space, because we usually want to access the depth texture at the same position (or at least a nearby position) to the pixel we are currently rendering.

I'm going to create a new shader file called "Silhouette.shader". I'll start off by replacing the entire contents with the following code, and I'll rename the shader at the top of the file as we have been doing with every new shader.

Listing 7-4. Renaming the Silhouette shader

```
Shader "Examples/Silhouette"
{
     Properties { ... }
     SubShader
     {
          Tags  { ... }

          Pass
          {
               HLSLPROGRAM
               #pragma vertex vert
               #pragma fragment frag

               struct appdata
               {
                    float4 positionOS : Position;
               };

               struct v2f { ... };

               v2f vert (appdata v) { ... }

               float4 frag (v2f i) : SV_Target { ... }
               ENDHLSL
          }
     }
}
```

First, we must edit the tags and include the correct library files to make this effect work. This works slightly differently between the built-in and Universal pipelines:

- In both pipelines, we must add two tags to the existing Tags block to enable transparent rendering. By using transparent rendering, we can ensure that all opaque objects have been rendered into the camera depth texture.

    - The RenderType tag and the Queue tag should both use "Transparent" as their value.

- In the built-in pipeline, we should include the "UnityCG.cginc" file.

- In URP, we should include Core.hlsl as usual, but we also require a file called DeclareDepthTexture.hlsl, which makes the camera depth texture available in the shader.

- In URP, we should also add a second Tags block within the Pass block and add a LightMode tag to it.

Here are the changes we must make in each pipeline.

Listing 7-5. Adding tags and include files in the built-in pipeline

```
Tags
{
        "RenderType" = "Transparent"
        "Queue" = "Transparent"
}

Pass
{
        HLSLPROGRAM
        #pragma vertex vert
        #pragma fragment frag

        #include "UnityCG.cginc"
```

Listing 7-6. Adding tags and include files in URP

```
Tags
{
        "RenderType" = "Transparent"
        "Queue" = "Transparent"
        "RenderPipeline" = "UniversalPipeline"
}

Pass
{
        Tags
        {
```

211

```
        "LightMode" = "UniversalForward"
    }

    HLSLPROGRAM
    #pragma vertex vert
    #pragma fragment frag

    #include "Packages/com.unity.render-pipelines.universal/
    ShaderLibrary/Core.hlsl"
    #include "Packages/com.unity.render-pipelines.universal/
    ShaderLibrary/DeclareDepthTexture.hlsl"
```

Next, let's deal with the shader properties. We will need only two properties for this shader, which represent the foreground and background colors. By default, the _ForegroundColor will be black, and the _BackgroundColor will be white.

Listing 7-7. Declaring Silhouette properties in the Properties block

```
Properties
{
    _ForegroundColor ("FG Color", Color) = (1, 1, 1, 1)
    _BackgroundColor ("BG Color", Color) = (1, 1, 1, 1)
}
```

Each property will need to be declared a second time in the HLSLPROGRAM block just below the v2f struct definition, and if you are using URP, make sure you follow the SRP Batcher rules by including them in the UnityPerMaterial constant buffer. Additionally, we must manually declare _CameraDepthTexture in the built-in pipeline, but it's already included in URP via the include files.

Listing 7-8. Declaring Silhouette properties in the HLSLPROGRAM block in the built-in pipeline

```
struct v2f { ... };

sampler2D _CameraDepthTexture;

float4 _ForegroundColor;
float4 _BackgroundColor;
```

Listing 7-9. Declaring Silhouette properties in the HLSLPROGRAM block in URP

```
struct v2f { ... };

CBUFFER_START(UnityPerMaterial)
     float4 _ForegroundColor;
     float4 _BackgroundColor;
CBUFFER_END
```

Now we can deal with the HLSLPROGRAM code block, starting with the structs. First, the appdata struct just needs to include the object-space position of each vertex; we don't need UVs because we are not performing texturing at all. In the v2f struct, we need the clip-space position of each vertex as usual, but we also need to access the screen-space position of the object in the fragment shader because we will use that position to sample the depth texture. We can derive that from the object-space position inside the vertex shader and pass it to the fragment shader via the v2f struct. There's no special semantic for screen-space positions, so we'll use the TEXCOORD0 semantic.

Listing 7-10. Adding clip-space and screen-space positions to the v2f struct

```
struct v2f
{
     float4 positionCS : SV_Position;
     float4 positionSS : TEXCOORD0;
};
```

Here's how the vertex shader will tie the two structs together:

- First, we will transform the vertex positions from object space (positionOS) to clip space (positionCS):

    - In the built-in pipeline, we use the UnityObjectToClipPos function.

    - In URP, we instead use the TransformObjectToHClip function.

- Using the clip-space position, we can obtain the screen-space position (positionSS):

213

- We use the ComputeScreenPos function, which is named the same way in the built-in and Universal pipelines.

- The screen-space position is required to sample the camera depth texture in the fragment shader. That's why we pass it via v2f.

Listing 7-11. The Silhouette vertex shader in the built-in pipeline

```
v2f vert (appdata v)
{
    v2f o;
    o.positionCS = UnityObjectToClipPos(v.positionOS);
    o.positionSS = ComputeScreenPos(o.positionCS);
    return o;
}
```

Listing 7-12. The Silhouette vertex shader in URP

```
v2f vert (appdata v)
{
    v2f o;
    o.positionCS = TransformObjectToHClip(v.positionOS.xyz);
    o.positionSS = ComputeScreenPos(o.positionCS);
    return o;
}
```

Now we come to the fragment shader. Inside the fragment shader, we first need to calculate screen-space UVs for sampling the depth texture. We do this by taking the screen-space positions and dividing the *xy*-components by the *w*-component, which puts the resulting UVs into the [0, 1] range in both axes. Once we have those UVs, we can use the tex2D function to directly sample the _CameraDepthTexture. This is a grayscale image, and we only need to access the first channel, which we can access with .r or .x.

Listing 7-13. Using screen-space UVs to sample the depth texture

```
float4 frag (v2f i) : SV_Target
{
    float2 screenUVs = i.positionSS.xy / i.positionSS.w;
    float rawDepth = tex2D(_CameraDepthTexture, screenUVs).r;
```

What do we do with the depth sample we have obtained? The raw values from the depth texture are nonlinear values between 0 and 1, so let's talk about different ways of using them.

Converting Depth Values

The depth values we can access in the depth texture can be converted into a few formats for common use cases. Since the values inside the depth texture are nonlinear, it's not always useful to use them directly, so we often convert them to different formats. The available formats are as follows:

- The *raw depth* is the value, between 0 and 1, taken from the depth texture as is with no modification. This is a nonlinear value that represents distance from the camera. In this representation, a depth value of 0.5 is not halfway between the near and far clip planes – it is actually fairly close to the camera to preserve precision for close-up distance comparisons.

- The *eye depth* is a linear value that represents the depth of a pixel in Unity units (i.e., meters) away from the camera. This format is useful for comparing depth values with world-space values, as it is possible to reconstruct world-space positions from the depth texture.

- It is possible to convert the nonlinear raw depth values to a linear representation. This is called the *Linear01 depth*, which is useful when we only care about how deep an object is in relation to others or when we are using depth values to mess with output colors. It is a value between 0 and 1.

Unity provides functions in HLSL and nodes in Shader Graph for converting from the "raw" representation to linear or eye depth. These functions are called `Linear01Depth`, which converts the raw values to a linear value between 0 and 1, and `LinearEyeDepth`, which converts the raw values to eye units. Both functions take the raw depth value as input, but in URP, we also need to pass in a second parameter called `_ZBufferParams,` which is declared automatically and contains values that help Unity perform the conversions.

Listing 7-14. Functions for converting depth values in the built-in pipeline

```
float scene01Depth = Linear01Depth(rawDepth);
float sceneEyeDepth = LinearEyeDepth(rawDepth);
```

Listing 7-15. Functions for converting depth values in URP

```
float scene01Depth = Linear01Depth(rawDepth, _ZBufferParams);
float sceneEyeDepth = LinearEyeDepth(rawDepth, _ZBufferParams);
```

With that in mind, let's continue with the Silhouette shader. We will be using the Linear01Depth function because we want a value between 0 and 1 to represent the distance between the near and far clip planes of whatever object was last rendered into the depth texture. Using that value, we will interpolate between _ForegroundColor and _BackgroundColor with the lerp function ("lerp" stands for "linear interpolation"). The lerp function takes two values – which can be colors, vectors, floats, and so on – and uses a third parameter between 0 and 1 to control the proportion of blending between the first two inputs. We will then output the resulting color as the final output of the fragment shader.

Listing 7-16. Completed fragment shader in the built-in pipeline

```
float4 frag (v2f i) : SV_Target
{
    float2 screenspaceUVs = i.positionSS.xy / i.positionSS.w;
    float rawDepth = SampleSceneDepth(screenspaceUVs);

    float scene01Depth = Linear01Depth(rawDepth);

    float4 outputColor = lerp(_ForegroundColor, _BackgroundColor,
    scene01Depth);

    return outputColor;
}
```

Listing 7-17. Completed fragment shader in URP

```
float4 frag (v2f i) : SV_Target
{
    float2 screenspaceUVs = i.positionSS.xy / i.positionSS.w;
```

```
float rawDepth = SampleSceneDepth(screenspaceUVs);

float scene01Depth = Linear01Depth(rawDepth, _ZBufferParams);

float4 outputColor = lerp(_ForegroundColor, _BackgroundColor,
scene01Depth);

return outputColor;
}
```

The shader is now complete, and if we attach the shader to an object in the scene via a material, then the object will display a silhouette of any opaque object located behind it. Figure 7-9 shows a cube with the Silhouette shader attached in front of the URP sample scene. Now that we have seen how this effect works in HLSL, let's see how it works in Shader Graph.

Silhouette Effect in Shader Graph

It is considerably easier to handle depth in Shader Graph than it is in HLSL code. To get started, create a new Unlit shader, name it "Silhouette.shadergraph", and open the Shader Graph editor.

Caution   If you are using URP, make sure you enable the depth texture (as seen in Figure 7-10). The Silhouette effect will not run properly if you do not enable it.

The first step is to make the shader use transparent rendering. We can do so by going to the Graph Inspector, selecting the Graph Settings tab, and changing the Surface from *Opaque* to *Transparent* (see Figure 7-11).

Figure 7-11. *The Surface option can be found under the Graph Settings tab of the Graph Inspector window. This is where we make the shader transparent*

This graph will require two Color properties, just like the HLSL version did, for tweaking the Foreground Color and Background Color. By default, I made them black and white, respectively. To sample the depth, all we need to add to the graph is a Scene Depth node, which will simultaneously sample the depth texture and handle any conversions we need. That's a lot easier than the code alternative! The *Sampling* option at the bottom of the node can be switched between three modes – *Linear 01*, which is the one we want, *Eye*, and *Raw*, corresponding to the three formats I described in the previous section. The screen-space UVs that we need are automatically used as input to this node, although we could use a different set of inputs if we wanted. The Screen Position node will be helpful if you want to modify the input.

We use a Lerp node to interpolate between the Foreground Color and Background Color. Those two properties should be connected to the first two inputs of Lerp, and the third input is the Scene Depth node's output. The output of Lerp, which is a mix of the two color inputs, should be used as the graph's *Base Color* output on the master stack. That's all that is required – the completed graph can be seen in Figure 7-12.

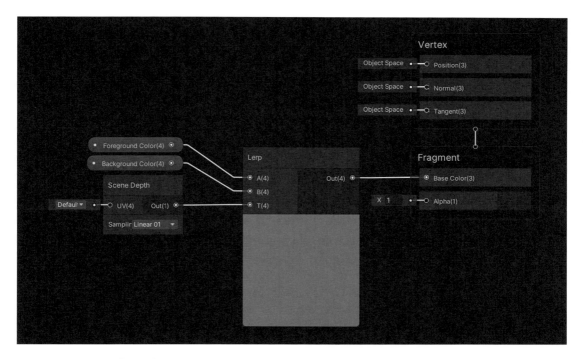

Figure 7-12. *The Silhouette graph is fairly small in size and can be created using just two properties and two extra nodes. An even slimmer graph could be made by outputting Scene Depth directly into Base Color if you don't need color customization*

Using this shader, you will see an effect much like in Figure 7-9. However, you may have noticed that sometimes, if you're using one of the custom HLSL-based shaders that we have written so far, it won't appear in the silhouette even if it is using the opaque rendering queue. This is a quirk of how Unity renders objects in the camera depth texture, which we will explore now.

Writing to the Depth Texture Using a Depth-Only Pass

Before we wrote the Silhouette effect, I mentioned that the camera depth texture is not made by merely copying the state of the depth buffer to a texture. Instead, Unity renders the opaque objects in the scene to the depth texture in a special pass that only renders depth information. We must manually add this pass to shaders if we want their depth information to be included in the depth texture, so let's see how that pass works in both the built-in pipeline and URP. Thankfully, Shader Graph handles the generation of the depth-only pass for us, so we will only need to handle this in our HLSL shaders.

Depth-Only Pass in the Built-In Pipeline

In the built-in pipeline, Unity does not support a dedicated depth-only pass. Instead, it uses the shadow-casting pass to determine which objects should be rendered into the depth texture. This pass looks the same for most objects, so a trick I like to use is to just copy the correct pass from the Standard shader.

- It's not easy to access the built-in shaders in the built-in pipeline from within the Editor. The best way to access them is through the Unity download archive:

    - Go to unity3d.com/get-unity/download/archive, select the version you are using, and use the drop-down boxes to pick "Built-in Shaders" to download them. The Standard shader will be included.

- In the source code for the Standard shader, you will find a shadow caster pass (with the name "ShadowCaster" inside the Pass block), so copy that pass to your own shader underneath the existing Pass but still inside the SubShader.

- We use the ShadowCaster pass because the built-in pipeline doesn't use a bespoke depth-only pass. Rendering depth information into the depth texture is just a side effect of the shadow-casting pass.

Note   We will be covering shadow casting in a later chapter, but we'll see a sneak peek here.

Listing 7-18. Adding a shadow caster pass to an existing shader

```
SubShader
{
    // Existing tags and other code.

    Pass
    {
        // Normal rendering pass here.
    }
```

```
Pass
{
    Name "ShadowCaster"
    Tags { "LightMode" = "ShadowCaster" }

    ZWrite On

    HLSLPROGRAM

    #pragma vertex vertShadowCaster
    #pragma fragment fragShadowCaster

    #include "UnityStandardShadow.cginc"

    #pragma multi_compile_shadowcaster
    #pragma multi_compile_instancing

    ENDHLSL
}
}
```

We don't need to discuss the ins and outs of shadow casting at this stage, but it is useful to outline generally what's going on in this pass:

- The ShadowCaster LightMode signals to Unity that this is the shadow-casting pass. The result of this pass will also be used for rendering the depth texture.

- ZWrite should be turned on.

- The vertShadowCaster and fragShadowCaster functions are exposed by the UnityStandardShadow built-in shader include file.

- The multi_compile_shadowcaster statement adds some keywords that are required for the shadow-casting pass.

- The multi_compile_instancing statement adds keywords related to instancing, which allows the GPU to process objects with this pass in batches for more efficient rendering.

When this pass is added to one of your custom shaders, we get two benefits: the object will cast shadows onto other objects (as long as the other objects handle receiving shadows), and they will be rendered into the depth texture, so any depth-based effect (such as the Silhouette shader) will feature them properly. However, we need to manually add support for shadows into every custom shader we write.

Now that we have seen how the built-in render pipeline handles rendering objects into the depth texture, let's see how URP handles it.

Depth-Only Pass in URP

In URP, we can look to the Unlit shader to see how it implements a depth-only pass. You can find the file in the Project View under *Packages* ➤ *Universal RP* ➤ *Shaders* ➤ *Unlit*. Unlike the built-in pipeline, URP supports a dedicated depth-only pass, which is separate from shadow casting, which gives us a lot more control over exactly how objects' depth is rendered.

The Unlit shader file is quite long and contains several Pass blocks; the one we are looking for is tagged with a LightMode called DepthOnly. Although it seems rather technical, thankfully we can just copy this pass over to our own shader and paste it underneath the existing Pass. I'll make a few modifications to trim down the code and then paste this into the existing TextureExample shader underneath the existing Pass but still inside the SubShader.

Listing 7-19. Adding a depth-only pass to an existing shader

```
SubShader
{
    // Existing tags and other code.

    Pass
    {
        // Normal rendering pass here.
    }
    Pass
    {
        Name "DepthOnly"
        Tags{"LightMode" = "DepthOnly"}
```

```
ZWrite On
ColorMask 0

HLSLPROGRAM

#pragma vertex DepthOnlyVertex
#pragma fragment DepthOnlyFragment

#include "Packages/com.unity.render-pipelines.universal/
Shaders/UnlitInput.hlsl"
#include "Packages/com.unity.render-pipelines.universal/
Shaders/DepthOnlyPass.hlsl"

#pragma multi_compile_instancing
#pragma multi_compile _ DOTS_INSTANCING_ON

ENDHLSL
    }
}
```

Let's very briefly deconstruct what's going on here:

- DepthOnly is one of the LightMode settings supported by URP, and it signals to the pipeline exactly what this pass is being used for. We should only include one pass that uses this LightMode tag.

- ZWrite must be on (obviously!), and we use ColorMask 0 to disable rendering to all color channels. This pass should not interfere with the screen at all.

- The DepthOnlyPass file contains the relevant vertex and fragment functions (DepthOnlyVertex and DepthOnlyFragment, respectively), while the UnlitInput file contains data that is required by DepthOnlyPass.

- The #pragma statements related to instancing allow the GPU to batch together objects that use this pass for more efficient rendering.

When we add this pass to our shaders, they will be rendered into the depth texture and show up in effects such as the Silhouette effect. We will need to copy a pass like this into every code shader if we want it to be included in the depth texture.

Note   The DepthOnlyVertex function is a regular vertex function that transforms vertices from object space to clip space. If you are performing any vertex deformation in your shader, then the DepthOnly pass will need to include the same vertex function as your existing forward pass (or a slimmed down version that only transforms vertex positions).

Now that we can render all our objects into the camera depth texture, even if they are using our own custom shaders, let's see another effect that utilizes depth.

Scene Intersections

It is useful in many shader effects to highlight portions of an object that are intersecting another object. For example, you could render a foamy shoreline on a beach where water pixels are close to the solid ground, or you could add highlights to the portions of a stylized energy shield that overlap physical objects. These shaders all require a technique that can detect which portions of a mesh are near other meshes. With the depth texture, we can devise a method for doing so.

Figure 7-13. *The black cube is intersecting the rest of the scene geometry, and the intersection points are visible. The material uses an intersection power value of 10, which results in a relatively thin intersection effect*

We will build a shader that calculates the distance from the camera of the pixel currently stored in the depth texture. For that, we can use the eye depth. By comparing that with the distance from the camera of the pixel we are about to render, we can work out the difference between the two. If the difference is small, then we class this as an intersection and color the pixel accordingly. Let's see how this works in HLSL and then in Shader Graph.

Scene Intersections in HLSL

I'll start by creating a new shader file and naming it "SceneIntersection.shader". This shader has a lot of overlap with the Silhouette shader we just wrote, so the starting code skeleton will look familiar; replace the file contents with the following code.

Listing 7-20. Skeleton code for the Scene Intersection effect

```
Shader "Examples/SceneIntersection"
{
    Properties { ...}
```

```
    SubShader
    {
        Tags
        {
            "RenderType" = "Transparent"
            "Queue" = "Transparent"
        }

        Pass
        {

            HLSLPROGRAM
            #pragma vertex vert
            #pragma fragment frag

            struct appdata
            {
                float4 positionOS : Position;
            };

            struct v2f
            {
                float4 positionCS : SV_Position;
                float4 positionSS : TEXCOORD0;
            };

            v2f vert (appdata v) { ... }

            float4 frag (v2f i) : SV_Target { ... }
            ENDHLSL
        }
    }
}
```

We will then make a series of pipeline-dependent changes to the code. These are the same changes we made when writing the Silhouette example, so make the following additions based on your pipeline:

- In the built-in pipeline, follow Listing 7-5 to set up the tags and include files properly. Then follow Listing 7-11 to set up the vertex shader.

- In URP, follow Listing 7-6 to set up the tags and include files required to make the shader work and then set up the vertex shader with Listing 7-12.

Once you've done that, then most of the shader will be set up appropriately. Next, we will deal with the properties:

- I will use a base color for the object, _BaseColor, which is black by default.

- A separate color, _IntersectColor, will be used to highlight parts of the object that intersect other objects and will be white by default.

- A float will be used to control the size of the intersections, which I will name _IntersectPower. It must be above zero, so I'll bound it between 0.01 and 100.

Listing 7-21. Adding properties to the shader in the Properties block

```
Properties
{
    _BaseColor("Base Color", Color) = (0, 0, 0, 1)
    _IntersectColor("Intersect Color", Color) = (1, 1, 1, 1)
    _IntersectPower("IntersectPower", Range(0.01, 100)) = 1
}
```

We then include these inside the HLSLPROGRAM block. In URP, include them all in the UnityPerMaterial constant buffer to meet the SRP Batcher requirements. We'll include these variables below the v2f struct definition.

Listing 7-22. Adding properties in the HLSLPROGRAM block in the built-in pipeline

```
struct v2f { ... };

sampler2D _CameraDepthTexture;

float4 _BaseColor;
float4 _IntersectColor;
float _IntersectPower;
```

Listing 7-23. Adding properties in the HLSLPROGRAM block in URP

```
struct v2f { ... };

CBUFFER_START(UnityPerMaterial)
      float4 _BaseColor;
      float4 _IntersectColor;
      float _IntersectPower;
CBUFFER_END
```

Now let's jump to the fragment shader. First, we will work out the scene eye depth, which is the distance from the camera of the object currently stored in the depth texture. We need to sample the depth texture using screen-space UVs, like we did in the Silhouette shader, so we can keep those lines of code. However, instead of using Linear01Depth, we will use the LinearEyeDepth function, which will convert the depth value into a distance (in Unity units) away from the camera. Remember that in URP only, LinearEyeDepth requires _ZBufferParams as an extra parameter.

Listing 7-24. Finding the eye-space distance of the depth texture sample in the built-in pipeline

```
float4 frag (v2f i) : SV_Target
{
      float2 screenUVs = i.positionSS.xy / i.positionSS.w;
      float rawDepth = SampleSceneDepth(screenUVs);
      float sceneEyeDepth = LinearEyeDepth(rawDepth);
```

Listing 7-25. Finding the eye-space distance of the depth texture sample in URP

```
float4 frag (v2f i) : SV_Target
{
      float2 screenUVs = i.positionSS.xy / i.positionSS.w;
      float rawDepth = SampleSceneDepth(screenUVs);
      float sceneEyeDepth = LinearEyeDepth(rawDepth, _ZBufferParams);
```

We want to compare sceneEyeDepth with the distance from the camera of the pixel we are currently rendering. This distance can be found in the *w* component of the screen position – thankfully, this is easy because we are already passing positionSS to the fragment shader.

Listing 7-26. Finding the distance of the currently rendered pixel

```
float sceneEyeDepth = LinearEyeDepth(...);
```

float screenPosW = i.positionSS.w;

From here, we can find the difference between these two distances and use whatever processing we want to make our object look nice. I'm going to produce a falloff effect where the _IntersectColor is most visible at the exact intersection point and gets weaker as pixels get further from the intersection point. In the following code example, the saturate function clamps the value between 0 and 1 so that I can correctly apply the _IntersectPower to control the size of the intersections.

Listing 7-27. Calculating the intersection strength

```
float screenPosW = i.positionSS.w;
float intersectAmount = sceneEyeDepth - screenPosW;
intersectAmount = saturate(1.0f - intersectAmount);
intersectAmount = pow(intersectAmount, _IntersectPower);
```

And finally, using the lerp function, I can blend between the _BaseColor (which is fully visible when there are no intersections) and _IntersectColor using the intersectAmount to control the blending between both colors. This gives us the return value of the fragment shader.

Listing 7-28. Using lerp to blend between two colors

```
intersectAmount = pow(intersectAmount, _IntersectPower);
```

return lerp(_BaseColor, _IntersectColor, intersectAmount);

If we were to apply this shader to an object through a material, then we would start to see the intersections as the object moves closer to other objects. The usefulness of this shader is somewhat limited in its current form, but you can incorporate this code into other shaders to introduce intersections to them. From there, you can style the intersections however you like. In Figure 7-13, the cube on the top-left has the Scene Intersection shader applied to it and is mostly black. It is intersecting the other scene geometry, and you can see a bright-white highlight where the intersections occur.

Now that we have seen how to use the depth texture to create scene intersections in HLSL, let's see how to do the same in Shader Graph.

Scene Intersections in Shader Graph

For this effect, I will be using a new Unlit graph, so right-click in the Project View and go to *Create* ➤ *Shader* ➤ *Universal Render Pipeline* ➤ *Unlit Shader Graph*. The first thing we must do is go to the Graph Settings tab and change the Surface mode to Transparent (as seen in Figure 7-14), which will allow us to access the Scene Depth node.

Figure 7-14. *Making the shader transparent in the Graph Settings*

Once we've done that, let's talk about the properties. As I outlined in the HLSL version of this effect, we need three properties, each of which is shown in Figure 7-15:

- A Color called Base Color, which is black by default.

- A Color called Intersect Color, which appears only where the object intersects another object.

- A Float called Intersect Power, which controls the size of the intersection effect. The higher this value is, the thinner the intersection glow is. This property should be bounded between 0.01 and a high value like 100.

Figure 7-15. *Adding properties to the graph*

With these properties in place, we will now calculate the two distances we want to compare, as shown in Figure 7-16:

- The first is the distance from the camera of the previous object drawn into the depth texture, which we can access by using a Scene Depth node in *Eye* mode.

- The second is the distance from the camera of the pixel we are currently rendering, which we can get using a Screen Position node in *Raw* mode – the value we want is the *w* component, which we access with a Split node.

- By subtracting the second value from the first, we get a distance metric that tells us how far away the pixel being rendered is from a floor, wall, or any other object.

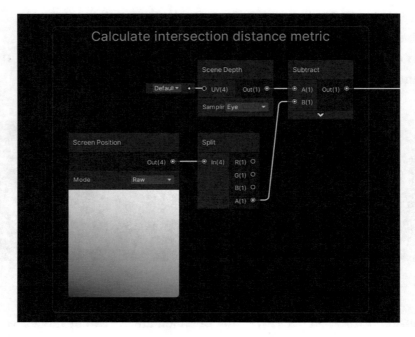

Figure 7-16. *Calculating a distance metric that tells us how far away a pixel is from other surfaces*

This value gives us the distance of the current pixel from other surfaces. I want this shader effect to use the Intersect Color when the pixel lies exactly on an intersection point and have a smooth blending falloff toward Base Color as pixels get further away from an intersection. With that in mind, I use the following nodes to modify the values we have obtained so far:

- I use a One Minus node to obtain a value that is 1 at the intersection point and falls as pixels get further from the intersection.

- The Saturate node is used to clamp values between 0 and 1, because negative values will prevent the next part from working as intended.

- The Power node lets us control the size of the falloff region by using the Intersect Power property. Since all values are between 0 and 1, taking a power higher than 1 will reduce the values, resulting in a thinner intersection falloff region.

- I use a Lerp node to blend between the Base Color and Intersect Color properties and then output the result to the graph's *Base Color* output.

The second half of the graph can be seen in Figure 7-17.

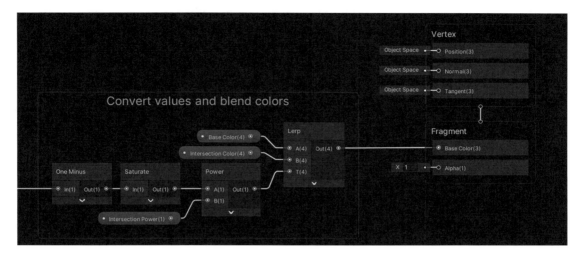

Figure 7-17. *Modifying the distance values and blending between output colors*

The result of this graph is identical to the HLSL version of the shader (seen in Figure 7-13).

We have now seen that the depth buffer is instrumental to correctly rendering opaque objects onto the screen and that the depth texture can be leveraged for some interesting effects in your games. Next, we will look at another buffer that is often stored alongside the depth buffer and can be used for even more effects: the stencil buffer.

The Stencil Buffer

The *stencil buffer* is an additional 2D data buffer that stores an integer value for each pixel on the screen. Using the stencil buffer, we can "remember" which parts of the screen were rendered by certain objects by changing their stencil values and, later, read the stencil buffer values back to customize how we render other objects. For example, we can mask certain portions of the screen so that other objects are prevented from being rendered there.

The stencil buffer is usually implemented as an extension to the depth buffer. Typically, we use 24 bits per pixel for the depth buffer and 8 bits per pixel for the stencil buffer, although these values can be lower on certain platforms such as mobile. Since the stencil buffer stores integers, this leaves us with possible stencil values between 0 and 255 – the default value is 0. Like with the depth buffer, we can also use *stencil testing* to determine how objects are rendered. Let's see how it works in HLSL.

> **Note**   Unfortunately, stencils are not yet supported in Shader Graph. That means you will have to rely on code shaders for any effects that read or write stencil buffer values. It's a shame because Shader Graph would be much more powerful with this functionality!

Stencil Testing in HLSL

A stencil test, much like a depth test, can be used to decide whether to render a pixel. If the stencil test passes, then Unity will carry out the depth test immediately afterward and render the pixel based on the outcome of *both* tests. If the stencil test fails, then the pixel is not rendered. Unlike the depth test, we have finer control over what happens when the stencil test fails; whereas the depth buffer will never be overwritten on a failed depth test, we can modify the stencil buffer on a failed stencil test. Let's see how this all works. To use the stencil buffer to its fullest potential, we need to create two shaders: one that writes values to the stencil buffer and one that reads values back from the buffer. With that in mind, let's create an effect that uses a stencil mask shader to write values to the stencil buffer and a second shader that only draws objects in the positions written by the mask shader.

Stencil Mask Shader

Let's create a new shader file and name it "StencilMask.shader". Inside this file, we are going to write a shader that will overwrite the stencil buffer value with a new value that we can customize. Since the purpose of this shader is only to write to the stencil buffer, we will not include a vertex or fragment shader, which means the object will be invisible.

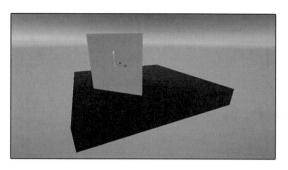 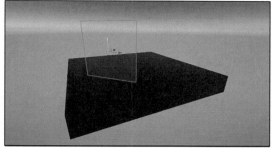

Figure 7-18. *A quad mesh selected in the Scene View, before adding the mask shader (on the left) and after (on the right)*

This shader will contain a single SubShader, which itself contains a single Pass. With that in mind, here is the skeleton shader I will be working with.

Listing 7-29. Skeleton stencil mask shader

```
Shader "Examples/StencilMask"
{
    Properties { ... }

    SubShader
    {
        Tags { ... }

        Pass { ... }
    }
    Fallback Off
}
```

When we use this mask shader on a material, it will be useful to be able to customize the stencil value we'll use to overwrite the existing stencil buffer value. We can use a shader property to do so. The stencil reference must be an integer between 0 and 255 inclusive, so I will use the Range type to bound the value and the [IntRange] attribute to force the value to be an integer. The _StencilRef property is the only property the shader requires.

Listing 7-30. Adding a reference property that is forced to be an integer between 0 and 255

```
Properties
{
        [IntRange] _StencilRef("Stencil Ref", Range(0, 255)) = 1
}
```

This stencil mask needs to render itself before we render opaque objects, because we may wish to use this mask to customize the way those opaque objects are rendered. We can force Unity to do that by modifying the Queue to be Geometry-1 inside the SubShader Tags. URP requires an extra RenderPipeline tag that is not required in the built-in pipeline.

Listing 7-31. Modifying the Queue to ensure the mask is rendered before other opaques in the built-in pipeline

```
Tags
{
        "RenderType" = "Opaque"
        "Queue" = "Geometry-1"
}
```

Listing 7-32. Modifying the Queue to ensure the mask is rendered before other opaques in URP

```
Tags
{
        "RenderType" = "Opaque"
        "Queue" = "Geometry-1"
        "RenderPipeline" = "UniversalPipeline"
}
```

Next, we will see a stencil inside a shader for the first time. Stencil is a block that contains many keywords that control this shader's interactions with the stencil buffer. This block should be added at the top of the Pass.

Listing 7-33. The Stencil block

```
Pass
{
    Stencil { ... }
}
```

The first thing we include in the Stencil block is the stencil reference value, for which we use the Ref keyword. For example, if we say Ref 1, then this shader will use a reference value of 1 to perform the stencil test. However, we created a property for this because we want to be able to edit the value, which will allow us to create several unique stencil masks if we want. We can use the _StencilRef property inside the Stencil block like the following.

Listing 7-34. Specifying a stencil reference value in the Stencil block

```
Stencil
{
    Ref[_StencilRef]
}
```

Next, we provide a comparison function with the Comp keyword. Like with the depth test, Unity will compare the reference value we provided with the value already in the stencil buffer at this pixel position. At the start of each frame, the entire stencil buffer is reset to 0, so assuming we are not writing a stencil before the Geometry-1 queue, 0 is the value we are comparing against. There are eight comparison functions, which are the same as the eight depth test functions: LEqual, Less, GEqual, Greater, Equal, NotEqual, Always, and Never.

For the stencil mask shader, we always want the stencil test to pass, so we will specify Comp Always.

Listing 7-35. Providing a comparison function for the stencil test

```
Stencil
{
    Ref[_StencilRef]
    Comp Always
}
```

Now we need to decide what happens on a successful or unsuccessful stencil test. Unlike the depth test, where the depth buffer value is overwritten automatically on a passed depth test (if ZWrite is On) and left alone on a failed test, with stencils, we can customize what happens in both circumstances. There is a higher degree of control with stencil testing than with depth testing.

We can do that with the Pass and Fail keywords, respectively. There are eight types of behavior that we can choose from:

- *Keep* – Do not modify the stencil buffer value.

- *Zero* – Change the buffer value to zero. Zero is the default value of the stencil buffer at the start of a frame.

- *Replace* – Overwrite the buffer value with the reference value, defined with the Ref keyword.

- *IncrSat* – Increase the buffer value by one. If it would exceed the maximum value, 255, it stays at 255 instead.

- *DecrSat* – Decrease the buffer value by one. If it would fall below zero, set it to zero instead.

- *Invert* – Invert each bit of the buffer value. Since the buffer contains unsigned 8-bit integers, this is the same as taking 255 minus the buffer value.

- *IncrWrap* – Increase the buffer value by one. If it would exceed the maximum value, 255, set it to zero instead.

- *DecrWrap* – Decrease the buffer value by one. If it would fall below zero, set it to 255 instead.

The default behavior for both the Pass and Fail cases is to Keep the existing value. In our case, we want to replace the buffer value when the stencil test passes, which we can do by saying Pass Replace. We don't care what happens on a failed stencil test in this scenario, since it will never happen with Comp Always.

Listing 7-36. Replacing the stencil value on a passed stencil test

```
Stencil
{
    Ref[_StencilRef]
    Comp Always
    Pass Replace
}
```

Finally, we must ensure that the mask does not write to the depth buffer, because this would prevent any opaque objects from appearing behind the mask if they are using the default z-testing behavior. We can do that with `ZWrite Off`, which we can specify just below the `Stencil` block.

Listing 7-37. Preventing the stencil mask from writing depth

```
Stencil { ... }
```
ZWrite Off

If we add a quad mesh to the scene and attach this shader to it using a material, then it should appear invisible regardless of the stencil reference we provide, as in Figure 7-18. No matter which direction you view the mesh from, it won't appear. Behind the scenes, however, it is modifying the stencil buffer; it's time to create a shader that will read from it.

Reading the Stencil Buffer

This will be a basic shader that samples a single texture and multiples the result by a base color value to obtain the output color of each pixel. The difference is this shader will also read from the stencil buffer and pixels will only be rendered if it finds certain values in the stencil buffer.

I will start by creating a new shader file, which I will name "StencilTexture.shader". I'll start with the following base code, which will look familiar if you followed the TextureExample section from Chapter 5.

Listing 7-38. The StencilTexture code skeleton

```
Shader "Examples/StencilTexture"
{
    Properties
    {
        _BaseColor ("Base Color", Color) = (1, 1, 1, 1)
        _BaseTex("Base Texture", 2D) = "white" {}
    }
    SubShader
    {
        Tags
        {
            "RenderType" = "Opaque"
            "Queue" = "Geometry"
        }

        Pass
        {
            HLSLPROGRAM
            #pragma vertex vert
            #pragma fragment frag

            struct appdata
            {
                float4 positionOS : Position;
                float2 uv : TEXCOORD0;
            };

            struct v2f
            {
                float4 positionCS : SV_Position;
                float2 uv : TEXCOORD0;
            };
```

```
v2f vert (appdata v) { ... }

float4 frag (v2f i) : SV_Target
{
        float4 textureSample = tex2D(_BaseTex, i.uv);
        return textureSample * _BaseColor;
}
ENDHLSL
            }
        }
}
```

Let's set up the parts of this shader that are pipeline dependent. In the built-in pipeline, we'll need to include the UnityCG.cginc library file. In URP, we'll include Core. hlsl and add a couple extra tags.

Listing 7-39. Setting up include files in the built-in pipeline

```
HLSLPROGRAM
#pragma vertex vert
#pragma fragment frag

#include "UnityCG.cginc"
```

Listing 7-40. Setting up tags and include files in URP

```
Tags
{
    "RenderType" = "Opaque"
    "Queue" = "Geometry"
    "RenderPipeline" = "UniversalPipeline"
}

Pass
{
    Tags
    {
        "LightMode" = "UniversalForward"
    }
```

```
HLSLPROGRAM
#pragma vertex vert
#pragma fragment frag
```

**#include "Packages/com.unity.render-pipelines.universal/
ShaderLibrary/Core.hlsl"**

We'll also need to sort out the vertex shader. It's a simple vertex shader that converts object-space vertex positions to clip space, but it requires a different function in each pipeline. Thankfully, the TRANSFORM_TEX macro for applying texture tiling and offset values to the UV coordinates exists in all pipelines.

Listing 7-41. The vertex shader in the built-in pipeline

```
v2f vert (appdata v)
{
    v2f o;
    o.positionCS = UnityObjectToClipPos(v.positionOS);
    o.uv = TRANSFORM_TEX(v.uv, _BaseTex);
    return o;
}
```

Listing 7-42. The vertex shader in URP

```
v2f vert (appdata v)
{
    v2f o;
    o.positionCS = TransformObjectToHClip(v.positionOS.xyz);
    o.uv = TRANSFORM_TEX(v.uv, _BaseTex);
    return o;
}
```

At this stage, we now have a fully functional shader that will sample a texture and display it on the object, so now we can introduce stencil support. We'll add a stencil reference value to the Properties block and modify the shader so that it only renders a pixel if the reference value equals the existing stencil value in the stencil buffer. We can use the same _StencilRef property we used for the stencil mask shader so that we can customize the reference value.

Listing 7-43. Adding a stencil reference property

```
Properties
{
     _BaseColor ("Base Color", Color) = (1, 1, 1, 1)
     _BaseTex("Base Texture", 2D) = "white" {}
     [IntRange] _StencilRef("Stencil Ref", Range(0, 255)) = 1
}
```

Note   The IntRange attribute makes it so that this property can only take on integer values in the specified range when modifying the property's value in the Inspector.

This shader already uses the Geometry rendering queue, which will be rendered after the stencil mask, so we can leave it as is. Let's now read from the stencil buffer. For this, we use the same syntax as before: we add a Stencil block at the very start of the Pass block and provide a reference value with the Ref keyword. Since we added the same _StencilRef property, we will use that as the reference value.

This time, however, we wish to only render pixels where the buffer value matches the reference value. For that, we can use Comp Equal. Regardless of whether the stencil test passes or fails, we want to preserve the value already in the stencil buffer. That's the default behavior if we don't specify Pass or Fail keywords, but I want to make this behavior explicit so I will use Keep for both.

Listing 7-44. Adding stencil support to the texture shader. Pixels are only drawn if the reference equals the buffer value, and the buffer value is left unchanged after the test

```
Pass
{
     Stencil
     {
          Ref[_StencilRef]
          Comp Equal
          Pass Keep
          Fail Keep
     }
```

We don't need to do modify ZWrite on this shader, as the default behavior is fine. Both shaders are now complete, so we can see what would happen if we attached the stencil-compatible version of the texture shader to a cube and placed it partially behind the stencil mask seen in Figure 7-18.

In Figure 7-19, we see two examples. In both examples, the stencil mask is writing a stencil value of 1. In the left example, the cube is also using a stencil reference value of 1, which means that only sections of the cube that are *inside* the mask will get drawn. Conversely, in the right example, the cube uses a stencil value of 0, which means parts of the cube *outside* the mask are drawn, since the rest of the scene has a stencil value of 0 by default. If we were to give the cube any other stencil reference value, none of it would be drawn.

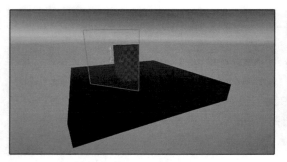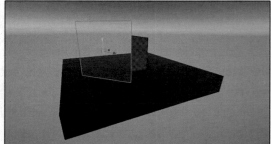

Figure 7-19. *In the left example, the cube and the mask (which is selected in Unity for clarity) have the same stencil reference. In the right example, they do not*

We have seen how modifying depth and stencil behavior in shaders can lead to some powerful effects. However, this often requires a lot of work to get working. If you want to add support for special depth or stencil effects, it requires you to retrofit existing shaders with new code, which is time-consuming if you have many shaders that require support for these features. In URP, there is a mechanism we can use that removes a significant amount of the hard work involved without needing to use shaders at all.

URP Renderer Features

URP Renderer Features can be used to inject custom render passes over the entire screen, among other things. So why am I bringing them up in the middle of a chapter about depth and stencils? As it turns out, URP includes a Renderer Feature called Render

Objects that lets us configure the depth and stencil settings on layers of objects without even needing to use shaders. With Render Objects, we can create a handful of powerful effects without needing to delve into HLSL or Shader Graph at all.

Note   The following effects will make use of Unity's layer system. If your project makes extensive use of layers for other purposes, keep in mind that there are only 32 available layers (some of which are reserved by Unity), so this may be a limiting factor preventing you from using these effects. In most games, it is unlikely you will reach the limit of 32 layers, however.

To use a Renderer Feature, first locate your project's Renderer Asset. In the URP template project, you can find this under *Assets* ➤ *Settings* ➤ *ForwardRenderer*, and it is next to the URP Assets. Clicking it will bring up the following information in the Inspector (shown in Figure 7-20).

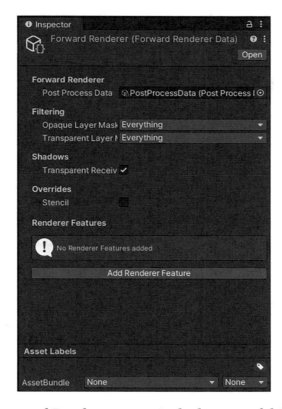

Figure 7-20. *The Forward Renderer asset. At the bottom of this window, we can add Renderer Features to customize certain aspects of the rendering loop*

It is possible to write your own Renderer Features (although that is out of the scope of this chapter), and Unity includes two out of the box. If you click the Add Renderer Feature button seen near the bottom of Figure 7-20, you can add either a Screen Space Ambient Occlusion feature, which you may find useful, or a Render Objects feature, which we are going to focus on.

Render Objects

The Render Objects feature is a powerful tool we can use to customize parts of the rendering loop, namely, depth and stencil testing. When you add one to your Renderer Asset, a new section will appear at the bottom, as seen in Figure 7-21. The feature has several options we will explore.

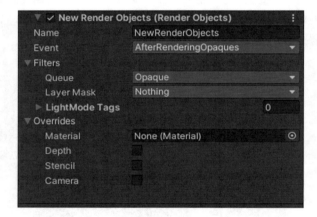

Figure 7-21. *A new Render Objects feature*

The first option is the *Name*, which we use to describe what the feature is for. It's best not to leave this as the default, as it will be difficult to remember what the feature is doing just by glancing at the settings.

The second option is the *Event*, which controls when this feature runs in the rendering loop. Renderer Features don't work quite the same as rendering objects in the standard way; instead, Unity exposes certain "milestones" throughout the rendering process and will render objects at those points in time. The name of each event is self-explanatory, and the possible values are

- BeforeRenderingPrepasses

- AfterRenderingPrePasses

- BeforeRenderingOpaques

- AfterRenderingOpaques

- BeforeRenderingSkybox

- AfterRenderingSkybox

- BeforeRenderingTransparents

- AfterRenderingTransparents

- BeforeRenderingPostProcessing

- AfterRenderingPostProcessing

- AfterRendering

The default value is AfterRenderingOpaques, which will run after Unity has finished rendering all opaque objects in the scene.

Next, there is a section for *Filters*, which lets us restrict which objects the Render Objects feature will run on. We can choose to run only on *Opaque* or *Transparent* objects using the *Queue* option, and we use the *Layer Mask* to restrict which layers the effect operates on. When using Render Objects, I often place all objects in a dedicated layer and use a layer mask containing only that layer. We can also choose to render only certain passes by specifying them in the *LightMode Tags* section.

The final drop-down section is the *Overrides* section. You can think of this section as "what the feature actually does." Here, we can choose to override the depth and stencil tests to use whatever behavior we want. This means that any objects within the layer mask and queue we specified will not use the depth and/or stencil settings contained in their own shader, but instead will use the values in the feature. There is the option to provide an override material; if you do, then Unity will swap out the material already on an object to the override material if the depth and stencil tests pass.

The *Camera* option inside Overrides lets us tweak the camera properties while rendering the layer. By changing the *Field Of View* and the *Position Offset*, we can act as if the camera has different settings from normal. If we tick the *Restore* option, then Unity will return the camera to the settings it had before this Render Objects feature ran.

Talking about Render Objects in abstract like this doesn't really illuminate the power of such feature, however. To show you what Render Objects (and Renderer Features in general) is capable of, let's create a couple of effects that use it and compare the process of using Render Objects with the workflow of manually writing shaders that do a similar thing.

X-Ray Effect Using Depth

Many games feature a mechanic that lets you see objects through walls. For example, some games have a scanner that lets you see valuable items in the vicinity of your character, while other games, such as stealth games, sometimes let you "tag" enemies so that you can continue to see them anywhere, even behind walls. In these games, the appearance of the object often changes when it is rendered behind a wall.

We can create this effect using the depth buffer. When an object is in front of all walls and other obstacles, we will use *less-equal* depth testing to render the object "normally," and when they are obstructed, we can detect that using *greater* depth testing and render the object with an x-ray shader.

Although we can create this effect with Render Objects, that won't help us if we're using the built-in pipeline! And besides, even if you are using URP, it will still be useful to compare the Render Objects approach with the classic shader approach. Let's see how the effect is made with shaders first.

X-Ray Effect with HLSL

To create this effect with HLSL shaders, we are going to require two shader passes. Right off the bat, this is going to cause problems; the built-in render pipeline supports multipass shaders for general rendering purposes, but URP does not. Therefore, we are going to use a different approach to create the shader for each pipeline using HLSL, but we will end up with the same result. We will also cover an alternative approach using URP Render Objects that you can take if you wish.

There are many ways you could visualize the x-ray objects when they are behind a wall – some games use a completely different style of shader from the "normal" shader for the objects – but we are going to keep things simple and use a block color for the x-ray objects.

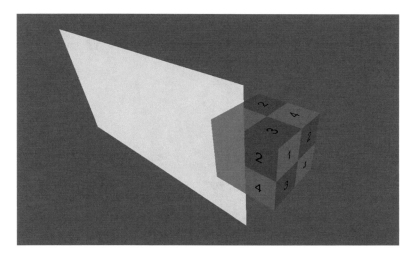

Figure 7-22. *The cube has the x-ray shader attached. The right-hand side of the cube is unobstructed, so it is textured. The left-hand part is occluded by the wall, so the cube is rendered in block red*

X-Ray Effect with HLSL in the Built-in Pipeline

This is our first multipass shader, unless you count the depth-only passes we worked with earlier! Don't worry – it's not overly complicated. I will start by creating a new shader and naming it "Xray.shader". It will include two passes:

- The first will render whenever the object is in front of all other objects. It will display the object normally (I'll use a simple texture shader to illustrate this).

- The second will render whenever the object is behind any other. It will render that part of the object in a block color.

With that in mind, here's the structure of the shader file I'll be starting with and making additions to.

Listing 7-45. The x-ray shader code skeleton

```
Shader "Examples/Xray"
{
    Properties
    {
```

```
        _BaseColor ("Base Color", Color) = (1, 1, 1, 1)
        _BaseTex ("Base Texture", 2D) = "white" {}
    }
    SubShader
    {
        Tags
        {
            "RenderType" = "Opaque"
            "Queue" = "Geometry"
        }

        Pass
        {
            HLSLPROGRAM
            #pragma vertex vert
            #pragma fragment frag

            #include "UnityCG.cginc"

            struct appdata { ... };

            struct v2f { ... };

            v2f vert (appdata v) { ... }
            float4 frag (v2f i) : SV_TARGET  { ... }

            ENDHLSL
        }

        Pass
        {
            HLSLPROGRAM
            #pragma vertex vert
            #pragma fragment frag

            #include "UnityCG.cginc"

            struct appdata { ... };
            struct v2f { ... };
```

```
            v2f vert (appdata v) { ... }
            float4 frag (v2f i) : SV_TARGET { ... }

            ENDHLSL
        }
    }
}
```

In multipass shaders, there is still only one set of `Properties`, which is shared between all passes, so I will add a new `Color` property called `_XrayColor` to control the color of the object when it is behind walls. This color is used in the second pass only. I'm going to make it pure red by default, so it will be obvious when it is being used.

Listing 7-46. Adding an x-ray Color property

```
Properties
{
    _BaseColor ("Base Color", Color) = (1, 1, 1, 1)
    _BaseTex ("Base Texture", 2D) = "white" {}
    _XrayColor("X-ray Color", Color) = (1, 0, 0, 1)
}
```

Inside a SubShader, it is possible to include multiple `Pass` blocks that carry out different shader code, and Unity will run each one in render queue order, from top to bottom. I've included two passes in this shader, so let's fill in the details for each pass separately.

Note   The render queues of the passes have an impact on rendering order. If two `Pass` blocks both use the `Geometry` queue, then they are rendered in top-to-bottom order. However, if the top pass uses the `Transparent` queue and the bottom one uses the `Geometry` queue, then the bottom one is still rendered first to maintain queue ordering.

Textured Pass

We will make the z-testing in the first pass explicit. Recall that, by default, a shader will use ZTest LEqual and ZWrite On if no ZTest or ZWrite is specified. However, it will be useful to anyone looking at this shader later to make this behavior explicit, since we will be using different behavior in the second pass. At the top of the first Pass, I will include the following code.

Listing 7-47. Making the z-testing in the first Pass explicit

```
Pass
{
        ZTest LEqual
        ZWrite On
```

> **Note**   Even though a lot of shader behavior is implicit, it is sometimes very helpful to write it explicitly in the code, like the z-testing behavior I've included here. When someone reads your shader code, it may help to make it easier to discern what your shader is doing and clarify the design decisions you made while writing the shader.

The rest of the pass is a straightforward texture sampling vertex and fragment shader pair that we have seen before, so I will just fill in the rest of the pass contents here.

Listing 7-48. The texture sampling shader pass

```
struct appdata
{
        float4 positionOS : POSITION;
        float2 uv : TEXCOORD0;
};

struct v2f
{
        float4 positionCS : SV_POSITION;
        float2 uv : TEXCOORD0;
};
```

```
float4 _BaseColor;
sampler2D _BaseTex;
float4 _BaseTex_ST;

v2f vert (appdata v)
{
    v2f o;
    o.positionCS = UnityObjectToClipPos(v.positionOS);
    o.uv = TRANSFORM_TEX(v.uv, _BaseTex);
    return o;
}

float4 frag (v2f i) : SV_TARGET
{
    float4 textureSample = tex2D(_BaseTex, i.uv);
    return textureSample * _BaseColor;
}
```

With that in mind, let's look at the second pass and see how it differs from the first.

X-Ray Pass

For the second pass, we want to use a different depth test. Although we will be drawing objects behind others, we don't want to replace the values in the depth buffer because that may interfere with the normal rendering of other objects. The new ZTest and ZWrite look like the following.

Listing 7-49. Using different depth testing and writing behavior in the second pass

```
Pass
{
    ZTest Greater
    ZWrite Off
```

In this pass, we won't be using any texturing, and the only property we need is
_XrayColor, so the appdata struct, v2f struct, and vert function will be stripped-down
versions of the corresponding ones from the first pass, missing all texture-related code.
Here's what they look like in the second pass.

Listing 7-50. Stripping away texture support and including the x-ray Color
property

```
struct appdata
{
	float4 positionOS : POSITION;
};

struct v2f
{
	float4 positionCS : SV_POSITION;
};

float4 _XrayColor;

v2f vert (appdata v)
{
	v2f o;
	o.positionCS = UnityObjectToClipPos(v.positionOS);
	return o;
}
```

That just leaves the frag function. All it needs to do is return _XrayColor
immediately.

Listing 7-51. Returning the x-ray color in the fragment function

```
float4 frag (v2f i) : SV_TARGET
{
	return _XrayColor;
}
```

The shader effect is now complete, and as you'll notice, the second pass looks a lot like the HelloWorld shader we wrote back in Chapter 3, except for the `ZTest` and `ZWrite` statements. If we attach the shader to an object, then we can see that it appears textured when unobstructed and block-colored when behind a wall, as in Figure 7-22.

Although we ended up with an effect that is rendered exactly as we wanted, this approach has a handful of limitations that might not make it an ideal choice for your game:

- The x-ray effect and the "normal" effect are tied together in a single shader. If you wanted to add x-ray support to several types of existing shader, you would have to manually add it to each shader.

- To enable and disable the x-ray effect on specific objects, you have two choices:

  - You can swap the material of the object from a version that does not include the x-ray pass to one that does or vice versa. This means you need to duplicate the number of shader files you have.

  - Or you can include a toggle somewhere in the x-ray pass that disables it at will. However, the pass will still be executed, which introduces overhead on all objects that you anticipate possibly enabling the x-ray feature on at any point.

If you want to create this same effect in URP with an HLSL-only approach, you avoid some of these problems, but others persist. Let's see how this effect can be created with HLSL with URP.

X-Ray Effect with HLSL in URP

URP does not support multiple "normal" shader passes in a single shader file due to intentional design constraints. Instead, we must use two shaders and attach them to an object using two materials. With that in mind, this is the approach I'll take in URP:

- For the "normal" texturing shader, I will use the TextureExample shader we wrote in Chapter 5. A material with this shader should be attached to one of the object's material slots.

- For the x-ray effect to be visible when the object is behind walls, we will write a shader in this section to do just that. A material with this shader should also be attached to a different material slot on the object.

I'll start by creating a new shader file and naming it "Xray.shader". This shader has a single pass, but it will look a lot like the second pass we wrote for the built-in pipeline version of this effect:

- We'll include a single property, _XrayColor, to tint portions of the object that are behind walls.

- We use ZTest Greater to test whether the object is behind a wall.

- We must turn ZWrite Off to prevent the x-ray pass from improperly interfering with the rendering of other objects.

Here is the complete shader.

Listing 7-52. The x-ray shader in URP

```
Shader "Examples/Xray"
{
    Properties
    {
        _XrayColor("X-ray Color", Color) = (1, 0, 0, 1)
    }
    SubShader
    {
        Tags
        {
            "RenderType" = "Opaque"
            "Queue" = "Geometry"
            "RenderPipeline" = "UniversalPipeline"
        }

        Pass
        {
            ZTest Greater
            ZWrite Off
```

```
Tags
{
     "LightMode" = "UniversalForward"
}

HLSLPROGRAM
#pragma vertex vert
#pragma fragment frag

#include "Packages/com.unity.render-pipelines.universal/
ShaderLibrary/Core.hlsl"

struct appdata
{
     float4 positionOS : POSITION;
};
struct v2f
{
     float4 positionCS : SV_POSITION;
};

CBUFFER_START(UnityPerMaterial)
     float4 _XrayColor;
CBUFFER_END

v2f vert(appdata v)
{
     v2f o;
     o.positionCS = TransformObjectToHClip(v.
     positionOS);
     return o;
}

float4 frag(v2f i) : SV_TARGET
{
     return _XrayColor;
}
```

```
                        ENDHLSL
                }
        }
}
```

Your objects should now look like Figure 7-22. With this approach, we no longer have the problem that our x-ray code is tied to the texturing shader code, so if we wanted to apply the x-ray functionality to an object using a different shader, we could just attach it as a second material. However, enabling and disabling the x-ray effect still requires managing the materials attached to a given object, which is cumbersome. In URP, there is a way around this with Render Objects.

X-Ray Effect with URP Render Objects (No Code)

Let's see an alternative approach that requires no code and uses Render Objects. Throughout this process, we can use shaders that we wrote in previous chapters (including ones we wrote with Shader Graph):

- Attach any shader you want to the object's material slots to render it "normally." We won't need to mess with adding or removing materials to or from any object. In this example, I will use TextureExample for this purpose.

- We will use the HelloWorld shader for the x-ray material. For now, just create the material and use any color you want, but don't attach it to anything.

We will need to use two Render Objects features for this effect.

Rendering Objects Behind Walls

Start by adding a dedicated new layer by selecting any GameObject and choosing *Layers ➤ Add Layer* at the top of the Inspector or by going to *Edit ➤ Project Settings ➤ Tags and Layers*. I'll call mine "Xray", as in Figure 7-23. Add a few objects to this layer – you should see no visual changes yet. These objects can use different materials if you'd like.

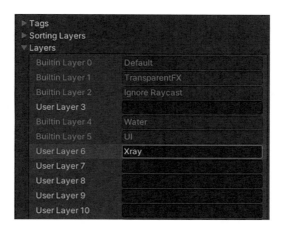

Figure 7-23. *Adding an Xray layer to the layer list*

Next, find your Renderer Asset (as shown in Figure 7-20). Near the top of the asset's options, you should see a *Filtering* section with an option called *Opaque Layer Mask*. We need to exclude the *Xray* layer from this mask, which will make any objects in the layer disappear from the Scene View. Then add a Render Objects feature to your Renderer Asset. I'm going to rename mine to something more descriptive like "Xray Objects Behind Wall", as shown in Figure 7-24.

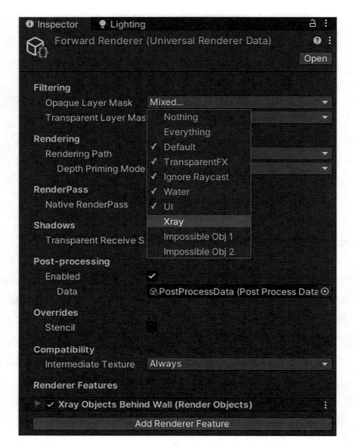

Figure 7-24. *Removing the Xray layer from the layer mask and adding a Render Objects feature*

Here's how the feature should work, as shown in Figure 7-25:

- Since we are dealing only with opaques currently, we can leave the *Event* as *AfterRenderingOpaques*.

- We need to change the *Layer Mask* to contain only the *Xray* layer, at which point all your objects should pop back into existence.

- When you expand the *Overrides* section and tick the *Depth* option, *Write Depth* is on by default, and the *Depth Test* option is set to *Less Equal*.

- These are the same as the default values in a shader, which is not what we want.

- If the objects wrote depth information while behind a wall, it would override the wall's depth from the depth buffer and potentially impact the rendering of any objects left to be rendered (such as transparents), so we need to untick *Write Depth*.

- We will also use a *Greater* depth test instead.

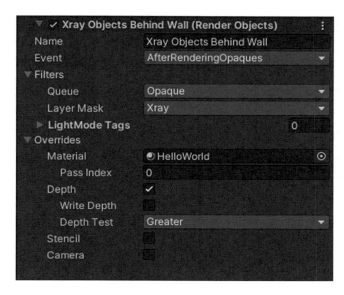

Figure 7-25. *The completed Xray Objects Behind Wall feature*

Now the object should be rendered where we want – only when behind a wall – but using its existing material, so I'll drag a material that uses the HelloWorld shader onto the *Material* slot under the *Overrides* section. All objects in the Xray layer now only appear when behind walls, as seen in Figure 7-26.

Figure 7-26. *Objects in the Xray layer can only be seen when obstructed by a wall or another opaque object. In this example, a cube can only be seen in the area where it is usually obscured by the wall – the override material uses the HelloWorld shader with a pure red color*

The first Render Objects feature is now complete, and it should look like Figure 7-26. Now that we can render objects that are hidden behind other objects, let's add back the normal rendering of the objects when they are unobstructed.

Rendering Unobstructed Objects

Add another Render Objects feature to your Renderer Asset and name it something descriptive like "Xray Objects Unobstructed". All we need to do on this one is to change the *Layer Mask* to *Xray* – everything else can be left alone. Since the default behavior on a Render Objects feature is to use ZTest LEqual and ZWrite On, we don't need to override the depth testing ourselves on the Xray Objects Unobstructed feature. The full feature settings can be seen in Figure 7-27.

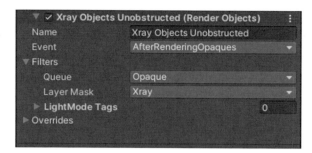

Figure 7-27. *The completed Xray Objects Unobstructed feature*

When you add this feature, the objects in that layer will appear again when unobstructed, and they will use their original materials since we have not provided an override material. See Figure 7-28.

Figure 7-28. *A cube is rendered with a red override material where it is obscured by the wall (on the left), but is rendered normally when it is unobscured (on the right)*

Note   If you are going to be drawing transparent objects with this method, then also remove the Xray layer from the Transparent Layer Mask on the Renderer Asset and include two additional Render Objects features that operate on the Transparent queue and use the AfterRenderingTransparents event.

Although the result of both approaches looks the same, there are some workflow advantages to using Render Objects for an effect like this:

- There is no code modification required for this method. Not only do we avoid needing to retroactively add support for a second pass or create new shaders but this also means you can create the effect entirely within the Unity Editor.

- You can use any material in the Override slot for the Xray Objects Behind Wall feature and swap it at any time if you want. With the multipass code shader approach, you might have to modify a shader file heavily to change the material like that.

- Toggling an object to use the x-ray effect is easy as adding or removing it to or from the Xray layer. With a code shader approach, you would have to access and change the material on the object's renderer component.

The Render Objects feature also has support for stencil overriding. In the next effect, we will exploit this functionality extensively to help create a room containing impossible geometry, where multiple objects possess the same physical space, but each can only be viewed from a certain direction.

Impossible Room Effect Using Stencils

The effect we are going to design next involves placing two sets of objects in the same room, such that they inhabit the same physical space. Using stencil masks, we can instruct Unity to render only one set of objects if we view the room from one angle and the other set of objects if we view the room from another angle. Using this trick, it will appear to a player as if a single space contains two disjoint sets of objects at the same time, which is, of course, impossible in the real world. For that reason, I call this the "impossible room" effect. Let's see how to build the effect in HLSL and then use Render Objects to make it easier to use *any* shader we want on the objects inside the room without needing to manually modify them to add stencil support.

Note   Remember that stencils are not available in Shader Graph, so we will be unable to create this effect using it.

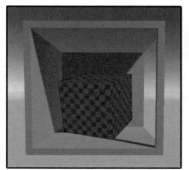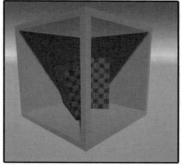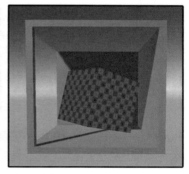

Figure 7-29. *An impossible room containing two cubes, seen from three different angles: in front of each of the two open faces and a view from the corner between the two faces*

Impossible Room Effect with HLSL

We have already created two shaders that we can use for this effect: the StencilMask shader, which can be used to write a specific value to the stencil buffer, and the StencilTexture shader (the modified stencil-compatible version of TextureExample), which we can force to only render if a specific stencil value is present in the stencil buffer. Let's see how to put together the effect.

First, we must set up a sample scene. I have created and imported a mesh, which looks like a cube with two open faces, which will act as the "impossible" room. Inside this room, I have added two rotated cubes, which each have a separate material with the original TextureExample shader. The two cubes overlap the same physical space, and you can see both cubes in the viewport, as seen in Figure 7-30.

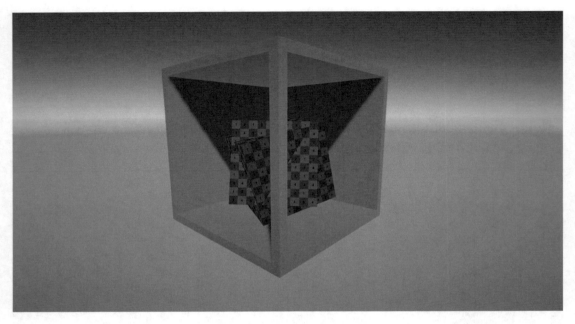

Figure 7-30. *An open-faced room containing two objects that overlap the same physical space*

Let's swap out the materials on these cubes. Both cubes will still use the color and texture values they are currently using, but I'll use the StencilTexture shader instead. If I give the red cube a stencil reference value of 1 and the blue cube a stencil reference value of 2, both will disappear from the Scene View, and all we'll see is the room mesh. We need to add a stencil mask over both open faces of the cube to render them again.

Create a new material using the StencilMask shader and give it a stencil reference value of 1. I will then add a quad mesh to the scene and line it up against the left open face of the room mesh and then assign the stencil mask material we just created to it. When you do, the red cube should appear visible in the Scene View again, but only in the places overlapping the stencil mask on the screen, as seen in Figure 7-31.

Figure 7-31. *The stencil mask mesh (which is selected for clarity) writes a stencil value of 1. The red cube uses a stencil reference of 1 and uses the Comp Equal function to only render in locations where the stencil buffer contains a 1*

Then, I will create a second material with the StencilMask shader and give it a stencil reference value of 2. I will add a second quad mesh, line it up with the right open face of the room mesh, and assign the second stencil mask material to it, and now both cubes should be visible, but only where their respective stencil reference value matches the value written by the stencil masks. Figure 7-29 shows the completed effect from three different angles.

This effect was relatively easy to put together, but only because we had already seen how to write the two required shaders in a previous section. Like the x-ray effect we previously created, the drawback of this approach is that you would have to add stencil support to each custom shader you want to use in the impossible room. If you wanted to use any of Unity's built-in shaders, you would have to duplicate them and add stencil support yourself. With Render Objects, we can avoid modifying shaders in URP altogether.

Impossible Room Effect with Render Objects

The key drawback to using a pure HLSL approach for this effect is the fact we need to add stencil support to the materials used by any object inside the room, which is time-consuming if you are going to include objects with several different shaders. However, we can still use the StencilMask shader to draw the stencil mask, since we only need to write that shader once. With that in mind, I'm going to set up my scene in a similar way to how I set up the scene for the HLSL version of this effect, except the cubes within the room will use the TextureExample shader and therefore will both appear in the Scene View even when the mask quads are active. Figure 7-32 illustrates the scene setup.

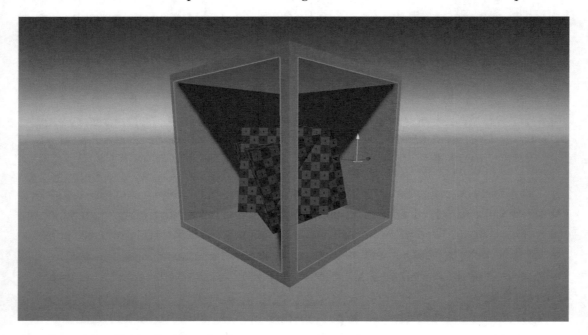

Figure 7-32. *The cubes inside the room are using the TextureExample shader, which does not have stencil support. The two mask quads, which are writing stencil values of 1 and 2, respectively, are selected in the Scene View for clarity*

Since we are using Render Objects, we will need to add the room objects to separate layers. Let's do the following steps:

- Add two new layers named "Impossible Obj 1" and "Impossible Obj 2".

- Assign the red cube to the "Impossible Obj 1" layer and the blue cube to the "Impossible Obj 2" layer.

- On your Renderer Asset, remove both these layers from the Opaque Layer Mask at the top of the asset. Both cubes should disappear from the Scene View.

Now we need to add back rendering both layers, which is where the Render Objects features come in. For each layer, we need to add a Render Objects feature that will override the stencil settings and only render the layer when a specific stencil value exists in the stencil buffer. We'll carry out the following process for the first feature:

- At the bottom of the Renderer Asset, select Add Renderer Feature and choose Render Objects.

- Rename the feature "Impossible Objects 1".

- Keep the Queue as Opaque and change the Layer Mask to only include the "Impossible Obj 1" layer.

- Open the Overrides section and tick the Stencil override.

- Change the reference value to 1 and use the Equal comparison function. Now, the red cube will pop back into existence.

- We don't need to change the Pass or Fail operations, because we don't want to change the stencil buffer value after the stencil test.

When you have completed these steps for the first feature, add a second feature with the same settings, except the name is "Impossible Objects 2", the layer mask uses the "Impossible Obj 2" layer, and the stencil reference value should be 2. Both features are shown in Figure 7-33.

Figure 7-33. *Settings for the two Impossible Objects Renderer Features*

When you have added both features, you will only be able to see the objects from the correct angle, as in Figure 7-34.

Figure 7-34. *The completed impossible room effect. The objects only appear behind the stencil mask with the matching stencil reference value*

Note   Like with other effects that use Render Objects, if you want to include transparent objects in this effect, you will need to remove the layers from the Transparent Layer Mask on your Renderer Asset, duplicate each Render Objects feature, and change the queue to Transparent and the event to AfterRenderingTransparents.

In this section, we saw that Render Objects is an effective alternative to shader modification in some scenarios. We did not cover the full range of functionality that Render Objects (or Renderer Features as a whole) provides, but you should have a good understanding of how we can use them to modify stencil and depth testing settings without needing to retrofit existing shaders with new features.

Summary

In this chapter, we learned about depth testing and how it is crucial to ensuring that objects are rendered to the screen in the correct order. The depth texture can be used for depth-based effects in shaders, although there is extra work involved if you want custom shaders to render their depth to the depth texture. Stencils are an extension of the depth buffer, which allow us to conditionally render objects based on stencil values that were rendered by previous objects.

In the next chapter, we will explore how Unity renders semitransparent objects and create shaders that are based on transparency. In summary, we learned the following in this chapter:

- The depth buffer stores the nonlinear distance of pixels from the camera. The highest depth value, 1, corresponds to the far clip plane; and the lowest depth value, 0, corresponds to the near clip plane.

- The ZTest and ZWrite keywords can be used to configure how shaders perform depth testing.

- Although many graphics APIs specify that depth testing should occur after the (expensive) fragment stage, early depth testing (and stencil testing) can occur before the fragment shader if it does not modify the final depth value of a pixel.

271

- Custom shaders require an extra pass to render depth into the camera depth texture. In the built-in pipeline, we add a ShadowCaster pass. In URP, we add a dedicated DepthOnly pass.

- The _CameraDepthTexture can be sampled in shaders to create depth-based effects. In Shader Graph, the corresponding node is called Scene Depth.

- Stencils can be used to conditionally render objects based on stencil values written by previously rendered objects.

- The stencil test operates immediately before the depth test. Although a failed depth test never writes to the depth buffer, a shader may write to the stencil buffer in several ways after a successful *or* failed stencil test.

- In URP, we can add Renderer Features to customize how certain parts of the rendering loop operate.

- One of the features supplied out of the box is called Render Objects, which lets us control the depth and stencil interactions of entire layers of objects at once.

CHAPTER 8

Transparency and Alpha

In computer graphics, opaque and semitransparent objects are handled very differently from one another. Rendering opaque objects is relatively easy, because every time we attempt to draw a pixel, we either fully replace the existing color value (if the depth test passes) or do not modify the existing value (if the depth test fails). With transparent rendering, the color of the pixel being rendered is *blended* with the existing value in the color buffer. When multiple transparent objects overlap on the same pixel, the order in which we render them matters, so we need to *sort* all transparent objects prior to rendering. Rendering transparent objects is more computationally intensive than rendering opaques, and in this chapter, we will see why.

How Rendering Transparent Objects Works

Once every opaque object in the game has been rendered using the techniques discussed in the previous chapter, we are left with transparent objects that are yet to be rendered. Whenever we want to draw a transparent object, it must first pass a depth test; if the transparent object is behind an opaque object in the scene, it won't be drawn. As with opaque objects, we can perform early depth testing if the fragment shader does not write depth information. After a successful depth test, the fragment shader will run and figure out the color of each pixel of the object.

When rendering a transparent object to the screen, we need to preserve some of the color that has already been stored in the color buffer and mix it with some of the color of the object being drawn. This is unlike opaque rendering, which overwrites the existing color entirely. The technique we use to mix these colors is called *alpha blending*.

Transparent objects each have an associated alpha value, which represents how transparent the object is; this is typically a value from 0 to 1, where 0 corresponds to an invisible object and 1 corresponds to a fully opaque object. In the shaders we have written so far, the fragment shader has output a four-element color, with the final

© Daniel Ilett 2022
D. Ilett, *Building Quality Shaders for Unity*®, https://doi.org/10.1007/978-1-4842-8652-4_8

element being the alpha, but it hasn't mattered because opaque objects ignore the alpha component. With alpha blending, the alpha value output by the fragment shader is used to control what proportion of the output color is taken from the transparent object and the color buffer, respectively. The order of rendering objects matters, so we sort all transparent objects from back to front before rendering them. The rendering loop for transparent objects looks like this:

- Sort all transparent objects back to front *relative to the camera* (objects with a higher depth value are rendered first).

  - Sorting occurs CPU-side and is not a shader operation.

  - Sorting is performed per object based on the origin point of the mesh.

- Pick the furthest object that has not yet been rendered and carry out the vertex shader on the object.

- Perform early depth testing (where appropriate) and discard any pixels that fail the depth test. By default, do not write depth on a passed depth test.

- Carry out the fragment shader on the object to obtain the final color value for the pixel, including an alpha value.

- Using the alpha value, blend together the color of the object with the color already in the scene.

- Pick the next object that has not been rendered and repeat the steps until all objects have been rendered.

There are many quirks to be aware of when using alpha-blended transparency, so let's break down in detail how alpha blending works.

How Alpha Blending Works

Blending is the process by which we take the color of a pixel we are rendering and, based on its alpha value, mix it with the color already in the color buffer. The result of the blending operation is that we can "see through" the pixel we just rendered by preserving some of the original color. Unity gives us control over how alpha blending works, so let's see a shader example in shader code.

Alpha Blending in HLSL

As with many of the shaders we have worked with, let's start by creating a new shader and naming it "TransparentTexture.shader". As a starting point, it'll look a lot like the TextureExample shader, except with a different name at the top of the file.

Listing 8-1. The TransparentTexture base shader

```
Shader "Examples/TransparentTexture"
{
    Properties
    {
        _BaseColor ("Base Color", Color) = (1, 1, 1, 1)
        _BaseTex("Base Texture", 2D) = "white" {}
    }
    SubShader
    {
        Tags { ... }

        Pass
        {
            HLSLPROGRAM
            #pragma vertex vert
            #pragma fragment frag

            struct appdata
            {
                float4 positionOS : Position;
                float2 uv : TEXCOORD0;
            };

            struct v2f
            {
                float4 positionCS : SV_Position;
                float2 uv : TEXCOORD0;
            };

            v2f vert (appdata v) { ... }
```

```
float4 frag (v2f i) : SV_Target
{
        float4 textureSample = tex2D(_BaseTex, i.uv);
        return textureSample * _BaseColor;
}
ENDHLSL
        }
    }
}
```

As with most of our shaders, we must make small changes to the base shader depending on the pipeline you are using.

Listing 8-2. Adding include files in the built-in pipeline

```
HLSLPROGRAM
#pragma vertex vert
#pragma fragment frag

#include "UnityCG.cginc"
```

Listing 8-3. Adding include files and tags in URP

```
Tags
{
        "RenderPipeline" = "UniversalPipeline"
}
Pass
{
    Tags
    {
            "LightMode" = "UniversalForward"
    }

    HLSLPROGRAM
    #pragma vertex vert
    #pragma fragment frag
```

```
#include "Packages/com.unity.render-pipelines.universal/
ShaderLibrary/Core.hlsl"
```

We'll also need to set up the vertex shader. The only difference is in the function we use to transform vertex positions from object space to clip space, as we have now seen many times before.

Listing 8-4. The vertex shader for alpha blending in the built-in pipeline

```
v2f vert (appdata v)
{
    v2f o;
    o.positionCS = UnityObjectToClipPos(v.positionOS.xyz);
    o.uv = TRANSFORM_TEX(v.uv, _BaseTex);
    return o;
}
```

Listing 8-5. The vertex shader for alpha blending in URP

```
v2f vert (appdata v)
{
    v2f o;
    o.positionCS = TransformObjectToHClip(v.positionOS.xyz);
    o.uv = TRANSFORM_TEX(v.uv, _BaseTex);
    return o;
}
```

The final bit of pipeline-dependent code is related to the variables in the Properties block. You'll hopefully be used to this by now, but URP requires most variable declarations to be in the CBUFFER block. These variables need to be declared inside the HLSLPROGRAM block, just below the v2f struct definition.

Listing 8-6. Variable declarations in the built-in pipeline

```
struct v2f { ... };

sampler2D _BaseTex;

float4 _BaseColor;
float4 _BaseTex_ST;
```

Listing 8-7. Variable declarations in URP

```
struct v2f { ... };

sampler2D _BaseTex;

CBUFFER_START(UnityPerMaterial)
    float4 _BaseColor;
    float4 _BaseTex_ST;
CBUFFER_END
```

Now we can start adding code to make this shader transparent. For transparent shaders, we need to set the Queue tag and RenderType tag used by the shader to Transparent inside the Tags block.

Listing 8-8. Changing the Queue and RenderType to Transparent

```
SubShader
{
    Tags
    {
        "RenderType" = "Transparent"
        "Queue" = "Transparent"

        // Other tags go here.
    }
```

If we used this shader on an object and changed the alpha channel of the _BaseColor property to below 1, then you might expect it to start turning transparent immediately, but alas, it will not. Without specifying the blend behavior, Unity will render this object in the Transparent queue, but it will not blend the fragment color with the color buffer value. For that, we must use the Blend keyword inside a SubShader or a Pass. The default behavior is Blend Off, which does not perform any blending.

Listing 8-9. Turning off blending

```
Pass
{
    Blend Off
```

What if we wanted to turn blending on? Blending is a relatively complex operation because we have a lot of control over exactly *how* blending occurs. Blend functions generally take two color values – a *source* and *destination* – and multiply the two by different amounts and then add them together. If we want to blend the fragment color with the color buffer value, we can specify what proportion of both colors will be used. The syntax for this is `Blend <source factor> <destination factor>`, where

- The "source factor" refers to the value we use to multiply the fragment color.

- The "destination factor" refers to the value we multiply the color buffer value by.

- The "source" is the fragment color itself.

- The "destination" is a render target, which in this case is the color buffer.

The final color value of the pixel, which is written into the color buffer, is calculated with the following formula:

Equation 8-1: Combining the source and destination colors

$$color = \left(source\ factor \times fragment\ RGB \right) + \left(destination\ factor \times color\ buffer\ RGB \right)$$

There are a limited number of values we can use for the source and destination factors, each of which acts as a multiplier on either the source or destination:

- *One* – Multiply the value by one.

- *Zero* – Multiply the value by zero.

- *SrcColor* – Multiply the value by the source color.

- *SrcAlpha* – Multiply the value by the source alpha.

- *DstColor* – Multiply the value by the destination color.

- *DstAlpha* – Multiply the value by the destination alpha.

- *OneMinusSrcColor* – Multiply the value by (1 – source color).

- *OneMinusSrcAlpha* – Multiply the value by (1 – source alpha).

- *OneMinusDstColor* – Multiply the value by (1 – destination color).

- *OneMinusDstAlpha* – Multiply the value by (1 – destination alpha).

That's a lot of values! To do traditional alpha blending, the combination of keywords is `Blend SrcAlpha OneMinusSrcAlpha`, which is doing the following calculation:

Equation 8-2: The traditional alpha-blended transparency equation

$$color = \left(fragment\ alpha \times fragment\ RGB \right) + \left(\left(1 - fragment\ alpha \right) \times color\ buffer\ RGB \right)$$

This line of code should be placed at the top of the `Pass`.

Listing 8-10. Traditional alpha blending in ShaderLab

```
Pass
{
        Blend SrcAlpha OneMinusSrcAlpha
```

With this line of code added, the shader will carry out alpha blending. Equation 8-2 may look familiar – this behavior *linearly interpolates* between the fragment color and the color buffer value, using the fragment alpha as the interpolation factor. Although there are many options we can use for blending, these options will blend colors in a way that looks natural for most physical objects, so you can think of this as the "default" way of doing things. Figure 8-1 shows the same cube rendered with different alpha values.

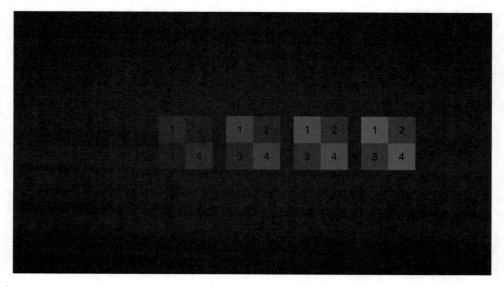

Figure 8-1. *Five cubes rendered with transparent materials*

From left to right, the cubes use alpha values 0, 0.25, 0.5, 0.75, and 1. The cube on the left is entirely invisible (you could be forgiven for thinking there are only four cubes!), and the cube on the right appears to be completely opaque. There are other ways of blending outside of "standard" alpha blending, some of which don't use alpha at all. Let's briefly explore some of the common methods.

Premultiplied Blending

So far, we have been using what's known as "straight alpha," where the RGB colors and the alpha channel are independent of one another. In other words, if you were to make changes to one, you wouldn't need to necessarily make changes to the other. With premultiplied alpha, the RGB colors and the alpha channel are linked; to make an object fully transparent, you must reduce the alpha *and* the RGB colors to zero. With that in mind, if you plan on using premultiplied alpha, when creating a texture, you usually ensure that all RGB values are multiplied by the associated alpha value before export (hence the name "premultiplied").

In the shader, we can use premultiplied blending by changing the `Blend` settings to `Blend One OneMinusSrcAlpha`.

Listing 8-11. Premultiplied blending

```
Pass
{
        Blend One OneMinusSrcAlpha
```

Under the hood, this is doing the following calculation:

Equation 8-3: The premultiplied blending equation

$$color = \big(fragment\ RGB + (1 - fragment\ alpha) \big) \times \big(color\ buffer\ RGB \big)$$

As you may have noticed, if we compare this with Equation 8-2, we are doing one less multiplication. As a result, premultiplied blending has the advantage of being slightly more efficient at runtime. However, you may not want to use premultiplied textures all the time, because you have "locked" the RGB channels of the texture together with the alpha channel, and it is difficult or impossible to revert to straight alpha, which you might need in other cases.

Note   In terms of the result, premultiplied blending ends up looking essentially the same as standard alpha blending. It just requires more setup work when creating textures.

Additive Blending

With *additive blending*, the alpha value is not used at all. Instead, colors are added together, well, *additively*. The fragment color's RGB component is added to the color buffer's RGB component, and that's it. For example, if the fragment value is red and the color buffer contains green, the output value will be yellow because mixing RGB colors works per channel. This property is useful in, say, a particle effect where you want it to look the brightest when many particles overlap each other on the screen. To use additive blending, the Blend setting should be Blend One One.

Listing 8-12.   Additive blending

```
Pass
{
        Blend One One
```

Unity will carry out the following calculation when you use this blend mode:

Equation 8-4: The additive blending equation

$$color = fragment\ RGB + color\ buffer\ RGB$$

It's like I said – we're just adding the two colors together! This is perhaps one of the easiest blend functions to understand. In Figure 8-2, I am rendering an opaque red cube in the background, with a transparent green cube in front of it, which uses additive blending. As a result, the overlapping region between the two cubes appears yellow.

Figure 8-2. *Additive blending is used on the front green cube*

Note   I've used a dark background here. If I used a white background with additive blending, then the leftmost section of the green (front) cube would appear invisible.

Multiplicative Blending

With *multiplicative blending*, not to be confused with premultiplied, the alpha channel is not used at all, just like with additive blending. The fragment color and color buffer value are multiplied together. This is useful for effects such as tinted glass, where the incoming light color is multiplied by the color of the glass to obtain the outgoing light color. For multiplicative blending, we use the `Blend DstColor Zero` function or the `Blend Zero SrcColor` function – they are equivalent.

Listing 8-13. Multiplicative blending version 1

```
Pass
{
    Blend DstColor Zero
```

Listing 8-14. Multiplicative blending version 2

```
Pass
{
    Blend Zero SrcColor
```

With this type of blending, Unity uses the following equation to calculate the final color of the pixel:

Equation 8-5: The multiplicative blending equation

$$color = fragment\ RGB \times color\ buffer\ RGB$$

We're just multiplying the two colors together, so the alpha value output by the fragment shader has no influence on the final color. In Figure 8-3, a transparent green cube with multiplicative blending is positioned in front of an opaque red cube. The front cube only appears green because the background is pure white (multiplying a color by white does not change the color), and the overlapping region between the two cubes is black because the multiplication operates per channel.

Figure 8-3. *Multiplicative blending is used on the front green cube*

Note   Likewise, I have used a light background here. With multiplicative blending, if I had used a dark background, then the leftmost section of the green (front) cube would not be easily visible.

We have now seen some of the most common blend functions used in Unity. So far, we have been specifying the blend factors directly in the shader file. However, in shader code, there is a way to turn them into properties so that we can customize blending however we want without needing to modify or duplicate the shader file.

Blend Mode Properties

It is useful to have the ability to change the source and destination blend factors on different material instances of the same shader effect. In our case, we have a transparent shader that can apply a texture to the object, but we originally hardcoded it to use Blend SrcAlpha OneMinusSrcAlpha. We have seen other types of blending that are quite useful, so let's turn the factors into properties.

The blend factors are available in the Unity scripting API as part of the UnityEngine. Rendering.BlendMode enum. We can add an integer property and instruct Unity to use the values from that enum as the possible property values using the Enum attribute, which causes a drop-down menu to appear on the Inspector for this property. The syntax looks like the following.

Listing 8-15. Source and destination blend factors as properties

```
Properties
{
     _BaseColor ("Base Color", Color) = (1, 1, 1, 1)
     _BaseTex("Base Texture", 2D) = "white" {}

     [Enum(UnityEngine.Rendering.BlendMode)]
     _SrcBlend("Source Blend Factor", Int) = 1

     [Enum(UnityEngine.Rendering.BlendMode)]
     _DstBlend("Destination Blend Factor", Int) = 1
}
```

The _SrcBlend and _DstBlend properties contain the source and destination blend factors, respectively. To use these within the shader, we can swap out the Blend SrcAlpha OneMinusSrcAlpha line of code to use the properties instead.

Listing 8-16. Swapping the source and destination blend factors for property versions

```
Pass
{
     Blend [_SrcBlend] [_DstBlend]
```

Now, we can specify any blend factor we want for the source and destination inside the Inspector window without needing to change the code each time. This only works with shader code – unfortunately, we can't do it in Shader Graph. Speaking of which, it's time to see how alpha blending works in Shader Graph.

Alpha Blending in Shader Graph

For this effect, I'll create a new Unlit graph and name it TransparentTexture.shadergraph. First, let's add transparency support. Go to the Graph Settings and change the *Surface* mode to *Transparent*, which will force Unity to use the *Transparent* rendering queue for this shader.

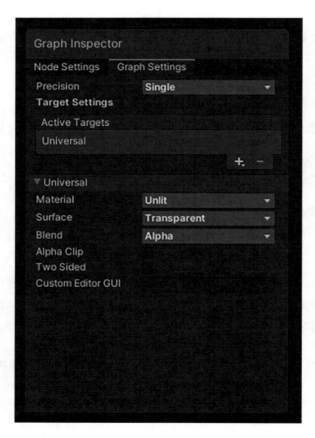

Figure 8-4. Changing the Surface mode to Transparent means that Unity will use transparent rendering for objects that use this shader

When you change this setting, an additional block called *Alpha* will appear on the master stack. This value is the one that Unity will use for alpha blending. Here's how the graph will work:

- This graph will use `Base Color` and `Base Texture` properties, which you will be familiar with by now.

- On the graph's surface, I'll sample the texture with a `Sample Texture 2D` node and multiply the result by `Base Color`.

- The result of that node should be output to the *Base Color* block on the master stack.

- Then, we'll `Split` the color and output only the *alpha* component (the fourth component) to the *Alpha* block on the master stack.

Figure 8-5 shows how these nodes should be connected.

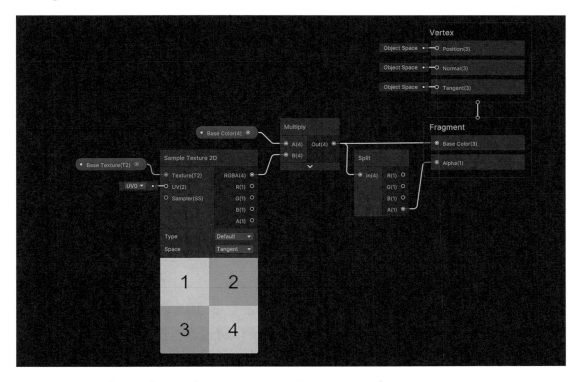

Figure 8-5. *The nodes in the TransparentTexture graph*

If you save the graph and use it on an object now, then you will see a result like in Figure 8-1. If we revisit the Graph Settings window (see Figure 8-4), you will see a *Blend* option, which by default uses the *Alpha* setting. Under the hood, this setting uses the same `Blend SrcAlpha OneMinusSrcAlpha` as the HLSL version of the shader we created. Let's see how some of the alternative blend modes work in Shader Graph.

Other Blend Modes

In shader code, we can put together any combination of blend modes we want. Shader Graph, on the other hand, supports a limited number of modes. In the Graph Settings (see Figure 8-4), if the graph uses the *Transparent* Surface mode, then there is a *Blend* option, which comes with four options: *Alpha*, *Premultiply*, *Additive*, and *Multiply*. These are the four blend settings that we saw in shader code. Table 8-1 lists each blend mode and the corresponding shader code that is generated by Shader Graph under the hood.

Table 8-1. *Blend modes and blend factors*

Blend Mode	Blend Factors
Alpha	`Blend SrcAlpha OneMinusSrcAlpha`
Premultiply	`Blend One OneMinusSrcAlpha`
Additive	`Blend One One`
Multiply	`Blend DstColor Zero` *or* `Blend Zero SrcColor`

Caution   I discovered that the Premultiply blend mode doesn't work as intended in many versions of Shader Graph. In practice, its behavior is like the Alpha blend mode. This bug is fixed in Unity 2022.1.0b1 – unfortunately, for versions before that, you may need to find a different workaround.

We have now seen that blend functions can be used to customize how Unity blends the fragment shader result with the objects previously rendered into the color buffer. For transparent objects, this is crucial to ensure that you can see other objects through them. However, this is not the only possible use of alpha. In the next section, we will see how to use alpha on opaque objects to clip pixels.

Alpha Clipping

Although transparent objects are an important part of the rendering process, they are not the only thing that we can use alpha for. When we are creating opaque shaders, you may have noticed that we still deal with RGBA colors; in HLSL, we return a color with an alpha component, and in Shader Graph, we only ditch the alpha value right at the end when we output to the RGB *Base Color* block. However, even opaque shaders can make use of alpha through *alpha clipping*.

Alpha clipping is a technique where we can cull pixels that have an alpha value below a customizable threshold value. Each pixel is either rendered completely opaque, or completely visible – as such, we can use opaque rendering for these objects. Let's see how alpha clipping works in both HLSL and Shader Graph by creating an alpha cutout shader. Figure 8-6 shows you the transparent circle texture we will apply to the mesh, and Figure 8-7 shows you what the mesh looks like with different alpha cutoff values.

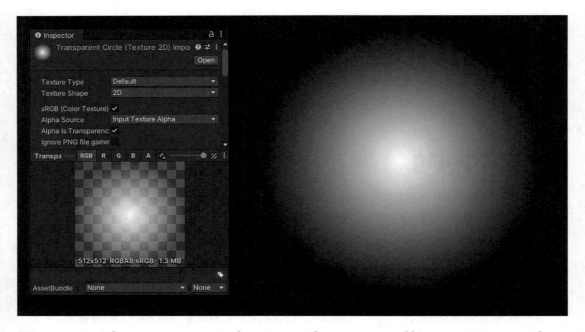

Figure 8-6. *The transparent circle texture. The texture itself is transparent, with no background, but I am showing it here on a dark-gray background to illustrate what it looks like*

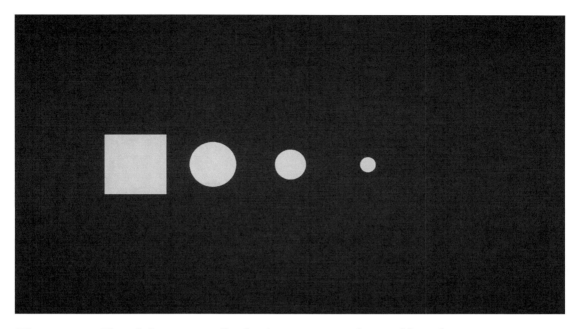

Figure 8-7. *The alpha cutout shader in action. Each quad has the same texture with different alpha cutoff values*

Alpha Cutout in HLSL

For this effect, I will create a new shader and name it "AlphaCutout.shader". The following code forms the starting point for the shader.

Listing 8-17. The AlphaCutout shader skeleton code

```
Shader "Examples/AlphaCutout"
{
    Properties
    {
        _BaseColor ("Base Color", Color) = (1, 1, 1, 1)
        _BaseTex("Base Texture", 2D) = "white" {}
    }
    SubShader
    {
        Tags { ... }
```

```
Pass
{
        HLSLPROGRAM
        #pragma vertex vert
        #pragma fragment frag

        struct appdata
        {
                float4 positionOS : Position;
                float2 uv : TEXCOORD0;
        };

        struct v2f
        {
                float4 positionCS : SV_Position;
                float2 uv : TEXCOORD0;
        };

        v2f vert (appdata v) { ... }
        float4 frag (v2f i) : SV_Target { ... }

        ENDHLSL
    }
  }
}
```

There are several pipeline-dependent changes you should make before we can start working on the shader:

- In the built-in pipeline, follow Listings 8-2, 8-4, and 8-6.

- In URP, follow Listings 8-3, 8-5, and 8-7.

Now let's start adding alpha cutout functionality to the shader. We need an additional property for this shader to control the cutoff value where we start culling pixels based on their alpha value. Since the alpha value will always be a float between 0 and 1, that will be the range for the _ClipThreshold property. Remember to define it in HLSLPROGRAM too.

Listing 8-18. The clip threshold property in the Properties block

```
Properties
{
    _BaseColor ("Base Color", Color) = (1, 1, 1, 1)
    _BaseTex("Base Texture", 2D) = "white" {}
    _ClipThreshold("Alpha Clip Threshold", Range(0, 1)) = 0.5
}
```

Listing 8-19. The clip threshold property in the HLSLPROGRAM code block

```
float4 _BaseColor;
float4 _BaseTex_ST;
float _ClipThreshold;
```

Unity reserves a queue for materials that use an alpha value to clip pixels called AlphaTest. This queue has a value of 2450, which is at the higher end of the queue values that Unity considers to be opaque (queues above 2500 are transparent). That's what we will use for this shader. However, it's important to note that the RenderType should be Opaque because this is an opaque shader.

Listing 8-20. The AlphaTest Queue

```
Tags
{
    "RenderType" = "Opaque"
    "Queue" = "AlphaTest"

    // Other tags go here.
}
```

Now we can turn our attention to the fragment shader, where we will carry out the alpha test. We will calculate the output color, but before the end of the shader, we will compare the alpha component against the _ClipThreshold property and discard the pixel if the alpha is below the threshold. There are two ways to do this.

The first method is to use the clip function. clip accepts a float parameter. If the value is below zero, the pixel is clipped; otherwise, it is rendered normally. We can utilize the _ClipThreshold property by subtracting it from the output color alpha and then passing it into the clip function.

Listing 8-21. The fragment shader using clip

```
float4 frag (v2f i) : SV_Target
{
      float4 textureSample = tex2D(_BaseTex, i.uv);
      float4 outputColor = textureSample * _BaseColor;

      clip(outputColor.a - _ClipThreshold);
      return outputColor;
}
```

The second method involves the discard statement. While the shader is being executed, if the GPU encounters the discard statement, the pixel is clipped, so we will use an if statement to check whether the pixel alpha is below the _ClipThreshold property.

Listing 8-22. The fragment shader using discard

```
float4 frag (v2f i) : SV_Target
{
      float4 textureSample = tex2D(_BaseTex, i.uv);
      float4 outputColor = textureSample * _BaseColor;

      if (outputColor.a < _ClipThreshold) discard;
      return outputColor;
}
```

Although one of these methods might be slightly faster on certain platforms, in practice, they usually have comparable performance, so don't worry too much about which one to use – just pick whichever one you want. In fact, the shader compiler could end up compiling them in the same way when they run on your GPU.

Let's see how the shader operates on objects in the Scene View. For this, I'm going to use a scene that contains a quad mesh, and I will use a texture with a smooth falloff from fully opaque to fully transparent pixels so I can illustrate the cutout functionality clearly. Figure 8-6 shows the texture on a dark background alongside its import settings – all pixels in the texture are white, and only the alpha value changes. Each quad uses the texture from Figure 8-6. As you can see, every pixel that is rendered is opaque white, because the original texture is full white with varying alpha values. The size of the circle changes due to the cutoff value changing. From left to right

- The first quad is rendered entirely because the cutoff value is 0. All pixels have an alpha value of at least zero, because that is the lowest possible value. Although the texture looks circular, this means the whole quad is rendered.

- The second quad has a cutoff value of 0.25. The outer parts of the circle have an alpha value below that, so they are culled.

- The third and fourth quads get smaller in size, because more pixels have alpha values that fall below their cutoff values of 0.5 and 0.75, respectively.

- The fifth quad is not rendered at all because its cutoff value is 1. None of the parts of the circle texture have an alpha value above 1, because it is the highest possible value, so all pixels are clipped.

Now that we have seen how alpha clipping can be used to create a cutout material in HLSL, let's see the same effect in Shader Graph.

Alpha Cutout in Shader Graph

For this effect, I will create another new Unlit graph and name it "AlphaCutout.shadergraph". The first change we need to make is to go to the Graph Settings and change the *Surface* to *Opaque* and then tick the *Alpha Clip* box, as shown in Figure 8-8. By doing this, the *Alpha Clip Threshold* block will appear on the master stack, and *Alpha* will be available, even though this is an opaque shader.

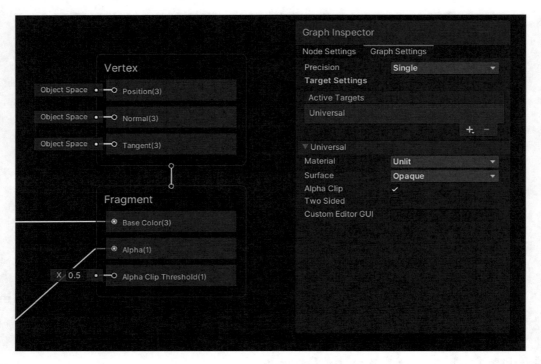

Figure 8-8. *By ticking Alpha Clip, the Alpha Clip Threshold block becomes* *available*

The combination of an *Opaque* surface and *Alpha Clip* being enabled means that Unity automatically puts this shader into the AlphaTest Queue under the hood. Next, we need to add properties to the graph:

- We'll add Base Color and Base Texture properties like we've seen on many graphs before.

- The Clip Threshold property will drive the effect. Make sure you bound the possible values the property can take between 0 and 1, as shown in Figure 8-9.

Figure 8-9. *The Clip Threshold property can take values between 0 and 1 inclusive*

Now we must handle the cutoff on the graph. For the *Base Color* and *Alpha* outputs, we can wire up the graph similarly to the TransparentTexture graph. Then, all we need to deal with is the Clip Threshold, which can be wired directly into the *Alpha Clip Threshold* block on the master stack. By doing this, Unity automatically reads the *Alpha* output and discards any pixel with a value below the *Alpha Clip Threshold* output. Figure 8-10 shows how the output nodes are connected.

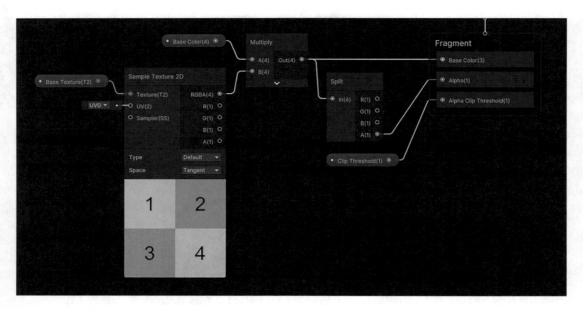

Figure 8-10. *The AlphaCutout graph*

Using this shader on objects in the Scene View will result in behavior identical to that seen in Figure 8-7. This effect is useful for masking out transparent portions of a texture without needing to use transparent rendering. Opaque rendering techniques are usually more efficient than equivalent transparent techniques, although it's worth mentioning that clipping out pixels in the fragment shader influences the depth value that gets written (if depth writing is enabled), so alpha clip shaders are unable to use early depth testing.

Note   Generally speaking, alpha clipping on opaque objects is faster than transparent rendering on desktop platforms. However, on mobile, this might be reversed. If in doubt, make sure you profile your game's performance often and choose whichever shader is faster if you have a choice between any two techniques.

This is just one possible consequence of using alpha clipping in your shaders. In the next case study, we will see an alpha clip rendering technique that can be used to "fake" a transparent appearance, despite all pixels being opaque.

Dithered Transparency with Alpha Clip

Transparent materials are generally more computationally expensive to render than opaque materials, and they can run into problems if you write depth because they are sorted per object, rather than per pixel like opaque objects. It would be useful to have a shader effect in our arsenal that can tie together the benefits of opaque rendering while still *appearing* as if the object were transparent. The *dithered transparency* effect, also known as *screen-door transparency*, can achieve that.

With dithered transparency, we use alpha clipping to render and cull pixels in a special pattern, which is based on the screen position of the pixel. On a screen with a sufficient pixel density, the pixels that are still being rendered will appear transparent, because some of the background is visible through the object. Figure 8-11 illustrates the effect we want to achieve.

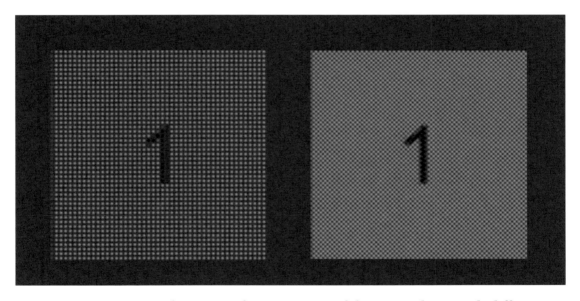

Figure 8-11. *A zoomed-in view of two versions of the same object with different alpha values*

In this zoomed-in example, the image on the left shows an object that has an alpha of 0.25. As a result, many of the object's pixels are not rendered at all. The image on the right shows the same object with an alpha of 0.5. About twice as many pixels of the object are shown, so fewer background pixels are visible through the object. Let's create this effect in HLSL and then again in Shader Graph.

Dithered Transparency in HLSL

This shader will pull together many of the concepts we've learned from specific shader effects that we have built so far. Let's create a new shader called "DitheredTransparency. shader" and then replace all the contents of the file with the following code.

Listing 8-23. The DitheredTransparency code skeleton

```
Shader "Examples/DitheredTransparency"
{
    Properties
    {
        _BaseColor ("Base Color", Color) = (1, 1, 1, 1)
        _BaseTex("Base Texture", 2D) = "white" {}
    }
    SubShader
    {
        Tags { ... }

        Pass
        {
            HLSLPROGRAM
            #pragma vertex vert
            #pragma fragment frag

            struct appdata
            {
                float4 positionOS : Position;
                float2 uv : TEXCOORD0;
            };

            struct v2f
            {
                float4 positionCS : SV_Position;
                float2 uv : TEXCOORD0;
            };

            v2f vert (appdata v) { ... }
```

```
                float4 frag (v2f i) : SV_Target { ... }

                ENDHLSL
            }
        }
}
```

As always, we need to get this shader up to speed with a few pipeline-dependent edits:

- In the built-in pipeline, follow Listings 8-2 and 8-6.

- In URP, follow Listings 8-3 and 8-7.

Now we can start to focus on the dithering effect. This shader will use the `AlphaTest` Queue since we will be using an alpha test to remove pixels along the dither pattern. Remember to set the `RenderType` to `Opaque`.

Listing 8-24. Using the AlphaTest Queue for the DitheredTransparency effect

```
Tags
{
        "RenderType" = "Opaque"
        "Queue" = "AlphaTest"

        // Other tags go here.
}
```

For this effect, we will generate the thresholds within the fragment shader itself and use the screen-space position of the pixel to obtain the correct one. To do this, we need to calculate the screen-space position inside the vertex shader and pass it to the fragment shader inside the `v2f` struct in a variable named `positionSS`. We first encountered screen-space positions in the previous chapter when we built a silhouette effect, and we will be using a similar approach here. Recall that there is no special semantic for screen-space positions, so we use the first unused texture coordinate interpolator, which is `TEXCOORD1` in this case.

Listing 8-25. The v2f struct

```
struct v2f
{
```

```
    float4 positionCS : SV_Position;
    float2 uv : TEXCOORD0;
    float4 positionSS : TEXCOORD1;
};
```

In the vertex shader, we must calculate positionSS. As we saw in the Silhouette shader, we can use the ComputeScreenPos function for this (thankfully, both the built-in pipeline and URP use the same function name). Some of the other code for the vertex shader is pipeline dependent, however, so pick the correct code listing for your pipeline.

Listing 8-26. Calculating screen-space positions using ComputeScreenPos in the built-in pipeline

```
v2f vert (appdata v)
{
    v2f o;
    o.positionCS = UnityObjectToClipPos(v.positionOS.xyz);
    o.uv = TRANSFORM_TEX(v.uv, _BaseTex);
    o.positionSS = ComputeScreenPos(o.positionCS);
    return o;
}
```

Listing 8-27. Calculating screen-space positions using ComputeScreenPos in URP

```
v2f vert (appdata v)
{
    v2f o;
    o.positionCS = TransformObjectToHClip(v.positionOS.xyz);
    o.uv = TRANSFORM_TEX(v.uv, _BaseTex);
    o.positionSS = ComputeScreenPos(o.positionCS);
    return o;
}
```

Now we can turn our attention to the frag function. The first thing we will do here is to sample _BaseTex using the standard set of UV coordinates and multiply by _BaseColor to work out the output color. The alpha channel of this color will be compared against the dither thresholds later to perform alpha clipping.

Listing 8-28. Sampling the texture to obtain the output color

```
float4 frag (v2f i) : SV_Target
{
    float4 textureSample = tex2D(_BaseTex, i.uv);
    float4 outputColor = textureSample * _BaseColor;
```

Next, let's calculate the screen-space UVs to use for sampling the dither pattern. In the Silhouette shader, we used screen-space UVs to sample the depth texture, where $(0, 0)$ referred to the bottom-left of the screen and $(1, 1)$ referred to the top right. This time, however, the dither thresholds will be contained in an array inside the fragment shader, and we will use the *integer position* of the pixels on screen to work out which dither threshold to use. This means we need to take those $[0, 1]$-ranged UVs and multiply them by the screen resolution to obtain UVs with a range of $[0, width]$ in the u-axis and $[0, height]$ in the v-axis. A built-in variable called `_ScreenParams` stores the width and height of the screen in its xy-components.

Listing 8-29. Converting screen-space UVs to screen-space pixel position UVs

```
float4 outputColor = textureSample * _BaseColor;

float2 screenUVs = i.positionSS.xy / i.positionSS.w * _ScreenParams.xy;
```

For the dither thresholds, I will be using the code generated by Unity behind the scenes when we use a `Dither` node in Shader Graph, which gives us a 16-element array that we can access as if it were a 4×4 array. Figure 8-12 shows the pattern that is generated by the `Dither` node in Shader Graph.

Figure 8-12. *The dither pattern that is generated by the Dither node in Shader Graph. We will use the same pattern of values for the dither thresholds in HLSL*

You could alternatively use a texture for this step so you could supply any dither pattern you want, but the approach we are taking here takes up far less graphics memory than a texture approach. We use the screenUVs we calculated earlier to obtain indices and then use those indices to get the correct dither threshold.

Listing 8-30. Obtaining the correct dither threshold value

```
float2 screenUVs = i.positionSS.xy / i.positionSS.w * _ScreenParams.xy;

float ditherThresholds[16] =
{
    16.0 / 17.0,  8.0 / 17.0, 14.0 / 17.0,  6.0 / 17.0,
     4.0 / 17.0, 12.0 / 17.0,  2.0 / 17.0, 10.0 / 17.0,
    13.0 / 17.0,  5.0 / 17.0, 15.0 / 17.0,  7.0 / 17.0,
     1.0 / 17.0,  9.0 / 17.0,  3.0 / 17.0, 11.0 / 17.0
};
uint index = (uint(screenUVs.x)%4)*4 + uint(screenUVs.y)%4;
float threshold = ditherThresholds[index];
```

In effect, we are using the pixel position of the object as an array index. I have slightly modified the code being used for the dither thresholds from the autogenerated code. Now, the threshold variable contains a grayscale value between 0 and 1, which represents an alpha threshold, so we need to compare this with the alpha component of outputColor. If outputColor.a is less than threshold, we will discard the pixel.

Listing 8-31. Discarding pixels based on their alpha value

```
float threshold = ditherThresholds[index];
```

if (outputColor.a < threshold) discard;

After discarding these pixels, the only thing left to do is return a value from the fragment shader, which will be the `outputColor`.

Listing 8-32. Returning a value from the fragment shader

```
    if (outputColor.a < threshold) discard;
```

**   return outputColor;**
```
}
```

The shader is now complete. If we attach materials that use this shader to a few objects and use different alpha values for each of their _BaseColor properties, we will see that the lower the alpha is, the fewer pixels of the object are rendered, as seen in Figure 8-13.

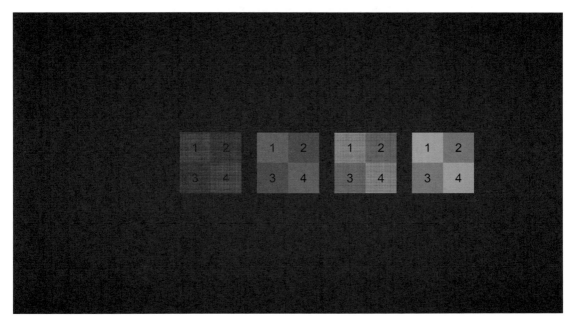

Figure 8-13. *A set of five cubes that use the DitheredTransparency shader. From left to right, the cubes use alpha values of 0, 0.25, 0.5, 0.75, and 1, respectively. The cube on the left is entirely invisible, and the cube on the right is fully opaque*

This effect looks best when viewed at native resolution on your screen, so Figure 8-13 may not do the effect justice! Because this effect uses opaque rendering, we get a performance boost over transparent rendering because any objects behind the opaque pixels of this one can be depth culled, and we avoid having to do any alpha blending at all. Let's see how to make this effect in Shader Graph too.

Dithered Transparency in Shader Graph

To make this effect in Shader Graph, I will create a new Unlit graph and name it "DitheredTransparency.shadergraph". First, we will go to the Graph Settings and change tick the *Alpha Clip* option, but make sure to keep the *Surface* option as *Opaque*.

Figure 8-14. *The Graph Settings for the DitheredTransparency graph*

For this graph, we only need to add the Base Color and Base Texture properties that we've come to know and love. We'll use a Sample Texture 2D node and a Split node to set up the *Base Color* and *Alpha* outputs of the graph, like we did for the AlphaCutout graph.

When we ticked *Alpha Clip*, the *Alpha* and *Alpha Clip Threshold* blocks should have been automatically added on the master stack (if not, you can add them by right-clicking the master stack and searching for the relevant block). For the *Alpha Clip Threshold* output, we will add a `Dither` node, with a value of 1 in its *In* setting, and output it directly to the *Alpha Clip Threshold* block, as seen in Figure 8-15.

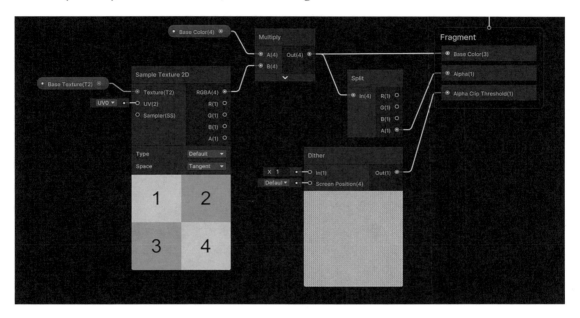

Figure 8-15. *The DitheredTransparency graph*

With that, the graph is complete, and it should look exactly like the HLSL implementation in Figure 8-13 when you attach it to objects in your game. Behind the scenes, Unity generates the threshold pattern seen in Figure 8-12 using similar code to Listing 8-21 in place of the `Dither` node and clips any pixel whose *Alpha* output was lower than the corresponding *Alpha Clip Threshold* output.

This is just one effect that is possible to make using alpha clipping. Next, we will look at a second case study which uses alpha clipping: the dissolve effect.

Dissolve Effect with Alpha Clip

There are several times in games where you may want to apply a dissolve effect to an object, such as when it is destroyed. There are several approaches you can take when designing a dissolve effect, and the technique we are about to implement involves using a cutoff threshold to cull all parts of the object above or below a certain position along one of the axes in object space. This would produce a clean cut, so we will modulate the position of each pixel using a small noise offset so that you can make the edges look a bit more chaotic if you want. Let's see the effect in HLSL and then in Shader Graph.

Figure 8-16. *Cubes with the Dissolve shader using different cutoff height values*

Dissolve Effect in HLSL

This effect will use TextureExample as a basis, so duplicate it and name the new file "Dissolve.shader" and rename it at the top of the file like the following.

Listing 8-33. The Dissolve shader code skeleton

```
Shader "Examples/Dissolve"
{
    Properties
    {
        _BaseColor ("Base Color", Color) = (1, 1, 1, 1)
        _BaseTex("Base Texture", 2D) = "white" {}
    }
```

```
SubShader
{
    Tags { ... }

    Pass
    {
        HLSLPROGRAM
        #pragma vertex vert
        #pragma fragment frag

        struct appdata
        {
            float4 positionOS : Position;
            float2 uv : TEXCOORD0;
        };

        struct v2f
        {
            float4 positionCS : SV_Position;
            float2 uv : TEXCOORD0;
        };

        v2f vert (appdata v) { ... }
        float4 frag (v2f i) : SV_Target { ... }

        ENDHLSL
    }
}
}
```

Like the other shaders in this chapter, we need to make a few edits depending on which pipeline you are using:

- In the built-in pipeline, follow Listings 8-2 and 8-6.

- In URP, follow Listings 8-3 and 8-7.

The cutoff itself is going to act like a plane in 3D space, which culls all pixels one side of it and preserves all pixels on the other side. There are several ways of implementing such a plane – for example, we could represent the plane in world space and provide properties that let us specify the plane mathematically using a normal vector and a point in space, and then the shader would compare the world-space position of each fragment against the plane to decide whether to cull them. However, a far easier method is to lock the cutoff plane to one of the cardinal axes and do the comparisons in object space. With this approach, the dissolve will always act along a single axis.

Let's deal with the graph properties. We are going to perform the cutoff along the object's y-axis, so we will specify the cutoff height as a property. We will be using noise to make the edge of the cutoff effect uneven, so we need to specify how granular the noise pattern will be and how strongly it will affect the edges of the mesh. We can keep the _BaseColor and _BaseTex properties, which are already here. Remember to declare them inside HLSL too.

Listing 8-34. Declaring Dissolve properties in the Properties block

```
Properties
{
    _BaseColor ("Base Color", Color) = (1, 1, 1, 1)
    _BaseTex("Base Texture", 2D) = "white" {}
    _CutoffHeight("Cutoff Height", Float) = 0.0
    _NoiseScale("Noise Scale", Float) = 20
    _NoiseStrength("Noise Strength", Range(0.0, 1.0)) = 0.5
}
```

Listing 8-35. Declaring properties in the HLSLPROGRAM block

```
float4 _BaseColor;
float4 _BaseTex_ST;
float _CutoffHeight;
float _NoiseScale;
float _NoiseStrength;
```

Like the DitheredTransparency shader, the Dissolve shader uses the AlphaTest Queue since we are performing an alpha test, but the RenderQueue is still Opaque. We specify these tags inside the Tags block.

Listing 8-36. Using the AlphaTest Queue for the Dissolve effect

```
Tags
{
        "RenderType" = "Opaque"
        "Queue" = "AlphaTest"

        // Other tags go here.
}
```

This shader will potentially be removing a large portion of the object. Recall that shaders render the "shell" of an object, so with the default settings, the object might look strange when viewed from certain angles because we'll see a huge void where the back faces of the mesh ought to be. With that in mind, we won't cull either the front or back faces of the mesh by specifying Cull Off inside the Pass, above the Tags block.

Listing 8-37. Turning off front and back face culling

```
Pass
{
        Cull Off
```

The fragment shader will require the object-space position to perform the alpha test. We need to pass this data from the vertex shader to the fragment shader inside the v2f struct. This is easy to do, because the vertex shader already receives the object-space position in the form of the positionOS variable inside the appdata struct, so we need to do a small modification to the vert function to pass the data along without modification. In the v2f struct, we will use the TEXCOORD1 semantic for the object-space position.

Listing 8-38. Addition to the v2f struct

```
struct v2f
{
        float4 positionCS : SV_Position;
        float2 uv : TEXCOORD0;
        float4 positionOS : TEXCOORD1;
};
```

Listing 8-39. The vertex shader for the dissolve effect in the built-in pipeline

```
v2f vert (appdata v)
{
    v2f o;
    o.positionCS = UnityObjectToClipPos(v.positionOS.xyz);
    o.uv = TRANSFORM_TEX(v.uv, _BaseTex);
    o.positionOS = v.positionOS;
    return o;
}
```

Listing 8-40. The vertex shader for the dissolve effect in URP

```
v2f vert (appdata v)
{
    v2f o;
    o.positionCS = TransformObjectToHClip(v.positionOS.xyz);
    o.uv = TRANSFORM_TEX(v.uv, _BaseTex);
    o.positionOS = v.positionOS;
    return o;
}
```

Now we need to think about the noise generator. A good choice for many shaders is *Perlin noise*, developed by Ken Perlin in the early 1980s for use in the movie *Tron*. The algorithm can be implemented in any number of dimensions, but in 2D, it works like this:

- Generate an evenly spaced grid of random unit vectors (vectors with a length of 1).

- For each point in space, including the space between those grid points

  - Find the four "corners" of the grid square you are in.

  - For each corner, calculate an offset vector between the point and that corner.

  - Calculate the dot product between each offset vector and the associated random unit vector of the corner.

- Once all four dot products have been calculated, interpolate between them (using the position of the point in 2D space as the interpolation factors) to obtain a single noise output value.

There is no built-in shader function that generates this type of noise for us, but we can turn our attention to Shader Graph, which has a built-in `Gradient Noise` node that generates Perlin noise behind the scenes. We can take the code that node uses behind the scenes and use it in our shader, with a bit of modification. It's a bit long; you don't need to know exactly what each line is doing, but I've added comments that may help.

Listing 8-41. Perlin noise generation in HLSL

```
v2f vert (appdata v) { ... }

// Generate a grid corner random unit vector.
float2 generateDir(float2 p)
{
    p = p % 289;
    float x = (34 * p.x + 1) * p.x % 289 + p.y;
    x = (34 * x + 1) * x % 289;
    x = frac(x / 41) * 2 - 1;
    return normalize(float2(x-floor(x+0.5), abs(x)-0.5));
}

float generateNoise(float2 p)
{
    float2 ip = floor(p);
    float2 fp = frac(p);

    // Calculate the nearest four grid point vectors.
    float d00 = dot(generateDir(ip), fp);
    float d01 = dot(generateDir(ip + float2(0, 1)), fp - float2(0, 1));
    float d10 = dot(generateDir(ip + float2(1, 0)), fp - float2(1, 0));
    float d11 = dot(generateDir(ip + float2(1, 1)), fp - float2(1, 1));

    // Do 'smootherstep' between the dot products then bilinearly
    interpolate.
```

```
fp = fp * fp * fp * (fp * (fp * 6 - 15) + 10);
      return lerp(lerp(d00, d01, fp.y), lerp(d10, d11, fp.y), fp.x);
}

// This function outputs in the range [-1, 1].
float gradientNoise(float2 UV, float Scale)
{
      return generateNoise(UV * Scale) * 2.0f;
}
```

I have modified Shader Graph's implementation so that the gradientNoise function outputs values in the range [–1,1]. Now that we can generate noise, let's fill in the fragment shader. The first thing we will do is calculate the object-space position of the fragment and displace its value along the y-axis slightly using noise.

Listing 8-42. Displacing the object-space position using noise

```
float4 frag (v2f i) : SV_Target
{
      float noiseSample = gradientNoise(i.uv, _NoiseScale) * _
      NoiseStrength;
      float noisyPosition = i.positionOS.y + noiseSample;
```

Next, we will perform the alpha thresholding step and discard any pixel whose noisyPosition is above the _CutoffHeight property.

Listing 8-43. Performing the alpha comparison

```
float noisyPosition = i.positionOS.y + noiseSample;

if (noisyPosition > _CutoffHeight) discard;
```

Finally, the fragment shader can end by sampling _BaseTex and multiplying by _BaseColor to obtain an output value. These lines won't have any effect if the pixel was already discarded due to failing the threshold check.

Listing 8-44. Sampling the base texture

```
if (noisyPosition > _CutoffHeight) discard;

float4 textureSample = tex2D(_BaseTex, i.uv);
return textureSample * _BaseColor;
}
```

There are no further changes that need to be made to the shader. Figure 8-16 demonstrates how different cutoff height values will appear in the game.

In Figure 8-16, the object-space positions along the y-axis of the top and bottom faces of the default Unity cube are 0.5 and –0.5, respectively. From left to right, these cubes use cutoff values of –0.5, –0.25, 0, 0.25, and 0.5; in each example, you can see a portion of the object is dissolving along the edge at the cutoff height. Each material uses a noise strength of 0.2 and noise scale of 20. In Figure 8-17, I keep the cutoff height consistently at 0 and change the noise scale instead.

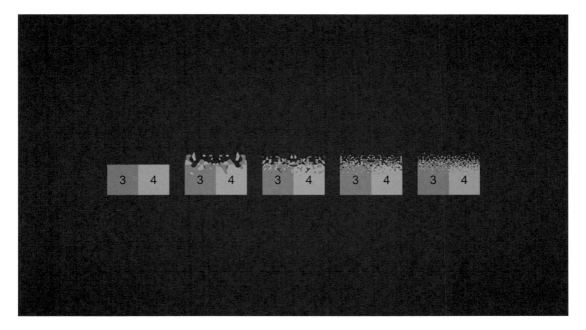

Figure 8-17. *Cubes with the Dissolve shader using different noise scale values*

From left to right, the cubes are using a noise scale of 0, 10, 20, 30, and 40, respectively. Interestingly, when the noise scale is 0, the shader applies a clean cut along the surface of the object. We can similarly achieve a clean cut when the noise strength is 0.

Now that we have seen how to implement the Dissolve shader in HLSL, let's see how it is done in Shader Graph.

Dissolve Effect in Shader Graph

We will start by creating another new Unlit graph and naming it "Dissolve.shadergraph". This graph uses *Alpha Clip*, so tick the option in the Graph Settings as in Figure 8-14. Once that has been dealt with, we can add properties to the graph. As with the HLSL version of this shader, we will be adding Base Color and Base Texture properties as usual, along with three additional Float properties called Cutoff Height, Noise Scale, and Noise Strength, respectively. The default values used by these properties can be seen in Figure 8-18.

Figure 8-18. *Dissolve graph properties*

The first addition we will make to the graph body itself is to wire up the Base Color and Base Texture properties using a Sample Texture 2D node in the same way we have seen in other graphs throughout this chapter. Figure 8-19 shows you how these properties should be connected to the graph outputs.

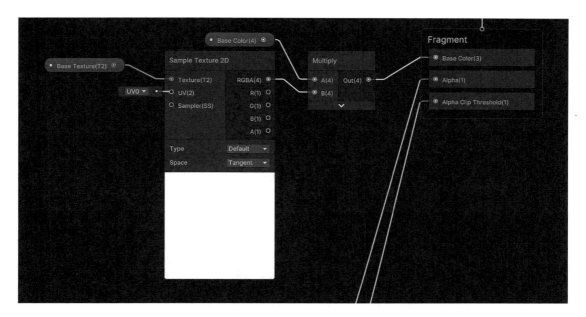

Figure 8-19. *Connecting the Base Color and Base Texture properties*

The next addition is to obtain the noise value and remap its values to the correct range. In the HLSL version, I changed the code of the Perlin noise generator so that it output values in the [–1, 1] range and then multiplied by _NoiseStrength. However, in Shader Graph, the Gradient Noise node outputs values in the [0, 1] range. The easiest method to get the values into the correct range is to use a Remap node and specify negative and positive _NoiseStrength and the min and max output values, respectively. Figure 8-20 shows you how these nodes should be connected.

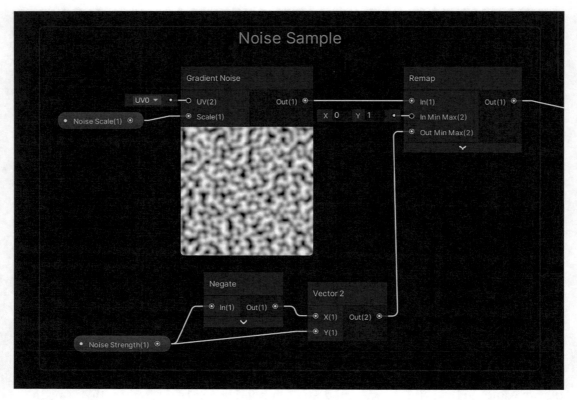

Figure 8-20. *Using Remap to obtain the correct range of values from the noise*

Next, we will perform the alpha test. For that, we need to add the noise values we just calculated to the y-component of the object-space position, which we can obtain with a `Position` node in *object* space. The result can be output to *Alpha Clip Threshold* on the master stack. The comparison value, `_CutoffHeight`, can be output directly into the *Alpha* output on the master stack. Behind the scenes, Unity will cull any pixel where the y-position, with added noise, is above `_CutoffHeight`. Figure 8-21 shows how the remaining nodes go together.

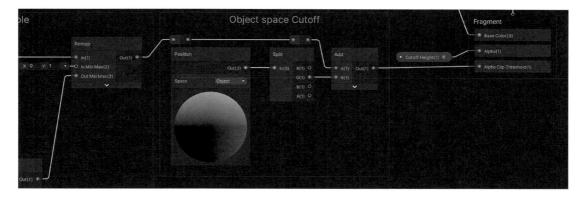

Figure 8-21. *Continuing from the previous nodes, the alpha test is performed*

If you use this shader on objects in the scene, you will see results like in Figures 8-16 and 8-17.

Summary

In this chapter, we learned about transparent rendering and how it differs from opaque rendering. Whereas opaque rendering ensures the correct order of objects using the depth buffer, transparent rendering requires us to sort the objects beforehand so that we can correctly blend their colors onto the screen. Alpha clipping can be used on both opaque and transparent shaders to completely remove pixels that fall below a specific alpha threshold – on opaque objects, this still lets us write to the depth buffer and use depth testing to cull objects behind the one being rendered. Here's what we learned in this chapter:

- Transparent objects must be sorted before rendering.

- We use blending to combine the result of the fragment shader of a transparent object with the color already present at the same location in the color buffer.

- Alpha-blended transparency uses Blend SrcAlpha OneMinusSrcAlpha.

- Other blend functions, such as premultiplied, additive, and multiplicative blending, use different blend settings.

319

- Alpha clipping can be used to cull pixels based on their alpha value. If the fragment alpha is lower than a specified threshold value, it is culled.

- The discard statement and the clip function can be used in HLSL to cull pixels. In Shader Graph, the Alpha Clip tick box combined with the Alpha and Alpha Clip Threshold outputs is used to control alpha clipping.

- Dithered transparency culls pixels according to a special dither pattern in screen space.

- Perlin noise can be used to generate organic-looking patterns, which are useful in shaders. One example is a dissolve effect.

CHAPTER 9

More Shader Fundamentals

We have covered many of the fundamental concepts in shaders in the previous chapters. However, there are concepts that don't fit neatly into a chapter of their own that are nonetheless important going forward. In this chapter, we will see the remaining core concepts that you should know about when writing shaders.

Interacting with C# Code

So far, we have built each shader in a way that lets us modify their properties inside the Unity Editor through the Inspector window. This is useful, because designers and other people who work with your shaders in the Editor can tweak the behavior of your shader without needing to edit the shader code or graph itself. However, there are many times where you need to change shader properties at runtime. In these circumstances, we can't just change the properties inside the Editor, but we can use *scripting* to change any property value at runtime. Let's see how it works.

Cycling Colors with the HelloWorld Shader

The HelloWorld shader and the HelloShaderGraph graph, which we created in Chapters 3 and 4, respectively, apply a flat unlit color to an object using the `_BaseColor` property. With scripting, let's see how we can change the color at runtime whenever we want. Note that I'll assume you know a bit of C# scripting in this section, so this won't be an in-depth guide to scripting in general. I'll start by creating a new C# script by right-clicking in the Project View and selecting *Create* ➤ *C# Script*, which I will name "ControlColor.cs". Double-click it to open it in your preferred text editor, which should present you with the boilerplate default script.

D. Ilett, *Building Quality Shaders for Unity*®, https://doi.org/10.1007/978-1-4842-8652-4_9

Listing 9-1. Default C# script

```
using System.Collections;
using System.Collections.Generic;
using UnityEngine;

public class ControlColor : MonoBehaviour
{
    // Start is called before the first frame update
    void Start()
    {

    }

    // Update is called once per frame
    void Update()
    {

    }
}
```

Let's assume we are working with an object that contains only one material and that material uses the HelloWorld shader. We will create an instance variable to keep track of the material, which we can assign in the Start method (or Awake if you prefer).

Listing 9-2. Keeping track of the material attached to the renderer

```
private Material material;

void Start()
{
    material = GetComponent<Renderer>().material;
}
```

If you were using an object with multiple materials attached, you could instead access the renderer's materials array and pick the correct material from it. The Material class lets you access many variables and methods related to materials, and the method we are interested in is SetColor. In fact, Unity exposes many methods that allow us to override the runtime material properties of several data types, some of which are listed in the following:

- *SetBuffer* – Set a ComputeBuffer or a GraphicsBuffer on the GPU.

- *SetColor* – Set an RGBA color on the GPU.

- *SetFloat* – Set a single floating-point number on the GPU.

- *SetInt* – Set a single integer on the GPU.

- *SetMatrix* – Set a 4 × 4 matrix on the GPU.

- *SetTexture* – Set a texture on the GPU. This can be a `Texture2D`, `Texture3D`, `Cubemap`, or any other type that inherits from the base `Texture` class.

- *SetTextureOffset* – For any texture, set the offset `Vector2` for that texture.

- *SetTextureScale* – For any texture, set the scale `Vector2` for that texture.

- *SetVector* – Set a `Vector4` on the GPU.

We can use any of these methods to pass data to the shader. Each one takes two parameters: the name of the property and the piece of data we want to assign to that property. We have been naming properties using similar syntax for the book so far, so it should be easy to identify the name of the shader because we have prefixed them all with an underscore (e.g., `_BaseColor`). We could configure our script to change `_BaseColor` to any color we want, so let's have a bit of fun and cycle through different hue values over time.

Each one of the preceding methods has a corresponding `Get` version, which returns the value currently attached to the material property. For example, we can call `GetColor` to obtain the `_BaseColor` value at any point. In the `Update` method, this is the first thing we will do.

Listing 9-3. Obtaining the base color in Update

```
private void Update()
{
        var color = material.GetColor("_BaseColor");

        // Remaining code will go here.
}
```

The first time this code runs, it will grab the color assigned to the Color in the Inspector. Next, we will shift the hue of the color over time. This is tricky to do in RGB color space, but the Color class contains a static method called RGBToHSV that converts our Color to hue, saturation, and value floats. Each one ranges from 0 to 1, so it will be easy to cycle the hue over time by setting its value to Time.time modulo 1 (Time.time is the time in seconds since the game started). If we multiply or divide the time, then the cycling will get faster or slower.

Listing 9-4. Cycling the hue over time

```
float hue, sat, val;
Color.RGBToHSV(color, out hue, out sat, out val);
hue = (Time.time * 0.25f) % 1.0f;
```

This code will cycle through the entire range of hue values every 4 seconds. Once we have changed the hue, we can set the value back on the material. That requires us to use Color.HSVToRGB to convert back to a traditional RGB color and then use SetColor to bind the color data to the _BaseColor property.

Listing 9-5. Converting to RGB and binding the color data

```
color = Color.HSVToRGB(hue, sat, val);
material.SetColor("_BaseColor", color);
```

The ControlColor script is now complete. If we attach it to a GameObject that uses the HelloWorld shader on its material, then the hue will cycle over time through the power of scripting. In Figure 9-1, the material and script are attached to a sphere. The _BaseColor starts full red, so when the hue shifts, the saturation and value will stay high, resulting in bright colors. From left to right, the color changes over time.

Figure 9-1. *The base color of the material changes over time*

With this example, we were able to change a single color over time, but scripting is capable of a lot more than that. Let's revisit another shader and see how we can change its behavior using scripting.

World-Space Dissolve

The dissolve effect uses alpha clipping to remove pixels above a specific y-position in object space. The limitation here is that the dissolve is locked to a specific axis. It would be useful to have a variant of this shader that works in world space instead and lets us configure the direction of the dissolve effect and change it at runtime – in other words, I want to position a plane in the world and automatically change the cutoff origin and direction of the material through scripting. Let's see how to do that.

World-Space Dissolve in HLSL

This will require modification of the shader because the functionality is going to be quite different from the original. Since there is considerable overlap with the original, I'm going to duplicate the Dissolve shader and name the new file "DissolveWorld.shader". Then we can make edits from here. The first thing we'll do is rename the shader at the top of the file.

Listing 9-6. Renaming the DissolveWorld shader

```
Shader "Examples/DissolveWorld"
```

Next, let's revisit the properties. We no longer need the _CutoffHeight property because we are going to use the world-space position and normal vectors to represent a plane instead, so we can remove it. However, since we are going to assign the plane position and normal in scripting instead of in the Inspector, we don't need to include them in the Properties block at all. Unity can set data on shader variables even if they are not exposed properties, but we still need to include those vectors inside the HLSL code. Remember to include these inside the `UnityPerMaterial` buffer in URP.

Listing 9-7. Adding plane variables inside HLSL

```
float4 _BaseColor;
float4 _BaseTex_ST;
float _NoiseScale;
float _NoiseStrength;
float3 _PlaneOrigin;
float3 _PlaneNormal;
```

Now let's look at the `v2f` struct and the vertex shader. Previously, we passed the object-space position of the mesh we were rendering to the fragment shader, but now we require the world-space position. Let's rename the variable inside the `v2f` struct from `positionOS` to `positionWS`.

Listing 9-8. Sending world-space position instead of object-space position

```
struct v2f
{
      float4 positionCS : SV_Position;
      float2 uv : TEXCOORD0;
      float4 positionWS : TEXCOORD1;
};
```

In the vertex shader, we will also replace the line of code that calculated the object-space position with a line that calculates the world-space position instead. Thankfully, both URP and the built-in pipeline use the same syntax for this.

Listing 9-9. Calculating the world-space position in the vertex shader

```
o.uv = TRANSFORM_TEX(v.uv, _BaseTex);
o.positionWS = mul(unity_ObjectToWorld, v.positionOS);
```

Now we can turn our attention to the fragment shader, which I will write from scratch. First, we can sample the noise using the `gradientNoise` function and add it to the fragment position. This time, instead of adding the noise offset to the y-position, we will add it along the plane normal direction. Just to note here, the plane normal should always be normalized, but we will make sure that's the case in the script, so we don't need to manually normalize it within the shader.

Listing 9-10. Adding noise to the fragment's world position

```
float4 frag (v2f i) : SV_Target
{
    float noiseSample = gradientNoise(i.uv, _NoiseScale) * _
    NoiseStrength;
    float3 noisyPosition = i.positionWS.xyz + _PlaneNormal * noiseSample;
```

Now we can check which side of the plane the fragment position is on. We do this by subtracting the plane origin from the fragment position and then computing the dot product between the result and the plane normal. If the result of the dot product is positive, the fragment position is on one side of the plane, and if it is negative, it is on the opposite side. If it is zero, then the point lies exactly on the plane. In our case, we will discard any pixel whose dot product is above zero.

Listing 9-11. Discarding pixels on one side of the plane

```
float3 noisyPosition = i.positionWS.xyz + _PlaneNormal * noiseSample;

float3 offset = noisyPosition - _PlaneOrigin;
if (dot(offset, _PlaneNormal) > 0.0f) discard;
```

All that remains to be done is to sample _BaseTex and multiply it by the _BaseColor like we did in the original Dissolve shader.

Listing 9-12. Sampling the base texture and multiplying by the base color

```
    if (dot(offset, _PlaneNormal) > 0.0f) discard;

    float4 textureSample = tex2D(_BaseTex, i.uv);
    return textureSample * _BaseColor;
}
```

Before we write the script, which is going to send the plane data to the shader, let's see how to make these changes in Shader Graph too.

World-Space Dissolve in Shader Graph

For the Shader Graph version of this effect, let's duplicate the Dissolve graph and rename the new one "DissolveWorld.shadergraph" and open it in the Shader Graph editor. We will change the properties first. As with the HLSL version of this shader, we no longer need the Cutoff Height property, and we can replace it with two new Vector3 properties called Plane Origin and Plane Normal. Make sure their reference strings are _PlaneOrigin and _PlaneNormal, respectively. However, by default, these will be visible in the material Inspector, so also untick the *Exposed* box in the Node Settings for both new properties, as in Figure 9-2.

Figure 9-2. *The plane properties for the DissolveWorld shader*

Now we will make changes to the nodes we used for the Dissolve graph. First, we must change the noise so that it is applied in the direction of the plane normal rather than in the object-space y-direction. We can do that by multiplying the noise value after the Remap node by the Plane Normal property as in Figure 9-3.

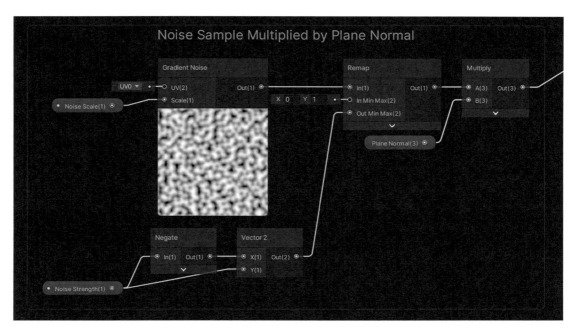

Figure 9-3. *Multiplying the noise by the plane normal*

After that, we can perform the cutoff. We need to add the noise value to the world-space fragment position, which we can obtain with a `Position` node in *world* space. Then, we can calculate which side of the plane the point is on using the same technique as the HLSL version of the shader: subtract the `Plane Origin` property and take the dot product with the `Plane Normal` property.

This value is negative when the fragment is on the side of the plane we want to keep, zero when it is exactly on the plane, and positive when it is on the side of the plane we want to discard. That means we can output it to *Alpha Clip Threshold* and then set the *Alpha* output to 0 as seen in Figure 9-4.

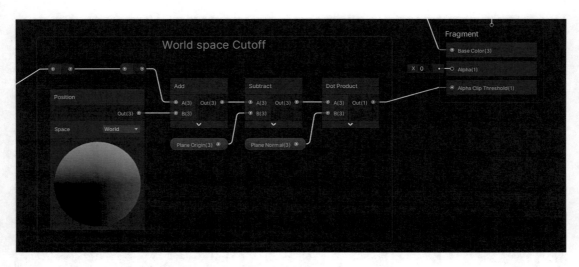

Figure 9-4. *Applying the cutoff in world space*

The graph is now complete, so let's see how to write a script that sends data about the plane to the shader.

World-Space Dissolve Scripting

Since we gave both the code and graph versions of the shader the same reference values for the plane origin and normal vectors, we just need to write one script that will work on both versions. I'm going to create a new C# script by right-clicking in the Project View and selecting *Create ➤ C# Script*, which I will name "DissolveWorld.cs". This will be a relatively short script. This script should be attached to a plane object in the scene, so the major difference between this and the new ControlColor script from the previous example is that we need to assign the Renderer that uses the dissolve material in the Inspector. With that in mind, I'll make the dissolveRenderer variable accessible to the Inspector and access its material in Start.

Listing 9-13. Accessing the renderer's material in Start

```
[SerializeField] private Renderer dissolveRenderer;
private Material material;

void Start()
{
    material = dissolveRenderer.material;
}
```

In Update, we will send the position and normal direction of the plane to the shader using the SetVector method. Although this method takes a Vector4 as its second parameter, the shader is using a float3 for these two variables. Thankfully, if we use a Vector3 as a parameter to the SetVector method, Unity converts it automatically to a Vector4, and on the shader side, it will ignore the fourth component to set the value of the float3. Unity does things in a bit of a roundabout way sometimes, but it works! The plane normal can be accessed through the up vector of the transform.

Listing 9-14. Sending the plane's position and up vector to the shader

```
void Update()
{
    material.SetVector("_PlaneOrigin", transform.position);
    material.SetVector("_PlaneNormal", transform.up);
}
```

The script is now complete. In the example scene I am about to show you, I have added a plane mesh to the scene through *Game Object ➤ 3D Object ➤ Plane*, then added a partially transparent material to its renderer, and attached the DissolveWorld script to it. That means we can't see it in the game, but it will still influence the dissolve effect on the sphere that is using the DissolveWorld shader. Figure 9-5 shows the Scene View and Game View side by side in Play Mode.

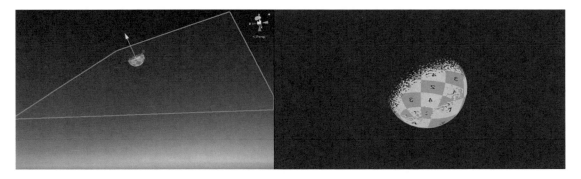

Figure 9-5. *On the left, the plane is selected in the Scene View. On the right, the dissolving object can be seen in the Game View*

If the plane is moved or rotated during runtime, then the sphere will update to reflect that, and different portions of the object will be discarded.

There are many effects that can be controlled through scripting. Sometimes, the state of the material will change in response to an event within the game, such as a collision or a user input. In other cases, you may wish to animate the properties of the material over time. Thankfully, Unity makes this easy with the use of its animation tools, which provide a high degree of control over shader properties, which we will explore next.

Controlling Shaders with Animations

Unity's animation tools can be used to control objects in many ways, including translating and rotating them, calling methods inside scripts, or playing sounds at certain points. It can also modify all public properties of materials at runtime. Like how scripts can modify properties using methods like SetFloat, animation clips in Unity can be used to control shader properties such as colors, floats, and vectors over time. Let's see how it works.

I'm going to create an animation that cycles the hue of the object through the range of values, as we did in the scripting example earlier in the chapter. However, it isn't possible to convert colors to HSV inside the animation window, so this effect will not be quite the same as the scripting example.

To start, open the Animation window. You can do this by right-clicking an existing window tab in the Editor and selecting *Add Tab* ➤ *Animation*. Then select an object in the scene that uses the HelloWorld shader. With the object selected, you should see a *Create* button in the Animation window, as seen in Figure 9-6. Click it and create a new animation clip called "Cycle".

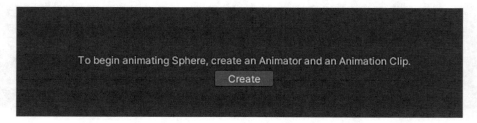

Figure 9-6. *Creating a new animation clip*

I'll keep this section brief since this is a shader book, not an animation book! Start by clicking the *Add Property* button, then select the Mesh Renderer drop-down, and choose the property called "Material._Base Color". Click the red button on the left of the animation toolbar, which will start recording our changes. We can then create a handful of key frames on the animation sheet, and for each one, make the object a different color – start with red, then orange, then yellow, and so on until you have about seven or so frames that cycle through the colors of the rainbow. The last frame should be the same as the start frame. Once you're finished, remember to click the red button again so that Unity stops recording the animation. Figure 9-7 illustrates the colors I used.

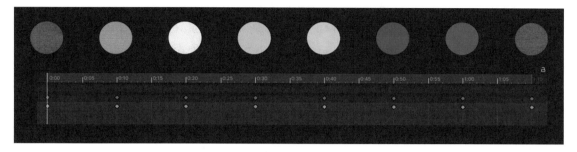

Figure 9-7.   *Animation key frames. Each key frame is 0:10 apart*

Running the game in Play Mode with this animation attached will exhibit similar behavior to Figure 9-1.

We can now control our shaders in Unity in several ways. Let's now see how to create shaders with different types of behavior that we can switch on and off at will.

Shader Keywords

Sometimes, you will write shader effects that require two or more distinct modes of operation. For example, you may be writing a game for several platforms that each support different shader features. In these cases, you could write each mode of operation in separate shader files, but this results in a lot of code duplication. Alternatively, we can use *shader keywords*. Keywords act as toggles that let you pick which portions of HLSL code should run depending on whether the keyword is turned on or not.

Broadly speaking, there are two types of keywords. The first type is like a switch, where the keyword is on or off. These types of keywords are useful when you have a feature that you'd like to turn on or off inside a shader at will. The second type is like an enumeration, where you have several different options and you pick only one. This type of keyword is useful when you have several modes of behavior that are mutually exclusive or when the shader can support multiple levels of quality with more intensive shader code being used at higher-quality levels.

Every time we add a keyword, Unity will compile multiple *shader variants* for each keyword value at build time. Each variant is a separate version of the shader file that gets included in the game build. If we are using one toggle keyword, then we end up with two variants, and if we introduced a second toggle keyword, then there would be two variants for each of those original variants, meaning four variants in total. In fact, each time you add a keyword, we multiply the total number of variants by the number of possible values that keyword can take – as you can imagine, we sometimes end up with a lot of variants! Later, we will see ways of reducing the number of variants that get included in the build.

Now that we have discussed what keywords are, let's see an example of using keywords in both HLSL and Shader Graph. We will introduce a keyword that, when active, will override whatever color the shader originally would have output, and instead, we will output the color red. This keyword acts as a toggle between two states. We will also see how to use scripting to toggle this keyword at runtime.

Shader Keywords in HLSL

For this example, I am going to use the HelloWorld shader as a starting point. With that in mind, I'll duplicate the HelloWorld shader file and name the new file "KeywordExample.shader". Like always, rename the shader at the top of the file.

Listing 9-15. Renaming the KeywordExample shader

```
Shader "Examples/KeywordExample"
```

We will want to turn the keyword on and off in the material Inspector, so we will start by discussing the syntax for adding a keyword to the Properties block.

Declaring Keyword Properties

Let's break this down into pieces:

- We use the Float type for properties that will be used for keywords.

- In this case, I will name the property _OverrideRed, but this is not the name of the keyword itself – only the property.

334

- Keywords use a different naming convention. The name of this keyword will be OVERRIDE_RED_ON. Keyword names use all caps and usually have underscores between each word.

- We specify that this property will be used for a keyword using an attribute. Since this keyword can either be on or off, we can use the Toggle attribute.

  - We name the keyword inside this attribute in a set of parentheses.

Bringing all these pieces together, we will add the following line of code to the Properties block.

Listing 9-16. Adding a togglable keyword property

```
[Toggle(OVERRIDE_RED_ON)] _OverrideRed("Force Red", Float) = 0
```

Once this property keyword has been added, it will appear in the material's Inspector window, as in Figure 9-8. This keyword is togglable, so you will see a checkbox next to it. This won't actually do anything to change the shader output yet, since we are not using the keyword anywhere inside the HLSL block, so the material still uses the value you set on Base Color.

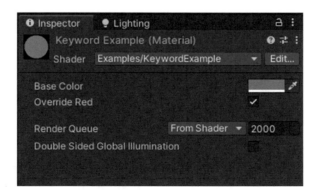

Figure 9-8. A property keyword in the material Inspector window

Now let's use the property in HLSL. We need to declare it before we can use it, which requires more special syntax.

Using Keywords

There are two main ways of declaring a keyword in HLSL, both of which are `#pragma` statements. The first is `#pragma multi_compile`, which takes a list of keyword values and automatically compiles every possible shader variant. You should use this approach if you will be enabling and disabling keywords at runtime (which we will cover shortly), but keep in mind that having many variants will increase the total build size of your game. When you list multiple keywords in a single list, they are mutually exclusive – only one can be active at a time. An example of its use is shown in Listing 9-17.

Note   Place these statements alongside existing `#pragma` statements, such as the ones we use to declare vertex and fragment shader functions.

Listing 9-17. Example multi_compile keyword declaration

```
#pragma multi_compile KEYWORD_A KEYWORD_B KEYWORD_C
```

In this example, only one of `KEYWORD_A`, `KEYWORD_B`, and `KEYWORD_C` is active at any one time. With `multi_compile`, we can also compile a variant in which none of the keywords in the list are active. We do this by specifying an extra keyword anywhere in the keyword list with a name that is at least one underscore. I usually use two underscores in the name for clarity, like the following.

Listing 9-18. Adding a blank keyword with multi_compile

```
#pragma multi_compile KEYWORD_A KEYWORD_B KEYWORD_C __
```

The second approach is `#pragma shader_feature`, which only builds shader variants that are being used when you build the game. This means you may have a reduced number of variants in your build, and therefore the build size will be reduced, but you will be unable to toggle keywords at runtime if some variants weren't included in the build. A good use case for `shader_feature` is if you are building shaders for multiple platforms that each require different sets of code – in that case, a game build for one platform never needs to include a variant intended for an incompatible other platform. An example of its use is shown in Listing 9-19.

Listing 9-19. Example shader_feature keyword declaration

```
#pragma shader_feature FEATURE_A FEATURE_B FEATURE_C
```

We can also specify the *scope* of the keyword here. Keywords can have *global* or *local* scope; global scope means that the keyword operates over every shader in the game, and local scope restricts the keyword to an individual material. By default, keywords use global scope, but we can restrict them to use local scope instead by appending _local to the directive you are using, like the following.

Listing 9-20. Using local scope with multi_compile

```
#pragma multi_compile_local KEYWORD_A KEYWORD_B KEYWORD_C __
```

We will use #pragma multi_compile_local for our shader. Later, we are going to toggle this keyword at runtime using scripting, so we must also include a variant where the keyword is inactive by adding a blank keyword to the list.

Listing 9-21. Using #pragma multi_compile to declare the OVERRIDE_RED_ ON keyword

```
#pragma vertex vert
#pragma fragment frag
```

`#pragma multi_compile_local OVERRIDE_RED_ON __`

We can now use OVERRIDE_RED_ON to change what the shader does based on whether it is turned on or off. We do this by encasing lines of code between #if and #endif directives, which means the encased code only runs when the keyword is active. We can also use #else, which means the code between that and #endif runs when the keyword is *not* active. It's just like an if-else statement in any other programming language.

Listing 9-22. A fragment shader using #if to pick between colors

```
float4 frag (v2f i) : SV_Target
{
#if OVERRIDE_RED_ON
    return float4(1.0f, 0.0f, 0.0f, 1.0f);
```

```
#else
        return _BaseColor;
#endif
}
```

This code is returning a hardcoded red color when the keyword is active and the user-defined _BaseColor otherwise, as in Figure 9-9.

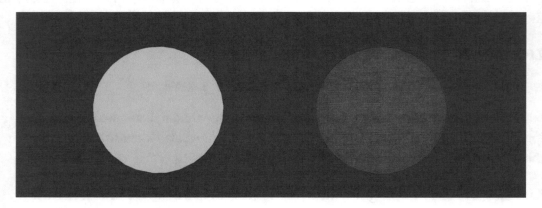

Figure 9-9. *On the left, the keyword is off. On the right, it is on*

On the left, the OVERRIDE_RED_ON keyword is off, so the object uses the Base Color defined on the material, which is green. On the right, the keyword is on, so the color is overridden, and the object becomes red. Let's now see how to do the same in Shader Graph.

Shader Keywords in Shader Graph

The Shader Graph interface makes it a little easier to work with keywords, because many of the fiddly bits present in the code are handled for us behind the scenes. Let's start by creating a new Unlit graph by right-clicking in the Project View and naming it "KeywordExample.shadergraph". This graph will include a Base Color property. Ordinarily we would wire this up to the *Base Color* output on the master stack, but not in this case.

Instead, we are going to use a keyword. We can add a keyword using the same drop-down on the Blackboard that we use for properties – at the bottom of the list, there will be a section for keywords with three options: Boolean, Enum, and Material Quality as shown in Figure 9-10.

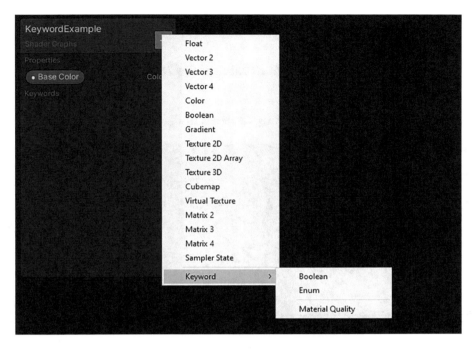

Figure 9-10. *Adding a keyword in Shader Graph*

The `Boolean` type is used for keywords that can be turned on or off. `Enum` is used for keywords that can take several mutually exclusive values, like those used for compiling shaders for multiple platforms. Finally, `Material Quality` is a predefined enum in URP that we can use to compile a graph for *Low*, *Medium*, and *High* preset quality levels. We'll pick `Boolean` for our shader.

In the Node Settings, we have a lot of control over how this keyword operates:

- The *Name* is used for the property name that will be visible in the material Inspector. I will name mine "Override Red".

- The *Reference* is the behind-the-scenes name of the keyword itself. I will name this "OVERRIDE_RED_ON". The convention is to use all caps with underscores between each word.

- The *Definition* lets us choose how Unity generates shader variants. The options are *Multi Compile* and *Shader Feature*, which are explained in the HLSL section. The *Predefined* option should be used if you want to use a keyword that is defined by URP for you. In our case, we will use Multi Compile.

- We can set the *Scope* of the shader to either *Global* or *Local*. Ours should be Local.

- We can specify what the *Default* value of the keyword is on a new material.

For our shader, we will use the settings as seen in Figure 9-11.

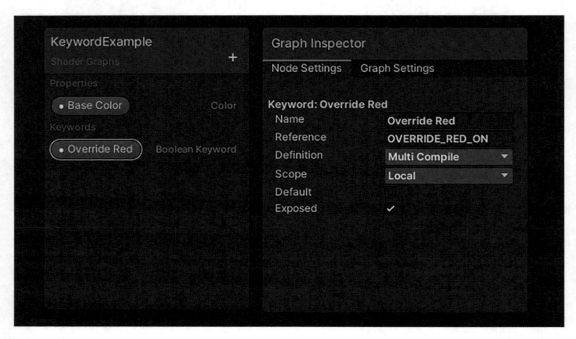

Figure 9-11. *Settings for the OVERRIDE_RED_ON keyword*

Now we can use this keyword on the graph to control the output. If we drag the `Override Red` property onto the graph, it will have two inputs labeled *On* and *Off* and one output vector. We can connect the `Base Color` property to the *Off* option, then hardcode a red color for the *On* option with the vector $(1, 0, 0, 1)$, and connect the output to the *Base Color* pin on the master stack, as seen in Figure 9-12.

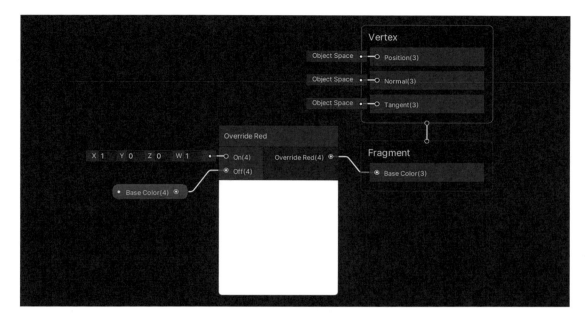

Figure 9-12. *Connecting the On and Off branches of a Boolean keyword*

When you do this and create a material using this shader, you will see an output just like in Figure 9-9. Now that we can use keywords in our shaders and modify their values in the material Inspector, let's briefly discuss how to change keywords at runtime using C# scripting.

Modifying Keywords Using C# Scripting

I am going to write a script that toggles the keyword value every second. Start by creating a new C# script by right-clicking in the Project View and choosing *Create* ➤ *C# Script*. This script should be called "KeywordControl.cs". Like we saw earlier in this chapter, the first step is to store a reference to the material itself, so replace the boilerplate Start method with the following code.

Listing 9-23. Getting a reference to the material

```
private Material material;

void Start()
{
    material = GetComponent<Renderer>().material;
}
```

Once we have this reference, we can start to modify the material's keyword values in the Update method. I'll use Time.time with the modulo operator to set up a clock that outputs a true or false value that switches every second. Then based on that Boolean output, I'll enable or disable the keyword. We can do that using the EnableKeyword and DisableKeyword functions, both of which take a string parameter for the name of the keyword.

Listing 9-24. Enabling and disabling a keyword in Update

```
void Update()
{
    bool toggle = Time.time % 2.0f > 1.0f;

    if(toggle)
    {
        material.EnableKeyword("OVERRIDE_RED_ON");
    }
    else
    {
        material.DisableKeyword("OVERRIDE_RED_ON");
    }
}
```

When you attach this script to an object that uses the KeywordExample shader, regardless of whether it uses the HLSL or Shader Graph version, it will toggle between colors every second.

We have now seen how keywords can be used in our shaders. Next, we will see a feature of ShaderLab that makes it easier to share passes between shaders.

UsePass in ShaderLab

The *UsePass* command, which is available in ShaderLab in all render pipelines, lets us take a Pass from one shader file and insert it into a different shader, provided the Pass is given a name. If you often find yourself reusing the same Pass in several shaders, then UsePass will save you the trouble of copying the code across several shader files. Let's see how it works in practice.

In Chapter 7, we saw that it is necessary to add a depth-only pass to shaders if we want objects to get copied to the camera depth texture. In those cases, we took the necessary passes from Unity's built-in shaders and copied them into our own shaders so that I could illustrate what they were doing under the hood. However, it isn't necessary to copy and paste them because we can use UsePass instead. To name a Pass so that we can access it with UsePass, we use the Name keyword at the top of the Pass and specify the name inside a string.

Listing 9-25. Naming a Pass

```
Pass
{
    Name "ExamplePass"
```

Unity helpfully names many of the Pass blocks in its built-in shaders. We can access them with UsePass, for which the syntax is to specify the shader name (the same one we define at the top of each shader file), followed by the pass name *in capitals*. UsePass works like any other Pass in that Unity evaluates the passes from top to bottom.

In Chapter 7 when we copied the ShadowCaster pass from the *Standard* shader for the built-in pipeline, we could use UsePass in its place instead.

Listing 9-26. Accessing the ShadowCaster pass with UsePass in the built-in pipeline

```
Pass { ... }

// Other passes may be present here.

UsePass "Standard/SHADOWCASTER"
```

And in the same chapter, when we copied the DepthOnly pass from the Unlit shader for URP, we can similarly use UsePass instead of copying and pasting the code.

Listing 9-27. Accessing the DepthOnly pass with UsePass in URP

```
Pass { ... }

// Other passes may be present here.

UsePass "Universal Render Pipeline/Unlit/DEPTHONLY"
```

Using these, you shouldn't notice a difference in results from the copy-paste method, but going forward, this will make it easier to use passes in multiple shaders. You might find it useful to build up your own collection of common passes and include them inside a single shader file so that you can include them in other shaders with UsePass.

Next, let's see another ShaderLab feature that makes it possible to use the previous state of the color buffer within shaders by copying it to a texture we can sample.

GrabPass in ShaderLab

GrabPass is a feature available by ShaderLab that lets Unity take the color buffer, which contains objects that have already been rendered, and copy it to a texture that you can sample in your shaders. GrabPass can execute at any point for any shader and is not locked to specific queues in the rendering pipeline, so it is very expensive if you use it often. On those platforms, Unity provides a scene color texture that we can sample, but it is only generated once after all opaques have been rendered. Let's see how GrabPass works in the built-in pipeline and then see the alternatives that are available in URP and Shader Graph. We will do this by creating a sepia tone effect, which takes the existing scene colors and applies an old yellowish photograph filter over the scene.

Note   GrabPass is not supported by URP, HDRP, or any custom SRP that you might write. This is a feature that is exclusive to the built-in render pipeline, but we will see alternatives for other pipelines shortly.

Figure 9-13. *Sepia tone in the URP default scene*

Sepia Tone Effect Using GrabPass in the Built-in Pipeline

The GrabPass command only works in the built-in pipeline. It is, however, a powerful tool that lets us access the state of the color buffer at *any* stage of rendering, no matter whether the shader uses opaque or transparent rendering, because it copies the color buffer into a special texture just before rendering the shader's other passes. With that in mind, let's see how to use it to create a sepia tone effect.

Note   This texture is available to any object that gets rendered inside the same batch as the first one during the same frame, which means GrabPass becomes very expensive if used in several different shaders, since Unity will be unable to batch them and therefore it will copy the color buffer into a texture several times per frame.

I'll start by creating a new shader file and naming it "SepiaTone.shader". A lot of the code will look familiar from other shaders we've written – the following code is the starting code I'll be working with.

Listing 9-28. The SepiaTone built-in shader code skeleton

```
Shader "Examples/SepiaTone"
{
    Properties
    {
    }
    SubShader
    {
        Tags
        {
            "RenderType" = "Transparent"
            "Queue" = "Transparent"
        }

        Pass
        {
            ZWrite Off

            HLSLPROGRAM
            #pragma vertex vert
            #pragma fragment frag

            #include "UnityCG.cginc"

            struct appdata
            {
                float4 positionOS : Position;
            };

            struct v2f
            {
                float4 positionCS : SV_Position;
                float4 positionSS : TEXCOORD0;
            };
```

```
v2f vert (appdata v)
{
    v2f o;
    o.positionCS = UnityObjectToClipPos(v.positionOS);
    o.positionSS = ComputeScreenPos(o.positionCS);
    return o;
}

float4 frag (v2f i) : SV_Target { ... }
ENDHLSL
            }
        }
}
```

The SepiaTone shader will use no properties, so we can keep the Properties block empty. I'll be using a transparent shader so that we can be sure all opaque objects are included in the grab texture, which is why I'm using Transparent tags in the Tags block.

Now that we have a starting point, let's discuss how GrabPass works. It works just like a regular Pass, insofar as it should be included inside a SubShader alongside other Pass blocks. You should include it *above* any other Pass blocks that need to use the scene color texture. The GrabPass block does not need to include anything inside its curly braces; if you leave it empty, Unity will copy the scene color details into a texture called _GrabTexture, which will become accessible to any subsequent shader pass.

Listing 9-29. Default GrabPass declaration

GrabPass { }

```
Pass { ... }
```

This method exhibits the slow batching behavior I described previously. However, we have the option of renaming the texture used by GrabPass. If we do, then Unity will only ever copy to the named texture once per frame – the first time we request Unity to write to that texture – which means that subsequent shaders that use GrabPass with the same named texture won't copy the color buffer into the texture again. This could result in a significant performance increase if you use GrabPass often. Let's name the texture used for the SepiaTone shader _SceneColorTexture.

Listing 9-30. GrabPass using a different texture name

```
GrabPass { "_SceneColorTexture" }

Pass { ... }
```

Now we can turn our attention to the Pass block. We must declare _
SceneColorTexture in HLSLPROGRAM before we can use it in the fragment shader. If we
didn't choose to specify an alternative name, we would declare _GrabTexture instead.

Listing 9-31. Declaring the GrabPass texture

```
struct v2f { ... };
sampler2D _SceneColorTexture;
```

In the fragment shader, we will sample _SceneColorTexture using the tex2D
function and apply a sepia tone filter to it. We do this using a 3 × 3 matrix of values,
where each row of the matrix represents how much one channel of the output color is
influenced by the channels of the original color. We use the mul function to multiply the
sepia tone matrix and the scene color.

Listing 9-32. Calculating the sepia-toned output in the fragment shader

```
float4 frag (v2f i) : SV_Target
{
    const float3x3 sepia = float3x3
    (
        0.393, 0.349, 0.272,   // Red.
        0.769, 0.686, 0.534,   // Green.
        0.189, 0.168, 0.131    // Blue.
    );

    float2 screenUVs = i.positionSS.xy / i.positionSS.w;
    float3 sceneColor = tex2D(_SceneColorTexture, screenUVs);

    float3 outputColor = mul(sceneColor, sepia);

    return float4(outputColor, 1.0f);
}
```

Since the sepia tone values always remain the same, I use the const keyword when declaring the matrix. The result of this shader is an effect that takes all pixels behind the object currently being rendered and applies a yellow-tinted filter to them. All objects drawn before the current object will have the filter applied to them because GrabPass can pull the contents of the color buffer at any point within a frame. The result is shown in Figure 9-14.

Figure 9-14. *Four colored rectangles behind a large rectangle that uses the SepiaTone shader*

From left to right, Figure 9-14 features four rectangles colored red, blue, yellow, and green. In front of the four rectangles, covering their lower halves, is a larger rectangle that uses the SepiaTone shader.

Although GrabPass is powerful, it can also be expensive when used often. It is also not supported by URP or Shader Graph, although there are alternatives with different restrictions that we can use instead. Let's see how the alternative method works in URP.

Sepia Tone Effect Using Camera Opaque Texture in URP

GrabPass does not work in URP, HDRP, or any other Scriptable Render Pipeline. However, that does not mean we are completely unable to use the previous state of the color buffer anywhere inside a URP shader. Like the _CameraDepthTexture, which we covered in Chapter 7, we have access to the _CameraOpaqueTexture inside our shaders. This texture represents the state of the color buffer after all opaque objects have been rendered (i.e., all objects with a render queue value of 2500 or below), so we are only able to use it in transparent shaders, and it will never contain any transparent objects. With those limitations in mind, let's see how the texture works in URP.

First, we must ensure that URP creates the texture for us. Like we did with the depth texture, find your project's URP Asset and enable the *Opaque Texture* option near the top, as seen in Figure 9-15.

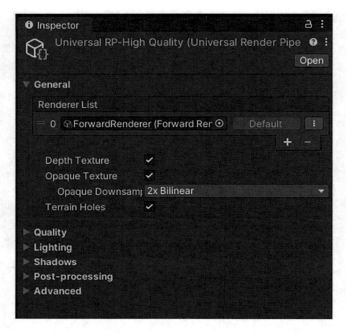

Figure 9-15. *The Opaque Texture option is below the Depth Texture option, which we have seen previously*

Once the Opaque Texture option has been ticked, Unity will generate the _ CameraOpaqueTexture for use inside our shaders. Now let's see what changes must be made to the built-in pipeline version of this shader to make it suitable for URP.

Let us again start by creating a new shader file and naming it "SepiaTone.shader". Here is the code I'll use as a starting point.

Listing 9-33. The SepiaTone URP shader code skeleton

```
Shader "Examples/SepiaTone"
{
    Properties
```

```
{

}
SubShader
{
      Tags
      {
            "RenderType" = "Transparent"
            "Queue" = "Transparent"
            "RenderPipeline" = "UniversalPipeline"
      }

      Pass
      {
            Tags
            {
                  "LightMode" = "UniversalForward"
            }

            HLSLPROGRAM
            #pragma vertex vert
            #pragma fragment frag

            #include "Packages/com.unity.render-pipelines.universal/
            ShaderLibrary/Core.hlsl"

            struct appdata
            {
                  float4 positionOS : Position;
            };

            struct v2f
            {
                  float4 positionCS : SV_Position;
                  float4 positionSS : TEXCOORD0;
            };
```

```
            v2f vert (appdata v)
            {
                  v2f o;
                  o.positionCS = TransformObjectToHClip(v.
                  positionOS.xyz);
                  o.positionSS = ComputeScreenPos(o.positionCS);
                  return o;
            }

            float4 frag (v2f i) : SV_Target { ... }
            ENDHLSL
        }
    }
}
```

Now we can make changes to the fragment shader to make the effect work in URP. The alternative method to GrabPass is to sample the _CameraOpaqueTexture instead, although URP provides a shader include file that contains functions to make this easier for us. Instead of including the *DeclareDepthTexture* file, which we used in the Silhouette shader to sample _CameraDepthTexture, we will instead include the *DeclareOpaqueTexture* file, which is contained inside the same folder.

Listing 9-34. Including the DeclareOpaqueTexture file

```
#include "Packages/com.unity.render-pipelines.universal/ShaderLibrary/
Core.hlsl"
#include "Packages/com.unity.render-pipelines.universal/ShaderLibrary/
DeclareOpaqueTexture.hlsl"
```

This include file will declare the _CameraOpaqueTexture for us and provide the SampleSceneColor function, which takes a set of UVs as input and returns a float3 color. In the fragment shader, we need to change the line where we read the scene color.

Listing 9-35. Reading the scene color using the SampleSceneColor function

```
float4 frag (v2f i) : SV_Target
{
      const float3x3 sepia = float3x3
```

```
    (
        0.393f, 0.349f, 0.272f,    // Red.
        0.769f, 0.686f, 0.534f,    // Green.
        0.189f, 0.168f, 0.131f     // Blue.
    );

    float2 screenUVs = i.positionSS.xy / i.positionSS.w;
    float3 sceneColor = SampleSceneColor(screenUVs);

    float3 outputColor = mul(sceneColor, sepia);

    return float4(outputColor, 1.0f);
}
```

With this approach, we can achieve almost the same effect as using GrabPass, with the caveat that _CameraOpaqueTexture can only be properly sampled inside a transparent shader and it will only contain opaques, whereas GrabPass could contain transparent objects too. Figure 9-13 shows what it looks like in the URP sample scene.

Now that we have thoroughly covered the sepia tone effect and using scene color in shader code, let's see how to do the same thing in Shader Graph.

Sepia Tone Effect Using the Scene Color Node in Shader Graph

Shader Graph exposes many useful nodes, and the Scene Color node is no exception; behind the scenes, it samples the very same _CameraOpaqueTexture as the URP code shader approach. Therefore, we must ensure the opaque texture is generated inside the URP Asset settings, as seen in Figure 9-15. Once that's done, create a new Unlit graph and name it "SepiaTone.shadergraph".

First, go into the Graph Settings and change the Surface mode to Transparent, as seen in Figure 9-16. Remember that the opaque texture is only generated between the opaque and transparent rendering queues, so we can only use it inside transparent shaders.

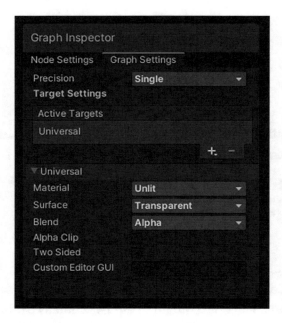

Figure 9-16. *Graph Settings for the sepia tone effect*

Next, we can go straight to the main graph surface since we don't need to include any properties. The Scene Color node samples _CameraOpaqueTexture and returns a float3 color. Like we did in the code versions of the shader, we will multiply this by a 3 × 3 matrix that contains the coefficients necessary to convert any RGB color into its sepia-toned equivalent. The Matrix 3x3 node will allow us to do that – we just need to insert the coefficients into the text entry fields on the node's body. The Multiply node carries out matrix multiplication as you would expect (take note of the order in which the two inputs are connected to it). Then the output can be connected to *Base Color* on the master stack. Figure 9-17 shows you how these nodes are connected.

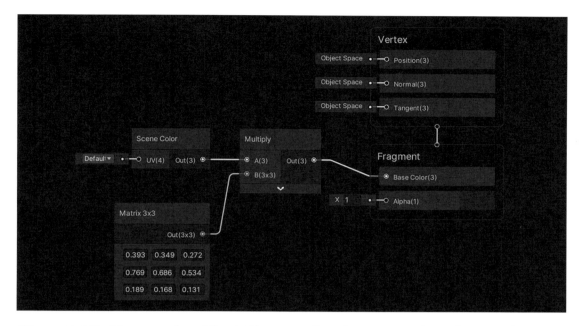

Figure 9-17. *The completed SepiaTone graph only requires these three nodes*

When you create a material that uses this shader and attach it to an object, you will see a result like Figure 9-13.

Summary

In this chapter, we have seen some more powerful and useful features of ShaderLab and Shader Graph. Scripting and animations can be used to completely control how materials act when playing a game, and features such as keywords and UsePass make it easier to work with shaders without needing to constantly duplicate code. GrabPass and the _CameraOpaqueTexture let us work with the color buffer inside shaders in the same way as the _CameraDepthTexture let us use depth. Here's what we learned in this chapter:

- C# scripts can be used to interface with shaders using functions like SetFloat, SetColor, and SetVector, all of which are part of the Material class.

- Unity's animation tools can also be used to control how materials look by modifying any public property of a material.

- Shader keywords can be used to pick between different sections of code inside the same shader file. Keywords cause multiple variants of the shader to be compiled when the game is built for a particular platform.

- UsePass can be used to copy named shader passes from other files without needing to manually duplicate the code.

- GrabPass can be used to capture the scene color at any arbitrary point, but it is only available in the built-in pipeline.

- The _CameraOpaqueTexture is available in Shader Graph and URP as an alternative to GrabPass. It allows the use of the opaque texture within transparent shaders.

CHAPTER 10

Lighting and Shadows

Lighting is one of the most important features to add to any shader if you want to add a sense of realism to your game. Players use visual cues such as size and shape to determine the relative position of objects in a 3D game, and lighting and shadows are two important cues that help players judge the depth of objects in relation to one another. That said, it's not just games with realistic graphics that rely on lighting – heavily stylized games also benefit from this added information. In this chapter, we will see how lighting can be added to objects, starting with relatively simple lighting models and gradually building up to a complicated lighting model based on the physical properties of your objects.

Lighting Models

A lighting model is our way of describing the way light sources interact with the surfaces of objects in the game. Typically, lighting models can't perfectly recreate the lighting from a real-world scene, but they are a close approximation. Broadly speaking, we can split the light falling onto an object into *local* or *direct illumination*, which is the result of a direct interaction between the surface of an object and a light source, and *global illumination*, which occurs when a proportion of light reflects off a surface and shines on another surface. Let's discuss several types of light before we work with them inside a shader.

Ambient Light

If you sit in an enclosed room in the daytime, even if your curtains are shut, the room will still be lit because the light will shine through the gaps in the curtains and bounce all over the room. As a result, most of the objects in the room will have roughly the same level of illumination despite none of them being directly illuminated by the sun. Similarly, even shadowed areas on a bright day will appear highly illuminated.

357

© Daniel Ilett 2022
D. Ilett, *Building Quality Shaders for Unity*®, https://doi.org/10.1007/978-1-4842-8652-4_10

Ambient lighting is our way of approximating global illumination. Generally speaking, methods that model global illumination are computationally expensive because they have to simulate not only the interactions between light sources and objects in the scene but also light bounces between objects and other objects. Ambient light, on the other hand, applies a flat amount of color to every object in the scene to simulate the effect of all those light bounces, particularly light that originated from the sun. Figure 10-1 shows an object illuminated only by ambient light.

Figure 10-1. *A sphere illuminated only by ambient light from the scene. The sky has slightly bluer reflected light than the ground*

The amount of ambient light applied to each object is a setting we can manually change at will. If our lighting model only considered ambient light, then the equation to calculate the final color of an object would look like this:

Equation 10-1: Lighting model containing only ambient light

$$L_{total} = L_{ambient}$$

That's not very interesting so far! It's worth noting at this point that the light can be any color, so this isn't just a single floating-point value – it's an RGB color, just like any other. To build a more interesting model, let's add different types of direct illumination.

Diffuse Light

A perfectly matte (non-shiny) surface tends to reflect light "evenly" – that is, the amount of reflected light depends on the properties of the surface and the angle between the light and the surface, and a small change in that angle causes a small change in the amount of reflected light. This is called *diffuse lighting*, which is a type of direct illumination. We use the vector between a point on the object's surface and the light source, called the *light vector* and denoted by *l*, and the *normal vector* at the same point on the surface, denoted by *n*, to calculate the amount of diffuse light falling onto an object. Diffuse light is not influenced at all by the position of the viewer (camera) relative to the object or the light source. Figure 10-2 shows the diffuse interaction between the light source and the surface.

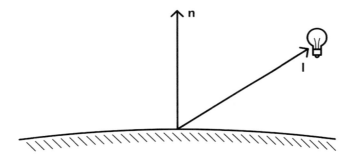

Figure 10-2. *Normal and light vectors for the diffuse light calculation*

The dot product between *n* and *l* gives us the proportion of ambient light acting on the surface. It's also worth mentioning that these vectors should be normalized prior to any lighting calculation, because that means the result will always be between –1 and 1. Since the dot product can be negative, we clamp negative values to zero; otherwise, we will encounter visual errors. This value is then multiplied by the color of the light source to give us the total diffuse lighting contribution. We can model the diffuse light with the following equation:

Equation 10-2: Diffuse lighting calculation

$$L_{diffuse} = L_{color} \times \max(0, n \cdot l)$$

In Figure 10-3, you'll see an object lit by both ambient and diffuse light. As you can see, diffuse lighting is characterized by a smooth falloff from a fully lit region, which is directly lit by the light source, to a shadowed region.

Figure 10-3. *A sphere illuminated by ambient and diffuse light. The scene's directional light is to the top left, hence the illumination from that direction*

Let's update our lighting model from Equation 10-1 to include diffuse lighting too. Lighting is additive, so all we need to do to calculate the total amount of lighting acting on the object is to sum the individual types of light.

Equation 10-3: Lighting model containing ambient and diffuse light

$$L_{total} = L_{ambient} + L_{diffuse}$$

Diffuse lighting is perhaps the most noticeable type of lighting, especially when you move the light source or the object. However, there are other types of lighting that depend on the position of the viewer.

Specular Light

When you view a shiny object, the position and strength of the reflective highlight changes whenever you move the object or the angle at which you look at it. This is called specular lighting, and it occurs when the surface of an object is smooth. With diffuse light, the surface typically has imperceptible bumps and other imperfections, which mean reflected light is scattered in all directions. With specular light, on the other hand, all or most of the light rays that reach the object's surface are reflected at the same angle. This means there is always a part of the surface that strongly reflects many rays directly into the viewer, which is why you see very bright highlights on a small section of the surface.

The amount of specular light is proportional to the dot product between two vectors: the vector between a point on the surface of the object and the viewer, denoted v, and the light ray reflected off the surface, denoted r. The reflected light ray, r, is itself the result of reflecting the incoming light ray, l, in the normal vector, n, which is computationally expensive to calculate. These vectors are shown in Figure 10-4.

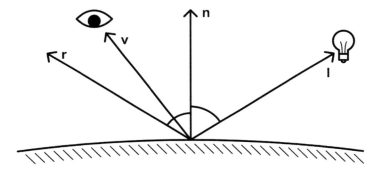

Figure 10-4. *View vector and reflected vector for specular light calculations. The angle between r and n is equal to the angle between l and n*

The result of the dot product is raised by a power, α, where a higher power represents a higher degree of shininess. This value is also multiplied by the light color to obtain the final specular light value.

Equation 10-4: Specular lighting

$$L_{specular} = L_{color} \times (r \cdot v)^{\alpha}$$

This is computationally expensive to calculate due to the reflection step. A slightly different approach, developed by Jim Blinn in the 1970s, removes the reflection vector calculation and uses a revised approach. Instead, we calculate the *half vector* between v, the viewer, and l, the light source – this is, comparatively, very easy to compute, so we use this calculation in shaders instead. The half vector is denoted by h, as seen in Figure 10-5.

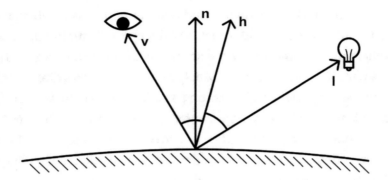

Figure 10-5. *Half vector and normal vector for specular light calculations using Blinn's method. The angle between v and h is equal to the angle between l and h*

Then, the specular lighting can be obtained using the dot product between n and h. We still need to raise the result by a power, α, although this method typically requires higher powers for a similar result to the first approach.

Equation 10-5: Specular lighting with Blinn's modification

$$h = \left(\frac{l + v}{|l + v|} \right)$$

$$L_{blinnSpecular} = L_{color} \times (n \cdot h)^{\alpha}$$

With specular lighting, we see a highlight on the object that moves in relation to the light source position and the viewer position. Figure 10-6 shows an object that is lit by ambient, diffuse, and specular lighting. This time, the base color of the object is red so that the specular highlight is easier to see.

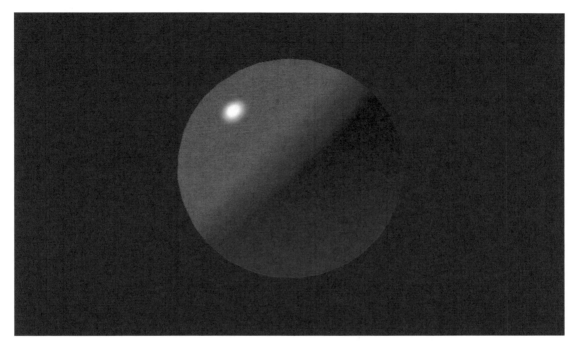

Figure 10-6. *A sphere lit by ambient, diffuse, and specular lighting. The specular highlight moves around depending on where the viewer is located*

Now that we can calculate specular highlights on our objects, we can add specular lighting to the lighting model.

Equation 10-6: Lighting model containing ambient, diffuse, and specular light

$$L_{total} = L_{ambient} + L_{diffuse} + L_{blinnSpecular}$$

Most basic lighting models would stop here and use only these types of light, but there is another type of light that I am quite fond of including in my shaders, so we will briefly cover it too.

Fresnel Light

When you view objects at a very shallow angle, sometimes they will appear bright. You may have seen this effect before in real life in places like large bodies of clear water or the surface of a polished table. The steeper the angle, the less bright the surface will appear. This is called *Fresnel lighting* (pronounced like "fruh-nell"). Fresnel light typically isn't included in many classical lighting models, but I like to include it in many of my shaders, especially if my game uses a stylized aesthetic.

Fresnel lighting is inversely proportional to the angle between the viewer and the surface normal. That means that when you view objects at a grazing angle, the Fresnel effect will be very prominent, but if you view the object face-on, there will be zero Fresnel light. As a result, we can calculate the amount of Fresnel light by taking the dot product between the view vector and the surface normal vector and then subtracting it from 1. Remember that n and v should be normalized before the calculation. These vectors can be seen in Figure 10-7.

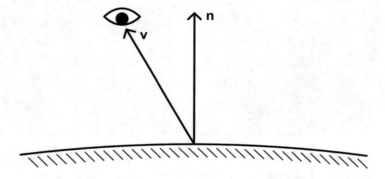

Figure 10-7. *View vector and normal vector for Fresnel light calculations*

In games, it is common to supply a power, β, to control the influence of Fresnel lighting, like we did for specular lighting. When you increase the power, the Fresnel light gets less prominent. Fresnel light is also multiplied by the light color, just like diffuse and specular light were.

Equation 10-7: Fresnel lighting

$$L_{fresnel} = L_{color} \times \left(1 - n \cdot v\right)^{\beta}$$

If you so choose, your lighting model can include Fresnel lighting in addition to the others.

Equation 10-8: Lighting model containing ambient, diffuse, specular, and Fresnel lighting

$$L_{total} = L_{ambient} + L_{diffuse} + L_{blinnSpecular} + L_{fresnel}$$

In Figure 10-8, you will see one sphere using material that has Fresnel and one that doesn't. The difference is most noticeable at the edges of the sphere where the angle between the viewer and the surface normal is the greatest.

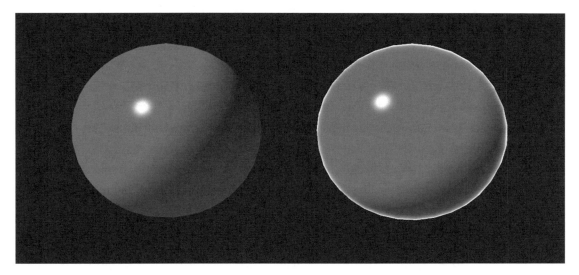

Figure 10-8. *The sphere on the left has no Fresnel. The sphere on the right does*

You should now know the theory behind several types of lighting that interact with the surface of an object. Now let's look at how to incorporate them into shaders.

Blinn-Phong Reflection Model

The *Phong reflection model* was developed by Bui Tuong Phong in the mid-1970s to model the way light interacts with the surface of an object, based on the properties of the object itself. It combines ambient, diffuse, and specular lighting to approximate how lighting operates in a real-world scene, as seen in Equation 10-6. The *Blinn-Phong reflection model* implements Blinn's alternative calculation of specular lighting into the existing Phong reflection model, as discussed previously. These reflection models work by taking the surface properties of many points on the object's surface (such as the base color, shininess, and normal vector) and the light vector, view vector, and half vector relative to those points and calculating the final color at each of those points.

Flat shading, *Gouraud shading*, and *Phong shading* are three methods for evaluating the amount of light on a surface. Each technique evaluates different locations on the object's surface and uses different interpolation techniques to obtain the final light amount on each pixel. Let's see how each of these techniques works.

Flat Shading

Flat shading methods use a single lighting value for each face of the mesh. Since every pixel in a triangle has the same amount of light falling on it, each face of the mesh appears flat, hence the name. To achieve flat shading, all pixels belonging to a particular triangle use the same vectors for the lighting calculations so that the final lighting value is the same for each of those pixels. However, we can still use textures for the base color of the object, so the pixels of a given face can still have different output colors.

We can choose any point on the surface of a triangle to serve as the "basis" point of lighting calculations for the whole triangle, as long as we consistently use the same method for all triangles. Usually, we pick either the first vertex or the centroid (middle point) of the triangle. Also, although the Blinn-Phong model contains specular lighting as a component, it's usually omitted when using flat shading because specular highlights on objects are typically very small and not captured well with flat shading techniques. Similarly, I will omit Fresnel lighting from the equation for flat shading.

Figure 10-9. *Flat shading. The sphere on the left has ambient, diffuse, specular, and Fresnel lighting, while the sphere on the right only has ambient and diffuse lighting*

Flat shading is a very efficient rendering technique, so it can be used to minimize the performance impact of your game, or when combined with low-poly meshes, flat shading can be used to achieve a stylized aesthetic in your game. Now that we know what flat shading is, let's see an example of how to use it in both HLSL shader code and Shader Graph. This shader will support basic texture mapping and will tint each triangle of the mesh based on its exposure to the primary directional light present in the scene. For now, this is the only light we will consider.

Flat Shading in HLSL

Let's create a new HLSL shader called "FlatShading.shader" and remove all its contents. At the top, name the shader "FlatShading" and open a Shader block. I've specified a skeleton set of code for this file that we can modify. For most of the shader, there are relatively minor differences between the code for the built-in pipeline and for URP.

Listing 10-1. Code skeleton for the FlatShading shader

```
Shader "Examples/FlatShading"
{
    Properties { ... }
    SubShader
    {
        Tags
        {
            "RenderType" = "Opaque"
            "Queue" = "Geometry"
        }
        Pass
        {
            Tags { ... }

            HLSLPROGRAM
            #pragma vertex vert
            #pragma fragment frag

            struct appdata { ... };
            struct v2f { ... };
            v2f vert(appdata v) { ... }
```

```
        float4 frag(v2f i) : SV_Target { ... }

        ENDHLSL
    }
  }
}
```

Let's handle the `Properties` block. We only need to define the surface properties of the mesh here – this isn't the place to put anything related to the lights in the scene. With that in mind, I'm going to add _BaseColor and _BaseTex properties for now.

Listing 10-2. The Properties block

```
Properties
{
    _BaseColor ("Base Color", Color) = (1, 1, 1, 1)
    _BaseTex("Base Texture", 2D) = "white" {}
}
```

Inside the `HLSLPROGRAM` block, we must declare those properties again. The code is slightly different between the built-in pipeline and URP because we must conform to the SRP Batcher rules in URP. Put the following lines of code for the pipeline you are using between the `v2f` struct definition and the `vert` function.

Listing 10-3. Declaring properties in HLSL in the built-in pipeline

```
struct v2f { ... };

sampler2D _BaseTex;
float4 _BaseColor;
float4 _BaseTex_ST;
```

Listing 10-4. Declaring properties in HLSL in URP

```
struct v2f { ... };

sampler2D _BaseTex;
```

```
CBUFFER_START(UnityPerMaterial)
    float4 _BaseColor;
    float4 _BaseTex_ST;
CBUFFER_END
```

Now let's look at the appdata and v2f structs. The appdata struct will take in the object-space position of each vertex, as well as a set of UV coordinates. We also require the normal vector for the lighting calculations, which comes with its own shader semantic, NORMAL. These normals are in object space, so I'll call the variable normalOS.

Listing 10-5. The appdata struct

```
struct appdata
{
    float4 positionOS : POSITION;
    float2 uv : TEXCOORD0;
    float3 normalOS : NORMAL;
};
```

The normalOS input takes the normal vectors attached to each vertex of the mesh and automatically uploads them to the shader for us to use.

The v2f struct requires the clip-space position and the UVs to be passed to the fragment shader. Since we are using flat shading, we can calculate all the lighting inside the vertex shader and send it to the fragment shader inside the v2f struct, so we won't need to also include the normal vector in v2f. However, flat shading requires us to only calculate the lighting once per triangle so we must prevent the lighting value being interpolated between each vertex of the triangle using the nointerpolation keyword. There is no special semantic to use for lighting values, so we'll just use the next available general-use interpolator, which is TEXCOORD1.

Note   Remember that TEXCOORD0, TEXCOORD1, and so on are known as "interpolators." However, this doesn't mean their values must be *interpolated* (mixed) between vertices. Shader terminology can often be confusing! The nointerpolation keyword prevents interpolation from taking place, which means the result from the first vertex of each triangle is used in the v2f struct and sent to every fragment for that triangle.

Listing 10-6. The v2f struct

```
struct v2f
{
        float4 positionCS : SV_POSITION;
        float2 uv : TEXCOORD0;
        nointerpolation float4 flatLighting : TEXCOORD1;
};
```

The flatLighting value inside v2f will contain the final light color that we can apply to objects inside the fragment shader. The fragment shader is identical in the built-in pipeline and URP, so let's handle it before discussing the vertex shader. All we need to do is sample _BaseTex and multiply by _BaseColor like usual, but now we have a flatLighting value to multiply by too.

Listing 10-7. The fragment shader

```
float4 frag (v2f i) : SV_Target
{
        float4 textureSample = tex2D(_BaseTex, i.uv);
        return textureSample * _BaseColor * i.flatLighting;
}
```

Finally, let's handle the vertex shader, which will be doing most of the heavy lifting for this shader. The code we'll use to access lighting information differs wildly between the built-in pipeline and URP, so let's deal with both versions separately.

Accessing Lights in the Built-In Pipeline

First, let's deal with some built-in pipeline specifics. We should specify that we are using forward rendering by supplying a LightMode tag called ForwardBase. This goes inside a new Tags block inside the Pass, rather than the existing Tags block that is inside the SubShader.

Listing 10-8. Using the ForwardBase LightMode in the built-in pipeline

```
Pass
{
        Tags
```

```
{
        "LightMode" = "ForwardBase"
}
...
```

Unity supplies a few helpful variables that we can use for lighting inside a file called "Lighting.cginc". We can include this file near the top of the HLSLPROGRAM block alongside the UnityCG.cginc file.

Listing 10-9. Including Lighting.cginc and UnityCG.cginc in the built-in pipeline

```
HLSLPROGRAM
#pragma vertex vert
#pragma fragment frag

#include "UnityCG.cginc"
#include "Lighting.cginc"
...
```

With that out of the way, we can move to the vert function. As with most vertex shaders, we must convert object-space positions to clip-space positions (which requires different functions between the built-in pipeline and URP), and since we're using textures, we must also pass the UV coordinates through. Here's a skeleton for the vert function in the built-in pipeline and in URP.

Listing 10-10. The vert function skeleton in the built-in pipeline

```
v2f vert (appdata v)
{
    v2f o;
    o.positionCS = UnityObjectToClipPos(v.positionOS.xyz);
    o.uv = TRANSFORM_TEX(v.uv, _BaseTex);

    ...
    return o;
}
```

Our calculations require the world-space normal vector, but we passed object-space `normals` to the vert function through `appdata`. We can convert from object to world space using the `UnityObjectToWorldNormal` function, which is included in UnityCG.cginc.

Listing 10-11. Converting from object- to world-space normals

```
o.uv = TRANSFORM_TEX(v.uv, _BaseTex);

float3 normalWS = UnityObjectToWorldNormal(v.normalOS);
```

Next, we will calculate the amount of ambient lighting acting upon the object. Unity makes the ambient light and the result from light probes available in the form of *spherical harmonics* coefficients. You don't need to know the specifics behind this – we just need to know that the `ShadeSH9` function can be used to obtain the ambient light, which includes light contributions from the skybox, as well as light probes.

Listing 10-12. Ambient lighting in the built-in pipeline

```
float3 normalWS = UnityObjectToWorldNormal(v.normalOS);

float3 ambient = ShadeSH9(half4(normalWS, 1));
```

The diffuse lighting comes next. We can access the color of the primary directional light with the `_LightColor0` variable, defined in Lighting.cginc, as well as its direction with the `_WorldSpaceLightPos0` variable. Since it is a directional light, the positioning of the light relative to the object doesn't matter. Once we have those values, we can use Equation 10-2 to calculate the amount of diffuse light.

Note   The name `_WorldSpaceLightPos0` might be confusing because it's called "pos" but it's getting the light *direction* in this example. Essentially, this variable contains details about the most prominent light in the scene. That's usually a directional light, in which case the variable returns its direction. If it is a different type of light, like a point light, this variable does indeed contain its position in world space.

Listing 10-13. Diffuse lighting with one directional light in the built-in pipeline

```
float3 ambient = ShadeSH9(half4(normalWS, 1));

float3 diffuse = _LightColor0 * max(0, dot(normalWS, _
WorldSpaceLightPos0.xyz));
```

Now all that's left is to combine each component of the lighting into a single value to be included in the v2f struct.

Listing 10-14. Adding together lighting components in the built-in pipeline

```
        float3 diffuse = _LightColor0 * max(0, dot(normalWS, _
        WorldSpaceLightPos0.xyz));

        o.flatLighting = float4(ambient + diffuse, 1.0f);

        return o;
}
```

You should now see flat shading in objects in your scene that look just like Figure 10-9. Now let's see how to do all this in URP instead.

Accessing Lights in URP

Let's deal with a few URP specifics before jumping into the vert function. Since we are using URP, we need to add a RenderPipeline tag specified as such in the Tags block inside the SubShader.

Listing 10-15. Specifying URP inside the Tags block in the SubShader

```
SubShader
{
    Tags
    {
        "RenderType" = "Opaque"
        "Queue" = "Geometry"
        "RenderPipeline" = "UniversalPipeline"
    }
    ...
```

Then, inside the Tags block in the Pass, we will be using the `UniversalForward`
`LightMode`.

Listing 10-16. Using UniversalForward in URP

```
Pass
{
    Tags
    {
        "LightMode" = "UniversalForward"
    }
    ...
```

In URP, many lighting helper functions are provided for us inside a file called
"Lighting.hlsl", which we will use extensively throughout the remaining portions of the
code. We can include it alongside the Core.hlsl file inside the `HLSLPROGRAM` block near
the top.

Listing 10-17. Including Core.hlsl and Lighting.hlsl

```
HLSLPROGRAM
#pragma vertex vert
#pragma fragment frag

#include "Packages/com.unity.render-pipelines.universal/ShaderLibrary/
Core.hlsl"
#include "Packages/com.unity.render-pipelines.universal/ShaderLibrary/
Lighting.hlsl"
...
```

As we did with the built-in pipeline example, let's create a skeleton `vert` function
that transforms positions from object to clip space and passes UV coordinates onto the
`frag` function.

Listing 10-18. The vert function skeleton in URP

```
v2f vert (appdata v)
{
    v2f o;
```

374

```
        o.positionCS = TransformObjectToHClip(v.positionOS.xyz);
        o.uv = TRANSFORM_TEX(v.uv, _BaseTex);

        ...
        return o;
}
```

The remaining code slots in place of the ellipsis in this skeleton code snippet. First, we must convert the normal vectors to world space using the `TransformObjectToWorldNormal` function.

Listing 10-19. Object- to world-space calculation for normals

```
o.uv = TRANSFORM_TEX(v.uv, _BaseTex);

float3 normalWS = TransformObjectToWorldNormal(v.normalOS);
```

Next, we can calculate the amount of ambient light acting upon the object. This requires us to sample the spherical harmonics coefficients like we did in the built-in pipeline example, except this time the function is called `SampleSHVertex` and it requires the world-space normal as a `float3`. There is a corresponding function called `SampleSHPixel` that is intended for the fragment shader, but we won't need it here.

Listing 10-20. Ambient lighting in URP

```
float3 normalWS = TransformObjectToWorldNormal(v.normalOS);

float3 ambient = SampleSHVertex(normalWS);
```

Next, we'll get the diffuse light contribution. We can access information about the main light using the `GetMainLight` function, which is included in Lighting.hlsl. It returns a `Light` object, which contains several helpful bits of information that we'll use to help calculate the lighting on our objects, such as its color and direction. We'll calculate the amount of diffuse light using Equation 10-2.

Listing 10-21. Diffuse lighting with one directional light in URP

```
float3 ambient = SampleSHVertex(normalWS);

Light mainLight = GetMainLight();
float3 diffuse = mainLight.color * max(0, dot(normalWS, mainLight.
direction));
```

Finally, we can add together each component of the light to obtain a value to pass to the fragment shader. We're only using ambient and diffuse lighting for flat shading, so those are the two values we'll add. The `flatLighting` variable is a `float4,` so we'll need to fill in the last component with a 1.

Listing 10-22. Adding together lighting components

```
float3 diffuse = mainLight.color * max(0, dot(normalWS, mainLight.
direction));

o.flatLighting = float4(ambient + diffuse, 1.0f);

return o;
}
```

With that, you should now see flat shading just like in Figure 10-9 in your scene. We have now seen how flat shading works in shader code, so let's move on to Shader Graph and see how we can implement flat shading there.

Flat Shading in Shader Graph

This graph is going to look a bit different from the ones we've made so far. In previous examples, each graph we have seen has been an *Unlit* graph, which means Unity does not automatically apply lighting to the object. However, now that we're starting to incorporate lighting into our shaders, it's time to start thinking about Shader Graph's *Lit* option. Let's create a new Lit graph and name it "FlatShading.shadergraph".

You should see two key differences. First, the master stack will contain several never-before-seen blocks. Second, the Graph Settings tab will have a few extra options in it, as seen in Figure 10-10.

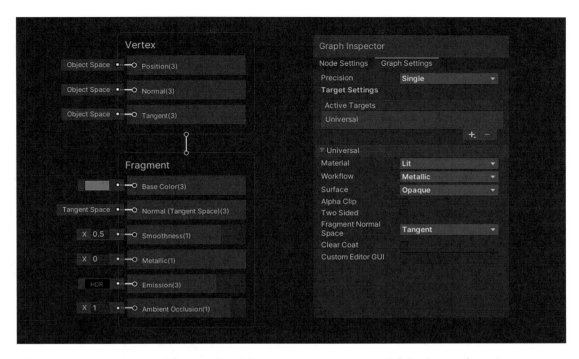

Figure 10-10. *A new Lit graph with unseen master stack blocks and options*

A Lit shader applies the lighting model automatically to objects, but instead of using the Blinn-Phong lighting model we've discussed previously, it uses *Physically Based Rendering* (PBR). We will explore PBR lighting later in this chapter, but for now we will focus on getting the flat shading effect to work. It is *a lot* of work to get true Blinn-Phong lighting to work inside Shader Graph, and it's a little bit overkill for this effect, so for now, we will implement flat shading using PBR. The upshoot is that the only thing we need to modify is the normal vector output in the *Fragment* section of the master stack. By replacing the normal vector, which by default is a per-pixel normal vector that has been interpolated across the surface of the mesh, with a per-triangle normal vector, which we can calculate, we'll end up with the flat shading we desire.

Here's how to do that. First, the graph requires `Base Color` and `Base Texture` properties, so I will include those on the Blackboard with the values seen in Figure 10-11 and wire them up to the *Base Color* output of the graph, as seen in Figure 10-12.

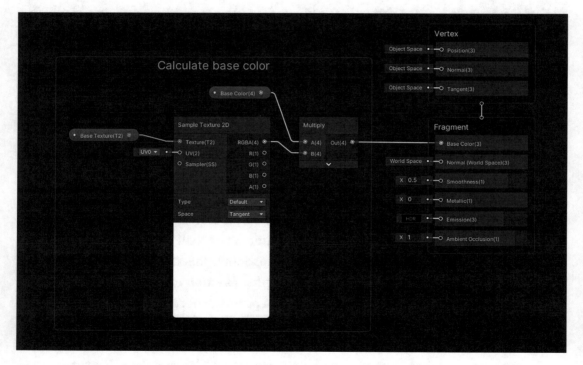

Figure 10-11. *Properties for the FlatShading graph*

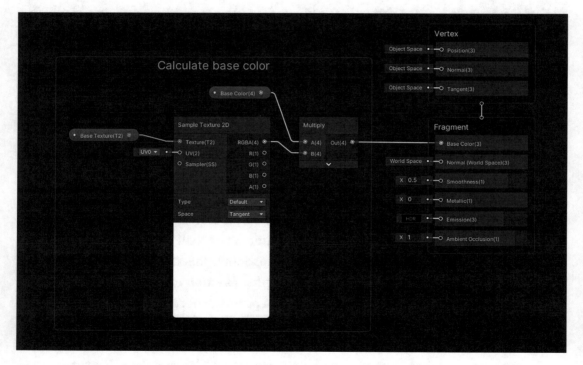

Figure 10-12. *Base Color output for the FlatShading graph*

Now we'll calculate the new normals. We don't have access to anything like the
`nointerpolation` modifier that we used in HLSL code, so we must calculate the per-
triangle normal vector ourselves inside the fragment stage. In this stage of rendering,
the shader has no knowledge of where the other vertices of the triangle are, so we can't
just calculate the normals based on that information. However, we do know that any

triangle face is always flat, and we can exploit that fact. The ddx and ddy functions in shaders, which are called *partial derivative functions*, can be used to calculate any input on the current pixel and an adjacent pixel (horizontally for ddx and vertically for ddy) to obtain two values and then return the difference between them. The equivalent nodes in Shader Graph are called DDX and DDY.

For example, if we input the world-space position to the ddx and ddy functions, we would obtain two small vectors, perpendicular to each other, that lie on the triangle's surface. The shrewd among you may have realized we can use the cross product on both those vectors to obtain the normal vector pointing away from the triangle, which is exactly what we wanted. The nice thing about this calculation is that, because the triangle is flat, we obtain the same normal vector for each pixel of the triangle, which results in a flat-shaded object. We just have to be careful with the order in which we use the two values with the cross product – the ddy comes first and then ddx.

This normal vector value is in world space. In Figure 10-10, you'll see that the Fragment stage *Normal* output, by default, expects a tangent-space vector, so we'll need to do a small modification. If we go into the Graph Settings (also seen in Figure 10-10), you'll notice the *Fragment Normal Space* option, which we can change to *World*, so that Unity swaps out the tangent-space *Normal* block with a world-space *Normal* block. If we take the result of the Cross Product node, pass it through a Normalize node, and output it to the *Normal (World Space)* block, we'll get the flat shading we desire. Figure 10-13 shows how these nodes are connected to each other.

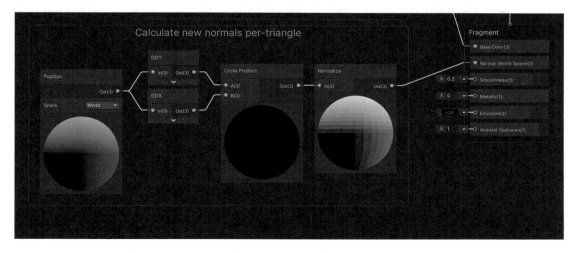

Figure 10-13. *Calculating per-triangle normals in Shader Graph*

This technique allows us to generate per-triangle normals in Shader Graph, but this is far more expensive than the HLSL equivalent, because rather than calculating them once for each triangle and passing that value to each fragment for the lighting calculations like HLSL does, in Shader Graph we must recalculate the normal vector for each fragment, which includes an expensive cross product calculation. However, it's not so prohibitively expensive that you would notice a significant slowdown in your game using this method.

You now know how to implement flat shading into your game, no matter whether you are using HLSL code or Shader Graph. Next, let's look at another type of shading: Gouraud shading.

Gouraud Shading

Gouraud shading is a technique that was developed in the early 1970s by Henri Gouraud. With Gouraud shading, the amount of light is evaluated at every vertex of an object and interpolated between those vertices to obtain lighting values for each pixel, as seen in Figure 10-14.

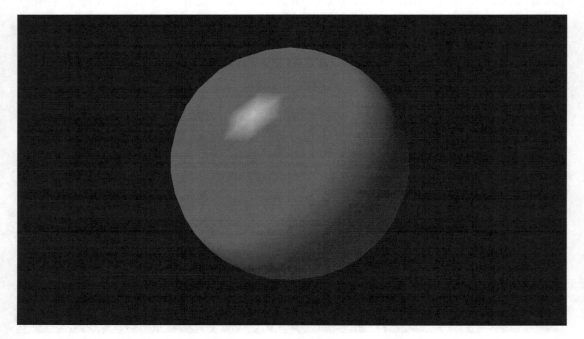

Figure 10-14. *Gouraud shading on a red sphere. The diffuse lighting looks smooth, but the specular highlight clearly shows where the individual vertices of the object are*

The advantage of Gouraud shading over flat shading is that we get a lighting gradient between each vertex due to the use of interpolation and we can implement specular lighting now. However, it's slightly more resource-intensive than flat shading, and specular lighting still suffers from severe artifacts that can be avoided by using a high-poly object to obtain higher-"resolution" reflections. That introduces problems of its own, however – when we cover Phong shading, we'll see that subdividing the geometry is unnecessary. But we're getting ahead of ourselves – let's see how Gouraud shading works in shader code and then in Shader Graph.

Note   The Gouraud shading effect is interesting as a curiosity or if you are explicitly going for a retro 3D look for your game, but otherwise, you will probably want to use Phong shading instead, which I cover next.

Gouraud Shading in HLSL

We'll start by creating a new shader file and naming it "GouraudShading.shader". Here's the skeleton for this shader.

Listing 10-23. Skeleton code for the GouraudShading shader

```
Shader "Examples/GouraudShading"
{
    Properties { ... }
    SubShader
    {
        Tags
        {
            "RenderType" = "Opaque"
            "Queue" = "Geometry"
        }
        Pass
        {
            Tags { ... }

            HLSLPROGRAM
```

```
            #pragma vertex vert
            #pragma fragment frag

            struct appdata
            {
                    float4 positionOS : POSITION;
                    float2 uv : TEXCOORD0;
                    float3 normalOS : NORMAL;
            };

            struct v2f { ... };
            v2f vert(appdata v) { ... }
            float4 frag(v2f i) : SV_Target { ... }

            ENDHLSL
        }
    }
    Fallback Off
}
```

Many parts of this shader are different from the FlatShading shader, so let's start with the Properties block. In addition to the _BaseColor and _BaseTex properties that we previously saw, we need a property to control the glossiness of the object. With Gouraud shading, we will be including the specular lighting component and raising it by a power. Therefore, we will add a _GlossPower property.

Listing 10-24. Gouraud shading properties

```
Properties
{
    _BaseColor ("Base Color", Color) = (1, 1, 1, 1)
    _BaseTex("Base Texture", 2D) = "white" {}
    _GlossPower("Gloss Power", Float) = 400
}
```

We need to declare these within the HLSLPROGRAM block between the v2f struct and the vert function – the syntax is slightly different between the built-in pipeline and URP.

Listing 10-25. Declaring properties in the built-in pipeline

```
struct v2f { ... };

sampler2D _BaseTex;
float4 _BaseColor;
float4 _BaseTex_ST;
float _GlossPower;
```

Listing 10-26. Declaring properties in URP

```
struct v2f { ... };

sampler2D _BaseTex;

CBUFFER_START(UnityPerMaterial)
     float4 _BaseColor;
     float4 _BaseTex_ST;
     float _GlossPower;
CBUFFER_END
```

The appdata struct is the same as the FlatShading shader – we need the object-space position and UVs like most of our shaders, plus the object-space normals. The v2f struct, on the other hand, looks a bit different. The lighting calculation will be more complicated because we're including the specular component. Typically, the ambient and diffuse light end up being multiplied by the object's base color, but the specular highlight does not. That means we can't just send the total light to the fragment shader inside a single variable in v2f like we did in the FlatShading shader – we'll need to split it into two parts. With that in mind, we'll include the clip-space position and the UVs in v2f as we would with a typical shader. Plus, we'll include the ambient and diffuse light inside a variable called diffuseLighting and the specular component in a variable called specularLighting.

Listing 10-27. The v2f struct with split lighting components

```
struct v2f
{
     float4 positionCS : SV_POSITION;
     float2 uv : TEXCOORD0;
```

```
    float4 diffuseLighting : TEXCOORD1;
    float4 specularLighting : TEXCOORD2;
};
```

Let's jump ahead to the fragment shader and incorporate those variables now. The frag function is fairly simple, as all we need to do is sample _BaseTex and multiply it by _BaseColor and diffuseLighting. Then we can add the specularLighting to obtain the final color of the object.

Listing 10-28. Fragment shader adding diffuse and specular lighting contributions

```
float4 frag (v2f i) : SV_Target
{
    float4 textureSample = tex2D(_BaseTex, i.uv);
    return textureSample * _BaseColor * i.diffuseLighting +
    i.specularLighting;
}
```

Now we come to the vertex shader, where most of the calculations take place. The code is very different between the built-in pipeline and URP, so I'll split the rest of the example into two sections.

Gouraud Vertex Shader in the Built-In Pipeline

The vertex shader is more complex than the FlatShading example because we're including the specular component and splitting the light contributions into two parts before sending them to the fragment shader in the v2f struct. We need to make a few additions to the shader as we saw in Listings 10-8 and 10-9. Then we'll start the vert function with the same skeleton we saw in Listing 10-10. Then we'll calculate the vectors we need for subsequent calculations. We need the world-space normals like we did with the FlatShading shader. Plus, we will be using the world-space view vector. Recall that the view vector is the vector between a point on the surface and the camera. Unity provides the WorldSpaceViewDir function for this purpose, which takes the object-space position as a parameter. This vector needs to be normalized.

Listing 10-29. Calculating vectors required for Gouraud shading in the built-in pipeline

```
v2f vert (appdata v)
{
    v2f o;
    o.positionCS = UnityObjectToClipPos(v.positionOS);
    o.uv = TRANSFORM_TEX(v.uv, _BaseTex);

    float3 normalWS = UnityObjectToWorldNormal(v.normalOS);
    float3 viewWS = normalize(WorldSpaceViewDir(v.positionOS));
```

Next come the ambient light and diffuse light calculations, which we can copy from Listings 10-12 and 10-13. After that we'll do the specular light calculation. We first need to calculate the half vector, which we can do by adding the view and light vectors together and normalizing the result. This works because both those vectors are normalized to begin with, so this has the same outcome as adding both and dividing by their combined length. Using the half vector, we can carry out the n-dot-h calculation that Blinn discovered and then raise it to the power of _GlossPower, before multiplying by the light color.

Listing 10-30. Half vector and specular lighting calculations in the built-in pipeline

```
float3 viewWS = normalize(WorldSpaceViewDir(v.positionOS));

float3 ambient = ShadeSH9(half4(normalWS, 1));

float3 diffuse = _LightColor0 * max(0, dot(normalWS, _
WorldSpaceLightPos0.xyz));

float3 halfVector = normalize(_WorldSpaceLightPos0 + viewWS);
float specular = max(0, dot(normalWS, halfVector)) * diffuse;
specular = pow(specular, _GlossPower);
float3 specularColor = _LightColor0 * specular;
```

The last thing we do in the vertex shader before returning is to set the value of diffuseLighting and specularLighting inside the v2f struct, ready for use in the fragment shader.

Listing 10-31. Setting diffuseLighting and specularLighting values

```
    float3 specularColor = _LightColor0 * specular;

    o.diffuseLighting = float4(ambient + diffuse, 1.0f);
    o.specularLighting = float4(specularColor, 1.0f);

    return o;
}
```

All the parts of the vertex shader are in place now, so the shader is complete for the built-in pipeline, and you will see Gouraud shading as in Figure 10-14 on your objects. Let's see how to write the vertex shader in URP.

Gouraud Vertex Shader in URP

The URP version of this shader needs to include the additions seen in Listings 10-15, 10-16, and 10-17. As with the built-in pipeline example, the URP version of the vertex shader now needs to include specular calculations. Starting with the vertex shader code skeleton from Listing 10-18, let's calculate the view vector. This uses a different function from the built-in pipeline: this time, the GetWorldSpaceNormalizedViewDir function is the one we want. This takes in a world-space vertex position as a parameter (whereas the built-in pipeline equivalent took an object-space position), so we'll also have to calculate that first.

Listing 10-32. Calculating vectors required for Gouraud shading in URP

```
v2f vert (appdata v)
{
    v2f o;
    o.positionCS = TransformObjectToHClip(v.positionOS.xyz);
    o.uv = TRANSFORM_TEX(v.uv, _BaseTex);

    float3 normalWS = TransformObjectToWorldNormal(v.normalOS);
    float3 positionWS = mul(unity_ObjectToWorld, v.positionOS);
    float3 viewWS = GetWorldSpaceNormalizeViewDir(positionWS);
```

The ambient light and diffuse light calculations are identical to the ones from the FlatShading shader in Listings 10-20 and 10-21. Then we come to the specular lighting calculations. The code for this is almost identical to Listing 10-30, except we use the `mainLight` variable in URP to access lighting information. We can round off the shader by passing the `diffuseLighting` and `specularLighting` values to the fragment shader through the `v2f` struct.

Listing 10-33. Half vector, specular lighting, and v2f lighting variables in URP

```
    float3 ambient = SampleSHVertex(normalWS);

    Light mainLight = GetMainLight();

    float3 diffuse = mainLight.color * max(0, dot(normalWS, mainLight.
    direction));

    float3 halfVector = normalize(mainLight.direction + viewWS);
    float specular = max(0, dot(normalWS, halfVector));
    specular = pow(specular, _GlossPower);
    float3 specularColor = mainLight.color * specular;

    o.diffuseLighting = float4(ambient + diffuse, 1.0f);
    o.specularLighting = float4(specularColor, 1.0f);

    return o;
}
```

The main differences between this and the built-in pipeline version of the shader are just a matter of different function and variable names, but the resulting visuals (as in Figure 10-14) should be almost identical. Let's see how this effect can be made in Shader Graph now.

Gouraud Shading in Shader Graph

Implementing Gouraud shading in Shader Graph entails more work than doing the same thing in HLSL. In fact, per-vertex lighting is impossible to achieve in Shader Graph versions prior to 12.0 (Unity 2021.2) because we only have access to three interpolators in the vertex stage: the *Position*, *Normal*, and *Tangent* vectors. With Shader Graph 12.0, we get access to *custom interpolators* that let us funnel custom data from the vertex stage to the fragment stage, like how the `v2f` struct in shader code gives us full control over the data passed between the `vert` and `frag` functions.

Note   Although I claim it's impossible, you probably *can* implement per-vertex lighting in older versions of Shader Graph. However, it will require "hacky" ways of getting round Shader Graph's limitations and will probably require injecting a lot of code using the Custom Function node, so it's de facto impossible using the intended behavior of Shader Graph. Regrettably, that means the GouraudShading effect only works in Shader Graph 12.0 (Unity 2021.2) and above.

Another roadblock we will encounter is the fact that Shader Graph does not yet have a built-in node that grabs lighting data such as position, direction, and color from the main light or any additional lights. Therefore, we will need to create a Custom Function node to obtain that information, for which we need to write a short section of shader code. Apologies to anyone wishing to avoid code entirely! We'll wrap that function inside a *Sub Graph* so that it's easy to access this behavior in any future graph that requires it. Using that Sub Graph, we can carry out the diffuse and specular lighting calculations required for the shader.

Note   A built-in Get Main Light node, or equivalent, has been "under consideration" by Unity for a while now. One day it might be available in the base Shader Graph package for URP! In lieu of this node, as of the writing of this book, a Get Main Light Direction node is available in Shader Graph 13.0 (for Unity 2022.1) and up. You still won't have access to the light color or shadowing, but it's a start.

GetMainLight Sub Graph

Let's do this step by step. First, I'm going to write a shader file containing the code to access the lighting information. Then, I'll create a Sub Graph with relevant inputs and outputs that we will be able to use in any graph that requires lighting information. Finally, I'll create a Custom Function node inside that Sub Graph, which accesses the custom HLSL code, and wire up the Sub Graph inputs and outputs to that node.

Start by creating a new file called "GetMainLight.hlsl". Unfortunately, there's no easy way to create a basic text file from within the Unity Editor, so you'll have to do this in an external text editor or IDE such as Visual Studio. This file will contain one function. Recall from all the way back in Chapter 4 that Custom Function nodes require a particular syntax for the function:

- We need to put the variable precision at the name after an underscore, that is, `FunctionName_float` or `FunctionName_half`.

- We put all the input and output variables inside the parameter list in the function signature:

  - Inputs look like any regular function parameter (such as "`float3 input`").

  - Outputs use the `out` keyword (such as "`out float3 output`").

- The function uses the `void` return type.

With that in mind, I'll write a function that returns similar information to the `GetMainLight` function that already exists in HLSL for URP. I'll use float precision for each variable, so with that in mind, here's the function signature.

Listing 10-34. GetMainLight custom function signature

```
void MainLight_float(float3 WorldPos, out float3 Direction, out
float3 Color,
      out float DistanceAtten, out float ShadowAtten)
{
    ...
}
```

This function takes the *world-space position* as input and outputs the *direction*, *color*, *distance attenuation*, and *shadow attenuation* of the main light at that position. In almost every case, the main light will be a directional light. We won't need the last two outputs just yet, but we'll include them here for completeness.

The first wrinkle we'll encounter is that Shader Graph is able to preview the output of any node inside a tiny window on the node itself, but that preview window doesn't have access to any lights, so we'll have to account for that in our code. We can use `#ifdef SHADERGRAPH_PREVIEW` to check if the code is being run inside a Shader Graph preview window, and if so, we'll return dummy values that simulate a white directional light.

Listing 10-35. Dummy values for inside a Shader Graph preview window

```
void MainLight_float(float3 WorldPos, out float3 Direction, out float3
Color, out float DistanceAtten, out float ShadowAtten)
{
#ifdef SHADERGRAPH_PREVIEW
    Direction = normalize(float3(0.5f, 0.5f, 0.25f));
    Color = float3(1.0f, 1.0f, 1.0f);
    DistanceAtten = 1.0f;
    ShadowAtten = 1.0f;
#else
    ...
#endif
}
```

Otherwise, the code is being run for real, and we'll need to access real values. We can use the very same GetMainLight function that we used in the HLSL version of this shader, except this time I'll pass shadow coordinates to the function that we can obtain using the TransformWorldToShadowCoord function. Don't worry too much about this just yet – we will discuss shadows later in the chapter. Using the Light object that is returned by GetMainLight, we can access the values we need for the function's outputs.

Listing 10-36. Using GetMainLight inside a custom function

```
#else
    float4 shadowCoord = TransformWorldToShadowCoord(WorldPos);
    Light mainLight = GetMainLight(shadowCoord);

    Direction = mainLight.direction;
    Color = mainLight.color;
    DistanceAtten = mainLight.distanceAttenuation;
    ShadowAtten = mainLight.shadowAttenuation;
#endif
```

That's all we need to do for the code. Let's now create the Sub Graph that will contain the Custom Function node that uses this code – name it "GetMainLight.shadersubgraph". You'll see an interface similar to a main graph, except the output stack will contain only a single `float4` output by default. The first thing we'll do is set up the inputs and outputs of the Sub Graph.

The inputs to a Sub Graph work the same as the properties of a main graph, so we'll add a `Vector3` input called `WorldPos` to the graph using the Blackboard window. The default value can be left as (0,0,0). The outputs are slightly different. If you click the `Output` node, which is exclusive to Sub Graphs, you will be able to add more outputs in the Node Settings window. Use the plus arrow to add more outputs, click any of the names to edit them, and use the type drop-down to change the type of the output. Wire up the outputs to match those used in the HLSL function we wrote, as seen in Figure 10-15.

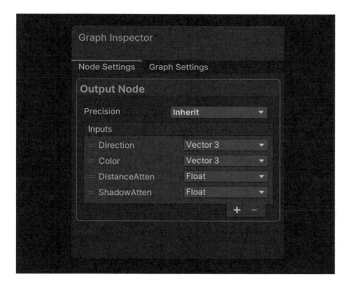

Figure 10-15. *Outputs for the GetMainLight Sub Graph*

Now that the inputs and outputs are sorted, let's add a `Custom Function` node to the graph. Similarly, we need to set up inputs and outputs to the function, which can all be done in the Node Settings. We also need to specify which HLSL function the node will be using. We do this by attaching the GetMainLight.hlsl file to the *File* slot and then typing in the name of the function without the precision suffix – in our case, we called it "MainLight". Figure 10-16 shows how the inputs, outputs, and file attachments should look in the Node Settings.

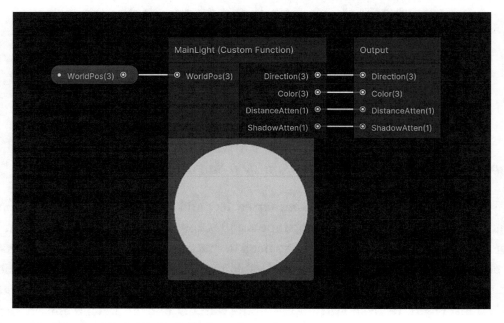

Figure 10-16. *Custom Function node settings for the MainLight function*

Then we can wire up the Sub Graph inputs to the `Custom Function` node inputs and the Sub Graph outputs to the `Custom Function` node outputs, as seen in Figure 10-17.

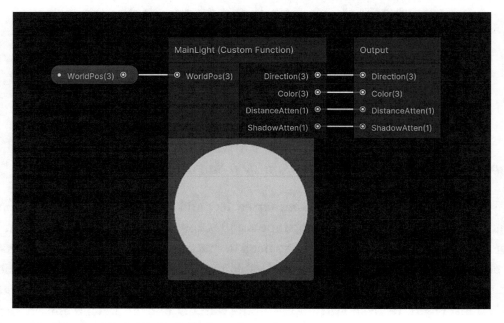

Figure 10-17. *GetMainLight Sub Graph nodes*

If you get red errors on the `Custom Function` node, you might need to go into the Graph Settings and change the *Precision* of the graph to *Single*. We can now use main light information in our graphs, which will be enough for the diffuse and specular lighting, but we still need to handle ambient light. We can use the same process to create a Sub Graph just for ambient light too. Although Shader Graph ships with an `Ambient` node, this only exposes three modes of ambient light – sky, equator, and ground – none of them work as well as the method we used in the HLSL version of the shader, so we're going to use the same code here.

GetAmbientLight Sub Graph

Since we've already seen much of this process at work, let's speed through this section. We'll create a new file called "GetAmbientLight.hlsl" in an external text editor and place the following code inside it.

Listing 10-37. GetAmbientLight function

```
void AmbientLight_float(float3 WorldNormal, bool IsVertex, out float3
Ambient)
{
#ifdef SHADERGRAPH_PREVIEW
	Ambient = 0.2f;
#else
	if(IsVertex)
	{
		Ambient = SampleSHVertex(WorldNormal);
	}
	else
	{
		Ambient = SampleSH(WorldNormal);
	}
#endif
}
```

The SampleSH and SampleSHVertex functions require the world-space normal as a parameter. I also added a Boolean switch to choose whether we want to calculate the ambient lighting per vertex or per fragment. Then follow these steps to set up the Sub Graph:

- Create the Sub Graph by right-clicking the Project View and choosing *Create* ➤ *Shader* ➤ *Sub Graph* and naming it "GetAmbientLight".

- Add a Custom Function node to the graph and change the *File* option to GetAmbientLight.hlsl and the *Function* option to "AmbientLight".

- Create a WorldNormal Vector3 input and an IsVertex Boolean input for both the Sub Graph and the Custom Function node.

- Create an Ambient Vector3 output for both the Sub Graph and the Custom Function node.

- Connect the input nodes and Output node to the Custom Function node as required.

The resulting graph should look like Figure 10-18.

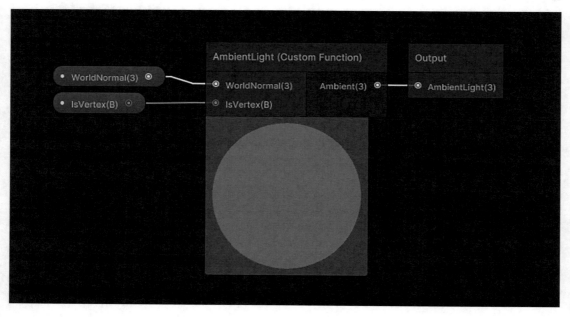

Figure 10-18. *The GetAmbientLight Sub Graph*

These Sub Graphs can now be used in any future graph that requires access to either main light or ambient light information. Without further ado, let's write a graph that can perform Gouraud shading.

Gouraud Shading with Custom Interpolators

Start by creating a new Unlit graph. This time, we're going back to an Unlit graph so that we can perform the lighting calculations ourselves in the vertex stage and avoid Unity applying a second layer of lighting to the object automatically. Name this graph "GouraudShading.shadergraph".

First, we'll set up the properties required for the graph. It requires three properties: a Color called Base Color, a Texture2D called Base Texture, and a Float called Gloss Power. These will work similarly to those we used in the HLSL version of the shader, and you can see them in Figure 10-19.

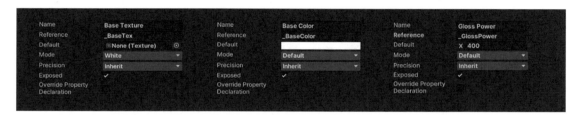

Figure 10-19. *Properties for the GouraudShading graph*

We will be doing the lighting calculations in the vertex shader and will need to pass them to the fragment shader. To do this, we need to make use of Shader Graph's *custom interpolator* feature. If you right-click inside the Vertex section of the master stack and choose *Add Block Node*, a *Custom Interpolator* option will show up. Add two of those and name them "DiffuseLighting" and "SpecularLighting", respectively, in the Node Settings. Both use the Vector3 type.

For the diffuse lighting, we'll carry out the following calculations:

- Perform the Dot Product between the Normal Vector and the *Direction* output of GetMainLight to obtain the amount of diffuse light.

- Saturate the result to remove any negative results.

- Multiply by the *Color* output of GetMainLight to tint the diffuse light with the main light's color.

- Add the GetAmbientLight result to the diffuse light.

- Output the result to the *DiffuseLighting* custom interpolator on the master stack's Vertex section.

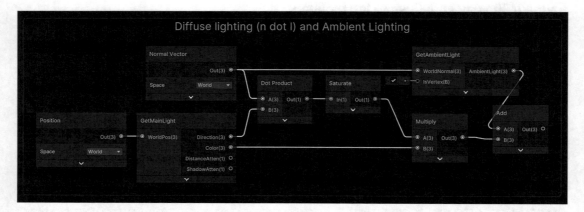

Figure 10-20.   *The DiffuseLighting calculation for the GouraudShading graph*

And for the specular lighting, we'll carry out these calculations:

- Add the View Vector and the *Direction* output of GetMainLight together and then Normalize the result to obtain the half vector.

- Take the Dot Product between the Normal Vector and that half vector to obtain the amount of specular light.

- Saturate the result to remove any negative results.

- Raise the result to the power of the Gloss Power property using a Power node.

- Multiply by the *Color* output of GetMainLight to tint the specular light with the main light's color.

- Output the result to the *SpecularLighting* custom interpolator on the master stack's Vertex section.

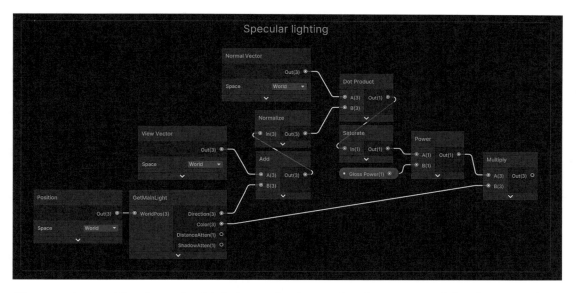

Figure 10-21. *The SpecularLighting calculation for the GouraudShading graph*

Now let's combine these types of light in the fragment stage. We can access the resulting values from the custom interpolators in the fragment stage using the DiffuseLighting and SpecularLighting nodes, respectively, as follows:

- Sample the Base Texture with a Sample Texture 2D node and multiply the output by Base Color.

- Multiply the result by the DiffuseLighting custom interpolator value.

- Add the SpecularLighting custom interpolator value.

- Output the result to the *Base Color* output on the master stack's fragment section.

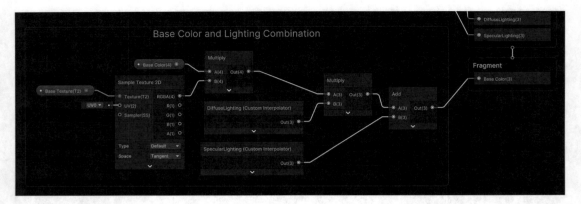

Figure 10-22. *Combining lighting information from the DiffuseLighting and SpecularLighting custom interpolators*

With those steps followed, you'll see a result just like in Figure 10-14. This is a relatively complicated graph, so the nodes might be hard to see all on-screen at once! Now that we have seen how Gouraud shading works in both HLSL and Shader Graph, let's see how Phong shading improves on Gouraud shading.

Phong Shading

First, let's clarify what we mean by Phong shading. We've talked about the Phong *reflection model*, where we add ambient, diffuse, and specular contributions at different points to calculate the amount of light incident on an object's surface. Phong *shading* is a different thing, but annoyingly we use the same terminology, which is often conflated.

Phong *shading* is an interpolation technique. With Gouraud shading, we calculated lighting *per vertex* and interpolated the result across fragments. With Phong shading, we instead interpolate the normal vector and view vector across fragments, renormalize them, and then calculate lighting *per fragment*. This technique is much more expensive than Gouraud shading, but it became the industry-standard approach for many years because it is produces results that are far more representative of a real-world scene. You can see an example in Figure 10-23.

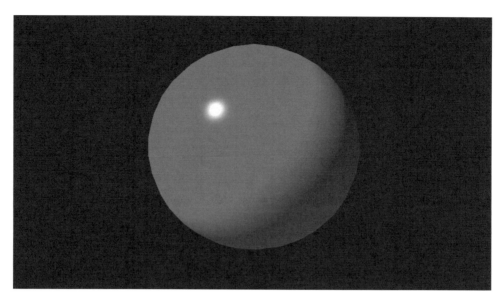

Figure 10-23. *Phong shading on a sphere. The specular highlight is far more realistic than with Gouraud shading*

The Phong reflection model incorporates ambient, diffuse, and specular light, but the Phong shading method is a good point to add Fresnel lighting to the model too. Recall that Fresnel light is inversely proportional to the dot product between the view vector and the normal vector. A modification of the effect that uses Fresnel lighting in addition to the other types of light can be seen in Figure 10-24.

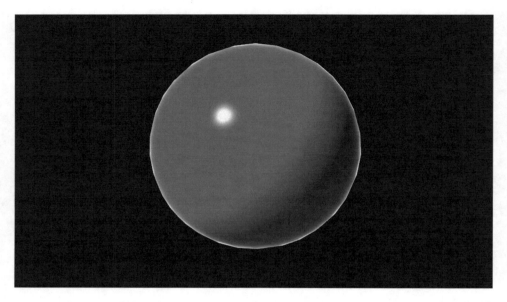

Figure 10-24. *A modification to Phong shading that incorporates Fresnel lighting*

Let's see how Phong shading can be implemented in HLSL and then in Shader Graph.

Phong Shading in HLSL

We'll start by creating a new shader and naming it "PhongShading.shader". The following code snippet is the skeleton shader we will develop in this section.

Listing 10-38. Skeleton code for the PhongShading shader

```
Shader "Examples/PhongShading"
{
    Properties
    {
        _BaseColor ("Base Color", Color) = (1, 1, 1, 1)
        _BaseTex("Base Texture", 2D) = "white" {}
        _GlossPower("Gloss Power", Float) = 400
    }
    SubShader
```

```
{
    Tags
    {
        "RenderType" = "Opaque"
        "Queue" = "Geometry"
    }
    Pass
    {
        Tags { ... }

        HLSLPROGRAM
        #pragma vertex vert
        #pragma fragment frag

        struct appdata
        {
            float4 positionOS : POSITION;
            float2 uv : TEXCOORD0;
            float3 normalOS : NORMAL;
        };

        struct v2f { ... }
        v2f vert(appdata v) { ... }
        float4 frag(v2f i) : SV_Target { ... }

        ENDHLSL
    }
}
}
```

You'll need to make a few changes based on which render pipeline you are using. In the built-in pipeline, you'll need to incorporate the following:

- Declare the properties inside HLSLPROGRAM by following Listing 10-25.

- Specify the correct tags by following Listing 10-8.

- Add the correct include files by following Listing 10-9.

And in URP, you'll need to do the following:

- Declare the properties inside HLSLPROGRAM by following Listing 10-26.

- Specify the correct tags by following Listings 10-15 and 10-16.

- Add the correct include files by following Listing 10-17.

Now let's explore how Phong shading differs from Gouraud shading. Most of the calculations will be moved from the vertex shader to the fragment shader, and the purpose of the vertex shader will be only to calculate the clip-space position, UVs, normal vector, and view vector required by the fragment shader. With that in mind, we no longer need to include lighting values inside the v2f struct, but we do need to include the normal vector and the view vector. We'll use TEXCOORD1 and TEXCOORD2 for those.

Listing 10-39. Modifying the v2f struct to include the normal vector and view vector

```
struct v2f
{
    float4 positionCS : SV_POSITION;
    float2 uv : TEXCOORD0;
    float3 normalWS : TEXCOORD1;
    float3 viewWS : TEXCOORD2;
};
```

The code looks very different between the built-in pipeline and URP from here on, so I'll split this section in two according to the render pipeline you're using.

Phong Shading in the Built-In Pipeline

In the vertex shader, we must calculate the clip-space position and UVs like usual. Then we must calculate the normal vector and view vector to include them in the v2f struct. We can use the same UnityObjectToWorldNormal and WorldSpaceViewDir functions we previously used in the GouraudShading example. This time, we won't need to normalize the view vector in the vertex shader for reasons we're about to see.

Listing 10-40. The vertex shader for Phong shading in the built-in pipeline

```
v2f vert (appdata v)
{
    v2f o;
    o.positionCS = UnityObjectToClipPos(v.positionOS);
    o.uv = TRANSFORM_TEX(v.uv, _BaseTex);

    o.normalWS = UnityObjectToWorldNormal(v.normalOS);
    o.viewWS = WorldSpaceViewDir(v.positionOS);

    return o;
}
```

The lighting calculations we had previously performed inside the vertex shader are nowhere to be seen. Instead, what's happening here is the normal and view vectors are being interpolated between each vertex so that we get per-fragment versions of those vectors. The snag here is that the interpolation step doesn't renormalize those vectors, so they can have a length less than one, which will mess up our lighting calculations. Therefore, the first thing we'll do in the fragment shader is renormalize them manually.

Listing 10-41. Renormalizing the normal and view vectors

```
float4 frag (v2f i) : SV_TARGET
{
    float3 normal = normalize(i.normalWS);
    float3 view = normalize(i.viewWS);
```

Once we've done that, the lighting code is largely a copy-and-paste job from the code we used in the vertex shader for Gouraud shading, except now the normal and view vectors don't come from the v2f struct.

Listing 10-42. Calculating lighting in the fragment shader in the built-in pipeline

```
float3 normal = normalize(i.normalWS);
float3 view = normalize(i.viewWS);

float3 ambient = ShadeSH9(half4(i.normalWS, 1));

float3 diffuse = _LightColor0 * max(0, dot(normal, _
WorldSpaceLightPos0.xyz));
```

```
float3 halfVector = normalize(_WorldSpaceLightPos0 + view);
float specular = max(0, dot(normal, halfVector));
specular = pow(specular, _GlossPower);
float3 specularColor = _LightColor0 * specular;

float4 diffuseLighting = float4(ambient + diffuse, 1.0f);
float4 specularLighting = float4(specularColor, 1.0f);

float4 textureSample = tex2D(_BaseTex, i.uv);
return textureSample * _BaseColor * diffuseLighting + specularLighting;
```

Once you've moved the lighting code to the fragment shader like this, you'll instantly notice a better specular highlight on objects, as seen in Figure 10-23. The diffuse lighting calculations are also more accurate, but generally they're not as noticeable as the specular highlight improvement. Let's see how this works in URP.

Phong Shading in URP

We'll start in the vertex shader by sending the clip-space position, UVs, normal vector, and view vector like we just did in the built-in pipeline example. We can use the TransformObjectToWorldNormal and GetWorldSpaceNormalizeViewDir functions like before, although we'll be renormalizing the view vector in the fragment shader anyway, so let's just use GetWorldSpaceViewDir instead.

Listing 10-43. The vertex shader for Phong shading in URP

```
v2f vert (appdata v)
{
    v2f o;
    o.positionCS = TransformObjectToHClip(v.positionOS.xyz);
    o.uv = TRANSFORM_TEX(v.uv, _BaseTex);
    o.normalWS = TransformObjectToWorldNormal(v.normalOS);

    float3 positionWS = mul(unity_ObjectToWorld, v.positionOS.xyz);
    o.viewWS = GetWorldSpaceViewDir(positionWS);

    return o;
}
```

Like with the built-in pipeline version of this shader, the problem with the normal and view vectors now is that they are not normalized due to the interpolation step, so the first thing we must do in the fragment shader is renormalize them with the `normalize` function as seen in Listing 10-41. Once that's done, we can carry out the lighting calculations in the fragment shader using slightly different variable names and round off the shader by adding together the lighting contributions like we did in both the FlatShading and GouraudShading examples. One key difference is that instead of the `SampleSHVertex` function, which we used to calculate the ambient light in the previous examples, we'll use `SampleSH` instead because it's running in the fragment shader this time.

Listing 10-44. Calculating lighting in the fragment shader in URP

```
float4 frag (v2f i) : SV_Target
{
    float3 normal = normalize(i.normalWS);
    float3 view = normalize(i.viewWS);

    float3 ambient = SampleSH(i.normalWS);

    Light mainLight = GetMainLight();

    float3 diffuse = mainLight.color * max(0, dot(normal, mainLight.
    direction));

    float3 halfVector = normalize(mainLight.direction + view);
    float specular = max(0, dot(normal, halfVector));
    specular = pow(specular, _GlossPower);
    float3 specularColor = mainLight.color * specular;

    float4 diffuseLighting = float4(ambient + diffuse, 1.0f);
    float4 specularLighting = float4(specularColor, 1.0f);

    float4 textureSample = tex2D(_BaseTex, i.uv);
    return textureSample * _BaseColor * diffuseLighting +
    float4(specularColor, 1.0f);
}
```

The URP version of the shader now works the same as the built-in pipeline version as seen in Figure 10-23, and you should see a huge improvement in the specular highlight on objects with this shader. We can add Fresnel light to the equation with small additions to the shader.

Fresnel Light Modification

Adding Fresnel light to the PhongShading shader requires only a few lines of code. Fresnel light is inversely proportional to the dot product between the view vector and the normal vector, which we already have access to in the fragment shader. It's also usually raised to a power of our choosing, so we can include that as a property. That'll be the first addition we make to the shader.

Listing 10-45. Adding a _FresnelPower property to the Properties block

```
Properties
{
        _BaseColor ("Base Color", Color) = (1, 1, 1, 1)
        _BaseTex("Base Texture", 2D) = "white" {}
        _GlossPower("Gloss Power", Float) = 400
        _FresnelPower("Fresnel Power", Float) = 5
}
```

Typically, the powers used for Fresnel lighting are far lower than those used for specular highlights. We also need to declare the _FresnelPower property inside the HLSLPROGRAM block alongside the existing properties. The built-in pipeline and URP property declarations look slightly different, so pick the one for your pipeline.

Listing 10-46. Declaring _FresnelPower in the built-in pipeline

```
float4 _BaseColor;
sampler2D _BaseTex;
float4 _BaseTex_ST;
float _GlossPower;
float _FresnelPower;
```

Listing 10-47. Declaring _FresnelPower in URP

```
CBUFFER_START(UnityPerMaterial)
      float4 _BaseColor;
      float4 _BaseTex_ST;
      float _GlossPower;
      float _FresnelPower;
CBUFFER_END
```

There are no changes that need making to the structs or the vertex shader, so let's jump straight to the fragment shader. The Fresnel calculation can slot in after the existing specular lighting calculation and just above the part where we add the lighting components together. The only difference between the code for the two pipelines is the variable used for the main light color.

Listing 10-48. Adding Fresnel lighting support in the built-in pipeline

```
float fresnel = 1.0f - max(0, dot(normal, view));
fresnel = pow(fresnel, _FresnelPower);
float3 fresnelColor = _LightColor0 * fresnel;

float4 diffuseLighting = float4(ambient + diffuse, 1.0f);
float4 specularLighting = float4(specularColor + fresnelColor, 1.0f);
```

Listing 10-49. Adding Fresnel lighting support in URP

```
float fresnel = 1.0f - max(0, dot(normal, view));
fresnel = pow(fresnel, _FresnelPower);
float3 fresnelColor = mainLight.color * fresnel;

float4 diffuseLighting = float4(ambient + diffuse, 1.0f);
float4 specularLighting = float4(specularColor + fresnelColor, 1.0f);
```

Once these lines of code are added, our objects will look like those in Figure 10-24. To round off this section, let's see how Phong shading works in Shader Graph, complete with Fresnel lighting support at the end.

Phong Shading in Shader Graph

Phong shading in Shader Graph looks a lot like Gouraud shading in Shader Graph, except the calculations can now be done in the fragment stage rather than the vertex stage. We'll also be adding Fresnel lighting support to the graph.

Start by creating a new Unlit graph and naming it "PhongShading.shadergraph". We want to make sure Unity doesn't automatically apply a second layer of lighting, so we can't use a Lit graph. We can quickly get up to speed by using the Sub Graphs we created for the GouraudShading effect, as well as the nodes we used on the GouraudShading graph itself. The main difference is that we will not be adding either of the custom interpolators that we used for the GouraudShading graph. Follow these steps to get yourself up to speed:

- Add the same properties as seen in Figure 10-19.

- Add the set of nodes seen in Figure 10-20 for the diffuse light and ambient light calculations. Do not connect those nodes to a custom interpolator.

- Add the set of nodes seen in Figure 10-21 for the specular light calculations. Do not connect those nodes to a custom interpolator either.

- Add the nodes seen in Figure 10-22 for the final lighting calculations, except

  - Replace the `DiffuseLighting` custom interpolator node with the output of the diffuse light node group.

  - Replace the `SpecularLighting` custom interpolator node with the output of the specular light node group.

- Output the result of the final addition to *Base Color* on the master stack.

At this stage we have achieved Phong shading in Shader Graph, but let's go one stage further and add Fresnel lighting support. First, we'll need to add a `Fresnel Power` property as shown in Figure 10-25.

Figure 10-25. *Fresnel Power property for the PhongShading graph*

Shader Graph has a `Fresnel Effect` node that automatically calculates Fresnel
lighting for us. Better still, the default vectors that are input to the node are exactly
the ones we need, and it has a *Power* input so that we don't need to manually add
a `Power` node after the `Fresnel Effect` node. Let's add one to the graph, connect
the Fresnel Power property, and add it to the existing diffuse and specular lighting
components before outputting the result to the Base Color output on the master stack.
Figure 10-26 shows how these nodes should be connected.

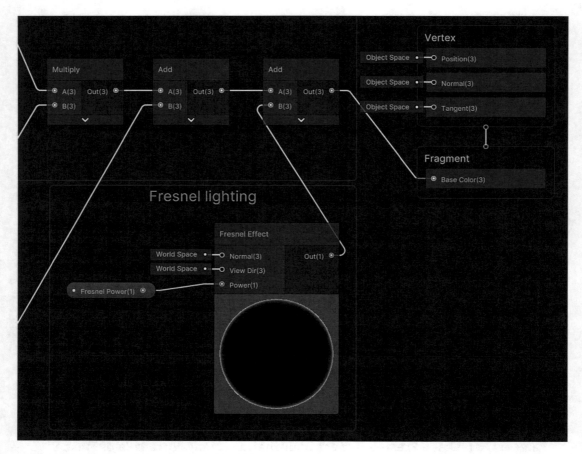

Figure 10-26. *Adding Fresnel lighting to the output of the PhongShading graph*

Now we have covered lighting objects in shaders by simulating the amount of ambient, diffuse, specular, and Fresnel lighting acting on the object. Next, we will see what functionality Unity provides out of the box to help us light objects without needing to calculate all the lighting ourselves.

Physically Based Rendering

Physically Based Rendering is exactly what it sounds like: rendering objects based on the physical properties of a surface, such as its albedo color, roughness/smoothness, and metallicity. Since 2015, with the release of Unity 5, the built-in pipeline has supported

PBR through the Standard shader, and in both URP and HDRP, the Lit shader supports PBR. Let's see the common features of a PBR shader and then create our own PBR shaders using the helper functions and macros provided by Unity.

Smoothness

Diffuse and specular light arise due to the way light reflects off a surface. Diffuse light occurs because incoming light rays get reflected in all directions due to complex interactions between the light and the surface of the object. A perfectly diffuse surface, one that reflects light equally in all directions, is called *Lambertian*; in fact, we have been using Lambertian reflectance as our model for diffuse light reflection in the shaders we have written. Although real-world materials don't reflect light equally in all directions, Lambertian reflection is still a good approximation for diffuse reflection.

Specular lighting, on the other hand, arises when light rays reflect off a flat surface, which means most of the outgoing rays point in the same direction. Incoming light rays are reflected in the normal vector of the surface, so if a viewer is positioned at the correct angle, it will receive those reflected rays, resulting in a specular highlight on the object's surface. Therefore, rough surfaces display almost no specular behavior, because the light rays are scattered rather than concentrated in a single direction. Mirrors are a special case of specular reflection, where almost all the light is reflected off the surface and almost none of it exhibits diffuse behavior. This is why shiny objects sometimes appear mirror-like. Figure 10-27 shows light rays reflecting off of a very smooth surface.

Figure 10-27. *On the left, a smooth surface. Light rays all get reflected in approximately the same direction. On the right, a rough surface. Light rays are scattered due to the surface details*

We can influence the amount of diffuse and specular light by modifying the smoothness of the surface. Objects with full smoothness will look very shiny – in other words, they have a high degree of specular reflection – and objects with low smoothness will primarily use the diffuse lighting component with little to no specular lighting. Very smooth objects may also appear mirror-like, as they reflect a large proportion of the environmental light, as seen in Figure 10-28.

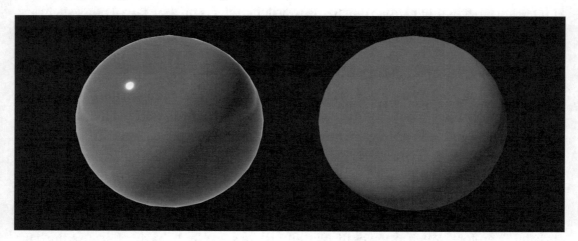

Figure 10-28. *On the left, a very smooth sphere that reflects environmental details and has a well-defined specular highlight. On the right, a rough sphere with no specular reflection*

Smoothness is only one part of PBR lighting. Typically, PBR shaders include two modes, which provide extra control over how an object is rendered: *metallic mode*, which lets us model objects on a scale between fully metallic and non-metallic, and *specular mode*, which gives us direct control over the color of specular reflections, rather than leaving it to other physical properties of the object. Let's see how both modes work.

Note   It's mostly down to personal preference which of the two workflows you choose. I prefer the metallic workflow because it is easier to design materials by looking up real-world values from lookup tables online, which list the metallic and smoothness ranges of real materials.

Metallic Mode

In metallic mode, we model the reflections of an object based on how much it acts like a metal. Fully non-metallic objects consist of a diffuse surface, with specular highlights visible on some parts of the object based on its smoothness. Fully metallic objects do not have a diffuse surface – the color of the object is based entirely on environmental reflections, although specular highlights still appear. A material in metallic mode will display specular reflections with a color that is based on the albedo of the object and the color of the incoming light. Figure 10-29 shows multiple objects with different levels of metallicity.

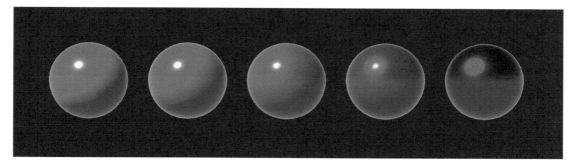

Figure 10-29.   *Spheres with increasing levels of metallicity. Starting on the left, the sphere is completely non-metallic. On the right, the sphere is fully metallic*

Metallic mode is only one of two workflows commonly used with PBR. Specular mode may provide benefits if you want direct control over the specular highlight.

Specular Mode

In specular mode, we have more control over the color of specular highlights than in metallic mode. Whereas in metallic mode, the color of specular reflections is a result of the albedo color of the object and the color of the light, with specular mode, we can tint the specular highlights a specific color. A material in specular mode with high smoothness and high specularity will still appear mirror-like, as does a material in metallic mode with high smoothness and high metallicity. However, a high-specularity material typically loses its albedo color, unlike high-metallicity materials. If you want to design a metal object in specular mode, you need to tint the specular color and keep the albedo color black. Figure 10-30 shows multiple objects with different specular colors.

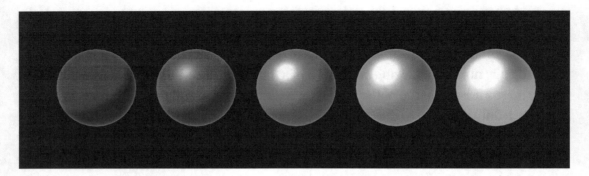

Figure 10-30. *Spheres with increasing specular colors. On the left, black is used for the specular color, meaning there is no specular highlight. On the right, full white is used, so the albedo color of the sphere has been overtaken by the specular color*

So far, we've seen that some components of our lighting models rely on the normal vector of the object's surface. The next feature we'll look at that is commonly featured in PBR shaders will let us modify the normal vector to simulate different surface shapes.

Normal Mapping

Normal mapping is a technique that lets us simulate detailed surfaces on an otherwise low-detail mesh using a texture (called a *normal map*). This allows us to add imperfections and other surface elements without needing to vastly increase the polygon count of the mesh. The advantage is that small details, which would otherwise require hundreds or even thousands of additional triangles to represent, can now be replaced by a texture that takes up comparatively little graphics memory, and we can use the same low-poly model with different normal maps if we want to swap out the surface details on an object easily.

Normal mapping works by modulating the normal vector at each point on the surface of an object. By doing so, lighting calculations produce a slightly different result, which makes the surface appear as if certain details existed, even if they are not physically present in the mesh. Figure 10-31 shows multiple versions of the same object with the same normal map, but different strengths.

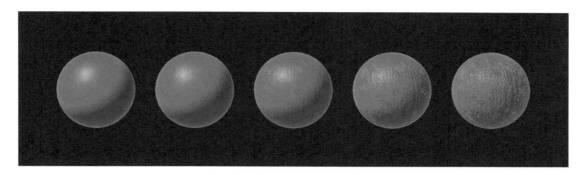

Figure 10-31. *Normal-mapped objects using a plywood texture from the URP sample scene. From left to right, the normal strength increases, starting at 0 (no normal mapping), then 1, 2, 4, and lastly 8. On the right sphere, the specular highlight is scattered by the normal map*

Although normal maps are not exclusive to PBR materials, they are certainly related to lighting, and they are used to mimic the physical properties of the surface, so I think it's useful to introduce them alongside PBR materials. That said, you could create a shader that uses normal mapping with Blinn-Phong lighting if you wanted to. Normal maps have an indirect influence on the way lighting gets applied to an object. There is another kind of texture we can use to *directly* control the strength of ambient light on the object.

Ambient Occlusion

Some parts of a mesh receive less ambient light than others. For example, small cracks on the surface or folds and corners naturally have less light falling on them due to their shape. Furthermore, some parts of objects will always be obscured by other objects, such as the inner layers of clothing, resulting in less light reaching them. *Ambient occlusion* is a term that refers to when ambient light is prevented from reaching parts of an object – in other words, the light is *occluded* by another object. We can provide a grayscale *occlusion map* to represent the amount of occlusion on each part of a surface, where a value of 1 represents areas that should receive full ambient lighting and 0 means an area should receive no ambient light at all. Figure 10-32 shows two objects with and without occlusion.

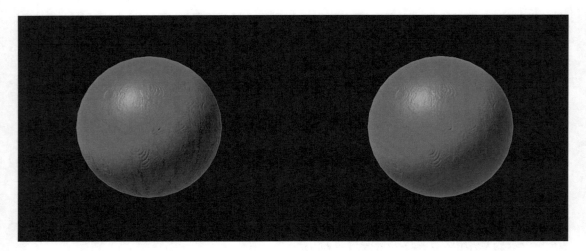

Figure 10-32. *Two spheres using a plywood normal map. The sphere on the left also uses an occlusion texture that matches the normal map, so you can see extra details in the shadowed regions. On the right, the sphere only has the normal map*

Now that we have seen a few textures that control the way external lights interact with the surface of the object, let's see how objects can directly control light emission from their own surface.

Emission

Some objects emit light of their own, such as screens or neon lights. These objects continue to appear bright even if placed in a dark area, although non-emissive parts of the same object can still be influenced by lighting and shadows. We can model this in a PBR shader using *emission* to represent which areas of the object should emit light of a particular color. This comes in two parts: we can apply an *emission map*, which represents the emissive parts of the object through texturing, and an *emissive color*, which uses HDR colors that can go beyond the standard 0–255 range of color values if we want to represent a very bright surface. If you don't apply an emission map, then the emission color will be applied to the entire object. Figure 10-33 shows multiple objects with increasing emissive strength.

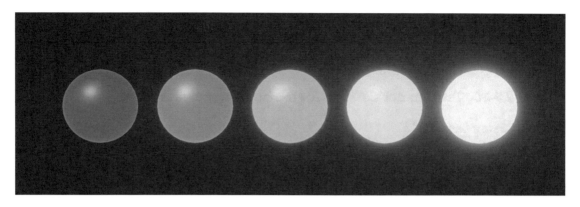

Figure 10-33. *Spheres that use only emissive light. Each object has a black albedo. From left to right, the spheres use red emissive light with intensity 0, 1, 2, 3, and 4, respectively*

Note   To see color bleeding from an emissive object, you must have a bloom filter attached to the camera. We will cover bloom and other post-process effects in the next chapter.

You should now know about the most common components of a PBR shader and how they work in theory. Using this knowledge, let's create a PBR shader in Unity for each pipeline in shader code and Shader Graph.

PBR in the Built-In Pipeline

In the built-in pipeline, we can use Unity's surface shaders to help us with the lighting. Surface shaders are a feature that are exclusive to the built-in pipeline that let us define a lighting model (or use one included with Unity) and then define the surface properties of the object (such as albedo color, smoothness, emission, and the other properties listed previously). Then Unity will automatically carry out the lighting calculations for us. Let's see how they work.

Note   Surface shaders are exclusive to the built-in pipeline. There isn't a direct parallel in code in any other pipeline as of the writing of this book.

417

Create a new shader via *Create ➤ Shader ➤ Standard Surface Shader* and name the new file "PBR.shader". This will generate a template surface shader. I've made some edits, so here is the shader we will be working on.

Listing 10-50. PBR shader skeleton for the built-in pipeline

```
Shader "Examples/PBR"
{
    Properties
    {
        _BaseColor ("Base Color", Color) = (1,1,1,1)
        _BaseTex ("Albedo (RGB)", 2D) = "white" {}
    }
    SubShader
    {
        Tags { "RenderType"="Opaque" }
        LOD 200

        CGPROGRAM
        #pragma surface surf Standard fullforwardshadows
        #pragma target 3.0

        struct Input
        {
            float2 uv_BaseTex;
        };

        sampler2D _BaseTex;
        float4 _BaseColor;

        void surf (Input v, inout SurfaceOutputStandard o)
        {

        }
        ENDCG
    }
    Fallback "Diffuse"
}
```

There's a lot of unfamiliar code in this snippet, so let's break down what's happening. The first key difference is that the shader code is encased in a CGPROGRAM block rather than an HLSLPROGRAM block. Typically, modern Unity shaders are written in HLSL entirely, but surface shaders were designed in a time where Cg was the primary shading language in Unity, and as such, many of the built-in surface shader features are designed around that. Some of the built-in structs use the fixed data type, which doesn't exist in HLSL. The fixed data type has at least 10 bits of fractional precision, although some hardware uses up to 32 bits, the same as a float. Otherwise, most shader syntax we've seen so far will work the same as in HLSL. Also, the code block is placed directly inside a SubShader rather than inside a Pass, because Unity may generate several shader passes based on the surface shader code.

Rather than using vertex and fragment functions, we define a single surface function, and Unity will automatically generate vertex and fragment functions behind the scenes for us. Let's break down the first #pragma statement, which looks like the following.

Listing 10-51. Surface shader #pragma statement

```
#pragma surface surf Standard fullforwardshadows
```

First, we define the name of the function, which in this case is surf – hence we start with #pragma surface surf. I've left the actual surf function empty for now because we'll be making significant edits to Unity's template. After this, we define the name of the lighting model we will use, of which there are several built-in choices:

- Lambert – Ambient and diffuse lighting only

- BlinnPhong – Ambient, diffuse, and specular lighting with the Blinn-Phong lighting model

- Standard – Physically Based Rendering in metallic mode

- StandardSpecular – Physically Based Rendering in specular mode

In the preceding example, the Standard lighting model was used, which means the object will automatically have PBR lighting applied to the object. After specifying the lighting model, we can optionally add other shader features. In this example, the fullforwardshadows option means that Unity will generate shadows for multiple lights (we will focus on shadows later in this chapter).

419

Next, let's think about data flow. Rather than using `appdata` and `v2f` structs in the same way as other shaders we've written so far, we'll use different structs. For inputs to the surface shader, we'll declare everything inside a struct named `Input`. Although the `Input` struct controls the data that gets used as input to the surface shader, it works slightly differently from `appdata` in a couple of ways. We don't need to declare shader semantics such as `TEXCOORD`. Because of this, there is a limited number of variables we can use in the `Input` struct, each of which has a predefined name, such as

- `float3 viewDir` – A vector in world space from the surface of the object to the camera

- `float4 screenPos` – The position of a point on the surface in screen space

- `float3 worldPos` – The position of a point on the surface in world space

UVs work slightly differently from regular shaders – to include them in `Input`, we must specify a `float2` with the name of a texture prefixed with "uv". For example, to include UVs that are set up to use the tiling and offset settings of the `_BaseTex` texture, we must include an entry in the `Input` struct called uv_BaseTex, which you can see in the preceding code snippet. In fact, we are going to include only this variable inside the `Input` struct.

Note   If you want, you can add sets of UVs for other textures to the Input struct, but I am going to use only one set of UVs, as you'll see. This means each texture supplied to a material using this shader should have all details lined up the same way on each texture.

The `Input` struct is used as an input to the surface shader function. The surface shader then outputs a struct that is then used by the lighting model under the hood to calculate the final lighting on the object. For example, if we're using the `Standard` lighting mode, then we will also use the `SurfaceOutputStandard` struct for the inputs and outputs of the surface shader, which looks like the following (you don't need to paste this code into your shader file).

Listing 10-52. The SurfaceOutputStandard struct

```
struct SurfaceOutputStandard
{
    fixed3 Albedo;
    fixed3 Normal;
    half3 Emission;
    half Metallic;
    half Smoothness;
    half Occlusion;
    fixed Alpha;
};
```

Although it's possible to declare a custom `SurfaceOutput` struct, we'll stick with the one used by Unity's Standard shader. Now that we have explored the flow of data inside a surface shader, it's time to start making changes to get the PBR lighting we're aiming for. First, let's focus on the properties. Properties work the same as traditional vertex-fragment shaders: we must first declare them inside the `Properties` block, and then we must declare them a second time inside the `CGPROGRAM` block. We need quite a few properties and keywords for this shader to encompass all the features of PBR:

- `_BaseColor` – This is a regular non-HDR `Color` property that controls the albedo color of the object.

- `_BaseTex` – A `Texture2D` that also controls the albedo color.

- `_MetallicTex` – A grayscale `Texture2D` that controls the metallicity of each part of the object. By default, it is white.

- `_MetallicStrength` – A `Float` between 0 and 1 that acts as a multiplier to the Metallic Map values. By default, it is 0.

- `_Smoothness` – A `Float` between 0 and 1 that defines how smooth the object is. By default, it is 0.5.

- `_NormalTex` – A `Texture2D` that can be used to add normal mapping to the shader. The default *Mode* option should be *Normal Map*, so that if no map is chosen, a flat normal map is used.

- _NormalStrength – A Float that acts as a modifier to the values sampled from the normal map. The higher the value is, the more strongly the normal map influences the lighting. By default, it is 1.

- USE_EMISSION_ON – This Boolean keyword property can be used to toggle emission on and off. We will use a Float property called _EmissionOn to control it.

- _EmissionTex – A Texture2D that controls whether any portions of the object glow, even in low-light conditions. By default, this is a white texture.

- _EmissionColor – A Color that acts as a multiplier to the values used for the emission map. It should be HDR-enabled so that it can use an extended range of color values. By default, it is black, corresponding to no emissive light.

- _AOTex – A Texture2D that is used to dim parts of the mesh that are obscured by small details. By default, this should be white, corresponding to full ambient lighting for all parts of the mesh.

Let's first declare these properties inside the Properties block. I'll overwrite the properties that were already there in the template file. Take note of the attributes in front of some of the properties.

Listing 10-53. The Properties block in the built-in pipeline

```
Properties
{
    _BaseColor("Base Color", Color) = (1,1,1,1)
    _BaseTex("Base Texture", 2D) = "white" {}
    _MetallicTex("Metallic Map", 2D) = "white" {}
    _MetallicStrength("Metallic Strength", Range(0, 1)) = 0
    _Smoothness("Smoothness", Range(0, 1)) = 0.5
    _NormalTex("Normal Map", 2D) = "bump" {}
    _NormalStrength("Normal Strength", Float) = 1
    [Toggle(USE_EMISSION_ON)] _EmissionOn("Use Emission?", Float) = 0
    _EmissionTex("Emission Map", 2D) = "white" {}
```

```
        [HDR] _EmissionColor("Emission Color", Color) = (0, 0, 0, 0)
        _AOTex("Ambient Occlusion Map", 2D) = "white" {}
}
```

Then we can define these same properties as variables inside the CGPROGRAM block.

Listing 10-54. Declaring properties inside the CGPROGRAM block for a surface shader

```
sampler2D _BaseTex;
float4 _BaseColor;
sampler2D _MetallicTex;
float _MetallicStrength;
float _Smoothness;
sampler2D _NormalTex;
float _NormalStrength;
sampler2D _EmissionTex;
float4 _EmissionColor;
sampler2D _AOTex;
```

The _EmissionOn property corresponds to the USE_EMISSION_ON keyword, which we need to declare separately in the code. I will include it below the #pragma statements at the top of the CGPROGRAM block.

Listing 10-55. Declaring the USE_EMISSION_ON keyword

```
#pragma surface surf Standard fullforwardshadows
#pragma target 3.0
#pragma multi_compile_local USE_EMISSION_ON __
```

Now, whenever we toggle the Boolean value of the _EmissionOn property on the material, Unity will turn the USE_EMISSION_ON keyword on or off according to the property's value. We can use that to control whether emission is used in the shader. Speaking of which, we can now turn our attention to the surf function.

The surf function accepts two parameters: the Input struct and a SurfaceOutputStandard struct. The latter uses the inout keyword because it is also the primary output of this function. The surf function is responsible for setting the value of the variables in the `SurfaceOutputStandard` struct seen in Listing 10-52. We'll calculate each value in turn by sampling each of the texture, color, and numerical properties we included. This is relatively simple for the `Albedo`, `Metallic`, `Smoothness`, `Occlusion`, and `Alpha` outputs.

Listing 10-56. Albedo, Metallic, and Smoothness outputs in a surface shader

```
void surf (Input v, inout SurfaceOutputStandard o)
{
    // Albedo output.
    float4 albedoSample = tex2D(_BaseTex, v.uv_BaseTex);
    o.Albedo = albedoSample.rgb * _BaseColor.rgb;

    // Metallic output.
    float4 metallicSample = tex2D(_MetallicTex, v.uv_BaseTex);
    o.Metallic = metallicSample * _MetallicStrength;

    // Smoothness output.
    o.Smoothness = _Smoothness;

    ...

    // Ambient Occlusion output.
    float4 aoSample = tex2D(_AOTex, v.uv_BaseTex);
    o.Occlusion = aoSample.r;

    // Alpha output.
    o.Alpha = albedoSample.a * _BaseColor.a;
}
```

All that remains are the `Normal` and `Emission` outputs. The `Normal` output requires us to sample `_NormalTex`, which stores normal vector information in the red and green channels. However, we need to convert the color information from the sample into a vector that Unity can use. The built-in `UnpackNormal` function helps us do just that. We can then take the result and multiply the red and green channels by `_NormalStrength`, which gives us a way to produce stronger or weaker normal mapping as desired. This code can be placed underneath the Smoothness output code.

Listing 10-57. Normal mapping in a surface shader

```
// Smoothness output.
o.Smoothness = _Smoothness;
```

```
// Normal output.
float3 normalSample = UnpackNormal(tex2D(_NormalTex, v.uv_BaseTex));
normalSample.rg *= _NormalStrength;
o.Normal = normalSample;
```

Finally, we come to the Emission output. When the USE_EMISSION_ON keyword is active, we can sample _EmissionTex and multiply by _EmissionColor, like how we calculated some of the other outputs. However, when the keyword is inactive, we need to return 0, corresponding to a black color, or no emission. We can use an #if directive to control which code gets used based on the keyword value. This code can be placed below the Normal output code and above the Ambient Occlusion output code.

Listing 10-58. Emission output in a surface shader

```
// Emission output.
#if USE_EMISSION_ON
    o.Emission = tex2D(_EmissionTex, v.uv_BaseTex) * _EmissionColor;
#else
    o.Emission = 0;
#endif
```

```
// Ambient Occlusion output.
float4 aoSample = tex2D(_AOTex, v.uv_BaseTex);
o.Occlusion = aoSample.r;
```

The surface shader is now complete, so you will now be able to attach it to a material and see PBR shading on your object. Try changing the material settings to see how different surface properties influence the appearance of the object. Now let's see how PBR works in URP.

PBR in URP

PBR lighting in URP can be pretty complicated. The Lit shader in URP is around 600 lines long, and it relies on include files that themselves contain many lines of code. However, we can leverage the same include files to produce our own version of the Lit shader, which we can modify at will. Start by creating a new shader file and naming it "PBR.shader". Then delete the entire contents of the file. Unlike the built-in pipeline, we don't have access to surface shaders, so we will write a classic vertex-fragment shader for URP. Here is the skeleton shader that we will modify.

Listing 10-59. PBR shader skeleton for URP

```
Shader "Examples/PBR"
{
    Properties { ... }
    SubShader
    {
        Tags
        {
            "RenderType" = "Opaque"
            "Queue" = "Geometry"
            "RenderPipeline" = "UniversalPipeline"
        }

        Pass
        {
            Tags
            {
                "LightMode" = "UniversalForward"
            }

            HLSLPROGRAM
            #pragma vertex vert
            #pragma fragment frag

            struct appdata { ... };
            struct v2f { ... };
```

```
            v2f vert (appdata v) { ... }

            SurfaceData createSurfaceData(...) { ... }
            InputData createInputData(...) { ... }

            float4 frag (v2f i) : SV_Target { ... }
            ENDHLSL
        }
    }
}
```

As you can see, there are a couple of unfamiliar functions and a lot of unfilled gaps, which we will get to soon. First, let's handle the properties. We'll use the same properties that we used for the built-in pipeline version of this, so let's include them in the Properties block at the top of the file using the code from Listing 10-53. Then we'll declare them inside the HLSL code block underneath the v2f struct.

Listing 10-60. Properties in HLSL in URP

```
struct v2f { ... };

sampler2D _BaseTex;
sampler2D _MetallicTex;
sampler2D _NormalTex;
sampler2D _EmissionTex;
sampler2D _AOTex;

CBUFFER_START(UnityPerMaterial)
      float4 _BaseColor;
      float4 _BaseTex_ST;
      float _MetallicStrength;
      float _Smoothness;
      float _NormalStrength;
      float4 _EmissionColor;
CBUFFER_END
```

Now let's talk about the flow of data within this shader:

427

- Inside the Lighting.hlsl file, which is included in this shader, Unity provides a function called `UniversalFragmentPBR` that calculates and applies PBR lighting for us.

  - The function takes two structs as input: `InputData` and `SurfaceData`, which themselves are included in the InputData. hlsl and SurfaceData.hlsl files, respectively.

  - We must include SurfaceData.hlsl ourselves, but InputData.hlsl is already included in Core.hlsl.

- The `InputData` struct can primarily be filled in with variables passed from the vertex shader. This means the `v2f` struct will contain many entries.

- The `SurfaceData` struct can be filled with similar data to the surface shader outputs we wrote for the built-in pipeline, such as albedo, emission, metallic, and so on. This should be calculated in the fragment shader.

- Shader features are turned on or off with `#pragma` keyword directives. We will include one of our own to control whether emission is active, plus a few that are required by Unity to add certain functionality to the shader.

We'll explore exactly what the `InputData` and `SurfaceData` structs contain later. First, let's add some shader functionality with `#pragma` keyword directives. Each keyword is used by the include files to control how the shader operates. For example, some keywords relate to lighting via the main light or additional lights, and others allow the object to receive shadows from other objects. We're going to use quite a few, so let's see what they all do. First, we have our own keyword:

- The `USE_EMISSION_ON` keyword is one we're adding to control whether emission should be used in the shader or not.

Then, we have keywords required for URP specifically:

- The `_MAIN_LIGHT_SHADOWS`, `_MAIN_LIGHT_SHADOWS_CASCADE`, and `_MAIN_LIGHT_SHADOWS_SCREEN` keywords all control how shadows from the main light interact with the object.

- The _ADDITIONAL_LIGHTS_VERTEX and _ADDITIONAL_LIGHTS keywords control how light from all lights *except* the primary light gets applied to the object.

- The _ADDITIONAL_LIGHT_SHADOWS keyword controls how shadows from the additional lights get applied to the object.

- _REFLECTION_PROBE_BLENDING and _REFLECTION_PROBE_BOX_ PROJECTION allow Unity to blend reflection probes if the object is between two probes.

- _SHADOWS_SOFT can be used to soften the edges of shadows. Otherwise, the object will have a hard border between shadowed and lit regions.

- The _SCREEN_SPACE_OCCLUSION keyword enables screen-space ambient occlusion. This is separate from our occlusion texture.

Finally, there are many keywords related to lightmapping:

- LIGHTMAP_SHADOW_MIXING, SHADOWS_SHADOWMASK, DIRLIGHTMAP_ COMBINED, LIGHTMAP_ON, and DYNAMICLIGHTMAP_ON all relate to lightmapping.

We'll include each of these keywords near the top of the HLSLPROGRAM block, just below the #pragma directives for the vert and frag functions. Recall that we can specify a blank (or "off") keyword by using underscores as the name of the keyword, which we'll include here if we want to turn any of these features off.

Listing 10-61. Lighting keywords in URP

```
#pragma vertex vert
#pragma fragment frag

#pragma multi_compile_local USE_EMISSION_ON __

#pragma multi_compile _ _MAIN_LIGHT_SHADOWS _MAIN_LIGHT_SHADOWS_CASCADE
_MAIN_LIGHT_SHADOWS_SCREEN
#pragma multi_compile _ _ADDITIONAL_LIGHTS_VERTEX _ADDITIONAL_LIGHTS
#pragma multi_compile_fragment _ _ADDITIONAL_LIGHT_SHADOWS
#pragma multi_compile_fragment _ _REFLECTION_PROBE_BLENDING
```

```
#pragma multi_compile_fragment _ _REFLECTION_PROBE_BOX_PROJECTION
#pragma multi_compile_fragment _ _SHADOWS_SOFT
#pragma multi_compile_fragment _ _SCREEN_SPACE_OCCLUSION

#pragma multi_compile _ LIGHTMAP_SHADOW_MIXING
#pragma multi_compile _ SHADOWS_SHADOWMASK
#pragma multi_compile _ DIRLIGHTMAP_COMBINED
#pragma multi_compile _ LIGHTMAP_ON
#pragma multi_compile _ DYNAMICLIGHTMAP_ON
```

Tip   When you see a giant pile of unfamiliar keywords like this, it's very easy to feel overwhelmed. When this happens, I try to bear in mind that each individual keyword is digestible, so rather than adding them all to the shader at the same time, try adding one or two and see how they impact the final shader. Then comment those out and add one or two others to see how they work. It's a lot easier to understand what each keyword does when you see individual changes like that.

Next, let's fill out the appdata and v2f structs. For the appdata struct, our shader will require the position and UVs as usual, but we also require the normal and tangent vectors associated with each vertex. They use the NORMAL and TANGENT semantics, respectively. The staticLightmapUV and dynamicLightmapUV are also required – these UVs are automatically generated by Unity for lightmapping purposes. If you've never encountered lightmaps before, they are textures generated by Unity's lightmapper when using baked lighting.

Listing 10-62. The appdata struct

```
struct appdata
{
        float4 positionOS : POSITION;
        float2 uv : TEXCOORD0;
        float3 normalOS : NORMAL;
        float4 tangentOS : TANGENT;
```

```
        float2 staticLightmapUV : TEXCOORD1;
        float2 dynamicLightmapUV : TEXCOORD2;
};
```

Recall that the normal vector points outward from the surface, while the tangent vector is parallel with the surface itself. Next, the v2f struct must pass a lot of data to the fragment shader because the InputData struct will require it. We need the clip-space position and UVs as with most shaders, but we also require several world-space vectors: the position, normal, tangent, and view vectors. We also require a shadowCoord variable for mapping shadows to objects and a few additional lightmap-related variables. The DECLARE_LIGHTMAP_OR_SH macro helps Unity to determine which interpolators are required. Most of these can be included via TEXCOORD interpolators. This is the highest number of interpolators we've seen so far inside a shader!

Listing 10-63. The v2f struct

```
struct v2f
{
    float4 positionCS : SV_POSITION;
    float2 uv : TEXCOORD0;
    float3 positionWS : TEXCOORD1;
    float3 normalWS : TEXCOORD2;
    float4 tangentWS : TEXCOORD3;
    float3 viewDirWS : TEXCOORD4;
    float4 shadowCoord : TEXCOORD5;
    DECLARE_LIGHTMAP_OR_SH(staticLightmapUV, vertexSH, 6);
#ifdef DYNAMICLIGHTMAP_ON
    float2  dynamicLightmapUV : TEXCOORD7;
#endif
};
```

Next, let's write the vert function, the vertex shader. It is responsible for calculating the values in v2f using the values supplied in appdata. Thankfully, this is made easier by a few helper functions:

- As we have seen previously, the TRANSFORM_TEX macro applies tiling and offset parameters of a given texture to the UVs.

- The `GetVertexPositionInputs` and `GetVertexNormalInputs` functions convert the position, normal, and tangent vectors to several different spaces for us.

- The `GetWorldSpaceNormalizedViewDir` function, which we have also seen before, converts the view vector to world space for us.

- The `OUTPUT_LIGHTMAP_UV` macro applies tiling and offset to the lightmap UVs using the values in `unity_LightmapST`. Think of it as `TRANSFORM_TEX` but for lightmaps instead.

- The `OUTPUT_SH` macro sets up spherical harmonics, which are used for ambient lighting evaluation.

Using these functions, we can put together the `vert` function.

Listing 10-64. The vert function

```
v2f vert (appdata v)
{
    v2f o;

    VertexPositionInputs vertexInput = GetVertexPositionInputs(v.
    positionOS.xyz);
    VertexNormalInputs normalInput = GetVertexNormalInputs(v.normalOS,
    v.tangentOS);

    o.positionWS = vertexInput.positionWS;
    o.positionCS = vertexInput.positionCS;

    o.uv = TRANSFORM_TEX(v.uv, _BaseTex);

    o.normalWS = normalInput.normalWS;

    float sign = v.tangentOS.w;
    o.tangentWS = float4(normalInput.tangentWS.xyz, sign);

    o.viewDirWS = GetWorldSpaceNormalizeViewDir(vertexInput.positionWS);

    o.shadowCoord = GetShadowCoord(vertexInput);

    OUTPUT_LIGHTMAP_UV(v.staticLightmapUV, unity_LightmapST,
    o.staticLightmapUV);
```

```
#ifdef DYNAMICLIGHTMAP_ON
    v.dynamicLightmapUV = v.dynamicLightmapUV.xy * unity_
    DynamicLightmapST.xy + unity_DynamicLightmapST.zw;
#endif
    OUTPUT_SH(o.normalWS.xyz, o.vertexSH);

    return o;
}
```

Before we deal with the fragment shader, let's now talk about the SurfaceData and InputData structs. The SurfaceData struct is responsible for representing the surface properties of the object in the same way that the SurfaceOutputStandard struct did for the surface shader for the built-in pipeline. Here's the struct definition, which is contained in SurfaceData.hlsl (you don't need to paste this struct into your own file).

Listing 10-65. The SurfaceData struct

```
struct SurfaceData
{
    half3 albedo;
    half3 specular;
    half  metallic;
    half  smoothness;
    half3 normalTS;
    half3 emission;
    half  occlusion;
    half  alpha;
    half  clearCoatMask;
    half  clearCoatSmoothness;
};
```

We don't need to populate all these values if we won't be using them. For example, I'm going to write a PBR shader that only uses metallic mode and not specular mode, so we can ignore the specular variable. In our shader, I've included a createSurfaceData function that takes a v2f parameter and will set up the struct values. We'll start by creating an instance of SurfaceData and zeroing each of its member variables.

Listing 10-66. Zeroing out the SurfaceData struct members

```
SurfaceData createSurfaceData(v2f i)
{
        SurfaceData surfaceData = (SurfaceData)0;

        ...
}
```

This ensures that all members are initialized to avoid errors and has the advantage that this code should still work if a future update to URP adds more members to the struct. After this, we can populate each of the members. The code is very similar to Listings 10-56 to 10-58 for the built-in pipeline, except the variables may have slightly different names.

Listing 10-67. The full createSurfaceData function

```
SurfaceData createSurfaceData(v2f i)
{
        SurfaceData surfaceData = (SurfaceData)0;

        // Albedo output.
        float4 albedoSample = tex2D(_BaseTex, i.uv);
        surfaceData.albedo = albedoSample.rgb * _BaseColor.rgb;

        // Metallic output.
        float4 metallicSample = tex2D(_MetallicTex, i.uv);
        surfaceData.metallic = metallicSample * _MetallicStrength;

        // Smoothness output.
        surfaceData.smoothness = _Smoothness;

        // Normal output.
        float3 normalSample = UnpackNormal(tex2D(_NormalTex, i.uv));
        normalSample.rg *= _NormalStrength;
        surfaceData.normalTS = normalSample;

        // Emission output.
#if USE_EMISSION_ON
        surfaceData.emission = tex2D(_EmissionTex, i.uv) * _EmissionColor;
#endif
```

```
    // Ambient Occlusion output.
    float4 aoSample = tex2D(_AOTex, i.uv);
    surfaceData.occlusion = aoSample.r;

    // Alpha output.
    surfaceData.alpha = albedoSample.a * _BaseColor.a;

    return surfaceData;
}
```

Next comes the InputData struct. This struct contains many variables that are required by URP to properly calculate lighting, such as positions, normals, and tangents. Here is part of the struct definition, which is contained in Input.hlsl (again, you don't need to copy this code into your own shader file).

Listing 10-68. The important members of the InputData struct

```
struct InputData
{
    float3   positionWS;
    float4   positionCS;
    half3    normalWS;
    half3    viewDirectionWS;
    float4   shadowCoord;
    half     fogCoord;
    half3    vertexLighting;
    half3    bakedGI;
    float2   normalizedScreenSpaceUV;
    half4    shadowMask;
    half3x3  tangentToWorld;
}
```

As with the SurfaceData struct, we don't need to populate every member of this struct, but it should give you a good idea of the features that you could add to the shader if you want. I've included a createInputData function to populate the struct. It takes a v2f as a parameter along with the tangent-space normal vector from SurfaceData. The most intensive part of this function is calculating the tangentToWorld matrix, which requires calculating the bitangent vector. Recall that the bitangent vector is perpendicular to both the normal and tangent vectors, and we can calculate it by taking the cross product of those two existing vectors.

The TransformTangentToWorld helper function lets us transform from tangent-space normal vectors to world-space normal vectors using the tangentToWorld matrix, and the NormalizeNormalPerPixel helper function works exactly as it sounds. The SAMPLE_GI macro helps with sampling global illumination data, and SAMPLE_SHADOWMASK is used to set up a shadow mask, which is used when combining baked and real-time lighting.

Listing 10-69. The full createInputData function

```
InputData createInputData(v2f i, float3 normalTS)
{
        InputData inputData = (InputData)0;

        // Position input.
        inputData.positionWS = i.positionWS;

        // Normal input.
        float3 bitangent = i.tangentWS.w * cross(i.normalWS,
        i.tangentWS.xyz);
        inputData.tangentToWorld = float3x3(i.tangentWS.xyz, bitangent,
        i.normalWS);
        inputData.normalWS = TransformTangentToWorld(normalTS, inputData.
        tangentToWorld);
        inputData.normalWS = NormalizeNormalPerPixel(inputData.normalWS);

        // View direction input.
        inputData.viewDirectionWS = SafeNormalize(i.viewDirWS);

        // Shadow coords.
        inputData.shadowCoord = TransformWorldToShadowCoord
        (inputData .positionWS);

        // Baked lightmaps.
#if defined(DYNAMICLIGHTMAP_ON)
        inputData.bakedGI = SAMPLE_GI(i.staticLightmapUV,
        i.dynamicLightmapUV, i.vertexSH, inputData.normalWS);
```

```
#else
    inputData.bakedGI = SAMPLE_GI(i.staticLightmapUV, i.vertexSH,
    inputData.normalWS);
#endif
    inputData.normalizedScreenSpaceUV = GetNormalizedScreenSpaceUV(i.
    positionCS);
    inputData.shadowMask = SAMPLE_SHADOWMASK(i.staticLightmapUV);

    return inputData;
}
```

Now that we have functions to set up the InputData and SurfaceData structs, we can finish the shader off with the frag function. The fragment shader is going to set up the SurfaceData and InputData structs using the createInputData and createSurfaceData functions, respectively, and then use those structs to call UniversalFragmentPBR. That last function returns a color, which will be the output of the fragment shader.

Listing 10-70. The frag function

```
float4 frag (v2f i) : SV_Target
{
    SurfaceData surfaceData = createSurfaceData(i);
    InputData inputData = createInputData(i, surfaceData.normalTS);

    return UniversalFragmentPBR(inputData, surfaceData);
}
```

With that, the PBR shader for URP is now complete, and you will see PBR lighting on any objects whose material uses this shader. As with the built-in pipeline version, try changing the properties of the material to see how the appearance of each object changes. Now that we have covered the PBR shader in shader code, let's move on to Shader Graph.

PBR in Shader Graph

Shader Graph is by far the easiest tool to use for custom PBR shaders because both URP and HDRP ship with a preset Lit option that uses PBR calculations under the hood for lighting. Most of the work to be done inside a PBR shader for Shader Graph is setting up the properties and wiring up a few basic nodes to read them. Let's create a new Lit shader and name it "PBR.shadergraph". When you open it in the Shader Graph editor, you will be met with the following blocks on the master stack as shown in Figure 10-34.

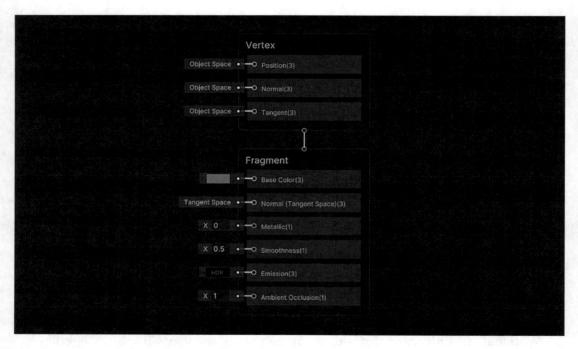

Figure 10-34. *The master stack of a new Lit graph*

You'll see that several of the blocks are based on concepts we have discussed in this chapter so far, such as *Normal, Metallic, Smoothness, Emission,* and *Ambient Occlusion.* By default, a material uses metallic mode, so if you want to switch to specular mode, go to the Graph Settings and change the *Workflow Mode* option from *Metallic* to *Specular.* The *Metallic* block will automatically swap out for a *Specular Color* block. I'll be using *metallic mode.* For this shader, we'll be adding a lot of properties and then connecting them to the master stack outputs one by one. We'll add the same properties to this graph that we added to the code versions of the shader, as seen in Figure 10-35.

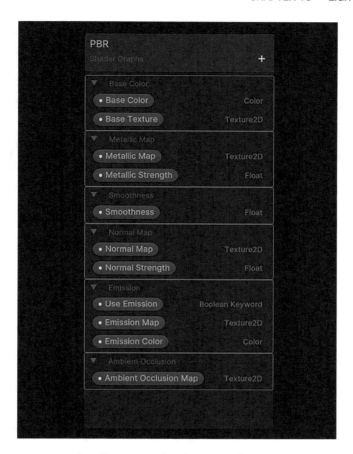

Figure 10-35. *Properties for the PBR Shader Graph*

Once these properties have all been added, we can sample each set of nodes and output them to the corresponding output on the master stack. Let's deal with each output in order, starting with the *Base Color* output. For this, we can sample the Base Texture property and multiply the result by the Base Color property as shown in Figure 10-36.

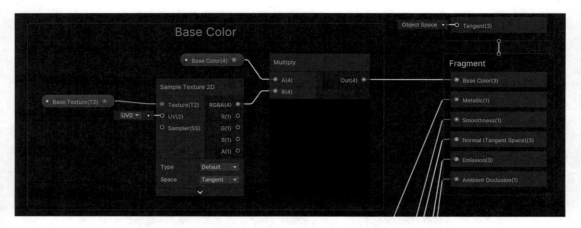

Figure 10-36. *Sampling the Base Texture and multiplying by Base Color*

Next is the *Metallic* output, which follows much the same process: sample the
Metallic Map and multiply the result by Metallic Strength. Figure 10-37 shows how
these nodes should be connected.

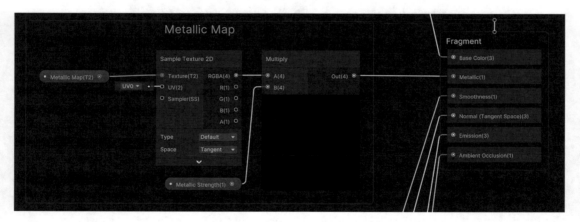

Figure 10-37. *Sampling the Metallic Map and multiplying by Metallic Strength*

After this, we can link up the Smoothness property to the *Smoothness* output,
as shown in Figure 10-38. This is the simplest output since we just need to link the
Smoothness property with the *Smoothness* block on the master stack.

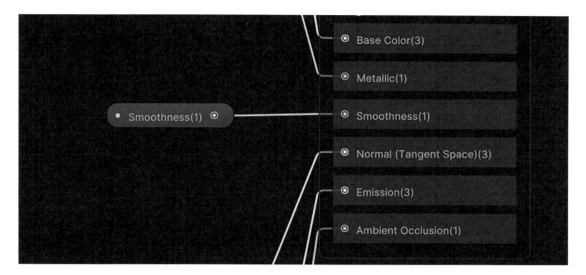

Figure 10-38. *Linking the Smoothness property to the Smoothness output block*

Next is the *Normal* output block. For this, we will sample the Normal Map texture using a Sample Texture 2D node. By changing the *Type* to *Normal* at the bottom of the node, Unity will output normal vectors rather than color values from the texture. After this, we can apply the Normal Strength property to these vectors using a Normal Strength node, which takes the input vector and makes it longer or shorter according to the *Strength* value used as an input. Figure 10-39 shows how this node should be connected to other nodes.

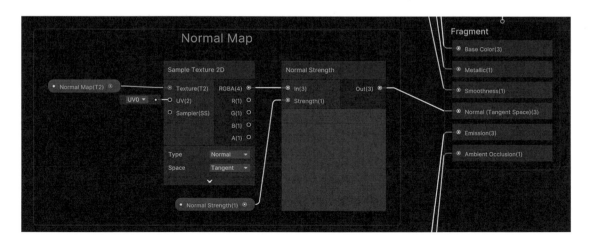

Figure 10-39. *Sampling the Normal Map and then modifying its strength with Normal Strength*

The penultimate output is the *Emission*, which requires slightly more work. To calculate the amount of emission, we can sample the Emission Map and multiply the output by Emission Color, like how we handled the *Base Color* output. However, we have also set up a property to turn emission on or off at will, so we'll need to incorporate that. Drag the Use Emission keyword property onto the graph and connect the existing emission nodes into the *On* slot so that those values are used when emission is turned on. In the *Off* slot, use a value of 0, corresponding to black, which means there is no emission. Connect the output of this keyword node to the *Emission* block on the master stack. Figure 10-40 shows how these nodes should be connected.

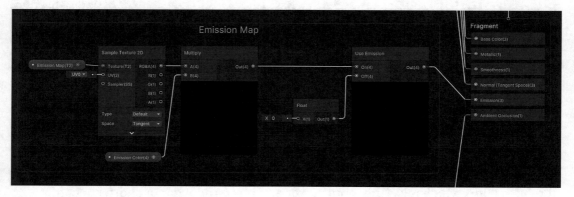

Figure 10-40. *Outputting different values for emission based on the value of the Use Emission keyword property*

The final output is the *Ambient Occlusion*, which is just a simple texture sample of Ambient Occlusion Map. Figure 10-41 shows how to connect these nodes to the output.

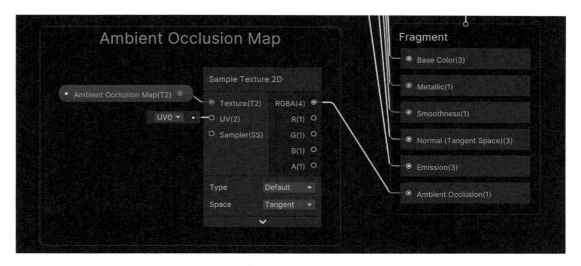

Figure 10-41. *Sampling the Ambient Occlusion Map for the Ambient Occlusion output*

Now that all these properties have been connected, you will see PBR lighting on objects. As with the code versions of this shader effect, try tweaking the material properties to see how the appearance of the object changes.

Thankfully, each of these PBR shaders applies shadows from other objects when calculating the amount of lighting on the object. However, some shaders are not yet able to cast shadows. In the next section, we'll see how to add shadow-casting support to our shaders.

Shadow Casting

Unity's render pipelines implement real-time shadow casting in slightly different ways. In this section, we won't necessarily write new shaders from scratch, but we'll see how to add shadow-casting support to existing shaders. Figure 10-42 compares an object that casts shadows with one that does not.

Figure 10-42. *The sphere on the left casts a shadow, while the sphere on the right does not. The floor below receives the shadow that is cast by the left sphere*

Shadow Casting in the Built-In Pipeline

When writing surface shaders, you can add the addshadow or fullforwardshadows compiler directive to make Unity generate a shadow-casting pass, which we already did in the PBR shader for the built-in pipeline. However, most of the shaders we wrote throughout the book were classic vertex-fragment shaders, which we'll need to manually add a shadow-casting pass to. In this section, we'll be writing a shader pass that you can add to any of those shaders to make them cast shadows. With that in mind, we won't create any new shader file – just include the pass we're about to write in a shader after any existing pass, like the following.

Listing 10-71. Adding a shadow caster pass to an existing shader

```
SubShader
{
    Pass
    {
        // Regular pass here.
        ...
    }
    Pass
    {
        Name "ShadowCaster"
```

```
        // Shadow caster pass here.
        ...
    }
}
```

You might recall that back in Chapter 7, we already wrote a shadow caster pass, because the built-in pipeline uses this pass to write depth information to the camera depth texture. We're going to use the same pass here. The pass is relatively simple since we use the UnityStandardShadow.cginc include file to import the vertShadowCaster and fragShadowCaster functions.

Listing 10-72. A shadow-casting pass in the built-in pipeline

```
Pass
{
    Name "ShadowCaster"
    Tags { "LightMode" = "ShadowCaster" }

    ZWrite On

    HLSLPROGRAM
    #pragma vertex vertShadowCaster
    #pragma fragment fragShadowCaster

    #pragma multi_compile_shadowcaster
    #pragma multi_compile_instancing

    #include "UnityStandardShadow.cginc"

    ENDHLSL
}
```

Here's a quick rundown of what's happening here:

- The ShadowCaster LightMode tells Unity that this pass is exclusively to be used as a shadow-casting pass.

- The vertShadowCaster function works like any other vertex shader and deals with the object position and texture offsets.

- The fragShadowCaster renders the object to the shadow map. The shadow map is then used by other objects to determine whether they should receive shadows.

- The multi_compile_shadowcaster directive sets up the macros that are required to make shadow casting work.

- The multi_compile_instancing directive makes this pass work with GPU instancing.

- The UnityStandardShadow.cginc include file is where most of these features are included.

Once you've added this pass to your shader, your objects should start to cast shadows, as seen in Figure 10-42. Now let's see how the process of adding real-time shadows differs in URP.

Shadow Casting in URP

Unlike the built-in pipeline, whose shadow caster pass is also used for rendering to the depth texture, URP's shadow caster pass is wholly used for shadow casting and nothing else. Therefore, we didn't see it in Chapter 7. However, just like we saw with the built-in pipeline, we can use URP's include files to help us set up this pass. The shadow caster pass should be added to an existing shader, as in Listing 10-71. This time, the code for the pass looks like the following.

Listing 10-73. A shadow-casting pass in URP

```
Pass
{
    Name "ShadowCaster"
    Tags { "LightMode" = "ShadowCaster" }

    ZWrite On
    ZTest LEqual

    HLSLPROGRAM
    #pragma vertex ShadowPassVertex
    #pragma fragment ShadowPassFragment
```

```
    #pragma multi_compile_instancing

    #include "Packages/com.unity.render-pipelines.core/ShaderLibrary/
    Common.hlsl"
    #include "Packages/com.unity.render-pipelines.core/ShaderLibrary/
    CommonMaterial.hlsl"
    #include "Packages/com.unity.render-pipelines.universal/
    ShaderLibrary/SurfaceInput.hlsl"
    #include "Packages/com.unity.render-pipelines.universal/Shaders/
    ShadowCasterPass.hlsl"
    ENDHLSL
}
```

Here's a breakdown of what's happening:

- The `ShadowCaster LightMode` tells Unity that this is a shadow-casting pass so that it can be run at the correct point in the graphics pipeline.

- The `ShadowPassVertex` function, the vertex shader, positions objects correctly on-screen and applies shadow biasing to ensure shadows render correctly.

- The `ShadowPassFragment` function, the fragment shader, renders values into the shadow map.

- The ShadowCasterPass.hlsl file contains these two functions and other helper functions used within. ShadowCasterPass.hlsl requires some of the contents of Common.hlsl, CommonMaterial.hlsl, and SurfaceInput.hlsl.

- The `multi_compile_instancing` directive makes this pass work with GPU instancing.

Once the shadow caster pass has been added to your shader, you will see shadows like those in Figure 10-42.

Shadow Casting in Shader Graph

In Shader Graph versions 11 and prior (for Unity 2021.1 and older), Lit and Unlit shaders automatically cast shadows. From our perspective, that's great because we have to put in no extra work to get shadows working. To turn off shadows, you must disable them on a per-object basis by selecting the object and setting *Cast Shadows* to *Off* in the *Lighting* section of its Mesh Renderer as seen in Figure 10-43.

Figure 10-43.   *Turning off shadows in Shader Graph 11.0 and earlier*

In Shader Graph 12.0 and up (for Unity 2021.2 and later), you can turn off shadow casting on a per-shader basis instead. In the *Graph Settings* of a Lit or Unlit shader, go to the *Cast Shadows* option and untick the box to prevent Unity from generating the shadow caster pass, as shown in Figure 10-44.

Figure 10-44. *Turning off shadows in Shader Graph 12.0 and later*

It's as easy as that – just untick a box! With that, you should know how to enable and disable shadow casting in each of Unity's pipelines and in Shader Graph.

Summary

Lighting helps you achieve a sense of realism in 3D games. By adding lighting, players have access to additional lighting cues that help them discern the position of objects within a 3D environment, which reduces the "artificial" look that players sometimes feel in an unlit environment. In this chapter, we learned how lighting models are made up of a few different types of light and that we could approximate the total light falling on an object by adding these individual light contributions from lights within the scene. The most popular lighting models are Blinn-Phong, which calculates light as a sum of ambient, diffuse, specular, and sometimes Fresnel light, and PBR, which models surfaces using physical properties such as smoothness, metallicity, specularity, and emission to simulate the way light interacts with that surface. Here's a brief rundown of what we learned:

- The total amount of light falling on a surface can be modeled as the sum of individual types of light, such as ambient, diffuse, specular, and Fresnel light.

- Ambient light is used to approximate global illumination from the environment.

- Diffuse light is proportional to the angle between the normal vector on the surface of an object and the light vector.

- Specular light is proportional to the angle between the reflected light vector and the view vector. The Blinn approximation removes the costly reflection step by using the dot product of the half vector and normal vector instead. The half vector is halfway between the view vector and light vector.

- Flat shading evaluates light once per triangle.

- Gouraud shading evaluates light once per vertex and interpolates the result across fragments.

- Phong shading interpolates the normal vector across fragments and calculates lighting per fragment for more realistic results.

- Physically Based Rendering uses the physical properties of a surface – its albedo color, smoothness, metallicity, specularity, normals, and occlusion – in the lighting calculation.

- Shadow casting can be enabled on objects by using Unity's built-in code or by using the tick boxes provided in Shader Graph.

CHAPTER 11

Image Effects and Post-Processing

Image effects, also known as *post-processing effects,* are a feature of many rendering systems that lets you take an image that has been rendered by the camera and perform extra processing steps to modify the appearance of the image. For example, you can modify the colors of the image or overlay new elements onto the image with post-processing. In this chapter, we will see how post-processing can be used in each pipeline to enhance the look of your game.

Render Textures

Render texture is the term we use for any texture that has been rendered by the camera, as opposed to traditional textures that are usually created in an external program. Typically, a render texture is the same size as the screen or window the game is running in, although it is possible to *downsample* a render texture so that it has a lower resolution and takes up less texture memory. Let's see how render textures work in Unity.

By default, Unity renders what each camera can see to the screen. However, cameras (including the main camera) can render to a texture instead, hence the term *render texture.* Broadly, there are two ways to do this: in the Editor and programmatically. To assign a target texture in the Editor, select your camera and drag a render texture onto the *Output Texture* slot on the Camera component (each pipeline styles the Camera component's variables slightly different, so what you see might not exactly match Figure 11-1).

© Daniel Ilett 2022
D. Ilett, *Building Quality Shaders for Unity*®, https://doi.org/10.1007/978-1-4842-8652-4_11

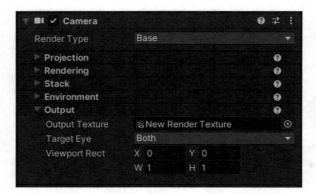

Figure 11-1. *A camera with a render texture assigned to its Output Texture slot. This component looks different between each pipeline*

Of course, we must get that texture somewhere. In the Project View, you can right-click and select *Create* ➤ *Render Texture* to create a new render texture asset. An example of such an asset can be seen in Figure 11-2. This asset can be attached to the *Output Texture* slot on your cameras, and it can be used as a texture on any material. At runtime, when the camera updates the texture, the material will update to reflect those changes.

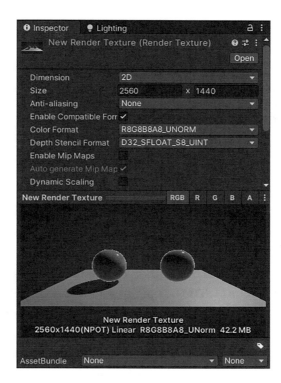

Figure 11-2. *A new render texture that has been assigned to the main camera. The preview at the bottom shows the camera's output*

There are a few settings you can change on the render texture, such as the format, which controls how many bits are used for each color channel, and the resolution. Play around with these options to see what happens. We can also create render textures at runtime and then assign those textures to cameras and materials. The following script provides simple usage examples.

Listing 11-1. Creating and using render textures with code

```
using UnityEngine;

public class RTExample : MonoBehaviour
{
    public Camera exampleCamera;
    public Material exampleMaterial;

    private RenderTexture rt;
```

```
private void Start()
{
    rt = new RenderTexture(1920, 1080, 32, RenderTextureFormat.ARGB32);
    rt.Create();

    exampleCamera.targetTexture = rt;
    exampleMaterial.SetTexture("_MainTex", rt);
}
}
```

In Start, the RenderTexture constructor is used to set up the format of the texture. This method can take many sets of parameters, but I've used one of the most important combinations here. The first two values are the width and height of the texture in pixels, respectively. Next is the number of bits in the depth buffer – 32 gives us a full-precision depth buffer with stencil support. The last parameter is the format. I've used ARGB32, which gives us 8 bits per channel including alpha, which is the default on most platforms if no value is supplied.

The constructor doesn't create any texture resource on the GPU by itself, so we must call the Create method on our texture to assign resources. Then, by setting the render texture to a camera's targetTexture variable, we can make that camera render into the texture rather than onto the screen. Likewise, we can assign the texture to any texture property on a material, and the material will update accordingly.

This is all useful, but what does it have to do with post-processing effects? In the background, Unity uses render textures to handle the state of the frame buffer during a frame before outputting the resulting image to the screen. At certain points in the rendering loop, which differ between render pipelines, Unity exposes the screen texture and lets us modify its contents. This is where image effect shaders come in! An image effect shader takes the screen texture as an input and modifies the colors within, returning a new color value. The modified texture is put back into the rendering loop before being output to the screen. Let's see how post-processing effects work in practice.

Post-Processing Effects

Post-processing effects in Unity come in two parts: the C# scripting side, which handles the render textures we are using and the materials we're applying to those render textures, and the shader side, which controls how the contents of a render texture are modified. We can use any shader syntax we're familiar with inside these shaders, but they should all sample the texture provided to them and modify the color of the texture in some way.

Note   Technically speaking, the shader isn't necessarily *forced* to read the source texture and modify it, but it would rather defeat the point of it being a post-processing effect if it didn't!

Post-processing effects work by supplying a quad mesh to the shader. This mesh has corners that line up exactly with the corners of the screen, and it has UV coordinates that exactly cover the [0,1] range in both axes. The vertex shader for a post-processing effect is very basic, as it just needs to position the quad mesh in the correct place and pass the UVs to the fragment shader. We also supply a render texture to the shader, called the *source texture*, which should be read and modified in some way inside the fragment shader. As a result, the fragment shader is where our focus will lie for post-processing effects.

Post-processing in Unity is a strange beast, as the level of support across the different render pipelines differs wildly:

- The built-in render pipeline supports post-processing fully.

- There is no official support for post-processing in URP, but we will see a workaround that lets us implement them with some effort. The shader side in URP is not much more complicated than the equivalent built-in pipeline shader.

- HDRP provides support for writing custom post-processing shaders, which is one of the few circumstances where custom code shaders in HDRP are encouraged.

- Shader Graph regrettably doesn't provide official support for post-processing shaders.

Important Note   Although it's technically feasible to put together some types of post-processing shader in Shader Graph, the lack of official support makes some common post-processing shader operations a lot more difficult to pull off, such as sampling multiple screen pixels in a loop. At that point, you lose the ease-of-use benefits that Shader Graph brings, and it stops being worth forcing it outside its capabilities. Therefore, we will not cover Shader Graph in this chapter.

It's a bit of a mess, but it's a mess we can navigate! As a starting point, let's create a post-processing effect that turns the screen grayscale based on the luminance of each color. This effect won't be very complicated on the shader side, but it will illuminate the significant difference in complexity between the pipelines on the C# programming side.

Grayscale Image Effect

The grayscale image effect is simple – it takes the color of each pixel in the image, and based on the luminance of the color, it outputs a grayscale value that is then displayed on-screen. The human eye is most sensitive to green light and least sensitive to blue light, so the calculation we'll use to obtain the grayscale luminance value is a dot product that looks like this:

Equation 11-1: The luminance equation

$$C_{output} = C_{input} \cdot \left(0.213, 0.715, 0.072 \right)$$

Although they look like magic numbers plucked from thin air, these are real-world values representing the relative sensitivity of your eyes to each color channel, which sum to 1. A fully white input results in a fully white output, and the same is true for black inputs and outputs. Figure 11-3 shows a scene before and after the Grayscale effect is applied (if you're viewing in black and white, both will look identical).

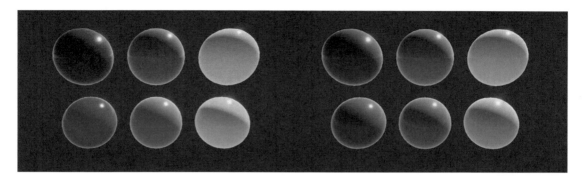

Figure 11-3. *Grayscale effect before (left) and after (right) being applied*

Now that we know how the grayscale calculation works, let's see how post-processing effects are made in each pipeline, starting with the built-in render pipeline.

Post-Processing in the Built-In Pipeline

As I mentioned, writing post-processing shaders comes in two distinct parts: the scripting side and the shader side. First, let's write the C# code that will be used to apply the shader effect to the screen.

Grayscale C# Scripting in the Built-In Pipeline

Create a new C# script by right-clicking in the Project View and selecting *Create* ➤ *C# Script*. We'll name it "GrayscaleEffect.cs". We can remove the boilerplate `Update` method and some of the `using` statements to be left with the following starting code.

Listing 11-2. GrayscaleEffect code skeleton

```
using UnityEngine;

public class Grayscale : MonoBehaviour
{
    void Start() { }
}
```

In the built-in pipeline, we can include a method called `OnRenderImage`, which automatically gets called on any script that is attached to a GameObject that has a Camera component attached. This method takes two `RenderTexture` parameters: the source texture, which contains the state of the screen after the camera has finished rendering objects and is one that we will send to the shader for modification, and the destination texture, which is the one that will be shown on-screen.

Inside OnRenderImage, we need to write code that will send the source texture to the shader, retrieve the result, and send it to the destination texture. We can do that with the Graphics.Blit method. Graphics.Blit takes any two textures as arguments and copies the first texture onto the second texture, with the option of supplying a material. If we call Graphics.Blit with only the source and destination textures as arguments, then we won't see any changes on-screen.

Listing 11-3. Graphics.Blit with no material specified

```
void Start() { }

void OnRenderImage(RenderTexture src, RenderTexture dst)
{
    Graphics.Blit(src, dst);
}
```

In this case, all we're doing is copying the screen contents onto the screen. Although this obviously isn't the behavior we want, this method is useful if we want to copy one render texture onto another in any other context. For the Grayscale effect, we're going to supply a material. In the script, we can create the material in the Start method and hold a reference to it and then modify the Graphics.Blit call to include the material. To create the material, we'll use Shader.Find, which lets us reference a shader by the name string we specify at the top of the shader file. We haven't created the shader file yet, but I'm going to use the name "Examples/ImageEffect/Grayscale", so we'll use that.

Listing 11-4. Referencing a shader by name with Shader.Find

```
Material mat;

void Start()
{
    mat = new Material(Shader.Find("Examples/ImageEffect /Grayscale"));
}
```

Caution   When using `Shader.Find`, be careful to make sure that the shader file you are referencing gets included in the final build. If a shader is used on a material in the project folder that is referenced in a scene, you're fine. Otherwise, if it is only ever referenced programmatically, make sure it is included in *Edit* ➤ *Project Settings* ➤ *Graphics tab* in the *Always Included Shaders* list. Unity also includes *any* assets in the game build if they're placed inside a folder named "Resources," no matter whether it is a subfolder or whether you have multiple folders called "Resources."

Now we can modify the `Graphics.Blit` method to use the material.

Listing 11-5. Using a material with Graphics.Blit

```
Graphics.Blit(src, dst, mat);
```

That's all we need to do for the script in the built-in pipeline. Now that we've completed it, let's move on to the shader file.

Grayscale Shader in the Built-In Pipeline

Unity provides a template file for image effects in the built-in render pipeline if you right-click in the Project View and select *Create* ➤ *Shader* ➤ *Image Effect Shader*. However, it will be useful to start from scratch to see which parts are important for an image effect shader. With that in mind, create a new shader file using that template, name the file "Grayscale.shader", and delete the contents of the file. From there, we can build up each part of the shader. First, rename the shader on the first line to match the name we used in the script.

Listing 11-6. Renaming the Grayscale shader

```
Shader "Examples/ImageEffect/Grayscale"
{

}
```

Next, we need to include the source texture as a property. The `Graphics.Blit` method copies the texture to the _MainTex property if one exists, so that's the name we'll use inside the shader. We don't need to include additional properties in this shader, although it is possible to include more in other image effect shaders if you need them.

Listing 11-7. Properties block for the Grayscale shader

```
{
    Properties
    {
        _MainTex ("Texture", 2D) = "white" {}
    }
}
```

Now we come to the SubShader. Inside the SubShader, we only need a single Pass block that contains the body of the shader. It's not too important to include a Tags block to specify the render queue, because this shader won't execute within the usual rendering loop anyway – it is executed specifically when the camera finished rendering everything on the screen. The Pass contains the HLSLPROGRAM block.

Listing 11-8. Structure of the rest of the shader

```
Properties { ... }
SubShader
{
    Pass
    {
        HLSLPROGRAM
        ...
        ENDHLSL
    }
}
```

Let's go through the contents of the HLSLPROGRAM block from top to bottom. First, we need #pragma statements to specify which functions we're using for the vertex and fragment shaders. After that, we'll #include the UnityCG.cginc file, which contains useful functions and macros.

Listing 11-9. Setup for the HLSL block

```
#pragma vertex vert
#pragma fragment frag

#include "UnityCG.cginc"
```

Next, let's add the appdata and v2f structs. The vertex shader needs to be passed the object-space position of the vertices of the screen quad that I mentioned, plus the UVs attached to it. The fragment shader only requires the clip-space position of each fragment and the associated UVs. As a result, both these structs are very basic.

Listing 11-10. appdata and v2f structs

```
struct appdata
{
    float4 positionOS : POSITION;
    float2 uv : TEXCOORD0;
};

struct v2f
{
    float2 uv : TEXCOORD0;
    float4 positionCS : SV_POSITION;
};
```

The vert function is also very short. We need to transform the vertex positions from object space to clip space using UnityObjectToClipPos. Then we can pass the UVs to the fragment shader without modification. Ordinarily, we might use TRANSFORM_TEX to apply scaling and offset to the UVs, but the _MainTex will never be scaled or offset, so there is no point.

Listing 11-11. The vertex shader

```
v2f vert (appdata v)
{
    v2f o;
    o.positionCS = UnityObjectToClipPos(v.positionOS);
    o.uv = v.uv;
    return o;
}
```

Next, let's declare _MainTex in HLSL. We have declared it in the Properties block in ShaderLab, but like all properties, we'll need to define it again in HLSL. I'll declare it between the vert and frag functions.

Listing 11-12. Declaring _MainTex in HLSL

```
sampler2D _MainTex;
```

Finally, we come to the fragment shader, which is the most important part of any post-processing effect. Here is where we sample the source texture and apply modifications to the colors within. The Grayscale shader is just a simple mapping from one set of colors to another, which requires passing the texture sample into a function that calculates the *luminance* of the color. Thankfully, UnityCG.cginc includes a function called Luminance, which converts an RGB color into a single grayscale float value based on the relative sensitivity of the human eye to red, green, and blue colors.

Listing 11-13. The fragment shader for the grayscale effect in the built-in pipeline

```
float4 frag (v2f i) : SV_Target
{
    float4 textureSample = tex2D(_MainTex, i.uv);

    float3 outputColor = Luminance(textureSample);

    return float4(outputColor, 1.0f);
}
```

With that, the shader is complete. If we attach the GrayscaleEffect script to the main camera (or any GameObject with a Camera component attached), then the output from the camera will have the Grayscale effect applied, as in Figure 11-3. Now that we have seen how this works in the built-in pipeline, let's look at how to make a post-processing effect in URP.

Post-Processing in URP

Unity does not yet officially support custom post-processing effects in URP. By that, I mean that there is no official template file or documentation for creating post-processing effects, as of Unity 2021.3. However, we can use the Renderer Features system to create them. Fair warning, though: The process is a lot more involved in URP than in the other pipelines. Hopefully, if you're reading this book in the far future, there will be an official (and simpler) way to create URP effects!

One powerful feature of URP is the volume system, which lets developers apply an effect or list of effects that we bundle together into profiles. We can create global volumes, which apply the effect regardless of where the camera is, or local volumes, which apply the effect only when the camera is positioned within a specific trigger volume in 3D space. We will write code that is compatible with the URP volume system.

Grayscale C# Scripting in URP

We need to write code to control how URP applies the Grayscale shader to the screen – this is where URP requires a lot more work than the built-in render pipeline. In URP, the OnRenderImage method doesn't get called at all, and we must use Renderer Features instead. At the end of Chapter 7, we saw how Renderer Features can be used in URP – this time, we will write our own custom Renderer Feature. The process to create a custom Renderer Feature for a post-processing effect is complicated, so let's set out the steps required to create one:

- We must create a class that holds the settings for the shader effect called GrayscaleSettings.

  - This class will inherit VolumeComponent and IPostProcessComponent, which allows our post-process to integrate with Unity's volume system.

- The settings that we define in this class will be visible on the Renderer Feature when we attach it to the features list on the Forward Renderer asset.

- We must create a second class that drives the effect called `GrayscaleRenderPass`.

  - This class inherits from `ScriptableRenderPass`, the base class for passes, and it is responsible for setting up the post-process effect's behavior and injecting the pass into the rendering loop.

- We must create a third class that creates and sets up the pass called `GrayscaleFeature`.

  - This class will inherit from `ScriptableRendererFeature`, the base class for all features. It is responsible for creating render passes for the post-process.

- Finally, we must write a shader file for the post-processing effect.

This workflow may seem complicated, but if we break each step down, you'll see that each part has its purpose. To start, let's create the settings script.

The GrayscaleSettings C# Script

Create a new C# script by right-clicking in the Project View and selecting *Create* ➤ *C# Script*, and name it "GrayscaleSettings.cs". As I briefly described before, the purpose of this file is to hold all the settings required to make our post-process work. Some shader effects will have more settings than others, but our Grayscale effect is relatively minimal. First, replace the contents of the file with the following skeleton.

Listing 11-14. GrayscaleSettings code skeleton

```
using UnityEngine;
using UnityEngine.Rendering;
using UnityEngine.Rendering.Universal;

public sealed class GrayscaleSettings : VolumeComponent, IPostProcessComponent
{
    public bool IsActive() { }

    public bool IsTileCompatible() { }
}
```

Now let's break down what's happening here:

- The script needs to use the UnityEngine.Rendering and UnityEngine.Rendering.Universal namespaces to be able to use URP's volume system.

- Inheriting from the VolumeComponent class is what allows us to plug into the URP volume system.

- The IPostProcessComponent interface is what makes GrayscaleSettings work as settings *for a post-processing effect* specifically. We are required to define the IsActive and IsTileCompatible methods from this interface.

When we want to add any post-processing effect to a volume profile, Unity will bring up a context menu to do so. We must add an attribute called VolumeComponentMenu to our class to define what name Unity will use for our effect in this menu. We also need to make the class serializable so that Unity can properly list the settings in the Inspector, which we can do with the System.Serializable attribute. Let's add those to the class now.

Listing 11-15. Adding attributes to the GrayscaleSettings class

```
[System.Serializable, VolumeComponentMenu("Examples/Grayscale")]
public sealed class GrayscaleSettings : VolumeComponent,
IPostProcessComponent { ... }
```

Next, let's add the setting variables required for this effect to work. Generally, these settings will match up with those used in the shader, with the exception of the _MainTex texture, which is supplied in the second C# script that we will write. In the case of our Grayscale effect, we'll only include one setting: the strength of the effect, which is a float between 0 and 1. We use special types for these settings, such as the following:

- FloatParameter – A single float that can take any value

- ClampedFloatParameter – A single float that can take a value between defined minimum and maximum values

- IntParameter – A single integer that can take any value

- `ClampedIntParameter` – A single integer that can take a value between defined minimum and maximum values

- `TextureParameter` – Any object that inherits the `Texture` base class, typically `Texture2D` or `RenderTexture`

Since the strength value should be bound between 0 and 1, let's use `ClampedFloatParameter` for it. It takes three parameters: the first is the default value when we first attach the setting to a volume, the second is the minimum value it can take, and the third is the maximum value it can take. I like to add tooltips to each setting variable to provide more context to end users about what this variable is for, which we can do with the `Tooltip` attribute. Remember: other people might be using these effects other than you! These variables can be defined just above the two methods.

Listing 11-16. Setting variables for the Grayscale effect

```
[Tooltip("How strongly the effect is applied. " +
        "0 = original image, 1 = fully grayscale.")]
public ClampedFloatParameter strength = new ClampedFloatParameter
(0.0f, 0.0f, 1.0f);

public bool IsActive() { ... }
```

Note   It's best practice to set up these effects so that the default values mean the effect is not active. If you don't, the volume system may not work properly, and your effect might be applied globally all the time, even if you don't have any volumes in the scene that use the effect.

Next, let's handle `IsActive`. We will use this method in the second C# script we'll write to decide whether to run the effect or not. We can define what "active" means for each effect – for the Grayscale effect, the strength should be higher than zero. On top of this, Unity will add a tick box onto every effect that lets us turn them on and off, even if they have no settings. For this, the `VolumeComponent` class (which we are inheriting from) exposes a variable called `active`.

Listing 11-17. The IsActive method for the grayscale effect in URP

```
public bool IsActive() => strength.value > 0.0f && active;
```

Finally, we'll handle the `IsTileCompatible` method. The Unity documentation doesn't provide any information on what this method does, so we will just make the method return `false`.

Listing 11-18. The IsTileCompatible method

```
public bool IsTileCompatible() => false;
```

The `GrayscaleSettings` script is now complete, so we can move on to the `GrayscaleRenderPass` script.

The GrayscaleRenderPass C# Script

This is the longest script we'll need to write to get the Grayscale effect working in URP. Create a new C# script via *Create* ➤ *C# Script* and name it "GrayscaleRenderPass". This script is going to control how URP interfaces between the shader, the settings we just created, and the renderer. This is effectively the "brain" of the post-process where we can customize exactly how it operates. Although a grayscale shader is one of the simplest post-processing effects we could create, this script still has many moving parts.

The `GrayscaleRenderPass` class inherits from `ScriptableRenderPass`, which is the base class for all render passes. We will need to override three methods from `ScriptableRenderPass`: namely, the `Configure`, `Execute`, and `FrameCleanup` methods. We will also supply a method called `Setup`. Here's the code skeleton for this class.

Listing 11-19. The GrayscaleRenderPass skeleton

```
using UnityEngine;
using UnityEngine.Rendering;
using UnityEngine.Rendering.Universal;

class GrayscaleRenderPass : ScriptableRenderPass
{
    public void Setup(...) { ... }
    public override void Configure(...){ ... }
```

```
    public override void Execute(...){ ... }
    public override void FrameCleanup(...){ ... }
}
```

Before we fill out these methods with code, let's add a few member variables, which we will place above all these methods. The pass needs to hold references to a few things:

- The material that will use the Grayscale shader

- A GrayscaleSettings object

- The source render texture supplied by the camera

- A temporary texture that we will use for applying the shader to the source texture

- A profiler tag that we can use to profile how many system resources the post-processing effect takes up

We will include each of these variables at the top of the class.

Listing 11-20. GrayscaleRenderPass instance variables

```
private Material material;
private GrayscaleSettings settings;

private RenderTargetIdentifier source;
private RenderTargetIdentifier mainTex;
private string profilerTag;

public void Setup(...){ ... }
```

Next, let's fill in each method in turn, starting with Setup. This method will be used to set up most of the member variables and attach this pass to the renderer. It takes a ScriptableRenderer and a profiler tag string as its two arguments.

Listing 11-21. The Setup method for the grayscale effect in URP

```
public void Setup(ScriptableRenderer renderer, string profilerTag)
{
    this.profilerTag = profilerTag;

    source = renderer.cameraColorTarget;
    VolumeStack stack = VolumeManager.instance.stack;
    settings = stack.GetComponent<GrayscaleSettings>();
    renderPassEvent = RenderPassEvent.BeforeRenderingPostProcessing;

    if (settings != null && settings.IsActive())
    {
        renderer.EnqueuePass(this);
        material = new Material(Shader.Find("Examples/ImageEffects/
        Grayscale"));
    }
}
```

The ScriptableRenderer is *the* object that controls rendering in URP. The cameraColorTarget member of a ScriptableRenderer is the color texture, which is the one we want to apply the Grayscale shader to. URP exposes several "events" throughout the rendering loop that we can attach our effects to; although the name doesn't necessarily suggest so, the one we want is BeforeRenderingPostProcessing, which runs just before any post-processing included in URP that you have active. Finally, we must check if the effect is active, and if it is, we can create the material that will drive the effect and attach the pass to the renderer.

Next up is the Configure method, which we use to set up any temporary textures that will be used for the effect. Unlike the built-in pipeline, which exposes handles to two textures, source and destination, URP only gave us a single handle to the source texture. Later in the Execute method, we must read from this texture and write back to it, but calling Blit when both texture arguments are the *same* texture may result in undefined behavior, so we'll create an intermediate texture and perform two Blit operations.

Listing 11-22. The Configure method for the grayscale effect in URP

```
public override void Configure(CommandBuffer cmd, RenderTextureDescriptor
cameraTextureDescriptor)
{
    if (settings == null) return;

    int id = Shader.PropertyToID("_MainTex");
    mainTex = new RenderTargetIdentifier(id);
    cmd.GetTemporaryRT(id, cameraTextureDescriptor);

    base.Configure(cmd, cameraTextureDescriptor);
}
```

The Execute method, which runs the effect, comes next. Inside this method, we create a CommandBuffer, which is an object that holds a list of rendering commands and attach commands to Blit the source and mainTex textures. Here's what this method does:

- First, we'll create the command buffer by supplying the profiler tag so that we can use the Profiler window to evaluate the performance of the shader.

- Next, we'll Blit the source texture onto the mainTex texture, which just copies it since we're not supplying a material. This step is important because we're unable to Blit between the source texture and itself.

- Then, we'll set up any material properties. For the Grayscale effect, we only have one property to worry about: _Strength.

- Next comes the all-important Blit in which we apply the material to mainTex and assign the results back to the source texture.

- Finally, we can execute the command buffer and clean up its resources.

The Execute method is run once per frame. If your post-processing effect had several properties or even multiple passes, then your command buffer could have many more commands attached to it.

Listing 11-23. The Execute method for the grayscale effect in URP

```
public override void Execute(ScriptableRenderContext context, ref
RenderingData renderingData)
{
    if (!settings.IsActive())
    {
        return;
    }

    CommandBuffer cmd = CommandBufferPool.Get(profilerTag);

    cmd.Blit(source, mainTex);

    material.SetFloat("_Strength", settings.strength.value);

    cmd.Blit(mainTex, source, material);

    context.ExecuteCommandBuffer(cmd);
    cmd.Clear();
    CommandBufferPool.Release(cmd);
}
```

Finally, we come to the FrameCleanup method, which runs at the end of each frame to clean up any temporary data that was created back in Configure. In the case of our Grayscale effect, that means the mainTex texture.

Listing 11-24. The FrameCleanup method for the grayscale effect in URP

```
public override void FrameCleanup(CommandBuffer cmd)
{
    cmd.ReleaseTemporaryRT(Shader.PropertyToID("_MainTex"));
}
```

The GrayscaleFeature C# Script

The final part of the puzzle is the Renderer Feature script, which will allow URP to run the effect in the first place. Start by creating a new C# script via *Create* ➤ *C# Script*, and name it "GrayscaleFeature.cs". The GrayscaleFeature class will inherit from ScriptableRendererFeature, which requires us to override two abstract methods called Create and AddRenderPass. Here's the code skeleton for the class.

471

Listing 11-25. The GrayscaleFeature code skeleton

```
using UnityEngine.Rendering.Universal;

public class GrayscaleFeature : ScriptableRendererFeature
{
    GrayscaleRenderPass pass;

    public override void Create() { ... }

    public override void AddRenderPasses(...) { ... }
}
```

The first thing to note is that we're including a variable called pass to hold our GrayscaleRenderPass. The Create method is called when GrayscaleFeature is first created, as the name suggests. Inside this method, we should create any render passes that the feature will use. We can also provide a name for the feature, which will be displayed when GrayscaleFeature is attached to the list of features on your Forward Renderer asset (we'll attach it when the script is complete). The name variable is a member of ScriptableRendererFeature, so we don't need to define it at the top of this class alongside pass.

Listing 11-26. The Create method

```
public override void Create()
{
    name = "Grayscale";
    pass = new GrayscaleRenderPass();
}
```

The AddRenderPasses method takes a ScriptableRenderer and a RenderingData object as parameters, and it is responsible for attaching passes to the ScriptableRenderer. We already wrote code inside the Setup method on GrayscaleRenderPass to attach itself to a renderer, so all we need to do here is call Setup and pass the correct parameters. The second parameter is a string tag, which will appear on the Profiler when we run this post-process.

Listing 11-27. The AddRenderPasses method

```
public override void AddRenderPasses(ScriptableRenderer renderer,
ref RenderingData renderingData)
{
    pass.Setup(renderer, "Grayscale Post Process");
}
```

With that, we have finally finished all the C# code required to run a post-processing effect in URP. It's *a lot* more complex than the built-in pipeline, isn't it! Now we'll deal with the shader code.

The Grayscale Shader

The Grayscale shader for URP, like the one for the built-in pipeline, is not too revolutionary and can use the same URP shader syntax we've been using throughout the book. Start by creating a new shader file and renaming it "Grayscale.shader". Then remove the contents of the file so we can write it from scratch. Here's the skeleton for this file.

Listing 11-28. The Grayscale shader for URP

```
Shader "Examples/ImageEffects/Grayscale"
{
    Properties
    {
        _MainTex ("Texture", 2D) = "white" {}
    }
    SubShader
    {
        Tags
        {
            "RenderType"="Opaque"
            "RenderPipeline"="UniversalPipeline"
        }
```

```
Pass
{
        HLSLPROGRAM
        #pragma vertex vert
        #pragma fragment frag

        #include "Packages/com.unity.render-pipelines.universal/
        ShaderLibrary/Core.hlsl"
        #include "Packages/com.unity.render-pipelines.core/
        ShaderLibrary/Color.hlsl"

        struct appdata
        {
                float4 positionOS : Position;
                float2 uv : TEXCOORD0;
        };

        struct v2f
        {
                float4 positionCS : SV_Position;
                float2 uv : TEXCOORD0;
        };

        sampler2D _MainTex;

        CBUFFER_START(UnityPerMaterial)
                float _Strength;
        CBUFFER_END

        v2f vert (appdata v) { ... }

        float4 frag (v2f i) : SV_Target { ... }
        ENDHLSL
        }
    }
}
```

Most of the code looks like a typical shader we would apply to an object, with only small differences. The first difference is that we don't need to include any shader properties in the Properties block besides the _MainTex texture, since we will be setting the values of any variables through scripting. That means we need to define _Strength in the constant buffer, but not the Properties block. Second, the vertex shader will not need to use TRANSFORM_TEX to apply an offset and scaling to the UVs, since _MainTex will always use the default scaling and offset settings.

Listing 11-29. The vert function

```
v2f vert (appdata v)
{
    v2f o;
    o.positionCS = TransformObjectToHClip(v.positionOS.xyz);
    o.uv = v.uv;
    return o;
}
```

Now we'll write the fragment shader, which is where the most important shader code for post-processing effects can be found. For this effect, we can use the Luminance function, contained in the Color.hlsl helper file, to convert the texture sample color values to grayscale based on the relative sensitivity of the typical human eye to red, green, and blue colors. We'll use the lerp function to mix the grayscale version with the original texture sample.

Listing 11-30. The frag function

```
float4 frag (v2f i) : SV_Target
{
    float4 textureSample = tex2D(_MainTex, i.uv);

    float3 outputColor = Luminance(textureSample);

    return lerp(textureSample, float4(outputColor, 1.0f), _Strength);
}
```

All the code is now complete for the Grayscale effect. The last step is to enable it in URP.

Using Volumes with Grayscale in URP

Post-processing effects in URP use the volume system. Let's add a new volume via *GameObject* ➤ *Volume* ➤ *Box Volume*. This type of volume applies effects only when the camera is within the box collider attached to the volume. We can also use a sphere and a convex mesh, which work similarly, or we can use a global volume that applies the effects constantly. Figure 11-4 shows a completed volume with the Grayscale effect attached.

Figure 11-4. *A volume with a profile attached that contains the Grayscale effect*

On the volume, you will notice a *Profile* option. A profile is a collection of effects with certain settings that a volume will read from; then the volume will apply those effects. Profiles are assets, so they can be reused on multiple volumes; by default, a volume has no profile attached, so click the *New* button to create one. We can then edit the profile's effects either by selecting the profile asset itself or on any volume with the profile attached (be aware that changing a profile's settings on one volume changes the profile's settings on *all* volumes using that profile).

To add the Grayscale effect, click the *Add Override* button and select the effect via *Examples* ➤ *Grayscale*. Tick the *Strength* option to override its default value and then change it to 1. Nothing will happen on-screen yet because there is one more step. Since we are using Renderer Features for this effect, we need to add it to URP's list of Renderer Features. Find your Forward Renderer asset (by default, it is in *Assets ➤ Settings*) and click the *Add Renderer Feature* button at the bottom. Then choose "Grayscale Feature." See Figure 11-5 for details.

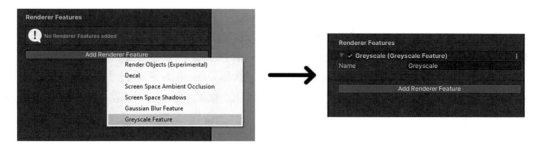

Figure 11-5. *Adding the Grayscale Feature to the Renderer Features list*

Note   If you are anything like me, you will constantly forget to do the last step and worry that some weird bug is preventing your effect from working. Try and drill it into your head as much as possible that you need to attach the effect to the Renderer Features list for it to work!

Now you should see a grayscale scene whenever your camera enters the volume, as in Figure 11-3. The great thing about the URP volume system is that these effects get applied in the Scene View as well as the Game View, which makes it very easy to test your effects and design scenes that use them! With that, we've finally finished the Grayscale post-processing effect for URP. Let's see how it works in HDRP.

Post-Processing in HDRP

Although Unity recommends using Shader Graph for almost every shader effect in HDRP rather than coding them by hand, post-processing effects are not officially supported by Shader Graph. As a result, Unity provides official support for post-processing effects in HDRP through the use of HLSL shader code, so this will be our first real look at shader code for HDRP.

Like in URP, post-processing effects in HDRP can make use of the volume system, which allows us to create collections of effects called profiles and attach them to trigger volumes in the world. Those volumes can be applied globally, so they are active

477

regardless of the position of the camera, or locally, so they are only active when the camera is inside the trigger. Unity can also blend between the effect being active and inactive using the volume system. Let's see how the Grayscale effect works in HDRP.

Grayscale C# Scripting in HDRP

HDRP still requires us to use C# scripting to set up our post-processing effects, but this time, Unity provides official support, so it is far easier than in URP. There's even a template script for it! Start by creating the script via *Create* ➤ *Rendering* ➤ *C# Post Process Volume*, which I will name "GrayscaleVolume.cs". Upon opening the file, you will see rather a lot of boilerplate code, so let's take the time to go through each part in turn. Listing 11-31 is a shortened version of the code you should see.

Listing 11-31. The C# Post Process Volume template file

```
using UnityEngine;
using UnityEngine.Rendering;
using UnityEngine.Rendering.HighDefinition;
using System;

[Serializable, VolumeComponentMenu("Post-processing/Examples/Grayscale")]
public sealed class GrayscaleVolume : CustomPostProcessVolumeComponent,
IPostProcessComponent
{
    [Tooltip("Controls the intensity of the effect.")]
    public ClampedFloatParameter intensity = new
    ClampedFloatParameter(0f, 0f, 1f);
    Material m_Material;

    public bool IsActive() => m_Material != null && intensity.value > 0f;

    public override CustomPostProcessInjectionPoint injectionPoint =>
    CustomPostProcessInjectionPoint.AfterPostProcess;

    const string kShaderName = "Hidden/Shader/GrayscaleVolume";
```

```
public override void Setup() { ... }

public override void Render(CommandBuffer cmd, HDCamera camera,
RTHandle source, RTHandle destination) { ... }

public override void Cleanup() { ... }
}
```

This script works very similarly to the scripts we wrote for URP (albeit with much of the boilerplate work removed), and you may notice some similarities between the workflows for the two pipelines. Approximately from top to bottom, here is what the script is doing:

- The script uses classes provided in the UnityEngine.Rendering and UnityEngine.Rendering.HighDefinition namespaces, so we must be using them.

- We use a VolumeComponentMenu attribute to add a custom menu on volumes that allows us to add this effect seamlessly.

- The CustomPostProcessVolumeComponent base class and the IPostProcessComponent interface make this script work with HDRP's volume system.

- We can define shader properties as variables here, which lets us tweak them when the effect is added to a volume. There are special wrapper types – such as ClampedFloatParameter – which are used for these properties.

- We hold a reference to the material that will be used to render the effect.

- The IsActive method, which is part of the IPostProcessComponent interface, lets us define what "active" means for our effect.

- We can specify the point in the rendering loop where this post-processing effect runs. By default, it runs AfterPostProcess, which means this custom effect runs after the effects built into HDRP.

- We must specify the shader name, which will be held in a variable called kShaderName. This variable is const because its value should never change.

- We must override methods from
  `CustomPostProcessVolumeComponent`:

  - The `Setup` method is used to create a material using the custom shader effect.

  - The `Render` method is used to send data to the shader based on the variables inside this script and instruct HDRP to render the effect.

  - The `Cleanup` method is used to remove any temporary resources, such as temporary render textures or materials, from memory.

Although the template file is a huge help and removes much of the boilerplate code that we otherwise had to write ourselves in URP, we'll need to make a handful of changes to match the Grayscale shader effect. Although we haven't yet written the shader, it's going to use the same `_Strength` property as the versions we wrote in the built-in pipeline and URP, so let's write the `GrayscaleVolume` script based on that knowledge.

First, let's change the variables. Instead of the `intensity` variable that the template file has, I'll use a variable called `strength` to match the `_Strength` property that the shader will use. This is the only shader property that we need to create a variable for. You can also change the `Tooltip` to provide more helpful information.

Listing 11-32. The strength variable

```
public sealed class GrayscaleVolume : CustomPostProcessVolumeComponent,
IPostProcessComponent
{
    [Tooltip("How strongly the effect is applied. " +
        "0 = original image, 1 = fully grayscale.")]
    public ClampedFloatParameter strength = new ClampedFloatParameter
    (0f, 0f, 1f);
```

Next, we'll update the `IsActive` method, which we can fix by replacing `intensity` with `strength`. In effect, this means the post-process only runs if the intensity is above zero.

Listing 11-33. The IsActive method for the grayscale effect in HDRP

```
public bool IsActive() => m_Material != null && strength.value > 0f;
```

Then we will change the name of the shader, which is stored in the kShaderName variable. This is the name that we declare on the very first line of the shader file, which in this case will be "Examples/ImageEffects/Grayscale". The Setup method will create a material that uses this shader and store it in a variable called m_Material.

Listing 11-34. Changing the shader name

```
const string kShaderName = "Examples/ImageEffects/Grayscale";
```

Note   The Setup method uses Shader.Find to obtain a reference to the shader, so make sure that the corresponding shader file is contained in the *Always Included Shaders* list or contained in any folder named "Resources" in your project.

The Setup and Cleanup methods don't need to change from the template script, which leaves us with the Render method. This method is responsible for taking a source render texture from the camera, applying a shader effect to it, and copying the result to a destination render texture, which gets applied back to the screen. The code is shorter than the URP equivalent because the command buffer is created for us and passed to the method as a parameter, which means we can focus entirely on moving data between the script and the shader and rendering the post-process effect.

We must first send the strength variable to the shader, which will allow it to fade between a partially grayscale and an entirely grayscale screen. Next, we need to send the source texture to the shader. In the other render pipelines, the Blit method automatically binds the source texture to the _MainTex property, but in HDRP, we need to manually use SetTexture instead. Conventionally, HDRP post-processing shaders use _InputTexture instead of _MainTex as the name of the source texture, so we'll use that instead. Finally, we can use the DrawFullscreen method in HDRP instead of Blit to draw the screen using the material that was created back in Setup.

Listing 11-35. The Render method for the grayscale effect in URP

```
public override void Render(CommandBuffer cmd, HDCamera camera, RTHandle
source, RTHandle destination)
{
    if (m_Material == null)
        return;

    m_Material.SetFloat("_Strength", strength.value);
    m_Material.SetTexture("_InputTexture", source);
    HDUtils.DrawFullScreen(cmd, m_Material, destination);
}
```

That's the C# scripting side dealt with, which leaves us with writing the shader for the effect.

Grayscale Shader in HDRP

As with the C# script, Unity provides an HDRP template for post-process shader files. Let's create a shader that uses the template via *Create* ➤ *Shader* ➤ *HD Render Pipeline* ➤ *Post Process*. Name it "Grayscale.shader". You should see a lot of boilerplate code, which I will briefly go over in the following.

Listing 11-36. HDRP template code for post process effects

```
Shader "Hidden/Shader/Grayscale"
{
    HLSLINCLUDE

    #pragma target 4.5
    #pragma only_renderers d3d11 playstation xboxone xboxseries vulkan
    metal switch

    #include "Packages/com.unity.render-pipelines.core/ShaderLibrary/
    Common.hlsl"
    #include "Packages/com.unity.render-pipelines.core/ShaderLibrary/
    Color.hlsl"
    #include "Packages/com.unity.render-pipelines.high-definition/
    Runtime/ShaderLibrary/ShaderVariables.hlsl"
```

```
#include "Packages/com.unity.render-pipelines.high-definition/
Runtime/PostProcessing/Shaders/FXAA.hlsl"
#include "Packages/com.unity.render-pipelines.high-definition/
Runtime/PostProcessing/Shaders/RTUpscale.hlsl"

struct Attributes { ... };

struct Varyings { ... };

Varyings Vert(Attributes input) { ... }

float _Intensity;
TEXTURE2D_X(_InputTexture);

float4 CustomPostProcess(Varyings input) : SV_Target { ... }

ENDHLSL

SubShader
{
    Pass
    {
        Name "Grayscale"

        ZWrite Off
        ZTest Always
        Blend Off
        Cull Off

        HLSLPROGRAM
            #pragma fragment CustomPostProcess
            #pragma vertex Vert
        ENDHLSL
    }
}
Fallback Off
}
```

I have condensed down the exact contents of the structs and functions, but most of these will stay the same between each post-process shader you make. You might also notice that this shader is structurally very different from the shaders we have written by hand so far – let's see how the shader works:

- This shader uses an HLSLINCLUDE block before the SubShader. Any code inside an HLSLINCLUDE block gets copied and pasted into every subsequent HLSLPROGRAM block, which makes HLSLINCLUDE useful if you have multiple passes.

- The Attributes and Varyings structs are used to pass data between shader stages. Attributes is equivalent to the appdata struct we've written in most of our shaders, and Varyings is equivalent to v2f.

- The Vert function is responsible for creating the full-screen quad and providing the correct texture coordinates for the fragment shader to use.

- The CustomPostProcess function is the fragment shader, which is where most of the customization can occur between post-processing shaders.

- Underneath the HLSLINCLUDE block, we can add a SubShader like usual. Inside the SubShader is a Pass, and inside that is the HLSLPROGRAM block where we declare which functions we are using for the vertex and fragment shaders.

This shader needs a few changes so that it matches up with the script we wrote earlier, so let's make those changes now. Firstly, we must rename the shader at the top of the file.

Listing 11-37. Renaming the shader

```
Shader "Examples/ImageEffects/Grayscale"
```

Next, let's handle the shader properties. You will notice that there is no Properties block, so we only need to declare variables inside HLSLINCLUDE. The only two properties are the _Strength float, which controls the proportion output between a normal and a grayscale image, and the _InputTexture. Here, we can use a special macro,

TEXTURE2D_X, which makes it easier to sample textures in a way that is compatible with VR, which requires one image for each eye. Although this book won't go into detail about VR rendering, it will be useful to use this macro anyway.

Listing 11-38. Shader variables in the `HLSLINCLUDE` block

```
float _Strength;
TEXTURE2D_X(_InputTexture);

float4 CustomPostProcess(Varyings input) : SV_Target { ... }
```

Finally, we come to the fragment shader, which is represented by the `CustomPostProcess` function. Here's what the function will do:

- The template code for this function uses the `UNITY_SETUP_STEREO_ EYE_INDEX_POST_VERTEX` macro (these names sure do roll off the tongue!) to enable *single pass instanced rendering*, making it possible to render both eyes in a single pass in VR for a significant performance boost.

- After that, we calculate the screen-space position of the current pixel based on the UVs that were passed to the fragment shader and the resolution of the screen.

  - Whereas UVs are in the range [0, 1] in both axes, the screen position is between [0, *width*] in the x-direction and [0, *height*] in the y-direction.

  - This is especially useful in post-processing effects, where the output color of one pixel often directly relies on the input colors of nearby pixels.

- Using those positions, we use another macro called `LOAD_ TEXTURE2D_X` to sample the texture in a VR-friendly way.

So far, the template code matches up with what we want to do for the Grayscale effect. We just need to add one line of code to convert `outColor` to grayscale before it is output by the shader. We can use the same `Luminance` function we used in the other two pipelines – it converts an RGB color to grayscale based on the relative sensitivity of the human eye to each of the three color channels.

Listing 11-39. The fragment shader for the grayscale effect in HDRP

```
float4 CustomPostProcess(Varyings input) : SV_Target
{
    UNITY_SETUP_STEREO_EYE_INDEX_POST_VERTEX(input);

    uint2 positionSS = input.texcoord * _ScreenSize.xy;
    float3 outColor = LOAD_TEXTURE2D_X(_InputTexture, positionSS).xyz;

    outColor = Luminance(outColor);

    return float4(outColor, 1);
}
```

Using Volumes with Grayscale in HDRP

Adding a volume in HDRP is very similar to the process we followed for URP. First, add a volume GameObject via *GameObject* ➤ *Volume* ➤ *Box Volume*, create a new profile by clicking the *New* button next to the *Profile* field, and add the Grayscale effect using the *Add Override* button (it's under *Post Processing* ➤ *Examples* ➤ *Grayscale*). This is the same process as in URP. Again, nothing will change on-screen, yet, even if the camera is in the volume. To fix this, we need to add the effect to HDRP's effect list, so go to *Edit* ➤ *Project Settings* ➤ *HDRP Default Settings* ➤ *Custom Post Process Orders*, which is near the bottom. You will see four lists, the bottom of which is labeled "After Post Process." Use the plus arrow button to add GrayscaleVolume to the list, as in Figure 11-6.

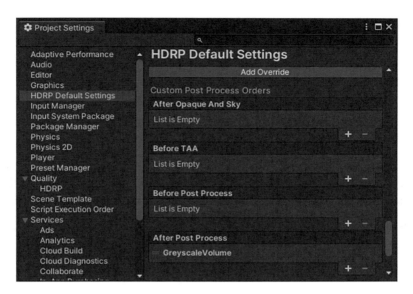

Figure 11-6. *Adding GrayscaleVolume to HDRP's list of post-process effects*

This list lets you customize the order of your custom effects, although in many cases it doesn't matter what order they are rendered in.

Note   If you notice graphical oddities when using multiple post-processing effects in a stack, then try switching the order. Occasionally, effects depend on each other in unexpected ways.

After this step, you should see the Grayscale effect in the scene when your camera enters the volume, as in Figure 11-3.

We have now seen how post-processing effects work in each of Unity's pipelines. The effect we wrote was relatively simple – amounting to very few lines of fragment shader code – so for the next effect, we will increase the complexity of the shader. We'll see that the complexity of the code in each pipeline does not increase by much.

Gaussian Blur Image Effect

One common type of post-processing effect is the blur effect, where the colors of adjacent pixels are mixed slightly to create a blurred version of the source image. A popular type of blur, called *Gaussian blur*, takes each pixel of the image and returns the weighted average of its color and the color of nearby pixels. Figure 11-7 shows a scene before and after a Gaussian blur effect is applied.

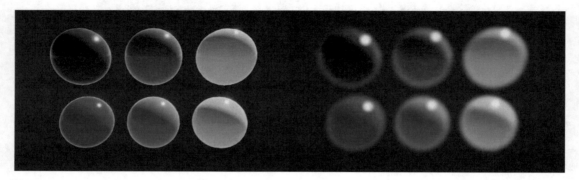

Figure 11-7. *A Gaussian blur effect before (left) and after (right) being applied to the screen*

Gaussian blur works by creating a 2D grid of weights, called a *convolution kernel*, and overlaying the center of the kernel onto a pixel of the image. Each value in the kernel is multiplied by the color of the pixel it overlaps, and the sum of those values becomes the output color of the center pixel. The kernel slides over the image until each pixel has an output. Figure 11-8 demonstrates how convolution works.

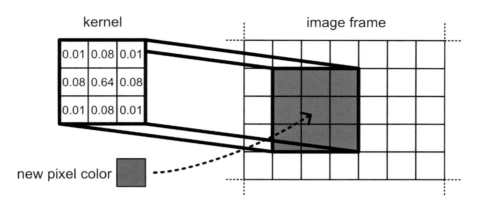

Figure 11-8. *Convolving a Gaussian kernel with an image. Each element of the kernel is multiplied by each pixel of the image, and the sum becomes the new center pixel color*

When the kernel overlaps the edge of the image, typically the edge pixel color is repeated across the "missing" pixels. The weights associated with each pixel are assigned according to a Gaussian function, named after Carl Friedrich Gauss, hence the name "Gaussian blur." Here's what the function looks like:

Equation 11-2: A one-dimensional Gaussian function

$$G(x) = \frac{1}{\sqrt{2\pi\sigma^2}} e^{\left(-\frac{x^2}{2\sigma^2}\right)}$$

If you've never seen this function before, then there is a lot going on, so let's explore what each part of the function is doing:

- This version of the Gaussian function operates in one dimension. We put in one value and get back one value.

- You don't need to understand every term in this function. You just need to know what x and σ do and the general shape of the graph.

- x is the distance from the center point. The pixel in the center of the kernel is at $x = 0$. If we evaluate on a pixel adjacent to the center pixel, x equals 1, and so on. This is the input to the function.

- σ is the *standard deviation*, which is a measure of spread. If this value is larger, then the convolution kernel gets larger, and the peak of the graph is smaller.

- As you get further from the center point, the values output by the function get lower. The shape of this curve is sometimes called a "bell curve." If you have used a normal distribution in statistics, then you've seen a Gaussian curve before.

Figure 11-9 shows the shape of the Gaussian function in one dimension.

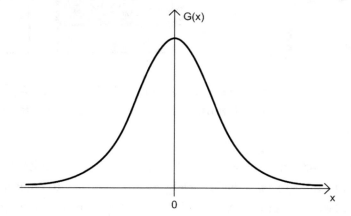

Figure 11-9. *The one-dimensional Gaussian function. As the value of x gets further from the mean value, 0, the value of G(x) decreases*

Of course, our images are in two dimensions. You can extend the Gaussian function to cover as many dimensions as you want by taking the product of the one-dimensional Gaussian functions in each dimension. In 2D, the Gaussian function looks like this:

Equation 11-3: A two-dimensional Gaussian function

$$G(x,y) = \frac{1}{2\pi\sigma^2} e^{\left(-\frac{x^2+y^2}{2\sigma^2}\right)}$$

One of the desirable features of the Gaussian kernel, as exposed by this equation, is that it is *separable* – that is, a 2D Gaussian kernel returns the same result as running a 1D Gaussian kernel horizontally and then running another 1D Gaussian kernel vertically on the result. In fact, running it this way is a lot more efficient. For example, with a 3 × 3 kernel, the 2D method requires nine multiplications per pixel, but the two-pass 1D method requires only six (three horizontally and then three vertically). However, this becomes slightly more complicated to implement on the shader side, since we need to write two shader passes and customize our code to run both those passes. Nonetheless, let's see how it can be done in each pipeline.

Gaussian Blur in the Built-In Pipeline

As with the Grayscale effect, the Gaussian Blur effect will require a script and a shader file to work. The difference here, apart from Gaussian blur being conceptually more complicated than grayscale, is that the Gaussian Blur effect will use a two-pass shader rather than Grayscale's one-pass shader. This will require more work on both the shader and script sides. Let's see how the script works first.

Gaussian Blur C# Scripting in the Built-In Pipeline

Start by creating a new C# script via *Create* ➤ *C# Script* and name it "GaussianBlurEffect.cs". This script will drive the Gaussian blur post-process by applying the two shader passes in the correct way. Let's start with the member variables. On top of holding a reference to the material, which the GrayscaleEffect script also did, we will add a public variable for the kernel size so that you can change the amount of blurring within the Unity Editor. As the kernel size increases, more surrounding pixels are sampled in the blur calculation for each pixel, which means there is more blurring. A kernel size of 1 is the same as no blurring. I've used the Range attribute to bound the value of the kernelSize variable between 1 and 101 – the kernel always needs to be at least 1 × 1, but my choice of upper bound is arbitrary so you can change it if you want.

Listing 11-40. Blur variables

```
using UnityEngine;

public class GaussianBlurEffect : MonoBehaviour
{
    [Range(1, 101)]
    public int kernelSize;
    private Material mat;
    ...
}
```

After declaring these variables, we'll use the Start method to create a material using the GaussianBlur shader (which we are yet to write), using the name "Examples/ImageEffect/GaussianBlur".

Listing 11-41. Finding the GaussianBlur shader

```
private Material mat;

void Start()
{
    mat = new Material(Shader.Find("Examples/ImageEffect/GaussianBlur"));
}
```

Lastly, let's handle the OnRenderImage method. The effect uses two passes, so we'll use a temporary RenderTexture, tmp, as an intermediate by using the RenderTexture. GetTemporary method. Then, we need to set the kernelSize value on the material. We'll be using a shader property called _KernelSize to do so. Next, by adding an integer fourth argument to Graphics.Blit, we can specify which shader pass to use, so we'll apply the horizontal pass (0) between src and tmp and then apply the vertical blur pass (1) between tmp (which has now been blurred horizontally) and dst. Once we're done, it's important to release the temporary texture we were using to avoid memory issues.

Listing 11-42. Applying a two-pass shader

```
void OnRenderImage(RenderTexture src, RenderTexture dst)
{
    RenderTexture tmp = RenderTexture.GetTemporary(src.descriptor);

    mat.SetInt("_KernelSize", kernelSize);

    Graphics.Blit(src, tmp, mat, 0);
    Graphics.Blit(tmp, dst, mat, 1);

    RenderTexture.ReleaseTemporary(tmp);
}
```

That's all we need for the script, so let's move on to the shader itself.

Gaussian Blur Shader in the Built-In Pipeline

There is a lot of overlap between the Gaussian Blur shader and the Grayscale shader, as the appdata and v2f structs are identical, as is the vert function. However, they are all required in both shader passes, so we will include them in an HLSLINCLUDE block in the SubShader. Recall that any code inside such a block gets copied for us to all HLSLPROGRAM blocks in subsequent Pass blocks, reducing the amount of repeated code. We will also be placing all variables and include files in HLSLINCLUDE, as well as a handful of constants and a function to help us calculate the Gaussian coefficients required in the shader passes. The shader looks like the following.

Listing 11-43. The GaussianBlur shader in the built-in pipeline

```
Shader "Examples/ImageEffect/GaussianBlur"
{
    Properties
    {
        _MainTex ("Texture", 2D) = "white" {}
    }
    SubShader
    {
        HLSLINCLUDE

        #include "UnityCG.cginc"

        static const float E = 2.71828f;
        static const float PI = 3.14159f;

        sampler2D _MainTex;
        float2 _MainTex_TexelSize;
        uint _KernelSize;

        float gaussian(int x, float sigma)
        {
            float twoSigmaSqu = 2 * sigma * sigma;
            return (1 / sqrt(PI * twoSigmaSqu)) * pow(E, -(x * x) /
            (2 * twoSigmaSqu));
        }

        struct appdata
        {
            float4 positionOS : POSITION;
            float2 uv : TEXCOORD0;
        };
```

```
        struct v2f
        {
                float2 uv : TEXCOORD0;
                float4 positionCS : SV_POSITION;
        };

        v2f vert(appdata v)
        {
                v2f o;
                o.positionCS = UnityObjectToClipPos(v.positionOS);
                o.uv = v.uv;
                return o;
        }

        ENDHLSL

        Pass { ... }

        Pass { ... }
    }
}
```

The gaussian function carries out Equation 11-2, given the pixel's distance from the center of the kernel, x, and the standard deviation, sigma. For that, we need to add two constants, E and PI, to represent Euler's constant, e, and pi, respectively. Let's now focus on the contents of the two passes, starting with the horizontal pass that blurs pixels along the x-axis. We'll name the pass "Horizontal" and then immediately open an HLSLPROGRAM block containing the fragHorizontal function. This function will loop over the kernel and multiply the values from the gaussian function by the underlying colors in the texture.

Listing 11-44. The horizontal blur pass for the Gaussian blur effect in the built-in pipeline

```
Pass
{
      Name "Horizontal"

      HLSLPROGRAM
      #pragma vertex vert
      #pragma fragment fragHorizontal
```

```
    float4 fragHorizontal (v2f i) : SV_Target { ... }
    ENDHLSL
}
```

Inside the function, we'll initialize variables for the color, the sum of all kernel values (they may not sum exactly to one, so we will correct for this after the loops), and the standard deviation. We want to calculate the standard deviation such that most of the Gaussian curve fits inside the kernel we've created – I found that dividing the _KernelSize by 8 works well. We'll also calculate the upper and lower bounds of the for-loop.

Listing 11-45. Preparing for the horizontal blur loop

```
float4 fragHorizontal (v2f i) : SV_Target
{
    float3 col = float3(0.0f, 0.0f, 0.0f);
    float kernelSum = 0.0f;
    float sigma = _KernelSize / 8.0f;

    int upper = ((_KernelSize - 1) / 2);
    int lower = -upper;
```

Next comes the loop. In each loop iteration, we'll calculate the Gaussian coefficient using the gaussian function and add that value to kernelSum. Then, we'll add a small offset to the UVs to sample a specific pixel along the x-axis, using _MainTex_TexelSize to step by one pixel each iteration. Using those UVs, we'll sample _MainTex and multiply by the Gaussian coefficient and then add the value to the col variable. I discovered that in some cases the screen texture can contain negative values, so I take the max with 0 to eliminate those cases. Once all loop iterations have executed, col will contain a blurred color value. To correct for kernels whose Gaussian coefficients don't quite sum to 1, we'll divide the resulting color by kernelSum and then return the color.

Listing 11-46. The horizontal blur loop

```
    int lower = -upper;

    for (int x = lower; x <= upper; ++x)
    {
        float gauss = gaussian(x, sigma);
```

```
            kernelSum += gauss;
            float2 uv = i.uv + float2(_MainTex_TexelSize.x * x, 0.0f);
            col += max(0, gauss * tex2D(_MainTex, uv).xyz);
            }

    col /= kernelSum;

    return float4(col, 1.0f);
}
```

Underneath the horizontal pass, we'll now deal with the vertical pass. The code is almost identical, except it's now named "Vertical" and the loop operates in the vertical axis instead.

Listing 11-47. The vertical blur pass for the Gaussian blur effect in the built-in pipeline

```
Pass
{
    Name "Vertical"

    HLSLPROGRAM
    #pragma vertex vert
    #pragma fragment fragVertical

    float4 fragVertical (v2f i) : SV_Target
    {
            float3 col = float3(0.0f, 0.0f, 0.0f);
            float kernelSum = 0.0f;
            float sigma = _KernelSize / 8.0f;

            int upper = ((_KernelSize - 1) / 2);
            int lower = -upper;

            for (int y = lower; y <= upper; ++y)
            {
                    float gauss = gaussian(y, sigma);
                    kernelSum += gauss;
                    float2 uv = i.uv + float2(0.0f, _MainTex_
                    TexelSize.y * y);
```

```
            col += max(0, gauss * tex2D(_MainTex, uv).xyz);
        }

        col /= kernelSum;

        return float4(col, 1.0f);
    }
    ENDHLSL
}
```

The shader is now complete. If you create a material with this shader and attach it to the camera via the material slot of the GaussianBlurEffect script, you'll see blurring like in Figure 11-7. Next, let's see how the effect works in URP.

Gaussian Blur in URP

As with the Grayscale effect, the Gaussian Blur effect is more difficult to write in URP than in the built-in pipeline. However, the scripting side of the Gaussian Blur effect is mostly the same as with the Grayscale effect for URP. Let's see how the scripting side works and then write the shader.

Gaussian Blur C# Scripting in URP

As with the Grayscale effect, we will be using three separate scripts for the Gaussian Blur effect as follows:

- A script called GaussianBlurSettings that controls the variables that will be visible when the effect is attached to a volume

- A script called GaussianBlurRenderPass that contains the logic for the effect, such as setting up render textures and applying materials to those textures

- A script called GaussianBlurFeature that instructs URP to use our custom render pass in the rendering loop

Since we already know what each type of script broadly does, let's jump straight into the GaussianBlurSettings script.

The GaussianBlurSettings C# Script

Create a new script via Create ➤ C# Script and name it "GaussianBlurSettings.cs". This script is responsible for setting up the variables used by the Gaussian Blur effect, which will be visible on any volume using the effect, and it will handle the conditions under which the effect is active. Let's start by replacing the script's entire contents with a boilerplate we can work with.

Listing 11-48. The GaussianBlurSettings skeleton script

```
using UnityEngine;
using UnityEngine.Rendering;
using UnityEngine.Rendering.Universal;

[System.Serializable, VolumeComponentMenu("Examples/Gaussian Blur")]
public class GaussianBlurSettings : VolumeComponent, IPostProcessComponent
{
    ...
    public bool IsTileCompatible() => false;
}
```

We will be able to add this effect to a volume via the drop-down by finding it under "Examples ➤ Gaussian Blur" due to the VolumeComponentMenu attribute. This script only requires one variable for the kernel size, for which we can use the ClampedIntParameter type to ensure its value is always at least 1, plus a Tooltip attribute to give the variable a nice description. After this, we'll add the IsActive method from the IPostProcessComponent interface. When the kernel size equals 1, that's the same as there being no blurring at all, so we'll only make the effect active when kernel size is strictly above 1. This code all goes above the IsTileCompatible method.

Listing 11-49. Variables and IsActive method

```
[Tooltip("How large the convolution kernel is. " +
    "A larger kernel means stronger blurring.")]
public ClampedIntParameter kernelSize = new ClampedIntParameter(1, 1, 101);

public bool IsActive() => kernelSize.value > 1 && active;

public bool IsTileCompatible() => false;
```

That's all we need for the GaussianBlurSettings script, so let's move on to GaussianBlurRenderPass.

The GaussianBlurRenderPass C# Script

This is still the longest of the three scripts, but there are a lot of similarities with the code from GrayscaleRenderPass, so we can go through a lot of it quickly. This script inherits from ScriptableRenderPass, so we must override the Configure, Execute, and FrameCleanup methods. Plus, we'll supply a Setup method to create some of the resources needed for the effect. Here's the base code that we'll be filling in.

Listing 11-50. The GaussianBlurRenderPass code skeleton

```
using UnityEngine;
using UnityEngine.Rendering;
using UnityEngine.Rendering.Universal;

public class GaussianBlurRenderPass : ScriptableRenderPass
{
    ...

    public void Setup(ScriptableRenderer renderer, string
    profilerTag) { ... }

    public override void Configure(CommandBuffer cmd,
    RenderTextureDescriptor cameraTextureDescriptor) { ... }

    public override void Execute(ScriptableRenderContext context, ref
    RenderingData renderingData) { ... }

    public override void FrameCleanup(CommandBuffer cmd)
    { ... }
}
```

Let's fill in the gaps, starting with the member variables. Like the Grayscale effect, we need a material, a settings object (this time, it's the GaussianBlurSettings we just wrote), handles to the source texture and main texture, and a profiler tag string. This time, we need an additional temporary texture to use as an intermediary between the two shader passes. I'll call it tempTex.

Listing 11-51. The member variables

```
public class GaussianBlurRenderPass : ScriptableRenderPass
{
    private Material material;
    private GaussianBlurSettings settings;

    private RenderTargetIdentifier source;
    private RenderTargetIdentifier mainTex;
    private RenderTargetIdentifier tempTex;
    private string profilerTag;
```

Next is the Setup method. This method retrieves a handle to the camera source texture, retrieves the effect's data from the active volume, and creates a material that uses the Gaussian Blur shader. We haven't written the shader yet, but its name will be "Examples/ImageEffects/GaussianBlur". The structure of this method is identical to the Setup method in GrayscaleRenderPass.

Listing 11-52. The Setup method for the Gaussian blur effect in URP

```
public void Setup(ScriptableRenderer renderer, string profilerTag)
{
    this.profilerTag = profilerTag;

    source = renderer.cameraColorTarget;
    VolumeStack stack = VolumeManager.instance.stack;
    settings = stack.GetComponent<GaussianBlurSettings>();
    renderPassEvent = RenderPassEvent.BeforeRenderingPostProcessing;

    if (settings != null && settings.IsActive())
    {
        material = new Material(Shader.Find("Examples/ImageEffects/
        GaussianBlur"));
        renderer.EnqueuePass(this);
    }
}
```

Now we come to the Configure method, which is overridden from the ScriptableRenderPass base. The primary responsibility of this script is to create the two render textures required to run the shader, which are called _MainTex and _TempTex, respectively. The method runs every frame, so we will need to deal with these textures later.

Listing 11-53. The Configure method for the Gaussian blur effect in URP

```
public override void Configure(CommandBuffer cmd, RenderTextureDescriptor
cameraTextureDescriptor)
{
    if (settings == null)
    {
        return;
    }

    int id = Shader.PropertyToID("_MainTex");
    mainTex = new RenderTargetIdentifier(id);
    cmd.GetTemporaryRT(id, cameraTextureDescriptor);

    id = Shader.PropertyToID("_TempTex");
    tempTex = new RenderTargetIdentifier(id);
    cmd.GetTemporaryRT(id, cameraTextureDescriptor);

    base.Configure(cmd, cameraTextureDescriptor);
}
```

Once the textures have been set up, we can move to the Execute method, which carries out the effect. The structure of the method is like the Execute method from GrayscaleRenderPass, except this is a two-pass effect, so we will need an additional call to Blit. The script will do the following:

- Immediately exit and do nothing if the settings' IsActive method returns false.

- Create the command buffer, cmd.

- Copy the source texture to mainTex ready to run the effect.

- Set the shader's _KernelSize property value to the kernelSize value from the volume settings.

501

- Perform the first `Blit` from `mainTex` to `tempTex` using shader pass 0.

- Perform the second `Blit` from `tempTex` back to `source` (which is also the output texture) using shader pass 1.

- Execute the command buffer, thereby running the steps outlined previously.

- Remove all commands from the buffer and release the command buffer back to the command buffer pool.

Listing 11-54. The Execute method for the Gaussian blur effect in URP

```
public override void Execute(ScriptableRenderContext context, ref
RenderingData renderingData)
{
    if (!settings.IsActive())
    {
        return;
    }

    CommandBuffer cmd = CommandBufferPool.Get(profilerTag);

    cmd.Blit(source, mainTex);

    material.SetInt("_KernelSize", settings.kernelSize.value);

    cmd.Blit(mainTex, tempTex, material, 0);
    cmd.Blit(tempTex, source, material, 1);

    context.ExecuteCommandBuffer(cmd);
    cmd.Clear();
    CommandBufferPool.Release(cmd);
}
```

Finally, we come to the `FrameCleanup` method, which we use to clean up all resources created temporarily during the frame. We already cleared the command buffer during `Execute`, so that just leaves the two textures we created back in `Configure`. The `ReleaseTemporaryRT` method will clean up the textures.

Listing 11-55. The FrameCleanup method for the Gaussian blur effect in URP

```
public override void FrameCleanup(CommandBuffer cmd)
{
    cmd.ReleaseTemporaryRT(Shader.PropertyToID("_MainTex"));
    cmd.ReleaseTemporaryRT(Shader.PropertyToID("_TempTex"));
}
```

The GaussianBlurRenderPass script is now complete. Hopefully, you found it a lot less complicated seeing it for a second time! Now we can move on to the final of the three scripts, GaussianBlurFeature.

The GaussianBlurFeature C# Script

Create this script via *Create* ➤ *C# Script* and name it "GaussianBlurFeature.cs". This is the simplest of the three scripts. It inherits from ScriptableRendererFeature, so we need to override the Create and AddRenderPasses methods. Create just needs to name the effect and instantiate a GaussianBlurRenderPass. Then the AddRenderPasses method can just call Setup on that pass, since we delegated all the setup code to the GaussianBlurRenderPass class.

Listing 11-56. The GaussianBlurFeature script

```
using UnityEngine.Rendering.Universal;

public class GaussianBlurFeature : ScriptableRendererFeature
{
    GaussianBlurRenderPass pass;

    public override void Create()
    {
        name = "Gaussian Blur";
        pass = new GaussianBlurRenderPass();
    }
```

```
public override void AddRenderPasses(ScriptableRenderer renderer, ref
RenderingData renderingData)
{
        pass.Setup(renderer, "Gaussian Blur Post Process");
}
}
```

The scripting side of the effect is complete, so we can move on to the Gaussian Blur shader itself.

Gaussian Blur Shader in URP

Create a new shader file and name it "GaussianBlur.shader". Then clear its contents entirely so we can write it from scratch. This post-processing shader uses two passes, so we will place all the common code for the two passes inside the HLSLINCLUDE block, so we don't need to type it all twice. This common code includes the appdata and v2f structs, the vert function, and the shader properties, plus the gaussian function that we'll use to calculate the Gaussian coefficients according to Equation 11-2. We'll need to include Euler's constant, e, as a constant variable, but pi is already contained in the Core include file, so we won't need to include it here unlike in the built-in pipeline.

Listing 11-57. The GaussianBlur shader in URP

```
Shader "Examples/ImageEffects/GaussianBlur"
{
    Properties
    {
        _MainTex ("Texture", 2D) = "white" {}
    }
    SubShader
    {
        Tags
        {
            "RenderType"="Opaque"
            "RenderPipeline"="UniversalPipeline"
        }
```

```
HLSLINCLUDE

#include "Packages/com.unity.render-pipelines.universal/
ShaderLibrary/Core.hlsl"

static const float E = 2.71828f;

float gaussian(int x, float sigma)
{
    float twoSigmaSqu = 2 * sigma * sigma;
    return (1 / sqrt(PI * twoSigmaSqu)) * pow(E, -(x * x) /
    (2 * twoSigmaSqu));
}

struct appdata
{
    float4 positionOS : Position;
    float2 uv : TEXCOORD0;
};

struct v2f
{
    float4 positionCS : SV_Position;
    float2 uv : TEXCOORD0;
};

sampler2D _MainTex;

    CBUFFER_START(UnityPerMaterial)
        float4 _MainTex_TexelSize;
        uint _KernelSize;
    CBUFFER_END

    v2f vert (appdata v)
    {
        v2f o;
        o.positionCS = TransformObjectToHClip
        (v.positionOS.xyz);
        o.uv = v.uv;
```

```
                            return o;
                    }

                    ENDHLSL
            }

            Pass { ... }

            Pass { ... }
        }
    }
```

For the two passes, the code is identical to Listings 11-45, 11-46, and 11-47 from the built-in pipeline version of the shader, so we will copy that code here.

Like we saw with the Grayscale shader, add the Gaussian Blur effect to a profile, attach the profile to a volume, and add Gaussian Blur to the Renderer Features list to see blurring like in Figure 11-7 in your scene. Finally, let's see how this effect works in HDRP.

Gaussian Blur in HDRP

As with the other render pipelines, the Gaussian Blur effect in HDRP has a C# scripting side and a shader side. We can use the same template files as the ones we used in the Grayscale effect. Let's see how each part works.

Gaussian Blur C# Scripting in HDRP

Unlike URP, we require only one C# script to drive the Gaussian Blur effect in HDRP. We can create it using the template at *Create* ➤ *Rendering* ➤ *C# Post Process Volume*, and I'll name it "GaussianBlurVolume.cs". I'll make a few changes to the template, so we're left with the following code as a starting point.

Listing 11-58. The GaussianBlurVolume code skeleton

```
using UnityEngine;
using UnityEngine.Rendering;
using UnityEngine.Rendering.HighDefinition;
using System;
```

```
[Serializable, VolumeComponentMenu("Post-processing/Examples/
Gaussian Blur")]
public sealed class GaussianBlurVolume : CustomPostProcessVolumeComponent,
IPostProcessComponent
{
    ...
    public override void Setup() { ... }
    public override void Render(...) { ... }
    public override void Cleanup() { ... }
}
```

We already saw how post-processing scripts broadly work in HDRP when we wrote the Grayscale shader, so let's quickly go through each part. First, we need to add a kernelSize member variable for the shader, plus a variable to store the material used by the effect. We will be using a temporary render texture because Gaussian Blur is a two-pass effect, so we will also store an RTHandle object called tempTex. Recall that RTHandle is a type that abstracts many of the features of a RenderTexture. We'll also add the IsActive method, which is true only when the material exists and the kernel size is above 1, the injection point for the effect, and the shader's name string.

Listing 11-59. Member variables

```
public sealed class GaussianBlurVolume : CustomPostProcessVolumeComponent,
IPostProcessComponent
{
    [Tooltip("How large the convolution kernel is. " +
        "A larger kernel means stronger blurring.")]
    public ClampedIntParameter kernelSize = new ClampedIntParameter
    (1, 1, 101);

    Material m_Material;
    RTHandle tempTex;

    public bool IsActive() => m_Material != null && kernelSize.value > 1;
```

```
        public override CustomPostProcessInjectionPoint injectionPoint =>
        CustomPostProcessInjectionPoint.AfterPostProcess;

        const string kShaderName = "Examples/ImageEffects/GaussianBlur";

        ...
}
```

The Setup method, which is responsible for creating the material used by the effect, is practically the same as the version we wrote for the Grayscale shader, except the error message is slightly different. This goes just below the variable declarations.

Listing 11-60. The Setup method for the Gaussian blur effect in HDRP

```
public override void Setup()
{
        if (Shader.Find(kShaderName) != null)
                m_Material = new Material(Shader.Find(kShaderName));
        else
                Debug.LogError($"Unable to find shader '{kShaderName}'. Post
                Process Volume Gaussian Blur is unable to load.");
}
```

Now we come to the Render method, which sets up the logic for the effect. We will be using a temporary render texture, which is a bit more finnicky in HDRP than URP. We use the RTHandles.Alloc method to retrieve a render texture from the pool. This method can accept many different optional arguments, but the one we are interested in is the first parameter, scale factor, which is a Vector2. A value of (1, 1) represents a render texture with the same dimensions of the screen; this syntax is helpful if you want to access textures smaller than the maximum screen size without needing to manually deal with accessing the screen size and performing the size divisions yourself. In our case, we want a texture the same size as the screen. Hence, we will use Vector2.one.

HDRP can act a bit strangely with temporary textures. Personally, I have run into many issues getting them to work, as there are several ways of creating and using them, and most of the methods I have tried result in a black or gray screen when trying to apply the effect. The following method works well:

- First, we'll send the source texture to a texture slot named _
  SourceTex in the shader.

- Then, apply the first shader pass with HDUtils.DrawFullScreen,
  saving the result in tempTex.

- Next, we'll send the tempTex texture to a new texture slot called
  _TempTex in the shader.

- Finally, we'll apply the second shader pass, saving the result in the
  destination texture.

This means the HDRP Gaussian Blur shader will use two texture names instead of one. This is because the format of the source texture is different from the format of tempTex, so we need to sample each one using slightly different functions – this will be important when we write the shader, so just bear it in mind for now. Here's the Render method.

Listing 11-61. The Render method for the Gaussian blur effect in URP

```
public override void Render(CommandBuffer cmd, HDCamera camera, RTHandle
source, RTHandle destination)
{
    if (m_Material == null)
        return;

    tempTex = RTHandles.Alloc(Vector2.one);

    m_Material.SetInt("_KernelSize", kernelSize.value);

    m_Material.SetTexture("_SourceTex", source);
    HDUtils.DrawFullScreen(cmd, m_Material, tempTex, shaderPassId: 0);

    m_Material.SetTexture("_TempTex", tempTex);
    HDUtils.DrawFullScreen(cmd, m_Material, destination, shaderPassId: 1);
}
```

Finally, we come to the Cleanup method. This method is responsible for cleaning up resources used by the shader each frame, which in this case are the material and the tempTex texture.

Listing 11-62. The Cleanup method

```
public override void Cleanup()
{
    tempTex.Release();
    CoreUtils.Destroy(m_Material);
}
```

Now that the code is complete, let's move on to the shader file.

Gaussian Blur Shader in HDRP

Create a new post-processing shader via *Create* ➤ *Shader* ➤ *HD Render Pipeline* ➤ *Post Process* and name it "GaussianBlur.shader". Much of the template will stay the same. In the HLSLINCLUDE block, we will add a gaussian function that calculates the Gaussian coefficients at a given distance from the center of the kernel. We will also be including the _KernelSize, _SourceTex, and _TempTex properties, but pay close attention to the type of those two textures. The fragment shader changes between the two passes, so we will remove it from HLSLINCLUDE and write the two new fragment shader functions in the corresponding Pass blocks.

Listing 11-63. The HLSLINCLUDE block

```
Shader "Examples/ImageEffects/GaussianBlur"
{
    HLSLINCLUDE

    #pragma target 4.5
    #pragma only_renderers d3d11 playstation xboxone xboxseries vulkan
    metal switch

    #include "Packages/com.unity.render-pipelines.core/ShaderLibrary/
    Common.hlsl"
    #include "Packages/com.unity.render-pipelines.core/ShaderLibrary/
    Color.hlsl"
    #include "Packages/com.unity.render-pipelines.high-definition/
    Runtime/ShaderLibrary/ShaderVariables.hlsl"
    #include "Packages/com.unity.render-pipelines.high-definition/
    Runtime/PostProcessing/Shaders/FXAA.hlsl"
```

```
#include "Packages/com.unity.render-pipelines.high-definition/
Runtime/PostProcessing/Shaders/RTUpscale.hlsl"

static const float E = 2.71828f;

float gaussian(int x, float sigma)
{
    float twoSigmaSqu = 2 * sigma * sigma;
    return (1 / sqrt(PI * twoSigmaSqu)) * pow(E, -(x * x) /
    (2 * twoSigmaSqu));
}

struct Attributes
{
    uint vertexID : SV_VertexID;
    UNITY_VERTEX_INPUT_INSTANCE_ID
};

struct Varyings
{
    float4 positionCS : SV_POSITION;
    float2 texcoord   : TEXCOORD0;
    UNITY_VERTEX_OUTPUT_STEREO
};

Varyings Vert(Attributes input)
{
    Varyings output;
    UNITY_SETUP_INSTANCE_ID(input);
    UNITY_INITIALIZE_VERTEX_OUTPUT_STEREO(output);
    output.positionCS = GetFullScreenTriangleVertexPosition
    (input.vertexID);
    output.texcoord = GetFullScreenTriangleTexCoord
    (input.vertexID);
    return output;
}
```

```
int _KernelSize;
TEXTURE2D_X(_SourceTex);
TEXTURE2D(_TempTex);

ENDHLSL

SubShader
{
        Pass { ... }
        Pass { ... }
}
}
```

The TEXTURE2D_X macro is used for VR games so that the shader can use separate textures for each eye – the template shader file uses this type of texture for the source texture by default. The TEXTURE2D type (without the X on the end) is just a regular texture. I'm using the latter type for _TempTex because this is the only method that seems to work reliably for multipass shaders. This means we'll need to make sure we use the correct sampling macro later too.

Let's move on to the two passes. The first pass, named "Horizontal", blurs the image horizontally. We'll use a similar approach as we saw in the Grayscale post-process shader by converting the UVs to screen-space coordinates, which are used by the LOAD_ TEXTURE2D_X macro to sample a texture, which in this case is _SourceTex. The loop for the blurring process is similar to the loops used in the built-in pipeline and URP versions of this shader.

Listing 11-64. The horizontal blur pass for the Gaussian blur effect in HDRP

```
Pass
{
        Name "Horizontal"

        ZWrite Off
        ZTest Always
        Blend Off
        Cull Off
```

```
HLSLPROGRAM
#pragma fragment HorizontalBlur
#pragma vertex Vert

float4 HorizontalBlur (Varyings input) : SV_Target
{
    UNITY_SETUP_STEREO_EYE_INDEX_POST_VERTEX(input);

    uint2 positionSS = input.texcoord * _ScreenSize.xy;

    float3 col = float3(0.0f, 0.0f, 0.0f);
    float kernelSum = 0.0f;
    float sigma = _KernelSize / 8.0f;

    int upper = ((_KernelSize - 1) / 2);
    int lower = -upper;

    for (int x = lower; x <= upper; ++x)
    {
        float gauss = gaussian(x, sigma);
        kernelSum += gauss;
        float2 uv = positionSS + float2(x, 0.0f);
        col += max(0, gauss * LOAD_TEXTURE2D_X(_SourceTex, uv).
        xyz);
    }

    col /= kernelSum;

    return float4(col, 1.0f);
}
ENDHLSL
}
```

Lastly, let's write the second pass, called "Vertical". It is much the same as the first pass, except it operates in the y-direction, so the loop is slightly different. Most importantly, make sure you use the LOAD_TEXTURE2D macro this time instead of the "X" version, because we are sampling a different type of texture in this pass.

Listing 11-65. The vertical blur pass for the Gaussian blur effect in HDRP

```
Pass
{
        Name "Vertical"

        ZWrite Off
        ZTest Always
        Blend Off
        Cull Off

        HLSLPROGRAM
        #pragma fragment VerticalBlur
        #pragma vertex Vert

        float4 VerticalBlur(Varyings input) : SV_Target
        {
                UNITY_SETUP_STEREO_EYE_INDEX_POST_VERTEX(input);

                uint2 positionSS = input.texcoord * _ScreenSize.xy;

                float3 col = float3(0.0f, 0.0f, 0.0f);
                float kernelSum = 0.0f;
                float sigma = _KernelSize / 8.0f;

                int upper = ((_KernelSize - 1) / 2);
                int lower = -upper;
                for (int y = lower; y <= upper; ++y)
                {
                        float gauss = gaussian(y, sigma);
                        kernelSum += gauss;
                        float2 uv = positionSS + float2(0.0f, y);
                        col += max(0, gauss * LOAD_TEXTURE2D(_TempTex, uv).xyz);
                }

                col /= kernelSum;

                return float4(col, 1.0f);
        }
        ENDHLSL
}
```

Now that the shader file is complete, we can set up the effect. We'll take the same steps as we did for the Grayscale shader: create a profile and add the Gaussian Blur effect to it and then attach the profile to a volume in your scene. Make sure the Gaussian Blur effect is included in the *Custom Post Process Orders* ➤ *After Post Processing* list in the HDRP Project Settings. Then your effect will appear in both the Scene View and Game View when the camera passes through the volume, as in Figure 11-7.

Summary

Post-processing effects can be used to add an extra layer of polish to your game or to create entirely new mechanics that rely on graphics. With post-processing shaders, also known as image effects, we can change the way the game looks in ways that are not possible with conventional object shaders. Image effect shaders operate on every pixel of the screen, changing their colors in any way you want. Each render pipeline in Unity deals with post-processing in different ways, so unfortunately each pipeline requires a unique approach to custom post-processing effects. In this chapter, we learned the following:

- Render textures are special types of texture that contain the output from a camera.

- You can create render textures in the Editor and assign them to a camera or create them programmatically and then use them in materials.

- A Grayscale effect takes the luminance of each pixel based on the real-world sensitivity of the human eye to red, green, and blue light and then outputs that luminance value as a grayscale color.

- An efficient type of blur called Gaussian blur uses the Gaussian function to assign coefficients to each entry in a kernel matrix.

  - The kernel is run over ("convolved with") each pixel of the image to produce an output color for the center pixel.

  - The Gaussian blur is separable, so we make performance gains by running two passes, one horizontally and the other vertically.

- URP and HDRP can make use of the SRP volume system, which is able to blend post-processing effects together or fade them in and out.

CHAPTER 12

Advanced Shaders

So far, we have primarily discussed vertex and fragment shaders that take meshes, transform their vertices onto the screen, and color the pixels. Most shaders take this form. We've already seen the power of these types of shaders and the broad range of capabilities they have, but they are not the only types of shaders. In the shader pipeline, there are two optional stages that we have not yet encountered: the tessellation shader and the geometry shader. On top of that, there are compute shaders, which operate outside the usual mesh shading pipeline and can be used for arbitrary calculations on the GPU. In this chapter, we will explore some of these strange and exotic new types of shaders and add ever-powerful new tools to our box of tricks.

Tessellation Shaders

Back all the way in Chapter 1, I presented a simplified diagram of the shader pipeline with six "stages," although in that diagram I lumped together tessellation and geometry shaders together into one box as "optional" stages to avoid complicating things (see Figure 1-1). Let's revisit and flesh out that diagram now in Figure 12-1 with a different example and split tessellation and geometry shaders into stages 3a and 3b. Then, let's discuss in detail what the tessellation stage is doing.

517

© Daniel Ilett 2022
D. Ilett, *Building Quality Shaders for Unity®*, https://doi.org/10.1007/978-1-4842-8652-4_12

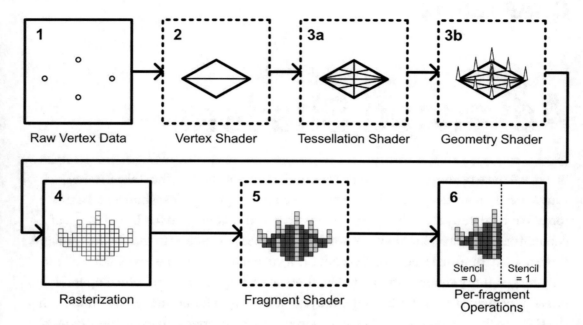

Figure 12-1. *The shader pipeline stages. In this example, a quad mesh is turned into a grassy mesh with blades – new geometry – growing out of new vertices created during the pipeline*

So what is changing between stage 2, the vertex shader, and stage 3a, the tessellation shader? Recall that the vertex shader just moves vertices around – it has no power at all to create or destroy vertices, and each vertex only knows about itself. On the other hand, here's what the tessellation shader does:

- The tessellation shader can create new vertices by *subdividing* an existing face of a mesh.

- The tessellation shader can create new vertices on the edges or within the face of each triangle of a mesh.

- Calling it a "tessellation shader" is slightly misleading because there are actually two programmable stages and one fixed-function stage involved in the process:

  - The *tessellation control shader* (TCS), also called the *hull shader*, defines how much tessellation should be applied to each face. This shader is not required for tessellation, although we will be including it in each example.

- It receives a *patch* made up of a small handful of vertices, and it can use information about those vertices to control the amount of tessellation. Unlike vertex shaders, hull shaders can access data about multiple vertices at once. We can configure the number of vertices in each patch.

- The *tessellation primitive generation* fixed-function stage, also called the "tessellator," is situated between the two programmable stages. It creates new primitives (i.e., triangles or quads) based on the hull shader output.

- The *tessellation evaluation shader* (TES), also called the *domain shader*, is responsible for positioning the vertices output by the tessellator.

- Although the domain shader is typically used to interpolate the position of new vertices based on the positions of existing vertices, you may change the position however you want. It is commonly used to offset the positions of vertices.

If some of this went over your head on the first read-through, don't worry – it clicked for me a lot more the first time after I worked through an example. There are many cases where tessellation can be used to achieve more aesthetically pleasing results, so let's start with a water wave effect.

Tip   Tessellation is often seen as a more advanced shader feature – after all, it's completely optional, and there are many moving parts to it. I've put it in the "Advanced Shaders" chapter for that reason. But keep in mind that, like any other shader, it's just made up of relatively small functions! Take the code I've written and try adding, removing, and hacking bits of it around to see what changes on-screen – hands-on experience will likely help you deepen your understanding of tessellation.

Water Wave Effect with Tessellation

Water is a common feature in games, and many of those games use a shader to apply waves that bob up and down to the water surface. These effects work by moving the vertices of the mesh up and down in world space over time to simulate waves rolling over the surface, and for this effect, we will do just that. Although this shader could be applied to any mesh, it will work best if applied to any flat plane mesh – Unity's built-in quad will do just fine. However, if we just displace the vertices, the effect will obviously look worse on a low-poly mesh than a high-poly one. That's where tessellation shaders come in. It would probably be wasteful to create a high-poly mesh in the Assets folder just for higher-quality water, so instead, we can take a basic quad and *subdivide* it with tessellation at runtime to end up with a high-poly mesh. That way, the waves will appear smoother, as seen in Figure 12-2.

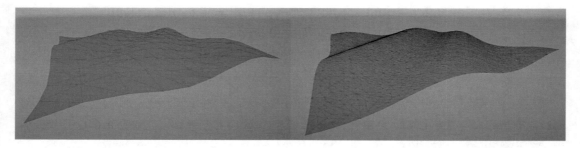

Figure 12-2. *Two instances of Unity's built-in plane mesh with a wave effect applied and different tessellation settings used. On the left, no tessellation is used. On the right, each quad is subdivided eight times, resulting in smoother waves*

To visualize the wireframe of a mesh in the Scene View as in Figure 12-2, you can change the Shading Mode from Shaded to either Wireframe or Shaded Wireframe (see Figure 12-3). This option is on the toolbar just above the Scene View window.

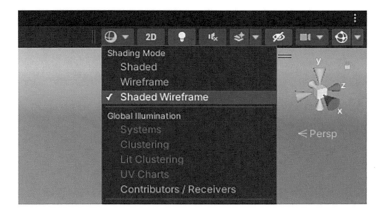

Figure 12-3. *Changing the Shading Mode to Shaded Wireframe*

We'll start by creating the effect in shader code and then see how it works in Shader Graph.

Note   In Unity 2021.3 LTS, tessellation is only compatible with HDRP Shader Graph, so unfortunately, we won't be able to use URP Shader Graph for this effect.

Wave Tessellation in Shader Code

Let's start with a skeleton shader file containing all the structs and functions and then fill them in one at a time. I'll explain each part of the shader in roughly the order they happen in the graphics pipeline. Create a new shader file called "Waves.shader" and replace its contents with the following code.

Listing 12-1. The wave tessellation shader skeleton

```
Shader "Examples/Waves"
{
    Properties
    {
        _BaseColor ("Base Color", Color) = (1, 1, 1, 1)
        _BaseTex("Base Texture", 2D) = "white" {}

        [Enum(UnityEngine.Rendering.BlendMode)]
        _SrcBlend("Source Blend Factor", Int) = 1

        [Enum(UnityEngine.Rendering.BlendMode)]
```

```
            _DstBlend("Destination Blend Factor", Int) = 1
    }
    SubShader
    {
        Tags
        {
            "RenderType" = "Transparent"
            "Queue" = "Transparent"
        }

        Pass
        {
            Blend [_SrcBlend] [_DstBlend]
            HLSLPROGRAM

            struct appdata { ... };
            struct tessControlPoint { ... };
            struct tessFactors { ... };
            struct v2f { ... };

            sampler2D _BaseTex;

            CBUFFER_START(UnityPerMaterial)
                float4 _BaseColor;
                float4 _BaseTex_ST;
            CBUFFER_END

            tessControlPoint vert( ... ) { ... }
            v2f tessVert( ... ) { ... }
            tessFactors patchConstantFunc( ... ) { ... }
            tessControlPoint tessHull( ... ) { ... }
            v2f tessDomain( ...) { ... }
            float4 frag(v2f i) : SV_Target { ... }

            ENDHLSL
        }
    }
    Fallback Off
}
```

This shader is set up to use transparent rendering, with _SrcBlend and _DstBlend properties to customize how transparency blending works. If you are using URP, then include the following tag inside the SubShader Tags block.

Listing 12-2. URP RenderPipeline tag

```
Tags
{
    "RenderType" = "Transparent"
    "Queue" = "Transparent"
    "RenderPipeline" = "UniversalPipeline"
}
```

Then also include a new Tags block inside the Pass, just under the Blend keyword.

Listing 12-3. URP forward pass tag

```
Blend [_SrcBlend] [_DstBlend]

Tags
{
    "LightMode" = "UniversalForward"
}
```

Finally, we'll include required files. In the built-in pipeline, we need the UnityCG. cginc file, and in URP, we need the Core.hlsl file.

Listing 12-4. Required files for the built-in pipeline

```
#include "UnityCG.cginc"

struct appdata { ... };
```

Listing 12-5. Required files for URP

```
#include "Packages/com.unity.render-pipelines.universal/ShaderLibrary/
Core.hlsl"

struct appdata { ... };
```

Next, let's add the properties for this shader. We need two `Float` properties called `_WaveStrength` and `_WaveSpeed` to control the height of the waves and the speed they move across the mesh, respectively. We will also include a third `Float` property called `_TessAmount` to control how much tessellation happens across the mesh – a higher value means more vertices get added to each triangle. The minimum amount is 1, meaning no vertices are added, and the maximum is 64, which is the highest number of subdivisions the hardware supports.

Listing 12-6. Wave shader properties

```
Properties
{
      _BaseColor ("Base Color", Color) = (1, 1, 1, 1)
      _BaseTex("Base Texture", 2D) = "white" {}
      _WaveStrength("Wave Strength", Range(0, 2)) = 0.1
      _WaveSpeed("Wave Speed", Range(0, 10)) = 1

      [Enum(UnityEngine.Rendering.BlendMode)]
      _SrcBlend("Source Blend Factor", Int) = 1

      [Enum(UnityEngine.Rendering.BlendMode)]
      _DstBlend("Destination Blend Factor", Int) = 1

      _TessAmount("Tessellation Amount", Range(1, 64)) = 2
}
```

We'll also need to add these properties in the `HLSLPROGRAM` block. The code looks slightly different between the built-in pipeline and URP.

Listing 12-7. Adding wave shader properties in the built-in pipeline

```
struct v2f { ... };

sampler2D _BaseTex;
float4 _BaseColor;
float4 _BaseTex_ST;
float _TessAmount;
float _WaveStrength;
float _WaveSpeed;
```

Listing 12-8. Adding wave shader properties in URP

```
struct v2f { ... };

sampler2D _BaseTex;

CBUFFER_START(UnityPerMaterial)
     float4 _BaseColor;
     float4 _BaseTex_ST;
     float _TessAmount;
     float _WaveStrength;
     float _WaveSpeed;
CBUFFER_END
```

Now we can move on to the HLSLPROGRAM block. As you can see in Listing 12-1, there are many structs and functions, some of which are familiar and others of which are brand-new. First, we'll tell Unity which functions correspond to which shaders with #pragma statements. The #pragma hull <name> and #pragma domain <name> statements tell Unity which functions make up the hull and domain shaders – in our case, these functions are called tessHull and tessDomain, respectively. We also need to say #pragma target 4.6, since 4.6 is the earliest of Unity's shader models that supports tessellation. It's roughly equivalent to OpenGL version 4.1 and DirectX 11.

Listing 12-9. #pragma statements for tessellation

```
HLSLPROGRAM
#pragma vertex vert
#pragma fragment frag
#pragma hull tessHull
#pragma domain tessDomain
#pragma target 4.6
```

Now, you may have noticed something strange in Listing 12-1. Not only do we have the vert function but I've added an additional function named tessVert, which looks suspiciously like an extra vertex shader function. Here's why. Ordinarily, the vertex shader is used to transform data about meshes from object space to clip space, but this shader will be different; I want to offset the vertices of the mesh upward in world space *after* the tessellation shader has run (indeed, the entire point of the shader is to smooth out the shape of those waves). However, the vertex shader always runs first. Therefore,

I'm supplying two vertex functions: one called vert, which is "officially" the vertex shader for this file, and another called tessVert, which I will run manually after all tessellation has been applied.

Wave Vertex Shader

The vert function will act as a pass-through; all the parameters it is passed in appdata will be unchanged and passed on to v2f. First, let's look at appdata. It's going to be very basic – the only data required by the shader is the object position and associated UV data of each vertex. We've seen this many times before.

Listing 12-10. The appdata struct for the wave effect

```
struct appdata
{
        float4 positionOS : Position;
        float2 uv : TEXCOORD0;
};
```

Before we write the vertex shader, let's think about what it will output. Usually, we would output a v2f struct containing clip-space positions and UVs, but as I mentioned, vert is going to output unchanged object-space positions and UVs. The next stage of the pipeline is the tessellation control shader, also called the hull shader. The hull shader expects to receive data about each *control point* (i.e., vertex) from the vertex shader. Therefore, I will create a struct called tessControlPoint to control what data gets passed between the vertex shader and the hull shader. The only difference is that the positionOS member of tessControlPoint uses the INTERNALTESSPOS semantic instead of POSITION. This struct is like any other, so you *could* add additional members if you wanted to do extra calculations in this vertex shader, such as generating normal vector information on the fly. However, I just want to use the vertex shader as a pass-through, so I will use the same members in tessControlPoint as in appdata.

Listing 12-11. The tessControlPoint struct for the wave effect

```
struct tessControlPoint
{
        float4 positionOS : INTERNALTESSPOS;
        float2 uv : TEXCOORD0;
};
```

Now let's write the vert vertex function. Each member of appdata will be copied into the tessControlPoint struct.

Listing 12-12. The vert vertex function

```
tessControlPoint vert(appdata v)
{
    tessControlPoint o;
    o.positionOS = v.positionOS;
    o.uv = v.uv;
    return o;
}
```

That's the vertex stage complete, and we can move on to the hull shader.

Wave Tessellation Control (Hull) Shader

The hull shader has two core responsibilities. First, it will output a list of control points that the tessellator uses as a base to perform subdivision on (in other words, we usually output the same geometric primitives that were input, like triangles). This can be done inside the body of the tessHull function. Second, it will output a set of *tessellation factors* that control how the inside portion and the edges of each primitive get subdivided. tessHull can't return two sets of data, so we specify these factors in a separate function called a *patch constant function*. Both stages run in parallel. We have a high degree of control over the inputs and outputs of the hull shader using attributes that get placed above the tessHull function – let's see how it all works:

- The tessHull function takes in a patch of control points.

- Think of a patch as a single polygon. It can be between 1 and 32 control points, but in our case, we'll just use 3, which is a triangle.

- The hull shader can access all control points in that patch.

- The first parameter to the hull shader is the patch itself. We specify what data each vertex holds (in our case, each one is a tessControlPoint) and how many vertices are in the patch (3).

- The second parameter is the ID of a vertex in the patch. The hull shader runs once per vertex and outputs one vertex per invocation.

- The output of `tessHull` will just be one vertex. We'll use the ID parameter to grab a vertex from the patch and then return that vertex.

- To tell Unity we are using triangles, we'll need a few attributes:

  - The `domain` attribute (not to be confused with the domain shader) takes the value `tri`. Other possible values are `quad` or `isoline` – these values depend on what type of mesh you have.

  - The `outputcontrolpoints` attribute is used to define how many control points are created per patch. We'll use the value 3.

  - The `outputtopology` attribute is used to define what primitive types should be accepted by the tessellator. This is also based on the mesh used. In our case, we'll use `triangle_cw`, which means triangles with clockwise winding order. Other possible values are `triangle_ccw` (i.e., counterclockwise winding order), `point`, and `line`.

Listing 12-13. The tessHull function

```
[domain("tri")]
[outputcontrolpoints(3)]
[outputtopology("triangle_cw")]
tessControlPoint tessHull(InputPatch<tessControlPoint, 3> patch, uint id :
SV_OutputControlPointID)
{
    return patch[id];
}
```

We're not done yet. We also need a `partitioning` attribute to define how the tessellator deals with the tessellation factors (we'll deal with those factors soon). Each partition mode defines how new subdivisions get formed when you change the tessellation factor associated with the inside or an edge. Here are the possible values:

- `integer` – Snap tessellation factors to the next highest integer value. All subdivisions are equally spaced.

- fractional_even – When using non-integer factors, an extra subdivision will appear when going between one even-numbered factor and the next. This subdivision is not equally spaced with nearby subdivisions – it grows as the tessellation factor increases until you hit an even number.

- fractional_odd – Same as fractional_even, but the changes apply to odd-numbered factors instead.

- pow2 – This seems to be the same as integer in the cases I tried out.

The final attribute is the patchconstantfunc attribute, which we use to specify the patch constant function that I mentioned before. We input the function name, which in our case is just patchConstantFunc.

Listing 12-14. Partitioning and patch constant function attributes

```
[domain("tri")]
[outputcontrolpoints(3)]
[outputtopology("triangle_cw")]
[partitioning("fractional_even")]
[patchconstantfunc("patchConstantFunc")]
tessControlPoint tessHull(InputPatch<tessControlPoint, 3> patch, uint id :
SV_OutputControlPointID)
{
    return patch[id];
}
```

With all the attributes in place, let's move on to the patch constant function. As I mentioned, the purpose of this function is to generate a set of *tessellation factors* that will be used by the tessellator to generate brand-new control points. For triangles, there are four factors: three of them are attached to each edge of the triangle, and the last one is for the center of the triangle. For example, if I were to give an edge a factor of 2, then Unity would split the edge into two segments by generating one new vertex in the middle of the edge and replacing the original triangle with two smaller triangles as necessary. If I give the inside a factor of 2, Unity adds one new vertex in the center of the triangle. Figure 12-4 shows you what objects look like using different factors.

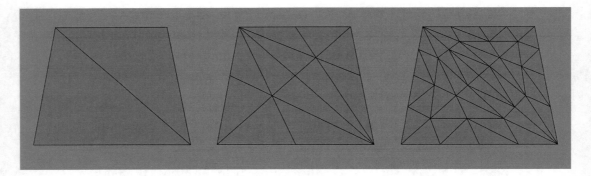

Figure 12-4. *Three versions of the default Unity quad with different tessellation factors. From left to right, the edges and the inside of the mesh use 1, 2, and 4 as their tessellation factors, respectively*

First, we will set up a struct for these factors called `tessFactors`. The edge factors are contained inside a small array of floats with three entries, which uses the `SV_TessFactor` semantic. The inside factor is a single float value with the `SV_InsideTessFactor` semantic.

Listing 12-15. The tessFactors struct

```
struct tessFactors
{
    float edge[3] : SV_TessFactor;
    float inside : SV_InsideTessFactor;
};
```

Now let's write the `patchConstantFunc` function. It takes in a patch and outputs a set of `tessFactors` for this patch. Although it's possible to give each edge a different factor, we'll give all three edges and the center the same factor, `_TessAmount`, to keep things simple.

Listing 12-16. The patch constant function

```
tessFactors patchConstantFunc(InputPatch<tessControlPoint, 3> patch)
{
    tessFactors f;
    f.edge[0] = f.edge[1] = f.edge[2] = _TessAmount;
    f.inside = _TessAmount;
    return f;
}
```

Now that we have handled both sides of the hull shader, we can move on to the domain shader.

Wave Tessellation Evaluation (Domain) Shader

The tessellator takes the control points output by the hull shader and the tessellation factors output by the patch constant function and calculates new control points, which it passes to the domain shader. The domain shader is invoked once per new control point; the parameters to the domain shader are the tessellation factors from the patch constant function, the patch output by the hull shader, and a set of coordinates. These are the *barycentric coordinates* of the new point, which denote how far the new vertex is from the original three control points on the triangle. For example, a vertex with barycentric coordinates (0.5, 0.5, 0) lies exactly on the halfway point of one of the triangle's edges. These coordinates use the SV_DomainLocation semantic.

The responsibility of the domain shader is to interpolate the new vertex data between each of the original triangle's vertices and return a v2f struct. Our domain shader uses the tessDomain function, so we will edit that. First, we'll add a domain attribute to it to specify we are using triangles. Then, in the function body, we'll create a new appdata struct and interpolate each of the members of the tessControlPoint between those barycentric coordinates and then put the results into appdata. Remember how this file has two vertex functions? We'll pass the appdata into the tessVert function and return that. tessVert takes in an appdata and returns a v2f, like most of the vertex shaders we saw in previous chapters.

Listing 12-17. The tessDomain function

```
[domain("tri")]
v2f tessDomain(tessFactors factors, OutputPatch<tessControlPoint, 3> patch,
float3 bcCoords : SV_DomainLocation)
{
    appdata i;

    i.positionOS = patch[0].positionOS * bcCoords.x +
        patch[1].positionOS * bcCoords.y +
        patch[2].positionOS * bcCoords.z;
```

```
    i.uv = patch[0].uv * bcCoords.x +
        patch[1].uv * bcCoords.y +
        patch[2].uv * bcCoords.z;

    return tessVert(i);
}
```

Remember that at this point, all the calculations have been operating in object space – it is still necessary to transform from object to clip space. That's what the tessVert function will do.

Wave Tessellation tessVert Function and Fragment Shader

We are now solidly out of the land of tessellation shaders and back onto familiar ground, working with just vertices and fragments. The tessVert function takes in an appdata struct and outputs a v2f struct. Rather than just transforming between object and clip space, as do most of the vertex functions we have written throughout the book, here's what this shader will do:

- We will transform the vertices to world space with unity_ ObjectToWorld, a matrix that is provided by Unity.

- Then, we'll apply a height offset based on the time since level start, the _WaveSpeed property value, and the x- and z-positions of the vertex in world space.

  - By applying a sine function to those variables, the waves will bob up and down over time.

- We'll then multiply the offset by _WaveStrength so that we have control over the physical size of the waves and add it to the y-position in world space.

- We can then transform the position from world to clip space with UNITY_MATRIX_VP. We need the positions to be in clip space before rasterization, so we're finished with positions now.

- Finally, we'll use TRANSFORM_TEX to deal with tiling and offsetting the UVs.

Listing 12-18. The `tessVert` function

```
v2f tessVert(appdata v)
{
    v2f o;

    float4 positionWS = mul(unity_ObjectToWorld, v.positionOS);
    float height = sin(_Time.y * _WaveSpeed + positionWS.x +
    positionWS.z);
    positionWS.y += height * _WaveStrength;

    o.positionCS = mul(UNITY_MATRIX_VP, positionWS);
    o.uv = TRANSFORM_TEX(v.uv, _BaseTex);
    return o;
}
```

The `tessVert` function is called inside the `tessDomain` function, which returns a `v2f` struct. Since we have no geometry shader, the next stage in the shader pipeline after the domain shader is the fragment shader, which receives the `v2f` struct as its input. The `frag` function is the simplest shader in this whole file – all it does is sample `_BaseTex` and multiply by `_BaseColor`.

Listing 12-19. The fragment shader

```
float4 frag(v2f i) : SV_Target
{
    float4 textureSample = tex2D(_BaseTex, i.uv);
    return textureSample * _BaseColor;
}
```

With that, you should be able to see tessellation on your objects using this shader, as in Figure 12-2. Obviously it's difficult to showcase the quality of an animation in a book, so play around with the tessellation factors in the code to see how it impacts the smoothness of the waves on your own computer. You will probably be able to find a sweet spot where the waves start looking smooth, and increasing the tessellation factors past that point has diminishing returns. Now that we have created tessellated waves in shader code, let's see how the same can be achieved with Shader Graph.

Wave Tessellation in Shader Graph

Tessellation became available in Shader Graph with HDRP version 12.0, corresponding to Unity 2021.2. Unfortunately, URP Shader Graph does not yet support tessellation, so this effect will only work in HDRP. On the flipside, tessellation is a lot easier to achieve with Shader Graph. Let's see how.

I'll start by creating an Unlit graph (you can use a Lit graph if you want – pick whichever looks best for your use case) and name it "Waves.shadergraph". We'll start by adding properties to the graph:

- A Color named Base Color that will provide a way to tint the albedo of the water.

- A Texture2D called Base Texture that will also affect the albedo.

- A Float called Wave Speed that is used to control how fast the waves spread across the surface of the water.

- A Float called Wave Strength that represents how high and low the waves travel in world space. A value of 1 means the waves travel one Unity unit up *and* down.

- A Float called Tess Factor (short for "tessellation factor") that we'll use to configure how many times the mesh gets subdivided. This property should use a slider between 1 and 64 (1 means no subdivisions, and 64 is the hardware limit).

With these properties in place, let's enable tessellation on the graph. Remember: this only works on HDRP in the latest LTS release of Unity as of the writing of this book (Unity 2021.3). Go to the Graph Settings tab of the Graph Inspector and expand the Surface Options section. Here, you will find settings such as opaque/transparent rendering (I'll use transparent for this graph, but you can use either), alpha clipping, double-sided rendering, and so on. One of the options is labeled *Tessellation*, and by ticking it, a few more options appear, and two new blocks appear on the vertex stage of the master stack. Those new options are as follows:

- *Max Displacement* – The maximum distance, in Unity units, that the tessellated triangles can be displaced from their original position. This isn't a hard limit, but it prevents triangles being improperly culled.

- *Triangle Culling Epsilon* – Higher values mean that more triangles are culled.

- *Start Fade Distance* – At this distance (in Unity units) from the camera, tessellation will start to fade by reducing the tessellation factor.

- *End Fade Distance* – At this distance (in Unity units) from the camera, tessellation stops (i.e., the tessellation factor is 1).

- *Triangle Size* – When a triangle is above this size, in pixels, HDRP will subdivide it. Lower values mean smaller triangles get subdivided, and therefore the resulting mesh will be smoother.

- *Tessellation Mode* – Choose between *None* and *Phong*. With *Phong* tessellation, Unity will interpolate the newly generated geometry to smooth the mesh.

I will set the Max Displacement to 1 and leave the other values with their defaults. The two new blocks on the vertex stage, which are of more interest to us, are

- *Tessellation Factor* – This is the same as the tessellation factor we saw in the code-based tessellation shader. This is the number of times a triangle is subdivided. However, there is no way to provide different edge factors for each edge or inside factors for the inside of the triangle – they all use the same value.

- *Tessellation Displacement* – This is the offset, in world space, of the vertices of the mesh. The offset is applied after tessellation, so it just happens to be perfect for the wave effect we're building.

With these blocks accessible on the master stack, we can get to work creating the wave effect. First, connect the `Tess Factor` property to the *Tessellation Factor* block. This will let us dynamically change the amount of tessellation on each material that uses this shader.

Next, we'll set up the output for the *Tessellation Displacement* block. As we did with the code-based wave shader, we'll add time multiplied by the `Wave Speed` property to the x- and z-positions of the vertex in world space and then apply a sine function to the result. We'll multiply that by the `Wave Strength` property and output it as a y-offset.

When we're accessing the vertex position with the Position node, be careful to change the *Space* to *Absolute World* instead of *World*, because the latter is relative to the camera position, which would cause the waves to move erratically when the camera moves! See Figure 12-5 to see how the nodes are set up.

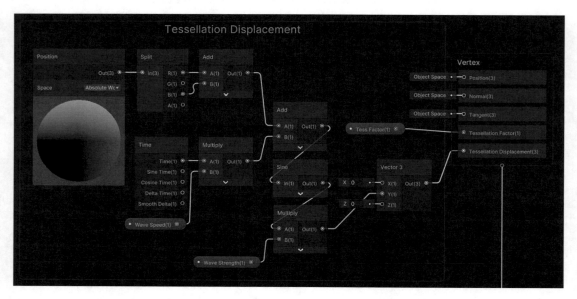

Figure 12-5. *Tessellation Factor and Tessellation Displacement in Shader Graph*

With these nodes in place, Unity will perform tessellation, add the tessellation offset to the vertices of the newly subdivided mesh, and then rasterize the mesh and apply the fragment stages to the pixels of the object. We'll deal with the fragment stage now. We'll use a node structure we've seen countless times before – sample the Base Texture with a Sample Texture 2D node, multiply the result by the Base Color property, output the result to the *Base Color* block, and then split off the alpha component and output it to the *Alpha* block on the master stack. See Figure 12-6 to see these nodes in action.

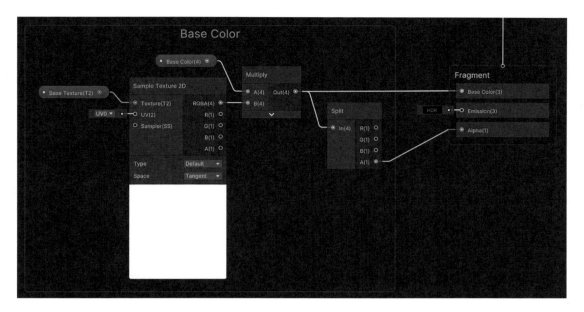

Figure 12-6. Outputting the Base Color

The graph is now complete, and you should see results just like those we saw with the code-based version of the shader (see Figure 12-2). Note that as you change the tessellation factor property, Unity will use `fractional_odd` subdivision behavior when using non-integer values, rather than the "integer" behavior we used with the code-based shader.

As you can see, tessellation is a powerful technique that can achieve things that are impossible with the vertex and fragment shaders we have used throughout the book so far. In the next example of tessellation, we will build a simplified LOD system that uses a high tessellation factor for objects close to the screen and a low tessellation factor when objects are far from the screen.

Level of Detail Using Tessellation

For the wave shader, we used a uniform amount of tessellation for each object – that is, every triangle of each object using a material with this shader used the same tessellation factor. That doesn't have to be the case. When a mesh is close to the camera, we want to use a high tessellation factor so that we get the most benefits out of the slightly increased processing time. But when a mesh is far away, we can get away with using a far lower tessellation factor. Even for large objects that exist both close to and far away from the camera, it is in our best interest to use lots of tessellations for the closest triangles and not as much for the furthest ones. In this shader example, we'll forget about waves and see how we can build a tessellation-based LOD system for a basic stationary mesh. Let's see how to do this in shader code and then in HDRP Shader Graph.

Level of Detail Tessellation in Shader Code

Let's go over the structure of the file. This time, I'll just use one vertex function at the start and do all the v2f processing in tessDomain. We'll be using the same set of functions as the wave shader, but the flow of data between the stages will be slightly different in ways I'll explain as we go. Start by creating a new shader file and naming it "TessLOD.shader". Here's the basic skeleton of the file.

Listing 12-20. The TessLOD shader skeleton

```
Shader "Examples/TessLOD"
{
    Properties
    {
        _BaseColor ("Base Color", Color) = (1, 1, 1, 1)
        _BaseTex("Base Texture", 2D) = "white" {}

        [Enum(UnityEngine.Rendering.BlendMode)]
        _SrcBlend("Source Blend Factor", Int) = 1

        [Enum(UnityEngine.Rendering.BlendMode)]
        _DstBlend("Destination Blend Factor", Int) = 1

        _TessAmount("Tess. Amount", Range(1, 64)) = 2
    }
    SubShader
    {
        Tags
        {
            "RenderType" = "Transparent"
            "Queue" = "Transparent"
        }
```

```
Pass
{
      Blend [_SrcBlend] [_DstBlend]

      HLSLPROGRAM
      #pragma vertex vert
      #pragma fragment frag
      #pragma hull tessHull
      #pragma domain tessDomain
      #pragma target 4.6

      struct appdata
      {
            float4 positionOS : Position;
            float2 uv : TEXCOORD0;
      };

      struct tessControlPoint { ... };

      struct tessFactors
      {
            float edge[3] : SV_TessFactor;
            float inside : SV_InsideTessFactor;
      };

      struct v2f
      {
            float4 positionCS : SV_Position;
            float2 uv : TEXCOORD0;
      };

      tessControlPoint vert(appdata v) { ... }

      tessFactors patchConstantFunc( ... ) { ... }

      [domain("tri")]
      [outputcontrolpoints(3)]
      [outputtopology("triangle_cw")]
      [partitioning("integer")]
```

```
            [patchconstantfunc("patchConstantFunc")]
            tessControlPoint tessHull(InputPatch<tessControlPoint, 3>
            patch, uint id : SV_OutputControlPointID)
            {
                    return patch[id];
            }

            [domain("tri")]
            v2f tessDomain( ... ) { ... }

            float4 frag(v2f i) : SV_Target
            {
                    float4 textureSample = tex2D(_BaseTex, i.uv);
                    return textureSample * _BaseColor;
            }
            ENDHLSL
        }
    }
    Fallback Off
}
```

There are a few key similarities between this and the Waves shader. The tessHull
and frag functions are identical, and most of the structs are the same. However, we're
going to make changes to the vert, patchConstantFunc, and tessDomain functions, as
well as the tessControlPoint struct. I've also removed all mentions of the properties
related to waves. There are also pipeline-specific changes that must be made:

- If you're working in the built-in pipeline, you'll need to follow
  Listing 12-4 to add the correct include file.

- In URP, instead follow Listing 12-5 for the relevant include file
  and then follow Listings 12-2 and 12-3 to add the correct tags to
  the shader.

With those small edits out of the way, let's add properties for this shader. We will need two new Float properties called _TessMinDistance and _TessMaxDistance, which do the following:

- When the distance of an edge (in Unity units) from the camera is less than _TessMinDistance, those edges use the full tessellation factor, defined in the _TessAmount property.

- When the distance is above _TessMaxDistance, the mesh uses a tessellation factor of 1, which means there is no tessellation at all.

- When the distance of an edge is between the two properties, the tessellation factor gets smaller the further from the camera you get.

With these properties, the Properties block looks like the following.

Listing 12-21. The Properties block

```
Properties
{
    _BaseColor ("Base Color", Color) = (1, 1, 1, 1)
    _BaseTex("Base Texture", 2D) = "white" {}

    [Enum(UnityEngine.Rendering.BlendMode)]
    _SrcBlend("Source Blend Factor", Int) = 1

    [Enum(UnityEngine.Rendering.BlendMode)]
    _DstBlend("Destination Blend Factor", Int) = 1

    _TessAmount("Tessellation Amount", Range(1, 64)) = 2
    _TessMinDistance("Min Tessellation Distance", Float) = 20
    _TessMaxDistance("Max Tessellation Distance", Float) = 50
}
```

We'll need to define them inside the HLSLPROGRAM block too. The code is slightly different between the built-in pipeline and URP.

Listing 12-22. Adding tessellation LOD properties in the built-in pipeline

```
struct v2f { ... };
```

```
sampler2D _BaseTex;
float4 _BaseColor;
float4 _BaseTex_ST;
float _TessAmount;
float _TessMinDistance;
float _TessMaxDistance;
```

Listing 12-23. Adding tessellation LOD properties in URP

```
struct v2f { ... };
```

```
sampler2D _BaseTex;
```

```
CBUFFER_START(UnityPerMaterial)
      float4 _BaseColor;
      float4 _BaseTex_ST;
      float _TessAmount;
      float _TessMinDistance;
      float _TessMaxDistance;
CBUFFER_END
```

With the properties in place, let's think about what the vertex shader needs to do by working backward. To work out the tessellation factors in `patchConstantFunc`, we will be working in world space because it makes the calculations far more intuitive. That means the `tessControlPoint` struct, which `patchConstantFunc` receives, must contain world-space positions. In turn, that means the `vert` function needs to calculate those world-space positions in the first place when constructing the `tessControlPoint` struct.

Listing 12-24. The tessControlPoint struct for the tessellation LOD effect

```
struct tessControlPoint
{
      float4 positionWS : INTERNALTESSPOS;
      float2 uv : TEXCOORD0;
};
```

Listing 12-25. The vert function for the tessellation LOD effect

```
tessControlPoint vert(appdata v)
{
    tessControlPoint o;
    o.positionWS = mul(unity_ObjectToWorld, v.positionOS);
    o.uv = TRANSFORM_TEX(v.uv, _BaseTex);
    return o;
}
```

The biggest part of this shader is the `patchConstantFunc`, which calculates the tessellation factors based on the distance of each edge from the camera. To do this, we'll do the following:

- Store the position of the three triangles in the patch in variables named `triPos0`, `triPos1`, and `triPos2`. I'll refer to variables with this naming system as `triPosX` from now on.

- Calculate the midpoint of each edge and store the result in variables called `edgePosX`.

- Get the world-space position of the camera from the built-in `_WorldSpaceCameraPos` variable.

- Calculate the distance of the three edges from the camera and store the result in `distX`.

- Use a bit of math to figure out an edge factor value for each edge, stored in `edgeFactorX`. These values are normalized between 0 and 1, where 0 corresponds to edges past the `_TessMaxDistance` and 1 corresponds to edges closer than `_TessMinDistance`.

- Calculate the actual edge tessellation factors, `f.edge[X]`, by squaring `edgeFactorX` and multiplying by the original `_TessAmount` (squaring is optional, but I found it looked better than not squaring). This could result in zero factors, which stop the triangle from being rendered, so take the `max` of this value and 1 so that the factor is always at least 1.

- Calculate the inside tessellation factor by taking the mean of the three edge factors.

The code looks like the following.

Listing 12-26. The patchConstantFunc function for variable tessellation based on distance

```
tessFactors patchConstantFunc(InputPatch<tessControlPoint, 3> patch)
{
    tessFactors f;

    float3 triPos0 = patch[0].positionWS.xyz;
    float3 triPos1 = patch[1].positionWS.xyz;
    float3 triPos2 = patch[2].positionWS.xyz;

    float3 edgePos0 = 0.5f * (triPos1 + triPos2);
    float3 edgePos1 = 0.5f * (triPos0 + triPos2);
    float3 edgePos2 = 0.5f * (triPos0 + triPos1);

    float3 camPos = _WorldSpaceCameraPos;

    float dist0 = distance(edgePos0, camPos);
    float dist1 = distance(edgePos1, camPos);
    float dist2 = distance(edgePos2, camPos);

    float fadeDist = _TessMaxDistance - _TessMinDistance;

    float edgeFactor0 = saturate(1.0f - (dist0 - _TessMinDistance) /
    fadeDist);
    float edgeFactor1 = saturate(1.0f - (dist1 - _TessMinDistance) /
    fadeDist);
    float edgeFactor2 = saturate(1.0f - (dist2 - _TessMinDistance) /
    fadeDist);

    f.edge[0] = max(pow(edgeFactor0, 2) * _TessAmount, 1);
    f.edge[1] = max(pow(edgeFactor1, 2) * _TessAmount, 1);
    f.edge[2] = max(pow(edgeFactor2, 2) * _TessAmount, 1);

    f.inside = (f.edge[0] + f.edge[1] + f.edge[2]) / 3.0f;

    return f;
}
```

We're left with only the tessDomain function to fill in now. As with the Waves shader, this function must interpolate each of the new control point properties using the barycentric coordinates supplied to the function. We'll use similar code to interpolate those properties, except tessControlPoint now uses world-space positions instead of object-space positions. tessDomain must output a v2f, so with that in mind, we'll use UNITY_MATRIX_VP to transform from world to clip space within tessDomain and populate the v2f struct in-place.

Listing 12-27. The tessDomain function interpolating properties and outputting v2f

```
[domain("tri")]
v2f tessDomain(tessFactors factors, OutputPatch<tessControlPoint, 3> patch,
float3 bcCoords : SV_DomainLocation)
{
    v2f o;

    float4 positionWS = patch[0].positionWS * bcCoords.x +
            patch[1].positionWS * bcCoords.y +
            patch[2].positionWS * bcCoords.z;

    o.positionCS = mul(UNITY_MATRIX_VP, positionWS);

    o.uv = patch[0].uv * bcCoords.x +
            patch[1].uv * bcCoords.y +
            patch[2].uv * bcCoords.z;

    return o;
}
```

The shader is now complete, and you will see a different number of subdivisions on some triangles as you move the camera closer to or further away from certain meshes, as shown previously in Figure 12-2. Try tweaking the min and max distances to see how the fade-out behavior of the tessellation works. Now let's see how this works in Shader Graph.

Level of Detail Tessellation in Shader Graph

Believe it or not, you already saw how this works in Shader Graph if you followed along with the Waves example for Shader Graph, as this functionality is built into Shader Graph directly! Remember that tessellation only works in HDRP Shader Graph. When tessellation is enabled for a Shader Graph, then a material that uses that shader will have a handful of tessellation-related options exposed in the Inspector. The relevant ones for us are *Start Fade Distance* and *End Fade Distance*, which I briefly explained previously.

When the camera is less than Start Fade Distance from any triangle of the mesh, then that triangle will use the tessellation factor defined in the shader. When the camera gets further away from the triangle than Start Fade Distance, the tessellation factor decreases linearly until it reaches End Fade Distance. When the camera is further than End Fade Distance, the triangle uses a tessellation factor of 1. With certain settings, it is possible to see a mesh that uses different tessellation factors on different parts of the mesh, as in Figure 12-7.

Figure 12-7. *The Start Fade Distance for this mesh is 5 units, and the End Fade Distance is 15 units, with a base tessellation factor of 64. This produces an extreme transition between high and low tessellation factors on the mesh*

We have now thoroughly explored tessellation factors and have seen how they can be used to increase the resolution of vertex-based effects for higher-quality effects. Next, let's explore another type of optional shader called geometry shaders.

Geometry Shaders

Geometry shaders are another optional stage in the rendering pipeline – see stage 3b in Figure 12-1. A geometry shader function receives an input primitive (such as a point or triangle) and a stream of all primitives in the mesh, and it can create brand-new primitives (based on the one it received as input) and add those to the stream. The original primitive is not automatically added back to the stream, so you may end up with completely new geometry from what you started with.

Although they are powerful, geometry shaders have some drawbacks. Often, they are quite slow, and many use cases for geometry shaders could be solved more efficiently with tessellation or compute shaders, albeit with potentially more complexity on the programmer's side. Also, hardware and API support for geometry shaders can be spotty, so be sure to check that your project's target devices will be able to support geometry shaders before diving into using them. Finally, geometry shaders are not supported by Shader Graph at all as of the writing of this book, so regrettably, we will not be able to create node-based geometry shaders.

There are many things you can do with geometry shaders, and in the following example, I will show you how to add small bits of geometry to any mesh to display the direction of the normals on the surface for that mesh.

Visualizing Normals with Geometry Shaders

Visualizing normals on the surface of an object is primarily useful for debugging, although with a bit of creativity I'm sure you could imagine how the effect could be adapted for spikes on the surface of an object. With this effect, we will generate two small rectangular quads, perpendicular to one another, on each vertex of the mesh in the direction of the normal vector at that point. The quads will use two-sided rendering, and due to using two perpendicular quads, they will be visible from all directions except directly face-on looking at the vertex down its normal vector. This shader will *only* render the normal vectors, not the original mesh, so you'll need to add a material with this shader in the second material slot on each object. The result will look like Figure 12-8.

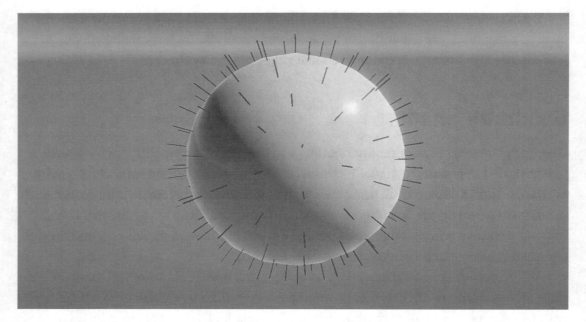

Figure 12-8. *Each "spike" emanating from the surface is used to visualize the direction of the normal vector at each vertex of the mesh*

Start by creating a new shader file called "NormalDebug.shader" and delete the file contents. Replace them with the following skeleton code.

Listing 12-28. The NormalDebug skeleton shader code

```
Shader "Examples/NormalDebug"
{
    Properties { ... }

    SubShader
    {
        Tags
        {
            "RenderType" = "Opaque"
            "Queue" = "Geometry"
        }
```

```
Pass
{
    HLSLPROGRAM
    #pragma vertex vert
    #pragma geometry geom
    #pragma fragment frag

    struct appdata { ... };
    struct v2g { ... };
    struct g2f { ... };

    v2g vert (appdata v) { ... };
    g2f geomToClip( ... ) { ... }
    void geom( ... ) { ... }
    float4 frag(g2f i) : SV_Target { ... }
    ENDHLSL
}
}
}
```

Already, you can see some of the structure of the file coming together. The `appdata` struct is used to supply input data to the vertex shader, but instead of a `v2f` struct, we have two new structs called `v2g` and `g2f`, meaning "vertex to geometry" and "geometry to fragment," respectively. That should make the flow of data through this shader clear! Alongside the familiar `vert` and `frag` functions, the `geom` function is the geometry shader function, and I've added a helper function called `geomToClip` that we'll explore later.

Before we explore these structs and functions, let's add three properties to this shader:

- A `Color` called `_DebugColor`, which is the color used to visualize the normal vectors at each point. We'll just use a block color for all normals.

- A `Float` called `_WireThickness,` which represents the width, in Unity units, of each visualized normal. This should be quite small, so I'll bound the value between 0 and 0.1.

- Another `Float` called `_WireLength`, which is unsurprisingly the height of each visualized normal. This can be slightly longer, so I'll bound the value between 0 and 1.

Each of these can be added to the Properties block at the very top of the file.

Listing 12-29. Properties for the NormalDebug shader

```
Properties
{
    _DebugColor("Debug Color", Color) = (0, 0, 0, 1)
    _WireThickness("Wire Thickness", Range(0, 0.1)) = 0.01
    _WireLength("Wire Length", Range(0, 1)) = 0.2
}
```

Each of these properties also needs to be declared in the HLSLPROGRAM block. The code differs between the built-in pipeline and URP, so pick the correct version for your pipeline. I'll place these declarations below the g2f struct definition.

Listing 12-30. Properties in HLSL in the built-in pipeline

```
struct g2f { ... };

float4 _DebugColor;
float _WireThickness;
float _WireLength;
```

Listing 12-31. Properties in HLSL in URP

```
struct g2f { ... };

CBUFFER_START(UnityPerMaterial)
    float4 _DebugColor;
    float _WireThickness;
    float _WireLength;
CBUFFER_END
```

As we've seen with other shader examples, that's not the only difference between code for these two pipelines. In the built-in pipeline, we need to include the UnityCG. cginc file.

Listing 12-32. The UnityCG.cginc include file for the normal debug effect in the built-in pipeline

```
#pragma fragment frag
```

#include "UnityCG.cginc"

In URP, we need to include the RenderPipeline = UniversalPipeline tag in the SubShader Tags block, the LightMode = UniversalForward tag in the Pass Tags block, and the Core.hlsl include file.

Listing 12-33. The Core.hlsl include file and relevant tags for the normal debug effect in URP

```
SubShader
{
    Tags
    {
        "RenderType" = "Opaque"
        "Queue" = "Geometry"
        "RenderPipeline" = "UniversalPipeline"
    }
    Pass
    {
        Tags
        {
            "LightMode" = "UniversalForward"
        }
        HLSLPROGRAM
        #pragma vertex vert
        #pragma geometry geom
        #pragma fragment frag

        #include "Packages/com.unity.render-pipelines.universal/
        ShaderLibrary/Core.hlsl"
```

Next, let's make sure the shader uses two-sided rendering so the visualized normals can be seen from all directions. For that, we can use the Cull Off keyword, which prevents Unity from culling the front or back faces of the mesh. Although we don't care what happens to the original mesh faces, since this shader won't render them, this culling option applies to all primitives output by the geometry shader. This keyword goes inside the Pass, just above HLSLPROGRAM.

Listing 12-34. Using the Cull Off keyword

```
Cull Off

HLSLPROGRAM
```

Now let's start filling some of the gaps in the code that I left in Listing 12-28, starting with the three structs. The appdata struct needs the vertex positions, as standard, plus the normals (after all, without these, we have nothing to visualize) and the tangents, which help us orient the new quad meshes properly. The normals and tangents use the NORMAL and TANGENT semantics, respectively.

Listing 12-35. The appdata struct for the normal debug effect

```
struct appdata
{
        float4 positionOS : POSITION;
        float3 normalOS : NORMAL;
        float4 tangentOS : TANGENT;
};
```

Next is the v2g struct, which we use to relay data from the vertex shader to the geometry shader. As we will see, the geometry shader will operate in world space because it makes calculations much easier, so the v2g struct just needs to contain the same data as appdata, but in world space instead. The normal and tangent vectors can use the same semantics as in appdata, but the position should use the SV_POSITION semantic instead.

Listing 12-36. The v2g struct

```
struct v2g
{
        float4 positionWS : SV_POSITION;
        float3 normalWS : NORMAL;
        float4 tangentWS : TANGENT;
};
```

Finally, the g2f struct is used to send data from the geometry shader to the fragment shader. The fragment shader won't be doing any texturing, so the only variable it requires is the clip-space position of each vertex, which needs the SV_POSITION semantic.

Listing 12-37. The g2f struct

```
struct g2f
{
    float4 positionCS : SV_POSITION;
};
```

With the structs out of the way, let's move on to the vertex shader. As I alluded to before, the vertex shader needs to transform the contents of appdata from object space to world space. For the positions and tangents, there's no built-in function to do this easily, so we should multiply those two inputs by the unity_ObjectToWorld matrix. For the normals, there is a built-in function called UnityObjectToWorldNormal in the built-in pipeline and TransformObjectToWorldNormal in URP.

Listing 12-38. The vert function in the built-in pipeline

```
v2g vert (appdata v)
{
    v2g o;

    o.positionWS = mul(unity_ObjectToWorld, v.positionOS);
    o.normalWS = UnityObjectToWorldNormal(v.normalOS);
    o.tangentWS = mul(unity_ObjectToWorld, v.tangentOS);
    return o;
}
```

Listing 12-39. The vert function in URP

```
v2g vert (appdata v)
{
    v2g o;
    o.positionWS = mul(unity_ObjectToWorld, v.positionOS);
    o.normalWS = TransformObjectToWorldNormal(v.normalOS);
    o.tangentWS = mul(unity_ObjectToWorld, v.tangentOS);
    return o;
}
```

Next in the pipeline comes the geometry shader. As I briefly mentioned, it receives two parameters: one is a single primitive shape – in our case, a *point* – and a triangle stream, which we can append triangles to. An important observation to make here is that the primitives we receive can be different from the primitives we create. Although we're receiving individual vertices, we will build triangles and add them to the stream. We must also specify what the maximum number of vertices each run of the geometry shader can create. We're going to generate a cross-patterned pair of quads pointing in the direction of the vertex normal, which means we'll generate eight new vertices each time, because each quad has four vertices. We specify this value with an attribute called `maxvertexcount`.

Listing 12-40. The geom function signature

[maxvertexcount(8)]
void geom(**point v2g i[1], inout TriangleStream<g2f> triStream**) { ... }

Now let's create those triangles inside the function body. First, we need to normalize the normal and tangent vectors and then use the cross product between them to obtain the bitangent vector, which is perpendicular to both. Using those vectors, we can create eight offset vectors that represent how far, in world space, the vertices of the new quads should be from the original point.

Listing 12-41. Calculating the normal, tangent, bitangent, and eight offset vectors

```
[maxvertexcount(8)]
void geom(point v2g i[1], inout TriangleStream<g2f> triStream)
{
        float3 normal = normalize(i[0].normalWS);
        float4 tangent = normalize(i[0].tangentWS);
        float3 bitangent = normalize(cross(normal, tangent.xyz) * tangent.w);

        float3 xOffset = tangent * _WireThickness * 0.5f;
        float3 yOffset = normal * _WireLength;
        float3 zOffset = bitangent * _WireThickness * 0.5f;
```

```
float3 offsets[8] =
{
    -xOffset,
     xOffset,
    -xOffset + yOffset,
     xOffset + yOffset,

    -zOffset,
     zOffset,
    -zOffset + yOffset,
     zOffset + yOffset
};

...
}
```

Using these offset values, we'll create new vertices and add them to the triangle stream, triStream, with the Append function. When we add vertices in this way, Unity will generate a triangle strip, which means the first three additions to the stream constitute a single triangle and every subsequent addition of a vertex results in the creation of one more triangle that shares two vertices with the previous triangle. Since we intend to create two quads, we'll append two sets of four vertices and separate the two groups with a call to triStream.RestartStrip, which stops building the current triangle strip and starts a new one when you add vertices afterward. The triStream requires instances of g2f, so we will use the geomToClip helper function, which takes the original vertex position and an offset vector as its two parameters, to build those. With that in mind, the rest of the geom function looks like the following.

Listing 12-42. Building two quads using triangle strips

```
float3 offsets[8] = { ... };

float4 pos = i[0].positionWS;

triStream.Append(geomToClip(pos, offsets[0]));
triStream.Append(geomToClip(pos, offsets[1]));
triStream.Append(geomToClip(pos, offsets[2]));
triStream.Append(geomToClip(pos, offsets[3]));
```

```
    triStream.RestartStrip();

    triStream.Append(geomToClip(pos, offsets[4]));
    triStream.Append(geomToClip(pos, offsets[5]));
    triStream.Append(geomToClip(pos, offsets[6]));
    triStream.Append(geomToClip(pos, offsets[7]));

    triStream.RestartStrip();
}
```

The geomToClip function takes the original vertex position of the point that was input to the geometry shader and one of the offset vectors we calculated inside that shader, adds them together, converts the result from world to clip space, and outputs a g2f struct instance containing that position. Although URP has a helper function called TransformWorldToHClip for the transformation step, the built-in pipeline does not, so we can make this function work on both pipelines by using UNITY_MATRIX_VP instead.

Listing 12-43. The geomToClip helper function

```
g2f geomToClip(float3 positionOS, float3 offsetOS)
{
    g2f o;
    o.positionCS = mul(UNITY_MATRIX_VP, positionOS + offsetOS);
    return o;
}
```

Finally, we come to the fragment shader. This is the easiest function in the entire file because it just needs to output _DebugColor.

Listing 12-44. The frag function for the normal debug effect

```
float4 frag (g2f i) : SV_Target
{
    return _DebugColor;
}
```

Now we have seen a handful of use cases for both geometry and tessellation shaders in Unity. Next, we'll explore another type of shader that exists outside the typical graphics pipeline, as it can be used for non-graphics purposes.

Compute Shaders

Compute shaders are a special type of shader, distinct from the rest, that exists outside the graphics pipeline in Figure 12-1. Compute shaders can be used for arbitrary code execution on the GPU, meaning that we don't have to use them for graphics purposes. With compute shaders, we can run a massively parallel application on the GPU, which is much better suited to certain tasks than the CPU. The best use cases are when you have thousands of small tasks that can run independently to each other – does that sound like vertex or fragment processing to you?

Compute shaders are a broad enough topic that they could fill an entire book by themselves. I will show you one example of how compute shaders can be used, even in a graphics context, to illustrate their power. I encourage you to take what you learn and explore other ways compute shaders can be used. In this example, we will take a terrain mesh and use a compute shader to generate data on each triangle of the terrain. Then, with scripting help, we will create a grass mesh instance on top of each terrain triangle using a second (non-compute) shader, using the parameters generated by the compute shader. The result can be seen in Figure 12-9.

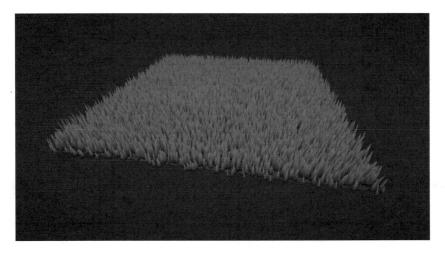

Figure 12-9. *A base terrain mesh with grass blades being generated on each triangle*

Grass Mesh Instancing

There are a couple of typical workflows related to compute shaders. The first involves sending data from the CPU (a C# script) to the GPU (the compute shader), doing some processing on the GPU, then reading the results on the CPU side, and doing something with those results. The second involves sending data from CPU to GPU, running the compute shader, and then reading the results inside a separate shader without needing to copy any data back to the CPU – both the shaders can share the same GPU memory. This second approach is useful because copying data between the CPU and GPU and back is time-consuming, so it's best to minimize the frequency of copying data back and forth as possible.

The grass effect is going to require the following:

- A terrain mesh and a grass blade mesh.

- A C# script to read data from both meshes and set up the data that needs to be sent to the compute shader.

- A compute shader that will receive a list of vertices and triangles of the terrain mesh and then generate a transformation matrix for each triangle.

- A "regular" shader for rendering each grass blade. The vertex shader reads one of the transformation matrices generated by the compute shader; applies it to the grass mesh to position, scale, and rotate it in object space; and then applies the MVP matrix to transform to clip space. The fragment shader blends two colors between the base and tip of the grass blade.

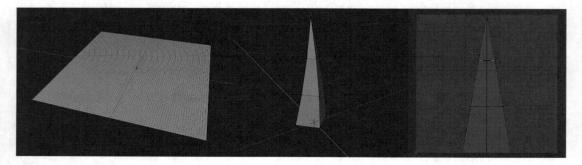

Figure 12-10. *From left to right: the high-poly terrain mesh, the low-poly grass blade mesh, and the UVs for the grass blade mesh. The base and tip of the grass blade mesh are at the bottom and top of the UV space, respectively*

Figure 12-10 shows the terrain and grass blade meshes that I am using for this effect, both of which were created in Blender. You can use a lower-poly terrain mesh if you want, but since we're going to generate a grass blade on every triangle of the terrain, I wanted mine to be high enough poly so that the grass would appear thick.

Before we can start the effect, we must ensure that reading and writing mesh data is enabled on both meshes – without doing so, the script will throw errors as it will be unable to read the mesh data. To enable read/write, select the mesh and tick the *Read/ Write* option in the Model tab. It should be about halfway down the list of options, as seen in Figure 12-11.

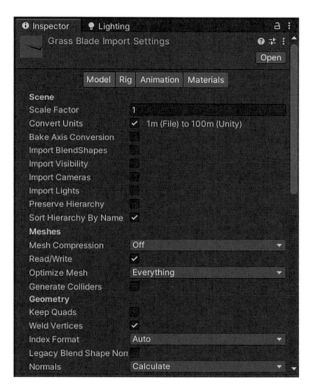

Figure 12-11. *Tick the Read/Write box in the mesh import settings; otherwise, the script will fail*

Now that we can read data from both meshes, let's start creating the effect by writing the C# script.

The ProceduralGrass C# Script

Create a new C# script and name it "ProceduralGrass.cs". There are many moving parts to this script, so I will go through them one at a time. Here is the script we will start with.

Listing 12-45. The ProceduralGrass C# script

```
using UnityEngine;

public class ProceduralGrass : MonoBehaviour
{
    private void Start() { ... }
    private void RunComputeShader() { ... }
    private void Update() { ... }
    private void OnDestroy() { ... }
}
```

Next, let's deal with the member variables of this class.

ProceduralGrass Properties

There are quite a lot of them, so I'll start by explaining what the unfamiliar types do. Then I'll outline the variables we'll need:

- The ComputeShader type is, unsurprisingly, the base type for all compute shaders. It's like the Shader type that we've seen previously. We will use a variable of this type to set parameters with which to run the compute shader.

- The GraphicsBuffer type is like another type, ComputeBuffer, which is typically used in compute applications. Both types of buffer store data in a format that can be sent to a compute shader, and they can contain most primitive types and even structs. The GraphicsBuffer type is specifically for graphics-related data, whereas ComputeBuffer is for arbitrary data.

- The Bounds type is used for bounding boxes that are used when culling objects. Unity won't be able to calculate this automatically with the technique we're using, so we will manually calculate the bounds.

Those are the types, so now let's see the variables we'll need:

- A ComputeShader object to store the compute shader used for the effect.

- Two Mesh objects to store the terrain mesh and the grass blade mesh. These are both meshes I created in Blender. The grass blade mesh must be assigned from the Editor, but the terrain mesh should be assigned to a MeshFilter component attached to the same object the script is on.

- A float to control the scale and a Vector2 to control the minimum and maximum height of the grass blades.

- Six different GraphicsBuffer objects – I'll explain these as I go through the code.

- A Bounds object for the combined bounding box of all the grass blade meshes, which will be generated on the terrain.

- Three integers related to the compute shader. I'll also explain these as I go.

Here are all the member variables we'll be needing.

Listing 12-46. Member variables for the ProceduralGrass script

```
public class ProceduralGrass : MonoBehaviour
{
    public ComputeShader computeShader;

    private Mesh terrainMesh;
    public Mesh grassMesh;
    public Material material;

    public float scale = 0.1f;
    public Vector2 minMaxBladeHeight = new Vector2(0.5f, 1.5f);

    private GraphicsBuffer terrainTriangleBuffer;
    private GraphicsBuffer terrainVertexBuffer;
```

```
        private GraphicsBuffer transformMatrixBuffer;

        private GraphicsBuffer grassTriangleBuffer;
        private GraphicsBuffer grassVertexBuffer;
        private GraphicsBuffer grassUVBuffer;

        private Bounds bounds;

        private int kernel;
        private uint threadGroupSize;
        private int terrainTriangleCount = 0;

        private void Start() { ... }
        private void RunComputeShader() { ... }
        private void Update() { ... }
        private void OnDestroy() { ... }
}
```

Let's now move on to the Start method.

ProceduralGrass Start Method

Inside Start, we will set up most of the data structures used by the compute shader.
First, let's get a reference to the compute shader *kernel* using the FindKernel method.
A kernel, in this context, is a function inside a compute shader. Compute shaders can
contain several of these kernels, and we're able to pick a specific one to run. For this
effect, I will be creating a kernel named "TerrainOffsets".

Listing 12-47. Accessing the kernel function

```
private void Start()
{
        kernel = computeShader.FindKernel("TerrainOffsets");
```

Next, let's start filling some of those buffers. Before we can do that, we need to
understand what kind of data makes up a mesh. To simplify, a mesh is made up of a
list of vertices, which are just three-dimensional vectors representing the position of
each vertex in object space. Then, there is a list of triangles, where each entry is an

index into the vertex list, and each set of three entries to the triangle list makes up one triangle. Figure 12-12 illustrates this idea. Meshes may also store up to eight sets of UV coordinates, normals, tangents, and colors associated with each vertex.

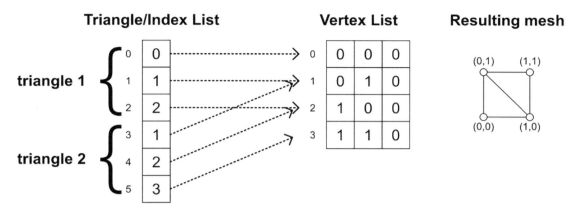

Figure 12-12. *Indexing into the vertex array. With meshes that share many vertices between multiple faces, this technique saves space over storing all shared vertices as duplicated three-component vectors in the vertex array*

We'll start with the terrain mesh, which we can get from the MeshFilter component attached to the object. First, we can access the vertex array through terrainMesh.vertices. Each entry in the list is a Vector3 representing the object-space position of a vertex. Then, we'll create a GraphicsBuffer for this array. There are three parameters to the GraphicsBuffer constructor:

- A *target*. This is just a type that tells Unity what we're using the buffer for. We'll use Target.Structured, because we will be using StructuredBuffer in the compute shader (more on that later).

- The number of entries in the buffer. For us, this is the same size as the vertex array.

- A *stride* value. The "stride" refers to the number of bits each entry in the array takes up, which we use to ensure Unity can pack all the data into the buffer without gaps. We can use the sizeof method to get the size of a float and then multiply by 3 because it's a Vector3.

We then use the SetData method on the buffer to bind the vertex array to the buffer, followed by the SetBuffer method on the compute shader to bind the buffer to a specific variable name in the compute shader. I'll use the name _TerrainPositions.

We'll do a similar thing for the triangle array, which we access through `terrainMesh.triangles`. This time, each entry is one integer, so we'll tweak the stride accordingly. The name of the buffer on the compute shader side will be `_TerrainTriangles`. We'll also keep a reference to the overall number of triangles, which is the size of the triangle array divided by three, in the `terrainTriangleCount` variable.

Listing 12-48. The terrain vertex and triangle buffers

```
kernel = computeShader.FindKernel("TerrainOffsets");

terrainMesh = GetComponent<MeshFilter>().sharedMesh;

Vector3[] terrainVertices = terrainMesh.vertices;
terrainVertexBuffer = new GraphicsBuffer(GraphicsBuffer.Target.Structured,
terrainVertices.Length, sizeof(float) * 3);
terrainVertexBuffer.SetData(terrainVertices);
computeShader.SetBuffer(kernel, "_TerrainPositions", terrainVertexBuffer);

int[] terrainTriangles = terrainMesh.triangles;
terrainTriangleBuffer = new GraphicsBuffer(GraphicsBuffer.Target.
Structured, terrainTriangles.Length, sizeof(int));
terrainTriangleBuffer.SetData(terrainTriangles);
computeShader.SetBuffer(kernel, "_TerrainTriangles",
terrainTriangleBuffer);

terrainTriangleCount = terrainTriangles.Length / 3;
```

Next comes similar data for the grass blade mesh. There's not much that's different, except that we won't need to bind any of this data onto the compute shader because the grass mesh doesn't ever interact with the compute shader directly and we'll be getting UV data too.

Listing 12-49. The grass vertex, triangle, and UV buffers

```
terrainTriangleCount = terrainTriangles.Length / 3;

Vector3[] grassVertices = grassMesh.vertices;
grassVertexBuffer = new GraphicsBuffer(GraphicsBuffer.Target.Structured,
grassVertices.Length, sizeof(float) * 3);
grassVertexBuffer.SetData(grassVertices);
```

```
int[] grassTriangles = grassMesh.triangles;
grassTriangleBuffer = new GraphicsBuffer(GraphicsBuffer.Target.Structured,
grassTriangles.Length, sizeof(int));
grassTriangleBuffer.SetData(grassTriangles);

Vector2[] grassUVs = grassMesh.uv;
grassUVBuffer = new GraphicsBuffer(GraphicsBuffer.Target.Structured,
grassUVs.Length, sizeof(float) * 2);
grassUVBuffer.SetData(grassUVs);
```

Next, let's deal with the output of the compute shader. As I mentioned, it will output one transformation matrix per terrain triangle (i.e., per three entries in the triangle array). We'll need to set up the buffer here on the CPU side, although we won't fill it with any data. We can then bind it to the variable _TransformationMatrices on the compute shader using SetBuffer. Each matrix is 4×4 in size, so for the stride, we'll use sizeof(float) multiplied by 16.

Listing 12-50. Creating the transformation matrix buffer

```
grassUVBuffer.SetData(grassUVs);

transformMatrixBuffer = new GraphicsBuffer(GraphicsBuffer.Target.
Structured, terrainTriangleCount, sizeof(float) * 16);
computeShader.SetBuffer(kernel, "_TransformMatrices",
transformMatrixBuffer);
```

Now we'll deal with the bounds. When Unity is culling objects that are outside of the camera's view, it compares against a bounding box around the object rather than the exact shape of the object, as it is efficient to calculate whether the bounding box is in view. Unity usually creates these automatically, but in this case, it can't know where the bounding box should be because we're generating the positions of the grass in a compute shader, so we must supply the bounds manually. This singular bounding box should cover all the grass geometry we create, so we'll take the terrain's bounds and expand them by the max grass height along the y-axis.

Listing 12-51. Creating the bounding box for the grass blade meshes

```
computeShader.SetBuffer(kernel, "_TransformMatrices",
transformMatrixBuffer);
bounds = terrainMesh.bounds;
bounds.center += transform.position;
bounds.Expand(minMaxBladeHeight.y);
```

The final thing to do in the Start method is run the compute shader, which I've separated into another method called RunComputeShader. Where you call this method depends on what the compute shader is doing. If the terrain mesh moves at runtime or you're doing any animation inside the compute shader, then call it in Update instead. However, for the effect I'm writing, I'll assume the terrain doesn't move so the transformation matrices only need to be calculated once at the start.

Listing 12-52. Calling the RunComputeShader method

```
        bounds.Expand(minMaxBladeHeight.y);

        RunComputeShader();
}
```

Let's now look at the RunComputeShader method.

ProceduralGrass RunComputeShader Method

This method binds all the remaining data to the compute shader before dispatching it. The compute shader requires the following data:

- The object-to-world matrix for the transform, which helps us put the grass blades in the correct preliminary position.

- The number of triangles in the mesh (i.e., the number of times the compute shader should run).

- The minimum and maximum height of each grass blade.

- The scale of the grass meshes. If we just used a scale of 1, the grass blades I made in Blender would be about 1 meter in height.

Listing 12-53. Setting parameters on the compute shader

```
private void RunComputeShader()
{
    computeShader.SetMatrix("_TerrainObjectToWorld", transform.
    localToWorldMatrix);
    computeShader.SetInt("_TerrainTriangleCount", terrainTriangleCount);
    computeShader.SetVector("_MinMaxBladeHeight", minMaxBladeHeight);
    computeShader.SetFloat("_Scale", scale);
```

In addition to sending these parameters, let's think about how many triangles the compute shader runs at a time and how many sets it will run in total. When we get to writing the compute shader itself, we will specify how many *threads* are contained in a *work group*. A single thread runs through the compute shader once, so if we specify, say, 64 threads to a work group, then that group runs through the compute shader 64 times in parallel, with slightly different inputs for each thread. We can divide a work group across one, two, or three dimensions, but we'll be sticking to one for this shader. We'll get on to setting the size of a work group later when we write the compute shader, but it's important to know this information for now.

On the C# scripting side, we must partition the data into work groups. The GetKernelThreadGroupSizes method will get us the number of threads in each group (we'll be setting this later). We can divide the number of terrain triangles by the number of threads per group to get the number of work groups – if these values do not perfectly divide, then the final group will contain some overshoot threads, which we'll deal with in the compute shader. Finally, we use the Dispatch method to create the work groups and invoke the compute shader. The first parameter to the function is the kernel ID, and the last three are the numbers of work groups in each dimension (we're only using one dimension).

Listing 12-54. Work groups and dispatching the compute shader

```
    computeShader.SetFloat("_Scale", scale);

    computeShader.GetKernelThreadGroupSizes(kernel, out threadGroupSize,
    out _, out _);
    int threadGroups = Mathf.CeilToInt(terrainTriangleCount /
    threadGroupSize);
    computeShader.Dispatch(kernel, threadGroups, 1, 1);
}
```

After the compute shader has finished running, the _TransformMatrices buffer will be full of usable data. This data can be shared between the compute shader and the conventional grass mesh shader. In the Update method, we will create those grass blades using GPU instancing.

ProceduralGrass Script Update Method

Unlike the compute shader, which we can run just once at the start of the game (if you don't want to move the terrain mesh or animate the grass in any way), we must tell Unity to render the grass blades every frame, so we'll do it in Update. Although you are familiar with setting properties on materials by this point, we will be doing things in a slightly different way, because we'll be using *GPU instancing*. Conventional rendering issues a draw call for every mesh in the scene, whereas GPU instancing can be used to draw multiple instances of the same mesh in a single draw call, removing a lot of overhead, and those instances can even use different properties as we will see. The only additional consideration in URP is that GPU instancing is incompatible with the SRP Batcher, so we won't need to include shader variables in a constant buffer – we'll deal with that later. Let's see how to run an instanced shader.

We'll start by creating a RenderParams object to contain all the settings for the rendering batch. This includes the bounds, which we already created, and a MaterialPropertyBlock, which contains all the buffers required by the shader. This includes the _TransformMatrices buffer, which is shared with the compute shader, plus the grass blade vertex and UV buffers, which will be referenced with the variable names _Positions and _UVs, respectively. Finally, we run the shader with the Graphics. RenderPrimitivesIndexed method. It takes the following arguments:

- The RenderParams object we just created.

- The topology of the mesh. This can be either Triangles, Quads, Lines, LineStrip, or Points – we'll choose Triangles.

- The index buffer. That's another name for the triangle buffer that is commonly used in computer graphics.

- The number of indices to get from the index buffer. We'll be using the entire buffer.

- The number of instances to render. This is the number of grass blades we'll have, equal to the number of transformation matrices inside _TransformMatrices.

Listing 12-55. The Update method

```
private void Update()
{
    RenderParams rp = new RenderParams(material);
    rp.worldBounds = bounds;
    rp.matProps = new MaterialPropertyBlock();
    rp.matProps.SetBuffer("_TransformMatrices", transformMatrixBuffer);
    rp.matProps.SetBuffer("_Positions", grassVertexBuffer);
    rp.matProps.SetBuffer("_UVs", grassUVBuffer);

    Graphics.RenderPrimitivesIndexed(rp, MeshTopology.Triangles,
    grassTriangleBuffer, grassTriangleBuffer.count, instanceCount:
    terrainTriangleCount);
}
```

With this method, Unity will render several grass blades. This could mean hundreds, thousands, or even millions of vertices being rendered with surprising efficiency. The final method to write in this script is OnDestroy.

ProceduralGrass Script OnDestroy Method

As with many graphics-related structures in Unity like compute buffers or temporary render textures, we must clear the memory used for the buffers on the CPU side manually. In our case, we'll do this when the terrain object is destroyed, since we need the buffers to be active for the entire life of the terrain. The Dispose method will do just what we need.

Listing 12-56. The OnDestroy method

```
private void OnDestroy()
{
    terrainTriangleBuffer.Dispose();
    terrainVertexBuffer.Dispose();
    transformMatrixBuffer.Dispose();

    grassTriangleBuffer.Dispose();
    grassVertexBuffer.Dispose();
    grassUVBuffer.Dispose();
}
```

The script is now complete, but if you attach it to an object right now, then nothing will happen (except maybe a flurry of errors and warnings) since we haven't written either of the shaders required for the effect. Let's start by writing the compute shader.

The ProceduralGrass Compute Shader

Compute shaders, which we write with HLSL syntax, are used for arbitrary computation on the GPU. Although this compute shader will serve a graphics purpose in the end, it won't be displaying any graphics on-screen in and of itself. Create a new compute shader via *Create* ➤ *Shader* ➤ *Compute Shader*, and name it "ProceduralGrass.compute". I'll remove all the contents for now, and we'll write the file from scratch.

First, we need to add a *kernel function*, which is the code we'll call from the C# scripting side. The kernel will be named TerrainOffsets, and it is a normal HLSL function with parameters and a return type, which is void. It takes one parameter, which is the float3 ID of the thread currently being run on one invocation of the function. For our shader, only the x-component of the ID will change. This parameter needs a semantic called SV_DispatchThreadID. We'll also specify the size of a work group with the numthreads attribute – I'll use the values (64, 1, 1), meaning each group has 64 threads in a 1D structure. Finally, we declare that this function is a kernel function using #pragma kernel TerrainOffsets at the top of the file.

Listing 12-57. Starting off the compute shader

```
#pragma kernel TerrainOffsets

[numthreads(64, 1, 1)]
void TerrainOffsets(uint3 id : SV_DispatchThreadID)
{ ... }
```

Note   The best number of threads in each work group and in each dimension depends heavily on the nature of the problem you are trying to solve. If the problem is 2D in nature, such as a 2D fluid simulation, then splitting your work groups across the x- and y-axes makes sense. You'd be tempted to see our problem as 2D or even 3D given the shape of the terrain mesh, but in reality, all we're receiving is 1D lists of vertices and triangles, so that's why I'm only using threads across one dimension. That said, you can try changing the value to see if performance increases – the optimal values are often hardware-dependent.

Let's also add a few properties. These are the same properties we set up on the C# scripting side, but we'll see a couple of unfamiliar types. The first type is `StructuredBuffer`, which is analogous to the `GraphicsBuffer` types we declared on the scripting side. A `StructuredBuffer<T>` is a read-only buffer that contains some number of T types (where T is a primitive type or a struct). The second type is `RWStructuredBuffer`, which is a read-write version of `StructuredBuffer`. By enabling read-write, this will make the buffer readable on the second shader that we will write later. The terrain triangle and vertex position buffers can use `StructuredBuffer`, but the `_TransformMatrices` buffer needs to be read-write.

Listing 12-58. Compute shader properties

```
#pragma kernel TerrainOffsets

StructuredBuffer<int> _TerrainTriangles;
StructuredBuffer<float3> _TerrainPositions;

RWStructuredBuffer<float4x4> _TransformMatrices;
uniform int _TerrainTriangleCount;
uniform float _Scale;
uniform float2 _MinMaxBladeHeight;
uniform float4x4 _TerrainObjectToWorld;
```

Before we dive into the `TerrainOffsets` kernel function, we need a couple of helper functions. The first function, `randomRange`, will accept three parameters – a `seed`, a `min` value, and a `max` value – and return a random float between the min and max. The seed is a `float2`, and I'll take a code snippet from Unity's `RandomRange` Shader Graph node for the body of the function. The second function, `rotationMatrixY`, will accept an angle parameter and return a rotation matrix that rotates a point around the y-axis by that angle, in radians (recall from Chapter 2 how rotation matrices are constructed). For that, I'll include a definition for `TWO_PI` just above the function definitions. All this should be defined just below the existing properties.

Listing 12-59. The randomRange and rotationMatrixY functions

```
uniform float4x4 _TerrainObjectToWorld;

#define TWO_PI 6.28318530718f

float randomRange(float2 seed, float min, float max)
{
      float randnum = frac(sin(dot(seed, float2(12.9898,
      78.233)))*43758.5453);
      return lerp(min, max, randnum);
}

float4x4 rotationMatrixY(float angle)
{
      float s, c;
      sincos(angle, s, c);

      return float4x4
      (
            c, 0, s, 0,
            0, 1, 0, 0,
           -s, 0, c, 0,
            0, 0, 0, 1
      );
}
```

Note   The HLSL `sincos` function, which you may not have seen before, takes three parameters. The first is the angle in radians. The latter two are output variables; this function simultaneously returns the sine and cosine of the input angle through those latter two parameters, respectively.

Now we can fill in the TerrainOffsets kernel function. Here's what the function will do:

- Any invocations with an ID higher than _TerrainTriangleCount should end immediately (recall that I talked about the possibility of overshooting if the number of triangles does not divide nicely by the size of each work group).

- Find the positions of the three vertices for the current triangle and calculate its center point (triangleCenterPos). This is the "base" position for placing the grass mesh.

- Generate two random seeds based on the ID. They are float2 seeds, so we'll shift the ID components around to get different seeds.

- Generate a scaleY value, which represents the height of the grass blade on the current triangle. We'll use the _MinMaxBladeHeight values to randomize the height.

- Generate a random offset value in the x- and z-directions using the two random seeds. This helps ensure the grass does not look too uniform.

- Create an initial transformation matrix, grassTransformMatrix, using the scale and offset values described previously. Recall from Chapter 2 how translation and scale can be represented in a 4 × 4 matrix.

- Create a random rotation matrix using the rotationMatrixY function. This will rotate each grass blade around the y-axis such that the direction they face is random.

- Multiply the randomRotationMatrix, grassTransformMatrix, and _TerrainObjectToWorld matrices together to obtain a single transformation matrix, which transforms one grass blade from object space to world space, adds an offset, scales it, and rotates it. This is stored in the _TransformMatrices buffer.

Listing 12-60. The TerrainOffsets kernel

```
[numthreads(64, 1, 1)]
void TerrainOffsets(uint3 id : SV_DispatchThreadID)
{
    if (id.x > _TerrainTriangleCount)
    {
        return;
    }

    int triStart = id.x * 3;
    float3 posA = _TerrainPositions[_TerrainTriangles[triStart]];
    float3 posB = _TerrainPositions[_TerrainTriangles[triStart + 1]];
    float3 posC = _TerrainPositions[_TerrainTriangles[triStart + 2]];

    float3 triangleCenterPos = (posA + posB + posC) / 3.0f;

    float2 randomSeed1 = float2(id.x, id.y);
    float2 randomSeed2 = float2(id.y, id.x);

    float scaleY = _Scale * randomRange(randomSeed1, _
    MinMaxBladeHeight.x, _MinMaxBladeHeight.y);

    float offsetX = randomRange(randomSeed1, -0.2f, 0.2f);
    float offsetZ = randomRange(randomSeed2, -0.2f, 0.2f);

    float4x4 grassTransformMatrix = float4x4
     (
        _Scale, 0, 0, triangleCenterPos.x + offsetX,
        0, scaleY,   0, triangleCenterPos.y,
        0, 0, _Scale, triangleCenterPos.z + offsetZ,
        0, 0, 0, 1
    );

    float4x4 randomRotationMatrix = rotationMatrixY(randomRange(randomSe
    ed1, 0.0f, TWO_PI));

    _TransformMatrices[id.x] = mul(_TerrainObjectToWorld,
    mul(grassTransformMatrix, randomRotationMatrix));
}
```

The compute shader gets run once per terrain triangle, so the `_TransformMatrices` buffer will contain one transformation matrix per terrain triangle. As we saw, our C# code then spawns one grass blade mesh instance for each of those transformation matrices. With that in mind, let's see the shader that is used to draw those grass blades.

The Grass Blade Shader

Start by creating a new shader file called "Grass.shader" and remove all its contents. Although this is a "conventional" graphics shader, it won't work the same as the other code shaders we have seen throughout the book. Typically, code shaders accept inputs to the vertex shader through the `appdata` struct (or similar), which we have created in each code shader so far. Unity automatically populates the members of that struct based on the vertex data attached to the mesh – positions, normals, UVs, and so on. However, we are passing these attributes inside `StructuredBuffer` instead, so we won't have any input struct. Let's see how it works. This shader still uses most of the same syntax as other HLSL code shaders, so let's set up a skeleton file to work from and then fill in the gaps.

Listing 12-61. Grass shader skeleton code

```
Shader "Examples/Grass"
{
    Properties { ... }

    SubShader
    {
        Tags
        {
            "RenderType" = "Opaque"
            "Queue" = "Geometry"
        }

        Pass
        {
            HLSLPROGRAM
            #pragma vertex vert
            #pragma fragment frag
```

```
            struct v2f
            {
                    float4 positionCS : SV_Position;
                    float2 uv : TEXCOORD0;
            };

            v2f vert ( ... ) { ... }

            float4 frag (v2f i) : SV_Target { ... }
            ENDHLSL

        }
    }
    Fallback Off
}
```

As you can see, we still use the same v2f struct as usual, as we are still passing data from the vertex shader to the fragment shader. It contains clip-space positions and UV coordinates, but you could add other variables such as normals if you wanted to incorporate lighting into this shader.

Next, let's add the properties. We'll use two Color properties for the base and tip of each grass blade, which we can declare in the usual way: declare them once inside the Properties block and then again in the HLSLPROGRAM block.

Listing 12-62. Declaring properties inside the Properties block

```
Properties
{
    _BaseColor("Base Color", Color) = (0, 0, 0, 1)
    _TipColor("Tip Color", Color) = (1, 1, 1, 1)
}
```

Declaring the properties inside HLSLPROGRAM looks slightly different between the built-in pipeline and URP. On top of the properties from the Properties block, we'll also add the three StructuredBuffer objects for the vertex positions, UVs, and transformation matrices that we received from the C# script and from the compute shader. They should be defined underneath the v2f struct.

Listing 12-63. Declaring properties in HLSL in the built-in pipeline

```
struct v2f { ... };

StructuredBuffer<float3> _Positions;
StructuredBuffer<float2> _UVs;
StructuredBuffer<float4x4> _TransformMatrices;

float4 _BaseColor;
float4 _TipColor;
```

Listing 12-64. Declaring properties in HLSL in URP

```
struct v2f { ... };

StructuredBuffer<float3> _Positions;
StructuredBuffer<float2> _UVs;
StructuredBuffer<float4x4> _TransformMatrices;

CBUFFER_START(UnityPerMaterial)
     float4 _BaseColor;
     float4 _TipColor;
CBUFFER_END
```

We'll also need to add tags and include files depending on which pipeline you are using. In the built-in pipeline, we'll only need to add the UnityCG.cginc include file.

Listing 12-65. The UnityCG.cginc include file for the grass blade effect in the built-in pipeline

```
#pragma fragment frag

#include "UnityCG.cginc"
```

When using URP, we'll need to include the RenderPipeline = UniversalPipeline tag in the SubShader Tags block, the LightMode = UniversalForward tag in the Pass Tags block, and the Core.hlsl include file.

Listing 12-66. The Core.hlsl include file and relevant tags for the grass blade effect in URP

```
SubShader
{
    Tags
    {
        "RenderType" = "Opaque"
        "Queue" = "Geometry"
        "RenderPipeline" = "UniversalPipeline"
    }

    Pass
    {
        Tags
        {
            "LightMode" = "UniversalForward"
        }

        HLSLPROGRAM
        #pragma vertex vert
        #pragma fragment frag

        #include "Packages/com.unity.render-pipelines.universal/
        ShaderLibrary/Core.hlsl"
```

Let's move on to the vert function. Unlike the other vertex shader functions we've seen so far, this one won't take an appdata as a parameter. Instead, it will have two parameters: the vertexID, which is unique for each vertex within a mesh and uses the SV_VertexID semantic, and the instanceID, which is different for each mesh being rendered and uses the SV_InstanceID semantic. These values will be used as indices to access the StructuredBuffer objects.

The vertex shader is surprisingly straightforward. Here's what it does:

- Access a transformation matrix from the compute shader via _TransformMatrices[instanceID]. There is one transformation matrix per instance.

- Create a v2f object.

- Access the vertex position from the _Positions buffer using vertexID as the index. Convert from float3 to float4 by adding a w component with a value of 1.

- Multiply the position by the transformation matrix. The position is now in world space.

- Convert from world space to clip space by multiplying the position by UNITY_MATRIX_VP.

- Get the correct UV coordinates from the _UVs buffer using vertexID as the index.

- Return the v2f.

Listing 12-67. The vert function for the grass blade effect

```
v2f vert (uint vertexID : SV_VertexID, uint instanceID : SV_InstanceID)
{
     float4x4 mat = _TransformMatrices[instanceID];

     v2f o;

     float4 pos = float4(_Positions[vertexID], 1.0f);
     pos = mul(mat, pos);
     o.positionCS = mul(UNITY_MATRIX_VP, pos);

     o.uv = _UVs[vertexID];

     return o;
}
```

The last thing to do is the fragment shader. Rasterization still happens between the vertex and fragment shaders, and we don't need to do anything different from usual to make this part of the shader work. The only thing the fragment shader does is use the UV's y-coordinate to interpolate between the _BaseColor and _TipColor.

Listing 12-68. The frag function for the grass blade effect

```
float4 frag (v2f i) : SV_Target
{
        return lerp(_BaseColor, _TipColor, i.uv.y);
}
```

With that, you should see grass blades appear on your terrain mesh. On my computer, with a well-used and aging Nvidia GTX 1070 graphics card, I was able to add many terrain meshes to the scene, each of which is running the C# script. In Figure 12-13, you will see *89.5 million* vertices being rendered at over 100 frames per second (less than 10ms processing time per frame) – that would be completely overkill for any project, but I hope that is indicative of the power of instancing!

Figure 12-13. *Although it is difficult to tell apart the grass blades at this distance, this screenshot contains millions of them*

There are many directions you could take this effect in, such as making the grass sway in the wind, which would require recalculating the transformation matrices every frame and providing a different matrix on any vertices touching the ground. You could also try mixing and matching different grass blade meshes, which would require multiple calls to `RenderPrimitivesIndexed`. This effect should give you a starting point, but the possibilities are endless!

Summary

Beyond the standard vertex and fragment shaders, there is a world of possibilities. Tessellation shaders help us increase the resolution of vertex-based effects by subdividing existing mesh geometry and creating new vertices between the old ones. Geometry shaders, while often limited by hardware or API support, are powerful shaders that can generate entirely new bits of geometry based on the properties of the existing geometry. Finally, compute shaders can be used for arbitrary processing of data on the GPU, but that doesn't mean they can't still be used for graphics purposes. Together with GPU instancing, we can generate data about thousands or even millions of vertices and generate new meshes on those vertices. Here's a rundown of what we learned in this chapter:

- The tessellation and geometry shader stages are optional stages that lie between the vertex and fragment shader stages.

- Tessellation involves creating new vertices between the existing ones, thereby subdividing the mesh into a higher-polygon version of itself. There are three major components:

  - The hull shader sets up the control points for the tessellator.

  - The patch constant function calculates the tessellation factors for the edges and the inside of each primitive.

  - The domain shader takes the new control points from the tessellator and interpolates vertex attributes from the original control points.

- The geometry shader takes a primitive shape and a stream of primitives and generates new primitives based on the properties of the input primitive and then adds them to the stream.

- Compute shaders can be used for arbitrary processing of large volumes of data on the GPU. They are best used for tasks where there are thousands or millions of small, similar tasks that are independent of one another. Graphics is an excellent example of such a problem.

  - Compute shaders can still be used for graphics-related problems, such as reading large amounts of mesh data and generating new data related to the mesh.

  - The `Graphics.RenderPrimitivesIndexed` method can be used to create thousands or millions of instances of a mesh, provided each instance uses the same shader.

CHAPTER 13

Profiling and Optimization

By now, if you've followed along with every chapter so far, you will be armed with the knowledge required to create a huge variety of shader effects. However, we have only focused on one aspect of shader writing so far: what shaders can do. Another hugely important aspect of shader writing is making your shaders run efficiently to ensure your game runs smoothly. It's all well and good writing beautiful shaders, but it's no use when they can't run well on your target hardware! In this chapter, we will explore ways of diagnosing performance issues and discuss common problems that arise when writing shaders. Then we'll look at solutions to those problems and some tricks you can use to eke out more frames from the hardware.

Profiling Shaders

Profiling an application is the act of measuring how much time it takes for each part of the application to run. Many engines, including Unity, have a built-in profiler that helps you visualize which parts of your game are taking the most time to process each frame. Taking a long time isn't inherently a bad thing – of course, some bits of code naturally take longer than others – but the profiler is an invaluable tool for finding parts of the code that are taking an abnormally large slice of the rendering time each frame. Let's explore how Unity's Profiler works.

To use the Profiler, we'll need to open the window, which we can do in two different ways:

- Right-click any active tab in the Editor and select *Add Tab* ➤ *Profiler*.

- Go to the *Window* tab on the Editor toolbar and pick *Analysis* ➤ *Profiler*.

© Daniel Ilett 2022
D. Ilett, *Building Quality Shaders for Unity®*, https://doi.org/10.1007/978-1-4842-8652-4_13

The Profiler window is dockable like any other window, so place it wherever you like. When you first open the window, it should look something like Figure 13-1.

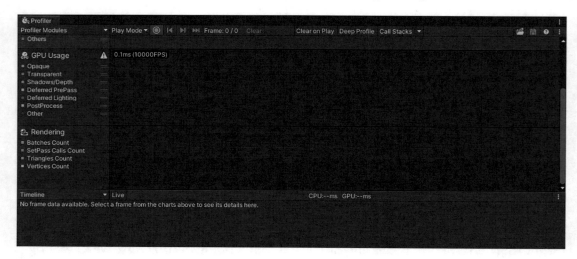

Figure 13-1. *An empty Profiler window*

On the left, you will see different modules, such as "CPU Usage," "GPU Usage," "Rendering," and so on. Using the *Profiler Modules* drop-down just above these sections, you can enable and disable as many of these modules as you want. Do experiment with these in your own time, but for now, I'll only be using the GPU Usage module so we can focus on shader-related performance. Keep the rest of the options on the top toolbar as the defaults, make sure the *Record Profiling Information* button – the little circle icon – is clicked so that it is red, and then go into Play Mode. When you do, the main body of the Profiler window will start to fill up with colorful graphs. If you pause the game, we can dig into which parts of the game took up the most processing time in a single frame. Figure 13-2 shows you what the Profiler looks like after running the game. I've left-clicked in the GPU Usage graph near the rightmost side of the window.

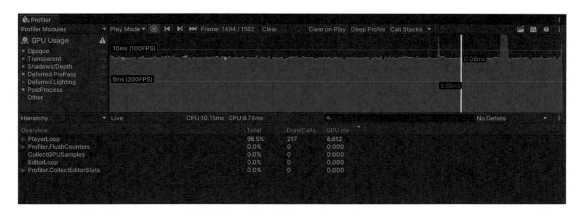

Figure 13-2. *An example capture from the Profiler window*

There's a lot to take in. The graph itself charts the time, in milliseconds (ms), that it takes for the GPU to process a single frame. On the frame I clicked, the GPU took 8.74ms in total to do everything it needed to during the frame. Panning left and right will give you information on the previous and next frames, respectively. You'll also see horizontal guidelines labeled with FPS values – in Figure 13-2, there are two: the top one is labeled "10ms (100FPS)," and the bottom one is labeled "5ms (200FPS)." These guidelines help you determine how far you are from your target frame rate. Almost all of the graph is color-coded reddish brown, meaning "Other."

You will also see an Overview section at the bottom with what appears to be a hierarchy of method calls, sorted from most to least intensive. In this case, each entry is related to the GPU usage, so each one displays the percentage of the frame that was taken up by that entry, as well as the number of draw calls made by that part of the code and the number of milliseconds taken to process it.

These entries can be clicked and expanded. For instance, in Figure 13-2, the PlayerLoop call took up a whopping 98.5% of the GPU's time this frame, which is suspiciously high! However, you might need to drill down several levels before you find the culprit within PlayerLoop. The Profiler window in Figure 13-2 was captured while I was running the compute shader grass example from the previous chapter in URP, with 144 instances of the terrain mesh, meaning there are over 30 million triangles in the scene at once – I expect my call to RenderPrimitivesIndexed to be taking up most of the GPU time this frame. Let's expand PlayerLoop a few levels, as seen in Figure 13-3.

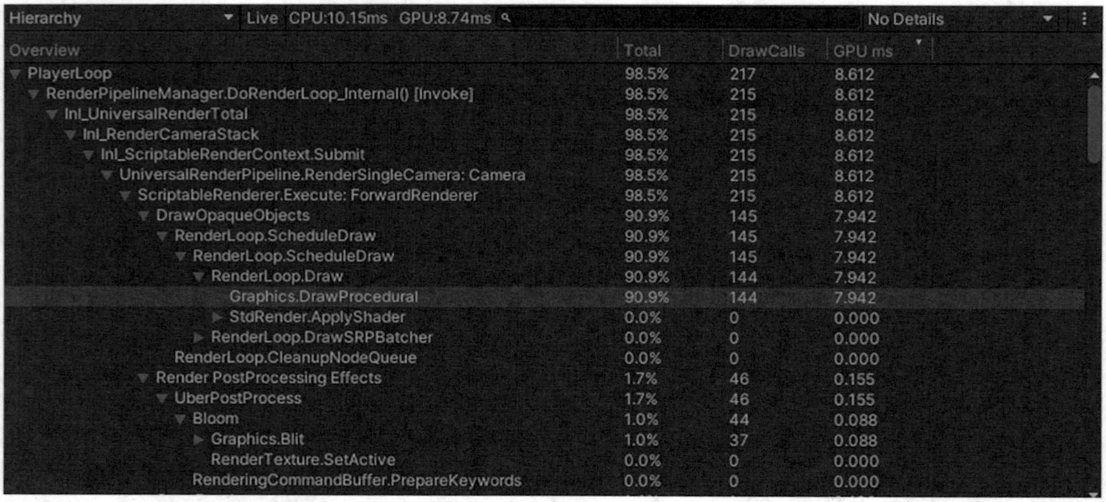

Figure 13-3. *Expanding an entry in the hierarchy exposes which sub-processes took the most computation time this frame*

Sometimes the names might be a bit long and not really mean much to you, so it helps to identify names you're familiar with. Since I'm on URP, `ScriptableRenderer.Execute: ForwardRenderer` stands out to me – I know that this must contain all GPU processing for the Forward Renderer. One of its child processes, `DrawOpaqueObjects`, took up 90.9% of the GPU time this frame – drilling down a few more layers brings us to `Graphics.DrawProcedural,` which can't be expanded further. This is responsible for 144 draw calls, which match the number of terrain instances exactly, so the grass meshes must be what is taking 90.9% of the GPU's processing power this frame. Although we actually called `Graphics.RenderPrimitivesInstanced` instead, Unity presumably calls `DrawProcedural` behind the scenes or uses the same profiler tag for both these method calls. Of course, in this example I already knew what would be taking up most of the processing time, but hopefully this example illustrates the basics of how to find problem spots in your own games. Next, we will discuss a few other considerations to make when profiling.

FPS or Milliseconds?

People often talk about the performance of a game in terms of its frames per second. The more frames you can see per second, the smoother the gameplay is, and the better the experience is for the player. Therefore, developers set a target frame rate to aim for to keep the game running smoothly, typically 60 or 30 frames per second (fps) for traditional games (this is a point of contention for many gamers!) and at least 90fps for VR games. However, this doesn't capture the full story.

Not all frames are created equal. Even if your game runs at an average frame rate of 60fps, you would notice *stuttering* if some of those frames took an abnormally long time to render. The "frames per second" measure is useless at identifying such frames. Instead, let's think about setting a 16.66ms budget for each frame – that's one-sixtieth of a second. Now, Unity must finish all calculations for each frame within 16.66ms. It's a subtle change, but now it becomes easier to think about what "smooth" gameplay means. After all, if, within 1 second, 59 of the frames each take 10ms to render and one of the frames somehow takes 410ms, this is still 60fps exactly, but that last frame has gone horrendously over budget. Therefore, if we want our game to run at 60fps, it is more useful from a profiling perspective to think about setting a frame time target of 16.66ms instead. To reach that number, just divide 1000ms by your target frame rate.

The other advantage of thinking in this way is that it becomes easier to compare the relative performance of your game under different conditions. Think about what it means for a game to take 1ms more GPU time to render each frame. "Taking 1ms longer to render a frame" always means the same thing, no matter what. Alternatively, if we used the frame rate to evaluate the game's performance, a 1ms slowdown would be the same as dropping from 60fps to 56.6fps. A 1ms slowdown is also the same as dropping from 30fps to 29.1fps or dropping from 120fps to 107.1fps. That 30fps slowdown looks tiny, but the 120fps slowdown seems huge. The point is all three of those scenarios look totally different from one another when talking in terms of frame rate, even though the *exact same* amount of extra work is being done per frame. Therefore, we'll talk in terms of frame time instead of frame rate.

You have now seen ways of using the Profiler to evaluate the performance of your game. In the next section, I'll introduce the Frame Debugger, another tool you can use to identify problems in your game.

The Frame Debugger

The Frame Debugger is an important tool in your arsenal that may help with debugging issues with your shaders. Unlike the Profiler, whose purpose is to help you identify how computationally intensive each part of the game is, the Frame Debugger breaks down each draw call in a single frame to tell you exactly what is being rendered, in order, and what keywords, properties, alpha test settings, and clip settings and which shader are active at every step of the process. This is of course useful for identifying why a shader isn't rendering properly, but it can also be used, among other things, to find draw calls being issued for objects that should have been culled or to find draw calls that could not be batched together. Figure 13-4 shows an example frame captured in the Frame Debugger.

Tip   Batching draw calls together typically improves the performance of your game, especially on mobile. With no optimizations, Unity would issue a new draw call for every object in the game, which requires setup on both the CPU and GPU sides. The setup can sometimes take longer than actually performing the draw command! However, batching can draw several objects in one draw call if they share the same mesh and material, which requires much less CPU-side preparation.

Figure 13-4. *The Frame Debugger window*

To enable the Frame Debugger window, go to *Window* ➤ *Analysis* ➤ *Frame Debugger*. It can be docked anywhere you want, like any other Unity window. To begin with, the window will be mostly empty, with an Enable button in the top left. Go into Play Mode; then, at any point, pause the game; and then click the Enable button in the Frame Debugger window to bring up the hierarchy view in Figure 13-4. Let's use the Frame Debugger to identify a problem in my game and fix it.

Identifying Problems with the Frame Debugger

Let's work with an alternative version of the grass effect. This time, I'm going to place thousands of GameObjects in the scene, each of which will use the same grass blade mesh and the same basic shader to color the blades (please don't do that in a real game – this is just an example, after all). I'm using URP for this example, which means the SRP Batcher can be used to batch together any objects that use the same mesh and the same shader, as long as the shader itself is compatible with the batcher. The result, as seen in Figure 13-5, appears similar to the compute shader instanced approach we used in Chapter 12. However, performance seems sluggish. The Profiler reports that the GPU takes 20.62ms to process the main thread – above the budget of 16.66ms we're aiming for – and the GPU thread takes 12.07ms. What gives?

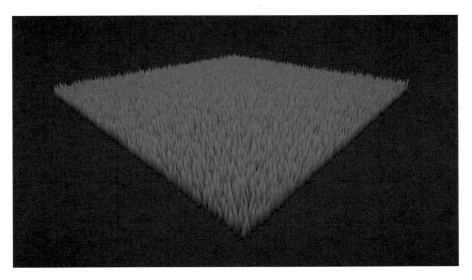

Figure 13-5. *A grassy field, where each blade is a separate GameObject*

When we run the game and look at the Frame Debugger and expand a couple of entries in the hierarchy, as seen in Figure 13-6, we can see what the issue might be. The `DrawOpaqueObjects` event is responsible for 9040 draw calls, which incidentally are how many grass blade meshes I added to the scene. If we expand that and its `RenderLoop.` `Draw` child, then each grass blade is listed in a separate draw call. I'll select one of those and look at the information on the right-hand side of the window, where the shader, alpha testing settings, and properties are listed.

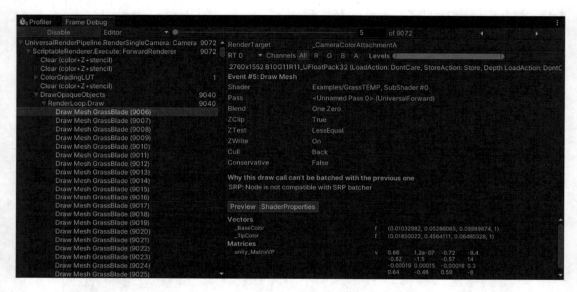

Figure 13-6. *The Frame Debugger breaks down exactly what is happening during each draw call during a frame*

There is a lot of information here, so it can be difficult to know exactly what to look for when diagnosing an issue like this, but let's recall some things we know about our scene. We know that each GameObject uses the same grass blade mesh and that they are all using the same material, which means these objects should be batched together while rendering. Given that there are 9040 draw calls for opaque objects (and the grass blades are the only opaque objects in the viewport), that is not currently the case. In Figure 13-6, I've selected one of the grass mesh draw calls. On the right-hand side of the window, in roughly the middle, there's a string of text that reads "Why this draw call can't be batched with the previous one, SRP: Node is not compatible with SRP batcher." That seems explanatory enough!

After digging into my shader, I discovered that the variables inside the HLSLPROGRAM block were not in a CBUFFER. After remedying the problem and running the game again, the Profiler shows that the CPU and GPU are taking 10.50ms and 2.82ms, respectively, far below the 16.66ms budget. Let's also see what the Frame Debugger says.

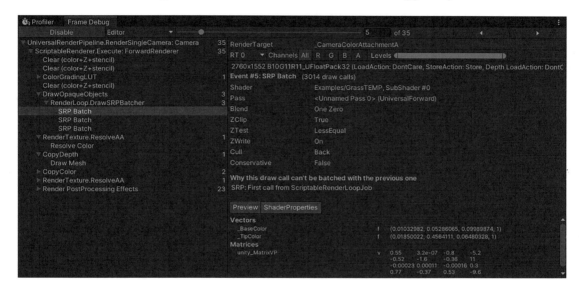

Figure 13-7. *The Frame Debugger also displays draw call batches whenever they are used and shows you how many draw calls were saved by being batched into one*

In Figure 13-7, the DrawOpaqueObjects event now takes up only three draw calls. It's still not down to one, so if we expand it, we can see that there are three SRP batches. Clicking each one displays the number of draw calls inside the batch on the right-hand-side information window near the top; these three batches contain 3014, 3014, and 3012 draw calls, respectively, which add up to 9040. Therefore, with the Frame Debugger, we can confirm that batching is working as intended. Now that you're aware of the Profiler and Frame Debugger and know how to use them to diagnose issues with your shaders, let's see some common pitfalls you may fall into when writing shaders and see ways of avoiding them.

Common Pitfalls and How to Fix Them

When developing shaders in Unity, there are some common problems that you will probably encounter that make your shaders less efficient than they could be. The good news is that, since they are so common, there are similarly common fixes! In this section, I'll go over a few of these problems and outline strategies for dealing with them. It's important to remember that these are not one-size-fits-all solutions and that you might come across scenarios that counterintuitively run less efficiently with these strategies.

Tip   When profiling shaders, it's a good idea to start with the most computationally expensive ones. It's easy to get into a mindset of wanting to squeeze every bit of performance out of *every* shader you write, and while it's great to have optimizations like these ones on your mind earlier rather than later, you will also want to avoid wasting hours and hours making your least expensive shader 5% more efficient. After all, once you've optimized the most expensive shaders first and ended up well under your GPU time budget, the rest of your time is most likely better spent on other parts of the game. It's a matter of perspective!

Overdraw

Overdraw occurs whenever we draw an object to the frame buffer and then later we draw over that pixel's color value with another color. With opaque objects, overdraw happens whenever a pixel passes the depth test, but an object had previously been rendered at that pixel this frame, so the color value is swapped out for the new one. With transparent objects, the process is similar, except transparency almost always results in overdraw by its nature – transparents are drawn after opaques, so every time a transparent pixel is blended with the existing pixel, that's overdraw. So why could overdraw cause problems?

Every time Unity needs to draw a color value into the frame buffer, it takes time and memory bandwidth to move the color data from the GPU to the frame buffer. It follows, then, that failing a depth test and not rendering anything is always quicker than passing a depth test and drawing to the frame buffer. Therefore, to combat overdraw, opaques are usually drawn starting with those closest to the camera and ending with those furthest away. The idea is that objects in the front obscure objects behind them, so drawing the closest object first and culling objects behind it is faster than rendering the hidden objects to the frame buffer, just to overwrite their values later anyway. That said, oddly shaped objects can still cause overdraw.

However, I'd advise you to keep in mind these three problem spots for overdraw: transparent objects (especially if you have many in the scene), particle effects, and post-processing shaders. Here's why:

- As I mentioned, transparent materials always incur overhead due to overdraw. That's not an inherently bad thing, but you should be careful to minimize cases where several transparent objects overlay each other on the screen. You can also try reducing the size of transparent objects if possible. Figure 13-8 illustrates the impact that overlapping objects may have in terms of overdraw.

- Particle effects also exhibit overdraw due to the relatively high number of objects, although particles are typically small so the amount of overdraw may be minimal in some cases. If you want to improve the performance of particle effects, try building the same effect with the minimal number of particles. Swapping out an effect with large numbers of tiny particles with an effect that uses fewer larger particles could reduce the amount of overdraw while still filling the space with particles.

- Post-processing effects also always exhibit overdraw because they render over the entire screen (unless you downsample the screen texture for the effect). Again, this may not be a problem, but you should be wary about adding a large stack of effects, because each one will add a level of overdraw.

Figure 13-8. *Overlapping transparent cubes rendered with 25% opacity black. The darkest parts of the image are where the most overdraw occurs, because the cubes' colors are being blended*

Take extra care on mobile platforms that tend to be heavily constrained by memory bandwidth. Next, let's talk about ways of reducing the performance impact of some fragment shaders.

Expensive Fragment Shaders

The vertex shader is unlikely to be a major source of performance issues in your game due to the relative difference in the total number of vertices in the scene compared with the total number of pixels or fragments on-screen. Put it this way: a 1920×1080-pixel screen contains just over two million pixels, but you rarely have even close to two million vertices. If you did, then you'd end up rendering multiple vertices per pixel, which is obviously wasteful. Therefore, you should try and minimize the amount of processing that you do in the fragment shader wherever possible because it will run a comparatively high number of times. This section will identify different problems related to the fragment shader and explore possible solutions. Bear in mind, however, that it will not always be possible to considerably cut down the performance impact – some effects are expensive by nature.

Moving Calculations to the Vertex Shader

Sometimes it is possible to move calculations from the fragment shader to the vertex shader. As I mentioned, far fewer vertices are typically processed for an object than fragments, so it follows that moving expensive operations to the vertex shader will reduce the amount of computation time. This won't be applicable in all cases. Try to find expensive calculations that don't require data about the fragment, such as interpolated UVs for a texture sample. Good candidates involve trigonometric functions such as sin, cos, or tan and other mathematical functions like sqrt and exp. Let's see an example. For this effect, the fragment shader builds a color in HSV space that cycles through the hue over time according to a sine wave and then converts the color to RGB space and outputs it. It's like the hue cycle script we wrote in Chapter 9, except now everything is implemented in the shader directly, and the hue cycles in a slightly different manner – see Figure 13-9.

Figure 13-9. *The hue cycles from red to orange and all the way to purple and then cycles in the reverse order to red again*

Let's see how this optimization works in shader code and then again in Shader Graph.

Moving Calculations in Shader Code

Here are the most important sections of the code.

Listing 13-1. A sine wave–based hue cycling shader effect

```
struct v2f
{
    float4 positionCS : SV_Position;
};
```

```
float3 hsv2rgb(float3 inHSV)
{
    float4 K = float4(1.0, 2.0 / 3.0, 1.0 / 3.0, 3.0);
    float3 P = abs(frac(inHSV.xxx + K.xyz) * 6.0 - K.www);
    return inHSV.z * lerp(K.xxx, saturate(P - K.xxx), inHSV.y);
}

v2f vert (appdata v)
{
    v2f o;
    o.positionCS = TransformObjectToHClip(v.positionOS.xyz);
    return o;
}

float4 frag (v2f i) : SV_Target
{
    float3 hsvColor = float3(0.0f, 1.0f, 1.0f);
    hsvColor.r = (sin(_Time.y) + 1.0f) * 0.5f;
    float3 rgbColor = hsv2rgb(hsvColor);

    return float4(rgbColor, 1.0f);
}
```

The code for the hsv2rgb function is taken from Unity's Colorspace Conversion node in Shader Graph. The fragment shader contains a sin function that is running for every fragment, but the value of _Time.y remains constant for each fragment, so it is wasteful to calculate it here. Instead, we can calculate the color in the vertex shader and send it to the fragment shader via the v2f struct. Here are the changes we need to make:

- Add an extra interpolator called hueShiftColor to the v2f struct. I'll use the COLOR semantic for it.

- Move the color calculation code to the vertex shader and use the result for the new hueShiftColor member of v2f.

- Remove the color calculation code from the fragment shader and return the value of hueShiftColor instead.

> **Tip**   When I need to write a shader function and I'm aware there is a Shader
> Graph node for that functionality, a trick I like to use is to go to the documentation
> page for that node. Unity lists a Generated Code Example for most nodes, so I copy
> that code and tweak it for my needs. I've used this trick a few times throughout the
> book, including here, for the `hsv2rgb` function.

Listing 13-2. Changes to the hue cycling shader effect

```
struct v2f
{
      float4 positionCS : SV_Position;
      float4 hueShiftColor : COLOR;
};

v2f vert (appdata v)
{
      v2f o;
      o.positionCS = TransformObjectToHClip(v.positionOS.xyz);

      float3 hsvColor = float3(0.0f, 1.0f, 1.0f);
      hsvColor.r = (sin(_Time.y) + 1.0f) * 0.5f;
      float3 rgbColor = hsv2rgb(hsvColor);

      o.hueShiftColor = float4(rgbColor, 1.0f);

      return o;
}
float4 frag (v2f i) : SV_Target
{
      return i.hueShiftColor;
}
```

By moving the calculations to the vertex shader in this alternative version, we'll be
doing far fewer calculations overall because there are fewer vertices than fragments. Let's
also see how this can be achieved in Shader Graph.

Moving Calculations in Shader Graph

We can also do this optimization with Shader Graph, but *only* in versions 12.0 and above (for Unity 2021.2 or later), by using custom interpolators. Figure 13-10 shows the same effect implemented in Shader Graph.

Note   There is no way to implement this optimization in Shader Graph in versions prior to Unity 2021.2 due to the absence of custom interpolators. There is no other way to pass custom data from the vertex shader to the fragment shader.

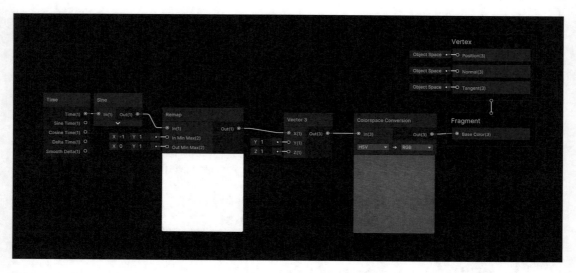

Figure 13-10.   *A Shader Graph for cycling the hue according to a sine wave*

All the calculations for building the HSV color and converting it to RGB are being done in the fragment stage. However, it is possible to move them to the vertex stage. Let's add a custom interpolator of type `Vector3` called *HueShiftColor* to the vertex stage of the master stack. Then we can connect the existing `Colorspace Conversion` node to the *HueShiftColor* block instead of the *Base Color* output block (you may need to delete the existing output wire first, as Shader Graph will not let you connect nodes to both output stages, even temporarily). Lastly, we can add a `HueShiftColor` node and connect it to the *Base Color* fragment output. Figure 13-11 shows how these nodes and blocks should appear.

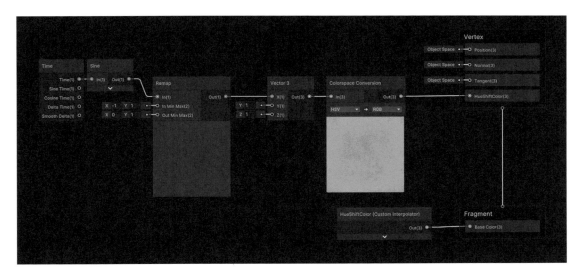

Figure 13-11. *Using a custom interpolator means we offset calculations to the vertex shader*

Keep an eye out in your own shaders for cases where you are doing unnecessary calculations in the fragment shader. Furthermore, you might find cases where moving the code results in a slightly different appearance, but the performance savings could be worth sacrificing visual quality slightly. Next, let's see another case where your fragment shader performance could be impacted.

Branching Logic

One piece of "common wisdom" passed around shader circles is "never do conditional branching in shaders." The idea behind this advice is that GPUs are bad at branching, so you should just never use branches in your shader code if you can help it. However, this is far from true, because not all branches are created equal. This topic is complicated, but I'll provide an overview here.

Let's think up an example shader and reason about what the shader compiler will do with our code. We'll have a property called `_ShouldInvertColor` – it's a `float` whose value will either be 0 or 1, which will be set on the material. When the value is above 0.5, all colors output by the shader will be inverted. Otherwise, they will remain unchanged. Here's the fragment shader.

Listing 13-3. Conditional inversion based on a property

```
float4 frag (v2f i) : SV_Target
{
      float4 outputColor = _BaseColor;

      if (_ShouldInvertColor > 0.5f)
      {
            outputColor = 1.0f - outputColor;
      }

      return outputColor;
}
```

In this fragment shader, we are using an if statement to check the value of _ShouldInvertColor and inverting the output color if it is above 0.5. In this code, there is an *implicit* else block that does nothing if _ShouldInvertColor is less than or equal to 0.5. What does the GPU do when it encounters code like this?

The GPU processes fragments concurrently by assigning the calculations for each fragment to a different thread. The threads are organized into groups called *wavefronts*, where one wavefront processes pixels that are spatially close to each other. When all threads in a single wavefront take the same path through a conditional statement, there is little to no impact on the performance of the shader, but if some pixels take one path and other pixels take the other path, then the GPU is forced to either compute the appropriate branch for each pixel (which is slow) or compute both branches for all pixels and pick the correct value (which is also slow).

What we have in Listing 13-3 is the first scenario, where all threads choose the same path through the code. Since we are using a property, whose value will not change throughout a frame, every single thread can use the same value for _ShouldInvertColor, so there is little additional impact to performance. While this is not a hard-and-fast rule, branching on uniform properties like this is typically safe to do (but you can still profile your shaders to check for issues).

Let's look at a second example. In this example, instead of using a property, a random float between 0 and 1 is generated in the fragment shader, with a seed value based on the fragment position and time. If the value is above 0.5, we invert the output color. The shader doesn't look great, but this is just a demonstration!

Listing 13-4. Conditional inversion based on random values

```
float rand(float2 seed)
{
     return frac(sin(dot(seed, float2(12.9898, 78.233)))*43758.5453);
}

float4 frag (v2f i) : SV_Target
{
     float4 outputColor = _BaseColor;

     float randomValue = rand(i.positionCS.xy + _Time.y);

     if (randomValue > 0.5f)
     {
          outputColor = 1.0f - outputColor;
     }

     return outputColor;
}
```

This code has the effect of scrambling the color output, as seen in Figure 13-12.

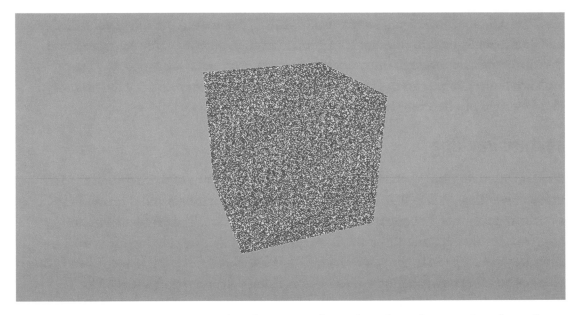

Figure 13-12. *This shader randomly inverts the color of pixels over time based on their position*

Now, many adjacent pixels will need to traverse different paths through the code, as roughly half the pixels get inverted. This is somewhat of a worst-case scenario for the GPU, because now it has no way to guarantee ahead of time which branch each thread should evaluate. This will certainly incur a performance penalty. Broadly speaking, this is the type of branching to look out for – you may want to consider rewriting the code in a way that doesn't require a branch.

That said, for a small fragment shader like this one, the code inside the branch is not that long. You might decide that the effort required to remove the branch and reformulate the code is not worth the potential performance gains – generally, the more code you put in a branch, the larger the performance impact will be. You might also have branching code where nearby pixels almost always traverse the same way through the branch, which has a minimal impact on the performance.

Caution   In Shader Graph, the `Branch` node *always* evaluates both sides of the branch. In that case, try to push as much code as possible outside of the branched logic to reduce the performance impact. Although not all shaders can be reformulated to remove branching, it's extra important to try and do so in Shader Graph.

The main idea I want you to take away is this: if you write a branch in your shader and you're really unsure whether it's a good idea, then *always profile your game* and decide for yourself whether the branch impacts performance too much. Next, let's look at a few tricks we can use to pack extra data into textures to reduce the memory bandwidth in our shaders related to texturing.

Texture Packing

Shaders often require grayscale textures. The naïve approach to writing such shaders involves sending a full RGBA texture with all four color channels and then reading, say, the red channel that encodes the relevant information. The problem with this approach is that the other three channels may be wasted if we're using more than one such grayscale texture in the same shader. After all, what's the point in using two RGBA textures, totaling eight channels, if we're only using two of those channels? Couldn't we just use one texture and include the data in the red and green channels?

Let's see an example. For this effect, we'll do the following:

- A base texture is used to apply an albedo color to the object. The shader is opaque, so this will use the red, green, and blue channels of the texture, but not the alpha channel.

- An emission mask texture is also applied to the object. This is a special emission texture we'll use to control which portions of the object have emissive light. The texture is grayscale – whenever it is white, it amplifies the base color to become emissive, and when it is black, there is no emission.

- An emission power property is used to control the maximum strength of the emission.

By now you're aware of how we can set up properties, so I'll skip straight to the fragment shader and explain what's going on here.

Listing 13-5. The emission mask fragment shader

```
float4 frag (v2f i) : SV_Target
{
    float3 baseColor = tex2D(_BaseTex, i.uv).rgb;
    float3 emissiveColor = baseColor * pow(2, _EmissionPower);

    float emission = tex2D(_EmissionMask, i.uv).r;

    float3 outputColor = lerp(baseColor, emissiveColor, emission);

    return float4(outputColor, 1.0f);
}
```

In this example, we are using two texture samples on two textures: one is used to grab the baseColor of the object from the _BaseTex, from which we can also derive the emissiveColor, and the other is used to access an emission mask value, emission, which we use to pick between baseColor and emissiveColor.

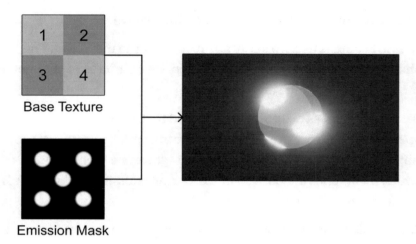

Figure 13-13. *An emission mask is used to determine which portions of the base texture should have their color ramped up dramatically to produce a light emission effect*

The problem here, as you might have seen, is that we are using two textures to sample four color channels in total, but you could pack four channels worth of data into a single texture. That has two effects. Firstly, the shader takes up more GPU memory than it needs to, and the build size of the game is higher than it could be, both of which are space considerations. Secondly, we're performing two texture samples for each fragment, which would be wasteful if we could use just one instead because texture sampling takes time. Let's remedy this by placing the grayscale emission mask in the alpha channel of _BaseTex. The specifics of doing this depend on your chosen graphics program, so you will need to figure out how to do that yourself. This process is called *packing*.

Once all the data has been packed into one texture, we can modify the shader to match. We no longer have an _EmissionMask texture, so we'll only sample _BaseTex and separate the two required bits of data from the sample. The fragment shader is now more efficient due to only needing one texture sample.

Listing 13-6. The emission mask fragment shader with texture packing

```
float4 frag (v2f i) : SV_Target
{
    float4 textureSample = tex2D(_BaseTex, i.uv);

    float3 baseColor = textureSample.rgb;
    float3 emissiveColor = baseColor * pow(2, _EmissionPower);

    float emission = textureSample.a;

    float3 outputColor = lerp(baseColor, emissiveColor, emission);

    return float4(outputColor, 1.0f);
}
```

By comparing Figure 13-13 to Figure 13-14, you can see that the shader still gives the same result if the value of _EmissionPower doesn't change.

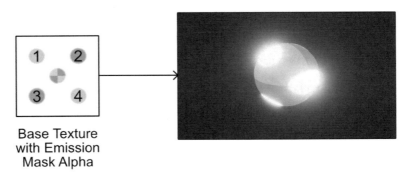

Base Texture
with Emission
Mask Alpha

Figure 13-14. *The emission mask is now baked into the alpha channel of the base texture*

This technique isn't an automatic win for all shaders, however. The biggest drawback is that the two textures are now "fused" together, so you have lost the ability to swap out just the base texture or just the emission mask without touching the other. You'll always need to go into your graphics program and redo the packing step whenever you want to swap in a new mask or new base texture. If you don't need to reuse these textures in other shaders for other objects, then this drawback might not matter to you.

Summary

Optimization is an important step in shader design, but we can't start adding optimizations before being sure they will provide a performance benefit to our game. That's where the Unity Profiler and Frame Debugger windows come in. These tools provide a means for us to identify problems with rendering and confirm that any optimizations we make have a meaningful impact on the game's performance. Although it is always useful to have a few optimization tricks up your sleeve, you should *always* profile the game before and after to make sure it did what you expect – after all, optimizations that work for one platform may have the opposite effect on another platform. Here's what we learned in this chapter:

- The Profiler window displays how long each frame of the game took to render in an easy-to-digest graphical format and then breaks down each frame into individual function calls (on the CPU side) and draw commands (on the GPU side).

- The Profiler contains many modules that let you profile different parts of the game, such as the CPU, GPU, memory, physics, and more. Each can be turned on and off at will.

- It's more useful to talk about performance in terms of frame time, in milliseconds, than frame rate, in frames per second. Relying only on FPS can result in a distorted view of the relative performance of your game.

- The Frame Debugger can be used to further break down each draw call during a frame. It is especially useful for finding draw calls that could be batched, as Unity provides the reason batching failed.

- Overdraw occurs when a frame buffer value is overridden during a frame, which could cause slowdown. Transparent objects, post-processing effects, and particles are especially susceptible to overdraw.

- We can optimize the shaders in our games in several ways:

    - Moving calculations from the fragment shader to the vertex shader

    - Removing costly dynamic branches wherever possible

    - Packing multiple grayscale textures into a single texture by moving individual color channels around

CHAPTER 14

Shader Recipes for Your Games

You've almost made it to the end of the book – congratulations! By now, your shader technique arsenal should be full to bursting. With the things we have learned throughout the book, you should be well equipped to make shader effects of all kinds in your own games. However, there are many shader effects and tidbits I keep coming back to, so I decided the final chapter of this book should unleash a handful of important case studies that you will be able to build on in your own games.

World-Space Scan Post-Process

When writing an image effect shader, you typically have access to a quad mesh that covers the width and height of the screen and a texture that was rendered by the camera. A result of this is that you don't have easy access to a way to get the world space of the objects in the scene, but this would be useful for many types of effect, such as a world scanner post-process or high-quality outlines. In this section, we will reverse engineer the world-space position of each pixel in the scene using the depth texture and then use it to build shader effects that couldn't be done outside of world space. As with the other post-process effects we saw in Chapter 11, the code will differ significantly between the built-in pipeline, URP, and HDRP, and we will be unable to write the effect in Shader Graph.

© Daniel Ilett 2022
D. Ilett, *Building Quality Shaders for Unity*®, https://doi.org/10.1007/978-1-4842-8652-4_14

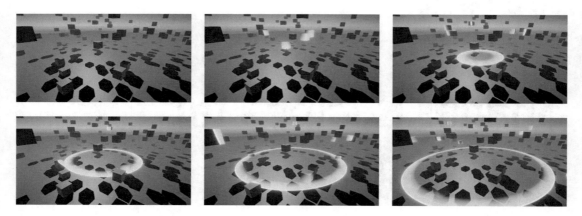

Figure 14-1. *The world-space scan effect. The effect starts small (top left) and gets progressively larger over time (from left to right, top to bottom)*

Note   The scan effect as I've written it for each pipeline will eventually continue until it reaches the skybox. That might be what you want, or you could add code to cut off the scan at certain depth values or fade the scan over time through scripting.

Across the three pipelines, we will use the same set of properties to control the effect, although they may take slightly different formats in each pipeline. The properties are as follows:

- `bool enabled` – The scan will only be visible and propagate across the scene when this is set to true.

- `Vector3 scanOrigin` – The world-space origin point of the scan. The scan will start here and travel outward away from this point.

- `float scanSpeed` – The speed, in meters, of the scan when it is enabled.

- `float scanDist` – The distance, in meters, that the scan has traveled from the origin point.

- `float scanWidth` – The width, in meters, of the scan visuals. We'll be using a ramp texture, so this value represents how much that texture gets stretched across the world during the scan.

- `Texture2D overlayRampTex` – The ramp texture representing the scan visuals. This texture is x-by-1, meaning that only the horizontal data matters.

- `Color overlayColor` – An additional tint color applied to the overlay texture. Using the `ColorUsage` attribute, we can make the color picker HDR-compatible and alpha-compatible.

With this in mind, let's delve into writing the effect for the built-in pipeline first.

World-Space Scan in the Built-In Pipeline

As we saw in Chapter 11, post-processing shaders come in two parts: the scripting side and the shader side. We'll be starting with the scripting side first.

World-Space Scan C# Scripting in the Built-In Pipeline

The world scan effect works by calculating the distance between the world-space position of each part of the scene and the origin point of the scan. Typical mesh shaders can get the world-space position of a vertex or fragment by multiplying the object-space position by the `_ObjectToWorld` matrix (also called `UNITY_MATRIX_M`), but that isn't possible in image effect shaders because we don't have access to the original object-space positions of each mesh in the scene. Image effect shaders only have access to a full-screen quad mesh, so we need to "reverse engineer" the data from the depth texture. Therefore, we will calculate the clip-space position of each pixel and then use the inverse view-projection matrix to obtain the original world-space position. I mention all this here rather than in the shader section because we'll need to pass the inverse view-projection matrix to the shader manually.

Note   As we'll see, in URP or HDRP, Unity declares a matrix for use in shaders called `UNITY_MATRIX_I_VP`, short for "inverse view-projection," which does precisely what we want. Frustratingly, this matrix isn't automatically available in built-in pipeline shaders, so we must create it in C# and pass it to the shader manually.

Start by creating a new C# script named "WorldScanEffect.cs". This script can be attached to any GameObject, but I prefer to attach it to the main camera. First, we will deal with the effect's properties. Alongside those listed when I first described the world scan effect, we also need private references to a material (which we'll use to apply the image effect) and a camera (which will be the main camera). In Listing 14-1, you'll see these properties, with descriptive tooltips, plus the empty method signatures for the rest of the class. We'll fill these methods in next.

Listing 14-1. The WorldScanEffect class and variables

```csharp
using UnityEngine;

public class WorldScanEffect : MonoBehaviour
{
        [Tooltip("Is the effect active?")]
        public new bool enabled = false;

        [Tooltip("The world space origin point of the scan.")]
        public Vector3 scanOrigin = Vector3.zero;

        [Tooltip("How quickly, in units per second, the scan propagates.")]
        public float scanSpeed = 1.0f;

        [Tooltip("How far, in meters, the scan has travelled from the origin.")]
        public float scanDist = 0.0f;

        [Tooltip("The distance, in meters, the scan texture gets applied
        over.")]
        public float scanWidth = 1.0f;

        [Tooltip("An x-by-1 ramp texture representing the scan color.")]
        public Texture2D overlayRampTex;

        [ColorUsage(true, true)]
        [Tooltip("An additional HDR color tint applied to the scan.")]
        public Color overlayColor = Color.white;

        private Material mat;
        private Camera cam;
```

```
    private void Start() { ... }
    private void Update() { ... }
    private void StartScan(Vector3 origin) { ... }
    private void StopScan() { ... }
    private void OnRenderImage(RenderTexture src, RenderTexture
    dst) { ... }

}
```

In Start, we must create a material instance and find the main camera. I'll also ensure the depth texture mode of the camera is set appropriately so that it generates a depth texture, because we'll be needing it in the shader. We haven't yet written the shader, so Shader.Find will fail to actually find anything if you run the code.

Listing 14-2. Creating the effect material and finding the main camera

```
private void Start()
{
    mat = new Material(Shader.Find("Examples/ImageEffect/WorldScan"));
    cam = Camera.main;

    cam.depthTextureMode = DepthTextureMode.Depth;
}
```

Next comes the Update method. To quickly test the scan, we'll use some of Unity's default input functionality to start the scan at the current position or stop the scan entirely. We will also increment the value of scanDist each frame so the scan can propagate further.

Listing 14-3. Starting, stopping, and propagating the scan

```
private void Update()
{
    if (Input.GetButtonDown("Fire1"))
    {
        StartScan(transform.position);
    }
    else if (Input.GetButtonDown("Fire2"))
```

```
    {
            StopScan();
    }

    if (enabled)
    {
            scanDist += scanSpeed * Time.deltaTime;
    }
}
```

The StartScan and StopScan methods themselves are very simple. They both set the value of enabled as appropriate, but StartScan also resets the scan distance and origin point.

Listing 14-4. The StartScan and StopScan methods

```
private void StartScan(Vector3 origin)
{
        enabled = true;
        scanOrigin = origin;
        scanDist = 0.0f;
}

private void StopScan()
{
        enabled = false;
}
```

And, finally, the juicy bit: the OnRenderImage method, where we apply the image effect. First, the method checks whether enabled is set to true and whether a ramp texture has been set – if either is not the case, then we won't apply the effect material. Otherwise, we'll calculate the inverse view-projection matrix by grabbing the view matrix and projection matrix separately from the camera, multiplying them, and then taking the inverse. Then, as we saw in other post-process scripts, we'll set all the shader properties and call Graphics.Blit to apply the effect with the material.

Listing 14-5. The OnRenderImage method

```
private void OnRenderImage(RenderTexture src, RenderTexture dst)
{
    if(!enabled || overlayRampTex == null)
    {
        Graphics.Blit(src, dst);
        return;
    }

    Matrix4x4 view = cam.worldToCameraMatrix;
    Matrix4x4 proj = GL.GetGPUProjectionMatrix(cam.
    projectionMatrix, false);

    Matrix4x4 clipToWorld = Matrix4x4.Inverse(proj * view);

    mat.SetMatrix("_ClipToWorld", clipToWorld);
    mat.SetVector("_ScanOrigin", scanOrigin);
    mat.SetFloat("_ScanDist", scanDist);
    mat.SetFloat("_ScanWidth", scanWidth);
    mat.SetTexture("_OverlayRampTex", overlayRampTex);
    mat.SetColor("_OverlayColor", overlayColor);

    Graphics.Blit(src, dst, mat);
}
```

Note   The camera's `projectionMatrix` member variable is different from the actual projection matrix that is uploaded to the GPU, hence the usage of the `GL.GetGPUProjectionMatrix` method. It's easy to overlook that and accidentally use the `projectionMatrix` variable directly, which will likely cause errors.

The script is now complete, so we can move on the shader file.

World-Space Scan Shader in the Built-In Pipeline

This is a rare case where the URP and HDRP versions of this shader may actually be slightly *easier* to write than the built-in pipeline version, because those two render pipelines have some handy library functions for calculating the world-space position that are unavailable in the built-in pipeline. However, let's not worry about that! Start by creating a new shader file called "WorldScan.shader" and fill it with the following code.

Listing 14-6. The WorldScan shader skeleton code

```
Shader "Examples/ImageEffect/WorldScan"
{
    Properties { ... }
    SubShader
    {
        Pass
        {
            HLSLPROGRAM
            #pragma vertex vert
            #pragma fragment frag

            #include "UnityCG.cginc"

            struct appdata
            {
                float4 positionOS : POSITION;
                float2 uv : TEXCOORD0;
            };

            struct v2f
            {
                float2 uv : TEXCOORD0;
                float4 positionCS : SV_POSITION;
            };

            v2f vert (appdata v)
```

```
        {
            v2f o;
            o.positionCS = UnityObjectToClipPos
            (v.positionOS.xyz);
            o.uv = v.uv;
            return o;
        }

        float4 frag (v2f i) : SV_Target { ... }
        ENDHLSL
    }
  }
}
```

Let's go through the usual procedure and start by filling in the shader properties, which match up with the variables we added to the C# script. Although post-processing shaders don't require you to add properties to the Properties block, I still like to include them there, and of course, we must add them inside the HLSLPROGRAM block. I'll add them underneath the v2f struct. The _ClipToWorld variable should only be added to the HLSLPROGRAM block, as should the _CameraDepthTexture, which is automatically generated by any camera that is set to record depth information (as ours is).

Listing 14-7. Adding properties to the Properties block for the world scan effect in the built-in pipeline

```
Properties
{
    _MainTex("Texture", 2D) = "white" {}
    _ScanOrigin("Origin Point", Vector) = (0, 0, 0, 0)
    _ScanDist("Scan Distance", Float) = 0
    _ScanWidth("Scan Width", Float) = 1
    _OverlayRampTex("Overlay Ramp", 2D) = "white" {}
    [HDR] _OverlayColor("Overlay Color", Color) = (1, 1, 1, 1)
}
```

Listing 14-8. Adding properties to the HLSLPROGRAM block

```
struct v2f{ ... };

sampler2D _MainTex;
sampler2D _OverlayRampTex;
sampler2D _CameraDepthTexture;

float3 _ScanOrigin;
float _ScanDist;
float _ScanWidth;
float4 _OverlayColor;

float4x4 _ClipToWorld;
```

The appdata and v2f structs and the vert function are all unremarkable versions we've seen countless times before, so we will move straight to the frag function. Inside this fragment shader, here's how we'll calculate and use the world-space position of the pixel:

- First, sample _CameraDepthTexture to obtain a depth value in clip space.

    - On Direct3D platforms, this value should be between 0 and 1. On OpenGL platforms, it's between –1 and 1. Our code uses the UNITY_REVERSED_Z and UNITY_NEAR_CLIP_VALUE macros to account for this.

- Next, reconstruct the clip-space position of the pixel based on this depth value and the UV coordinate.

- Multiply the clip-space position by _ClipToWorld to transform it into world space and then divide its xyz components by its w component to obtain a final world-space coordinate for the pixel.

- Then, calculate the distance between the pixel position and the scan origin point.

    - If this distance is less than _ScanDist, we can sample _OverlayRampTex and apply it to the world, stretched over a distance of _ScanWidth.

- Return a final color value by overlaying the scan texture sample value (if there is one) onto the original image.

We can put the following sequence of steps into action using the following shader code.

Listing 14-9. The frag function for the world scan effect in the built-in pipeline

```
float4 frag (v2f i) : SV_Target
{
        float depthSample = tex2D(_CameraDepthTexture, i.uv).r;

#if UNITY_REVERSED_Z
        float depth = depthSample;
#else
        float depth = lerp(UNITY_NEAR_CLIP_VALUE, 1, depthSample);
#endif

        float4 pixelPositionCS = float4(i.uv * 2.0f - 1.0f, depth, 1.0f);

#if UNITY_UV_STARTS_AT_TOP
        pixelPositionCS.y = -pixelPositionCS.y;
#endif

        float4 pixelPositionWS = mul(_ClipToWorld, pixelPositionCS);

        float3 worldPos = pixelPositionWS.xyz / pixelPositionWS.w;

        float fragDist = distance(worldPos, _ScanOrigin);

        float4 scanColor = 0.0f;

        if (fragDist < _ScanDist && fragDist > _ScanDist - _ScanWidth)
        {
                float scanUV = (fragDist - _ScanDist) / (_ScanWidth * 1.01f);

                scanColor = tex2D(_OverlayRampTex, float2(scanUV, 0.5f));
                scanColor *= _OverlayColor;
        }

        float4 textureSample = tex2D(_MainTex, i.uv);

        return lerp(textureSample, scanColor, scanColor.a);
}
```

That's a fairly large chunk of code! However, much of the code was spent calculating the clip-space position of the pixel and transforming it into world space. It's a lot more complex than you perhaps first imagined, but my hope is that you will be able to take this code and implement it in other post-processing effects that rely on world-space positions.

You will notice that we use dynamic branching in the shader. At first glance it appears as if this type of branching might suffer from performance issues, especially as we are doing a texture sample within the branched code, but I reasoned that the GPU is extremely likely to go down the same side of this branch on adjacent pixels, so the performance impact is minimal – see Chapter 13 for more details on branching in shaders.

With this code in place, you should see a scan propagate across the scene when you left-click in Play Mode. To obtain results like in Figure 14-1, I used a bright HDR-enabled blue overlay color (see Figure 14-2) and an overlay texture that transitions from completely clear to blue and to bright white (see Figure 14-3).

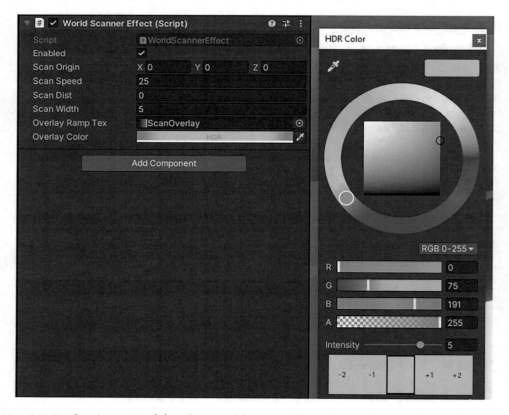

Figure 14-2. *Settings used for the world scan effect. Some properties will be modified at runtime*

620

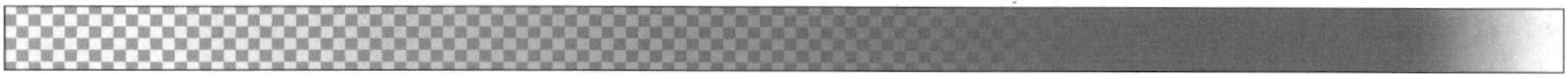

Figure 14-3. *The overlay ramp texture. The y-axis has been exaggerated for clarity, and a checkerboard backdrop has been added to highlight which parts are transparent*

Now that we have created the effect in the built-in pipeline, let's see how to reconstruct world-space positions in image effects in URP.

World-Space Scan in URP

As was the case with the URP post-processing effects we wrote in Chapter 11, the world-space scan effect requires multiple scripts and a single shader file. We'll start by writing the scripts, followed by the shader.

World-Space Scan C# Scripting in URP

I'm going to split this effect into four script files. That sounds like a lot, but don't let it daunt you – most of these files are quite short, and each one serves a different purpose! For the built-in pipeline scan effect, we managed to package everything into a single script because the code to read inputs, act on them, and update values each frame and the code to set up and run the shader all needed to be attached to a GameObject, so it made sense to package the whole thing into one script and put it on a single GameObject. However, with URP, it's a different story – here's why.

The code to set up and run the shader in URP is made up of three classes with different purposes, none of which can be attached to a GameObject in the usual way. Therefore, I'm going to create a fourth script containing the code that runs an update loop to read the player's inputs and update the effect's parameters appropriately. Let's run through each script in order.

The WorldScanSettings C# Script

Create a new C# script named "WorldScanSettings.cs". This script is responsible for handling the effect's properties, which will be visible on the volume profile. Hence, this script inherits from `VolumeComponent` and `IPostProcessComponent`. By and large, this class contains the same variables and some similar methods as the built-in pipeline version (see Listing 14-1 for more context).

Listing 14-10. The WorldScanSettings variables and method signatures

```
using UnityEngine;
using UnityEngine.Rendering;
using UnityEngine.Rendering.Universal;

[System.Serializable, VolumeComponentMenu("Examples/World Scanner")]
public class WorldScanSettings : VolumeComponent, IPostProcessComponent
{
        [Tooltip("Is the effect active?")]
        public BoolParameter enabled = new BoolParameter(false);

        [Tooltip("The world space origin point of the scan.")]
        public Vector3Parameter scanOrigin = new Vector3Parameter
        (Vector3.zero);

        [Tooltip("How quickly, in units per second, the scan propagates.")]
        public FloatParameter scanSpeed = new FloatParameter(1.0f);

        [Tooltip("How far, in meters, the scan has travelled from the
        origin.")]
        public FloatParameter scanDist = new FloatParameter(0.0f);

        [Tooltip("The distance, in meters, the scan texture gets applied
        over.")]
        public FloatParameter scanWidth = new FloatParameter(1.0f);

        [Tooltip("An x-by-1 ramp texture representing the scan color.")]
        public Texture2DParameter overlayRampTex = new
        Texture2DParameter(null);

        [Tooltip("An additional HDR color tint applied to the scan.")]
        public ColorParameter overlayColor = new ColorParameter(Color.white,
        true, true, true);

        public void StartScan(Vector3 origin) { ... }

        public void UpdateScan() { ... }

        public void StopScan() { ... }
```

```
    public bool IsActive() => ... ;

    public bool IsTileCompatible() => false;
}
```

The StartScan, UpdateScan, and StopScan methods are exposed to allow other scripts to control the behavior of the effect without needing to access the variables directly. Here's what each one does:

- StartScan enables the effect, changes the origin point of the scan, and resets the scan distance to zero.

- UpdateScan should be called every frame. It increments the scan distance based on the scan speed.

- StopScan simply disables the effect.

We also have the IsActive method, which should return true if enabled is set to true *and* if a ramp texture is assigned for the effect.

Listing 14-11. The StartScan, UpdateScan, StopScan, and IsActive methods

```
public void StartScan(Vector3 origin)
{
    enabled.Override(true);
    scanOrigin.Override(origin);
    scanDist.Override(0.0f);
}

public void UpdateScan()
{
    scanDist.value += scanSpeed.value * Time.deltaTime;
}

public void StopScan()
{
    enabled.Override(false);
}

public bool IsActive() => overlayRampTex.value != null && enabled.value
&& active;
```

You'll notice here that sometimes I'm just updating a setting directly and other times I'm calling Override to update a value. By default, Unity will use whatever default values you've set on each variable. To override the default values in the Inspector, you must tick the box to the left of a setting before Unity will allow you to make changes. Override does a similar thing in scripting. By calling Override, Unity will let you start changing the value of a setting programmatically, so I've made sure the code within StartScan and StopScan uses Override – from that point onward, just changing the setting value directly works as expected. The settings for the effect are all set up now, so we can move on to writing the render pass, which drives the effect.

The WorldScanRenderPass C# Script

Create a new C# script called "WorldScanRenderPass.cs". This script is responsible for creating the material for the effect, setting up the render textures that will be used each frame, grabbing the effect settings from the WorldScanSettings object attached to the volume, and running the effect each frame, as well as cleaning up resources used during the frame. Much of this script will be familiar if you followed Chapter 11, so for the sake of brevity, I'll just list most of the code here.

Listing 14-12. The WorldScanRenderPass class

```
using UnityEngine;
using UnityEngine.Rendering;
using UnityEngine.Rendering.Universal;

public class WorldScanRenderPass : ScriptableRenderPass
{
    private Material material;
    private WorldScanSettings settings;

    private RenderTargetIdentifier source;
    private RenderTargetIdentifier mainTex;
    private string profilerTag;

    public void Setup(ScriptableRenderer renderer, string profilerTag)
    {
        this.profilerTag = profilerTag;

        source = renderer.cameraColorTarget;
```

```
        VolumeStack stack = VolumeManager.instance.stack;
        settings = stack.GetComponent<WorldScanSettings>();
        renderPassEvent = RenderPassEvent.BeforeRenderingPost
        Processing;

        if (settings != null && settings.IsActive())
        {
                material = new Material(Shader.Find("Examples/
                ImageEffects/WorldScan"));
                renderer.EnqueuePass(this);
        }
    }

    public override void Configure(CommandBuffer cmd,
    RenderTextureDescriptor cameraTextureDescriptor)
    {
        if (settings == null)
        {
                return;
        }

        int id = Shader.PropertyToID("_MainTex");
        mainTex = new RenderTargetIdentifier(id);
        cmd.GetTemporaryRT(id, cameraTextureDescriptor);

        base.Configure(cmd, cameraTextureDescriptor);
    }

    public override void Execute(ScriptableRenderContext context, ref
    RenderingData renderingData) { ... }

    public override void FrameCleanup(CommandBuffer cmd)
    {
        cmd.ReleaseTemporaryRT(Shader.PropertyToID("_MainTex"));
    }
}
```

That gets us most of the way there, but keep in mind that we haven't written the shader file yet, so the call to Shader.Find in the Setup method will currently fail to find anything. Next, let's see what happens in Execute:

- If the IsActive method on the settings returns false, then we shouldn't run the effect.

- Else, we'll need to create a command buffer with the profiler tag specified in the class variables.

- Then, before anything else, we should copy the original camera texture, source, to a temporary render texture, mainTex.

- Next, we can set each of the shader properties on the material. Unlike the built-in pipeline version, we don't need to calculate the inverse view-projection matrix manually and send it as a shader property.

- We apply the effect with the Blit method, sending the result back to the source texture.

- Finally, we can execute the command buffer and release its resources back to the command buffer pool.

Listing 14-13. The Execute method

```
public override void Execute(ScriptableRenderContext context, ref
RenderingData renderingData)
{
    if (!settings.IsActive())
    {
        return;
    }

    CommandBuffer cmd = CommandBufferPool.Get(profilerTag);

    cmd.Blit(source, mainTex);

    material.SetVector("_ScanOrigin", settings.scanOrigin.value);
    material.SetFloat("_ScanDist", settings.scanDist.value);
    material.SetFloat("_ScanWidth", settings.scanWidth.value);
```

```
material.SetTexture("_OverlayRampTex", settings.
overlayRampTex.value);
material.SetColor("_OverlayColor", settings.overlayColor.value);

cmd.Blit(mainTex, source, material);

context.ExecuteCommandBuffer(cmd);
cmd.Clear();
CommandBufferPool.Release(cmd);
}
```

With that, the WorldScanRenderPass class is complete, and we can move on to the
WorldScanFeature class.

The WorldScanFeature C# Script

Create a new C# script called "WorldScanFeature.cs". This script is used to set up a
Renderer Feature, and it is responsible for telling URP which render passes should be
used for the feature. Accordingly, it inherits from ScriptableRendererFeature, and it is
the shortest of the scripts we need to write for the world scan effect. Here is the script in
its entirety.

Listing 14-14. The WorldScanFeature script

```
using UnityEngine.Rendering.Universal;

public class WorldScanFeature : ScriptableRendererFeature
{
    WorldScanRenderPass pass;

    public override void Create()
    {
        name = "World Scanner";
        pass = new WorldScanRenderPass();
    }
```

```
    public override void AddRenderPasses(ScriptableRenderer renderer, ref
    RenderingData renderingData)
    {
            pass.Setup(renderer, "World Scan Post Process");
    }
}
```

There's not much to discuss regarding this class, so we can move on to the fourth and final C# script.

The Scanner C# Script

The three scripts we have written so far do not get attached to GameObjects, because they are not components. That means there isn't an easy way to control the settings based on user input or over time from within the scripts themselves. Therefore, we need another script that *can* be attached to a GameObject so that we have control over when and how the scan gets triggered. To that end, create a C# script named "Scanner.cs" and attach it to any GameObject in the scene – the player character object or the main camera are both good choices.

The script is relatively straightforward, although you may not have come across the TryGet method on volume profiles, which we use to check whether a certain effect is attached to the profile and output it if so. It returns true if the effect exists. I'll also be using the null conditional operator, ?., in the Update method to only run each method on scanSettings if it is not null. It's a handy operator you might not have encountered before, which helps to avoid null reference exceptions!

Listing 14-15. The Scanner script

```
using UnityEngine;
using UnityEngine.Rendering;

public class Scanner : MonoBehaviour
{
        public Volume volume;
        private WorldScanSettings scanSettings = null;

        private bool isScanning = false;
```

```
private void Start()
{
    if(volume == null || volume.profile == null)
    {
        return;
    }

    if(volume.profile.TryGet(out scanSettings))
    {
        scanSettings.StopScan();
    }
}

private void Update()
{
    if(Input.GetButtonDown("Fire1"))
    {
        isScanning = true;
        scanSettings?.StartScan(transform.position);
    }
    else if(Input.GetButtonDown("Fire2"))
    {
        isScanning = false;
        scanSettings?.StopScan();
    }

    if(isScanning)
    {
        scanSettings?.UpdateScan();
    }
}
}
```

Finally, that's all the scripting out of the way, so let's move on to the shader.

World-Space Scan Shader in URP

Start by creating a new shader file called "WorldScan.shader". Much of the shader is
similar to the built-in pipeline version, so I'll list much of the code here (except the frag
function) and mention the key features and differences.

Listing 14-16. The WorldScan shader file

```
Shader "Examples/ImageEffects/WorldScan"
{
    Properties
    {
        _MainTex ("Texture", 2D) = "white" {}
        _ScanOrigin("Origin Point", Vector) = (0, 0, 0, 0)
        _ScanDist("Scan Distance", Float) = 0
        _ScanWidth("Scan Width", Float) = 1
        _OverlayRampTex("Overlay Ramp", 2D) = "white" {}
        [HDR] _OverlayColor("Overlay Color", Color) = (1, 1, 1, 1)
    }
    SubShader
    {
        Tags
        {
            "RenderType"="Opaque"
            "RenderPipeline"="UniversalPipeline"
        }

        Pass
        {
            HLSLPROGRAM
            #pragma vertex vert
            #pragma fragment frag

            #include "Packages/com.unity.render-pipelines.universal/
            ShaderLibrary/Core.hlsl"
            #include "Packages/com.unity.render-pipelines.universal/
            ShaderLibrary/DeclareDepthTexture.hlsl"
```

```
struct appdata
{
    float4 positionOS : Position;
    float2 uv : TEXCOORD0;
};

struct v2f
{
    float4 positionCS : SV_Position;
    float2 uv : TEXCOORD0;
};

sampler2D _MainTex;
sampler2D _OverlayRampTex;

CBUFFER_START(UnityPerMaterial)
    float3 _ScanOrigin;
    float _ScanDist;
    float _ScanWidth;
    float4 _OverlayColor;
CBUFFER_END

v2f vert (appdata v)
{
    v2f o;
    o.positionCS = TransformObjectToHClip(v.
    positionOS.xyz);
    o.uv = v.uv;
    return o;
}

float4 frag (v2f i) : SV_Target { ... }

ENDHLSL
        }
    }
}
```

Here's a rundown of the code so far:

- Unlike the built-in pipeline version, we don't need to include a _ClipToWorld matrix as a variable.

- We also don't need to declare _CameraDepthTexture. That and all depth-related macros and helper functions are found in the DeclareDepthTexture.hlsl helper function, which is included.

- Otherwise, all the other properties are declared in Properties and inside the HLSLPROGRAM block. All variables, apart from the textures, are declared inside a constant buffer.

- The appdata and v2f structs and the vert function are all unremarkable, standard versions we've seen before.

The most interesting part of the code is the frag function. Most of it is the same as in the built-in pipeline version, except we now have access to a ComputeWorldSpacePosition function that takes the UVs, depth texture value, and inverse view-projection matrix as parameters and returns the world-space position. From that point, we can calculate the distance of the pixel position from the scan origin point, both in world space, and map the ramp texture onto the original camera texture depending on that distance value.

Listing 14-17. The frag function for the world scan effect in URP

```
float4 frag (v2f i) : SV_Target
{
#if UNITY_REVERSED_Z
    float depth = SampleSceneDepth(i.uv);
#else
    float depth = lerp(UNITY_NEAR_CLIP_VALUE, 1, SampleSceneDepth(i.uv));
#endif

    float3 worldPos = ComputeWorldSpacePosition(i.uv, depth, UNITY_MATRIX_I_VP);

    float fragDist = distance(worldPos, _ScanOrigin);

    float4 scanColor = 0.0f;
```

```
    if (fragDist < _ScanDist && fragDist > _ScanDist - _ScanWidth)
    {
        float scanUV = (fragDist - _ScanDist) / (_ScanWidth * 1.01f);

        scanColor = tex2D(_OverlayRampTex, float2(scanUV, 0.5f));
        scanColor *= _OverlayColor;
    }

    float4 textureSample = tex2D(_MainTex, i.uv);

    return lerp(textureSample, scanColor, scanColor.a);
}
```

Now that the shader code is finished, you can see the effect in action by following these steps, which should end up looking like Figure 14-1:

- Attach the world scan feature to your Forward Renderer asset. By default, this is in *Assets ➤ Settings* – use the *Add Renderer Feature* button at the bottom.

- Add the world scan effect to a volume profile and then add that to a volume somewhere in your scene.

- Modify the settings to use a bright HDR blue for the overlay color and an overlay texture that goes from totally transparent to blue and to full white – the same as the one I used for the built-in pipeline. See Figure 14-4 for the settings I used and Figure 14-5 for the ramp texture.

Figure 14-4. *Settings used for the world scan effect in URP. Some properties will be modified at runtime, but you can test out settings in the Scene View*

Figure 14-5. *We'll use the same ramp texture as we used in the built-in render pipeline*

Finally, with the built-in pipeline and URP out of the way, let's see how the effect works in HDRP.

World-Space Scan in HDRP

Although HDRP has a couple of extra quirks we'll need to work around, the effect is built similarly to the other two render pipelines. We'll require two scripts, one that is attached to the volume and drives the effect and one that is attached to a GameObject to control the scan at runtime, and one shader file. Let's jump right in.

World-Space Scan C# Scripting in HDRP

As we saw in Chapter 11, HDRP comes with a template file for custom post-processing effects, which condenses everything into a single class, unlike URP. However, like URP, this class is not associated with a GameObject directly, so it is difficult to read input and run an update loop inside the volume's class directly. Therefore, we will create a second script that will end up looking extremely similar to the Scanner class we wrote for URP. But let's start with the volume script first.

The WorldScanVolume C# Script

Start by creating a new post-processing script via *Create* ➤ *Rendering* ➤ *HDRP C# Post Process Volume* and name the new script "WorldScanVolume.cs". Many parts of the script will be filled out by you, and most of it should be familiar if you followed Chapter 11, so I'll start with the template seen in Listing 14-18. I'll add a few methods, which we will modify as we go.

Listing 14-18. The WorldScanVolume script

```
using UnityEngine;
using UnityEngine.Rendering;
using UnityEngine.Rendering.HighDefinition;
using System;

[Serializable, VolumeComponentMenu("Post-processing/Examples/WorldScan")]
public sealed class WorldScanVolume : CustomPostProcessVolumeComponent,
IPostProcessComponent
{
    ...

    Material m_Material;

    public bool IsActive() => { ... }
    public override CustomPostProcessInjectionPoint injectionPoint =>
    CustomPostProcessInjectionPoint.BeforePostProcess;

    const string kShaderName = "Examples/ImageEffects/WorldScan";

    public override void Setup()
```

```
    {
        if (Shader.Find(kShaderName) != null)
            m_Material = new Material(Shader.Find(kShaderName));
        else
            Debug.LogError($"Unable to find shader '{kShaderName}'.
            Post Process Volume WorldScanVolume is unable to load.");
    }

    public override void Render(CommandBuffer cmd, HDCamera camera,
    RTHandle source, RTHandle destination) { ... }

    public override void Cleanup()
    {
        CoreUtils.Destroy(m_Material);
    }

    public void StartScan(Vector3 origin) { ... }

    public void UpdateScan() { ... }

    public void StopScan() { ... }
}
```

Those of you with a keen eye might have noticed that we're using the BeforePostProcess injection point, rather than AfterPostProcess as we have previously seen. I chose this injection point specifically because I want the bloom effect to be applied to the scan effect (if you have chosen to use bloom in your game), as it permits us to use HDR colors to make the scan glow as it travels across the scene. AfterPostProcess would run after bloom has been applied.

Let's add the effect's properties at the very top of the class. These will be the same properties as the URP version of the effect, covering the origin point, speed, width, texture, and color of the scan visuals.

Listing 14-19. The scan effect properties

```
[Tooltip("Is the effect active?")]
public BoolParameter enabled = new BoolParameter(false);

[Tooltip("The world space origin point of the scan.")]
public Vector3Parameter scanOrigin = new Vector3Parameter(Vector3.zero);

[Tooltip("How quickly, in units per second, the scan propagates.")]
public FloatParameter scanSpeed = new FloatParameter(1.0f);

[Tooltip("How far, in meters, the scan has travelled from the origin.")]
public FloatParameter scanDist = new FloatParameter(0.0f);

[Tooltip("The distance, in meters, the scan texture gets applied over.")]
public FloatParameter scanWidth = new FloatParameter(1.0f);

[Tooltip("An x-by-1 ramp texture representing the scan color.")]
public Texture2DParameter overlayRampTex = new Texture2DParameter(null);

[Tooltip("An additional HDR color tint applied to the scan.")]
public ColorParameter overlayColor = new ColorParameter(Color.white, true,
true, true);
```

```
Material m_Material;
```

Next comes the IsActive method, which should return true only when enabled is set to true and the overlayColor texture is assigned.

Listing 14-20. The IsActive method

```
public bool IsActive() => m_Material != null && overlayRampTex.value !=
null && enabled.value;
```

The Render method is responsible for sending data to the shader via the material and instructing Unity to render the effect with a call to DrawFullscreen or Blit. We don't do anything unusual in Render in this effect.

Listing 14-21. The Render method

```
public override void Render(CommandBuffer cmd, HDCamera camera, RTHandle
source, RTHandle destination)
{
      if (m_Material == null)
            return;

      m_Material.SetVector("_ScanOrigin", scanOrigin.value);
      m_Material.SetFloat("_ScanDist", scanDist.value);
      m_Material.SetFloat("_ScanWidth", scanWidth.value);
      m_Material.SetTexture("_OverlayRampTex", overlayRampTex.value);
      m_Material.SetColor("_OverlayColor", overlayColor.value);

      m_Material.SetTexture("_InputTexture", source);
      HDUtils.DrawFullScreen(cmd, m_Material, destination);
}
```

Finally, I've added three new methods: StartScan, UpdateScan, and StopScan. Each one is intended to be called externally; this means that the WorldScanVolume script is not responsible for handling user input, but an external script does not need to change the volume parameters directly. We'll use the same code as the URP version.

Listing 14-22. The StartScan, UpdateScan, and StopScan methods

```
public void StartScan(Vector3 origin)
{
      enabled.Override(true);
      scanOrigin.Override(origin);
      scanDist.Override(0.0f);
}

public void UpdateScan()
{
      scanDist.value += scanSpeed.value * Time.deltaTime;
}
```

```
public void StopScan()
{
    enabled.Override(false);
}
```

That's all we need for this script, so let's move on to the script we'll use to read user input.

The Scanner C# Script

This script will be almost identical to the URP version. Start by creating a new C# script called "Scanner.cs". The script is very straightforward – in Start, we use the TryGet method to grab a reference to the WorldScanVolume if one exists on the volume profile, and if it does, then we will start, stop, and update the scan accordingly in Update. We can use the null conditional operator, ?., to only run each method if TryGet succeeded.

Listing 14-23. The Scanner class

```
using UnityEngine;
using UnityEngine.Rendering;

public class Scanner : MonoBehaviour
{
    public Volume volume;
    private WorldScanVolume worldScan = null;

    private bool isScanning = false;

    private void Start()
    {
        if(volume == null || volume.profile == null)
        {
            return;
        }
```

```
            if(volume.profile.TryGet(out worldScan))
            {
                worldScan.StopScan();
            }
    }

    private void Update()
    {
        if (Input.GetButtonDown("Fire1"))
        {
            isScanning = true;
            worldScan?.StartScan(transform.position);
        }
        else if (Input.GetButtonDown("Fire2"))
        {
            isScanning = false;
            worldScan?.StopScan();
        }

        if (isScanning)
        {
            worldScan?.UpdateScan();
        }
    }
}
```

If you attach this to a GameObject such as the player object or the main camera, then you can control the volume settings at runtime. Just one small problem: We haven't written the shader yet, so let's do that next.

World-Space Scan Shader in HDRP

Start by creating a new post-processing shader via *Create* ➤ *Shader* ➤ *HDRP Post Process* and name it "WorldScan.shader". Most of this template will stay intact, but I'll post my starting point here in case Unity decides to change the template in a future Unity version.

Listing 14-24. The WorldScan shader skeleton

```
Shader "Examples/ImageEffects/WorldScan"
{
    HLSLINCLUDE

    #pragma target 4.5
    #pragma only_renderers d3d11 playstation xboxone xboxseries vulkan
    metal switch

    #include "Packages/com.unity.render-pipelines.core/ShaderLibrary/
    Common.hlsl"
    #include "Packages/com.unity.render-pipelines.core/ShaderLibrary/
    Color.hlsl"
    #include "Packages/com.unity.render-pipelines.high-definition/
    Runtime/ShaderLibrary/ShaderVariables.hlsl"
    #include "Packages/com.unity.render-pipelines.high-definition/
    Runtime/PostProcessing/Shaders/FXAA.hlsl"
    #include "Packages/com.unity.render-pipelines.high-definition/
    Runtime/PostProcessing/Shaders/RTUpscale.hlsl"

    struct Attributes
    {
        uint vertexID : SV_VertexID;
        UNITY_VERTEX_INPUT_INSTANCE_ID
    };

    struct Varyings
    {
        float4 positionCS : SV_POSITION;
        float2 texcoord   : TEXCOORD0;
        UNITY_VERTEX_OUTPUT_STEREO
    };

    Varyings Vert(Attributes input)
    {
        Varyings output;
        UNITY_SETUP_INSTANCE_ID(input);
```

```
        UNITY_INITIALIZE_VERTEX_OUTPUT_STEREO(output);
        output.positionCS = GetFullScreenTriangleVertexPosition(input.
        vertexID);
        output.texcoord = GetFullScreenTriangleTexCoord(input.
        vertexID);
        return output;
    }

    // List of properties to control your post process effect
    TEXTURE2D_X(_InputTexture);

    ...
    float4 CustomPostProcess(Varyings input) : SV_Target
{ ... }

    ENDHLSL

    SubShader
    {
        Pass
        {
            Name "WorldScan"

            ZWrite Off
            ZTest Always
            Blend Off
            Cull Off

            HLSLPROGRAM
            #pragma fragment CustomPostProcess
            #pragma vertex Vert
            ENDHLSL
        }
    }
    Fallback Off
}
```

To access the depth texture in HDRP, we'll need to add one more include file: NormalBuffer.hlsl. We can add this line below the other include statements.

Listing 14-25. Including the NormalBuffer.hlsl file

```
#include "Packages/com.unity.render-pipelines.high-definition/Runtime/
Material/NormalBuffer.hlsl"
```

Next, let's add the shader properties. Recall from Chapter 11 that HDRP custom post-process shaders don't have a Properties block, so we just need to declare them once inside HLSLINCLUDE. I'll put them just below the _InputTexture definition. For the overlay ramp texture, we'll be sampling this later in a slightly different way that we haven't used in a post-processing shader before. In addition to declaring the texture with TEXTURE2D(_OverlayRampTex), we must separately declare a sampler that will be used to sample the texture properly. We use the SAMPLER macro to declare this sampler.

Listing 14-26. Shader properties in HLSLINCLUDE

```
TEXTURE2D_X(_InputTexture);

TEXTURE2D(_OverlayRampTex);
SAMPLER(sampler_OverlayRampTex);

float3 _ScanOrigin;
float _ScanDist;
float _ScanWidth;
float4 _OverlayColor;
```

Finally, let's fill in the fragment shader, which is represented by the CustomPostProcess function. This will look very similar to Listing 14-17 from the URP version of the shader, with a couple of key differences:

- We use the LOAD_TEXTURE2D_X macro to sample both the _CameraDepthTexture and _InputTexture. This macro requires UV coordinates in the range [0, width] along the u-axis and [0, height] along the v-axis, instead of the typical [0,1] range along both. Multiply the texture coordinates by _ScreenSize.xy to get the correct new UVs.

- HDRP uses camera-relative rendering, which means the values from ComputeWorldSpacePosition give us a world-space position *relative to the camera position*. To correct this and obtain an *absolute* world-space position, pass the result through the GetAbsolutePositionWS function.

- We use SAMPLE_TEXTURE2D to sample _OverlayRampTex. This macro *does* use the typical [0, 1] range for UV coordinates. In this shader, we're calculating the UVs from scratch.

Here's the full fragment shader.

Listing 14-27. The CustomPostProcess function

```
float4 CustomPostProcess(Varyings input) : SV_Target
{
     UNITY_SETUP_STEREO_EYE_INDEX_POST_VERTEX(input);

     uint2 positionSS = input.texcoord * _ScreenSize.xy;

     float depthSample = LOAD_TEXTURE2D_X(_CameraDepthTexture,
     positionSS).r;

#if UNITY_REVERSED_Z
     float depth = depthSample;
#else
     float depth = lerp(UNITY_NEAR_CLIP_VALUE, 1, depthSample);
#endif

     float3 worldPos = ComputeWorldSpacePosition(input.texcoord, depth,
     UNITY_MATRIX_I_VP);
     worldPos = GetAbsolutePositionWS(worldPos);

     float fragDist = distance(worldPos, _ScanOrigin);

     float4 scanColor = 0.0f;
```

```
    if (fragDist < _ScanDist && fragDist > _ScanDist - _ScanWidth)
    {
        float scanUV = (fragDist - _ScanDist) / (_ScanWidth * 1.01f);

        scanColor = SAMPLE_TEXTURE2D(_OverlayRampTex, sampler_
        OverlayRampTex, float2(scanUV, 0.5f));
        scanColor *= _OverlayColor;
    }

    float4 textureSample = LOAD_TEXTURE2D_X(_InputTexture, positionSS);

    return lerp(textureSample, scanColor, scanColor.a);
}
```

With that, all the components of the effect should be completed. By following these steps, you should be able to see the effect running in your own game:

- Go to *Project Settings* ➤ *Graphics* ➤ *HDRP Global Settings* ➤ *Custom Post Process Orders* (near the bottom of the window) and add WorldScanVolume to the *Before Post Process* list. Without doing so, the effect will not render.

- Add a volume to your scene via *GameObject* ➤ *Volume* ➤ *any Volume option*, add a profile to that volume, and tweak the settings however you want. Figure 14-6 shows the settings I used, and Figure 14-7 shows the ramp texture.

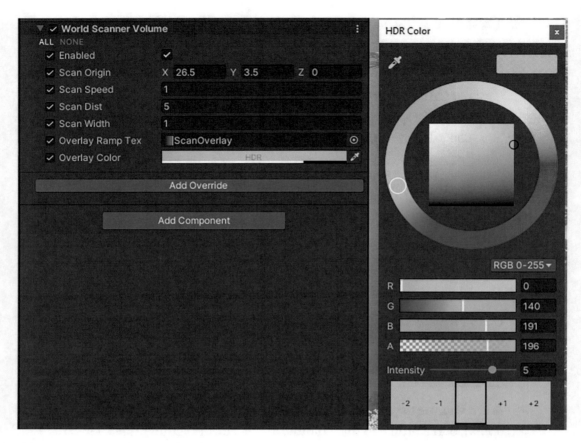

Figure 14-6. *Settings used for the world scan effect in HDRP*

Figure 14-7. *The overlay ramp texture, which we previously used in the built-in pipeline and URP versions of this effect*

You should now have the knowledge required to create a world scan effect in each of Unity's render pipelines. Furthermore, the code used to reconstruct world-space positions in a post-processing shader can be ported to other shaders – I'm sure you can think of other effects that could benefit from processing in world space rather than clip space! Next, let's revisit the concept of lighting that we explored in Chapter 10 and introduce a new, stylized way to render objects.

Cel-Shaded Lighting

Cel-shading is a very popular lighting style used in games, sometimes called *toon lighting* or just "a cartoonish aesthetic." With cel-shading, the light falling on an object is subjected to a cutoff, meaning that objects don't have smooth lighting – a part of the object is either fully lit or unlit (although sometimes there may be a *very small* falloff range). The good news is that this effect can be incorporated into many existing shaders, as we can access the amount of light falling on an object and perform a cutoff on those values. The concepts we learned in Chapter 10 will be essential for this effect.

Note   In HDRP, the concept of lighting is fundamentally handled very differently from the other pipelines. Put simply, it is extremely difficult to customize the way lighting works in HDRP without considerable effort. Unfortunately, that means I won't be able to make this cel-shading effect work in HDRP.

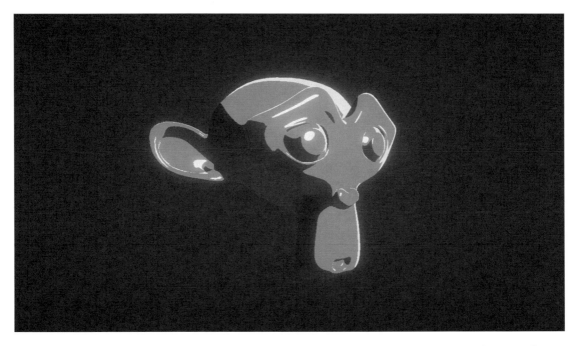

Figure 14-8. *The cel-shading effect applied to Blender's Suzanne monkey mesh*

For this example, I will create a cel-shading effect that uses only the main light in the scene. We can create this effect in both shader code and Shader Graph based on what we learned earlier in the book, so let's do both.

Cel-Shaded Lighting in HLSL

Much of this effect is going to look like the PhongShading shader we wrote in Chapter 10, with a couple of additions and changes. Start by creating a new shader called "CelShading.shader" and then replace the template code with the following code.

Listing 14-28. The CelShading shader code skeleton

```
Shader "Examples/CelShading"
{
     Properties { ... }
     SubShader
     {
          Tags
          {
               "RenderType" = "Opaque"
               "Queue" = "Geometry"
          }

          Pass
          {
               HLSLPROGRAM
               #pragma vertex vert
               #pragma fragment frag

               ...

               struct appdata
               {
                    float4 positionOS : POSITION;
                    float2 uv : TEXCOORD0;
                    float3 normalOS : NORMAL;
               };
```

```
struct v2f
{
        float4 positionCS : SV_POSITION;
        float2 uv : TEXCOORD0;
        float3 normalWS : TEXCOORD1;
        float3 viewWS : TEXCOORD2;
};

...

v2f vert (appdata v) { ... }

float4 frag (v2f i) : SV_Target { ... }
ENDHLSL
        }
    }
    Fallback Off
}
```

First, let's set up the correct tags and include files for your chosen pipeline. In the built-in pipeline, we'll include UnityCG.cginc as usual, plus Lighting.cginc for access to light information, and then add a LightMode tag required for the pipeline. In URP, we need to include Core.hlsl as standard and Lighting.hlsl for light information and then add a couple of tags specific to the pipeline.

Listing 14-29. Include files and tags for the built-in pipeline

```
Pass
{
    Tags
    {
        "LightMode" = "ForwardBase"
    }

    HLSLPROGRAM
    #pragma vertex vert
    #pragma fragment frag

    #include "UnityCG.cginc"
    #include "Lighting.cginc"
```

Listing 14-30. Include files and tags for URP

```
SubShader
{
      Tags
      {
            "RenderType" = "Opaque"
            "Queue" = "Geometry"
            "RenderPipeline" = "UniversalPipeline"
      }

      Pass
      {
            Tags
            {
                  "LightMode" = "UniversalForward"
            }

            HLSLPROGRAM
            #pragma vertex vert
            #pragma fragment frag

            #include "Packages/com.unity.render-pipelines.universal/
            ShaderLibrary/Core.hlsl"
            #include "Packages/com.unity.render-pipelines.universal/
            ShaderLibrary/Lighting.hlsl"
```

Next, let's add the shader properties. Alongside the properties I used in the PhongShading example, I'll be adding two cutoff values:

- The _LightCutoff property determines at what point light crosses over from complete darkness to complete light. In other words, if we set the cutoff at 0.1, then any lighting value above 0.1 becomes 1, and any value below 0.1 becomes 0. This applies to the n-dot-l diffuse light and n-dot-h specular light, but not the ambient light. The value must be above 0.

- The _FresnelCutoff property does a similar thing, but only applies to the Fresnel light. I made this a separate property because I feel that cutoff values that look good for diffuse and specular light are generally lower than values that look good for Fresnel light. This must also be above 0. I'll make the default value for this one slightly higher than the other.

We can add these properties to the Properties block as usual, alongside four other properties that were included in the PhongShading example. Then we'll declare them inside the HLSLPROGRAM block just below the v2f struct definition. The code for that is slightly different for each pipeline.

Listing 14-31. Shader properties in the Properties block

```
Properties
{
    _BaseColor ("Base Color", Color) = (1, 1, 1, 1)
    _BaseTex("Base Texture", 2D) = "white" {}
    _GlossPower("Gloss Power", Float) = 400
    _FresnelPower("Fresnel Power", Float) = 5
    _LightCutoff("Lighting Cutoff", Range(0.001, 1)) = 0.001
    _FresnelCutoff("Fresnel Cutoff", Range(0.001, 1)) = 0.085
}
```

Listing 14-32. Declaring properties in the HLSLPROGRAM block for the cel-shading effect in the built-in pipeline

```
struct v2f { ... };

sampler2D _BaseTex;
float4 _BaseColor;
float4 _BaseTex_ST;
float _GlossPower;
float _FresnelPower;
float _LightCutoff;
float _FresnelCutoff;
```

Listing 14-33. Declaring properties in the HLSLPROGRAM block for the cel-shading effect in URP

```
struct v2f { ... };

sampler2D _BaseTex;

CBUFFER_START(UnityPerMaterial)
      float4 _BaseColor;
      float4 _BaseTex_ST;
      float _GlossPower;
      float _FresnelPower;
      float _LightCutoff;
      float _FresnelCutoff;
CBUFFER_END
```

The vertex shader is responsible for passing the clip-space position and UVs to the fragment shader as usual, but the lighting code also requires the world-space position and view vector. I already covered the built-in functions that help us do this in Chapter 10, but to recap

- The built-in pipeline gives us the UnityObjectToWorldNormal and WorldSpaceViewDir functions to get those vectors, for which we can just pass in the object-space normal and position vectors, respectively.

- In URP, we use TransformObjectToWorldNormal to obtain the world-space normal vector from the object-space normal vector. The GetWorldSpaceViewDir function requires the world-space position as input and returns the world-space view vector.

Listing 14-34. The vertex shader in the built-in pipeline

```
v2f vert (appdata v)
{
      v2f o;
      o.positionCS = UnityObjectToClipPos(v.positionOS);
      o.uv = TRANSFORM_TEX(v.uv, _BaseTex);
```

```
        o.normalWS = UnityObjectToWorldNormal(v.normalOS);
        o.viewWS = WorldSpaceViewDir(v.positionOS);

        return o;
}
```

Listing 14-35. The vertex shader in URP

```
v2f vert (appdata v)
{
        v2f o;
        o.positionCS = TransformObjectToHClip(v.positionOS.xyz);
        o.uv = TRANSFORM_TEX(v.uv, _BaseTex);
        o.normalWS = TransformObjectToWorldNormal(v.normalOS);

        float3 positionWS = mul(unity_ObjectToWorld, v.positionOS);
        o.viewWS = GetWorldSpaceViewDir(positionWS);

        return o;
}
```

Finally, we come to the fragment shader – like so many of the shaders we have written so far, this is where all the fun happens! First, let's calculate the normal, view, and light direction vectors that will be required for the lighting calculations, plus the light color. While we're at it, let's also throw in the ambient light calculation, since that won't actually be using a cutoff. I'm also including that because up until this point, the fragment shader code differs between the built-in and Universal pipelines, but after this, all our code is renderer-agnostic. All the code should look familiar if you followed the PhongShading example.

Listing 14-36. Calculating vectors and ambient light in the built-in pipeline

```
float4 frag (v2f i) : SV_TARGET
{
        float3 normal = normalize(i.normalWS);
        float3 view = normalize(i.viewWS);
```

```
    float3 lightColor = _LightColor0;
    float3 lightDir = _WorldSpaceLightPos0.xyz;

    float3 ambientColor = ShadeSH9(half4(i.normalWS, 1));
    ...
```

Listing 14-37. Calculating vectors and ambient light in URP

```
float4 frag (v2f i) : SV_Target
{
    float3 normal = normalize(i.normalWS);
    float3 view = normalize(i.viewWS);

    Light mainLight = GetMainLight();

    float3 lightColor = mainLight.color;
    float3 lightDir = mainLight.direction;

    float3 ambientColor = SampleSH(i.normalWS);
    ...
```

Now we can calculate the diffuse, specular, and Fresnel light. Here's what the remainder of the fragment shader will do:

- First, we'll calculate the "raw" diffuse light using the n-dot-l calculation, which results in a value between –1 and 1. We'll need the diffuse variable value later.

- Next, perform the diffuse lighting cutoff with _LightCutoff using a step function. If you recall, step takes two inputs and returns 1 if the second input is higher than the first and 0 otherwise. Then, multiply by the light color to obtain the final diffuse color.

- Calculate the half vector and perform the n-dot-h calculation. Then clamp negative values to zero. Raise the result by the _GlossPower. Then multiply by diffuse because specular highlights can't appear where there is no diffuse light.

- Then, perform the specular lighting cutoff with _LightCutoff in a similar step function and multiply by the light color to get the final specular color.

- Do a similar thing for the Fresnel light: do the 1-minus-n-dot-v calculation, raise it to the _FresnelPower, multiply by diffuse to remove it from unlit parts of the object, take a step function – this time with _FresnelCutoff instead – and multiply by the light color to obtain the final Fresnel color.

- Sample the base texture and apply all the lighting values appropriately.

Listing 14-38. Lighting calculations in the fragment shader

```
float3 ambientColor = <platform dependent code>;

float diffuse = dot(normal, lightDir);

float diffuseAmount = step(_LightCutoff, diffuse);
float3 diffuseColor = lightColor * diffuseAmount;

float3 halfVector = normalize(lightDir + view);
float specular = max(0, dot(normal, halfVector));
specular = pow(specular, _GlossPower);
specular *= diffuse;

float specularAmount = step(_LightCutoff, specular);
float3 specularColor = lightColor * specularAmount;

float fresnel = 1.0f - max(0, dot(normal, view));
fresnel = pow(fresnel, _FresnelPower);
fresnel *= diffuse;

float fresnelAmount = step(_FresnelCutoff, fresnel);
float3 fresnelColor = lightColor * fresnelAmount;

float4 diffuseLighting = float4(ambientColor + diffuseColor, 1.0f);
float4 specularLighting = float4(specularColor + fresnelColor, 1.0f);

float4 textureSample = tex2D(_BaseTex, i.uv);
return textureSample * _BaseColor * diffuseLighting + specularLighting;
```

If you attach this shader to a material and add it to an object in your scene, then you should see results like those in Figure 14-8. Now that we have covered cel-shading in HLSL, let's move on to Shader Graph.

Cel-Shaded Lighting in Shader Graph

Start by creating a new Unlit graph and naming it "CelShading.shadergraph". Like the code version of this effect, the graph is going to use many of the same properties and nodes as the PhongShading graph we wrote in Chapter 10. In this example, the graph I make uses opaque rendering.

Note   In particular, this effect will use the GetMainLight and GetAmbientLight subgraphs that we created during Chapter 10. It would be useful to read that chapter first, because those subgraphs are crucial for the cel-shading effect.

First, let's deal with the properties. Alongside the Base Color, Base Texture, Gloss Power, and Fresnel Power properties that I've lifted from the PhongShading example, I'm also adding two Float properties called Lighting Cutoff and Fresnel Cutoff. These properties are detailed in Figure 14-9. Both represent the cutoff point where light transitions from complete darkness to full lighting, but I use two separate values because Fresnel light looks best with a higher cutoff point than the diffuse or specular light. Both values should be greater than zero.

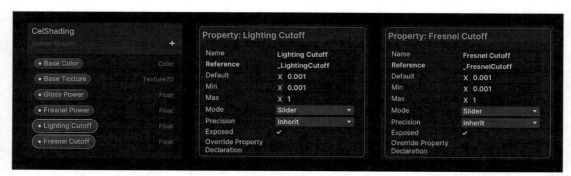

Figure 14-9. *The Lighting Cutoff and Fresnel Cutoff properties*

Now let's carry out the key calculations for this effect, starting with the diffuse light. This comes in two parts. First, we'll calculate the "raw" diffuse lighting value using the n-dot-l calculation with the help of the GetMainLight subgraph as shown in Figure 14-10. We'll need the result of this later for both the specular and Fresnel light calculations, because neither of those types of light should appear where diffuse light is absent. The Dot Product node outputs a value between –1 and 1.

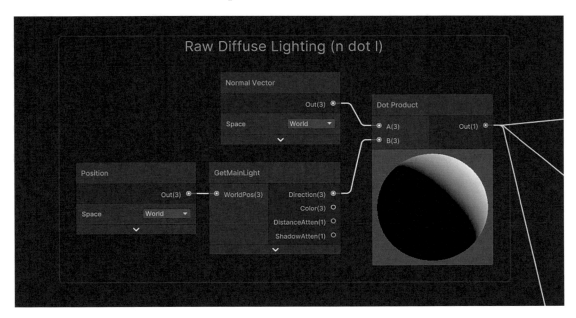

Figure 14-10. *The "raw" diffuse calculation, n-dot-l*

The second part of the diffuse calculation takes the n-dot-l result and then applies the cutoff, for which we use a Step node. Recall that the Step node returns 1 when its *In* input is higher than its *Edge* input and 0 otherwise. After that, we multiply by the light color. This is also a good place to incorporate the ambient light, too, which we can add to the diffuse cutoff result, as shown in Figure 14-11.

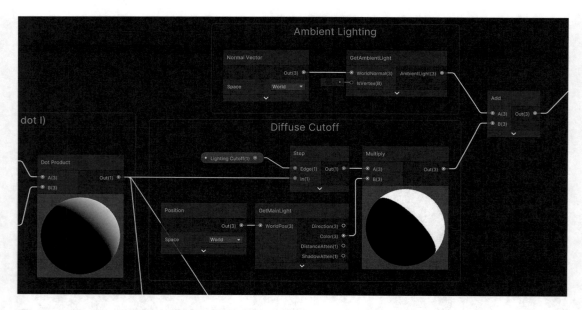

Figure 14-11. *Adding the cutoff diffuse and ambient light together*

Next, let's calculate the "raw" specular light before any cutoff gets applied. This calculation will look familiar from the PhongShading example. We'll calculate the half vector by adding the light and view vectors, then normalizing the result, and using it for the specular n-dot-h calculation. We'll Saturate the result and then raise it to the Gloss Power as shown in Figure 14-12.

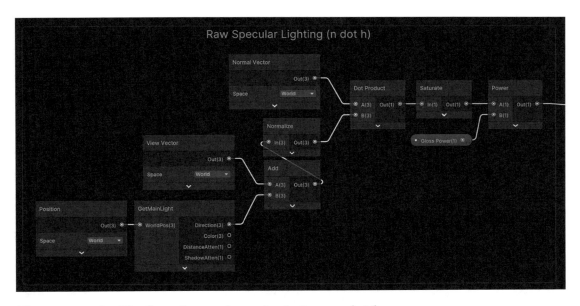

Figure 14-12. The "raw" specular calculation, n-dot-h

Next comes the specular lighting cutoff. Before we can do that, multiply the raw specular value by the raw diffuse value, because specular light should never appear where there is no diffuse. I choose to use the pre-cutoff diffuse value so that the specular highlight gradually gets smaller as you approach the cutoff point; otherwise, using the post-cutoff diffuse value results in the specular highlight being cut in half, which looks odd. Use Step to perform the cutoff with Lighting Cutoff once again and then multiply the result by the light color as shown in Figure 14-13.

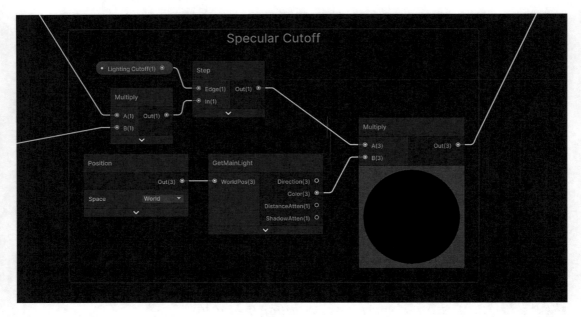

Figure 14-13. *The specular light cutoff calculation. The inputs to the left-hand Multiply node are the results of the raw diffuse and raw specular node groups*

The last type of lighting to incorporate is Fresnel. For this, we can use the handy Fresnel Effect node with the Fresnel Power property in its *Power* input (instead of manually doing the 1-minus-n-dot-v calculation), multiply by the raw diffuse value, and then apply the Fresnel Cutoff with a Step node as shown in Figure 14-14.

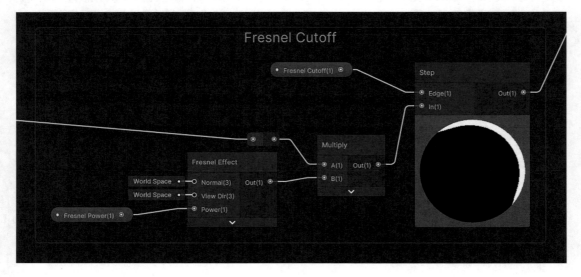

Figure 14-14. *The Fresnel lighting cutoff calculation*

The last step is to tie everything together. Let's sample the Base Texture and multiply by Base Color and then multiply by the diffuse-plus-ambient value that we calculated earlier. This would give us a matte object. After that, just add the cutoff specular and cutoff Fresnel light values and output the result to the *Base Color* block on the master stack. Figure 14-15 shows how these nodes should be connected.

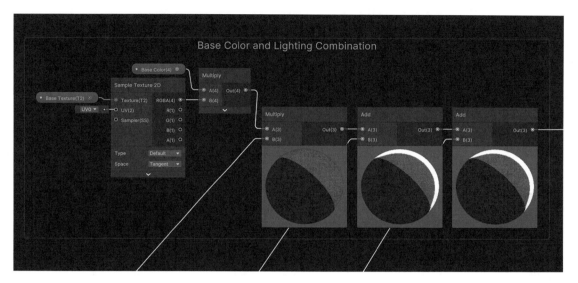

Figure 14-15. *Piecing everything together. In this example, I used red for the Base Color to make the different types of lighting easier to see*

As with the code version, you can now attach this via a material to any object in your scene, and you should see results like in Figure 14-8. As long as there is at least one light in the scene, you'll start to see cel-shaded lighting on your objects, thanks to the lighting cutoff point! The cel-shaded aesthetic typically works best on objects without too much texture detail due to the relative simplicity of the lighting, although you may find success with detailed textures if you play around with the effect a little.

In the next example shader, we'll see a technique that brings together many different shader concepts we've seen throughout the book to create a complex interactive effect that can be modified to fit several different aesthetics.

Interactive Snow Layers

Most of the time, you'll write a shader and attach it to an object, and it'll just end up as something nice to look at in your game, but that doesn't have to be the end of the story; shaders can have an *interactive* component to them. Personally, I enjoy it when games incorporate shaders that you can influence yourself, and in this section, I'll show you how to make one such shader. If your game has thick layers of snow, then it will feel satisfying for your players if they leave a trail through the snow when walking through it. The same is true for walking through water and leaving ripples in your path or wading through thick liquids like slime or mud or even walking through thick waist-high fog and making the fog dissipate as you fight your way through it, all of which are slightly different takes on the same basic premise. Here's what my snow implementation looks like.

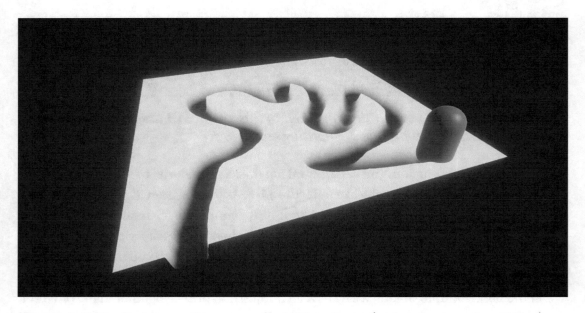

Figure 14-16. *An interactive snow effect. The player (a simple capsule collider) has left a trail through the snow as they walked through it*

Tip   It's very subtle, but I'm using a snow texture from ambientCG on this mesh. The incredibly permissive Creative Commons CC0 license is used for all works on the ambientcg.com website, which allows you to copy, modify, and distribute the work, including for commercial purposes, without requesting permission or giving credit. There are PBR textures available for many common surface types, so you will save a lot of time prototyping with resources from the site.

As you can see, we are using actual mesh deformation for this effect. Consequently, it will have many moving parts. To make sure the ground mesh is sufficiently high resolution to get good-quality trails like these, we will use tessellation to increase the number of vertices in the mesh, since mesh deformation only operates on individual vertices, not fragments. There are several ways we can bake the position of the player and other objects into the heightmap, but I'm going to use a RenderTexture alongside a compute shader to generate the values in that texture. That's mostly because I find compute shaders extremely powerful and interesting, and I think that seeing them in another context will help you understand just how flexible they can be.

Note   Compute shaders can only be created via code at the moment, and Unity doesn't seem to have plans for a "Compute Shader Graph." Furthermore, since we will be using tessellation in the snow mesh shader, we can't build a Shader Graph version of that shader in URP. However, we can still build the effect in every pipeline by taking a "fully code" approach for the built-in pipeline and URP, and HDRP permits us to use tessellation in Shader Graph.

With this effect, we'll have a ground mesh that makes up the snow and "actors" that can move around the scene. When one of these actors intersects with the snow, it will displace some amount of the snow. An effect like this is quite tricky to write in a way that generalizes to any shape or size of mesh, whether that's the ground mesh or the actor mesh, so I'm going to list a few caveats with this specific approach first:

- I will assume that the ground mesh is perfectly flat and square. The mesh should also have its local Y facing upward when unrotated. The Unity default plane follows these rules, but the Unity default quad is rotated 90 degrees the wrong way. Meshes that break these rules require rewriting some of the code.

- The surface of your mesh should cover the [0,1] UV range exactly. Tiling or offsetting the UVs in any way may break the effect.

- The intersection logic relies on colliders, so I will only consider capsule colliders walking through the snow, and I will assume they are oriented standing upward. You can add support for other shapes of collider as an extension, but again, the code will be slightly different.

- I also assume that the actors are always taller than the maximum height of the snow. The effect will still work if that's not true, but the actors will just walk at ground height and delete snow above them, which will probably look strange.

This effect broadly has three parts: the C# scripting side, the compute shader side, and the snow mesh shader side. When using compute shaders, I often find that the C# scripting ends up rather prevalent because there is a lot of setup regarding the data used by the compute shader. With that in mind, we'll start with the scripting side.

Interactive Snow C# Scripting

We will write two C# scripts, both of which work in each pipeline. One will be relatively short and is attached to each actor in the scene that can interact with the snow, and the other is much longer and is attached to the snow mesh directly. We'll start with the snow actor script.

The SnowActor C# Script

Start by creating a new C# script and naming it "SnowActor.cs". The purpose of this script is to provide a way for the snow mesh to get data about actors that are standing in the snow. We'll be detecting which actors are currently stood in the snow using Unity's collision system, but the logic for that will be contained entirely within the other C# script attached to the snow mesh. Therefore, the SnowActor class just needs to expose a few methods to get information about each actor. Here's the kind of data we'll need access to:

- The "ground position" of the actor, that is, the position of the actor's "feet."

- The radius of the actor. Remember, we're just using capsules to represent each actor.

- Whether the actor is currently moving. We don't need to update an actor's contribution to the snow level if it isn't currently moving.

Here's the script in its entirety. We're not doing anything too fancy here, so it should be straightforward to understand what it's doing just by reading it.

Listing 14-39. The SnowActor script

```
using UnityEngine;

public class SnowActor : MonoBehaviour
{
    public Vector3 groundOffset;
    private CapsuleCollider capsuleCollider;

    private Vector3 lastFramePos = Vector3.zero;
    private bool isMoving;

    private void Start()
    {
        capsuleCollider = GetComponent<CapsuleCollider>();
    }
```

```
public Vector3 GetGroundPos()
{
        return transform.position + groundOffset;
}

public float GetRadius()
{
        Vector3 localScale = transform.localScale;
        float scaleRadius = Mathf.Max(localScale.x, localScale.z);
        return capsuleCollider.radius * scaleRadius;
}

private void Update()
{
        isMoving = (transform.position != lastFramePos);
        lastFramePos = transform.position;
}

public bool IsMoving()
{
        return isMoving;
}
}
```

For the GetRadius method, I've added a check so that if you scale along the x- or z-axis, then that gets properly accounted for. All you need to do now is add a default capsule to your scene (*Create ➤ 3D Object ➤ Capsule*), attach the SnowActor script, and set the groundOffset value to (0, –1, 0), since the midpoint of the capsule is one Unity unit in the air. The capsule primitive already comes with a capsule collider, but Unity only registers collisions if at least one of the parties in the collision has a Rigidbody attached, so go ahead and add one to your capsule. The Rigidbody can be kinematic if you plan to move it using raw code or non-kinematic if you'll be using forces to move it. However, I'll leave the movement code out of this example because it's already very lengthy. Figure 14-17 shows the components attached to the capsule. Let's move on to the more interesting InteractiveSnow script.

Figure 14-17. *To register collisions, the snow actor GameObject needs a collider and Rigidbody attached*

The InteractiveSnow C# Script

Create another C# script and name it "InteractiveSnow.cs". The purpose of this script is to set up a texture to keep track of which bits of the snow have been walked on and then handle the compute shader, which will be used to modify that texture. The InteractiveSnow script will keep track of the position of all actors currently inside the snow and then send data to the compute shader to update the texture whenever any of the actors move. Here's the code we'll be filling in.

Listing 14-40. The InteractiveSnow class code skeleton

```
using System.Collections.Generic;
using UnityEngine;

public class InteractiveSnow : MonoBehaviour
{
    ...

    struct SnowActorInfo { ... }

    private void Start() { ... }

    private void Update() { ... }
```

```
        private void ResetSnowActorBuffer() { ... }

        private void OnTriggerEnter(Collider other) { ... }

        private void OnTriggerExit(Collider other) { ... }

        private void OnDestroy() { ... }
}
```

We'll get into the struct and those methods soon, but first, there are a lot of class variables to get through. Here are the public variables that can be changed in the Inspector:

- *Snow Resolution* – A `Vector2Int` that stores the resolution of the `RenderTexture`. A value of about 1024 is plenty for the Unity built-in plane mesh, although you can decrease it to enhance the performance or increase it if you need finer details or if you're using a larger surface.

- *Mesh Size* – This `float` is the physical size of the plane in meters. The default value will be 10 since that's the size of the Unity built-in plane mesh. We use this value to convert the actors' world-space positions to UV-space positions.

- *Max Snow Height* – This `float` is the height, in meters, that the snow will reach when the texture is white. This is the starting height of the snow.

- *Snow Falloff* – This `float` represents the transition between full height and full depression of the snow when an actor walks through it. Without a falloff, the depressions made in the snow would have completely straight vertical walls.

- *Snow Engulf* – Alongside the Snow Falloff, this float artificially reduces the radius of each actor so some of the snow "engulfs" them. This makes the actors look slightly more like the snow is engulfing them.

- *Max Snow Actors* – We must impose a strict limit on the number of snow actors because we will be using fixed-length buffers to send actor data to the compute shader.

- *Snow Offset Shader* – The compute shader itself. We'll be writing this later.

On top of that, there is a whole host of private variables required to keep track of state and drive the effect:

- *Snow Offset Tex* – This is the `RenderTexture` that stores the height of each bit of the snow.

- *Snow Material* – This is the material that is attached to the snow mesh. We store a reference to it so that we can bind properties to it during runtime.

- *Box Collider* – We'll be using Unity's collision system to detect actors. The snow mesh will have a `BoxCollider` tagged as a trigger attached for this purpose. The collider will reach from the ground level to the max height of the snow.

- *Snow Actors* – We will keep track of which snow actors are inside the collider via this `List`.

- *Snow Actor Buffer* – We can't send the snow actors themselves to the compute shader, and it wouldn't make much sense to do so because we only need two bits of data: the position and radius of each actor. This `GraphicsBuffer` will contain that data.

Each of these variables can be included at the top of the script.

Listing 14-41. The InteractiveSnow variables

```
public class InteractiveSnow : MonoBehaviour
{
        public Vector2Int snowResolution = new Vector2Int(1024, 1024);
        public float meshSize = 10.0f;
        public float maxSnowHeight = 0.5f;
        public float snowFalloff = 0.25f;
        public float snowEngulf = 0.1f;
        public int maxSnowActors = 20;
        public ComputeShader snowOffsetShader;
```

```
private RenderTexture snowOffsetTex;
private Material snowMaterial;
private BoxCollider boxCollider;

private List<SnowActor> snowActors = new List<SnowActor>();

private GraphicsBuffer snowActorBuffer;

struct SnowActorInfo { ... }
```

Next, let's look at the SnowActorInfo struct and the ResetSnowActorBuffer method. We'll be sending data about each actor to the compute shader, but it's not possible to send a reference to the entire GameObject. Nor would that make any sense, because we only need the position and radius of each of those actors. Instead, we'll use this struct. Every time we want to send actor data to the GPU, we'll build an instance of this struct for each actor and package them inside the snowActorBuffer. We do that inside the ResetSnowActorBuffer method, which iterates through the actor list, checks the actor is moving, then calculates its position and radius in UV space, and creates the struct.

Listing 14-42. The SnowActorInfo struct

```
struct SnowActorInfo
{
    public Vector3 position;
    public float radius;
}
```

Listing 14-43. The ResetSnowActorBuffer method

```
private void ResetSnowActorBuffer()
{
    var snowActorInfoList = new SnowActorInfo[snowActors.Count];

    for(int i = 0; i < snowActors.Count; ++i)
    {
        var snowActor = snowActors[i];
        Vector3 relativePos = transform.InverseTransformPoint
        (snowActor.GetGroundPos());
```

```
    if (snowActors[i].IsMoving() && relativePos.y >= 0.0f)
    {
        relativePos.x /= meshSize;
        relativePos.z /= meshSize;
        relativePos.y /= maxSnowHeight;
        relativePos += new Vector3(0.5f, 0.0f, 0.5f);

        var snowActorInfo = new SnowActorInfo()
        {
            position = relativePos,
            radius = (snowActor.GetRadius() - snowEngulf) /
            meshSize
        };

        snowActorInfoList[i] = snowActorInfo;
    }
}

snowActorBuffer.SetData(snowActorInfoList);
}
```

Here, the InverseTransformPoint method transforms the actor position to the snow mesh's local space. Only actors that are moving and are positioned above the mesh get included in the buffer. From there, we divide the x- and z- components by meshSize to transform the position to snowOffsetTex's UV space and divide the y-component by the maxSnowHeight – we'll be using that value to determine the snow's new height at this position. We'll need to add an offset of 0.5 along the x- and z-directions because the snow mesh center point was misaligned with the UV coordinate origin point.

Now we'll fill in the OnTriggerEnter, OnTriggerExit, and OnDestroy methods. The first two of those methods register and deregister instances of SnowActor whenever they enter and exit the trigger, respectively. The OnDestroy method exists to clean up the snowActorBuffer when we don't need it anymore.

Listing 14-44. The OnTriggerEnter, OnTriggerExit, and OnDestroy methods

```
private void OnTriggerEnter(Collider other)
{
      var snowActor = other.GetComponent<SnowActor>();

      if(snowActor != null && snowActors.Count < maxSnowActors)
      {
            snowActors.Add(snowActor);
      }
}

private void OnTriggerExit(Collider other)
{
      var snowActor = other.GetComponent<SnowActor>();

      if (snowActor != null)
      {
            snowActors.Remove(snowActor);
      }
}

private void OnDestroy()
{
      snowActorBuffer.Dispose();
}
```

Let's now explore the Start method, which is the longest one in the file. This method is responsible for setting up the many moving parts of the effect and setting the initial state of the shaders. Here's what the code will do, in order:

- Create the snowOffsetTex texture. It is crucial to enable reading and writing the texture so that we are able to update it whenever actors interact with the snow.

- Get references to the BoxCollider component and the material attached to the snow mesh's Renderer component.

- Resize the box collider and reposition its center point accordingly.
  The bottom face of the collider intersects the ground level, and the
  top face intersects the max snow level.

- Create the GraphicsBuffer that will be used to hold actor data for the
  compute shader.

- Set properties on both the compute shader and the regular shader
  that do not need updating at runtime.

- Run a kernel on the compute shader called "InitializeOffsets". This
  kernel sets the initial color values of snowOffsetTex.

Listing 14-45. The Start method

```
private void Start()
{
        snowOffsetTex = new RenderTexture(snowResolution.x, snowResolution.y,
        0, RenderTextureFormat.ARGBFloat);
        snowOffsetTex.enableRandomWrite = true;
        snowOffsetTex.Create();

        snowMaterial = GetComponent<Renderer>().material;
        boxCollider = GetComponent<BoxCollider>();

        Vector3 size = boxCollider.size;
        size.y = maxSnowHeight;
        boxCollider.size = size;

        Vector3 center = boxCollider.center;
        center.y = maxSnowHeight / 2.0f;
        boxCollider.center = center;

        snowActorBuffer = new GraphicsBuffer(GraphicsBuffer.Target.
        Structured, maxSnowActors, sizeof(int) * 4);

        snowOffsetShader.SetFloat("_SnowFalloff", snowFalloff / meshSize);
        snowOffsetShader.SetVector("_SnowResolution", (Vector2)
        snowResolution);
```

```
        snowMaterial.SetFloat("_MaxSnowHeight", maxSnowHeight);
        snowMaterial.SetTexture("_SnowOffset", snowOffsetTex);

        int kernel = snowOffsetShader.FindKernel("InitializeOffsets");
        snowOffsetShader.SetTexture(kernel, "_SnowOffset", snowOffsetTex);
        snowOffsetShader.Dispatch(kernel, snowResolution.x / 8,
        snowResolution.y / 8, 1);
}
```

That leaves just the Update method to fill in. This method first checks if there are any actors inside the snow actor list, and if not, then the Update method returns immediately to avoid unnecessary computation. If there are, then it updates the snow actor buffer. Then it finds the "ApplyOffsets" kernel; sends the actor buffer and offset texture to that kernel, as well as the number of snow actors; and finally dispatches the kernel. This kernel is the most important one in the entire effect, as it displaces the snow height at each actor position.

Listing 14-46. The Update method

```
private void Update()
{
        if (snowActors.Count == 0)
        {
            return;
        }

        ResetSnowActorBuffer();

        int kernel = snowOffsetShader.FindKernel("ApplyOffsets");
        snowOffsetShader.SetTexture(kernel, "_SnowOffset", snowOffsetTex);
        snowOffsetShader.SetBuffer(kernel, "_SnowActors", snowActorBuffer);
        snowOffsetShader.SetInt("_SnowActorCount", snowActors.Count);
        snowOffsetShader.Dispatch(kernel, snowResolution.x / 8,
        snowResolution.y / 8, 1);
}
```

This script is now complete. To set up the snow mesh, attach the `InteractiveSnow` script to it and ensure it has a box collider attached with the *Is Trigger* option ticked. You can add other colliders to the mesh to avoid objects clipping through the floor – in Figure 14-18, I've also attached a mesh collider – but make sure there is only one box collider, because we're modifying its size via scripting.

Figure 14-18. *Components attached to the snow mesh. We haven't yet written the InteractiveSnow shader that will be attached to the material*

It's time to write the compute shader that will update the snow offset texture each frame.

Interactive Snow Compute Shader

The compute shader includes two kernels. One is used to set the original snow level, and the other is used to apply the influence of the snow actors to modify the snow level. Start by creating a new compute shader via *Create* ➤ *Shader* ➤ *Compute Shader* and naming it "InteractiveSnow.compute". Here's the code we'll start with.

Listing 14-47. The InteractiveSnow compute shader code skeleton

```
#pragma kernel InitializeOffsets;
#pragma kernel ApplyOffsets

struct SnowActorInfo { ... };

RWTexture2D<float4> _SnowOffset;
uniform float2 _SnowResolution;
uniform float _SnowFalloff;

StructuredBuffer<SnowActorInfo> _SnowActors;
uniform int _SnowActorCount;

[numthreads(8,8,1)]
void InitializeOffsets(uint3 id : SV_DispatchThreadID) { ... }

float inverseLerp(float a, float b, float t)
{
        return (t - a) / (b - a);
}

[numthreads(8,8,1)]
void ApplyOffsets (uint3 id : SV_DispatchThreadID) { ... }
```

First, let's set up the SnowActorInfo struct. The members of this struct should match up with the members of the corresponding SnowActorInfo struct that we wrote in the C# script, except instead of using C# variable types, we use HLSL variable types.

Listing 14-48. The SnowActorInfo struct

```
struct SnowActorInfo
{
    float3 position;
    float radius;
};
```

It is possible to mix and match regular functions and multiple kernel functions inside a single compute shader file, so we specify the kernel functions using the #pragma kernel statement. You'll notice that the variables inside this file are direct parallels of those from the InteractiveSnow script – these are the exact variables we sent data to from within that script. We've encountered StructuredBuffer previously, so the other variable type of note is RWTexture2D, which is just a rewritable and readable variant of the standard Texture2D.

The first kernel function is called InitializeOffsets. This kernel function runs over each texel of the texture once, so if the texture has a resolution of 1024 by 1024, then the thread ID will run from 1 to 1024 in the x- and y-directions. All we do in this function is set every entry in the texture to white, or 1. Although this is perhaps a bit overkill, this leaves room for you to tweak the initial offset values if you'd like.

Listing 14-49. The InitializeOffsets kernel function

```
[numthreads(8,8,1)]
void InitializeOffsets(uint3 id : SV_DispatchThreadID)
{
    _SnowOffset[id.xy] = 1.0f;
}
```

The second kernel function is called ApplyOffsets. In this function, we'll iterate over the _SnowActors list, and for each one, we will compute the distance of the actor from the UV position of the texel associated with the thread. If that distance is less than the radius plus falloff, then we can modify the height of the snow and store the new value in the _SnowOffset texture.

Here, the inverseLerp function will help. Where lerp takes two input values and returns a new "result" value between them based on the third input value called the interpolation factor, the inverseLerp function takes two input values and a "result" value and returns what interpolation factor *would have* returned that "result" value in a lerp. That's why it's the "inverse" of lerp!

Listing 14-50. The ApplyOffsets kernel function

```
[numthreads(8,8,1)]
void ApplyOffsets (uint3 id : SV_DispatchThreadID)
{
    for (int i = 0; i < _SnowActorCount; i++)
    {
        float2 currentUV = float2(id.x, id.y) / _SnowResolution;

        float dist = distance(currentUV, 1.0f - _SnowActors[i].
        position.xz);

        if (dist < _SnowActors[i].radius + _SnowFalloff)
        {
            float heightMod = inverseLerp(0, _SnowFalloff, dist - _
            SnowActors[i].radius);
            heightMod = saturate(heightMod);

            float newHeight = lerp(_SnowActors[i].position.y, _
            SnowOffset[id.xy], heightMod);
            _SnowOffset[id.xy] = min(newHeight, _SnowOffset[id.xy]);
        }
    }
}
```

This compute shader is now complete. The two kernels are called from the InteractiveSnow C# script, as you saw. Whenever the compute shader makes a change to the snow offset texture, those changes can also be seen by any other shader that references that texture. In that same C# script, we already bound that texture to the snow mesh's material, so the final step is to see how that material's shader works.

Interactive Snow Mesh Shader

This shader works by displacing the vertices of the mesh in the y-direction according to the value in the snow offset texture. To draw snow trails in the ground, the mesh needs to have a sufficiently high vertex resolution, so we will use tessellation in the shader to achieve that. That causes a couple of issues that we covered in Chapter 12. Recall that in Shader Graph, only HDRP supports tessellation – URP does not. However, both the built-in pipeline and URP can support tessellation with code-based shaders, so you're not completely out of luck in URP! I'll show you how to write the shader in HLSL and then in Shader Graph.

Snow Shader in HLSL

Start by creating a new shader file and naming it "InteractiveSnow.shader". Although we've named several files for this effect "InteractiveSnow", the file extensions are all different, so don't worry about conflicts arising from that. As I mentioned, we'll be using tessellation for this effect, but we won't be doing anything regarding tessellation that we didn't already see in Chapter 12, so I won't explain it in detail here. With that in mind, here's the code we'll be starting with.

Listing 14-51. The InteractiveSnow mesh shader skeleton

```
Shader "Examples/InteractiveSnow"
{
    Properties { ... }
    SubShader
    {
        Tags
        {
            "RenderType" = "Opaque"
            "Queue" = "Geometry"
        }

        Pass
        {
            HLSLPROGRAM
            #pragma vertex vert
            #pragma fragment frag
```

```
#pragma hull tessHull
#pragma domain tessDomain
#pragma target 4.6

...

struct appdata
{
      float4 positionOS : Position;
      float2 uv : TEXCOORD0;
};

struct tessControlPoint
{
      float4 positionOS : INTERNALTESSPOS;
      float2 uv : TEXCOORD0;
};

struct tessFactors
{
      float edge[3] : SV_TessFactor;
      float inside : SV_InsideTessFactor;
};

struct v2f
{
      float4 positionCS : SV_Position;
      float2 uv : TEXCOORD0;
};

...

tessControlPoint vert(appdata v) { ... }
v2f tessVert(appdata v) { ... }
tessFactors patchConstantFunc( ... ) { ... }
tessControlPoint tessHull( ... ) { ... }
v2f tessDomain( ... ) { ... }
float4 frag (v2f i) : SV_Target { ... }
ENDHLSL
```

```
        }
    }
    Fallback Off
}
```

First, let's deal with tags and include files, which are different between the built-in pipeline and URP.

Listing 14-52. Tags and include files for the snow effect in the built-in pipeline

```
Pass
{
    Tags
    {
        "LightMode" = "ForwardBase"
    }

    HLSLPROGRAM
    #pragma vertex vert
    #pragma fragment frag
    #pragma hull tessHull
    #pragma domain tessDomain
    #pragma target 4.6

    #include "UnityCG.cginc"
```

Listing 14-53. Tags and include files for the snow effect in URP

```
Tags
{
    "RenderType" = "Opaque"
    "Queue" = "Geometry"
    "RenderPipeline" = "UniversalPipeline"
}
```

```
Pass
{
        Tags
        {
                "LightMode" = "UniversalForward"
        }

        HLSLPROGRAM
        #pragma vertex vert
        #pragma fragment frag
        #pragma hull tessHull
        #pragma domain tessDomain
        #pragma target 4.6

        #include "Packages/com.unity.render-pipelines.universal/
        ShaderLibrary/Core.hlsl"
```

Next, we will add the shader properties, of which some we have seen briefly before in the C# script and others were present in the compute shader. Here's what each property will do:

- *Low Color* – The `Color` assigned to parts of the snow mesh that have been fully stood on.

- *High Color* – The `Color` shown on the parts of the snow at the maximum height. These two colors will both use the [HDR] attribute, which is particularly important on the high color where the snow will be brightest, as snow tends to brightly reflect the sun and we can artificially boost the brightness using HDR.

- *Base Tex* – The albedo `Texture` for the snow surface.

- *Snow Offset* – The `Texture` containing the offset at each point on the snow's surface. This is the same texture that was generated by the compute shader.

- *Max Snow Height* – The maximum height that the snow will be offset by in world space along the y-axis.

- *Tess Amount* – The number of tessellation subdivisions applied to the mesh. The hardware maximum value is 64.

We must declare these in the Properties block in all pipelines using ShaderLab syntax.

Listing 14-54. Declaring properties for the snow effect in the Properties block

```
Properties
{
        [HDR] _LowColor ("Low Snow Color", Color) = (0, 0, 0, 1)
        [HDR] _HighColor("High Snow Color", Color) = (1, 1, 1, 1)
        _BaseTex("Base Texture", 2D) = "white" {}
        _SnowOffset("Snow Offset", 2D) = "white" {}
        _MaxSnowHeight("Max Snow Height", Float) = 0.5
        _TessAmount("Tessellation Amount", Range(1, 64)) = 2
}
```

After, we must then redeclare them in the HLSLPROGRAM block, which requires slightly different code between the built-in pipeline and URP. These declarations can go beneath the v2f struct definition.

Listing 14-55. Declaring properties in HLSLPROGRAM in the built-in pipeline

```
struct v2f { ... };

sampler2D _BaseTex;
sampler2D _SnowOffset;
float4 _LowColor;
float4 _HighColor;
float _MaxSnowHeight;
float _TessAmount;
```

Listing 14-56. Declaring properties in HLSLPROGRAM in URP

```
struct v2f { ... };

sampler2D _BaseTex;
sampler2D _SnowOffset;

CBUFFER_START(UnityPerMaterial)
        float4 _LowColor;
        float4 _HighColor;
```

```
    float _MaxSnowHeight;
    float _TessAmount;
CBUFFER_END
```

For the rest of the shader, the code is identical between the two pipelines. First, let's deal with the tessellation-specific code. As I mentioned, nothing here will look any different from what we learned about tessellation in Chapter 12. To recap

- The vertex function, vert, converts instances of appdata into tessControlPoint instances.

- Then, the hull shader function, tessHull, and patch control function, patchConstantFunc, are responsible for positioning the input control points and supplying tessellation factors, respectively; both these stages happen in parallel.

- Then, the tessellator (which is not a programmable stage) creates the new control points, which get fed to the domain shader function, tessDomain.

- The tessDomain function interpolates properties about the new control points between the old control points.

Listing 14-57. The vertex shader and tessellation-specific functions

```
tessControlPoint vert(appdata v)
{
    tessControlPoint o;
    o.positionOS = v.positionOS;
    o.uv = v.uv;
    return o;
}

tessFactors patchConstantFunc(InputPatch<tessControlPoint, 3> patch)
{
    tessFactors f;
    f.edge[0] = f.edge[1] = f.edge[2] = _TessAmount;
    f.inside = _TessAmount;
    return f;
}
```

```
[domain("tri")]
[outputcontrolpoints(3)]
[outputtopology("triangle_cw")]
[partitioning("integer")]
[patchconstantfunc("patchConstantFunc")]
tessControlPoint tessHull(InputPatch<tessControlPoint, 3> patch, uint id :
SV_OutputControlPointID)
{
    return patch[id];
}

[domain("tri")]
v2f tessDomain(tessFactors factors, OutputPatch<tessControlPoint, 3> patch,
float3 bcCoords : SV_DomainLocation)
{
    appdata i;

    i.positionOS = patch[0].positionOS * bcCoords.x +
        patch[1].positionOS * bcCoords.y +
        patch[2].positionOS * bcCoords.z;

    i.uv = patch[0].uv * bcCoords.x +
        patch[1].uv * bcCoords.y +
        patch[2].uv * bcCoords.z;

    return tessVert(i);
}
```

That leaves us with only the tessVert and frag functions. Although this shader officially uses vert as its vertex function, the only purpose of that is to funnel data to the tessellation stages. We'll run the tessVert function on the outputs from tessDomain, so it acts like a *post-tessellation* vertex shader. For this function, we can sample _SnowOffset with tex2Dlod to obtain the normalized height for the current vertex. Recall that in the vertex stage, we must specifically use tex2Dlod, as the regular tex2D function won't work. We'll use the height value to apply a world-space offset in the y-direction, capped at _MaxSnowHeight. After that, we'll convert from world space to clip space and output a v2f instance, outputting the same UVs that were input.

Listing 14-58. The tessVert function

```
V2f tessVert(appdata v)
{
    v2f o;
    float heightOffset = tex2Dlod(_SnowOffset, float4(v.uv, 0, 0));

    float4 positionWS = mul(unity_ObjectToWorld, v.positionOS);
    positionWS.y += lerp(0, _MaxSnowHeight, heightOffset);

    o.positionCS = mul(UNITY_MATRIX_VP, positionWS);
    o.uv = v.uv;
    return o;
}
```

Finally, we come to the frag function, which is run last in the graphics pipeline. By sampling the same _SnowOffset texture as the tessVert function (this time using tex2D), we can lerp between _LowColor and _HighColor to calculate a tint color based on the strength of the snow depression at the current position. We then sample _BaseTex to obtain the snow's albedo color and multiply by the tint color to get our shader output.

Listing 14-59. The frag function for the snow effect

```
float4 frag (v2f i) : SV_Target
{
    float snowHeight = tex2D(_SnowOffset, i.uv).r;
    float4 textureSample = tex2D(_BaseTex, i.uv);
    return textureSample * lerp(_LowColor, _HighColor, snowHeight);
}
```

This shader is now finished, so you can attach it to a material and apply it to the snow mesh GameObject. If the InteractiveSnow and SnowActor scripts are correctly applied to objects in the scene, then you will see results like in Figure 14-16 if you run the game in Play Mode. If you are using HDRP, then you'll need to write this shader in Shader Graph instead, which we'll cover next.

Snow Shader in Shader Graph

Start by creating a new Unlit graph and name it "InteractiveSnow.shadergraph". Open it in the Shader Graph editor, and in the Graph Settings, expand the *Surface Options* section and tick *Tessellation*. You should see the *Tessellation Factor* and *Tessellation Displacement* blocks appear on the vertex stage of the master stack, which we will need soon. Before we can use them, we'll need to add some shader properties.

The properties for this graph will be the same as in the HLSL version of the shader – each one is described in that section. Figure 14-19 shows the properties required for this graph, particularly the _LowColor, _HighColor, and _TessAmount properties that use special settings.

Figure 14-19. *The InteractiveSnow graph properties*

With the properties in place, let's tessellate the mesh and apply an offset to each vertex of the mesh along the y-axis according to the values in the Snow Offset texture. For that, we must use the Sample Texture 2D LOD node, because the standard Sample Texture 2D node does not work in the vertex stage. The values from the texture are between 0 and 1, so we will use a Lerp node to change the range to between 0 and Max Snow Height. We'll use a Vector 3 node to construct the offset vector and output it to the *Tessellation Displacement* block on the master stack. For the *Tessellation Factor* block, we'll connect our Tess Amount property as shown in Figure 14-20.

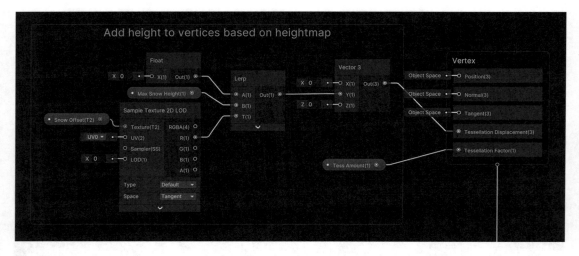

Figure 14-20. *Applying a height offset to the vertices of the tessellated mesh*

Unity will then handle the tessellation for us – we won't need to tweak any of the default tessellation settings in the Graph Settings window. We can now move to the fragment stage of the graph. In this stage, we will sample the Snow Offset texture and use the result – a value between 0 and 1 – as the interpolation factor of a Lerp node to pick between Low Color (when the value is 0) and High Color (when the value is 1). Then, we'll multiply it by the albedo color, which we get by sampling Base Tex. The result is used for the *Base Color* output of the graph. Figure 14-21 shows how these nodes should be connected.

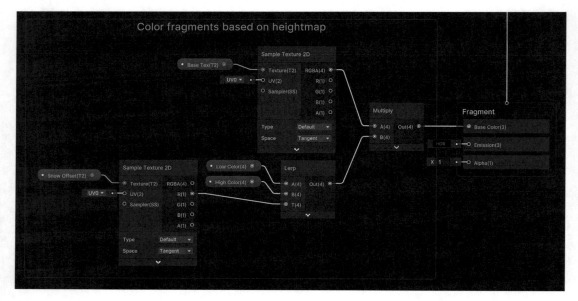

Figure 14-21. *Determining the snow tint color that influences the albedo color*

This graph is now complete, so you can use it in a material and attach the material to the snow mesh. If you've set everything else up as I described, then you will be able to move a snow actor through the trigger attached to the mesh, and trails will start to appear in the snow as the actor walks through it, as seen in Figure 14-16.

Although interactive shader effects are exciting, it can be just as exciting to make pretty shaders that the player can't interact with, so next, we'll create a hologram shader that can be used to visually enhance games with a futuristic setting.

Holograms

A surefire way to make your game look more futuristic is to add holograms to it. Holograms are essentially a projection of a mesh into the world using bright light, so typically, holograms in games give off a soft colorful glow. Although there are several different directions you could go in, I'll make a hologram effect by supplying a black and white texture that encodes which parts of the mesh should be cut out. The idea is if you want a hologram that looks like scan lines, then you can supply a texture full of alternating black and white lines and if you want a hologram that looks speckled like white noise, then you can supply a texture made up of scattered white dots on a black background. The texture will be sampled in screen space. Then we'll apply an HDR color to the white parts and cull the black parts. Figure 14-22 shows you the kinds of effect you can make using this approach.

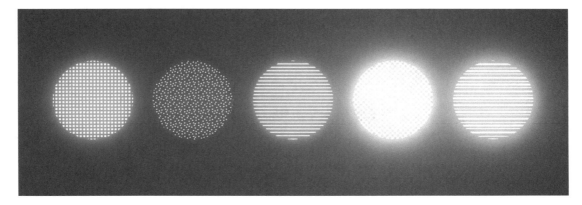

Figure 14-22. *Five holograms with different hologram textures and colors. This effect looks best when viewing the effects at native resolution, as resizing can impact the sampling*

One key thing to keep in mind is that you must have a bloom filter attached to your camera to see the color bleeding present in Figure 14-22 – this effect is available in each pipeline's built-in post-process effect stack. We'll be making this effect in both HLSL and Shader Graph.

Holograms in HLSL

Start by creating a new shader and naming it "Hologram.shader". We'll be using alpha testing to cull the gaps between the holographic pixels, so make sure the Queue tag for this shader is set to AlphaTest. Here's the code we'll be starting with.

Listing 14-60. The Hologram shader code skeleton

```
Shader "Examples/Hologram"
{
    Properties { ... }
    SubShader
    {
        Tags
        {
            "RenderType" = "Opaque"
            "Queue" = "AlphaTest"
        }

        Pass
        {
            Tags
            {
                "LightMode" = "UniversalForward"
            }

            HLSLPROGRAM
            #pragma vertex vert
            #pragma fragment frag
```

```
        struct appdata
        {
                float4 positionOS : Position;
                float2 uv : TEXCOORD0;
        };

        struct v2f { ... };

        v2f vert (appdata v) { ... }
        float4 frag (v2f i) : SV_Target { ... }

        ENDHLSL
    }
}
Fallback Off
}
```

The first addition we'll make is to add the correct tags and include files for the pipeline you are using. This code should be familiar to you by now!

Listing 14-61. Tags and include files for the hologram effect in the built-in pipeline

```
Pass
{
    Tags
    {
        "LightMode" = "ForwardBase"
    }

    HLSLPROGRAM
    pragma vertex vert
    #pragma fragment frag

    #UnityCG.cginc"
```

Listing 14-62. Tags and include files for the hologram effect in URP

```
SubShader
{
    Tags
    {
        "RenderType" = "Opaque"
        "Queue" = "AlphaTest"
        "RenderPipeline" = "UniversalPipeline"
    }

    Pass
    {
        Tags
        {
            "LightMode" = "UniversalForward"
        }

        HLSLPROGRAM
        #pragma vertex vert
        #pragma fragment frag

        #include "Packages/com.unity.render-pipelines.universal/
        ShaderLibrary/Core.hlsl"
```

Next, let's deal with the shader properties. I briefly described what kind of data the shader requires in the introduction to this shader, but let's go into more detail here:

- *Base Tex* – The albedo texture that would usually be applied to an object. If this texture has fully transparent portions, then this will be important when we cull pixels later.

- *Hologram Tex* – A texture that should contain only black and white. We'll sample this texture in screen space, take only the red channel, and use it as a "mask" to determine which areas of the object should emit glowing light and which areas should be culled.

- *Hologram Color* – A tint color applied to the holographic pixels. This is an HDR color, which facilitates the glowing effect.

- *Hologram Size* – This float is used to scale the hologram texture.

We'll need to declare each of these properties in the Properties block.

Listing 14-63. Declaring properties for the hologram effect in the Properties block

```
Properties
{
    _BaseTex("Base Texture", 2D) = "white" {}
    _HologramTex("Hologram Texture", 2D) = "white" {}
    [HDR] _HologramColor("Hologram Color", Color) = (0, 0, 0, 0)
    _HologramSize("Hologram Size", Float) = 1
}
```

We'll need to then declare them once more in the HLSLPROGRAM block, where the code is slightly different depending on the pipeline you are using. We'll declare each of these properties underneath the v2f struct definition. I'm going to be using the texel size of _HologramTex in a later step, so we need to include the _HologramTex_TexelSize variable here too.

Listing 14-64. Declaring properties in the HLSLPROGRAM block for the hologram effect in the built-in pipeline

```
struct v2f { ... };

sampler2D _BaseTex;
sampler2D _HologramTex;
float4 _BaseTex_ST;
float4 _HologramTex_TexelSize;
float4 _HologramColor;
float _HologramSize;
```

Listing 14-65. Declaring properties in the HLSLPROGRAM block
for the hologram effect in URP

```
struct v2f { ... };

sampler2D _BaseTex;
sampler2D _HologramTex;

CBUFFER_START(UnityPerMaterial)
     float4 _BaseTex_ST;
     float4 _HologramTex_TexelSize;
     float4 _HologramColor;
     float _HologramSize;
CBUFFER_END
```

Next, let's look at the v2f struct itself. Most basic shaders like this one don't need anything inside the v2f struct besides clip-space positions and UV coordinates, but as I mentioned, I want to sample _HologramTex in screen space. Therefore, we require screen-space coordinates for use in the fragment shader. For that, we can calculate them in the vertex shader and send them to the fragment shader via the v2f struct. I'll name the variable positionSS, to fit our naming scheme, and use the TEXCOORD1 semantic for it.

Listing 14-66. The v2f struct

```
struct v2f
{
     float4 positionCS : SV_Position;
     float2 uv : TEXCOORD0;
     float4 positionSS : TEXCOORD1;
};
```

Now we can move on to the vert function, that is, the vertex shader, where we will calculate the value of positionSS, as well as everything else that needs to go in the v2f struct. We've seen how to calculate positionCS and uv before – the calculation for positionCS requires pipeline-specific code. To calculate positionSS, we can use the ComputeScreenPos function, which is included in all pipelines; this function takes the clip-space position as a parameter and returns the screen-space position.

Listing 14-67. The vert function for the hologram effect in the built-in pipeline

```
v2f vert (appdata v)
{
    v2f o;
    o.positionCS = UnityObjectToClipPos(v.positionOS.xyz);
    o.positionSS = ComputeScreenPos(o.positionCS);
    o.uv = TRANSFORM_TEX(v.uv, _BaseTex);
    return o;
}
```

Listing 14-68. The vert function for the hologram effect in URP

```
v2f vert (appdata v)
{
    v2f o;
    o.positionCS = TransformObjectToHClip(v.positionOS.xyz);
    o.positionSS = ComputeScreenPos(o.positionCS);
    o.uv = TRANSFORM_TEX(v.uv, _BaseTex);
    return o;
}
```

That just leaves us with the frag function, which is the fragment shader. Here's a rundown of what the fragment shader needs to do:

- Calculate the screen-space UVs to use for _HologramTex.

    - We need to take the positionSS variable from v2f and perform the perspective divide, where we divide the xy components by the w component.

    - Then, multiply by the screen resolution. This value is contained in _ScreenParams.xy, which is a built-in variable.

    - Finally, divide by the size of _HologramTex. This value is contained in _HologramTex_TexelSize.zw, but we must multiply the value by _HologramSize.

- Use the screen-space UVs to sample _HologramTex to get a hologram value from the red channel. Then use the standard set of UVs to sample _BaseTex.

- Calculate the alpha value for the pixel by multiplying the base texture alpha by the hologram sample value.

  - If this value is below 0.5, then discard the pixel.

- Multiply the hologram sample by _HologramColor to get the final hologram color.

- Add the hologram color and the base texture sample together to get the final output color for the shader.

Listing 14-69. The frag function for the hologram effect

```
float4 frag (v2f i) : SV_Target
{
    float2 screenUV = i.positionSS.xy / i.positionSS.w * _ScreenParams.xy
    / (_HologramTex_TexelSize.zw * _HologramSize);

    float hologramSample = tex2D(_HologramTex, screenUV).r;
    float4 textureSample = tex2D(_BaseTex, i.uv);

    float alpha = textureSample.a * hologramSample;

    if (alpha < 0.5f) discard;

    float4 hologramColor = hologramSample * _HologramColor;
    float4 outputColor = textureSample + hologramColor;

    return outputColor;
}
```

The shader is now complete, so you should be able to see objects like those in Figure 14-22 if you create a material with this shader and attach it to objects in your scene. Let's see how this effect works in Shader Graph too.

Holograms in Shader Graph

Start by creating a new Unlit graph and naming it "Hologram.shadergraph". Start by going into the Graph Settings and ticking the *Alpha Clipping* setting – besides doing that, you can keep using *Opaque* rendering. The properties we'll need for this graph are the same as the ones we used in the HLSL version of the effect, so check out that section for a full description of each property. Figure 14-23 lists the properties we need and their types.

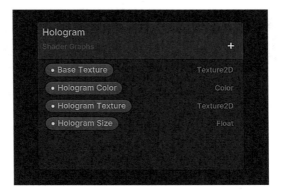

Figure 14-23. *The properties for the Hologram effect*

On the graph itself, the first thing we need to do is calculate the screen-space UVs with which we'll sample the Hologram Texture. This is a little easier to do in Shader Graph than in HLSL code because Shader Graph comes with a Screen Position node that we can use. Multiply that by the screen resolution to obtain a position in what I like to call "pixel space." Then, multiply the `Hologram Texture`'s `Texel Size` by the `Hologram Size`, and use that value to divide the pixel-space position. Figure 14-24 shows how these nodes should be connected.

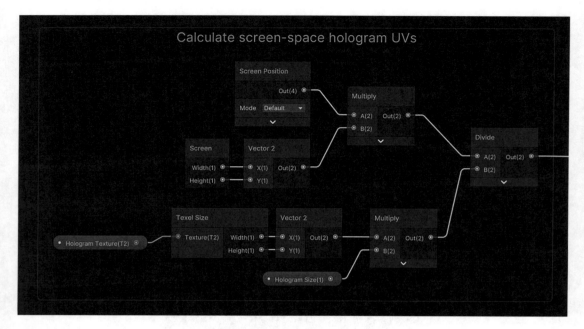

Figure 14-24. *Calculating the UVs for sampling the Hologram Texture*

Finally, we can sample the Hologram Texture using these screen-space UVs. Also sample the Base Texture using the standard set of UVs. For the *Base Color* output on the master stack, take the hologram sample's *R* component, multiply by Hologram Color, and add the base sample color. For the *Alpha* output on the master stack, simply add the *R* component of the hologram sample to the *A* component of the base sample. Connect these nodes as shown in Figure 14-25.

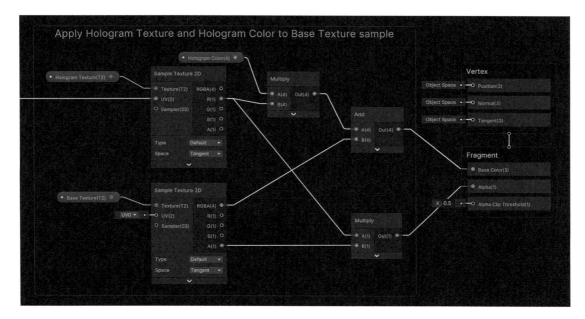

Figure 14-25. *Using the Hologram Texture and Base Texture for the graph outputs*

With that, the effect is complete! Attach this shader to a material and use it on objects in your scene to make them glow, as shown in Figure 14-22. As I mentioned, there are so many ways you can build a holographic effect, so try swapping out the hologram texture with all kinds of patterns to see how they affect the outcome. You could also try sampling the hologram texture in world space or object space instead of screen space, which produces rather different results, or try animating the hologram texture over time. There's really no limit to futuristic holograms! In the next section, we'll be building a couple of shaders specifically for 2D sprites.

Sprite Effects

So far in the book, we have focused almost entirely on 3D objects. While a lot of the concepts can be translated to 2D and several of the shaders will still work on 2D objects with some modification, I want to focus on some 2D effects in this section. To round off the book, we'll create a few fun effects that make your sprites look snazzy!

Each of these effects will be built with the default Sprite Renderer in mind. The Sprite Renderer has two fields we are primarily interested in: the *Sprite* field and the *Material* field. When we attach a material to this Sprite Renderer, then whichever sprite is attached to the Sprite field will automatically get sent to the shader the material uses in the _MainTex slot. Therefore, it is important to base our shaders on that _MainTex texture. With that in mind, let's move on to the first effect.

Sprite Pixelation

Let's start off simple to get the hang of sprite-specific shaders. With this effect, we will introduce the ability to pixelate a sprite based on a slider value, as seen in Figure 14-26.

Figure 14-26. *The same sprite shown five times, with increasingly higher levels of pixelation as you go from left to right*

Note   The sprites I'll be using in this section are by Kenney. These Creative Commons CC0 assets and many more can be found at kenney.nl/assets.

There's one important thing you must do on all sprites you want to use with this effect. In the import settings for the original texture, make sure that *Generate Mip Maps* is ticked – the option is about halfway down the list of settings. Once you've done that, we can move on to writing the shader – we'll cover the effect in HLSL code and then in Shader Graph.

Sprite Pixelation in HLSL

Start by creating a new shader and naming it "SpritePixelate.shader". This will be a basic vertex-fragment shader, so here's the code we'll be starting with.

Listing 14-70. The SpritePixelate shader code skeleton

```
Shader "Examples/SpritePixelate"
{
    Properties { ... }
    SubShader
    {
        Tags
        {
            "RenderType" = "Transparent"
            "Queue" = "Transparent"
        }

        Pass
        {
            Cull Off
            Blend SrcAlpha OneMinusSrcAlpha
            ZTest LEqual
            ZWrite Off

            HLSLPROGRAM
            #pragma vertex vert
            #pragma fragment frag

            struct appdata
            {
                float4 positionOS : Position;
                float2 uv : TEXCOORD0;
            };

            struct v2f
            {
                float4 positionCS : SV_Position;
                float2 uv : TEXCOORD0;
            };
```

```
                v2f vert (appdata v) { ... }
                float4 frag (v2f i) : SV_Target { ... }

                ENDHLSL
        }
    }
    Fallback Off
}
```

Sprite shaders typically use transparent rendering with two-sided rendering, so I've set up the shader tags appropriately and added the correct Blend, Cull, ZTest, and ZWrite keywords. Next, let's set up include files and other tags, which are required in each pipeline. This code is probably second nature to you by now!

Listing 14-71. Tags and include files for the sprite pixelation effect in the built-in pipeline

```
Pass
{
    Tags
    {
        "LightMode" = "ForwardBase"
    }

    Cull Off
    Blend SrcAlpha OneMinusSrcAlpha
    ZTest LEqual
    ZWrite Off

    HLSLPROGRAM
    #pragma vertex vert
    #pragma fragment frag

    #include "UnityCG.cginc"
```

Listing 14-72. Tags and include files for the sprite pixelation effect in URP

```
Tags
{
        "RenderType" = "Transparent"
        "Queue" = "Transparent"
        "RenderPipeline" = "UniversalPipeline"
}

Pass
{
        Tags
        {
                "LightMode" = "UniversalForward"
        }

        Cull Off
        Blend SrcAlpha OneMinusSrcAlpha
        ZTest LEqual
        ZWrite Off

        HLSLPROGRAM
        #pragma vertex vert
        #pragma fragment frag

        #include "Packages/com.unity.render-pipelines.universal/
        ShaderLibrary/Core.hlsl"
```

Next, let's add the shader properties. For this shader, instead of using _BaseTex as our name for the base texture as we usually do, we will instead use _MainTex, because Unity automatically binds this name to the sprite attached to the Sprite Renderer. Additionally, I will include a _BaseColor property to tint the texture and an _LOD property to control the level of pixelation seen on the sprite.

Listing 14-73. Adding properties to the Properties block for the sprite pixelation effect

```
Properties
{
    _BaseColor ("Base Color", Color) = (1, 1, 1, 1)
    _MainTex("Main Texture", 2D) = "white" {}
    _LOD("LOD", Int) = 0
}
```

As usual, we must also declare these properties inside the HLSLPROGRAM code block. However, we'll be doing something slightly different with _MainTex. In Chapter 5, I gave an overview of how custom SamplerState objects can be added to shaders, and here we have a prime example of where to use them, because I want to force the sprite to use blocky pixel rendering, rather than bilinear filtering. To use a custom SamplerState to sample the texture, we need to use the Texture2D type and declare a new SamplerState separately rather than using the sampler2D type we're accustomed to. The name of the SamplerState will be sampler_point_repeat, which Unity will automatically interpret to mean "point sampling, repeat wrapping." We can declare these, alongside the other properties, underneath the v2f struct definition.

Listing 14-74. Declaring the properties in HLSLPROGRAM in the built-in pipeline

```
struct v2f { ... };

Texture2D _MainTex;
SamplerState sampler_point_repeat;
float4 _BaseColor;
float4 _MainTex_ST;
int _LOD;
```

Listing 14-75. Declaring the properties in HLSLPROGRAM in URP

```
struct v2f { ... };

Texture2D _MainTex;
SamplerState sampler_point_repeat;

CBUFFER_START(UnityPerMaterial)
```

```
    float4 _BaseColor;
    float4 _MainTex_ST;
    int _LOD;
CBUFFER_END
```

Now we come to the vertex shader, vert. This vertex function is just like any other – just because we're using a sprite doesn't mean it is special. Unity automatically generates a mesh to fit your sprite, so we can use UnityObjectToClipPos in the built-in pipeline or TransformObjectToHClip in URP to transform vertex positions from object space to clip space and TRANSFORM_TEX in both pipelines to account for UV tiling and offset settings on _MainTex.

Listing 14-76. The vert function for the sprite pixelation effect in the built-in pipeline

```
v2f vert (appdata v)
{
    v2f o;
    o.positionCS = UnityObjectToClipPos(v.positionOS.xyz);
    o.uv = TRANSFORM_TEX(v.uv, _MainTex);
    return o;
}
```

Listing 14-77. The vert function for the sprite pixelation effect in URP

```
v2f vert (appdata v)
{
    v2f o;
    o.positionCS = TransformObjectToHClip(v.positionOS.xyz);
    o.uv = TRANSFORM_TEX(v.uv, _MainTex);
    return o;
}
```

That leaves us with the fragment shader, frag. Recall from Chapter 5 that you can sample a texture using the Sample function rather than the tex2D function; there is another function, SampleLevel, that allows you to sample the texture with a specific mip level. We'll use that to sample _MainTex and then multiply the result by _BaseColor.

Listing 14-78. Sampling a texture with SampleLevel

```
float4 frag (v2f i) : SV_Target
{
        float4 textureSample = _MainTex.SampleLevel(sampler_point_repeat,
        i.uv, _LOD);
        return textureSample * _BaseColor;
}
```

This code works in both the built-in and Universal pipelines, so we're now done with the shader, and you'll be able to see results like in Figure 14-26 if you use this shader with a sprite. Let's cover the effect in Shader Graph next.

Sprite Pixelation in Shader Graph

Start by creating a new graph and naming it "SpritePixelate.shadergraph". Here, your choice of graph type depends on which render pipeline you are using. In URP, rather than using the standard *Unlit* type that we've used previously for 3D objects, you can use the *Sprite Unlit* type instead. This type of graph automatically uses transparent, double-sided rendering. In HDRP, there is no such graph type, so we'll have to make do with the *Unlit* type. You'll have to manually change the *Surface Type* to *Transparent* and tick the *Double-Sided* option in the Graph Settings too. With these settings, both pipelines will have the same blocks on the master stack (except HDRP will have an additional *Emission* block, which we can ignore). Once you've sorted the graph type out, we can move on to the shader properties.

We will use the same three properties as the HLSL version of the effect, plus one extra, as detailed in Figure 14-27:

- A Color called Base Color. The default value should be white with full alpha.

- A Texture2D called Main Texture. You must set the reference value to _MainTex to ensure Unity automatically binds the sprite attached to the Sprite Renderer to this texture slot.

- A Float called LOD. We can set this property's *Mode* to *Integer*.

- A SamplerState, which we can just name Sampler State. The *Filter*
  mode should be set to *Point,* and the *Wrap* mode should be *Repeat.*
  This property is unable to be exposed to the Inspector, so think of it
  as a "local variable."

Figure 14-27. *Properties for the SpritePixelate effect. The LOD and Sampler State properties are highlighted as we must change a couple of settings on them*

The surface of the graph itself is incredibly simple. We'll use a Sample Texture 2D LOD node with the Main Texture property in its *Texture* slot, the LOD property in its *LOD* slot, and the Sampler State property in its *Sampler* slot. We can then multiply the *RGBA* output by Base Color, output the full result to the *Base Color* block on the master stack, then separate out the alpha with a Split node, and output that to the *Alpha* output on the master stack, as shown in Figure 14-28.

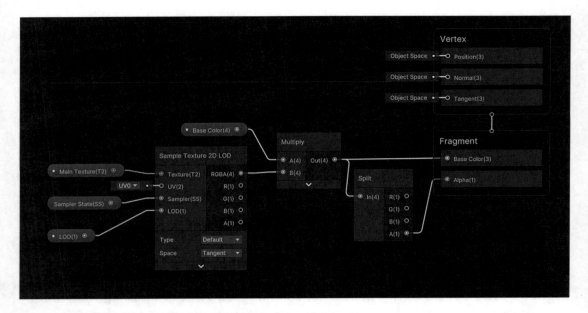

Figure 14-28. *The SpritePixelate graph surface*

With that, the shader is complete, and you can now use this effect in every pipeline and get results like in Figure 14-26. Although you could use this shader for purely utilitarian reasons, I said we would be making *fun* shaders in this section, so I like to use effects like this one to fade out sprites in a sort of "pixelated explosion" effect by increasing the LOD setting while decreasing the alpha component of Base Color. It makes things look a lot more interesting than just an alpha falloff! Now let's see how another sprite-based effect works.

Sprite Ripples

For this effect, we'll modify the UVs to make the sprite appear as if ripples emanated from the center outward. To do this, we will measure the distance of each pixel from the center of the sprite, create a clock, and then feed both values into a sine function. Based on the result, which should give us a radial pattern, we'll add a UV offset and sample _MainTex, resulting in the effect shown in Figure 14-29.

Figure 14-29. *From left to right, the ripples distort the sprite over time. The effect is far more evident in motion, but it's easiest to see on the face here, as the facial features expand outward and then contract inward*

Let's build this effect in HLSL code and then in Shader Graph.

Sprite Ripples in HLSL

Start by creating a new shader file called "SpriteRipples.shader". Here's the code we will start out with.

Listing 14-79. The SpriteRipples shader code skeleton

```
Shader "Examples/SpriteRipples"
{
      Properties { ... }
      SubShader
      {
            Tags
            {
                  "RenderType" = "Transparent"
                  "Queue" = "Transparent"
            }

            Pass
            {
                  Cull Off
                  Blend SrcAlpha OneMinusSrcAlpha
                  ZTest LEqual
                  ZWrite Off
```

```
HLSLPROGRAM
#pragma vertex vert
#pragma fragment frag

struct appdata
{
        float4 positionOS : Position;
        float2 uv : TEXCOORD0;
};

struct v2f
{
        float4 positionCS : SV_Position;
        float2 uv : TEXCOORD0;
};

v2f vert (appdata v) { ... }
float4 frag (v2f i) : SV_Target { ... }

ENDHLSL
    }
  }
  Fallback Off
}
```

First, we need to add the appropriate tags and include files for the pipeline you're working in. If you are using the built-in pipeline, add the code from Listing 14-71, or if you're working in URP, add the code from Listing 14-72. Similarly, the vertex shader is the same as the SpritePixelate shader example, but it differs between pipelines, so add the vert function from Listing 14-76 if you are working in the built-in pipeline or from Listing 14-77 if you are working in URP.

Next, let's deal with the shader properties. Alongside the _MainTex property that we must include to have access to the sprite attached to the Sprite Renderer and the _BaseColor property we include in most of our shaders, we'll also add three properties to configure the ripples:

- *Ripple Density* – This float represents how close each ripple is to the next. Increasing it will cause more ripples on the sprite at any one time.

- *Speed* – This `float` acts as a time multiplier. Increasing it causes ripples to expand outward faster.

- *Ripple Strength* – This `float` controls how strongly each ripple distorts the UVs.

We must add each property to the Properties block at the top of the file.

Listing 14-80. Adding properties to the Properties block for the sprite ripple effect

```
Properties
{
    _BaseColor ("Base Color", Color) = (1, 1, 1, 1)
    _MainTex("Main Texture", 2D) = "white" {}
    _RippleDensity("Ripple Density", Float) = 1
    _Speed("Speed", Float) = 1
    _RippleStrength("Ripple Strength", Float) = 0.01
}
```

We must then declare each property in the HLSLPROGRAM block, which requires slightly different code between the built-in and Universal pipelines. We will place these declarations just below the v2f struct definition.

Listing 14-81. Declaring properties in the HLSLPROGRAM block for the sprite ripple effect in the built-in pipeline

```
struct v2f { ... };

sampler2D _MainTex;
float4 _BaseColor;
float4 _MainTex_ST;
float _RippleDensity;
float _Speed;
float _RippleStrength;
```

Listing 14-82. Declaring properties in the HLSLPROGRAM block for the sprite ripple effect in URP

```
struct v2f { ... };

sampler2D _MainTex;

CBUFFER_START(UnityPerMaterial)
     float4 _BaseColor;
     float4 _MainTex_ST;
     float _RippleDensity;
     float _Speed;
     float _RippleStrength;
CBUFFER_END
```

Now we come to the heart of the effect, the `frag` function. Here's what this function will do:

- Calculate the offset between the current pixel and the center point by remapping the UVs from the [0, 1] range to the [–1, 1] range.

- From that value, calculate the distance of the pixel from the center.

- Create a clock that takes the time multiplied by `_Speed` and adds the distance we just calculated. Multiply the distance by `_RippleDensity` to influence the number of visible ripples.

- Use a sine function to create an undulating effect, where the offset values will go from 1 to –1 back to 1 over time.

- Normalize the offset value from before to obtain a direction value, then multiply by both the sine clock and `_RippleStrength`, and then add the value to the UVs. This gives us a new set of UVs with an offset that ripples over time, like we wanted.

- Use those UVs to sample `_MainTex` and then multiply by `_BaseColor` to obtain the final color value.

All the code in the frag function works in both the built-in pipeline and URP, so go ahead and use the following code, no matter which one you are using.

Listing 14-83. The frag function for the sprite ripple effect

```
float4 frag (v2f i) : SV_Target
{
    float2 offset = (i.uv - 0.5f) * 2.0f;
    float dist = distance(offset, float2(0.0f, 0.0f));

    float time = _Time.y * _Speed;
    float clock = time + dist * _RippleDensity;
    float sineClock = sin(clock);

    float2 direction = normalize(offset);
    float2 newUV = i.uv + sineClock * direction * _RippleStrength;

    float4 textureSample = tex2D(_MainTex, newUV);
    return textureSample * _BaseColor;
}
```

That's all we need to include in the shader, so you should see results like in Figure 14-29 if you attach the shader to a material and use it on a Sprite Renderer. Note that you should use very low values for _RippleStrength, in the ballpark of about 0.01, or else the ripples will be *very* chaotic. Next, let's see how the effect works in Shader Graph.

Sprite Ripples in Shader Graph

Start by creating a new graph called "SpriteRipples.shadergraph". As with the SpritePixelate effect, we can use the Sprite Unlit graph type if working in URP, but in HDRP, you will have to use the Unlit graph type and manually set the shader to use transparent, double-sided rendering.

We'll be using the same properties as the HLSL version, so we can start by adding those to the Blackboard. Remember that it's a good idea to set sensible default values; Ripple Density should be about 10; Speed depends on what kind of effect you're going for, but 5 is a good default value; and Ripple Strength should be very low, around 0.01. Figure 14-30 details the values you should use for each property.

Figure 14-30. *Properties for the SpriteRipples graph*

The first thing we'll do on the graph surface is calculate the offset vector between the current pixel and the center of the sprite, which we do by using a Remap node to remap the UV coordinates from the [0, 1] range to the [–1, 1] range. We'll need this offset vector later. We'll also calculate the distance from the center with a Distance node.

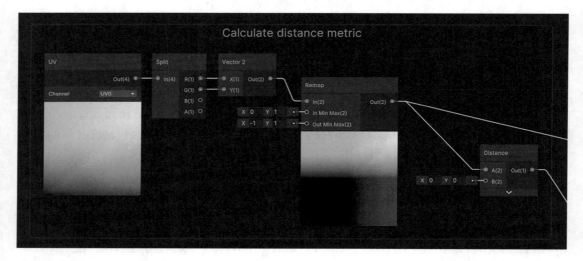

Figure 14-31. *Calculating the offset and distance from the center of the sprite*

We'll then multiply the distance metric by the Ripple Strength property to ensure several ripples are visible on the sprite at any one time and then add a timer that is influenced by the Speed property. This forms a clock, which we feed into a Sine node to create an undulating output that runs from –1 to 1 over time in a ripple pattern.

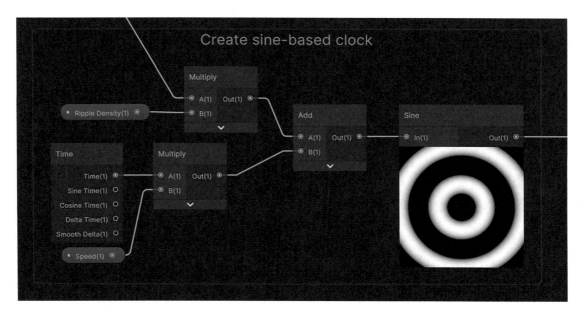

Figure 14-32. *Creating a sine wave clock*

Next, `Normalize` the offset vector from Figure 14-31 (i.e., the `Remap` node output) and multiply by `Ripple Strength` to obtain a small vector pointing in the direction away from the center and then multiply by the sine wave from Figure 14-32 to give us our final UV offset value. Use a `Tiling And Offset` node to apply the offset to the original set of UVs, as shown in Figure 14-33.

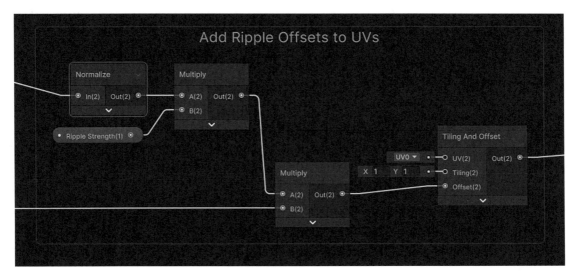

Figure 14-33. *Applying the offset to the UVs*

Finally, we can use these UVs to sample the Main Texture and then multiply by the Base Color property to apply a tint. The result of that multiplication gets output to the *Base Color* block on the master stack, and we can use a Split node to get the alpha channel and output that to the *Alpha* block on the master stack. Figure 14-34 shows how these nodes should be connected to the graph outputs.

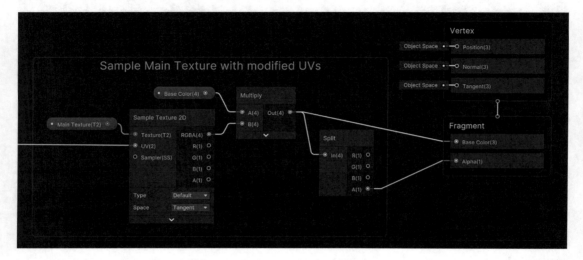

Figure 14-34. *Sampling the Main Texture, combining with the Base Color, and outputting*

The graph is now complete, and you can attach this shader via a material to any Sprite Renderer you want. Although this effect appears niche at first, you can apply it in many situations, such as when you use a psychic attack on an enemy or perhaps if the object is jelly-like. Perhaps you could color the sine clock values and apply those to the final albedo color as an extra tint!

Summary

Shaders let you create practically any visual effect you can think of! If you've made it all this way, then congratulations are in order – you should be well equipped to make the shaders you need for any game you're making. In this chapter, we saw versatile shaders that can be adapted into several aesthetics and shaders that I haven't had the chance to touch on so far but are nonetheless important when making games. In this chapter, we learned the following:

- It is possible to reconstruct world-space positions in image effect shaders using the depth buffer alongside the clip-space position of the pixel.

- World-space positions can be used for post-processing effects such as a world scanner.

- Cel-shaded lighting introduces a cutoff point into lighting before applying it to an object. There are several methods for introducing the cutoff.

- Some shaders are just used for aesthetic purposes, but others can be interactive and have a direct gameplay impact.

- You can use compute shaders and tessellation shaders together to create a snow mesh effect.

  - The compute shader can be used to read data from characters inside the snow and calculate a heightmap texture from it.

  - The tessellation shader, and associated vertex shader, can be used to read the heightmap and modify the height of the vertices of the mesh.

- Holograms are a common effect seen in "futuristic" games, whereby objects are seemingly made up of pure light.

  - By delegating the hologram pattern to a texture and applying HDR colors to it, you end up with a versatile effect where you can easily just swap out the texture.

- It is possible, in both HLSL and Shader Graph, to create effects that work specifically on 2D sprites.

  - The Sprite Renderer component automatically sends the sprite attached to it to any shader attached to it via the _MainTex property.

Index

A

Alpha blending
    blending (*see* Blending operation)
    clipping (*see* Clipping)
    definition, 273
Ambient lighting
    flat shading methods, 375
    lighting models, 358–359
Animations, 332–333

B

Base shader, 141–145, 151, 275
Bilinear filtering, 135, 138, 176
Blending operation
    HLSL shaders
        additive, 282–283
        built-in pipeline, 276, 277
        calculation, 280
        formula, 279
        linearly interpolates, 280
        multiplicative, 283–284
        premultiplied
          alpha, 281–282
        properties, 285–286
        Queue and RenderType, 278
        ShaderLab, 280
        transparent materials, 280
        TransparentTexture, 275
        turning off, 278
        URP tags, 276
        variable declarations, 277
    Shader Graph
        modes/factors, 288
        surface mode, 286
        TransparentTexture graph, 287
    working process, 274
Blinn-Phong reflection model, 365
    flat shading methods, 366–380
    gouraud shading, 380–398
    phong shading, 398–410
Blinn's method, 362

C

Cartesian coordinates, 33, 44, 155, 156, 160
Cartesian mapping, 155
Cel-shading lighting, 647
    Blender's Suzanne monkey mesh, 647
    graph
        base texture/color, 661
        diffuse/ambient light, 658
        fresnel lighting cutoff
          calculation, 660
        lighting/fresnel cutoff
          properties, 656
        PhongShading graph, 656
        raw diffuse calculation, 657, 659
        specular calculation, 660
    HLSL shader
        built-in pipeline, 649
        fragment shader, 653–655
        HLSLPROGRAM block, 651
        properties, 650

D, E

F

Printed in the United States
by Baker & Taylor Publisher Services